TEACHING AT ITS BEST

TEACHING AT ITS BEST

A Research-Based Resource for College Instructors

Third Edition

Linda B. Nilson

JOSSEY-BASS
A Wiley Imprint
www.josseybass.com

Published by Jossey-Bass
A Wiley Imprint
989 Market Street, San Francisco, CA 94103-1741—www.josseybass.com

Library of Congress Cataloging-in-Publication Data
Nilson, Linda Burzotta.
   Teaching at its best : a research-based resource for college instructors / Linda B. Nilson. — 3rd ed.
      p. cm.
   Includes bibliographical references and index.
   ISBN 978-0-470-40104-0 (pbk.)
  1. College teaching. 2. Effective teaching. I. Title.
   LB2331.N55 2010
   378.1′7—dc22
                  2010000722
Printed in the United States of America
THIRD EDITION

PB Printing 10 9 8 7 6 5 4

The Jossey-Bass
Higher and Adult Education Series

CONTENTS

To Greg,
the man behind the woman

THE AUTHOR

Linda B. Nilson is the founding director of Clemson University's Office of Teaching Effectiveness and Innovation. In addition to writing the first two editions of *Teaching at Its Best: A Research-Based Resource for College Instructors* (1998, 2003), she has authored *The Graphic Syllabus and the Outcomes Map: Communicating Your Course* (Jossey-Bass, 2007) and edited a number of volumes: *Enhancing Learning with Laptops in the Classroom* (with Barbara E. Weaver, Jossey-Bass, 2005) and Volumes 25 through 28 of *To Improve the Academy: Resources for Faculty, Instructional, and Organizational Development* (with Douglas Reimondo Robertson, Anker, 2007, 2008; with Judith E. Miller, Jossey-Bass, 2009, 2010). Her other publications are articles and book chapters on teaching with learning objects and mind maps, designing a graphic syllabus, improving student-peer feedback, teaching large classes, getting students to do the readings, critical thinking, scholarly writing and publishing, and graduate student professional development, along with book-length instructional handbooks for three universities. One of her papers (with Ernest N. Biktimirov) won the 2002 Financial Management Association Competitive Paper Award in Financial Education.

Dr. Nilson presents faculty and graduate student workshops and keynotes at colleges, universities, consortia, and conferences in the United States and internationally. Among her faculty development activities was developing and directing the week-long 2008 Institute for Teaching and Learning in Higher Education, sponsored by the South Carolina Teaching Excellence Network. Her workshop repertoire spans every teaching and learning chapter in this book—course design and development, teaching strategies for small and large classes, assessment, classroom management, and student evaluations—along with career development topics, such as preparation of a teaching philosophy, peer assessment of teaching for promotion and tenure, early academic career management, faculty time management, and scholarly writing and publishing.

Before coming to Clemson in 1998, Dr. Nilson directed the Center for Teaching at Vanderbilt University and the Teaching Assistant Development Program at the University of California, Riverside. At the latter institution, she developed the disciplinary cluster approach to training teaching assistants (TAs), a cost-effective way for a centralized unit to provide disciplinary-relevant instructional training. This approach received coverage in the *Chronicle of Higher Education,* and she similarly structured TA training at Vanderbilt. Her entrée into educational development came in the late 1970s while she was on the sociology faculty at UCLA. After she distinguished herself as an excellent instructor, her department selected her to establish its Teaching Assistant Training Program. She supervised it for four years, and it still follows her original organization. As a sociologist, she conducted research in the areas of occupations and work, social stratification, political sociology, and disaster behavior. Her career also included several years in the business world as a technical and commercial writer, a training workshop facilitator, and the business editor of a southern California magazine.

Dr. Nilson is active in the Professional and Organizational Development (POD) Network in Higher Education, which honored her work with the 2000 Innovation (Bright Idea) Award, and the Society for Teaching and Learning in Higher Education. She has held leadership positions in the POD Network, the Southern Regional Faculty and Instructional Development Consortium, and Society for the Study of Social Problems, the Public Relations Society of America, Toastmasters International, and Mensa.

A native of Chicago, Dr. Nilson was a National Science Foundation fellow at the University of Wisconsin, Madison, where she received her Ph.D. and M.S. degrees in sociology. She completed her undergraduate work in three years at the University of California, Berkeley, where she was elected to Phi Beta Kappa.

Whatever their Carnegie classification, institutions with high standards of instructional excellence, in particular at the undergraduate level, should warmly welcome this third edition, as so many did the first and second editions. It has been updated and expanded to serve the same audience of new and experienced instructors who are sincerely dedicated to learner-centered teaching at its best. They should find it useful whether they teach young, adult, or highly diverse students and whether they rely on traditional classroom or hybrid formats.

Liberal arts and community colleges as well as other teaching-centered institutions have always promoted high standards of teaching excellence. But time was that no one really cared much what instructors in more research-oriented universities did in the classroom, as long as it was legal. No one—not the students, their parents, colleagues, administrators, accrediting agencies, employers, or any levels of government—scrutinized a faculty member's teaching methods, which was usually straight lecture, or sought evidence of student learning. Departments barely considered the quality of one's teaching in hiring, tenure, and promotion decisions. Of course, some instructors deeply cared about their student evaluations, but they usually were the ones who received high ratings and grateful student comments. Otherwise they were rarely rewarded. In fact, these "popular" faculty were suspect. So were those who broached the subject of teaching enhancement with their colleagues.

This time was not a hundred years ago but more like thirty or forty. It was in this chilly environment that Wilbert J. McKeachie was writing and publishing the earliest editions of *Teaching Tips*. His was the only book of its kind on the market. Of course, the research literature on college teaching and learning was sparse back then. Today that literature would fill rooms, and *Teaching Tips* is in its twelfth edition, with plenty of competition, including this book you are reading. College instructors across all types of institutions now face a host of internal and external stakeholders; it seems that everyone cares about what they do in the classroom and how they affect students. Who says the academy never changes?

This book has gathered together the fruits of these changes—literally thousands of research-based methods, policies, and practices for being effective in all aspects of teaching, course management, and assessment—and serves them in readily consumable portions so you can confidently try them out in your next class.

The research on college-level teaching is the foundation of and inspiration for this book. It has blossomed into the fertile body of literature called the scholarship of teaching and learning. It encompasses not only the impact of different instructional methods and learning experiences on student achievement, satisfaction, and knowledge retention, but also recommendations on how to implement these strategies most successfully. Because few faculty have the time to keep abreast of this literature as well as their own discipline, the concise summary of hundreds of teaching options presented here is essential for time saving.

You should use this book as a toolbox for both classroom and technology-enhanced instruction. The tools include not only teaching methods and moves but also face-to-face and online activities and exercises, practices to enhance instructor-student rapport, strategies to make learning easier, and guidelines for designing and grading assignments and papers. With physical tools, you may have to find the right tool for the job. But you usually have the choice of several right tools for a given teaching job, whatever your goals for students. Therefore, I present plenty of alternatives. I avoid playing champion for certain methods over others and the latest innovations over the tried-and-true. Rather, I present the how-to's and why-do's for many teaching tools, along with their trade-offs, just as the research reports them, and leave the choices to frontline faculty.

Guiding my decisions on the organization and the writing style was my intention to write this book for people like you who don't have time to read a book. To ensure easy accessibility and allow rapid reading, the writing style is concise and informal, the paragraphs are relatively brief, most of the thirty-two chapters are short and generously subdivided into sections, and the Contents page is detailed with chapter section headings. In addition, the six major parts are sequenced according to your likely chronological need for the material. Still, you can read the chapters in any order, and the text makes numerous cross-references to other chapters that elaborate on a given subject. So you can casually browse, quickly locate specific topics, and skip over the tools with which you are already familiar.

I wrote this book in the second person and the first-person plural. These writing conventions both personalize the text and make it easier to read. In addition, the second person facilitates presenting the directions, rules, and formulas that some techniques follow. My goal has been to demystify the method, simplify the instructions, and equip you with a new tool right away.

While preserving the most appreciated features of the second edition, this third edition incorporates more and new material—from extensive updates of every topic that new research has addressed to three brand-new chapters, plus a line-by-line editing to further improve the writing. I describe these changes for each part of the book:

Part One, "Laying the Groundwork for Student Learning," guides you through the tasks to complete before the term begins. Understanding your students and how they learn anchors all your plans, so it is dealt with in the first chapter. The section on how people learn brings in more principles and findings from cognitive psychology, as well as their concrete implications for teaching. It is followed by a lengthy new section on the importance of mental structure in learning, retention, and retrieval. Finally, another new section addresses reaching and teaching the millennial generation. Along with updating the term *learning objectives* to *learning outcomes,* Chapters Two and Three on, respectively, course design and the syllabus add Anderson and Krathwohl's revision of Bloom's taxonomy of cognitive operations, Fink's six kinds of learning essential for creating "significant learning experiences," and a section on developing an outcomes map to show students the learning process you have planned for them. The advice in Chapter Four for your first class meeting adds preclass physical and vocal exercises for enhancing your persona and nonverbal communication. Chapter Five on motivation greatly expands the literature review, explicating four theories of motivation and the evidence for them, and it offers more strategies for motivating students, most of which must be planned into a course. Finally, the sections on inclusive teaching and equity in the classroom offer many more ways to create fertile learning environments in diverse settings.

Part Two, "Managing Your Courses," targets the administrative side of teaching: the copyright guidelines to follow, recommended course policies regarding student conduct and academic integrity, and the routines to establish for office hours and with teaching assistants. All of the material on copyright is up-to-date, and the chapter on academic honesty incorporates the latest incidence and prevalence statistics, addresses electronic forms of cheating, and examines the prospect of changing students' values. Chapter Nine includes more novel ideas for places and settings for office hours, and Chapter Ten adds new literature on the faculty-teaching assistant relationship.

Part Three, "Choosing and Using the Right Tools for Teaching and Learning," opens with a new chapter on selecting the teaching formats, methods, and moves that are known to help students achieve specific cognitive outcomes. The rest of the chapters (and those in Part Four) describe well-researched instructional methods and lay out ground rules for setting up and managing them to ensure powerful learning experiences. The menu is extensive, varied, and applicable across the disciplines. It also includes many new topics: using clickers (that is, personal response systems or classroom response systems) to add interactive learning value to the lecture; teaching and motivating students to take good lecture notes; fostering civility and managing conflict during discussions; advancing discussion through Bloom's hierarchy using a question template; posing Brookfield and Preskill's "momentum" questions; implementing academic games; designing and debriefing your own simulations; acquainting students with small-group dynamics; integrating group processing and self-assessment into group work; and administering group tests.

Part Four, "More Tools: Teaching Real-World Problem Solving," extends the menu to major methods that help students acquire various problem-solving skills: to resolve the type of open-ended, realistic problems that good cases and problem-based learning present; solve closed-ended quantitative problems; and tackle challenging scientific questions in both lectures and labs. All of the methods covered fall under the general umbrella of inquiry-guided learning, the focus of Chapter Eighteen, which

opens this part. This completely new chapter explains the competing definitions of inquiry-guided learning, the evidence for its effectiveness, the best practices in implementing it, possible objects and modes of inquiry, and all the many variations on the inquiry-guided theme. Other new sections in Part Four address peer assessment in quantitative problem solving, the principles of successful science instruction, and an inspiring array of recent innovations in science education, all of which are inquiry guided, problem focused, collaborative, and more successful in promoting learning than the traditional lecture. Some of these innovations call for minor changes in the traditional lecture format, such as peer instruction, the case method, problem-based learning, just-in-time-teaching, and experimental demonstrations, while others transform the entire learning process—for example, the "studio course," process-oriented guided inquiry learning (POGIL), and student-centered active learning environment for undergraduate programs (SCALE-UP). Research also finds that students similarly benefit from labs that require inductive reasoning to derive scientific principles and nonroutine problem solving.

Part Five, "Making Learning Easier," groups together types of assignments, class activities, skill development lessons, ways of presenting material, and technology applications that help ensure students learn and retain as much of your material as possible. These strategies include ensuring students do the readings, explaining how your discipline thinks, teaching in different modes and media, adding visual learning aids, and using technologies—from the traditional to the latest Web 2.0 tools—appropriately. Chapter Twenty-Six on teaching with visuals is new. First, it summarizes the research on how the brain processes graphic representations to learn and store more knowledge. Then it provides everything you need to know to incorporate concept maps, mind maps, and concept circle diagrams into your classes: how other faculty have used them successfully (research and examples), how you and your students can create them, and how you can assess your students' products. Other chapters also present new material:

ways to teach students how to read and comprehend academic material; Felder and Silverman's Index of Learning Styles; the validity and reliability of learning style models; recent enhancements to learning management systems; updated research on the effects of posting presentation slides online; Web resources for assignments and activities, including learning objects; effective uses of podcasts and vodcasts; and the latest instructional applications of blogs, wikis, social networking tools, and Second Life.

Finally, Part Six, "Assessing Learning Outcomes," offers guidance first on assessing student learning through activities, tests, and assignments and then on evaluating teaching effectiveness and documenting it for review. New material appears throughout the chapters on first-time topics: writing multiple true-false items for tests (and why you should use them); developing objective test items to assess higher-order thinking skills; grading mechanics quickly while making students learn them; using a new version of contract grading to motivate students; and helping them use your feedback to improve (and why they don't). Other topics have been expanded or updated: formative feedback methods, ways to prepare students for tests, techniques for grading essay questions and writing assignments, approaches to writing a teaching philosophy, and the complexities of evaluating teaching. The lengthy section on student evaluations offers additional analyses on what they actually measure, how instructor behaviors affect them, how to interpret and improve them, and how they should and shouldn't be used in personnel decisions.

If you are familiar with an earlier edition of this book, you may also notice that the information on the instructional support and resources that campuses typically offer has been moved from the first chapter to the appendix. In addition, many of the chapters now include Web addresses of particularly valuable resources for you and your students.

I welcomed Jossey-Bass's invitation to write this third edition and accepted it as an honor. But, of course, it kept me at the computer after hours and on weekends for over a year. My laptop became my faithful travel companion in many airports and on many flights. Unfortunately, the writing and revising cut into precious time with loved ones, especially my dear husband, Greg Bauernfeind. Yet he was my head cheerleader during the entire process of "eating the elephant." He encouraged my efforts, celebrated my progress, and took care of business on the home front. I lovingly dedicate this edition to him.

LINDA B. NILSON
Clemson, South Carolina
November 2009

TEACHING AT ITS BEST

PART 1

LAYING THE GROUNDWORK FOR STUDENT LEARNING

CHAPTER 1

Understanding Your Students and How They Learn

Whenever we prepare an oral presentation, a publication, or even a letter, the first issue we consider is our audience. The person or people for whom we intend our message influence our content, format, organization, sentence structure, and word choice. The same holds true in teaching. The nature of our students—their academic preparation, aspirations, and cognitive development—affects our choices of what and how to teach. We need to think of our job not as teaching art, biology, English, history, math, psychology, and so on but as teaching *students*.

Yet another consideration, this one unique to teaching, is how the human mind learns. For any given subset of knowledge, some types and styles of delivery are simply more effective means of communication than others—that is, they make it easier for people to attend to, grasp, and remember. Yet in spite of the fact that we are all responsible for encouraging human minds to learn, it seems that only cognitive or educational psychologists know how the human mind works.

Knowing both who your students are and how their minds learn is the starting point for teaching at its best.

■ YOUR UNDERGRADUATE STUDENT BODY PROFILE

If you're not already familiar with your student audience, or your experience tells you that its composition has changed, your institution's admissions or student affairs office can provide the type of student data you need. At a minimum, you should find out the distributions and percentages on these variables: age; marital and family status; socioeconomic background; race and ethnicity; full-time and part-time employed; campus residents versus commuters; native versus international; geographical mix; and special admissions. If your students are primarily young, on-campus residents, for instance, you can afford to make more collaborative out-of-class assignments. You might also benefit from finding out about the leadership positions and activities that individuals in a given class engaged in when they were in high school.

You also need to know your students' level of academic preparation and achievement. You can assess your institution's selectivity by comparing the number of applicants each year with the number of those accepted (a two-to-one ratio or above is highly selective). For each entering class, you can find out about its average scholastic test scores (SATs, ACTs), the percentage ranked at varying percentiles of their high school graduating classes, the percentage of National Merit and National Achievement Finalists (over 5 percent is high), and the percentage that qualified for Advanced Placement credit (over a third is high). For several hundred American colleges and universities, almost all of this information is published every summer in the "America's Best Colleges" issue of *U.S. News & World Report*.

Another question you might want to answer is where your students are headed in life. Your institution's career center should have on file the percentage of students planning on different types of graduate and professional educations, as well as the immediate employment plans of the next graduating class. Often departments and colleges collect follow-up data on what their students are doing a few years after graduation.

■ HOW PEOPLE LEARN

Whatever your student body profile, certain well-researched principles about how people learn will apply:

- People are born learners, beginning from infancy with an insatiable curiosity and an increasing awareness of their learning. They absorb and remember untold billions of details about objects, other people, their language, and things they know how to do (Bransford, Brown, & Cocking, 1999; Spence, 2001).
- People learn through elaborative rehearsal, which means connecting new knowledge to what they already know and believe (Bransford et al., 1999; Tigner, 1999).
- People learn what they regard as relevant to their lives (Svinicki, 2004).
- People learn socially by constructing knowledge in a group (Stage, Kinzie, Muller, & Simmons, 1999), but they otherwise learn one-on-one and on their own (Spence, 2001).
- People learn when they are motivated to do so by the inspiration and enthusiasm of other people in their lives (Feldman, 1998b).
- People don't learn well when their major learning context is teacher centered—that is, when they passively listen to a teacher talk. Rather, they learn when they are actively engaged in an activity, a life experience. The human brain can't focus for long when it is in a passive state (Bligh, 2000; Bonwell & Eison, 1991; Hake, 1998; Jones-Wilson, 2005; McKeachie, 2002; Spence, 2001; Svinicki, 2004).
- People learn best when they receive the new material multiple times but in different ways—that is, through multiple senses and modes that use different parts of their brain (Kress, Jewitt, Ogborn, & Charalampos, 2006; Tulving, 1985; Vekiri, 2002).
- People learn when they actively monitor their learning and reflect on their performance—a mental operation called *metacognition* or *self-regulated learning* (Bransford et al., 1999).
- Relatedly, people learn less by reviewing material and more from being tested or testing themselves on it, as the latter involves greater cognitive processing and practice retrieving (Dempster, 1996, 1997; Roediger & Karpicke, 2006).
- People learn better when the material evokes emotional and not just intellectual or physical involvement. In other words, a lasting learning experience must be moving enough to make the material memorable or to motivate people to want to learn it. This learning pattern mirrors the biological basis of learning, which is the close communication between the frontal lobes of the brain and the limbic system. From a biological point of view, learning entails a change in the

brain: the establishment of desirable new synapses (Leamnson, 1999, 2000; Mangurian, 2005).

These key learning principles have some complementary teaching principles, and they echo through the rest of this book:

- Hold your students to high expectations. But be reasonable, and don't use yourself as the standard. Very few students will learn your field as quickly as you did or choose the life of the mind as you have.
- Start where your students are. Find out what they already know and don't know and what they believe to be true, and become familiar with their lifestyles. Then relate the new content, skills, and abilities you are helping them learn to what is familiar to them, both cognitively and experientially. Use examples and analogies out of their lives and their generational experience.
- Make the material relevant to the students' lives, which for today's concrete learners means connecting your material to their day-to-day experience, future careers, or real-world problems.
- Demonstrate enthusiasm and passion for your subject and for teaching it, as these are contagious emotions. If these don't come naturally to you, learn how to use your voice and body to convey them.
- Assign creative, inventive, and challenging tasks to small groups and more routine learning tasks, such as first-exposure reading and standard problem sets, as individual homework. Some students will need tutoring after their individual attempts at learning, which you, a teaching assistant (TA), or group members can provide. Reflection and writing are also individual learning activities, even though they can be very challenging and creative.
- Use active learning techniques, and when you do lecture, do so interactively—that is, with frequent breaks for student activities.
- When possible, use experiential methods: those that place students in real-life problem-solving situations, simulated or genuine.

- Teach in multiple modalities. Give students the opportunities to read, hear, talk, write, see, draw, think, act, and feel new material into their system. In other words, involve as many senses and parts of the brain as possible in your teaching and their learning. If, as is commonplace, the students are reading or listening to the material, have them take notes on it, discuss it in pairs or groups, concept- or mind-map it, freewrite about it, solve problems with it, complete a classroom assessment exercise on it, or take a quiz on it.
- Teach your students how to learn your material, and build in assignments that make them observe, analyze, and assess how well they are learning.
- Build into your course plenty of assessment opportunities, including low-stakes quizzes, practice tests, in-class exercises, and homework assignments that can tell students how much they are really learning, as well as provide them with retrieval practice.
- Motivate and reinforce learning with emotions. Make a learning experience dramatic, humorous, surprising, joyous, maddening, exciting, or heart-wrenching. Integrate engaging cases and problems to solve, simulations and games, role plays, service-learning, and other experiential learning opportunities into your courses. Let students reflect, debate, consider multiple points of view, write down their reactions to the material, and work cooperatively in groups. Any emotion will aid learning by inducing more enduring changes—that is, the generation of new, lasting synapses—in the brain.

■ HOW STRUCTURE INCREASES LEARNING

Structure is so key to how people learn and has such far-reaching implications for teaching that it deserves an entire section of its own. In fact, without it, there is no knowledge.

Students are always talking about "information" when they refer to what they are learning. After all, this is the "information age," and abundant information is constantly available. It's a snap to find people's phone numbers, the capitals of countries, the years of events, directions from one place to another, an area's major industries, economic figures, political leaders, and election results, to name just a few common pieces of information. But all of these are only facts: isolated bits of information that do not add up to any generalizations or conclusions about the way the world works.

What isn't so available is knowledge, that is, organized bodies of knowledge, which is what we academics have to offer that information-packed websites do not. Knowledge is a structured set of patterns that we have identified through observation, followed by reflection and abstraction—a grid that we have carefully superimposed on a messy world so we can make predictions and applications (Kuhn, 1970). Knowledge comprises useful concepts, agreed-on generalizations, well-grounded inferences, strongly backed theories, reasonable hypotheses, and well-tested principles and probabilties. Without knowledge, science and advanced technology wouldn't exist.

Unfortunately, our students come to our courses, and usually leave them, viewing our material as a bunch of absolute, disconnected facts, supplemented by technical terms—about as well organized, meaningful, and memorable as a phone book. These facts and "things" were out there. Human beings "discovered" them; we didn't construct them. From this perspective, memorization is the only learning strategy that makes sense.

Students are not stupid; they are simply novices in our discipline. They lack a solid base of prior knowledge and may harbor misconceptions and faulty models about the subject matter (Svinicki, 2004). Being unable to identify the central, core concepts and principles (Kozma, Russell, Jones, Marx, & Davis, 1996), they wander somewhat aimlessly through a body of knowledge, picking up and memorizing what may or may not be important facts and terms and using trial-and-error to solve problems and answer questions (Glaser, 1991). They do not see the big picture of the patterns, generalizations, and abstractions that experts recognize so clearly. As a result, they have trouble figuring out how to classify and approach problems at the conceptual level (Arocha & Patel, 1995; DeJong & Ferguson-Hessler, 1996).

Without that big picture, students face another learning hurdle as well. The mind processes, stores, and retrieves knowledge not as a collection of facts but as a logically organized whole, a coherent conceptual framework, with interconnected parts. In fact, it requires a big picture. That framework is what prior knowledge is all about. New material is integrated not into an aggregate of facts and terms but into a preexisting structure of learned knowledge. Without having a structure of the material in their heads, students fail to comprehend and retain new material (Anderson, 1984; Bransford et al., 1999; Rhem, 1995; Svinicki, 2004).

The mind structures knowledge based on patterns and relationships it recognizes across observations. In fact, it is driven to generalize about and simplify reality. If it did not, we would experience repetitive events as novel every time they occurred and would learn and remember nothing from them. No doubt, we would find reality too complex to operate within and would perish. Animals too have the need and capacity to recognize patterns. They learn to obtain what they need and survive not just by instinct but by learning—for instance, learning to hide, judge distances, time their strikes, and fool their prey—and they get better with practice. The behaviorists call learning by pattern recognition *operant conditioning,* and they have demonstrated that mammals, birds, reptiles, and probably fish learn this way.

Human thinking is so wired to seek and build structure that we make up connections to fill in the blanks in our understanding of phenomena if we don't already have a complete explanatory "theory" handy. Some of these made-up connections that pan out under scrutiny are elevated to science. Charles Darwin, for example, did not observe mutations happening in nature; rather, he hypothesized their occurrence to fill in the explanatory blanks for species diversity. No one was around to watch the big bang, but the theory fills in quite a few missing links in cosmology. Astronomers have never observed what they believe to make up 30 percent of the universe: dark matter. This term refers to undetectable matter or particles that are hypothesized to account for unexpected gravitational effects on galaxies and stars. Scientists have inferred its existence to explain anomalies in calculations of the total mass of a galaxy cluster. In these calculations, the total mass of the composite galaxies can be determined by comparing their dynamic mass (dispersion speeds) with their luminous mass, which is calculated from the amount of light the cluster emits. These two measurements of total mass should be similar, but the dynamic mass, which is affected by gravity, is often hundreds of times larger than the luminous mass. Dark matter "explains" this otherwise inexplicable finding.

Not all imagined connections, however, stand the test of time or science. Superstitions and prejudice exemplify false patterns. The belief of many people, including many of our students, that one's intelligence is fixed and immutable also fails under careful study.

Faculty are now recognizing and beginning to address the misconceptions about natural and social phenomena that students bring into their science and social science courses. Consider the now-classic videotape, *A Private Universe* (Schneps & Sadler, 1988). It dramatically shows that Harvard graduates and even professors carry around incorrect theories about the causes of the seasons and the phases of the moon if they have not deep-processed the scientific explanation. It also shows that a sharp, young, presumably open mind has a hard time abandoning and replacing a flawed but familiar explanatory structure with a new and better one. The new one has to be easy to grasp, plausible, more useful, and convincing enough to make the learner see the failures of the old one (Baume & Baume, 2008; Posner, Strike, Hewson, & Gertzog, 1982).

The kind of deep, meaningful learning that moves a student from novice toward expert is all about acquiring the discipline's hierarchical organization of patterns, its mental structure of knowledge (Alexander, 1996; Anderson, 1993; Carey, 1985; Chi,

Glaser, & Rees, 1982; Reif & Heller, 1982; Royer, Cisero & Carlo, 1993). Only then will the student have the structure on which to accumulate additional knowledge. By their very nature, knowledge structures must be hierarchical to distinguish the more general and core concepts and propositions from the condition specific and derivative. Experts move up and down this hierarchy with ease.

What are the odds that a learner will develop such a structure of knowledge on his or her own in a few weeks, months, or even years? How long did it take us? Most, if not all, of our time in graduate school—or longer? People require years of specialized study and apprenticeship to internalize the structure of the discipline and become expert. Unfortunately, many, if not most, of our students pass through our discipline for only a term or two—not nearly enough time to notice its patterns and hierarchical structure. Yet without having a mental structure for organizing what they learn, they process our course content superficially and quickly forget it. Is it not our responsibility as teaching experts to help our students acquire a structure quickly, so our short time with them is not wasted? Should we not make the organization of our knowledge explicit by providing them an accurate, ready-made structure for making sense of our content and storing it?

What then are the complementary teaching principles to the central role that structure plays in learning?

- Very early in the term, give students activities and assignments that make them retrieve, articulate, and organize what they already know (or think they know) about your course material. Then identify any evident misconceptions and address in class how and why they are wrong.
- Again, very early, give students the big picture—the overall organization of your course content. The clearest way to show this is in a graphic syllabus (see Chapter Three). Carry through by presenting your content as an integrated whole, that is, as a cohesive system of interpreting phenomena—not as an aggregate of

small, discrete facts and terms. Keep referring back to how and where specific topics fit into that big picture.

- Give students the big picture of their learning process for the term—that is, the logical sequencing of your learning outcomes for them. A flowchart of the student learning process for a course is called an *outcomes map* (see Chapter Two).

- Help students see the difference between information and knowledge. The previous discussion of the topic, as well as the next section of this chapter, supplies some useful concepts and vocabulary for explaining the difference.

- Teach students the critical thinking structures that your discipline uses—for example, the scientific method, the diagnostic process, the rules of rhetoric, basic logic (the nature of fact, opinion, interpretation, and theory), and logical fallacies. Where applicable, acquaint them with the competing paradigms (metatheories) in your field, such as the rational versus the symbolic interpretive versus the postmodern perspectives in English literature, pluralism versus elitism in political science, functionalism versus conflict theory in sociology, and positivism (or empiricism) versus phenomenology in social science epistemology.

- Design exercises for your students in pattern recognition and categorical chunking to help them process and manage the landslide of new material. These thinking processes will help them identify conceptual similarities, differences, and interrelationships while reducing the material to fewer, more manageable pieces. The fewer independent pieces of knowledge the mind has to learn, the more knowledge it can process and retain. Cognitively speaking, less is more.

- In addition to showing your students a graphic syllabus and outcome map of your course, furnish them with graphic representations of theories, conceptual interrelationships, and knowledge schemata—such as concept maps, mind maps, diagrams, flowcharts, comparison-and-contrast matrices, and the like—and then have them develop their own to clarify their understanding of the material. Such visuals are powerful learning aids because they provide a ready-made, easy-to-process structure for knowledge. In addition, the very structures of graphics themselves supply retrieval cues (Svinicki, 2004; Vekiri, 2002). Chapter Twenty-Six deals with this topic in more detail.

■ THE COGNITIVE DEVELOPMENT OF UNDERGRADUATES

No matter how bright or mature your students may be, do not expect them to have reached a high level of cognitive maturity in your discipline. Almost all students, especially freshmen and sophomores, begin a course of study with serious misconceptions about knowledge in general and the discipline specifically. Adult learners are no exception. Only as these misconceptions are dispelled do students mature intellectually through distinct stages. As an instructor, you have the opportunity—some would say the responsibility—to lead them through these stages to epistemological maturity.

Psychologist William G. Perry (1968, 1985) formulated a theory of the intellectual and ethical development of college students. In its simple four-stage version, students begin college with a dualistic perspective and may, depending on their instruction, advance through the stages of multiplicity, relativism, and commitment (definitions are given below). The research supporting it accumulated rapidly, making Perry's the leading theory on the cognitive development of undergraduates. Baxter Magolda's (1992) four levels of knowing—absolute, transitional, independent, and contextual—roughly parallel Perry's, with most females following a relational pattern and most males the abstract. Table 1.1 displays both models.

While Perry's framework of development applies across disciplines, a student's level of maturity may be advanced in one and not in another. So we shouldn't assume, for example, that a sophisticated senior in a laboratory science major has a comparable

Table 1.1   Stages/Levels of Student Cognitive Development

Perry's Stages of Undergraduate Cognitive Development	Baxter Magolda's Levels of Knowing
3. Relativism: All opinions equal • Standards of comparison	Independent Knowing
1. Duality: Black and white thinking; authorities rule • Uncertainty	Absolute Knowing
2. Multiplicity: Poor authorities or temporary state • Uncertainty as legimate, inherent	Transitional Knowing
4. Commitment (tentative) to best theory available	Contextual Knowing

understanding of the nature of knowledge in the so-cial sciences or the humanities.

The more elaborate version of Perry's theory posits nine positions through which students pass on their way to cognitive maturity. (The stages in Perry's simpler model are italicized.) How far and how rapidly students progress through the hierarchy, if at all, depend largely on the quality and type of instruction they receive. It is this flexible aspect of Perry's theory that has made it particularly attractive and useful. The schema suggests ways that we can accelerate undergraduates' intellectual growth.

Let us begin with position 1, the cognitive state in which most first-years arrive. (Of course, many sophomores, juniors, and seniors are still at this level.) Perry used the term *dualism* to describe students' thinking at this stage because they perceive the world in black-and-white simplicity. They decide what to believe and how to act according to absolute standards of right and wrong, good and bad, truth and false-hood. Authority figures, like instructors, supposedly know and teach the absolute truths about reality. Fur-thermore, all knowledge and goodness can be quan-tified or tallied, like correct answers on a spelling test.

At position 2, students enter the general cog-nitive stage of *multiplicity*. They come to realize that since experts don't know everything there is to know, a discipline permits multiple opinions to compete for acceptance. But to students, the variety merely reflects that not all authorities are equally legitimate or competent. Some students don't even give these competing opinions much credence, believing

them to be just an instructor's exercise designed ulti-mately to lead them to the one true answer. As they advance to position 3, they accept the notion that genuine uncertainty exists, but only as a temporary state that will resolve itself once an authority finds the answer.

Entering position 4, which marks the broader stage of *relativism,* students make an about-face and abandon their faith in the authority's ability to iden-tify "the truth." At this point, they either consider all views equally valid or allow different opinions within the limits delineated by some standard. In brief, they become relativists with no hope of there ever being one true interpretation or answer.

Students at position 5 formalize the idea that all knowledge is relativistic and contextual, but with qualifications. They may reserve dualistic ideas of right and wrong as subordinate principles for special cases in specific contexts. Thus, even in a relativistic world, they may permit certain instances where facts are truly facts and only one plausible truth exists.

At some point, however, students can no longer accommodate all the internal inconsistencies and am-biguities inherent in position 5. They may want to make choices but often lack clear standards for doing so. As a result, they begin to feel the need to ori-ent themselves in their relativistic world by making some sort of personal commitment to one stance or another. As this need grows, they pass through posi-tion 6 and into the more general cognitive stage of *commitment.* When they actually make an initial, ten-tative commitment to a particular view in some area, they attain position 7. Next, at position 8, they experience and examine the impacts and implications of their choice of commitment. That is, they learn what commitment means and what trade-offs it carries.

Finally, at position 9, students realize that trying on a commitment and either embracing or modifying it in the hindsight of experience is a major part of personal and intellectual growth. This process is, in fact, a lifelong activity that paves the road toward wisdom and requires an ever open mind.

■ ENCOURAGING COGNITIVE GROWTH

Nelson (2000), a leading authority on developing thinking skills, contends that we can facilitate students' progress through these stages by familiarizing them with the uncertainties and the standards of comparison in our disciplines. He and many others (Allen, 1981, in the sciences, for example) have achieved excellent results by implementing his ideas. (Kloss, 1994, offers a somewhat different approach tailored to literature instructors.)

Exposure to uncertainties in our knowledge bases helps students realize that often there is no one superior truth, nor can there be, given the nature of rational knowledge. This realization helps lead them out of dualistic thinking (position 1) and through multiplistic conceptions of knowledge (positions 2 and 3). Once they can understand uncertainty as legitimate and inherent in the nature of knowledge, they can mature into relativists (positions 4 and 5).

Instructive examples of such uncertainties include the following: (1) the range of viable interpretations that can be made of certain works of literature and art; (2) the different conclusions that can be legitimately drawn from the same historical evidence and scientific data; (3) a discipline's history of scientific revolutions and paradigm shifts; (4) unresolved issues on which a discipline is currently conducting research; and (5) historical and scientific unknowns that may or may not ever be resolved.

Our next step is to help students advance beyond relativism through positions 6 and 7, at which point they can make tentative commitments and progress toward cognitive maturity. To do so, students need to understand that among all the possible answers and interpretations, some may be more valid than others. They must also learn why some are better than others—that is, what criteria exist to discriminate among the options, to distinguish the wheat from the chaff.

Disciplines vary on their criteria for evaluating validity. Each has its own metacognitive *model*—that is, a set of accepted conventions about what makes a sound argument and what constitutes appropriate evidence. Most students have trouble acquiring these conventions on their own; they tend to assume that the rules are invariable across fields. So Nelson advises us to make our concepts of evidence and our standards for comparison explicit to our students.

By the time students reach position 5, they are uncomfortable with their relativism, and by position 6, they are hungry for criteria on which to rank options and base choices. So they should be highly receptive to a discipline's evaluative framework.

To encourage students to reach positions 7 and 8, we can provide writing and discussion opportunities for them to deduce and examine what their initial commitments imply in other contexts. They may apply their currently preferred framework to a new or different ethical case, historical event, social phenomenon, political issue, scientific problem, or piece of literature. They may even apply it to a real situation in their own lives. Through this process, they begin to realize that a commitment focuses options, closing some doors while opening others.

We should remind students that they are always free to reassess their commitments, modify them, and even make new ones, but with an intellectual and ethical caveat: they should have sound reason to do so, such as new experiences or data or a more logical organization of the evidence—not just personal convenience. With a clear understanding of this final point, students achieve position 9.

Bringing Perry's and Nelson's insights into our courses presents a genuine challenge in that students in any one class may be at different stages, even if they are in the same graduating class. Almost all first-year students fall in the first few positions, but juniors and seniors may be anywhere on the hierarchy. It may be wisest, then, to help students at the lower positions catch up with those at the higher ones by explicitly addressing knowledge uncertainties and disciplinary criteria for selecting among perspectives and creating opportunities for students to make and justify choices in your courses.

Keep your students' cognitive growth in mind as you read this book. If you use the outcomes-centered approach to designing a course (see Chapter Two), you may want to select a certain level of cognitive maturity as a learning outcome for your students.

You will find more strategies for teaching uncertainty and alternative explanations in later chapters. Chapter Twenty-Four on teaching your students to think and write in disciplinary contexts revisits the notion of metacognitive models and examines some crucial differences in argumentation and evidence across major disciplinary groups.

■ TEACHING THE MILLENNIAL GENERATION

If you are teaching traditional-age students, you need to know some basics about this generation, which has come to be called generation Y, the Net generation, the NeXt generation, and most commonly, the millennial generation. A great deal has been written about it, and this section provides a quick synthetic summary (Bureau & McRoberts, 2001; Carlson, 2005; Featherstone, 1999; Frand, 2000; Hersch, 1998; Howe & Strauss, 2000; Levine & Cureton, 1998; Lowery, 2001; Nathan, 2005; Oblinger, 2003; Plotz, 1999; Raines, 2002; Strauss & Howe, 2003; Taylor, 2006; Tucker, 2006). The generalizations seem to apply to at least the bulk of middle- and upper-middle-class millennials.

This generation comprises children born between 1982 (some say 1980) and 1995 to the late baby boomers. These parents kept their children's lives busily structured with sports, music lessons, club meetings, youth group activities, and part-time jobs. In their spare time, young millennials spent many hours on the computer, often the Internet, interacting with peers, doing school work, playing games, shopping, and otherwise entertaining themselves. Unless they attended private or college-town schools, they received a weaker K–12 education than previous generations. Still, they flooded into colleges and universities starting around 2000. Their combined family and school experience, along with their heavy mass media exposure, made them self-confident, extremely social, technologically sophisticated, action bent, goal oriented, service or civic minded, and accustomed to functioning as part of a team. On the flip side, they are also impatient, demanding, stressed out, sheltered, brand oriented, materialistic, and self-centered. They use—and abuse—alcohol and prescription drugs more than street drugs. Although skeptical about authority, they tend not to be particularly rebellious, violent, or promiscuous. With so much activity in their lives as well as frequent interaction with friends and family (much on computers and cell phones), they have little time or inclination for reflection, self-examination, or free-spirited living. Another feature of this generation, one that distinguishes it from so many preceding ones, is that millennials do not hunger for independence from their parents. Quite the contrary, they stay close to the parents through college (and often beyond) and turn to their parents for help when organizations don't meet their needs. These parents have earned the descriptor of "helicopter parents" for hovering over their grown children to ensure their well-being and competitive advantage in life.

For college faculty, this generation can be challenging to deal with. Millennials view higher education as an expensive but economically necessary consumer good, not a privilege earned by hard work and outstanding performance. They (or their parents) "purchase" it for the instrumental purpose of opening well-paying occupational doors on graduation, so they feel entitled to their degree for the cost of the credits. As many of them did little homework for their good grades through high school, they anticipate the same minimal demands in college and are often resentful about the amount of reading, research, problem solving, and writing that we assign them and about the standards that we hold for their work. Those whose grades slip in college feel their self-esteem threatened and may react with depression, anxiety, defensiveness, and even anger against us. In addition, they hear a lot a "bad news" from us in their classes: that they didn't learn enough in high school to handle college, that knowledge bases are full of holes and unsolved mysteries, that their beliefs and values are subject to question and debate, and that both college and the real world demand that they work and prove their worth.

Not only are we bearers of bad news, however inadvertently, but we are also very different from them and difficult to fathom and identify with. We prize the life of the mind, we love to read, and we work long hours for relatively little money. We must remember that this generation values money and what it can buy. Aside from the materialism that their parents and the mass media promoted, these young people face the prospect of being the first generation, at least in the United States, that cannot afford a standard of living comparable to that of their parents, let alone higher. So while some observers call millennials hopeful, others point to their economic anxiety (Levine & Cureton, 1998).

In any case, our modest material status, coupled with all our education, does not inspire a great deal of their respect. To them, we render customer service, a somewhat menial calling, to a society that doesn't value abstraction, intellectual discourse, or knowledge for knowledge's sake. There's just no money in them. Therefore, if they are dissatisfied with our services (usually workload, grades, or our responsiveness to their desires), they complain to our "bosses," often involving their parents to bolster their power. They sense they have the upper hand: that instructors are subject to being disciplined or even fired at administrative will and that institutions want to retain students and keep them happy. In this quasi-corporate model, the customer is always right, whether she is or not. So millennials can be demanding, discourteous, impatient, time-consuming, and energy sapping. For the same reason, colleges and universities have been upgrading their residence halls, food services, recreational and workout facilities, tutoring programs, computing, and teaching (with an eye toward boosting student ratings).

Despite the difficulties millennials may present, this generation can be easy to reach if we make a few adjustments. After all, they have career goals, positive attitudes, technological savvy, and collaborative inclinations. In addition, they are intelligent enough to have learned a lot, even if it is not the knowledge that we value. Our adjustments need not include lowering our own standards.

Although millennials are understandably cynical about authority (so are we) and don't assume we have their best interests at heart, they value communication and information and respond well when we explain why we use the teaching and assessment methods we do. We can "sell" them on the wisdom of our reading selections, assignments, in-class activities, and rubrics, reinforcing the fact that we are the experts in our field and in teaching it. As experts, we *should* have solid, research-based reasons for our choices. Why not show our students the respect of sharing these reasons?

Millennials also want to know that we care about them. Remember that they are still attached to their parents and not far from the nest. They are also accustomed to near-constant interaction, so they do want to relate to us. Showing that we care about their learning and well-being—by calling them by name, asking them about their weekend, promising we will do whatever it takes to help them learn, stating how much we want them to be successful, and voicing our high expectations of them—will go very far in earning their loyalty and trust.

Finally, having led a tightly organized childhood and adolescence and not being rebellious, they respond well to structure, discipline, rules, and regulations. If you set up or have them set up a code of classroom conduct (see Chapter Seven), they will generally honor it. If you promise that you will answer their email at two specific times each day and you follow through, they will not expect you to be available 24/7. Whatever course policies your syllabus states, as long as they are clear and airtight, the students will generally respect them, though a few may try to pressure you to bend your rules. Even their parents will usually withdraw their demands for grade information if you clearly explain any applicable restrictions under the Family Educational Rights and Privacy Act. What millennials consider unprofessional is an instructor's (apparent) disorganization, ill preparation, or inability to stick to her own syllabus.

Of course, blanket statements about an entire generation always apply to only a portion of its members. Biggs (2003) has another take on it. He describes an undergraduate profile applicable to both the British Commonwealth nations and the United States, and he puts a face on it—two faces, actually. There is "Susan," the archetypal "good" student—intelligent, well prepared, goal oriented, and motivated to master the material. Susan came to college with solid thinking, writing, and learning skills. While about three-quarters of today's college students were like her in 1980, only about 42 percent are like her today (Brabrand & Andersen, 2006). The rest (almost 60 percent) are like "Robert," who is much less academically talented, college ready, and motivated to learn (Brabrand & Andersen). He just wants to get by with the least amount of learning effort so he can parlay his degree into a decent job. He will rely on memorizing the material rather than reflecting on and constructing it. "Good teaching," according to Biggs, is "getting most students to use the higher cognitive level processes that the more academic students use spontaneously" (p. 5)—that is, changing Roberts into Susans.

When you divide the student population the way Biggs does, the millennial generation doesn't look so monolithic, and no matter where we teach, we find both types of students in our classes. A sizable minority of them are interested in learning

and know something about how to do it, even if they are also materialistic, tied to their parents, and on Facebook. While we can generalize about millennials, we must not forget that they are the most diverse generation—economically, politically, ethnically, racially, and culturally—that North American institutions of higher learning have ever welcomed.

THE ADULT LEARNER

Adults learn the same way as traditional-age students, but they respond somewhat differently to certain instructor behaviors, teaching strategies, and content emphases. They are less forgiving about an instructor's shortage of experience, expertise, teaching savvy, and suitable supplementary materials. For good reason, they value their own life experience and want to share and apply it in class, assignments, and group work. They know the world to be complex, and therefore they expect to learn multiple ways of solving problems and to have discretion in applying the material. They need the opportunity for reflection after trying out a new application or method. Rote learning just won't work with them. Finally, adult learners are practical and usually quite disinterested in theory. They demand that the materials have immediate utility and relevant application (Aslanian, 2001; Vella, 1994; Wlodkowski, 1993). None of this implies that they are difficult learners. In fact, they are often highly motivated, eagerly participatory, and well prepared for class.

INCLUSIVE INSTRUCTING

Age is but one variable on which students vary. Add gender, race, ethnicity, national origin, sexual orientation, and religion. Time was when only well-to-do white males attended college in the United States. But now over 60 percent of all undergraduates are female, and in 2003–2004, only 63.7 percent were white, 14.1 percent African American, 11.9 percent Hispanic, 5.4 percent Asian American,

0.9 percent Native American, 0.5 percent Pacific Islander, and 2.1 percent multiracial. In addition, 11.3 percent had a disability ("Profile of Undergraduate Students, 2003–4," 2007).

While all people learn by the same basic processes described earlier, some of these groups educationally thrive under circumstances that are not always typical in the American classroom. In addition, they often share distinctive values, norms, background experiences, and a sense of community that set them apart and make them feel set apart—and not always in a positive way. Traditionally underrepresented groups are more likely to struggle emotionally in college and to leave before attaining a degree.

As an instructor, you are also an ambassador of the academy to these groups, and you are close enough to them to reach out and include them. How you relate to these students has a powerful impact on their performance and retention (Ferguson, 1989; Grant-Thompson & Atkinson, 1997; Guo & Jamal, 2007; Jones, 2004; Kobrak, 1992). Here are some guidelines, and you'll find more in the section "Equity in the Classroom" at the end of Chapter Five:

- Assign and mention the scholarly and artistic contributions of diverse groups where appropriate (Toombs & Tierney, 1992).
- Call a group by the name that its members prefer.
- Develop a personal rapport with your African American, Native American, Hispanic, and female students. Their style of thinking and dealing with the world tends to be relational and interpersonal, which means intuitive, cooperative, holistic, subjective, relationship focused, motivated by personal loyalty, and oriented to socially relevant topics (Anderson & Adams, 1992; Baxter Magolda, 1992). This style contrasts with the analytical, which values analysis, objectivity, logic, reason, structure, sequence, the abstract, debate, challenge, competition, and economic practicality. It is prevalent among European and Asian American males and in the academy in general

(Anderson & Adams). How closely and easily you relate to your diverse and female students will strongly affect their motivation to learn, their trust in your intentions for them, and their overall satisfaction with college (Allen, Epps, & Haniff, 1991; Gonsalves, 2002; Grant-Thompson & Atkinson, 1997; Kobrak, 1992; Nettles, 1988).

- Be aware that most international students stand physically closer to others than do Americans, that many Asian American women are taught to avoid eye contact, and that many Asian Americans and Native Americans have learned to listen quietly rather than jumping into discourse.
- Don't avoid course-appropriate topics related to diverse groups because they are sensitive, controversial, or applicable to only a minority of people. Some students will see your avoidance as prejudicial.
- Don't avoid giving timely, constructive feedback to diverse students about their work out of fear of injuring their self-esteem or being accused of racism. Indeed, diverse students may interpret your criticisms as racially motivated disrespect, so you should bring up this possibility yourself and explicitly ask them rather than sweeping the issue under the rug. Be very sure that the students really understand your criticisms and recommendations for improvement (Gonsalves, 2002).
- Don't make so much of their successes that you imply you didn't expect them to succeed.
- Don't let any students get away with insensitive remarks in class. Such incidents open up teachable moments for you to lead an open discussion about cultural differences and stereotyping. Before launching a potentially controversial discussion, it is also a good idea to explain what a civil intellectual discourse comprises and to set up ground rules for it.
- Don't ask diverse students to speak in class as representatives of their group. Whatever the group, it is too internally diverse to be represented by one or a few members.

■ THE CHALLENGE

With such a varied student population on so many dimensions, including academic background, instructors sometimes wonder at what level of student to aim their courses. Unfortunately, there is no clear answer. Some of us find peace aiming at the top 20 percent, where we know our efforts will be intellectually productive. Others of us aim at the broad middle, hoping to bring as many students along with us as possible. Of course, where the top 20 percent and broad middle lie varies by type of institution.

This dilemma rarely presented itself over forty years ago. Back then, higher education was largely a screening device for privileging the best and the brightest—and often the wealthiest—over the rest of the socioeconomic pack. The more selective colleges and universities welcomed only the top performers, regardless of cultural and economic background, and they shamelessly discouraged or flunked out students who did not thrive on the lecture method. In fact, most institutions with a high attrition rate were proud of it. The society did not hold them accountable for effective teaching and achieving learning outcomes; the term *learning outcome* did not even exist. Students were solely responsible for their learning, and those who survived college had to have strong study skills, cognitive abilities, and self-motivation. Under this old system, many of today's students would never have completed college—if they ever gained admission.

During the 1980s and 1990s, higher education started to adopt a different and rather novel goal: to educate as many as possible rather than to screen. At the time, which wasn't long ago, this was quite a radical notion, but it also was a pragmatic response to the changing demographics of our society. This shift in the mission of higher education generated teaching and learning centers, higher faculty standards for teaching effectiveness, and an explosion of research on how students learn and respond to different instructor behaviors, teaching methods, and instructional settings. This book draws on and integrates much of this research into a practical reference on the most effective approaches to use for different types of learning outcomes.

CHAPTER 2

Outcomes-Centered Course Design

Teaching has only one purpose, and that is to facilitate learning (Cross, 1988). Learning can occur without teaching at no loss to anyone, but teaching can and unfortunately does occur without learning. In the latter case, the students obviously lose time, money, potential gains in knowledge and cognitive development, and perhaps confidence in themselves or the educational system (or both). But less obviously, instructors lose faith in their students and in themselves. For our own mental health as well as that of our students, we need to make teaching and learning synonymous sides of the same coin.

The first step toward this goal is to design your courses wisely. Whether you are teaching an established course for the first time, developing a brand-new course, or revising a course you currently teach, first ask yourself what you are trying to accomplish. No doubt, you want your students to learn certain things, to master a body of material. But you can't assess how well you've met this goal, or your students' learning, unless you have them do something with that material that demonstrates their learning. What they do may involve writing, discussing, acting, creating a graphic or visual work, conducting an experiment or demonstration, making an oral presentation, designing a Web page, or teaching a lesson. Any display of learning will do, as long as you can perceive it though your senses and appraise the quality of the performance. How else can you determine their internal state—what they know, realize, and understand?

■ WHY OUTCOMES-CENTERED COURSE DESIGN?

This chapter proposes starting the course design process with what you want your students to be able to do by the end of the course. But other approaches exist. You can develop a course around a list of content topics you consider important to cover. In fact, before 1990, a course was always characterized by its range of content, such as "a comprehensive survey of vertebrate animals including their taxonomy, morphology, evolution, and defining facets of their natural history and behavior" or "an introduction to the process of literary criticism." Course catalogues and many syllabi still contain these descriptions. You can also organize a course around your favorite textbook or the one you've been told to use. However, such approaches will not ensure that your course is student active, which we know is essential for learning, or acceptable to your institution's and your school's accrediting agencies.

Outcomes-centered course design guarantees a high level of student engagement because the process steers you toward student-active teaching strategies. It also conforms to the accountability requirements of an increasing number of accrediting agencies. These agencies hold a unit accountable for its students' achieving certain learning outcomes, as well as for formally assessing its students' progress toward that goal. In other words, they require departments and schools to determine what they want their students to be able to do, at least on graduation, and to produce materials that show what the students can do. Some agencies even take it on themselves to specify exactly what abilities and skills the graduates of a certain area should demonstrate.

■ WRITING OUTCOMES

A learning outcome is a statement of exactly what your students should be able to do after completing your course or at specified points during the course. Some faculty set outcomes for individual classes and units of the course. Outcomes are written from a student's point of view—for example, "After studying the processes of photosynthesis and respiration, the student should be able to trace the carbon cycle in a given ecosystem." Of course, they are promises, and you should make it clear that students have to do their part to make this promise come true. So you might state verbally and in your syllabus something like this: "Students may vary in their competency levels on these abilities. You can expect to acquire these abilities only if you honor all course policies, attend classes regularly, complete all assigned work in good faith and

on time, and meet all other course expectations of you as a student."

Before you start composing outcomes, find out from your dean or department chair whether an accrediting agency has already mandated them for your course. For instance, the National Council for the Accreditation of Teacher Education lists the required outcomes for many education courses. The Accreditation Board for Engineering and Technology provides program outcomes, some of which may be useful and even essential for your course.

If you, like most other instructors, are free to develop your own outcomes, you might first want to research the history of the course. Why was it proposed and approved in the first place, and by whom? What special purposes does it serve? What other courses should it prepare students to take? Often new courses emerge to meet the needs of a changing labor market, update curriculum content, ensure accreditation, or give an institution a competitive edge. Knowing the underlying influences can help you orient a course to its intended purposes for student learning (Prégent, 1994).

Second, get to know who your students are so you can aim your course to their needs and level. Refer to the first part of Chapter One for the types of student data you will need—all of which should be available from your institution's admissions office, student affairs office, and career center—to find out the academic background, interests, and course expectations of your likely student population. Ask colleagues who have taught the course before about what topics, books, teaching methods, activities, assignments, and so on worked and didn't work well for them. The more relevant you can make the material to the target group, the more effective your course will be.

If you cannot gather much information in advance, keep your initial learning outcomes and course design somewhat flexible. On the first day of class, use index cards and icebreakers to learn more about your students and their expectations (see Chapter Four); then adjust and tighten the design accordingly.

Technically an outcome has three parts to it, though usually only the first part appears in the outcomes section of a syllabus. Sooner or later, however, you will have to define the second and third parts as well:

Part 1: A statement of a measurable performance. Learning outcomes center on action verbs (for example, *define, classify, construct, compute;* see Table 2.1) rather than nebulous verbs reflecting internal states that cannot be observed (for example, *know, learn, understand, realize, appreciate*). For example: "The student will be able to classify given rocks as igneous or metamorphic." "The student will be able to describe the most important differences between sedimentary and metamorphic rocks." Table 2.2 later in the chapter offers many more examples.

Part 2: A statement of conditions for the performance. These conditions define the circumstances under which the student's performance will be assessed. Will she have to demonstrate that she knows the differences among igneous, metamorphic, and sedimentary rocks in writing, in an oral presentation, or in a visual medium (drawings, photographs)? Will he be able to identify the parts of a computer system on a diagram or in an actual computer?

Part 3: Criteria and standards for assessing the performance. By what criteria and standards will you evaluate and ultimately grade a student's performance? What will constitute achieving an outcome at a high level (A work) versus a minimally competent level (C work)? For example: "For an A on essay 3, the student will be able to identify in writing at least three differences between igneous and metamorphic rocks, at least three between igneous and sedimentary rocks, and at least three between metamorphic and sedimentary—for a total of at least nine differences. For a B, the student will be able to identify at least six differences. For a C, the student will be able to identify at least four differences," and so on. Rubrics have such criteria and standards built into them.

TYPES OF LEARNING OUTCOMES

Virtually every college-level course has *cognitive* outcomes—those pertaining to thinking. But other types exist that may be pertinent to your courses. *Psychomotor* skills—the ability to manipulate specific objects correctly and efficiently to accomplish a specific purpose—constitute another type that is important in art, architecture, drama, linguistics, some engineering fields, all laboratory sciences, nursing and other health-related fields, and foreign languages. *Affective* outcomes specify emotional abilities you want your students to develop, such as receiving, responding, and valuing (Krathwohl, Bloom, & Masia, 1999). Of course, you cannot observe your students' inner feelings, but you can observe their demonstration of emotions. For example, in nursing, counseling, and the ministry, students must learn to show empathy and open-mindedness toward patients and clients, and performances can be assessed in a role play or a case analysis. Such abilities are also very useful in management, medicine, human resources, marketing, psychology, and architecture. A wide range of disciplines integrate *social* learning outcomes to their courses, since the workplace relies on teamwork and group learning is now widely accepted. Many instructors want their students to be able to collaborate effectively in a team, and they consider both the group product and peer evaluations of the group members' social behavior in assessing students' performance. With new ethics-across-the-curriculum programs, *ethical* outcomes have come to the fore. Some institutions and schools want their students to take into account the moral considerations and implications of various options in making professional, scientific, technical, and business decisions. The case method, simulations, role plays, service-learning, fieldwork, and internships provide both learning and assessment contexts for ethical objectives. Exhibit 2.1 gives more specific examples of all five types of outcomes.

Exhibit 2.1   General Types of Learning Outcomes

Psychomotor—physical performance; may involve eye-hand coordination. *Examples:* medical and nursing procedures; laboratory techniques; animal handling or grooming; assembling, operating, testing, or repairing machines or vehicles; singing; dancing; playing musical instruments; use of voice, face, and body in public speaking.

Affective—demonstration of appropriate emotions and affect. *Examples:* demonstrating good bedside manner and empathy with patients; showing trustworthiness and concern for clients, customers, subordinates, or students; showing tolerance for differences; showing dynamism, relaxed confidence, conviction, and audience responsiveness in public speaking.

Social—appropriate, productive interaction and behavior with other people. *Examples:* cooperation and respect within a team; leadership when needed; assertive (not aggressive, passive, or passive-aggressive) behavior in dealing with conflict; negotiation and mediation skills.

Ethical—decision making that takes into account the moral implications and repercussions (effects on other people, animals, environment) of each reasonable option. *Examples:* medical and nursing decisions involving triage, transplants, withholding care, and prolonging life; lawyers' decisions about whether and how to represent a client; managerial decisions involving social, economic, political, or legal trade-offs.

Cognitive—thinking about facts, terms, concepts, ideas, relationships, patterns, conclusions. *Examples:* knowledge and remembering; comprehension and translation; application, analysis, synthesis, and creating; evaluation.

Fink (2003) takes a somewhat different approach in his model of six categories of learning, which encompass cognitive, affective, and social outcomes. His categories are cumulative and interactive, and the ideally designed course incorporates all six of them as outcomes. In fact, Fink claims that all six kinds of learning are essential to create a genuinely significant learning experience. These are his categories of learning:

- *Foundational knowledge:* Students recall and demonstrate understanding of ideas and information, providing the basis for other kinds of learning.
- *Application:* Students engage in any combination of critical, practical, and creative thinking; acquire key skills; and learn how to manage complex projects, making other kinds of learning useful.

- *Integration:* Students perceive connections among ideas, disciplines, people, and realms of their lives.
- *Human dimension:* Students gain a new understanding of themselves or others, often by seeing the human implications of other kinds of learning.
- *Caring:* Students acquire new interests, feelings, and values about what they are learning as well as motivation to learn more about it.
- *Learning how to learn:* Students learn about the process of their particular learning and learning in general, enabling them to pursue learning more self-consciously, efficiently, and effectively. (Reprinted with permission of John Wiley and Sons, Inc.)

In the "Helpful Frameworks for Designing a Course" section later in this chapter, we consider how an instructor can create learning experiences that interrelate all these categories synergistically.

For the time being, we will focus on writing cognitive outcomes, since they are universal in higher education courses.

TYPES OF COGNITIVE OUTCOMES

Bloom (1956) developed a useful taxonomy for constructing cognitive outcomes. His framework posits a hierarchy of six cognitive processes, moving from the most concrete, lowest-level process of recalling stored knowledge through several intermediate cognitive modes to the most abstract, highest level of evaluation. (Depending on your field, you may prefer to make application the highest level.) Each level is defined:

- *Knowledge:* The ability to remember and reproduce previously learned material
- *Comprehension:* The ability to grasp the meaning of material and restate it in one's own words
- *Application:* The ability to use learned material in new and concrete situations
- *Analysis:* The ability to break down material into its component parts so as to understand its organizational structure
- *Synthesis:* The ability to put pieces of material together to form a new whole
- *Evaluation:* The ability to judge the value of material for a given purpose

This handy taxonomy is popular to this day, but Anderson and Krathwohl (2000) offer a few "friendly amendments" to it in their newer model. They use more action-oriented gerunds, update the meaning of "knowledge" and "synthesis," and rank "creating" above "evaluating":

- *Remembering* = Knowledge (lowest)
- *Understanding* = Comprehension
- *Applying* = Application
- *Analyzing* = Analysis
- *Evaluating* = Evaluation
- *Creating* = Synthesis (highest)

All of these conceptual terms become more concrete in Table 2.1, which lists common student performance verbs for each of Bloom's and Anderson and Krathwohl's cognitive operations. Once you select the cognitive operations that you'd like to emphasize in a course, you may find it helpful to refer to this listing while writing your outcomes. Another good reference is Table 2.2, which gives examples of outcomes at each cognitive level in various disciplines.

Bear in mind that the true cognitive level of an outcome depends on the material students are given in a course. If they are handed a formal definition of iambic pentameter, then their defining it is a simple recall or, at most, comprehension operation. If, however, they are provided only with examples of poems and plays written in it and are asked to abstract a definition from the examples, they are engaging in the much higher-order process of synthesis.

As you check key verbs and draft outcome statements, think about what cognitive operations you are emphasizing. We can foster critical thinking and problem-solving skills only by setting outcomes above the knowledge/remembering and comprehension/understanding levels. Although these lower levels furnish foundations for learning, they are not the end of education. Therefore, it is wise to include some higher-order outcomes to challenge students to higher levels of thinking. We will revisit Bloom's and Anderson and Krathwohl's combined taxonomy in Chapter Fourteen, as it is also very useful for framing questions.

Once you draft your outcomes, go to Table 2.3, on the last page in this chapter. It presents a rubric for evaluating and revising learning outcomes.

DESIGNING THE LEARNING PROCESS

When you list all your learning outcomes, you will probably notice that some have to precede others. Students have to achieve some of them early in the term to prepare them to achieve more advanced ones

Table 2.1   Student Performance Verbs by Level of Cognitive Operation in Bloom's Taxonomy and Anderson and Krathwohl's Taxonomy

1. Knowledge/Remembering		2. Comprehension/Understanding	
Arrange	Omit	Arrange	Paraphrase
Choose	Order	Associate	Outline
Define	Recall	Clarify	Recognize
Duplicate	Recite	Describe	Rephrase
Find	Recognize	Explain	Report
Identify	Relate	Express	Restate
Label	Repeat	Grasp	Review
List	Reproduce	Identify	Select
Match	Select	Indicate	Summarize
Memorize	Spell	Interpret	Translate
Name	Tell	Locate	Visualize

3. Application/Applying		4. Analysis/Analyzing	
Apply	Illustrate	Analyze	Distill
Break down	Interpret	Calculate	Distinguish
Calculate	Make use of	Categorize	Divide
Choose	Manipulate	Classify	Examine
Compute	Operate	Compare	Experiment
Demonstrate	Practice	Contrast	Identify assumptions
Determine	Schedule	Criticize	Induce
Dramatize	Sketch	Deduce	Inspect
Employ	Solve	Derive	Investigate
Give examples	Use	Differentiate	Model
	Utilize	Discriminate	Probe
		Discuss	Question
		Dissect	Simplify
			Test

5/6. Synthesis/Creating		6/5. Evaluation/Evaluating	
Adapt	Imagine	Agree	Dispute
Arrange	Infer	Appraise	Evaluate
Assemble	Integrate	Argue	Judge
Build	Invent	Assess	Justify
Change	Make up	Award	Prioritize

Table 2.1 (*Continued*)

5/6. Synthesis/Creating		6/5. Evaluation/Evaluating	
Collect	Manage	Challenge	Persuade
Compose	Modify	Choose	Rank
Conclude	Originate	Conclude	Rate
Construct	Organize	Convince	Recommend
Create	Plan	Criticize	Rule on
Design	Posit	Critique	Score
Develop	Predict	Debate	Select
Discover	Prepare	Decide	Support
Estimate	Produce	Defend	Validate
Extend	Propose	Discount	Value
Formulate	Set up	Discredit	Verify
Forward	Suppose	Disprove	Weight
Generalize	Theorize		

Note. Depending on the use, some verbs may apply to more than one level.

Table 2.2 Examples of Outcomes Based on Bloom's Taxonomy and Anderson and Krathwohl's Taxonomy

Level	The Student Should Be Able to...
Knowledge /Remembering	• Define iambic pentameter. • State Newton's laws of motion. • Identify the major surrealist painters.
Comprehension /Understanding	• Describe the trends in the graph in his or her own words. • Summarize a passage from Socrates' *Apology*. • Properly translate into English passages from Voltaire's *Candide*.
Application/Applying	• Describe an experiment to test the influence of light and light quality on the Hill reaction of photosynthesis. • Scan a poem for metric foot and rhyme scheme. • Use the Archimedes principle to determine the volume of an irregularly shaped object.
Analysis/Analyzing	• List arguments for and against human cloning. • Determine the variables to be controlled for an experiment. • Discuss the rationale and efficacy of isolationism in the global economy.
Synthesis/Creating	• Write a short story in Hemingway's style. • Compose a logical argument on assisted suicide in opposition to his or her personal opinion. • Construct a helium–neon laser.
Evaluation/Evaluating	• Assess the validity of certain conclusions based on the data and statistical analysis. • Critically analyze a novel with evidence to support a critique. • Recommend stock investments based on recent company performance and projected value.

later in the course. If they cannot perform the prerequisite outcomes, they won't be able to achieve the latter ones. For instance, if you want your students to be able to develop a research proposal near the end of the course, they will have to be able to do several other things beforehand:

- Frame a research problem or hypothesis.
- Justify its significance.
- Conduct and write up an adequate literature review.
- Devise an appropriate research design.
- Describe the data collection procedures.
- Outline the steps of the analysis (which is premised on some methodological expertise).
- Explain the importance of the expected results.
- Develop a mock budget.

If your course or its prerequisite courses do not include these skills as outcomes, the students will be ill equipped to achieve the outcome of writing a decent research proposal.

From this perspective, a course is a learning process of advancing through a logical succession of outcomes. This sequencing of outcomes serves as scaffolding for the entire course design.

Ultimate Outcomes

The easiest way to develop this logical succession of student learning outcomes is to formulate your end-of-term, or ultimate, outcomes first. These are likely to be the most challenging skills and cognitively advanced learning. No doubt they require high levels of thinking (application, analysis, synthesis, or evaluation) and a combination of skills and abilities that students should have acquired earlier in the course. Often assessment takes the form of a major capstone assignment or a comprehensive final, or both, to assess student achievement of these outcomes.

Mediating Outcomes

From here you work backward, determining what your students will have to be able to do before they can achieve your ultimate outcomes. These are

your mediating outcomes, and you will probably have quite a few of them, each representing a component or lower-level version of one of your ultimate outcomes. You might want to visualize the working-backward process by picturing a branching tree that grows from three or more main trunks (ultimate learning outcomes) on the far right and branches back to the left. These branches represent your mediating and foundational (the very first) outcomes, which students must achieve before attempting the more advanced outcomes to the right.

Your challenge now is to figure out the most logical and efficient order in which students should acquire these mediating abilities. These outcomes may have a logical internal order of their own. The skill-building logic is probably clearest in cumulative subjects such as mathematics, physics, and engineering. However, many courses, especially those within a loosely organized curriculum, allow instructors a lot of discretionary room in sequencing the mediating outcomes. Textbooks may follow a certain order, but the topical sequencing may be largely arbitrary. In introductory survey courses, literature courses, and even certain science and health science courses, the topics students study and the skills they acquire can be logically organized in different ways.

Foundational Outcomes

Once you work your way back to the beginning of your course, you will reach your foundational learning outcomes: those on which the learning process of the course is predicated. These will involve one or more of the following:

- Your students will master the lowest-level cognitive operations on the subject, recalling and paraphrasing basic facts, processes, and definitions of essential terms and concepts.
- They will identify, question, and abandon the misconceptions about the subject matter that they brought into the classroom at the beginning of the term.

- They will identify, question, and abandon their dualistic thinking about the subject matter (a particularly prevalent epistemological misconception) as they come to recognize uncertainties in the field.

These are perhaps the most basic learning objectives we can set for students. After all, they can't apply, analyze, synthesize, or evaluate a discipline's knowledge if they cannot speak or write the discipline's language and summarize or paraphrase the basics. If you organize a course into modules of knowledge that have different sets of basic facts, terms, concepts, or theories, you will probably have foundational outcomes at the start of each module.

Moreover, students cannot accurately map new, valid knowledge onto existing knowledge that is riddled with misconceptions and misinformation. A faulty model will not accommodate the new material you intend for them, so they will not be able to assimilate it, at least not at more than a surface level. To bring about a major shift in your students' worldview, you must create learning situations that reveal the errors in their mental models and the explanatory superiority of your discipline's model.

Let us consider some discipline-specific examples of essential shifts. To master physics on a serious level, students must replace their Aristotelian or Newtonian model of the physical world, both of which are serviceable in everyday life, with Einstein's model. To think like a sociologist, a learner must relinquish an individualistic free-will view to explain people's life courses and replace it with the deterministic, probabilistic theory that their location in the social structure at birth stacks the deck in favor of or against possible life courses and the acquisition of various rewards. To understand evolutionary biology, students have to stop viewing *Homo sapiens* as the purpose and destination of epochs of evolution and see our species as just another temporarily successful adaptation among millions of others.

In addition, to begin to internalize any body of knowledge, students must acquire an understanding of what knowledge actually is and what it isn't.

As discussed in Chapter One, knowledge is simply a mental grid that human beings have created and imposed over a more complex reality to try to understand and manipulate it. This grid encompasses all the major patterns we have identified through our observations, along with our best-evidenced interpretations of them at this point in time. The fact that that reality is inherently messy and conforms only so far to any grid we can construct is the underlying source of the uncertainty in all disciplines. Because all grids are more or less flawed, disciplines have evolved standards of comparison for distinguishing the better ones. To bring students to these insights, dualism is the first misconception we should discredit before escorting them into our subject matter.

■ HELPFUL FRAMEWORKS FOR DESIGNING A COURSE

Three frameworks—Bloom's (1956) and Anderson and Krathwohl's (2000) hybrid taxonomy cognitive operations, Perry's (1968) and Baxter-Magolda's (1992) theory of undergraduate cognitive development, and Fink's (2003) categories of learning—offer schemata, alone and in combination, for designing courses. You may find one or more of them useful as heuristic devices.

Bloom's and Anderson and Krathwohl's Framework

Both Bloom's (1956) and Anderson and Krathwohl's (2000) taxonomies of cognitive operations are hierarchical, from lower order to higher order. They posit that to be able to perform one level of thinking, learners must be able to perform all the lower-order thinking operations. By extension, a well-designed course should sequence the learning outcomes to lead students up the hierarchy.

It is self-evident that a student has to be able to define certain concepts, state certain principles, and recall certain facts before thinking about them in a more complex way. But beyond that, both Bloom's and Anderson and Krathwohl's hierarchy breaks down. For instance, the practice of medicine, law, and other professions is all about *applying* knowledge to new, often complicated situations. But before applying knowledge, professionals have to *analyze* the elements of the problematic situation, *evaluate* what knowledge and disciplinary algorithms are most useful and relevant to the situation, and *synthesize* (or *create*) a problem-solving strategy—for example, a legal approach or a medical diagnosis and treatment plan.

Perry's and Baxter-Magolda's Framework

"The Cognitive Development of Undergraduates" section in Chapter One summarizes both Perry's (1968) and Baxter-Magolda's (1992) parallel frameworks. As a course design heuristic, the idea is to sequence your learning outcomes as students progress through each of the stages or levels, whether nine or four, as far as you think you can lead your class. For the primary foundational outcome, which is moving beyond dualism, students would have to explain the multiple competing interpretations or theories for some disciplinary phenomenon or issue, demonstrating that they realize that authorities don't have all the answers or the one right answer on the matter. To achieve a major mediating outcome (moving through multiplicity and relativism), students would have to analyze and critique these interpretations or theories. For the ultimate outcome (tentative commitment), they would have to embrace one of the interpretations or theories and justify their choice, as well as qualify it by explicating the limitations of the chosen viewpoint.

While this schema may not apply well to an undergraduate science or engineering course, it can work very effectively in high-uncertainty and interpretive disciplines, such as literature, the arts, and philosophy. I used it to design a freshman seminar I taught in the past, Free Will and Determinism. While anchored in philosophy, it featured readings from clinical and behaviorist psychology, sociology, political science, genetics, biochemistry, and sociobiology. Rather than list them in the learning outcomes in the syllabus—at the time, they were called "objectives," not "outcomes," and were rarely listed—I wrote them in the paragraphs below, starting with the ultimate outcome:

> By the end of this course, you will have developed a well-reasoned, personal position on the role of free will, determinism, compatibilism, fatalism, and spiritual destiny in your own and others' lives. You will be able to express, support, and defend your position orally and in writing while acknowledging its weaknesses and realizing that it can never be validated as "the right answer" and that it may change over time [Ultimate Outcome: Tentative Commitment]. Hopefully, you will also begin to feel comfortable with the uncertainty and tentativeness of knowledge and with making decisions in spite of it.

> To help you attain these major objectives [outcomes], you will also acquire these supporting abilities: to sift out the various positions on free will and determinism (as well as compatibilism, fatalism, and spiritual destiny) in the assigned literature, along with their implicit premises and "givens," and to express them accurately in writing and orally [Foundational Outcome: Uncertainty]; to draw sound comparisons and contrasts among them; to evaluate their strengths, weaknesses, and limitations [Mediating Outcome 1: Uncertainty as Inherent and Legitimate]; and to distinguish among the stronger and the weaker positions [Mediating Outcome 2: Standards for Comparison].

The ultimate outcome closely reflected the final paper and the two mediating outcomes, the tasks required in the first two papers.

Fink's Framework

Fink's (2003) categories of learning do not offer a built-in sequencing of outcomes as do the other two frameworks. His approach is not hierarchical but cumulative and interactive. An ideally designed and developed course promotes all six kinds of learning, resulting in a genuinely "significant" learning experience. The goal is not to order the kinds of learning but to help students interrelate and engage in them synergistically. So a course design based on Fink's framework might start with foundational knowledge and then progressively add outcomes addressing each of the other five kinds of learning one or more times during the course, ensuring that all six kinds are represented by the end.

According to Fink, his framework can accommodate courses of all levels and disciplines, whether face-to-face or online, and he provides a comprehensive, step-by-step procedure for applying it to any course. Here is one generic example. After students acquire some foundational knowledge, have them apply this new knowledge to solve a problem of relevance to them (application) or to a situation where they can see how some phenomenon affects them and others (human dimension). This learning experience should promote their interest in the subject matter (caring). With their interest piqued, they should begin to notice the relationships between the new material and other things they have learned (integration). As they recognize more linkages, they should start drawing additional implications for their own and others' lives (human dimension) as well as other ways to apply the material to improve the quality of life (application). At this point, they should want to learn still more (caring) and realize their need to acquire stronger learning skills (learning how to learn). This illustration shows that a well-designed course can generate a mutually reinforcing relationship between learning and motivation.

■ SHOWING STUDENTS THEIR LEARNING PROCESS

The younger generation of students is not as facile with text as it is with visuals, so a wise idea is to illustrate your course design to your students so they can see where your course is going in terms of their learning. You can illustrate your course design in an *outcomes map,* which is a flowchart of the learning outcomes, starting from your foundational outcomes, progressing through your mediating outcomes, and finally arriving at your ultimate outcomes. In other words, it is a visual representation of the sequence, progression, and accumulation of the skills and abilities that students should be able to demonstrate at various times in the term. It shows how achieving one or more outcomes should enable students to achieve subsequent ones.

As I have written extensively on charting an outcomes maps elsewhere (Nilson, 2007a), I will furnish here just a couple of examples that I have developed. Figure 2.1 is an outcomes map for my Free Will and Determinism course. Following Perry's (1968) framework, it contains just a few outcomes that build up to the ultimate "commitment" outcome. These outcomes parallel those copied from the course syllabus above. Figure 2.2 is the outcomes map for my graduate course, College Teaching. It does not follow any course design framework. It has a genuine flowchart look and feel, clearly showing how achieving one outcome equips students to achieve later ones. The students' major assignment is an individual course design and development project, after which they write a statement of teaching philosophy. I make it clear to my students that, of course, I won't be able to assess them on two of the ultimate outcomes—obtaining a teaching position and meeting institutional assessment requirements and goals—but they will leave knowing how to meet these crucial career goals in their fast-approaching future.

While these two examples look very different, they cannot possibly illustrate the dozens of ways that outcomes maps can vary: the directions in which they flow, their spatial arrangements, their enclosures and connectors, and their use of type sizes, type styles, shadings, and colors. Outcomes maps may or may not reflect one of the three course design frameworks discussed earlier. They may or may not supply a time schedule—such as the week or class number that you

Figure 2.1   Outcomes Map for a Freshman Seminar: Free Will and Determinism

ULTIMATE LEARNING OUTCOME

To develop and explain in writing a well-reasoned personal position on the role of free will, determinism, compatibilism, and fatalism (including spiritual destiny) in your own and others' lives, and to defend it while acknowledging its weaknesses and limitations (capstone paper 3)

MEDIATING LEARNING OUTCOMES

To assess how research supports or refutes each position (study questions and in-class discussions, weeks 6–12; paper 2 on scientific findings versus clinical reports due week 12)

To assess how one's own life experiences support or refute each position (journaling and in-class discussions, weeks 6–14)

To refute positions from the viewpoints of other positions (simulation/mock trial week 6, based on paper 1)

To apply the positions to interpret and assess a situation (paper 1 on criminal case, due week 6)

FOUNDATIONAL LEARNING OUTCOMES

To express accurately, both orally and in writing, the free willist, determinist, compatibilist, and fatalist positions, along with their assumptions and justifications (readings, study questions, in-class writing exercises, in-class discussions, weeks 1–5)

expect students to achieve each outcome. But however they look, they all furnish students with far more information about how their learning will progress through the course than a simple list of outcomes.

If you decide to chart an outcomes map for any of your courses, the process will probably make you reexamine your outcomes and their sequencing. You might realize that you've previously missed a step or two in your students' logical learning process or that a different ordering of some of your outcomes would make more sense. So you may find that you get as much out of your drawing the map as your students do.

■ OUTCOMES-CENTERED COURSE DEVELOPMENT

Your course design is a skeleton. With that in place, you have to start developing the course into a more detailed plan—that is, filling it out by putting muscle and connective tissue on the bone structure.

Course Content

Only after formulating your learning outcomes should you begin to select the content that will help your students achieve those outcomes. The challenge is to limit the content to only this purpose. If you

Figure 2.2 Outcomes Map for a Graduate Course, College Teaching
Note: CATs = classroom assessment techniques.

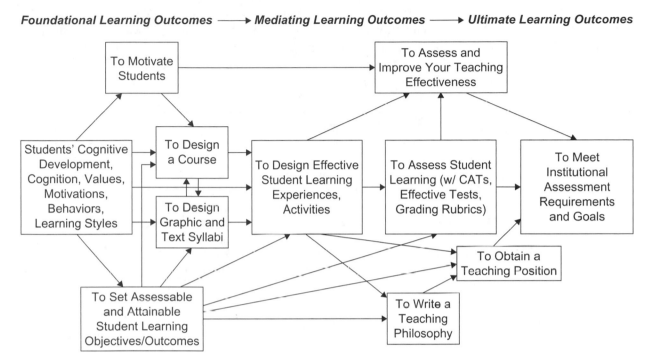

specialize in the content area, it will be difficult to narrow it. Prégent (1994) advises brainstorming as many topics and themes as possible. For help, you can consult Contents pages of reputable texts, course catalogues and syllabi from other institutions, and your colleagues. Then rank-order the topics according to their relevance to your outcomes.

Do not hesitate to eliminate topics entirely. Instructors, especially new ones, tend to pack too much material into a course. It is better to teach a few topics well than merely to cover the material with a steamroller and wind up teaching very little of anything.

You can draw a graphic of the interrelationships among your course topics just as you can draw one about the organization of your student learning outcomes. We look at the graphic syllabus in the next chapter.

Readings

Choose books in line with your learning outcomes and content. If you are looking specifically for a textbook, you will be fortunate to find one that reflects your general philosophy and preferences. If you're not so lucky, consider selecting the best available option for some of your reading assignments and supplementing it with handouts, reserve readings, websites, and a class packet. Try to avoid making students purchase more than one expensive text.

It is one thing to assign readings and another to get students to read them. If you have found students' reading compliance or even comprehension to be a problem, then consider yourself in excellent company and refer to Chapter Twenty-Three for solutions.

In-Class Activities, Assignments, and Assessments

Your learning outcomes should direct all the other elements of your course. Let's start with graded assignments and assessments. Your ultimate outcomes should suggest questions and tasks or at least foci, themes, or formats for your final exam, final paper assignment, or capstone student project. After all, these outcomes delineate what you want your students to be able to do by the end of the course. Then move backward through the course and devise assignments and tests that have students performing your mediating and, finally, your foundational outcomes. Once you've written sound outcomes, you've at least outlined your assignments and assessments. It's just that simple—almost anyway. The chapters in Part Six offer good advice about constructing these instruments and assessing student performance on them.

Table 2.3   Rubric for Evaluating and Revising Student Learning Outcomes

Dimension	Excellent	Common Errors	Needs Revision	Missed the Point
Outcomes are observable, assessable, and measurable.	Outcomes are assessable and measurable. The instructor can observe (usually see or hear) and evaluate each learner's performance by clear standards—for example, how well, how many, to what degree.	Some outcomes use verbs that refer to a learner's internal state of mind, such as *know, understand,* or *appreciate,* which an instructor cannot observe and assess. Or some outcomes are too general to specify standards for evaluation.	Outcomes do not describe (1) observable performances that are assessable and measurable and/or (2) what the learners will be able to do.	Outcomes list the topics the course will cover or what the instructor will do. Or outcomes use verbs that refer to a learner's internal state of mind, which an instructor cannot observe and assess.
Most outcomes require high levels of cognition.	Most outcomes reflect high levels of cognition (application, analysis, synthesis, and evaluation).	All or almost all the outcomes require low levels of cognition (knowledge and comprehension), such as *recognize, identify, define,* or *describe.*	Not enough outcomes address higher levels of cognition, given the level of the course and the learners.	Some outcomes consistently use verbs that refer to a learner's low-level internal state of mind, such as *know, understand,* or *appreciate.*
Outcomes are achievable.	Outcomes are realistic for the course length and credit hours and the level of the learners.	Outcomes are too numerous for the instructor to assess or the learners to achieve.	Outcomes are too advanced for the course length or credit hours for the learners.	Outcomes don't use action verbs to describe what the learners will be able to do.
Outcomes are relevant and meaningful to the learners.	Outcomes are relevant to the learners and their personal or career goals.	Not all the outcomes and their benefits are clear to the learners.	The learners can't make sense out of the outcomes.	Outcomes don't indicate what the learners will be able to do.

Selecting in-class activities and learning-focused assignments is a more complex process because you have so many possibilities to choose from and so little time to manage and give feedback on them. So all of Chapter Eleven is devoted to helping you make the best decisions—that is, selecting the most effective methods for your outcomes—and the chapters in Parts Three and Four describe your major options and how to implement them. You will find the class-by-class bricks and mortar for building a successful learning experience for your students, ensuring that your teaching translates into learning.

Indeed, your outcomes can and should guide your choice of activities down to the individual class level. If you want your students to be able to write a certain type of analysis by a certain week of the term, then structure in-class activities and assignments to give them practice in writing that type of analysis. If you want them to be able to solve certain kinds of problems, then design activities and assignments to give them practice in solving such problems. If you want them to research and develop a point of view, and argue it orally, then select activities and assignments to give them practice in research, rhetoric, and oral presentation, if they don't already have it.

Figure 2.1 of my Free Will and Determinism course shows not only the relationships among the learning outcomes but also the activities and assignments that helped students achieve those outcomes and assessed their progress. These activities and assignments are listed in parentheses after each outcome, followed by the weeks in the term that they occurred. They included three papers, readings, in-class and online discussions, journaling, a simulation, study questions, and in-class writing exercises. While this does not provide a class-by-class schedule, it served well as a general outline for developing the schedule and detailed descriptions of the activities and assignments.

Once you have a sound course design, your syllabus almost writes itself. The next chapter presents a concise checklist of all the information that can and usually should be included in this important course document.

CHAPTER 3

The Complete Syllabus

A syllabus is most simply defined as a concise outline of a course of study. But it is also the students' introduction to the course, the subject matter, and *you*. In addition to providing a schedule of class assignments, readings, and activities, it should give students insight into the material and your approach to teaching it. In a sense, then, it is not only the road map for the term's foray into knowledge but also a travelogue to pique students' interest in the expedition and its leader.

While syllabi of just a couple of pages are common, students always have many more questions than a brief syllabus can answer. In addition, some courses call for a great deal of first-day information. A comprehensive, well-constructed syllabus may easily run five, six, or even ten pages, and this isn't necessarily too long. The original "learning-centered syllabus" can go on for twenty, thirty, or fifty pages or more, becoming in effect a "course handbook" (Grunert, 1997). So this chapter presents a suggested checklist for developing a shorter but comprehensive syllabus (Altman & Cashin, 1992; Grunert O'Brien, Millis, &

Cohen, 2008), whether printed or online. The more information you include, the less you have to improvise or decide on the run, and the fewer student questions you will have to answer. If you doubt that your students will read such a lengthy document, see the penultimate section in this chapter on inducing your students to read it.

■ APPROPRIATE SYLLABUS ITEMS

Following is an annotated list of all the information that you should put in a course syllabus. For examples of the recommended information and further detail, Grunert O'Brien et al. (2008) is by far the best resource. At the end of this section is a box on the items that can protect you from student complaints, grievances, and even lawsuits:

1. *Complete course information:* The course number and title; days, hours, and location of class meetings; credit hours; any required or recommended prerequisites, including permission of the instructor

for enrollment; any required review sessions; any required laboratories or recitation or discussion sections, with the same information as given for the course; and the titles and location of any online course materials, exercises, assignments, exams, and supplementary materials that are on the Web (give the URL) or in your course management system (give the folder).

2. *Information about yourself:* Your full name and title, the way you wish to be addressed, your office hours, your office location, your office phone number, email address, and home page URL (if you have one). If you decide to give students your home or cell phone number, you may wish to limit calls to certain days and hours. So your students do not expect you to be on email 24/7, specify the days and hours that you will be answering their email.

3. *The same information about other course personnel,* such as teaching assistants (TAs), technicians, and other assistants. You might encourage your section and lab TAs to develop their own syllabi.

4. *A briefly annotated list of reading materials,* such as assigned books, journal articles, class packets, and Web materials with full citations (including edition), price, location (bookstore, library, reserve status, URL, or course management system folder), identification as required or recommended, and your reasons for selecting them. If you do not plan to give regular assignments from the text, consider making it a recommended supplementary source. If commercially prepared notes are available, say how helpful they might be.

5. *Any other materials required for the course,* including cost estimates and where to find them at a good price. (Don't forget eBay for pricier items.) For example, some science labs require students to have a personal stock of cleaning supplies and safety equipment. Art and photography classes usually expect students to furnish their own equipment, supplies, and expendable materials. If special types of calculators, computers, or software are called for, describe these in detail. If the materials won't be used immediately, specify when in the term they will be.

6. *A complete course description,* including the organization or flow of the course, your rationale for it, and the major topics it will address. You may even want to list topics it will *not* cover, especially if your course has too much popular appeal and tends to attract less-than-serious students.

7. *Your student learning outcomes for the course—* not just your ultimate outcomes (what students should be able to do or do better at the end of the course) but also your mediating and foundational outcomes. Chapter Two gives guidance on developing solid learning outcomes, designing a course around them, and charting an outcomes map to show students your plan for their learning process. However, you don't want your outcomes to be interpreted as binding promises, and you know your students have to apply themselves to achieve these outcomes. So consider adding the caveats and disclaimers recommended in the box on legal issues in the syllabus.

8. *All graded course requirements and a complete breakdown of your grading scale,* preferably buttressed by a rationale. Nothing is so annoying as hearing half your students bargain for points or ask for a curve after an exam. Detail the point values of all graded work: in-class and homework assignments, peer group evaluations, class participation, discussion, electronic communication, tests, papers, projects, and so on. Also comment on the expected number and types of tests and quizzes, homework assignments, and papers. Specify whether lowest-scoring work can be thrown out. Finally, state the grading system you will use (criterion-referenced or a curve), along with percentage breakdowns.

9. *The criteria on which each written assignment, project, and oral presentation will be evaluated,* including your grading system (see Chapter Thirty-One) and your policies regarding revisions and extra credit. As with grade protests that often follow returning exams, the choral call for extra credit can be a nuisance unless your position is firmly established from the start.

10. *Other course requirements aside from those computed in the grade.* If you expect students to participate in class discussions, you must tell them. If you plan to give unannounced, ungraded quizzes to monitor

comprehension, then let it be known from the beginning. It is better to ensure that all students understand your expectations from the start than to spring new rules on them later in the term.

11. *Your policies on attendance and tardiness.* Instructors occasionally debate whether to grade on attendance. As one side argues, how can students learn and contribute to the class without being there? (As Woody Allen once put it, over 90 percent of life is just showing up.) No question, taking and grading on attendance does increase class attendance (Friedman, Rodriguez, & McComb, 2001). But others argue that students should be free to learn as much or as little as they choose by whatever means they choose. However you decide, your syllabus should state your policy.

Including attendance and even tardiness in the final grade (some instructors incorporate it under class participation) is no longer unusual. Absences are a problem at many institutions, especially in required courses (Friedman et al., 2001). Some colleges and universities require instructors to report students who are excessively absent, so you may have to keep attendance even if you don't intend to grade on it. (Check the academic regulations in your institution's course catalogue.) However, most instructors do not count certain absences, such as those for documented medical reasons, documented court obligations, and athletic team commitments

12. *Your policies on missed or late exams and assignments.* Students occasionally have good reasons for missing a deadline or a test, as they do for some absences, and you may want to ask for documentation for the reason given. State whether students can drop one quiz or grade during the term or if a makeup is possible. If you assess penalties for late work, describe them precisely to put to rest any later disputes.

13. *A statement of your and your institution's policies on academic dishonesty, as well as their applications to your course.* Cheating and plagiarism are all too common on campuses, as Chapter Eight documents. Unless you make a strong statement about your intolerance of them, your students may assume that you

are naive or will look the other way. This statement may include a summary of the official procedures you will follow in prosecuting violations and the sanctions a student may suffer. (See your institution's course catalogue, student handbook, or faculty handbook for details.) If your institution has an honor code, state that you will strictly adhere to and enforce it. Another reason to address academic honesty policies is to spell out how you will apply them to cooperative learning activities and products. Instructors have to devise their own rules on small-group work. If you don't detail your rules, one of two things is likely to happen: your students may inadvertently violate your and your institution's policies, or they may not work as cooperatively as you'd like.

14. *A statement of your institution's policies on Americans with Disabilities Act (ADA) accommodations.* The office at your institution that provides these accommodations should be able to furnish you with such a statement.

15. *Policies on classroom decorum and academic discourse.* Classroom and general social incivility has increased in recent years, and having policies and ground rules defining appropriate and inappropriate behavior can go far in preventing class disruptions, name-calling, personal attacks, and other demonstrations of disrespect. State any consequences for disruptive behavior specifically and clearly, and explain the nature of, value of, and rules for civil discussion. Chapter Seven sets out recommended policies.

16. *Proper safety procedures and conduct for laboratories.* While you would hope that students would have the common sense to apply good safety habits to their work, you cannot assume that these habits are intuitive. Specify strict rules for lab dress and procedures. If you threaten to exact penalties for safety violations, then stand ready to make good on your word. Remember that it is better to take away a few lab points than to risk the safety of the entire section. (See Chapter Twenty-Two.)

17. *Relevant campus support services for students and their locations* for assistance in mastering course software, doing computer assignments, writing papers

or lab reports, learning study skills, and solving homework problems. The Appendix identifies these resources on the typical campus.

18. *Other available study or assignment aids.* If you plan to distribute study guides, review sheets, practice problems, practice essay questions, or advance grading rubrics, students find it helpful to know about them from the start.

19. *A weekly or class-by-class course schedule* with as much of the following as possible: topics to be covered; in-class activities and formats (lecture, guest speaker, class discussion, group work, demonstration, case study, field trip, role play, simulation, game, debate, panel discussion, video, computer exercise, review session, and so on); dates of announced quizzes and exams; and due dates of all reading assignments, written homework, papers, and projects. Be sure to accommodate holidays and breaks.

20. *A concluding legal caveat or disclaimer.* In our litigious society, a few students have filed grievances and even sued faculty for failing to follow the syllabus schedule and policies. Although you may not intend your syllabus to be a legally binding contract, students may think they are not getting their money's worth if you significantly diverge from the syllabus during the course or fail to get through it. Therefore, for your own protection, take note of the last entry in the box, "The Legal Side of the Syllabus."

Three other syllabus items are recommended:

21. *Curricular requirements your course satisfies,* such as general education; writing-, speaking-, or ethics-across-the-curriculum; various majors; and any other graduation requirements that your institution or department has.

22. *Background information about yourself,* such as your degrees, universities you attended, other universities where you have taught or conducted research, and your areas of research. After all, you may be asking your students for some personal and academic information. In addition, most students are keenly interested in you as a professional and a person and appreciate knowing something about you. A little sharing about yourself can also help build their sense of personal loyalty to you.

23. *Your teaching philosophy.* So many faculty write such a statement for job applications and reviews that you might want to append yours to your syllabus or include an abbreviated version in the document, preferably within the first page or so. It can express your commitment to education, your hopes and objectives for your students, your knowledge of how people learn, your view of the mutual rights and obligations between instructors and students, the rapport with students you aim to develop, and your preferred teaching and assessment methods. With it, you can set a fruitful, congenial tone for the term.

The Legal Side of the Course Syllabus

Your course syllabus is generally regarded by your students, your institution, and the courts as a legally binding contract. To protect yourself and meet student needs, you must supply certain information. If you desire flexibility, you must build it into the document. Including the items that follow will help you avoid student complaints, grievances, and even lawsuits:

- Prerequisite courses student should have successfully completed to pass this course—*whether or not* these are stated in the course catalogue.
- How often and when you will answer student email.
- Days and hours you will be accessible to students by phone.
- Policies of your institution on ADA accommodations.

- Policies on missed and late exams and assignments. Describe any penalties clearly and precisely, and state a "no exceptions" policy clearly. Check the academic regulation in your institution's course catalogue so your penalties don't exceed what is allowed.
- Policies on attendance and tardiness. If you require class attendance and on-time arrival and take off any points for lack of attendance or tardiness, you should state academic reasons for your requirements (for example, you conduct learning activities or lecture important materials not in the readings).
- Policies on class participation. If you grade on class participation, be sure you have some sort of written record to back up this part of the grade.
- Policies on academic integrity, including in collaborative work specific to the course. Typically it is best to follow, and to state that you follow, your institution's policy on academic integrity: that you refer all cases of suspected cheating and plagiarism to whatever administrative office is in charge of the matter. Multiple incidents of academic dishonesty therefore have a cumulative impact on students.
- Policies and procedures on lab safety and health if they are applicable.
- Policies on classroom decorum and academic discourse if needed. State any consequences for classroom incivility specifically and clearly, justifying your policies as necessary for optimal student learning.
- Policies on extra credit, even if you will allow none. Your course grading breakdown, such as, 91–100 = A, 81–90 = B, and so on. Assume nothing.
- Caveat or disclaimer regarding your student learning outcomes. You can't guarantee that students will learn to do anything unless they do their part as learners. Therefore, add this or a similar statement after you list your outcomes: "(1) Students may vary in their competency levels on these outcomes, and (2) they can expect to achieve these outcomes *only if* they honor all course policies, attend classes regularly, complete all assigned work in good faith and on time, and meet all other course expectations of them as students."
- Caveat or disclaimer regarding changes to the course. Adding this statement or one like it at the end of your syllabus will give you the flexibility you may need during the term: "The above schedule, policies, procedures, and assignments in this course are subject to change in the event of extenuating circumstances, by mutual agreement, and/or to ensure better student learning."

In addition to these twenty-three items, Grunert's (1997) learning-centered syllabus contains the content of course handouts, such as instructions for assignments, that most instructors distribute during the term. It can also include much more: a letter from the instructor; reading, studying, note-taking, writing-style, and exam-taking tips and aids; a learning-styles inventory and interpretation key; a learning contract; team-building suggestions; and detailed directions for projects, papers, presentations, and portfolios. This type of syllabus can become so long that it deserves and requires a title page and a contents page. To its credit, it provides students with all the tools they need to succeed in your course from the start, and you have all the elements of your course in place.

■ THE GRAPHIC SYLLABUS

A graphic syllabus, like an outcomes map, is a visual tool to communicate your course to students more effectively. Specifically, it is a flowchart, graphic organizer, or diagram of the sequencing and organization of your course's major topics through the term. It may also note the calendar schedule of the topics, the major activities and assignments, and the tests. But however much information it contains, it can't include everything that a regular text syllabus should, so it is meant to be a supplement to, not a replacement for, it. As I have already written extensively about the graphic syllabus (Biktimirov & Nilson, 2003; Nilson, 2002, 2007a), the discussion here will be brief.

Perhaps the best way to understand the concept is to see an example of it. Figure 3.1 displays the

Figure 3.1 Graphic Syllabus of Social Stratification Course

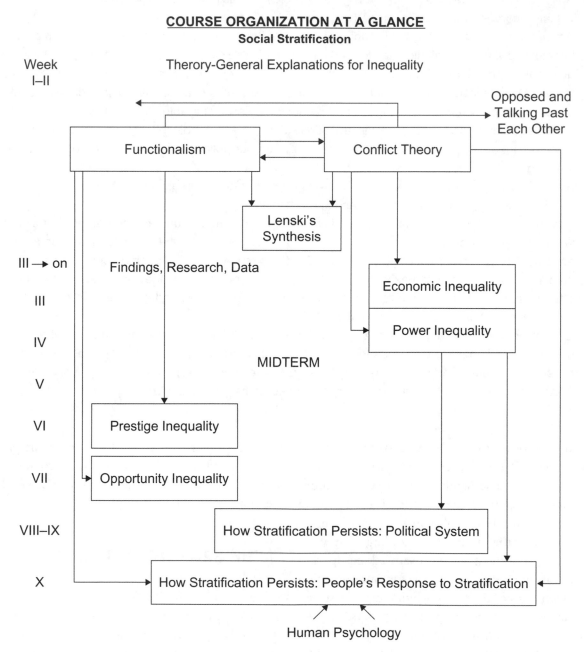

graphic syllabus of an undergraduate Social Strati-fication course I taught at UCLA some years ago. It is fairly simple and unadorned, but it helped my students *see* the complex interrelationships of the weekly topics. For instance, it makes clear that the first three weeks addressed theory and the rest of the course empirical research. It illustrates that one of the two major theories has spawned research on two types of inequality (which support *this* theory), while the other major theory has generated research on two other types of inequality (which support *that* theory). During the last few weeks on how social stratification persists, the graphic shows that one explanation derives only from one major theory and its research, while the second one integrates both major theories and their findings, as well as psychology. The flow of course topics takes on a logic and internal cohesion that a list cannot capture.

Aside from clarifying complex relationships among topics, a graphic syllabus offers many other learning benefits. As explained in Chapter One, it gives students an additional level of understanding of the course material by providing the big pic-ture of your course content—the structure of the knowledge as an integrated whole, a cohesive system of interpreting phenomena. With a knowledge structure already in hand, students are better able to deep-process and retain the material. In addition, a graphic syllabus reveals why you organized the course the way you did. No doubt you put substantial time and mental effort into your course design and topical organization, but without any background in the field, students can't possibly follow your sophisticated logic. They don't know what many of the words mean or how one concept or topic may relate to another. A graphic shows such relationships using spatial arrangements and arrows.

Additional advantages accrue from a graphic syllabus by virtue of its being a visual represen-tation. Students are more likely to comprehend and remember materials they receive both verbally and visually. In addition, they need not expend as much cognitive energy interpreting a graphic as they do interpreting text because visuals require less working memory and fewer cognitive transfor-mations. Graphics especially benefit students with learning styles that reading materials and lectures don't reach effectively—those known as "visual," "concrete," "holistic," "global," "divergent," and "intuitive-feeling," depending on the learning style framework used. (See Chapter Twenty-Five for summaries of some of these frameworks.) Since these learning styles are increasingly common, perhaps dominant, among younger students but relatively rare among college faculty (Schroeder, 1993), it is easy to overlook our students' needs for visuals. Moreover, graphics communicate better than text across cultural and language barriers, so they help meet the learning needs of a diverse student population. Graphics also showcase alternative ways of taking notes, outlining papers, and organizing concepts that students with the learning styles above can really use. Chapter Twenty-Six explains and references the evidence for these learning advantages as they apply to visual representations in general.

One final benefit of designing a graphic syllabus is for you. Not only is the activity a creative right-brain outlet, but it can help you identify any snags in your course organization, such as topics that are chronologically misplaced or missing or don't fit at all.

Bear in mind that a graphic syllabus shows the structure of your course, not the field, its history, or a theoretical model. These may make fine graphics, but under a different name. In addition, a graphic syl-labus should flow in only one direction, as a course does through time. A final warning: Don't make it too complex, cluttered, or detailed. Its intent is to clarify. And do refer to it during the course as you would to a map during a trip.

■ THE ONLINE "LIVING SYLLABUS"

All distance learning instructors have an online syl-labus, and even many classroom instructors have one in addition to a hard-copy version. The beauty of an online syllabus is that it gives you the option to make it dynamic, growing, "living," as Mark A. Wilson at the College of Wooster (2008, p. 1) put it. In the first paragraph on his website for his classroom-based course, History of Life, he informs his students that he will be adding links, images, alternative perspectives on controversial issues, and other information on a weekly basis as the term proceeds, and he requires them to check the site at least once a week.

Those of us who post our course materials on a course management system also add materials during the term—from lecture outlines to homework assignments to review questions. But we usually add them to various folders on our course site and rarely, if at all, put them into the syllabus. The advantage to doing the latter is that students wind up reviewing the syllabus again and again. Depending on where we locate the new material in the document, students may be reminded of the various course requirements, policies, schedule, and previously learned content. Wilson (2008) maximizes the potential value of his students' scrolling through his syllabus by having two content-rich sections of text (350 to 900 words) for each week's topic—Web resources for that week and "Geology in the News"—each studded with links to more information on concepts, proper names, and other subjects he mentions. On the way to the new material he has added for the week, students glance through prior material.

■ GETTING STUDENTS TO READ YOUR SYLLABUS

A solid syllabus says good things about you to your class. Among them, it says that you understand students, how they abhor surprises and last-minute assignments, and how they appreciate a tightly organized, explicit course structure around which they can plan the next few months. It says that you respect them, as well as the subject matter of the course.

Even so, you can't expect students to really study your carefully constructed document. Regularly during the term, instructors field student questions that

are answered in the syllabus. So the challenge is getting students to focus on the document. Although they may not remember every aspect of the course, they should remember where they can look up information. Just reading through the syllabus out loud during your first class meeting isn't enough, and besides, you have other matters to tend to during that class period (see Chapter Four). Here are four more effective options.

First, if your syllabus is not too long, have your students read it in class; then break into small groups to do one of several possible syllabus activities. For instance, they can simply discuss the document and answer each other's questions about it. Alternatively, you may want to structure their discussion around some question, such as: "Compared to the other courses you've taken in college, do you expect this one to be more or less difficult [or require more or less time], and why?" For another possible activity, Ballard (2007) had her students make a list of questions that they should never ask her, since the answers are in the syllabus. Perhaps the most gamelike alternative is to send the groups on a scavenger hunt for certain critical information in the document. You might want to bring some small rewards for the students in the quickest and most thorough group.

Another option is to assign the syllabus as homework, answer questions about it the second day of class, then have each student sign a contract with statements like these: "I have thoroughly read the course syllabus and understand its contents. I understand the course requirements and the grading and attendance policies stated in the syllabus" (T.I.D. Campbell, personal communication, September 27, 2001).

A third alternative, especially for a long syllabus, is to assign it as homework and give a graded test on it the second day of class (Raymark & Connor-Greene, 2002). The test items need not be all factual questions on the number of tests, the point value of assignments, and the like. You can ask interesting and thought-provoking short-answer and short-essay questions, such as: "Which of the student learning objectives for this course are most important to you personally, and why?" "Of the four papers assigned, which are you least (or most) looking forward to writing, and why?" "Which of the grading criteria for your oral presentation play most to your strengths as a learner or a speaker?" Answers to these questions will give you insights into your students' aspirations, interests, insecurities, and self-assessments. Such questions will also motivate your students to think about the value of your course to them personally and professionally.

One final option is to distribute your syllabus the first day but wait to review it in class until the third week of the term or so, after your enrollment stabilizes and students start to care about the course requirements, assignments, and grading (F. A. McGuire, personal communication, October 12, 2007). This is just-in-time learning at its purest, and you are almost guaranteed an interested audience. Of course, you will still have to refer your class to immediately

needed information on the first day, such as course prerequisites, your office hours and contact information, ADA accommodations, safety procedures and conduct (if applicable), classroom conduct policies, and early reading assignments.

■ THE EVOLVING SYLLABUS

Over the past few decades, the syllabus has evolved from a short, sterile list of required readings, topics, assignments, and dates to an elaborate, detailed blueprint for a carefully constructed learning experience. The document has even added several opportunities for instructors to place their personal trademarks, as well as graphic counterparts and dynamic online possibilities. It is rare for an official document to undergo such a radical transformation so quickly.

CHAPTER 4

Your First Day of Class

Whether you are teaching for the first time or are a seasoned classroom veteran, the first day of class can evoke anxiety as well as excitement. Like no other day, it affects the tenor of the entire term. It may also represent innovations and experiments in course content, organization, and design; teaching formats and techniques; and assessment methods—not to mention all those new student faces. This chapter suggests ways to reduce the anxiety, heighten the excitement, and start off the course on a positive, professional, and participatory note. It should be particularly useful to newer instructors. With some adaptation, these strategies apply to online courses as well.

■ BEFORE THE FIRST CLASS

You probably prepared your course materials well before the start of the term. If you have posted materials on your course management site or independent website, check that everything that you want to be there *is* there. Avoid the copying machine bottleneck (and the often resulting malfunctions) by making copies of your first-day handouts as far in advance as you can.

Along with course materials, prepare your agenda for the first class. This chapter contains a range of productive activities to choose from. It may be wise to divide your selections into "essential" and "desirable as time remains." Practice your first-day presentations and your directions for the activities in advance.

A day or two before your first class, tend to some classroom details. First, inspect the room to ensure that all of the technology that you will need (hardware, software, overhead projector) is there and in working order and that you know how to access and operate it. Don't forget low-tech needs like chalk, whiteboard markers, and erasers. Check the lights, the clock (if any), and the heating and air-conditioning system as well. If anything is missing or awry, ask your department to correct the problem. Then take a few moments to orient yourself to the setting. Stand in

43

the front of the room and imagine the seats filled with your students. Make eye contact with the sectors of your imaginary class, walk out toward them, move about the room, and practice smiling.

At least a half-hour before the first class, start preparing yourself—specifically, your body and your voice. You want to project a successful instructor persona to your class—one of relaxed confidence, goodwill, and an in-command, no-nonsense presence. This will inspire your students' respect for your authority, their confidence in you, their goodwill in return, and their willingness to honor your rules and policies. Plus, you want to convey enthusiasm, passion, dynamism, and charisma so you can get their attention and keep them engaged for the entire class. If you don't think you're naturally relaxed, confident, in command, and charismatic, take heart in knowing that you can look as if you are by practicing certain behaviors that are listed in Chapter Seven under "Preventing Incivility: Your Classroom Persona." Furthermore, you can make these behaviors come more easily and naturally by performing a few exercises shortly before class.

To make your body more relaxed, more fluid, looser, and seemingly larger—meaning that you will fill up your life space—do the following in this order:

- Ground yourself by standing up straight with your feet about a foot apart, and feel them securely anchored in the ground.
- Breathe slowly and deeply from your diaphragm three or more times. As you inhale, you should feel your ribs and stomach expanding. Breathe in through your nose (which cleanses the air) and out through your mouth (to exhale more completely). Oxygen works wonders for shaky nerves and cloudy brains.
- Stretch every part of your body in every direction. It is best to stretch slowly until you feel a twinge of strain, then hold the pose for a moment. For your spine, bend over all the way forward, then backward and to each side. Roll your neck and your shoulders, stretch out your arms, and do a few squats and lunges for your legs and thighs.

Stretching relaxes and loosens your muscles while increasing circulation and your overall energy.
- Shake out your hands and feet as though you were shaking off tension.
- Move your eyes from side to side and up and down to prepare for making eye contact all over a room.

This next series of exercises will increase your vocal variety, resonance, articulation, and projection:

- Sing scales up and down a few times.
- Say one or more words at alternating high and low pitches, as high and low as your voice can go.
- Read a children's book aloud with all the exaggeration in vocal variety and speaking pace that you can muster.
- Stretch your mouth and lips in every direction, or exaggerate their movement while saying long, complex words.

Actors and singers do similar exercises every time before they perform. Teaching involves performance as well, and our bodies and voices are our instruments. These exercises may be most important before your first class of the term, but you will enhance your classroom presence by doing them before your first class every teaching day.

If you are new to teaching, have strategies at hand to combat any sudden case of stage fright. (Of course, there is no substitute for having practiced your first-day presentation and directions in advance.) Just before you begin class, take a few long, slow, deep breaths and balance yourself by focusing on some spot on the wall or an inanimate object in the room. You might also try looking just over the heads of your students for the first few minutes (but no longer, or students will notice). Or visualize yourself conducting a one-on-one tutorial instead of talking to a class. Always feel free to take a quiet moment to breathe and collect your thoughts. Remember that many students are impressed by anyone with the courage to speak in public and are forgiving of the occasional lapse of continuity.

■ FIRST IMPRESSIONS

What you do and do not do the first day of class will affect your students' and even your own expectations and behavior for the rest of the term. So think ahead of time about the expectations and behaviors you want to establish in your classroom for the next ten to fifteen weeks. Lay out these expectations and lead the kind of class activities that model the level of student engagement you have in mind for the rest of the course. For example, if you hope for considerable discussion, engage your students in discussion, perhaps about their expectations of the course or their current conceptions of the subject matter. If you intend to have several in-class writing exercises, start with a short one that first class. If you plan on using cooperative learning, have a small-group activity the first day.

No doubt you want to establish a serious, professional classroom atmosphere, and you communicate this tenor in several ways. First, have a comprehensive, well-structured syllabus ready to distribute (see Chapter Three). It tells your class that you are careful, well organized, conscientious, and serious about teaching. Make extra copies for last-minute enrollees, and bring extras with you during the first two weeks of class.

Second, say a few words to market the course and the material. Enthusiasm is contagious. Showing some of your own for the subject matter and the opportunity to teach it will motivate your students' interest in learning it and inspire their respect for you as a scholar.

Third, dress a little more formally than you normally would, at least if you're inclined to more casual attire. A touch of formality conveys professionalism and seriousness. It also gives instructors who are female, youthful looking, or physically small an aura of authority and a psychological edge that help separate them from their students (Johnston, 2005; Roach, 1997).

Since you expect students to be prompt, set a good example from the start. Arrive in the classroom early, and set a welcoming tone by chatting with students informally as they arrive. Make students feel comfortable with you as a person as well as an instructor, but don't confuse your roles; remember the difference between being friendly and being friends.

Not only are you not friends, but students expect you to maintain an orderly, civil classroom, with or without their voluntary cooperation. If you don't, your teaching effectiveness and their respect for you will suffer. In fact, many students were never socialized to arrive to class on time, stay seated the whole period, speak only when sanctioned by the instructor, or show respect to both the instructor and their peers. You have to give them—and enforce—your rules of classroom decorum. The first (or second) day of class is the optimal time to set up a code of conduct for the term, and the students who come already motivated to learn will love you for it. Chapter Seven offers several effective approaches to getting this somewhat unpleasant job done without alienating your class.

Finally, make productive use of the entire class period. The rest of this chapter suggests several social and content-oriented activities that you can organize, even if the students have no background in the subject matter. The most important point is not to waste the first class—not to treat it as a throwaway day or dismiss it early. Only if you treat class time like the precious commodity that it is will your students do so as well.

■ EXCHANGING INFORMATION

Information flow should be a two-way street, even (and perhaps especially) on the first day. But you as the instructor initiate the exchange, first by displaying the following information before class convenes: the name and number of your course, the section number (if appropriate), the meeting days and times, your name, your office location, and your office hours. This information assures students that they are in the right place.

The next several activities need not come in the order presented, but they are strongly recommended for setting an open and participatory as well as professional tone for the rest of the term.

Student Information Index Cards

Get to know your students, and let them know that you are interested in them personally, by passing out blank index cards and asking them to write down this information for you: their full name, any preferred nickname, their year in school, their major, and their previous course work in the field. Additional information such as hometown, outside interests, and career aspirations may help you relate class material to your students on a more personal level. Consider also asking them to write out what they expect from this course, why they are taking it (again, aside from requirements), or what topics they would like to see addressed. You may be able to orient the material toward some of their interests and advise those with erroneous expectations to take a more suitable course.

Your Background

Since you're asking students about themselves, it's only fair to tell them something about yourself. (They *are* interested.) You needn't divulge your life history, but giving them a brief summary of your educational and professional background, orally or in your syllabus, helps reinforce your credibility as an instructor and your humanness as a person. A bit of openness also enhances your students' personal loyalty to you.

Include some information about your own research and interests, what attracted you to your discipline, why you love teaching it, and the implications and applications of the subject in the world. See this as an opportunity to make the material more relevant to your students.

Course Information

Mark on your copy of the syllabus the points you want to elaborate, clarify, and emphasize. For instance, do mention your office hours and urge students to seek your help outside class (see Chapter Nine). But

rather than reading through the whole document, consider choosing one of the options under "Getting Students to Read Your Syllabus" in Chapter Three. The first one describes several syllabus activities in which small groups of students discuss the document, raise questions about it, or find information in it. These are ideal for the first day of class. Two other options are to assign the syllabus as homework and follow up with a test or a contract at the next class meeting. Don't otherwise expect students to read the syllabus carefully.

Whether you share your teaching philosophy, explain why you've chosen the teaching and assessment strategies you plan to use and what benefits they have over other reasonable options, especially if your methods are innovative or collaborative. Your explanation will not only reassure students of your professionalism and commitment to their learning but also reduce their resistance to unusual formats. They will also see your effort as a sign of respect for them.

In turn, clearly state your expectations of students and their responsibilities for preparing for class and participating. For example, if your course calls for considerable discussion, emphasize the importance of their doing the readings, your rules for calling on them, and your criteria for assessing their contributions. Also, offer them some advice on how to take notes on discussion; this remains a mystery even to the most verbal students (see Chapter Thirteen). If you plan to lecture at all, give students some pointers on your lecture organization and good note-taking strategies (see Chapter Twelve). You might also share some helpful reading and study skills and problem-solving strategies appropriate to your subject matter.

You cannot possibly anticipate all the questions that students will have, especially about your testing and grading procedures. But here are some likely ones that you should be prepared to field:

- How will you make up the tests?
- What types of questions will they have?
- What kinds of thinking will they require?
- How should students best prepare for them?
- Will you distribute review sheets?

- Will you hold review sessions?
- How will you evaluate papers and other written assignments?
- How many As, Bs, Cs, and so on do you usually give?
- How possible is it for all students to get a good grade?

Reciprocal Interview

This two-way interview, which takes about fifty minutes in small classes, is a structured activity for you and your students to exchange course-related information (Case et al., 2008). You distribute a handout that asks questions like these:

1. What do you hope to gain from this course?
2. How can I help you reach these goals?
3. What concerns do you have about this course?
4. What resources and background in the subject matter do you bring to it?
5. What student conduct rules should we set up to foster the course's success?
6. What aspects of a class or an instructor impede your learning?

Students write their answers to these questions as individuals for the first five minutes and discuss them in groups for the next ten minutes. Then each group spokesperson reports these responses aloud to the class (fifteen minutes). For the second part of the exercise, your handout should also suggest questions to pose to you about your course goals, student expectations, and views on grading. (Students can ask other questions as well.) First as individuals, then back in their groups, students select and develop questions for you, which requires about ten minutes. Then each group spokesperson reads these questions aloud, which you answer over the next ten minutes.

According to student feedback (Case et al., 2008), this activity establishes a comfortable class environment, fosters a sense of community, communicates your openness and commitment to student success, and serves as a social icebreaker. Minority students especially appreciate it. If you plan on a lot of group work and class discussion during the term, this exercise will prepare students to participate.

Learning Students' Names

Most students, especially at smaller and private colleges and universities, expect their instructors to learn their name. Students expect less personal treatment in very large classes (over one hundred students), in which case learning their names will make you a legend. To borrow an old cliché, learning your students' names shows you care. So begin learning and using names to address students early. If you have trouble remembering names, here are some strategies to help you.

You can seat students in specific places and make a seating chart. Students may not prefer a seating chart, but they will tolerate it graciously if you say the reason is to learn their names. Seating them in alphabetical order will probably make learning their names easiest for you, and it ensures that proximity-based small groups will be randomly mixed. In addition, it will facilitate your taking attendance (just look for the empty chairs).

Some instructors learn names by taking notes about each student's physical appearance on the class roster—information such as body shape and size, hair color and length, dress style, age, and any distinguishing physical traits. It is best to conceal such notes from your students' view.

Taking roll in every class helps you learn names as well as take attendance. While learning names, you can also use the roll to call on students more or less randomly as long as you tell your class what you'll be doing. Or you may use the index cards to call on students. Just shuffle them as you would a deck of cards every so often.

Still another strategy is to have students wear name tags or badges or display name cards or tents on their desks. To avoid the hassle of making new name tags or cards for every class, print up permanent, convention-style tags or cards, distribute them at the start of each class, and collect them at the end of each session. This is also a subtle way to take attendance.

If you want to become a legend in a large class, your most effective strategy may be collecting photographs of your students with their names attached and reviewing them over and over. First check to see whether your institution makes the ID photos of the students enrolled in your classes available to you on your course management site. If not, you or your teaching assistant can take digital photographs of individual students or small groups of students; just be sure each person is associated with the right name. Or you can ask your students to give you a picture of themselves with their name on it. Using photographs, you can probably master the names of over a hundred students within a few weeks.

■ SOCIAL ICEBREAKERS: GETTING TO KNOW YOU

If your class size allows it, try to incorporate one or two icebreaker activities on the first day. There are two types: the social or getting-to-know-you variety, which gets students acquainted, and subject matter icebreakers, which motivate students to start thinking about the material. Feel free to move beyond the popular examples given here and devise your own.

Let's first consider some social icebreakers. If you plan on discussion or group work, these smooth the way for broad participation and cooperative group interaction. First-year students in particular appreciate the opportunity to meet other students, including more senior ones, who can serve as role models.

Simple Self-Introductions

Perhaps the simplest social icebreaker is to have students take turns introducing themselves to the class by giving their name, major, maybe their reason for taking the course (once again, aside from fulfilling some requirement), and perhaps something about them that they are proud of having done or become. This activity may work best in a smaller class, however, as

the prospect of speaking in front of a large group of strangers can mildly terrify some students. If you will have your students make speeches or oral presentations in front the class during the term, this first-day exercise can help them get used to the assignments to come.

Three-Step Interviews

Students can share the same type of information with a neighbor. Then, without knowing beforehand the second part of the task, each partner can introduce his or her counterpart to another pair or to the class as a whole. This exercise has the added benefit of teaching careful listening skills (Kagan, 1988).

Class Survey

For an informal class survey like this icebreaker, you do *not* want to use clickers (personal response systems, explained in Chapter Twelve) because you want your students to see who is giving this or that answer. So begin by asking students to raise their hands in response to some general questions: How many students are from [various regions of the country]? East/west of the Mississippi? First year, sophomores, juniors, seniors? How many work full-time? How many are married? How many have children? How many like golf? Reading? How many have traveled abroad? To Europe? To Asia? Then you may venture into opinion questions, perhaps some relevant to the course material. Students soon start to form a broad picture of their class and to see what they have in common. They will find it far easier to interact with classmates who share their interests and backgrounds.

Scavenger Hunt

In this more structured activity, give students a list of "requirements" and tell them to move about the classroom seeking fellow students who meet each one. No one may use a given student for more than one requirement. Some possible requirements are "has been to Europe," "prefers cats to dogs," "has a birthday in the same month you do," "can speak two or more languages fluently," and "cries at movies." The "found" students sign their name next to the requirement they meet. You might give prizes to the three fastest students.

Human Bingo

This icebreaker is a variation on scavenger hunt. Instead of a list of requirements, make a page-size four-by-four table with a different requirement in each box, and give one copy of the table to each student. Be sure your class as a whole can meet all the requirements. As in the scavenger hunt, no one may use a given student for more than one requirement. When a student has all the boxes signed by qualified fellow students, she shouts out, "Bingo!" and gets a prize. Bring a few prizes in case of ties.

The Circles of _____.

Give each student a sheet of paper with a large central circle and other smaller circles radiating from it. Students write their names in the central circle and the names of groups with which they identify most strongly (such as gender, age group, religious, ethnic, racial, social, political, ideological, athletic) in the satellite circles. Then have students move around the room to find the three classmates who are the most or the least similar to themselves.

Like Scavenger Hunt and Human Bingo, this exercise helps students appreciate the diversity in the class, as well as meet their fellow students. This icebreaker also generates homogeneous or heterogeneous groups of four if you need them for another activity.

■ SUBJECT MATTER ICEBREAKERS

This second type of icebreaker stimulates your students' interest in the subject matter and informs you about what they know, think they know, and know they don't know about it. Some of these can also help you identify or confirm their faulty models and misconceptions about the subject matter.

Classroom Assessment Techniques

Classroom assessment techniques (CATs) are ungraded activities and exercises that you assign to your students (often anonymously) so you can appraise their academic skills, intellectual development, self-awareness as learners, reactions to the material, and understanding of the material (Angelo & Cross, 1993). Chapter Twenty-Eight examines CATs as tools to assess student learning in progress, but several of them are designed for the first day of class or the day you introduce a new topic. The Background Knowledge Probe, for example, is a diagnostic test and a stimulus to recall previously learned material. Focused Listing also activates students' prior knowledge. And in a Self-Confidence Survey, students assess how secure they feel about their cognitive and learning skills or their mastery of a body of knowledge, depending on how you design the survey. Such an exercise enhances students' self-awareness as learners along with giving you insight into their cognitive and psychological preparation for your course.

Problem Posting

To whet students' appetites for the material, one particularly useful first-day activity is problem posting (McKeachie, 2002). First, ask students to think about and jot down either problems they expect to encounter with the course or issues they think the course should address. Then act as the facilitator, recording student responses on the board, a slide, or an overhead transparency. To build trust with your class, avoid seeming judgmental, and check the accuracy of your understanding by restating the students' comments and requesting their confirmation.

As the frequency of student suggestions begins to decline, propose stopping. Make sure, however, that the whole class has a chance to contribute, even if you have to coax the quiet members. If some students wish to speculate on how to address any of the points listed, keep a close rein on the discussion so that it does not stray too far afield. Tell students which of their questions the course will address—this gives them something to look forward to—but also be honest about the ones it will not.

Problem posting is useful not only at the beginning of the course, but also later when broaching a particularly difficult topic. The exercise accomplishes several purposes. First, it opens lines of communication between you and your students, as well as among students. Second, it lends validity to their concerns and assures them they're not alone. Third, it reaffirms that you are approachable and as capable of listening as you are of talking. Finally, it encourages students to devise solutions to problems themselves, reducing their reliance on you for the definitive answers.

Commonsense Inventory

Another way to break students into the subject matter, as well as help them grasp its relevance, is to have them respond to a brief inventory or pretest (Nilson, 1981). Assemble five to fifteen commonsense statements directly related to the course material, some or all of which run counter to popular beliefs or prejudices—for example: "Suicide is more likely among women than men." "Over half of all marriages occur between persons who live within twenty blocks of each other." Then have students individually mark each statement as true or false and share their answers in pairs or small groups. You can let your students debate their differences among themselves, or you can thicken the plot by making

each pair or group reach a consensus around certain statements. Have a spokesperson from each group explain and defend its position. After these presentations, you can give the correct answers, which may spark even more debate, or take the cliff-hanger approach and let the class wait for them to unfold during the term.

■ DRAWING CLASS TO A CLOSE

At the end of this first class, you may want to ask students to write down their reactions and hand them in anonymously (McKeachie, 2002). Pose general questions such as: What is the most important thing you learned during this first day? How did your expectations of this course change? What questions or concerns do you still have about the course or the subject matter? Such questions show your interest in students' learning and their reactions to you and your course. You should also give them plenty of time to ask you questions in class.

Finally, and it's worth repeating, do not dismiss the first class early. If you conduct some of the activities in this chapter, the time will be more than adequately filled and productively spent. Not only will your students enjoy an introduction to the course and its subject matter, but they will also have a chance to get acquainted with you and their classmates.

CHAPTER 5

Motivating Your Students

I n the context of education, the term *motivating* means stimulating the desire to learn something. When we in academe use the term, we're usually talking about stimulating students' interest in the subject matter—in other words, *intrinsic* motivation. We want to induce a genuine fascination with the subject, a sense of its relevance and applicability to life and the world, a sense of accomplishment (for its own sake) in mastering it, and a sense of calling to it. But this is only one type of motivation.

Extrinsic motivators are external to one's feelings about the subject matter, and we see them operating in our students strongly enough to eclipse their intrinsic motivation. Among the most powerful are the expectations of significant others, such as parents, spouses, employers, and teachers. Many of today's younger students pursue a major because of its earning potential. For them, high achievement in the form of top grades may mean entrance into a professional or business school and ultimately a high-paying occupation. Other students may care about grades only so they can stay in school or have

someone else pay for it. A few just want to extend their adolescence and put off adult responsibilities. Returning students often have their eye on a promotion or a favorable career change. In the 1960s, some male students were motivated to excel at least in part to stay out of the military during the Vietnam War. To them, their lives depended on decent grades.

While we can't always affect extrinsic forces, we can enhance our subject matter's intrinsic appeal to students, and intrinsic motivators are often more potent than extrinsic ones (Hobson, 2002; Levin, 2001; Svinicki, 2004). We know that motivation isn't fixed, but it isn't easily modified in the short term either (Frymier, 1970). How can we enhance students' intrinsic motivation? Most of us don't feel very successful at doing it. It seems that students come to us either motivated or not, and they leave the same way. Do we have to reduce their extrinsic drive for good grades first? If we do, how can we? If we don't, why can't we be more effective at getting students engaged in our material?

In spite of a huge literature about motivation in psychology and education psychology, we know precious little about the topic. In the educational context, we don't seem to know how to manipulate people's values, attitudes, and belief systems very well, at least not as well as politicians and advertisers seem to know. Yet if it is true that when all is said and done, learning is "an inside job," motivating students is our primary task.

■ WHAT WE KNOW ABOUT MOTIVATION IN LEARNING

The vast body of literature on the relationships among intrinsic motivation, extrinsic motivation, and student performance comes to no clear conclusions. One stance claims that extrinsic rewards undercut intrinsic motivation (Deci, Koestner, & Ryan, 1999; Kohn, 1993), but some say only under certain circumstances: not if the reward is positive feedback and verbal reinforcement (Deci, 1971) and only if the person was intrinsically motivated to begin with (Svinicki, 2004). These findings have been used to argue against grading, but think about it: Does the fact that you get paid for teaching make it less appealing to you? Another contingent finds almost the opposite: that extrinsic rewards have either no effect or an enhancing one on intrinsic motivation (Cameron & Pierce, 1994; Eisenberger & Cameron, 1996). Still others say the two types of motivators have interactive curvilinear effects on student performance, which is optimized by moderate extrinsic motivation coupled with high intrinsic motivation (Lin, McKeachie, & Kim, 2001). Yet another position is that autonomy of action trumps intrinsic-extrinsic distinctions (Rigby, Deci, Patrick, & Ryan, 1992; Ryan & Deci, 2000). On the extreme end is the argument that intrinsic motivation simply doesn't exist ("Intrinsic Motivation Doesn't Exist, Researcher Says," 2005). A related body of research has addressed the impact of performance goals. Performance-avoidance goals (to avoid looking incompetent) clearly undermine motivation, but the effects of performance-approach goals (to look competent) on both motivation and performance have been positive in some studies and negative in others (Urdan, 2003).

Fortunately, a couple of studies have solicited college students' opinions of what makes them want to learn, so we have a good idea of what students think motivates them. Sass (1989) found the critical factors to be the instructor's enthusiasm for the material and teaching it, the high relevance of the material, the clear organization of the course, the appropriateness of the difficulty level, active learning strategies, variety in the instructor's teaching methods, the instructor's rapport with the students, and the use of appropriate examples. These are all known to be highly effective in enhancing both student learning and student ratings. More recently, Hobson (2002) identified the most powerful positive and negative motivators for students. In order of descending importance, the former are the instructor's positive attitudes and behaviors, a cohesive course structure, a student's prior interest in the material, the relevance of the course content, and the appropriateness of the performance measures. The most potent demotivators are the instructor's negative attitudes and behaviors and a disorganized course structure. Further down on the list are a poor learning environment, boring or irrelevant course content, and a student's prior disinterest in the material.

To the extent students perceive themselves accurately, these findings are good news. Although we cannot control students' attitudes about our material before they come into our courses, we definitely have control over our own attitudes and behavior and the learning environment, and we usually determine the course organization, course content, and assessment measures.

■ CREDIBLE THEORIES OF MOTIVATION

Before we explore concrete strategies for enhancing students' motivation, let's consider the major theories that anchor these strategies. In everyday practice, these models work best when two or more are applied together.

Behaviorism

Behaviorism posits two types of reinforcement as powerful shapers of behavior. In the positive variety, students get (are rewarded with) something they want for their behavior, and in the negative type, they avoid something they don't want for the behavior. Either way, the students are the acting agents, and the reinforcement makes them more likely to repeat the behavior. Punishment following a behavior will tend to decrease that behavior's likelihood in the future, but with less effectiveness than reinforcement. Again there are two types. In one type, students get something they don't want for their behavior, and in the other, they are deprived of something they do want for the behavior. The problem is that punishment teaches students what not to do, but it tells them nothing about what they should do.

While behaviorist theory is straightforward and rings true, the key to applying it is determining what students (and people in general) do and do not want. All around the world, the educational system rests on grades as the universal student currency, but even they don't always motivate and they certainly aren't sufficient. But this is not to say that were it not for our institutional obligation to give grades, we should abandon behaviorism in teaching.

In fact, Darby Lewes applies behaviorist principles very effectively in her English literature courses at Lycoming College, a small, private liberal arts institution (Lewes & Stiklus, 2007), and her secret has nothing to do with grades. At the beginning of every course, she confronts her students' natural aversion to the subject matter—one rooted in their fear of failure, a fear they acquired over years of schooling. Until we conquer this aversion, she contends, students will not learn the material at a deep level no matter what we do or don't do. So early in the term she motivates students to think about a piece of literature and participate in class discussion about it by rewarding each good-faith contribution with a quarter—yes, a

twenty-five-cent piece. Money is a more universal currency than grades. A quarter isn't much, and it's only a secondary reinforcer (of value only when exchanged), but it motivates her students to partake in literature from the beginning, which is no mean feat.

Lewes doesn't give out quarters willy-nilly all term. First, she doesn't always give one out for a second contribution during a class, thereby inducing the talkative students to hang back and the quiet ones to speak out. Second, since the effect of pure positive reinforcement weakens over time, she soon replaces regular reinforcement with the selective variety, rewarding only high-quality contributions with a quarter. At this point, the reward provides informational feedback about the relative strength of varying responses, and by this time, she has overcome students' natural aversion to literature. In addition, the delay students encounter in earning the next quarter enhances their motivation to work harder and develop their answers more fully. Third, she incorporates regularly scheduled negative reinforcers—in the form of daily quizzes on the readings—to ensure her students are keeping up. Finally, she reserves a jackpot of a ten-dollar bill for extremely special occasions, such as when especially resistant or fearful students volunteer worthy responses. The prospect of earning ten dollars has made Lewes legendary among students at her college, and anyone who has ever observed gambling knows how the possibility of a jackpot positively reinforces behavior. But rather than risking money, these students are learning.

Lewes's approach may be controversial, but her students respond well to it and give her teaching high ratings. They acquire confidence and pride as they learn. Many of them even acquire a taste for literature. It's hard to argue with this kind of success.

Goal Orientation

Students who work primarily for good grades have what is called a *performance goal* orientation. They aim to display higher competency than others and to avoid making mistakes and "failing" in front of others. Given the stakes, they tend to eschew risk taking.

For them, learning often exerts stress on their self-esteem and induces insecurity. By contrast, students who work out of a desire to learn have a *learning goal* orientation. Because they don't care about what others may think of their performance, they willingly take risks, make mistakes, and seek feedback so they can improve. As instructors, we want to foster this type of goal orientation because it engenders deeper learning and retention of our material than does the former (Dweck & Leggett, 1988).

Using this model, we can encourage learning over performance goals by doing what we can to create a safe and secure classroom environment, reduce students' stress over tests and assignments, deemphasize grades and competition, allow alternate ways to satisfy course requirements, reward risk taking and persistence, and role model a learning goal orientation (Svinicki, 2004). Specific ways to implement these recommendations are under "Strategies for Motivating Students" below.

Relative Value of the Goal

This social cognitive model posits that the more value students give to learning our material, relative to meeting other needs in life, the more motivated they will be to learn (Bandura, 1997). Therefore, we have to create experiences in which their learning serves important needs. In other words, we must add value to their learning.

The purest value we add to our material is to make it more stimulating, interesting, and emotionally engaging—that is, more intrinsically motivating. But we shouldn't stop there. We can also enhance its value by giving students some control and choice over the course content, their learning strategies, and their performance options. In addition, we can highlight its practical utility to students, for now and in the future. Going deeper into the human psyche, we can position our material to meet some immediate psychological needs, such as those for cognitive balance, social affiliation and approval, and self-esteem. For instance, we can help students put their learning toward resolving inconsistencies in their beliefs, values,

and worldview. We can also make their learning more of a social than an individual enterprise. Finally, we can give students a taste of achievement by encouraging them to tackle some genuine learning challenges and rewarding them accordingly (Svinivki, 2004). Again, more specifics are in the section on strategies later in this chapter.

Expectancy of Goal Achievement

Expectancy theory rests on a pragmatic premise: Why aspire to achieve something you know you can't get? Students won't even try to learn something that seems impossibly difficult. To set and pursue a goal, students need to believe they have the agency and the capability. Agency depends on their sense of self-efficacy and their beliefs about the malleability of intelligence and locus of control. Students with low self-confidence, the view that intelligence is fixed by heredity, or the fatalist belief in an external locus of control have a weak sense of agency and a low expectancy of goal achievement. Capability depends on their perception that the goal is reachable and that they have (or soon will have) the skills, prior experience, and support to reach it. Students feel capable when they view the learning task as doable, given their abilities, academic background, and resources: time, encouragement, assistance, and so on (Wigfield & Eccles, 2000).

Although it can be hard to find the right balance, we have to try to make our readings, assignments, and tests just right—that is, neither too long and hard nor too short and easy. But just as important, we must foster our students' beliefs that they have the agency and capabilities to achieve. Too many students sailed through the K–12 system and never had to meet an academic challenge before coming to college. While they may have high self-esteem, they may have a weak sense of self-efficacy at the college level. They may even sabotage their own success by not studying in order to protect their self-esteem since, if they do poorly, they can blame their lack of studying rather than their lack of ability. It is likely that such students also believe that they can't raise their intelligence.

Other students don't believe they have control over their academic fate. In their experience, studying and working hard seems to make little difference in their grades. They feel they just get lucky when they encounter readings they can understand, test questions they can answer, and assignments they can handle. In their view, most of the control resides in us. Sometimes they get an instructor who likes them and what they produce, but most instructors don't. With this belief system, students don't perceive themselves earning an A, a C, or an F; rather, they truly think that we give them an A, a C, or an F. While it is true that faculty grading criteria and standards may vary, many of these students lack basic learning skills. They don't know how to focus their mind, read carefully, take decent notes, think critically, study effectively, and write clearly. Without these skills, they may fall short—not on the agency but on the capability to achieve an academic goal. To foster their success, we need to refer them to the campus resources that can help them learn how to learn and to communicate (see the Appendix) and to do what we can to help them.

Many other specific suggestions for enhancing students' sense of agency and capability, and therefore their expectancy to achieve, are set out in the next section.

■ STRATEGIES FOR MOTIVATING STUDENTS

Happily, effective motivational techniques and effective teaching techniques greatly overlap. Of course, by definition, more motivated students want to learn more, so they achieve more. But it is also true that better teaching generates more rewarding learning experiences, which beget more motivation to learn. It is not surprising, then, that you motivate students using the same methods and formats that you do to teach them effectively. To reach as many students as possible, use as many of the following strategies as you can (Biggs, 2003; Cashin, 1979; Ericksen, 1974; Gigliotti & Fitzpatrick, 1977; Hobson, 2002; Levin,

2001; Marsh, 1984; Owens, 1972; Panitz, 1999; Paulsen & Feldman, 1999; Sass, 1989; Svinicki, 2004; Theall & Franklin, 1999; Watson & Stockert, 1987).

Your Persona

- Deliver your presentations with enthusiasm and energy. Strive for vocal variety and constant eye contact. Vary your speaking pace, and add dramatic pauses after major points. Gesture and move around the class. Be expressive. To your students, be they right or wrong, your dynamism signifies your passion for the material and for teaching it. As a display of your motivation, it motivates them (see Chapters Seven and Twelve).

- Explain your reasons for being so interested in the material, and make it relevant to your students' concerns. Show how your field fits into the big picture and how it contributes to society. In so doing, you also become a role model for student interest and involvement.

- Make the course personal. Find out your students' birthdays, and when one comes along, put up a slide with "Happy Birthday, ___!" on it. Email students with your concern if they haven't been in class for a couple of days. Write students congratulatory letters when they do well on a test.

- Get to know your students. Ask them about their majors, interests, and backgrounds. This information will help you tailor the material to their concerns, and your personal interest in them will inspire their personal loyalty to you (see Chapter Four).

- Foster good lines of communication in both directions. Convey your expectations and assessments, but also invite your students' feedback in the form of classroom assessment exercises (see Chapter Twenty-Eight) and some form of midterm evaluation (for example, your own questionnaire or some type of class interview conducted by your institution's teaching center).

- Use humor where appropriate. A joke or humorous anecdote lightens the mood and has the synapse-building benefits of emotional intensity (see Chapter One). Just be sensitive to context, setting, and audience.

- Maintain classroom order and civility to earn your students' respect as well as to create a positive learning environment (see Chapter Seven).

Your Course

- Design, structure, and develop your course with care, and explain its organization and your rationale for it to your students (see Chapter Two).
- Allow students some voice in determining the course content, policies, conduct rules, and assignments. If they have input, they will feel more invested and responsible for their learning.
- Build in readings and activities that will move students beyond their simplistic dualistic beliefs about your field (see Chapters One and Two). The constricted, naive view of "learning" as memorizing definitions and facts isn't very motivating.
- Highlight the occupational potential of your subject matter. Inform students about the jobs and careers that are available in your discipline, what attractions they hold, and how your course prepares students for these opportunities. Whenever possible, link new knowledge to its usefulness in some occupation.
- For numerous ways to motivate students to do the readings on time, see Chapter Twenty-Three. When students come prepared, you can fill class time with engaging and intrinsically motivating activities.

Your Teaching

- Explain to your class why you have chosen the teaching methods, readings, assignments, in-class activities, policies, and assessment strategies that you are using.
- Help students realize that they can transfer skills they have learned in other courses into yours and vice versa.
- Make the material and learning activities meaningful and worthwhile to students by connecting them to their futures and the real world.

- Use examples, anecdotes, and realistic case studies freely. Many students learn inductively, experientially, and concretely.
- Use a variety of presentation methods to accommodate various learning styles (see Chapter Twenty-Five).
- Teach by inquiry when possible. Students find it satisfying and intrinsically motivating to reason through a problem and discover underlying principles on their own (see Chapter Eighteen).
- Use a variety of student-active teaching formats and methods, such as discussion, debates, press conferences, symposia, role playing, simulations, academic games, problem-based learning, the case method, problem solving, writing exercises, and so on—all covered in later chapters. These activities directly engage students in the material and give them opportunities to achieve a level of mastery for achievement's sake.
- Share strategies and tips for them to learn your material, including reading, studying, and thinking about it. Also teach students relevant problem-solving strategies.
- Use cooperative learning formats. They are student active and add the motivational factor of positive social pressure. But be sure you set up and manage the groups properly (see Chapter Sixteen).
- Bring the arts into your teaching to stir student emotions. This is a standard culture-learning strategy in the foreign languages, but it has far broader application. In mathematics courses, you can show the utility of concepts and equations in visual design and musical composition. In history, anthropology, literature, and comparative politics courses, you can acquaint students with the art of the age or place. If possible, you can have them read native literature and listen to native music. Such experiences give students an intuitive feel for other times and places.
- Make the material accessible. Explain it in common language, avoiding jargon where possible.
- Hold students to high expectations. Refuse to accept shoddy work. Give it back to them ungraded

and tell them they have to do the assignment again at a high level of quality to get credit.

- Use Lewes's progressive behaviorist method to overcome your students' aversion to the material and reinforce their thoughtful contributions to discussion.

Assignments and Tests

- Reinforce the idea that all students can improve their cognitive and other abilities with practice and are in control of their academic fates. In other words, build up their sense of self-efficacy and their belief in an internal locus of control.
- Provide many and varied opportunities for graded assessment so that no single assessment counts too much toward the final grade.
- Give students plenty of opportunity to practice performing your learning outcomes before you grade them on the quality of their performance.
- Sequence your learning outcomes and assessments to foster student success.
- Give students practice tests.
- Provide review sheets that tell students what cognitive operations they will have to perform with key concepts on the tests. In other words, write out the learning outcomes you will be testing them on.
- While students must acquire some facts and terminology to master the basics of any discipline, focus your tests and assignments on their conceptual understanding and ability to apply the material, and prepare them for the task accordingly. Facts are only tools with which to construct broader concepts and are thus means to a goal, not goals in themselves.
- Set realistic performance goals, and help students achieve them by encouraging them to set their own reasonable goals. Striving to exceed a personal best is a mighty motivator.
- Design assignments that are appropriately challenging given the experience and aptitude of the class. Those that are either too easy or stressfully difficult are counterproductive.

- Assess students on how well they achieve the learning outcomes you set for them, and remind them that this is what you are doing.
- Allow students options for demonstrating their learning, such as choices in projects and other major assignments.
- Design authentic assignments and activities—those that give students practice in their future occupational and citizenship activities.
- Give assignments that have students reflect on their progress. For example, have students write a learning analysis of their first test in which they appraise how they studied and how they can improve their studying.
- Evaluate work by an explicit rubric (a specific set of criteria with descriptions of performance standards) that students can study and ask questions about before they tackle an assignment.
- Place appropriate emphasis on testing and grading. Make tests fair, which means consonant with your learning outcomes, topical emphases, and previous quizzes and assignments. Tests should be a means of showing students what they have mastered, not what they haven't.
- Give students prompt and constant feedback on their performance, as well as early feedback on stages and drafts of major assignments.
- Accentuate the positive in grading. Be free with praise and constructive in criticism and suggestions for improvement. Acknowledge improvements made. Confine negative comments to the particular performance, not the performer.
- Let students assess themselves. Of course, you must teach them how to do this first.
- Show your students instances of peers who have succeeded.
- Reduce the stress level of tests by lowering the stakes—for example: Test early and often. Drop the lowest quiz or test score. Let students write explanations for their multiple-choice and true-false item answers. Provide chances for them to earn back some of their lost points.

- Use criterion-referenced grading instead of norm-referenced grading (see Chapter Thirty-One). The former system allows all the students in a class to get high grades.
- Use contract grading for some of your assignments or your entire course. Contract grading (or contract learning) means assigning grades according to how well students fulfill certain work requirements (as specified in the syllabus or an appendix to it)—not according to what grade they aspire to earn. To get higher grades, they have to successfully complete either more work that shows evidence of more learning or more challenging work that shows evidence of more advanced learning. Under these conditions, students are often more motivated to learn because they have a greater sense of choice of assignments, self-determination, and responsibility for their grade, as well as less fear about creative risk taking and grade anxiety (see Chapter Thirty-One).
- Give extra credit or bonus points (or the chance to earn back lost points) only for work that depends on students' having done their regular assigned work. For example, Golding (2008) increased her class attendance and on-time homework turn-ins by giving students bonus problems to work on at the beginning of class in exchange for their assigned homework problems.

▮ EQUITY IN THE CLASSROOM

Equity and its opposite have a powerful impact on student motivation, and thus achievement. Not that instructors purposely show favoritism, but research documents that some have, however unconsciously. K–12 teachers have sometimes praised (or at least have failed to punish) boys for being aggressive but have discouraged girls from acting similarly. Many college instructors have expressed this same bias by allowing males more time to respond to discussion questions and giving disproportionate approval to males' marginal answers. Females, as well as minority and disabled students, have been more likely to be ignored or interrupted and their correct answers merely accepted (Hall & Sandler, 1982; Krupnick, 1985; Sadker & Sadker, 1992).

No doubt classrooms have become more equitable over recent years. But this progress began as instructors became aware of the unconscious dynamics just described. The following guidelines translate this awareness into behavior (Guo & Jamal, 2007; Jones, 2004; Toombs & Tierney, 1992):

- Create a safe climate for the expression of different points of view. Set ground rules for civil discussion in class, and intervene if any students act disrespectfully to others (see Chapter Seven).
- Give attention to all students as equally as possible. After asking a question, lengthen your wait time by ten to fifteen seconds to allow more students to mentally prepare their responses before you call on anyone. This will help you broaden participation.
- Praise students equally for equal-quality responses.
- Use nonstereotypical examples in presentations. If you use a female in an example, make her a scientist, an accountant, or a surgeon rather than a nurse, a teacher, or a secretary.
- When possible, integrate course content that includes the contributions and perspectives of both genders and all cultural, ethnic, and racial groups that may be represented in your classes.
- Use gender-neutral language. Try to avoid using the pronouns *he* and *him* exclusively when discussing people in general.
- Use pedagogical strategies that appeal to multiple learning styles (see Chapter Twenty-Five). When possible, allow students to choose the mode in which you will assess their learning (paper, poster, Web page, video, oral presentation, art form, concept or mind map, and so on).
- Resist falling into reverse discrimination. Do not give inordinate attention to minority and disabled students, as this may appear to reflect your expectation of their failure.
- Discretely ask your students with disabilities and non-English-speaking backgrounds whether you

can do something in class to make their life easier, such as facing the class when you are talking.

- Be sensitive to difficulties your students may have in understanding you. International, English as a Second Language, and hearing-impaired students may have trouble with idiomatic expressions and accents. Ask such students privately if they do, and urge them to watch your lips and to request clarification.

The "Inclusive Instructing" section in Chapter One and all of Chapter Thirteen on discussion offer many more suggestions for ensuring equity in the classroom. Equity is really about increasing and broadening student participation, not only in discussion but in higher education and beyond. In fact, it is a by-product of the best practices in teaching, so just about every chapter in this book provides recommendations that, at least indirectly, enhance equity.

PART 2

MANAGING YOUR COURSES

CHAPTER 6

Copyright Guidelines for Instructors

As you prepare to teach a course—classroom, online, or hybrid—you will likely bump into the issue of copyright. No doubt you will want to assign, play, or show works of other people beyond the required books, CDs, and DVDs you expect your students to buy.

If so, you have just entered the through-the-looking-glass world of "fair use," "educational purposes," and other such Cheshire categories that make most of us instructors think twice before we press the start button on a copying machine or even consider showing a videotape in class. This is the unwieldy wonderland in which the only legally correct answer to your simplest query may be "probably," "unlikely," and "it depends on the specific case." For example, *Q:* Is a classroom a public place? (This issue may affect the legality of showing a videotape in class.) *A:* Experts disagree and the courts have not yet settled the issue.

In the absence of simple, clear rules of thumb, it is little wonder that we tend to pick up copyright law by word of mouth—and wind up swapping myths and misconceptions. The legal ambiguities only feed our fears of what might happen to us if we were actually caught by the copyright enforcers (whoever they may be) violating their rules, even unknowingly.

The laws, guidelines, and enforcement policies are not well publicized in the academic world and may surprise you. Many of them are highly technical, make questionable sense, and are frankly difficult to absorb and remember. Those governing newer technologies also change as lawsuits are resolved and the U.S. Copyright Office issues new regulations and exemptions, some of which have expiration dates.

All of the legal information in this chapter comes ultimately from Title 17 of the United States Code, which includes the Copyright Act of 1976 and its subsequent amendments—literally dozens of them. The Conference on Fair Use (CONFU, 1995–1997), the Digital Millennium Copyright Act of 1998 (DMCA, one of the amendments to the 1976 law), and the Technology Harmonization and Education Act of 2002 (TEACH Act, another such amendment) set the guidelines for multimedia use and online and distance learning, some of which have an ambiguous legal status. I focus on the fair use exemptions that are granted for educational purposes.

Laws, statutes, and guidelines are written to obfuscate, so credit is due those who interpreted them and served as invaluable factual sources for this chapter: Brinson and Radcliffe (1996), Davidson (2008), Emett and New (1997), Foster (2008a), Harper (2001), Jordan (1996), Nemire (2007), and Orlans (1999).

WHERE COPYRIGHT DOES AND DOES NOT APPLY

Copyright law does not protect facts, ideas, discoveries, inventions, words, phrases, symbols, designs that identify a source of goods, and some U.S. government publications (you must check on each one). This doesn't mean we don't cite the sources of our facts, other people's ideas, and certain key phrases, for example. We just need not ask permission or purchase a license to use them. Many inventions are protected by patent law, yet another realm of intellectual property.

Copyright law does protect creative works, whether literary (fiction and nonfiction), musical (including lyrics), dramatic (including accompanying music), choreographic, sculptural, pictorial, graphic, architectural, audiovisual (including motion pictures), and sound recorded.

COMMON COPYRIGHT MISCONCEPTIONS

Let me dispel some popular misconceptions. First, giving credit to the author of a work is not a way around or substitute for copyright law compliance. All a citation exempts you from is plagiarism. Second, the absence of a copyright notice does not mean the work is not protected. While most works have

a notice, those published on or after March 1, 1989, are protected even without one. Third, changing someone else's copyrighted work here and there will not make it legally yours. In fact, such action may make you doubly liable: for infringement of copying right *and* of the copyright holder's modification right.

Finally, flattering or showcasing a work is not likely to allay the copyright owner's objections to your free use of the work. This is especially true of multimedia works; their producers view licenses as a new source of income. Freelance writers, music publishers, and musical performers have successfully sued major companies like the *New York Times* for the unauthorized publication or distribution of their work on online computer services.

FREE USE: FAIR USE, FACTS, AND PUBLIC DOMAIN

"Free use" means no license or written permission from the copyright holder is required to copy, distribute, or electronically disseminate the work. However, whether a given case qualifies depends on three rather gray criteria: (1) your use is "fair use," (2) the material you wish to use is factual or an idea, and (3) the work you wish to use is in the public domain.

In general, fair use means use for noncommercial purposes and specifically for purposes of teaching, scholarship, research, criticism, comment, parody, and news reporting. The courts are most likely to find fair use where the copied work is a factual as opposed to a creative work. However, no legal guidelines are available to distinguish factual material or an idea from something else; determinations are made on a case-by-case basis. Another consideration is whether the new work poses market or readership competition for the copyrighted work.

The amount and the significance of the protected work used also figures into the determination of fair use. Use of a tiny amount of the work should not raise concerns unless it is substantial in terms of importance—such as the heart of the copied work.

For instance, a magazine article that used 300 words from a 200,000-word autobiography written by President Gerald Ford was found to infringe the copyright on the autobiography. Even though the copied material was only a small part of the autobiography, it included some of the most powerful passages in the work.

Public domain is a clearer legal concept but is sometimes redefined. If published in the United States, a work is now in the public domain if (1) it was published on or before 1923, (2) ninety-five years have elapsed since its publication date if it was published between 1923 and 1977, or (3) seventy years have elapsed since the author's death if it was published after 1977. However, if a work was published between 1923 and 1963 and the copyright owner did not renew the copyright after the twenty-eight-year term that once applied, the work has come into public domain. Corporate works published after 1977 enter the public domain ninety-five years after publication.

The fair use exemption does not permit unlimited copying and distribution. The "privilege" is highly restricted by "guidelines" with legal force, though they are often ambiguous and arcane, and they do not cover all situations. They were negotiated among educators, authors, and publishers. Of course, no copyright exemption excuses you from citing and crediting your sources.

■ PRINTED TEXT

While you may find it restrictive, print media is the realm that most liberally allows fair use. It is, of course, the oldest realm.

Single Copying

As an instructor, you may make single copies, including a transparency or slide, of the following for teaching purposes without obtaining prior permission: a chapter of a book; an article from a periodical or newspaper; a short story, essay, or poem; a diagram, graph, chart, drawing, cartoon, or picture from a book, periodical, or newspaper.

Multiple Copying

You may make multiple copies—specifically, one copy per student in a course—without first obtaining permission if the work meets the criteria of brevity, spontaneity, and cumulative effect and if each copy contains a copyright notice.

The guidelines define the "brevity" criterion in this way: (1) an entire poem printed on no more than two pages or an excerpt from a longer poem, not to exceed 250 words copied in either case; (2) an entire article, story, or essay of fewer than 2,500 words or an excerpt of fewer than 1,000 words or less than 10 percent of the work, whichever is less, but in either event, a minimum of 500 words to be copied; or (3) one chart, graph, diagram, drawing, cartoon, or picture per book or periodical issue. Multiple copying meets the "spontaneity" criterion when you do not have a reasonable length of time to request and receive permission to copy. What a "reasonable length of time" may be is not specified.

The "cumulative effect" is considered acceptably small (permission not required) when your copying is for only one course, and you do not make multiple copies in more than nine instances per term per course. Furthermore, you may not make multiple copies of more than one short poem, article, story, essay, or two excerpts from the same author or more than three from the same collective work or periodical volume in one term.

If you want to copy and distribute entire or multiple works that in any way violate the rules above, you must first obtain permission.

Copying Short Works

Short works such as children's books are often fewer than 2,500 words, and you may not copy them as a whole. All you may reproduce without permission is an excerpt of no more than two published pages containing not more than 10 percent of the total words in the text.

Additional "Privileges" and Prohibitions

You are allowed to incorporate text into your multimedia teaching presentations, as can your students into their multimedia projects.

Notwithstanding the guidelines above, your intentions and the specific work also come into play. You may not make copies under these conditions to create, replace, or substitute for anthologies, compilations, or collective works; substitute for replacement or purchase of "consumable" works such as workbooks, exercises, standardized tests, or answer sheets or of the same item term after term; or if you charge students beyond the copying cost or on direction of a higher authority. In addition, you may make copies for your students in only nine instances per term.

Course Packets

You must limit the materials to single chapters, single articles from a journal issue, and small parts of a work, such as several illustrations, charts, or graphs. Those who sell the packets must put copyright notices on the originals you provide and limit sales to students enrolled in the course for that term. These packets are being replaced by course management systems and electronic reserves, which are governed by somewhat different rules (see below).

■ VISUAL MATERIALS

The guidelines in this section apply only to photographs and illustrations not in the public domain, which never require permission to use. However, if the one you want to use is part of a copyrighted collection, you should obtain permission for use from the copyright holder. Go to www.mpa.org or www.loc.gov to check.

You may use entire single images but no more than five by a single artist or photographer. If you are taking images from a collection, you may use no more than fifteen images or 10 percent of those in the collection, whichever is fewer.

If an image is not designated for sale or license, you may digitize and use it if you obtain prior permission and limit access (password-protect) to enrolled students and other instructors of the course. Furthermore, your students may download, print out, and transmit it for personal academic use, including course assignments and portfolios, for up to two years. You may also use the image at a professional conference.

An alternative to obtaining permission to show copyrighted visual materials is to take and display photographs of them. This option is legal for fair use as long as the quality of the photographic reproductions is lower than that of commercial reproductions, such as professionally produced slides and prints—in other words, as long as the amateur photographs can't compete in the same market (University of Minnesota Libraries, 2007).

Academic art librarians know where to locate specific pictorial, graphic, artistic, and architectural works and what the restrictions for their use may be. The library may already have permission or a license to display certain works. You can find unrestricted fair use materials (no permission required) at the Creative Commons (www.creativecommons.org).

■ IN-CLASS PERFORMANCES

Assuming your institution is accredited, you and your students can freely show videos, play music, recite poetry, read and perform plays, and project slides in a classroom setting. You can show websites or videos off the Web in a live class. None of these actions requires permission. Copying sheet music, however, is restricted to out-of-print music and performances "in an emergency."

You can also play, without prior permission, a DVD, videotape, or musical CD (or excerpts from it) in class that you have legally bought or rented. But here is the murky part: if a videotape or DVD carries the warning "For Home Use Only," the law is unclear on whether you may show it in your classroom. If the classroom is considered a "public place," you may not, but the courts have not resolved this issue. Legal experts reason that you probably can because instructors are clearly permitted to display or perform works in face-to-face teaching situations. Of course, you may show any rented videotape or DVD that has been cleared for public presentation as long as it serves a purely instructional objective. Even the hint of entertainment purposes, such as the presence of nonstudents in the classroom, can raise a legal flag.

Movie studios have built the home video and DVD industry into a multibillion-dollar business, in part by strictly enforcing the distinction between instruction and entertainment. To illustrate, in 1996 the Motion Picture Licensing Corporation, a Los Angeles copyright policing agency representing the studios, sent threatening letters to fifty thousand day care centers across the nation. The letters demanded up to $325 per year for what they termed "a public-performance video license" for showing children's videos (for example, *Pooh and Scrooge*) to their "public" of toddlers. Apparently Hollywood does not regard its standard products as educational and therefore exempt from licensing fees under the fair use (Bourland, 1996).

The rules are also ambiguous about whether you can record a television program off-the-air at home and then show it in class. If it is a commercial program, some experts consider this illegal, while others recommend that you demonstrate compliance with the spirit of the law by following the guidelines for campus media units in the next section.

■ RECORDING BROADCAST PROGRAMMING

The guidelines given here specify what educational institutions (campus media units) can record off-the-air for educational purposes without obtaining a permission or license from the copyright holder.

Broadcast Programming (Major National and Local Stations)

These guidelines apply only to off-the-air recording by nonprofit educational institutions, which are responsible for ensuring compliance:

- DVDs or videotapes may be kept for only forty-five calendar days after the recording date. After this time, they must be erased.
- The recording may be shown to students only during the first ten class days after the recording date and may be repeated only once for reinforcement.
- Off-the-air recordings may be made only at the request of an individual instructor and not in anticipation of an instructor's request. The same instructor can request that the program be recorded only once.
- Duplicate copies may be made if several instructors request the recording of the same program.
- After the first ten classes allowed for showing, the recording may be used only for evaluation, such as for a test.
- Off-the-air recordings may not be edited or combined with other recordings to create a new work or an anthology.
- All videotapes, including copies, must contain a copyright notice when broadcast.

Public Television

The Public Broadcasting Service, the Public Television Library, the Great Plains National Instructional Television Library, and the Agency for Instructional Television have somewhat less restrictive rules for off-the-air recording for educational purposes:

- Recordings may be made by instructors or students in accredited, nonprofit educational institutions.
- Recordings may be used only for instruction in a classroom, lab, or auditorium but are not restricted to one classroom or one instructor.

- The use of recordings is restricted to one institution and may not be shared outside it.
- Length of allowed retention varies.

Cable Channel Programs

Cable channels require you to ask permission to show any of their programming, even for fair use purposes, but instructors may be allowed to keep their recordings for much longer. The rules vary by program.

■ ONLINE/ELECTRONIC MATERIALS AND DISTANCE LEARNING

Course management systems and electronic reserves have pretty much replaced course packets and hard copy library reserves, and millions of courses are delivered in part or entirely online. As with print, online content must be accessible only to the students enrolled in the class and only for that term. But because these materials are digitized, the fair use laws governing them are somewhat different, often murky, and more restrictive than those governing course packets.

For starters, the readings on e-reserve should not comprise more than a small amount of all the assigned reading for the course. As specified in the Digital Millennium Copyright Act of 1998, copyright-protected digital materials also include a wide range of content you might not expect: print and electronic books, analog and digital musical recordings, websites, works embedded in websites, print and email messages and attachments, and possibly even databases. In addition, the Technology Harmonization and Education Act of 2002 requires instructors to add a legal notice in your syllabus that online materials "may" be copyright protected.

Most legal and library authorities argue that you or your institution's library must obtain permission to post any copyrighted digital course content, even when it is available elsewhere on the Internet, is being used in a course for the first time, or is supplemental, unless you get your general counsel's approval to skip obtaining permission. In fact, some university lawyers contend that fair use protection makes permissions unnecessary (Foster, 2008a). Libraries, however, tend to err on the conservative side and routinely obtain permissions.

Probably your easiest alternative is providing your class with links to materials that are already available online through your institution's library, which already has a license or permission to make the materials available. But what if you want to link to sites not in your library? Here again the law is cloudy. Some say you "may" need the permission of the website owner, and others claim you don't. Another safe bet is to use vendor-provided digital content that is sold along with many textbooks (course cartridges, CDs, DVDs). Because the cost includes the copyright license, no restrictions apply to its use.

The legal area surrounding copyright and fair use of electronic materials is the most volatile as well as the most restrictive. Recall that in the traditional face-to-face classroom, you and your students can listen to music, read poems aloud, perform plays, display slides, or play excerpts from a DVD, all without prior permission, as long as the purpose is educational. Between 1997 and 2002, you and your students could not do any of these things electronically under fair use protection. The CONFU guidelines required you to obtain a license. Finally, Congress closed this odd legal gap in mid-2002 when it passed the TEACH Act without debate (after the bill languished for an entire year in the House Judiciary Committee). As the rules stand now, you may without prior permission download images from the Internet for your teaching, and students may do so for their projects. You may do the same for sound and video files, but they are subject to severe length limitations: videos to three minutes or 10 percent, whichever is shorter, and music to 10 percent of the composition, up to a maximum of thirty seconds. The same length limits apply if you or your students take excerpts from a lawfully purchased or rented videotape, DVD, or CD. Permission is required only when you or a student wants to exceed these length limits or to post or repost any of the files online.

Don't even think about trying to get permission to put an entire commercially produced motion picture or musical CD on electronic reserve or online. This would require a very costly license.

Electronic copyright law is unsettled, ambiguous, and subject to challenge from both commercial and educational interests. So stay tuned to the news media, especially the *Chronicle of Higher Education* and the websites listed at the end of this chapter, to keep abreast of the latest legal developments and clarifications. Another good idea is to make materials available in ways that avoid potential trouble. For example, refer your students to URLs rather than incorporating Internet-based text, images, and performances into your online course materials. Also make the most of any vendor-provided digital content that may accompany your textbooks.

OBTAINING PERMISSION OR A LICENSE

Perhaps you wish to reproduce, display, or play a work or a portion of a work that exceeds the length limits or otherwise violates the guidelines just discussed. Or perhaps your campus library or copy center cannot obtain the necessary permissions or licenses in time for you or your students to use the work. You and your students may follow these procedures to obtain them on your own.

Request in writing (email is okay) the permission of the copyright holder (which is not necessarily the author or creator) to reprint, display, or post online, identifying the exact portion of the work, the number of copies you wish to make and distribute or the planned location on the Internet, the expected readership or viewership, and the purpose or planned use of the work (for example, instruction in a given course for a specific term at a given institution). A permission granted for classroom use applies only to one course during one term. Or you can contact the Copyright Clearance Center at www.copyright.com. It offers an electronic service that usually obtains your permission in a day or two.

Or you can request a license of the copyright holder in writing, giving the same precise information as above. Licenses are often required to show a work or portion of a work or to include some nontrivial portion of it in your own scholarship or multimedia production. Licenses always entail fees, but they may be negotiable.

HOW COPYRIGHT VIOLATIONS ARE ACTUALLY HANDLED

So what if you forgot to put a long, important journal article on e-reserve, and you decide to make copies of the whole thing and hand them out to your students in class? What penalties might you face?

The laws state that you face a judgment of up to $100,000 for each willful infringement, and ignorance of the law won't get you off. What may get you off is a convincing argument that you were acting in good faith, believing on reasonable grounds that your case qualified as fair use. Your institution will probably defend you if you follow its fair use policies.

However, the law doesn't always operate by the law. In the educational arena, institutions, not individuals, are usually sued, and very few of these have been over the past several decades. Obviously colleges, universities, school systems, and private K–12 schools have much deeper pockets than their teaching staff. So copyright enforcers send them threatening letters every once in a while to remind them of the law and potential penalties. Sometimes a threat is based on a tip that violations have occurred. (Some enforcement agencies maintain tip hotlines.) But even in this case, the designated agent-for-service receives not a summons but a cease-and-desist order. Educational institutions have generally induced its violators to cease and desist immediately and have avoided further legal action.

Historically, the most aggressive copyright enforcer has been the Software Publishers Association, which patrols software pirating (installation or reproduction without site licenses), and even it confines its efforts to organizations and stays out of people's at-home offices.

Corporations, which can rarely claim fair use protection, have never enjoyed such gentle treatment. But then they have the most to gain financially by copyright violations. The copyright cops have ensured that they also have the most to lose. So be aware that publishing houses, which are corporations no matter how academic they may be, interpret fair use very conservatively (Orlans, 1999).

■ FOR FURTHER AND FUTURE REFERENCE

These resources provide further detail on copyright protections, restrictions, and exemptions, as well as the latest changes in the laws and guidelines. All websites were retrieved November 18, 2009:

U.S. Copyright Office: www.copyright.gov; Address: 101 Independence Ave. S.E., Washington, DC 20559–6000; Public information phone services, 8:30 a.m. to 5:00 p.m. Eastern Time, Monday through Friday: (202) 707-3000, (202) 707-5959. Circulars and forms are available free at www.copyright.gov/circs.

Copyright Website LLC: www.benedict.com.

Copyright Clearance Center Campus Guide to Copyright Compliance for Academic Institutions: www.copyright.com/Services/copyrightoncampus.

Indiana University Information Policy Office: http://copyright.iu.edu/about.

Cornell University Copyright Information Center: www.copyright.cornell.edu/resources.

Hall Davidson Copyright Resources: www.halldavidson.com/downloads.html#anchor923173.

University of Minnesota Libraries Copyright Information and Education: www.lib.umn.edu/copyright.

University of Texas System Crash Course in Copyright: www.utsystem.edu/OGC/intellectualproperty/cprtindx.htm.

CHAPTER 7

Preventing and Responding to Classroom Incivility

Classroom incivility has become a national and even international problem in higher education. The topic includes preventing and sanctioning disciplinary problems and maintaining a controlled, orderly environment that is conducive to learning. Knowing preventive measures and constructive responses to disruption can greatly enhance your relationship with your students because even minor incivilities can mar the atmosphere, break your concentration, and really get under your skin. And losing your temper is not an option. How effectively you control your classes may even affect your life in general. Boice (2000) found this ability to be the best single predictor of junior faculty persistence and success in an academic career.

■ WHAT IS INCIVILITY?

Students surveyed at Wright State University cited six common classroom behaviors that they found annoying (Ballantine & Risacher, 1993):

1. Talking in class
2. Noisily packing up early
3. Arriving late and leaving early
4. Cheating
5. Wasting class time—a general category spanning being unprepared for class, dominating discussion, repeating questions, and asking for a review of the last class meeting
6. Showing general disrespect and poor manners toward the instructor and other students

Instructors surveyed at Indiana University, Bloomington, also identified these student behaviors as unacceptable (Royce, 2000):

7. Eating in class
8. Acting bored or apathetic
9. Making disapproving groans
10. Making sarcastic remarks or gestures
11. Sleeping in class
12. Not paying attention
13. Not answering a direct question
14. Using a computer in class for nonclass purposes

15. Letting cell phones and pagers go off in class
16. Cutting class
17. Dominating discussion
18. Demanding makeup exams, extensions, grade changes, or special favors
19. Taunting or belittling other students
20. Challenging the instructor's knowledge or credibility in class
21. Making harassing, hostile, or vulgar comments to the instructor in class
22. Making harassing, hostile, or vulgar comments or physical gestures to the instructor outside class
23. Sending the instructor inappropriate emails
24. Making threats of physical harm to the instructor.

While the most extreme forms of incivility are rather rare, the Indiana University faculty reported that all the other behaviors listed above occurred at least "sometimes" in their classes (Royce, 2000).

We can always add a few, such as talking on a cell phone, listening to music, coming to class in pajamas or beachwear, putting on makeup, reading a newspaper or magazine, chewing and popping gum loudly, doing work for another class, refusing to participate, acting entitled, coming on sexually to the instructor or another student, and leaving trash in the classroom. But none of the above compares with the ultimate incivility we've been seeing with increasing frequency: faculty being murdered in cold blood. Whether major or minor, these students behaviors were almost unheard of up through the mid-1980s.

■ WHY THE INCREASE?

Over the past four decades, the academy has changed in many ways that have no doubt exacerbated behavioral and disciplinary problems. Increasing diversity has brought in many students who don't share traditional academic values, norms, and communication styles. The student-instructor chasm has also widened as faculty have become older and increasingly specialized. In addition, as universities have grown in size, they have become more transient and impersonal, generating an atmosphere of distrust and indifference (Baldwin, 1997–1998; Leatherman, 1996).

Other changes have contributed as well. Colleges and universities have been working harder than ever before to retain students, so they now sanction only the most seriously offensive behaviors. Unfortunately, the same is true in the K–12 system, which does little to enforce discipline or nurture a love of learning. In addition, the factors that are associated with classroom incivility have become more common in the academy: large classes and instructors who are young, female, and low status—adjuncts, lecturers, and TAs (Royce, 2000). Large classes taught by low-status instructors are also often required courses, which breed incivility as well.

Kristensen (2007) offers a list of other reasons collected from several sources: the "dumbing down" of K–12 education, indifferent or indulgent parenting, dysfunctional families, students living at home and not maturing, media violence, upward mobility pressures in a weak economy, students' indifference to learning, their sense of entitlement, and their consumer attitude.

This last reason deserves some elaboration because it has two facets. The first is students' view of higher education as a high-priced commodity that they or their parents are purchasing. This attitude feeds into their feelings of entitlement to good grades; after all, they think, they bought them. The second facet is students' regard for faculty. From the consumers' point of view, instructors are just well-educated service workers who are supposed to cater to students (Rice, Sorcinelli, & Austin, 2000). In fact, despite their education, instructors aren't very well-paid service workers either. No doubt the high valuation that the millennial generation places on a lucrative career and material possessions also lowers its respect for faculty and for education.

Then again, the entire American culture has lost trust in and respect for authority in general. Too many business, religious, and political leaders have proven themselves to be dishonest, greedy, immoral, and indifferent to the interests of their customers, congregations, and constituencies. Moreover, they have profited from their lack of integrity and corrupt behavior. So while the public has grown cynical of authority, some sectors, including many students, still view these leaders as role models and believe that corruption, dishonesty, and greed help people get ahead. Therefore, this book devotes all of Chapter Eight to preserving academic honesty.

Another change in the culture has been increasing informality in most forms of self-expression, including dress, language, and behavior. This trend is evident in churches, restaurants, stores, offices, airports, and schools, as well as artistic reflections of the culture, such as popular music, television, and movies. A few decades ago, public and private schools at all levels enforced strict dress codes for both students and teachers. Similarly, offices permitted only business suits, dresses, and skirts and blouses, all with dress shoes. People expected and encouraged displaying a sense of propriety in behavior much more than they do today.

Of course, that was then, and this is now. The rest of this chapter suggests strategies for minimizing and responding to specific types of incivilities in and out of the classroom. Of course, prevention is the preferred outcome, but this behavior is not always in your control. So acceptable ways to stop the behaviors are also covered. Unfortunately, none of these strategies are absolutely foolproof given the unpredictability of human behavior. Still, your well-considered efforts at both prevention and response are likely to inspire the respect of the vast majority of your students, as they too are bothered by their peers' annoying behaviors and expect you to quell such distractions (Ballantine & Risacher, 1993; Young, 2003).

■ PREVENTING INCIVILITY: YOUR CLASSROOM PERSONA

What kind of personality do you project in the classroom? Is it at all weak, timid, and self-effacing? Is it innocent and naive about students' instrumentalist attitudes toward education and their efforts to cut

corners and do minimal work for their grades? Is it laid back, anything-goes, and permissive? If you are a mature female, do you convey a sweet maternal image, specifically one of a protective and overly nurturing pushover who will show endless mercy toward irresponsible student behavior? Or perhaps you project quite the opposite—that of a cold, distant, condescending professor, possibly with a cynical attitude, a sarcastic sense of humor, an uncaring heart, or a mean, critical streak? (Remember that students are very sensitive and prone to overinterpret small slights.) If your students perceive you as any of these types, you are likely to encounter a disproportionate amount of classroom incivility. In the first four cases, many students will feel free to take advantage of your apparent vulnerability or tolerance and will walk all over you. In the last case, they will feel justified in returning your seemingly "bad attitude" in kind.

Your students will see you as having one persona or another, whether you put any energy into constructing one or not. This is a good part of the performance dimension of teaching (Carroll, 2003b). So why not consciously project a persona that will command students' respect—and perhaps just a touch of fear—and inspire their trust and loyalty? Why not exude relaxed confidence, goodwill, and an in-command, no-nonsense attitude—the elements of a successful faculty image? It is not difficult to do; all it requires is certain concrete behaviors, some verbal and some nonverbal. Whether or not you carry this aura naturally, it is not dishonest to behave in ways that will make you more effective in the classroom. After all, aren't we willing to do almost anything to help our students learn?

Balancing Authority and Approachability

Most students accept the authority of a tenure-track faculty member without question. But some students are reluctant to accord the same respect to an adjunct, a graduate student, a TA, or an instructor who violates the traditional professorial stereotype of the mature, white male with an imposing stance and a low, deep voice. Clearly if you look young, are physically small, have a relatively high voice, are nonwhite, or female, you may well encounter some student resistance. If you project any weakness, nervousness, softness, or too easy-going an attitude, you're likely to find students pushing the envelope with you, behaving discourteously, and expecting special favors of you. A few of these simple strategies will add the air of authority to your persona and help you take stronger control of your classes (Nilson, 1981):

- Stand up in front of your class instead of sitting, move around the room, and use broad gestures. The dramatic effect is to make you appear larger than life. Increasing one's apparent size is a common aggressive and defensive posture throughout the animal kingdom.
- Try to deepen your voice slightly and to project it farther by speaking from your diaphragm. Also avoid ending a declarative sentence with a questioning rise in pitch.
- Favor more formal dress to convey that you are serious and business minded, especially if you are female (Johnston, 2005; Roach, 1997).
- Add an air of formality and dignity to your classroom. For instance, address students by their last names, and ask that they address you by your title (Dr. or Professor) and last name.
- Refer in class to your own scholarship where appropriate. This establishes you as an authority on the subject and elevates you in your students' eyes.

Female instructors, in particular, must take measures to reinforce their legitimacy and authority. Students tend to underestimate the educational attainment of female instructors, even controlling for many other instructor characteristics (Miller & Chamberlin, 2000). Students are also more likely to challenge female and minority instructors about their legitimacy, expertise, opinions, and teaching methods (Moore, 1996; Turner & Myers, 2000). In addition, many students expect females to display an empathetic softness that they think they can take advantage of. While research shows that female

gender does not depress student evaluations of teaching in any consistent or significant way, it very well may in more male-dominated fields, such as engineering (Feldman, 1992, 1993; Marsh & Roach, 1997; Nilson & Lysaker, 1996).

Other instructors face the opposite problem of intimidating students. They can do so by too perfectly matching the somewhat chilly professorial stereotype or by coming off as domineering. From your students' viewpoint, you may fall in this category if you are male and are some combination of very tall, physically large, deep-voiced, rugged looking, serious and reserved, or have an aggressive or curt social style. The following behaviors can warm up your persona, making you seem more approachable and likable (Nilson, 1981):

- Assume a relaxed posture in the classroom. Sit down or perch casually on the corner of a desk.
- Speak more softly in class, as long as everyone can still hear you. Also interact with the class more, perhaps by tossing out more questions to answer or problems to solve.
- Dress down slightly—for example, wear a loosened tie and a sports jacket or a two-piece suit rather than a three-piece suit.
- Chat casually with students before and after class so they can see you as friendly, warm, and personable. Address students by their first names. (If you are a TA, consider asking them to call you by your first name.) Consciously practice social immediacies (see the next section).
- Smile whenever appropriate.
- If you are a TA or a faculty member still taking courses, mention that you too are a student, so you can identify with the academic demands they are facing.

Showing That You Care

Wherever your persona falls on the authority-approachability continuum, you can help prevent class incivility and conflict by practicing social immediacies—that is, conveying both verbally and nonverbally that you care about your students as learners and as people. Like everyone else in the world, students want to be loved on some level. You can verbally express, for example, concern for their learning and future success, high expectations for them, interest in their activities outside class, empathy with their learning challenges and stress, and your availability to help them outside class. You can also learn and use their names. Nonverbally, you can communicate your respect for and interest in them by making regular eye contact, speaking with energy and enthusiasm, listening intently without interrupting, standing with an open body posture, and smiling frequently. When students raise a problem in the course, you can clarify your course objectives and schedule and enlist students to help resolve the issue.

All of these instructor behaviors, along with teaching interactively, are associated with more civil student conduct and greater student attentiveness in class (Meyers, 2003; Meyers, Bender, Hill, & Thomas, 2006; Wilson & Taylor, 2001). They may even override the negative effects of being female, young, less experienced, and a member of a racial/ethnic minority group (Meyers et al., 2006).

Setting Ground Rules

All the literature on classroom management considers setting ground rules essential (Baldwin, 1997–1998; Ballantine & Risacher, 1993; Boice, 1996; Brooks, 1987; Feldmann, 2001; Gonzalez & Lopez, 2001; Nilson, 1981; Sorcinelli, 1994). Most students respond very well to them; they want to know what is expected of them. In addition, ground rules convey that you are in command and no-nonsense Therefore, announce on the first day, especially in a large class, exactly what disruptive behaviors you will not tolerate in your course—and why. Your most convincing reason—and one that is research based—is that such behaviors annoy the other students in the class. This conveys your goodwill. (Reiterate this reason when handling a noisy disruption.)

Some rules also belong in your syllabus, especially your expectations and any grade-relevant

policies regarding attendance, tardiness, class participation, extension requests, missed assignment deadlines, and makeup exams (see Chapter Three). You may want to add statements forbidding sleeping in class, eating in class, side conversations, live cell phones and pagers, and displays of disrespect for fellow students. (Focus on the most common incivilities you encounter; don't make the list too long.) Then be prepared to ask any offenders to stop the behaviors immediately or leave the room.

You may prefer to emphasize appropriate behaviors rather than disruptive ones. If so, express your rules in a positive way—for example, "Students are expected to hand in assignments on time" rather than "Students will be penalized for late assignments." Even so, you must specify the consequences for violating the rules.

Some instructors have reduced incivilities by having their students collectively draw up a classroom-conduct contract, or set of rules for behavior to which they will agree. Here's the procedure. On the first day of class, lead a discussion on the student behaviors that genuinely bother the members of the class. As a member, you can add one or two behaviors to the list. Then from the notes you take, type up a contract for all students to sign at the next class meeting in which they promise not to engage in the disruptive behaviors listed. If someone refuses to sign it, let the other students decide what to do; after all, it's their contract. Instructors who use contracts claim that for the rest of the semester, students pretty much police themselves, keeping even minor violations to a minimum (Baldwin, 1997–1998; Ballantine & Risacher, 1993). Some institutions publish a student code of conduct, but students often don't buy into what they don't feel they own.

A variation on a class contract starts out as a student bill of rights and leads to a larger life lesson (Nilson & Jackson, 2004). Students should have no problem coming up with rights for themselves, and you should ensure these are written down. A few will quickly realize, however, that rights come with responsibilities. In fact, each right comes with at least one responsibility. For instance, the right to be evaluated fairly obligates students to hand in work that accurately reflects their best abilities. The related right to receive timely and consistent feedback from the instructor requires that they hand in work on time and use that feedback in improving their work. The right to be safe to express their opinions in turn commits them to respect the opinions of other students and the instructor. For a final example, the right to a well-organized course with well-organized, well-prepared classes obligates students to come to class prepared to make the most of the course. Because students generate these rights and responsibilities themselves, they are likely to police themselves, as in the case of a contract. When they don't, all you have to do to enforce the rules is to smile at the offenders and gently remind them by saying *contract* or *bill of rights*.

Rewarding Civil Behavior

As we saw in the case of motivating students (Chapter Five), applying behaviorism wisely can change student behavior for the better. Of course, setting ground rules and course policies and ensuring violators face unpleasant consequences, whether social pressure or lost points, represent the negative reinforcement and punishment side of the equation. But what about using positive reinforcement, which is more powerful than negative reinforcement and punishment, to discourage such violations?

In addition to noticing and sanctioning misbehavior, we can notice and reward good behavior. We can compliment a class when everyone arrives on time or when attendance is especially high. (This shows that you do see these things.) When a student is often late, we should not only correct the behavior by speaking to her in private about it but also thank her when she does arrive on time. When a noisy class quiets down, express your appreciation. Research shows that these little positive reinforcers are effective at the workplace as well as in the classroom. They also help create a pleasant and fruitful learning atmosphere (Daniels, 2000; Daniels & Daniels, 2004; Wiesman, 2006, 2007).

Modeling Correct Behavior

Sometimes classroom incivility starts with the instructor's behavior toward the students, such as being rude, sarcastic, condescending, indifferent, insensitive, or inflexible (Boice, 1996; Gonzalez & Lopez, 2001). Your efforts to model good manners do not guarantee that students will always imitate you. But students will consider your standards and requirements fairer if your behavior reflects them, and no doubt more students will honor them. For instance, if you don't want students to interrupt one another during discussions, judiciously try not to interrupt students yourself. If you value punctuality, come to class ahead of the bell and complete your board work before class begins. If you want assignments turned in on time, return papers promptly. If you expect students to come to your office hours, keep to your schedule faithfully. These constitute instructor rights and matching responsibilities.

However, students may have somewhat different conceptions of unacceptable faculty behavior than we do. The Teaching Assistant Program at Michigan State University conducted a small ($N = 50$) but revealing survey of undergraduate perceptions of irritating instructor behaviors. More than 20 percent of the students mentioned these six:

1. Showing up late for class
2. Not showing up for office hours
3. Making students feel stupid (put down, inferior, dumb) or showing lack of respect
4. Not getting to know students
5. Writing on the board while blocking the information or talking to the board
6. Not following the syllabus

Less frequently mentioned were not preparing for class, being disorganized, giving inadequate explanations of difficult material, not controlling the class, assigning busywork, lecturing too quickly, speaking too softly or in a monotone, reading lecture notes, starting class early and ending it late, not grading assigned work, and assigning too much homework

(Teaching Assistant Program, Michigan State University, n.d.). We may not think of talking to the board, straying from the syllabus, or talking fast as offensive, but it is to students. In fact, after a first-day-of-class discussion of what *they* shouldn't do, we should ask them in turn what they don't want *us* to do.

From the students' point of view, defining and modeling correct behavior means meeting their learning needs and showing them respect by living up to their professional expectations of us. We can start by reversing all the don'ts above into do's. For instance, we should display a brief agenda, outline, or list of student outcomes at the beginning of every class. Not only will we appear well prepared and organized; we will also communicate nonverbally that we are in command of the classroom.

We should also explain why we have chosen the readings, teaching methods, class activities, and assignments that we have without students having to ask. They don't assume that we do what we do for their own good or because of our knowledge of how people learn, so we need to convince them. We can tell them how many other inferior textbooks we reviewed, how much research stands behind the effectiveness of our methods, and how well our assignments will prepare them for their future careers. We might even summarize our teaching philosophy (see Chapter Thirty-Two on writing one).

Yet another way to show respect for students is to hold them to high expectations. Communicating this point may initially require some tough love, such as refusing to accept shoddy work (in this case, you quickly return it to the student and require him to revise it up to standard before you will grade it). The work may be docked for being late, but at least it will merit some points. Taking this strong action early in the term will motivate students to stretch their abilities, and you'll probably not have to take it again.

Commanding Class Attention

Sometimes students become restless, apathetic, and potentially disruptive because their attention is wandering or they're bored. Your practicing good

platform (public speaking) skills both projects a strong persona—one who is relaxed, confident, in command, and no-nonsense—and enables you to command student attention and engagement for longer periods of time. These skills come up briefly again in Chapter Twelve because they strongly influence the motivational and teaching effectiveness of a lecture. They also affect how easily you can keep students awake, quiet, orderly, and on task for all or part of a class period. Aristotle had good reason for evaluating rhetorical oratory on not only invention (content) and arrangement (organization) but also style (sentence structure and word use), delivery (vocal and physical performance), and memory (freedom from notes).

Excellence in public speaking encompasses many different behaviors. Because Chapter Twelve addresses invention and arrangement and since you are probably gifted with respect to style, let us proceed directly to delivery. It too comprises many different behaviors, most of them "small," so to speak. But they add up to a tremendous difference in the way the speaker and the message are received and regarded. Following is a simple listing of major platform skills (adapted from Toastmasters International speech manuals and related materials):

- *Effective use of voice:* Volume adjusted to be audible for the room and audience; words enunciated clearly; rich, resonant voice quality, projected from chest and diaphragm; vocal variety (changes in intonation to complement content and for emphasis); volume variety (either extreme for emphasis); varied and appropriate speaking pace (never hurried and dramatically slower for more important content); pregnant pauses for emphasis before and after major points; imagery plays on words (for example, drawing out "slow" and "long," saying "icy" in an icy tone, saying "soft" softly, saying "strong" with especially deep resonance).
- *Effective use of body:* Solid, natural stance (unless moving, legs comfortably apart, knees slightly bent, arms hanging at sides, shoulders relaxed, and

back straight); natural movement around lectern or stage and out toward audience (for emphasis and to complement content); abundant gestures to complement content (especially broad ones before large audiences); word dramatization (for example, momentarily acting out "timid," "angry," "anxious," "huge"); varied facial expressions (more dramatic in a large room), including smiles where appropriate; only occasional glances, if any, at notes; steady eye contact with the audience (at least three seconds per audience sector or quadrant are recommended).

- *Effective use of visual aids and props:* In addition to rehearsing their use to avoid awkwardness, see Chapters Twenty-Six and Twenty-Seven for pointers.

- *Emotions to project:* Relaxed confidence, conviction; enthusiasm, excitement, passion, a sense of drama, curiosity; sincerity, concern, honesty, openness, warmth, goodwill, caring, a sense of humor.

- *Minimization or elimination of distracting behaviors:* Um, uh, you know, sort of, kind of, and-and, that-that; mispronunciations; false sentence starts; midsentence switches to the start of a new sentence; volume fade-outs at end of sentences; pacing, swaying, or other repetitive movements; leaning on the lectern, against the wall, against the chalkboard; lengthy checks of notes; ritual apologies to audience (for example, "I hoped to have prepared this lecture more carefully").

- *Not speaking for too long.* As you will read in Chapter Twelve, students have a rather short attention span for lecture. Unless you already project a charismatic persona, you're inviting disruptions if you lecture beyond ten to twenty minutes at a time. Whenever you spot a bored expression or glazed eyes while you are lecturing, pause and change the pace. Pose a question, open the floor for questions, or use any of the student-active breaks suggested in Chapter Twelve. If you don't shift your students' attention to a learning activity, they will shift their attention to a nonlearning activity.

Of course, all of these skills assembled together seem impossibly numerous and precise to master. But you probably have inadvertently learned most of them already and may need to polish only a few. If your institution has a teaching center, it probably will videotape you teaching a class and offer you the chance to view your tape with a trained specialist. This service can help you assess your platform skills and identify ways to hone your public speaking effectiveness.

For now, the most important skill you should check is your eye contact with your students. It is a powerful form of crowd control. In large classes, it is easy to forget the far half of the class, and that is exactly the half you usually need to control the most. Eye contact also personalizes your comments, encourages students to return your attentiveness to them in kind, and enables you to read their faces to gauge their interest and understanding.

Another key skill to monitor is your voice. Its tonal variety and pace reflect your level of engagement in the material and your enjoyment of teaching. A voice can sound monotone to an audience because the person speaks at the same pitch or at the same pace for long periods of time. If you find yourself droning this way through a dry section of your lecture, try consciously to modulate your voice and vary your speaking pace to keep student interest.

Singers and actors have something to teach us. They do warm-up exercises for their voices and bodies before they perform, and as performers in our own right, we might consider doing the same to get ready for class. These exercises are described in detail in Chapter Four because they also relieve first-day jitters, so a brief summary should suffice here.

For example, to enhance your vocal variety, resonance, and projection, you can sing scales, alternate high and low pitches, and read children's books aloud with exaggerated changes in pitch and pace. To loosen up, relax, and eliminate tension from your body, take three or four slow, deep breaths all the way into your diaphragm and pushing out all the old air before inhaling again. This breathing is also good for your vocal resonance and projection as well as your brain, since oxygen enhances cognitive functioning.

Another excellent exercise is standing with your legs about a foot apart and stretching every part of your body in every direction you can. It's best to stretch slowly, stop when you feel any strain, and hold the position for a few moments. Finally, extend your arms out in front of you and send energy along them and out your fingertips. This mental practice enhances your ability to send energy out to your audience. Taken together, these physical exercises will help you fill up your life space in front of your class. Your relaxed state, coupled with your improved blood flow, will make an open body posture feel natural and will add energy, spring, and flow to your movements. You will seem larger, more animated, and more dynamic. Add greater vocal variety and richer voice quality, and your persona will begin to take on charisma. If you observe a charismatic speaker closely, you will see that charisma can be broken down into a number of small but powerful behaviors carefully orchestrated in combination.

■ RESPONDING TO INCIVILITY

If you encounter a discipline problem in your classroom, stay calm and in control. Count to ten, breathe deeply, visualize a peaceful scene—anything to keep you from losing your temper. No matter how much an offensive student tries to bait you, you lose credibility if you lower yourself to his level. If you keep your composure, you win the sympathy and support of the other students. They may even start using social pressure to discipline the offenders themselves.

In fact, whenever you sanction a student for mild, garden-variety uncivil behavior, smile through your firmness. A smile conveys not only warmth and approachability but also unflappable cool and relaxed confidence. It says you don't take the misconduct personally, that you are just doing your job to maintain a productive learning environment, and that student misbehavior doesn't get under your skin. With this kind of cool, students sense they can't bait you, so they won't.

Keeping your composure, however, does not mean accepting and tolerating the abuse. It is critical that you do not ignore or otherwise tolerate the behavior. You must respond immediately. The worst thing you can go is to ignore the behavior (Meyers et al., 2006). The longer you let the incivility continue, the higher the level of response you will have to take later (Feldmann, 2001; Gonzalez & Lopez, 2001). Here are some specific, appropriate measures you can take in response to disruptive behaviors (Baldwin, 1997–1998; Ballantine & Risacher, 1993; Boice, 1996, 2000; Feldmann, 2001; Gonzalez & Lopez, 2001; Nilson, 1981; Sorcinelli, 1994; Watkins, 1982). Always be especially strict in enforcing the rules early in the term.

Talking in Class

Occasional comments or questions from one student to another are to be expected. However, chronic talkers bother other students and interfere with your train of thought. To stop them, you have several options. The simplest is simply to pause, allowing their voices to fill the silence. You may also want to accompany your pause with a long stare at the offenders. Staring at them with a smile suggests you're nonplussed by the violation. Another option is to walk over to the offenders while you continue to teach. Still another, and an especially classy alternative, is to handle it with a little humor, such as an invitation to share the conversation with the class. If appropriate, refer to the classroom conduct contract or bill of rights and responsibilities that the class authored and signed. If you don't have a contract, pleasantly say something like, "I really think you should pay attention to this; it will be on the test" or "You are disturbing your classmates." If the problem persists, get stern with the offenders outside class. Public embarrassment is a last resort that should be avoided, since it can turn some students against you.

Packing Up Early

Routinely reserve some important points or classroom activities—quizzes, writing exercises, clarification of the upcoming readings, study guide distribution, a classroom assessment technique (as in Chapter Twenty-Eight)—until the end of class. Or have students turn in assignments at the end of class. Paper rustling and other disruptive noise making during class can be stopped the same way as talking in class.

Arriving Late or Leaving Early

State your policies clearly on these offenses in your syllabus and on the first day of class and never reteach material for the tardy. You can insist that students inform you in advance of any special circumstances that will require them to be late to class. You can even subtract course points for coming late and leaving early as long as you set this policy at the start. You might draw attention to offenders by pausing as they walk in and out. Alternatively, you can set aside an area near the door for latecomers and early leavers. Finally, as you can do to discourage packing up early, you can routinely schedule important class activities at the beginning and the end of class.

Chronic offenders of these policies deserve their day in court—that is, talk to them or email them privately about the problem. They may be late because the previous hour's class tends to run late or is a long walk away. Or they may have to leave your class a little early to get to their job on time.

Cheating

Academic dishonesty is such a serious and widespread problem in higher education today that the entire next chapter is devoted to preventing and responding to it.

Coming to Class Unprepared

This problem too is so widespread that all of Chapter Twenty-Three addresses getting students to do the readings.

Dominating Discussion

If certain students habitually try to monopolize class time, tell them to speak with you after class to clarify their questions and discuss more of the issues. You can also broaden the discussion and call attention away from the disruptive student by asking the rest of the class for the answers.

If a student is rambling around or off the subject, take control by seizing the chance to interrupt her and paraphrase whatever meaning you can salvage. Then supply an answer and move along. Alternatively, you can defer answering it for the sake of saving class time and advise her to raise it outside class.

Asking Questions You've Already Answered

A student asks you about the procedure for doing an assignment that you've already explained. Rather than putting down the student ("Where were you when I gave the assignment?"), just answer the question civilly and quickly, or say that you already answered the question and will repeat the answer only outside class. Another option is to refer that student to the written instructions you've provided and ask exactly which part needs clarification.

Asking Wheedling Questions

Occasionally students try to wheedle answers out of you to avoid having to work out the answer for themselves. In class, you can invite other students to suggest leads and possibly get a discussion going. But one-on-one, the best way to avoid giving in is to answer each of the student's questions with another question that should help him think through the answer. A student who is asking questions solely to pry answers out of you will soon tire of your questions and go away.

Asking Argumentative Questions

A student who tries to entrap you in an argument for the sake of arguing either wants attention or has an authority problem. Just acknowledge his input and quickly move on. To lower yourself to the bait jeopardizes your credibility with the class. If another incident occurs, tell the student you will discuss the issue outside class. After class, inform him in private that you do not appreciate and will not tolerate such uncalled-for hostile behavior in your classroom. Also mention that it disturbs other students and wastes their class time.

Another strategy is to handle questions through a different medium. You can collect written questions in a box and briefly address some of them at the next class meeting. You can also encourage students to email their questions to you or put them on the course website. While less personal, these options offer a less confrontational format.

Asking Loaded Questions

The rare nefarious student may design a question just to embarrass you and put you on the defensive. Like the argumentative student, this type is also probably seeking attention and respect from his peers and deserves the same response. You may also be able to turn the loaded question back on the student asking it:

Student: You're not really saying . . . ?

Instructor: What I'm saying is . . . Now, what is your perspective on this topic?

Demanding a Grade Change

To discourage this situation from happening often, set a policy in your syllabus that if a student wants to protest a grade, either you will regrade the entire test or assignment, or better yet, you will not accept a grade protest unless the student submits a written justification for the change, citing exact book pages and class period dates, within forty-eight hours. Do not accept email messages; they are too informal.

If a student still comes to you demanding a grade change, try to neutralize her emotion and delay dealing with the issue until she calms down. Schedule an appointment with her in your office at least a day or two later. Then open with a positive, empathetic statement: "I understand your frustration. Let's take a look at your paper [or test] and talk about the grading." Have the student read her answer aloud to help her hear her errors. Maintain eye contact and try to agree with her whenever possible. If necessary,

explicitly disassociate the grade from her worth as a person. Even if you can't turn the student's opinion around, you can reduce both your own and her anxiety levels by showing yourself to be an ally (at least partially). Finally, try to give her a graceful way to retreat from the situation. Just don't be intimidated into changing the grade.

It is very rare that an instructor feels physically threatened by a hostile student, and it invariably happens when others are not around. While verbal hostility calls for a private approach, the physical version requires quite the opposite: try to move yourself and the student into as public a place as possible, even if just the hallway. A colleague or student may call campus security on your behalf.

Using a Computer in Class for Nonclass Purposes

Some students claim they are facile at multitasking, so they can read and respond to their email, text or "messenger" with a friend, participate in a chatroom, make purchases, surf the Web, *and* pay attention in class at the same time. But if this were true, people could simultaneously talk on their cell phones and drive safely (a low-concentration cognitive task), and we know that no one can do this.

Unfortunately, it is impossible to monitor students' screens unless you teach from the back of the room, and you may or may not be able to roam around to see what students are doing. But you can take measures to reduce the behavior drastically. When you assign an in-class computer task, keep your students extra busy by giving them minimal time to complete it. Also have them work in small groups, each group at one laptop or terminal. Chances are that three or four students won't be able to agree on a renegade site. Between computer assignments in class, have students turn off their computers or close their laptops.

Of course, discouraging this behavior is the best approach. In your syllabus, have a policy that students engaging in renegade computer activities will be marked absent for that day.

Cutting Classes

These are the top three reasons students give for cutting class: (1) attendance is not taken or does not affect the grade, (2) the instructor does not see or care if a student is missing, or (3) the class content is available elsewhere. We also know that attendance drops off in required, large, and more lecture-oriented classes (Friedman, Rodriguez, & McComb, 2001).

From these findings, the best ways to increase attendance, especially when used in combination, suggest themselves: basing part of the course grade on attendance; taking attendance regularly (even if you don't calculate it in the grade); basing part of the course grade on participation in discussion (see Chapter Thirteen); making the class more interactive and participatory; giving frequent, graded quizzes; regularly taking up homework to be graded; covering in class a great deal of material that isn't in the readings; not allowing commercial production of your lecture notes; not putting your lecture notes on the Web (skeletal outlines are okay); requiring students to catch up with any classes they have missed on their own; conducting cooperative learning group activities in class and grading students in part on peer performance evaluations (see Chapter Sixteen); and conducting other frequent, graded in-class activities.

Asking for Extensions and Missing Assignment Deadlines

In your syllabus, specify penalties for late work (for example, docking a portion of the grade), with or without an "approved" extension. Some instructors feel comfortable strictly enforcing this policy, while others prefer to be flexible. Students occasionally have good reasons for not meeting deadlines, but they also occasionally lie. You must assess each extension request and excuse on a case-by-case, student-by-student basis, perhaps allowing a single, documented incident but drawing the line at the second.

A student with a habitual problem deserves a private talk and the full penalties. You might ask other instructors in your department for the names of any chronic cases that they have encountered.

Showing Disrespect in General

If your prevention measures fail, talk to offenders privately and explain that their behavior is affecting their fellow students' ability to learn. Avoid showing or inciting anger by keeping your voice low. Be aware that sometimes students show disrespect to get the attention they believe they can't get through any other means. They want to vent their anger toward authority or express some other deep-seated emotional problem. Leave such cases to the professionals, and refer them to your institution's psychological or counseling center.

If your warnings fail or you face grievous and repeated displays of disrespect and abuse, don't hesitate to order the offenders out of the classroom, at least for that day. Should they refuse to leave, call campus security. After the incident, review it with the students in class so they can serve as witnesses, tell your department chair, and make a written record of the verbal exchange. While calling security is a last-resort response, it's a good idea to memorize the number or have it on speed dial. Taking this tack should end your incivility problems in the course for the rest of the term (Carroll, 2003a).

■ SEEKING ASSISTANCE

You are not alone in having to deal with student incivilities. Ask your more respected colleagues how they handle them. Requesting their advice will not lead them to believe you are an ineffective teacher. Another source of strategies is the student affairs staff. These officers usually understand students and their worlds and how to communicate with them better than most faculty, and the dean of student affairs should know about even mildly threatening incivilities. In addition, refer students with ego, authority, or anger management problems to your institution's psychological or counseling center. Finally, speak outside class with your best-behaved students, enlisting them to help you keep an orderly learning environment.

CHAPTER 8

Preserving Academic Integrity

The term *cheating* refers to a wide variety of behaviors generally considered unethical (Barnett & Dalton, 1981), at least by faculty. In its basic form, it is misrepresenting one's knowledge and effort. Plagiarism, a type of cheating, is claiming the ideas or words of others to be one's own, if just passively by not referencing their true source—in short, theft of intellectual property. A student who plagiarizes a report, fails to cite sources, copies an answer on a test, or pays someone to write a term paper has dishonestly obtained information and has lied in passing off the product as her own original work.

■ HOW PREVALENT IS CHEATING?

Since the late 1980s, surveys have documented that cheating is a way of life for American college students. Over two decades ago, 45 percent of undergraduates nationwide reported having cheated at some time in college, and an additional 33 percent copped to being habitual or "hard-core" cheaters—that is, they cheated in eight or more classes while in college (Collison, 1990a). The figures were comparable at thirty-one highly selective American universities, where 67 percent of the students admitted to cheating (Kibler, 1992). Plagiarizers numbered fewer: only about 10 percent (Collison, 1990b).

A more recent survey shows that little has changed. Seventy-five percent of American college students reported having cheated (Center for Academic Integrity survey cited in Hutton, 2006), the major differences being the use of cell phones for test answers and the Internet for purchased papers and stolen sources (Altschuler, 2001). But plagiarism increased a great deal, no doubt due to the Internet. One-quarter of the students said that they at least sometimes copied and pasted text from the Web without attribution, and 28 percent admitted lifting text from printed material (Kellogg, 2002). As shocking as these figures may seem, other sources have reported even higher ones (Kleiner & Lord, 1999). In one survey 90 percent of the students admitted that they use the Internet to cheat (Berry,

Thornton, & Baker, 2006). Even worse, not even 30 percent of those who cheat regret doing it, and getting caught deters only 7 percent of them from doing it again, according to a survey conducted by CollegeHumor (cited by Poythress, 2007).

We know that cheating in high school bears a strong relationship to cheating in college (Harding, Mayhew, Finelli, & Carpenter, 2007), so let's look at a 2006 national survey of high school students to project to more contemporary college students. Sixty percent admitted to cheating on at least one test, one-third to plagiarizing at least one assignment from the Internet and 62 percent to lying to a teacher about a significant matter—all within the previous year. This behavior reflects their perceptions of the real world. Fifty-nine percent believe that "successful people do what they have to do to win, even if others consider it cheating," and nearly one-quarter agree that "people who are willing to lie, cheat, or break the rules are more likely to succeed than people who do not." Yet 92 percent claim to be "satisfied with my own ethics and character," and 84 percent say that most of the people who know them would count them among the most ethical people they know (Josephson Institute, 2008). Cheating and lying are so entrenched in this generation that most of its members consider them ethical.

■ WHO CHEATS, AND WHY?

Student cheating mirrors the ethics and behavior of the broader society. An overall decline of public morality started in the self-centered 1970s and 1980s and has just gotten worse. Media depictions of the good life whet students' appetites for something that they are not sure they will be able to afford. Moreover, the now commonplace scandalous antics of business and political leaders make amoral and immoral behavior seem normal, and the small price these leaders pay makes it look profitable (Collison, 1990a; Josephson Institute, 2008). In fact, 90 percent of college students don't think that cheaters ever pay the price (Kleiner & Lord, 1999). As one student put it, "Cheating is a very common practice in our country. Everyone wants to make a lot of money, and cheating is a way to beat out other people" (Collison, 1990b, p. A31).

When asked why they cheat, 32 percent of students cite laziness, 29 percent better grades, and 12 percent pressure to succeed (Center for Academic Integrity survey cited in Hutton, 2006). In an earlier survey, some students mentioned grade competition and peer pressure from fellow fraternity and sorority members (Collison, 1990b). Disinterest in the material explains why students may cheat in certain courses but not others (Kleiner & Lord, 1999).

Some student demographics and activities are related to the prevalence of cheating. While religious affiliation and major are not (Nowell & Laufer, 1997), the findings are mixed on the relationship to gender and grade point average (Barnett & Dalton, 1981; Hutton, 2006; Kerkvliet, 1994; Nowell & Laufer, 1997). However, cheating does seem to be associated with younger age (Hutton, 2006; McCabe & Trevino, 1997; Nowell & Laufer, 1997), fraternity or sorority membership, extensive extracurricular involvement, heavy drinking and partying behavior (Hutton, 2006; Kerkvliet, 1994; McCabe & Trevino, 1997; Nowell & Laufer, 1997), and being employed (Nowell & Laufer, 1997).

Still, the most important determinants of cheating are student perceptions. If they anticipate peer disapproval for the behavior, they are less likely to do it. If, however, they see cheating as widespread and acceptable among their peers, the likelihood rises (Anderman, Freeman, & Mueller, 2007; Barnett & Dalton, 1981; Bunn, Caudill, & Gropper, 1992; Hutton, 2006; McCabe & Trevino, 1997; Mixon, 1996). Another critical perception is the opportunity to cheat. The lower the chances of getting caught (low supervision) and the lower the sanctions for getting caught (low threat)—as students size up their odds—the more prevalent cheating is. So not surprisingly, the behavior is related to class size and the use of multiple-choice tests (Barnett & Dalton, 1981; Kerkvliet & Sigmund, 1999; Mixon, 1996; Nowell & Laufer, 1997). Anonymity no doubt plays a role with respect to both class and institutional size. Cheating is more common in classes taught by non-tenure-track and graduate student instructors (Kerkvliet & Sigmund, 1999; Nowell & Laufer, 1997), a situation that frequently occurs in larger, research-oriented public universities.

Sadly enough, faculty play a role in setting student perceptions as well. According to surveys, half of the instructors admit to ignoring at least some of the cheating they are aware of (McCabe, 2005; Nadelson, 2007). After all, pursuing a cheating case takes time and yields no rewards for faculty. In general, colleges and universities turn a blind eye to much of the cheating that goes on and understate the prevalence of the behavior (Bok, 2006; Haney & Clarke, 2007).

Even so, student perceptions are malleable, and institutions and instructors can influence them. Colleges and universities with honor codes weave academic integrity into the student culture (see the section on honor codes below), and with or without an honor code, small private institutions nurture bonds of trust and caring between students and faculty. In these contexts, cheating is less acceptable and, as a result, less prevalent (Hutton, 2006). How much you as an instructor emphasize academic honesty and how dedicated you seem to teaching and your students have a sizable impact as well. If students view you as lax or indifferent about integrity, if they consider your tests confusing and unfair, or if they can't see the relevance of your material, some will feel entitled to cheat (Hutton, 2006; Kerkvliet & Sigmund, 1999; Whitley, 1998). In other words, if you don't seem to care, they won't either.

DETECTING CHEATING

Catching incidences of cheating is not rocket science. During tests, an observant eye can often see wandering glances and students passing notes, cheat sheets, and even bluebooks to one another. Sometimes you can spot a ringer by an unfamiliar face. Other tip-offs are a heavily erased exam, suspicious behavior (for example, leaving the room during the exam, rustling through one's things, hiding a cell phone in one's lap, repeatedly looking at one's hands and arms), and, of course, a considerable number of identical answers,

even incorrect ones, across exams. Be concerned, too, if a student improves his exam performance meteorically without having seen you or your teaching assistant (TA) for extra help.

Plagiarism is possible when a student hands in a paper (1) without quotations or references, (2) with references that don't fit with the text, (3) with odd, esoteric, or inaccessible references, (4) on a topic other than the one assigned, (5) with a format different from your requirements, (6) with a cover page typeface different from the text's, (7) late, (8) on a recently changed topic, (9) with a shifting writing style, (10) with familiar-sounding sections, (11) heavy on facts not tied together, (12) very similar to another student's paper, (13) that is photocopied, or (14) that is just too perfect and mature for the student in question.

Realize that you may not be able to trace all purchased papers to their source, and there are dozens of paper mills on the Web. However, you can uncover most cases of plagiarism by using one of several online text-matching services (for a fee) or by typing, in quotation marks, a distinctive suspect phrase or sentence into one or more Web search engines (for free).

PREVENTING CHEATING

Except for your instructor status, the crucial determinants of cheating are within your control. So you can stop or at least drastically reduce academic dishonesty in your classes with proven prevention measures. Most of these either make cheating more difficult or heighten students' perceived chances of getting caught and facing dire consequences, and the rest reduce students' motivation to cheat (Barnett & Dalton, 1981; Brauchle, 2000; Hutton, 2006; Johnson & Ury, 1998, 1999; Kerkvliet & Sigmund, 1999; Kleiner & Lord, 1999; McCabe & Trevino, 1996, 1997; Office of Educational Development, 1985; Whitley, 1998; Wilhoit, 1994):

1. Motivate your students' interest in your subject, and help them understand its relevance to their careers and the broader world so they will want to learn it (see Chapter Five).

2. Define cheating and plagiarism to your students, and give examples and hypothetical cases. Your students may not understand these terms. Also teach them how to cite sources correctly.

3. State verbally and in writing your own and your institution's policies on academic dishonesty and their applications to each assignment and test you give. State that you strictly enforce these policies and will check for plagiarism electronically. Include statements in your syllabus (see Chapter Three).

4. If you're a graduate student or adjunct instructor, be especially assertive. Students may think they can get away with more in your class since you're supposedly less savvy and more sympathetic to students than regular faculty are.

5. Make your exams as original as possible to reduce student reliance on old tests for study. Solicit potential new test questions from TAs and students.

6. Ensure equal access to study aids by placing a file of old tests and assignments on your course website for all students to use. Fraternities and sororities often keep test files for their members.

7. Make up different forms of tests, especially multiple-choice tests, by varying the order of the questions. The test tools in course management systems such as Blackboard will usually do this for you.

8. Firmly remind your class before each test that academic integrity is important to you, your institution, and the larger society, and that you will enforce it using all the institutional means you have available.

9. Although even good students don't want to "squeal," appeal to their social ethics and their desire to protect their own intellectual property to report cheating.

10. During tests, if the room permits, seat students with space between them and place their personal belongings, especially cell phones, far away from them (for example, at the front of the room).

11. In large lecture halls, have assigned test seats, and keep a chart of students' names.

12. Supply scratch paper if needed.

13. Clear all calculators before passing out a test.

14. If blue books are used, have students turn theirs in just before the test, then redistribute them randomly.

15. Proctor tests judiciously, enlisting the aid of your TAs and colleagues. Don't allow yourself or your assistants to work on any other project while proctoring. Charge only one proctor (perhaps yourself) with answering any questions during the test.

16. Check for cheat notes in nearby restrooms, on the underside of baseball cap bills, on students' skin (perhaps visible only through a hole in their jeans), on the labels of beverage bottles, and in other highly imaginative places.

17. Collect tests from students individually to avoid a chaotic rush at the end of class.

18. When grading tests manually, clearly mark incorrect answers with an X or a slash in ink. Also place a mark at the end of each answer to make any later additions obvious.

19. Return exams, papers, and assignments to students in person or electronically.

20. Collect your test questions after you review the tests. If the test question forms are separate from the answer sheets, have students put their names on the forms to ensure you can account for all of them.

21. Assign paper topics that are unique and specific and require original critical thinking or critical self-examination.

22. Give explicit collaboration rules for all out-of-class assignments.

23. Change your writing assignments as often as possible to discourage paper recycling.

24. Take class time to discuss difficulties in the assignments and how to overcome them.

25. Make specific format requirements, and grade in part on adherence to them.

26. Require a certain combination of sources—so many from the Web, so many from print material in the campus library, so many from videos in the campus collection, and so on.

27. Teach students how and when to cite sources.
28. Warn students that you will be checking the originality of their papers with plagiarism-detection software. This deterrent is much more effective that just cautioning them against plagiarism (Braumoeller & Gaines, 2001).
29. Require a personal interview as a source, preferably taped or conducted over e-mail, with the documentation to be turned in.
30. Meet with students early and often to monitor their progress on a major assignment and to gauge the development of their ideas.
31. Guide and monitor students through the process of researching and writing. Have them complete assignments in stages and turn in progress reports.
32. Require students to submit first drafts. This ensures you see a work in progress and allows you to provide early feedback.
33. Require students to turn in photocopies of the print and Web material they use, at least the first page.
34. Require students to turn in the original of their paper and a copy for your files. You can refer to the file copy if you suspect piracy later.
35. Strive to be fair, clear, and authentic in all the ways you assess. Explain to students your rationales behind your assessment instruments and grading standards.

If you suspect any form of academic dishonesty, take swift, decisive action. Know your institution's policies and the person to whom to report the violation. (Ask your dean or chair, or refer to your institution's faculty handbook, student handbook, or course catalogue.) Our hope is that the judicial process won't be discouragingly time-consuming, laborious, and biased in the student's favor. Some instructors don't take the official route instead and handle cases quietly on their own—for example, giving an F to papers and tests where plagiarism or cheating is evident (Schneider, 1999). Ask senior colleagues how much de facto discretion you have and should take. Usually an instructor's ad hoc penalties are more lenient than institutional ones and don't go on a student's record.

We don't know very much about the incidence of cheating in online classes, but what we do know is discouraging. Milliron and Sandoe (2008) uncovered evidence of cheating on low-stakes online quizzes involving 20 percent of the three hundred students in their hybrid introductory information systems course. Most frequently, students were taking the quizzes in groups or giving one another answers. After their hybrid course ended, Haney and Clarke (2007) surveyed their students about their quiz-taking practices, 54 percent of whom admitted to exchanging answers and 79 percent of whom were aware of online cheating. Perhaps the intimacy of small, online courses counteracts the anonymity, and older students who don't know each other outside the course are probably less likely to cheat. But it's almost impossible to know who is taking an online exam unless the students have Webcams on their computers or a remote proctor is available (Carnevale, 1999).

HONOR CODES

Campuses with a well-established and well-enforced honor code have a somewhat lower incidence of cheating, by as much as 25 percent, than those that do not (Collison, 1990a; Gordon, 1990; McCabe & Trevino, 1996; McCabe, Trevino, & Butterfield, 1999). Students are responsible for policing one another, and cheating violations usually carry a heavy penalty, such as expulsion. However, these codes only reflect the real reason for the difference, which lies in the campus culture's high regard for academic integrity and honor (McCabe & Trevino, 1996; McCabe et al., 1999). Typically students pledge their adherence to the honor code in writing on every graded test and assignment, which serves to remind them of the code and reinforce their commitment to it. Such campuses are predominantly private.

In the hopes of changing the culture, several large, public institutions are testing the efficacy of modified honor codes. While instructors still take precautions such as proctoring tests and checking for plagiarism, students take an honor pledge and to an extent police themselves (Wasley, 2008). For instance, a student-dominated judicial board is often established to try alleged violators and decide their fate. Thus far, various forms of cheating have dropped to rates about midway between those of honor-code campuses and those of no-code campuses on the campuses that have adopted modified codes (McCabe & Pavela, 2000).

Another quite new and little-used strategy to change the campus culture or begin a transition to an institutional honor code is to encourage faculty to introduce classroom honor codes. Students are required to sign the code at the beginning of the course and again on each piece of graded work. Preliminary results are promising but are based on small classes (Pavela, 2008).

The success of traditional, modified, and classroom honor codes is modest yet shows that the student culture has an impact independent of the larger societal culture. But it only makes sense that cheating will remain prevalent as long as the larger culture tolerates unethical behavior.

■ CHANGING STUDENT VALUES

What about the future of this larger culture? As studies cited early in this chapter found, younger students feel little remorse about cheating, and they consider themselves ethical in spite of it. We are facing the prospect that this generation's culture of cheating will carry over into the broader society and economy. In fact, those who cheat in college intend to violate norms and rules in the future to get ahead (Lovett-Hooper, Komarraju, Weston, & Dollinger, 2007). It seems many, if not most, students don't perceive cheating as wrong. Can we possibly convince them that it is?

No doubt, we can convince some. According to a survey by Staats, Hupp, Wallace, and Gresley (2009), only 24 percent of the students definitely planned to cheat in the future, and almost 30 percent were uncertain. Perhaps this undecided group can be swayed.

Wueste (2008) is even more optimistic. He believes that we can persuade as many as 60 percent of our students by pointing out the damaging consequences, the injustice, and the character implications of cheating. He offers these specific arguments to share with students:

- Cheating misleads employers into thinking you have mastered knowledge and skills that you haven't. What harm will you do to the world lacking that knowledge and those skills?
- Relatedly, cheating cheapens your degree. If you graduate poorly prepared, you will lower your institution's regard among employers and your fellow citizens.
- Cheating undermines the faculty's ability to give you honest feedback and evaluation of your work.
- Cheating gives you an unfair advantage over your fellow students who do not cheat.
- Cheating violates the social contract that you voluntarily enter into with your institution when you arrived here.
- Cheating damages your character. If you cheat now in college, you will cheat later in other contexts—in the workplace, on your taxes, in your marriage, and so on.
- Cheating obstructs any hope of your achieving excellence in whatever matters to you. You will never accomplish what you are capable of; you won't even know what you're capable of.

We can add to Wueste's list Staats et al.'s hopeful findings (2009): compared to cheaters, academically honest students hold a higher opinion of others and score higher on measures of courage, empathy, and honesty in general.

Will reasoning this way with students change their values? If we have taught long enough, we know firsthand that we indeed have the power to create learning experiences that induce students to change their values. Our prevention and policing efforts haven't solved the cheating problem, and Wueste's and Staats et al.'s approach has barely been tried. Its time has come.

CHAPTER 9

Making the Most of Office Hours

When you think of your role as an instructor, you may picture yourself lecturing, facilitating discussion, managing student groups, answering questions, and the like in a classroom or laboratory—in any case, interacting with and helping a number of students to learn. During office hours, however, you interact with and help individual students. This is a golden teaching opportunity because one-on-one tutoring yields more learning by far than does class instruction (Bloom, 1984). Yet we rarely discuss or conduct research on holding effective office hours. Face-to-face and in private, students share their confusions, misunderstandings, and questions more candidly and completely than they do in class, and you are in the best position to give them the individual attention and help they need. The problem is getting them in your office.

Find out the number of office hours per week that your institution or department requires or expects of instructors. You may want to add another hour when you have a relatively large class or a writing-intensive course or if you are a professor without a teaching assistant (TA).

GETTING STUDENTS TO SEE YOU

Students see TAs during their office hours with little hesitation. But most of them, freshmen in particular, are intimidated by the prospect of visiting even the most kind-hearted, hospitable faculty member. If you're a TA who teaches your own course, you may be mistaken for faculty and face the same problem.

Students have their reasons for avoiding office hours. Those most likely to seek individual help tend to be getting middle-range grades in a course, in the B− to C+ range; those least likely are either doing quite well or doing very poorly and in most need of individual tutoring. The latter students have apparently decided that they are incapable of succeeding and are beyond help (Karabenick & Knapp, 1988). Other types of thinking may keep students away from your door. For instance, some personalities and cultures view help seeking as demeaning—threatening to either their self-esteem (Nadler, 1983) or perceived autonomy (Ryan, Pintrich, & Midgley, 2001). Spending your office hours alone with your research and writing may seem attractive at first, but it won't after you see those disappointing first papers, lab reports, or quizzes. So you have to make efforts to induce the students to see you. These efforts include finding the right place, establishing the right setting, scheduling the right times, and giving a lot of encouragement.

The Right Place

Office hours need not always be in your office. Richardson (2006) moved his office hours to a bench under a shade tree (he lives in a warm, sunny climate) and found the change energized his scholarship and his connection to students and the campus. Some years back, Gogel (1985) conducted an informal experiment that broadened the location possibilities. During a three-year observation period, he scheduled his office hours in a remote office building for the first and third years and in a common study area in the medical library the second year. In the first and third years, only one student showed up each year, predictably just prior to an exam. In the second year, a full 20 percent of his students paid him visits at various times during the semester to discuss the material and ask questions.

Could it be that students are more intimidated by your office than by you? Or perhaps the issue is the convenience of your office location. Does this mean you should move your office hours out of your office? If your office is out of the way for your students, the idea is worth considering, especially before exams and paper deadlines.

You might even split your office hours between two locations—some in your office and some in the student union or an appropriate library.

The Right Setting

Chung and Hsu (2006) experimented with supplementing their office hours with a weekly one- or two-hour "course center" in a regular classroom. With a course instructor or TA present, students could come to ask questions or just study on their own or in small groups for as long as they wanted. Some weeks no one came, and at other times (before

major tests and project due dates), almost 20 students (out of 150 enrolled one semester and 185 enrolled another semester) showed up. The researchers then administered surveys to the students asking where they sought help with the class. Almost 60 percent used the course center, versus 36 percent office hours, and almost 80 percent said the course center increased the likelihood of their getting help. Furthermore, 54 percent preferred the help offered by the course center over office hours, due in part to the group-work option and the informal, collegial atmosphere. Students could study or work on their homework and get an answer to a question as soon as it arose. Those struggling with the material could see that they were in good company and make visible progress.

No doubt the course center is a successful draw for students needing help, and it is worth your consideration as a supplement to your office hours. You may even be able to share center staffing duties with other instructors or TAs teaching different sections of the same or a similar course.

The Right Times

Be careful and considerate in scheduling your office hours. If you are available only briefly during prime class time—that is, when students are attending their other classes—then you immediately reduce your students' ability to see you. To maximize your availability to students, straddle your office hours over two class periods, allowing students with a class over one period the chance to see you during the other time slot. If you teach a discussion, recitation, or laboratory section, make sure that your office hours do not overlap with the lecture portion of the course. If you run out of hours in the day, consider scheduling an early evening office hour, perhaps in the student union, an appropriate library, or another student-friendly location. Also, consider the day. Try to schedule at least an hour on Mondays or Tuesdays, when students are most likely to have questions from the readings and other homework they did over the weekend. During the term, remind your classes periodically that you also meet by appointment.

The Right Encouragement

Start out by publicizing your office hours, first in your syllabus, then on the board or a slide during the first day of class, and intermittently during the term before high-traffic weeks, such as before tests and major assignment deadlines. Put a supportive statement in your syllabus graciously offering your willing counsel and urging students to take advantage of your office hours. Perrine, Lisle, and Tucker (1995) found this effort effective in attracting younger students (under age twenty-five) to seek help. You might have your students write your office hours and locations on the front of their course notebooks. In addition, post your hours prominently outside your office door.

It also helps to establish a friendly classroom atmosphere on the first day of class by having students fill out index cards on themselves, conducting icebreaker activities, and sharing highlights of your own background (see Chapter Four). On that day and throughout the rest of the term, warmly invite students to stop by your office to talk about the course as well as the material.

But even the warmest series of invitations may not provide enough encouragement. You may have to require the pleasure of their company. Here are several acceptable ways:

- Make it a regular course requirement for each student to schedule a time to meet with you as early in the term as possible. The first meeting will pave the way for future voluntary visits.
- Have students schedule individual meetings while they are writing the first paper. You can use this opportunity to review their first draft and clarify your expectations for the paper.
- Have students turn in papers, problem sets, lab reports, extra-credit work, and other assignments not in class but in your office during certain hours of a nonclass day.
- Have students schedule meetings with you to get their grades on their papers or written assignments. You can return their marked papers or assignments in class for them to review before meeting with you, but hold the grades hostage.

(This strategy works better during the term than after it ends.)
- If you divide your class into small groups or assign group projects, you might have each group schedule at least one appointment with you to give a progress report.

When students arrive, especially the first time, try to make them feel welcome and at ease. After all, they're on your turf, and it takes courage for them to be there. You might spend the first minute or two finding out how they are, how the course is going for them, and how they are experiencing college in general. In this day and age, however, too warm an approach can be misunderstood. If you are meeting in your office, close the door for privacy but leave it slightly ajar. Also maintain a respectable seating distance from the student.

Should an emergency or illness prevent you from making your office hours, leave a note or ask your department staff to leave a note, apologizing for your unavoidable absence.

■ MAKING THE TIME PRODUCTIVE

Most students who come to your office hours do so with a definite purpose in mind, often one that you have defined in class. So it is worth a little class time, if not a section in your syllabus, to advise students on how to prepare for meetings with you. You cannot be expected to read their minds. For instance, you might instruct them to come with appropriate materials: their journals or lecture notes, their lab books, their homework problems, drafts of their papers, or the readings with troublesome passages marked. You might even tell them to write out their questions or points of confusion as clearly as they can. If the issue is a homework problem, insist that they work it out as far as they can, even if they know their approach is faulty. If the issue is a grade, tell them to bring in a written justification—with citations to the readings, lectures, discussions, labs, or other materials—for changing their grade. Reserve the right to terminate and reschedule a meeting if a student is not adequately prepared. Why waste your time and your student's time? In addition, counsel students that they are not to use your office hours to get a condensed version of the classes they have missed or to get you to write their papers or do their homework problems for them. (Chapter Eight offers suggestions on handling problematic student demands and questions.)

When students do come properly prepared, try to give them your undivided attention. If you cannot prevent intrusive phone calls, keep them brief. If other students are waiting outside your door, work efficiently without letting their presence distract you.

■ STUDENT-ACTIVE TUTORING

To maximize the value of your consultation, make it as student-active as possible. Refer to Chapter Fourteen on questioning techniques for recommendations on how to help students work through their confusions as much on their own as possible. Although some students resent this strategy, you can often be most helpful by responding to their questions with other questions that will lead them to answers. After all, they won't really learn what you tell them—only what they themselves realize (Bonwell & Eison, 1991). Usually the single most informative (to you) and helpful (to them) question that you can pose to students you are tutoring is why they chose the answer or problem-solving approach that they did (especially if it's an incorrect one), why they came to the conclusion they did (have them reason it through), or why they stopped solving the problem, researching, reasoning, or writing, for example, where they did. This question should lead both of you to the key misconception, misunderstanding, missing step, or error in reasoning. Sometimes students want to see you to give them a sense of security. For instance, they have revised their paper according to your or their peer group's specifications, but they lack confidence in their writing. Or they have done their homework problems but want you to

check them over. Rather than giving just perfunctory affirmations, you can help them acquire their own sense of security by having them explain and justify to you their revisions or problem solutions. If they can "teach" their rationales, they have earned the right to feel confident.

Identifying student errors calls for extra gentleness. Students who come to you for extra help are probably feeling somewhat insecure and self-conscious. So praise their smallest breakthroughs generously, and let them know you appreciate their coming to see you. You want them to feel welcome to come back.

If a student fails to show up on time for an appointment, call to remind her and reschedule if necessary. If she simply forgot, counsel her that your time is too valuable a commodity to be forgotten.

■ STUDENTS IN ACADEMIC OR EMOTIONAL TROUBLE

Dealing with students in serious trouble is beyond the scope of an instructor's responsibility. Students who seem overwhelmed by the material or lack basic writing, reasoning, and mathematical skills should be referred to the learning skills or academic assistance center on your campus. As described in the Appendix, a unit of this type usually offers individual tutoring and workshops on a range of academic skills, such as textbook reading, writing, studying, problem solving, note taking, critical thinking, test preparation, and general learning.

Emotionally distressed students usually need professional help. For your own peace of mind, it is important to remember that you are neither the cause of nor the solution to their problems, even if they try to attribute them to a grade in your course. You can be most helpful by knowing how to identify such students, approaching them about their apparent problem in a nonjudgmental and caring way, referring them to your institution's psychological or counseling center (walk them there, if need be), and informing the center about the encounter. Here are some classic warning signs (Western Kentucky University Counseling and Testing Center, 2008):

- Angry challenges to your authority
- Physical aggression, either real or threatened
- Uncharacteristically animated or agitated behavior
- Complaints of rejection or persecution
- Distorted perceptions of reality
- Unjustified demands on your time
- A sudden drop in academic performance
- A sudden extended absence from class
- Repeated missed assignments
- Social withdrawal or isolation
- Deteriorations in physical appearance or personal hygiene
- Visible changes in weight
- Self-injurious behavior (for example, cutting oneself)
- Apparent drug or alcohol abuse
- Impaired speech or disjointed thoughts
- Dramatic mood swings or erratic behavioral changes
- Continual lack of energy, sleepiness, listlessness, or depression
- Expressions (oral or written) of hopelessness, worthlessness, loneliness, emotional pain, or the desire to end it all
- Expression of concern by a fellow student

The most immediate proper responses to aggressive behaviors are simple and easy to remember: when dealing with verbal aggression, make arrangements to meet with the student later in a private place to allow the emotions to defuse (verbal, private). If you sense the situation may elevate to physical abuse, move yourself and the student into a public area (physical, public). In any case, do not ignore the behaviors listed above if you see them.

It is impossible to anticipate all the different kinds of help that your students may need. The Appendix will help you refer them to the right office.

CHAPTER 10

Course Coordination Between Faculty and Teaching Assistants

The ideal relationship between faculty and teaching assistants (TAs) is a mutually beneficial exchange. The professor receives an invaluable staff member in return for supervising a graduate student's apprenticeship in college teaching. The TA in turn performs an array of vital support services, under the professor's direction, while preparing for his future career. Through the TA, the students benefit from the opportunity for personalized consultation and additional, often more participatory instruction than is possible in a large class with a single faculty member. It is an all-around win–win arrangement.

But often the faculty-TA relationship isn't as productive and mutually rewarding as it can be. Few professors are trained in supervisory techniques, and TAs may be afraid to reveal their ignorance by asking too many questions. In addition, the relationship requires time and effort that one or both parties may not be willing to give.

Like all other professional relationships, the successful TA-faculty team thrives on respect, trust, cooperation, and communication. This chapter suggests specific ways for both parties to foster these qualities in their working relationship.

■ BEFORE THE TERM: COURSE REVIEW AND ROLE SPECIFICATIONS

TA assignments should be made as early as possible, preferably well before the start of the term. Early assignments allow time for the faculty and TAs to discuss the course and their mutual responsibilities, as well as to prepare to meet them. This extra time is crucial for first-time TAs and for experienced TAs taking on new assignments. TAs also need the assurance that they will have support and guidance when the need arises.

If you are faculty, count yourself very fortunate to have one or more TAs, as only a handful of other faculty nationwide have them. But realize that they are university employees as well as graduate students. It is your professional obligation and duty to supervise them, which means that you are largely responsible for their performance (Perlmutter, 2008b). Supervising means assigning work to them, instructing them on how to perform the work, monitoring the quality of their performance, and giving them feedback on their performance. This feedback may not always be a pat on the back. It may involve additional instruction or even disciplining. When necessary, you will have to be tough, like a boss.

Hold an introductory staff meeting at least a few days before classes begin. Start this meeting by explaining the institutional policies and rules related to their employment, such as those pertaining to sexual harassment, the privacy of student records, and laboratory safety (Perlmutter, 2008b). Then hand out your syllabus and present your course objectives, organization, and schedule. Review general mechanics, such as grading policies and grade complaint procedures, even if TAs will not be conducting sections. Students' opinions of the course are influenced greatly by the efficiency and proficiency of the instructional staff.

Next, firmly establish the work roles that you and your TAs will play. TAs must know what is expected of them, as well as what they can expect of their faculty supervisors. To ensure clarity, issue a written statement of mutual responsibilities, and make sure everyone understands and agrees.

When allocating course duties, try to divide tasks fairly, equitably, and efficiently. TA responsibilities may include assisting in course preparation, preparing or instructing (or both) in laboratories, leading discussions, conducting help and review sessions, attending lectures, guest lecturing, taking roll, assisting in assignment and test preparation, being available during tests, grading, calculating grades, and holding office hours. More experienced TAs, those whom Nyquist and Wulff (1996) call "colleagues-in-training" and "junior colleagues," can take on more important tasks than can "senior learners," who just hope to survive their TAship and get the students to like them. The former can try their hand at designing activities and assignments, preparing handouts, constructing tests, writing rubrics, and taking over the lecture part of the class.

Faculty responsibilities typically involve constructing quizzes, tests, and assignments, supervising TAs doing these tasks, advising TAs on discussion sections or laboratory content and methods, coaching them in presentation and teaching skills, providing them with feedback on their teaching effectiveness, scheduling and directing TA staff meetings, and ensuring TAs have whatever supplies they need.

Depending on the size of the class and the number of TAs involved, you may wish to assign an experienced TA to act as a head TA in charge of facilitating communication among all course TAs. Strong interpersonal skills are essential here, as the head TA must maintain a good rapport with both you and fellow TAs.

Finally, try to give realistic estimates of the expected time and effort required of the TAs to perform their job well. While these estimates will vary from person to person and from week to week, they will allow TAs to plan their schedules more efficiently. Be sure you know the number of hours per week that each TA assignment involves.

◼ DURING THE TERM: REGULAR MEETINGS AND TEACHING FEEDBACK

Once you and your TAs reach a clear understanding on duties and expectations, everyone must first and foremost maintain open lines of communication. If a TA cannot approach you or the head TA with a problem, the situation may very well worsen and sour the student's learning experience. You and the head TA should actively invite TAs to seek your problem-solving advice.

Of course, communication is a two-way street. If you are a TA and you fail to seek or follow good counsel, openly disagree with your supervising faculty in front of your students, or otherwise are insubordinate, you are likely to get in trouble with the class and eventually your faculty. Clear, open communication is everyone's responsibility and is vital to the success of the course.

The easiest and most reliable means of maintaining good communication is the regular, usually weekly, staff meeting. (A chatroom meeting is a high-tech alternative to face-to-face.) Scheduling these meetings is the faculty's or head TA's charge. They are essential to the smooth coordination of multisection courses, which are so common at the introductory levels of the laboratory sciences, mathematics, English, and the foreign languages. These meetings should follow a fairly standard agenda of reviewing current and upcoming material, discussing TAs' lesson plans, and assessing students' learning. Let us take each major topic in turn.

Agenda Item 1: Course Content

If you are faculty, you must ensure that your TAs have enough background in the course material to teach or tutor it. If you don't require them to attend your lectures, you might give them copies of your lecture notes. Some TAs may benefit from supplementary readings as well. You should also provide your TAs with leads on the student trouble spots they can anticipate and should address in section and office hours. Especially in the lab sciences, TAs must be well versed in the principles, procedures, hazards, and typical pitfalls of the next laboratory. In addition to your TAs' reputation with students, safety may be at stake here.

If you are a TA, you are responsible for coming to these weekly meetings having read the upcoming readings, including the lab manual section, where applicable. Raise all your questions; reserve the "dumb" ones for your fellow TAs if you prefer. You too should anticipate student stumbling blocks and ask for help in leading your students over them. Whether your supervising faculty requires it, do attend all lectures. Students often complain on their teaching evaluation forms about TAs who do not. Always rehearse a lab you've never done before, preferably with a TA who has.

Agenda Item 2: TAs' Lesson Plans

The second major item is what the TAs should do with the upcoming material in their discussion sections, labs, or help sessions. What teaching techniques and formats will give students the most productive chance to actively work with and play with the material? Should the TAs start off with a quiz or a warm-up writing exercise on the major points of the reading, the lab procedures, or the last lecture? If discussion is appropriate, what questions should the TAs pose, and in what order? Should they be written on the board, on an overhead transparency, or in a handout? Or should they be handed out in advance and serve as a study guide? If reviewing homework problems is scheduled, should the TAs have students present their solutions on the board? Should the TAs have new problems for the students to solve in small groups? How about a short simulation, a case study, or role playing to actively engage students in the material? If a preexam review session is planned, what review questions would be helpful? How should the students address them? By writing practice answers individually, outlining them in small groups, or playing academic game like Jeopardy or Millionaire? In any case, the TAs should not be giving the answers themselves.

The options are more numerous than the techniques and formats covered in this book, and appropriate ones deserve discussion. This way, the weekly meetings can function as a teaching methods seminar for the TA staff.

The purpose that supplementary sections and help sessions should not serve is to introduce new material. As this book emphasizes throughout, few students can master material only through passive activities like reading and listening, even when supplemented with note taking. Students must also talk about it, write about it, apply it to problems, use it in experiments, act it out, see it demonstrated, or demonstrate it themselves—in essence, do something with it. The TA's most important role is to design and facilitate opportunities for students to work actively with material already introduced.

In addition to covering teaching techniques and formats for the coming week, these TA meetings should review what did and didn't work last time. TAs need not repeat one another's mistakes, and they can help each other solve their problems.

Occasionally, too, a classroom failure may call for some damage control, while a genuine success merits recognition, even imitation.

Agenda Item 3: Student Learning

The final item of business, assessing students' learning, has two parts. The first part is openly discussing how well students are learning the material. This information may come from homework assignments, quizzes and tests, classroom participation, classroom assessment exercises, consultations with students, and general impressions. By identifying areas of student weakness, all parties know what to review before proceeding to new material.

If you're a TA, you probably have an inside track on how the students are doing. Generally students talk more often and more candidly with you than with faculty. So you have a clearer picture of their involvement and difficulties with the material. You are also probably better positioned to identify individual students who are having academic or emotional trouble. When such cases arise, advise your supervising faculty. But for the students' sake, tell them about the campus units that can help them (see Chapter Nine and the Appendix).

The second part of assessing students' learning is planning the next stage of assessment and testing. Whether you are faculty or a TA, have other members of the course staff review a draft of any assignment, quiz, test, or grading rubric you have drafted. It is amazing what another set of eyes can pick up—not just typos but also double-barreled multiple-choice items, ambiguous essay questions, unclear performance descriptions on rubrics, awkward sentence structure, confusing word use, and all the other verbal land mines that are so hard to avoid. Sometimes, too, instructors forget to model their test questions on the homework and in-class exercises to which they accustomed their students. It is also easy to overlook important material covered just a few weeks ago. Assignments, quizzes, tests, and grading rubrics are important enough to ask others to review.

If you are a supervising faculty member fortunate enough to have all experienced TAs for a particular course, you may be tempted to shorten or forgo the weekly staff meetings. But resist the temptation. Your holding these meetings demonstrates your commitment to teaching excellence and staff morale.

One more faculty responsibility—an essential facet of supervision—is to observe and give constructive feedback to each of your TAs who appears before a class. The fact that you care enough to do so reinforces your TAs' loyalty and morale, along with the value of teaching in general. It is best to follow up each observation with a one-on-one consultation focusing on strategies for professional growth and improvement. For obvious reasons, do not delegate this task to a head TA.

■ EXTENDING MANAGING TO MENTORING

Beyond supervising TAs, you will no doubt become a mentor to certain graduate students. The mentoring relationship is complex enough to deserve discussion.

The role of the mentor is a multifaceted one that extends beyond the role model (Murray, 1991). For example, the mentor serves as a source of information about the profession, and she tutors the protégé (or mentee) in specific professional skills. During times of personal turmoil, the mentee seeks advice and a sympathetic ear, casting the mentor in a confidant role. The mentor also helps the protégé plot a suitable career path.

However, the mentoring relationship is a two-way street. As such, the protégé must accept responsibility for and be willing to advance his own growth and development. In addition, he must test his abilities against new challenges and honestly evaluate them in view of career options. Finally, he must be receptive to the mentor's instruction, coaching, and constructive criticism.

The mentoring relationship reaps returns for the mentor as well. According to some mentors, it heightens their motivation. While some senior personnel face burnout, mentors are constantly reminded of what they first found interesting and exciting about their profession. They become more inspired leaders, enhancing overall group and organizational productivity.

Here are some practical guidelines for both faculty and graduate students (Blandford, 2000; Cameron, 1993; Nicholls, 2002; Perlmutter, 2008a):

- *Mentors,* reasonably pace your training and advising. Remember that you didn't learn everything at once or the first time through.
- *Protégés,* regard your relationship as a college teaching tutorial, and budget time for it. If you feel overwhelmed, let your mentor know.

- *Mentors,* do not ask or expect your protégés to provide you with personal services, such as babysitting, house-sitting, running errands for you, or driving you around, except in an emergency.
- *Protégés,* respect the boundaries of the relationship and both your mentor's and your own limited time. Resist asking your mentor to do too much for you. Focus your meetings on professional business, not issues in your personal life.

- *Mentors,* be aware that your protégés are probably unfamiliar with various university and department regulations, office procedures, routine deadlines, and endless other professional protocols that are now second nature to you. Do convey this information explicitly.
- *Protégés,* take what your mentor tells you seriously, even if some of it sounds silly or strange.

- *Mentors,* give fair, encouraging, and caring feedback on your protégés' job performance on a regular basis. They may not know when they have done well and when they haven't, and they need to know, for both your and their sakes. Critical remarks can evoke a defensive, even fearful reaction. So couch them in terms of ways to improve and expectations for future success.

- *Protégés,* ask for regular feedback, and don't expect to hear you're doing a perfect job. There is always a lot to learn and plenty of room for improvement. If you find it hard to believe, just trust for now that your mentor's constructive criticism has nothing to do with her not liking you as a person or not believing in you as a junior professional. In fact, it's a compliment: it means she considers you strong enough to hear the truth and make improvements. If your mentor's counsel sounds inappropriate, ask for clarification, ponder it for while, and pass judgment later.

- *Mentors,* cultivate an environment where temporary lapses and setbacks, fears, and failures can be shared, forgiven, overcome, and filed away as learning experiences. Give your protégés as many chances as your course can afford. Whenever appropriate, counsel them on how to avoid or conquer the problem. For instance, advise an anxious protégé to visualize a worst-case classroom scenario, and together brainstorm ways to defuse the situation. (Your institution's teaching center can help.)
- *Protégés,* bring your performance fears out in the open. Your mentor can help you calm your adequacy anxieties, control your stage fright, and feel capable of handling your worst-case teaching nightmare. Remember that your mentor faced similar fears at one time. She hasn't forgotten, and she wants to help you.

- *Mentors,* resist the natural temptation to mold your protégés into your clones. Each must find and explore his own potential.
- *Protégés,* try on and borrow elements of your mentor's teaching and testing style that fit you, but also shop around. Great teaching takes many forms. Developing your own unique excellence is a creative, long-term process.

- *Mentors,* expect to feel occasionally that your time and wisdom are going unappreciated. Your protégés probably lack the experience to put your good counsel and training into perspective at the moment. Know that they will acquire that perspective and gratitude over time.

- *Protégés,* thank your mentor for her time, advice, instruction, and caring. Credit her when appropriate. Don't forget that while supervising a course is an assigned task, the more personal attention your mentor is giving you is purely voluntary and its own reward.

- *Mentors and protégés,* review your relationship periodically. Bear in mind that if it should endure, it is designed to self-destruct over the long run as the protégé evolves into a colleague. In the meantime, expect occasional tensions and imbalances. Mentors can find it hard both to accept and relinquish their superior role; protégés can vacillate between dependency and the desire to break away. Talking about these stresses informally can resolve them.

These same principles apply to mentoring relationships between faculty and undergraduates and between senior faculty and junior colleagues. At any level, the positive effects of the relationship are mutually substantial and the material costs minimal.

PART 3

CHOOSING AND USING THE RIGHT TOOLS FOR TEACHING AND LEARNING

CHAPTER 11

Matching Teaching Methods with Learning Outcomes

Your selection of teaching methods is critical to your students' learning. Derek Bok (2006) argues that it is even more important than the content you select, and he bemoans that faculty discussions neglect the topic of pedagogy. He points out the discouraging research finding that the average student cannot remember most of the factual content of a lecture within fifteen minutes after it ends. However, he notes, lessons learned through more active teaching methods can leave students changed forever:

> In contrast, interests, values, and cognitive skills are all likely to last longer, as are concepts and knowledge that students have acquired not by passively reading or listening to lectures but through their own mental effort.... The residue of knowledge and the habits of mind students take away from college are likely to be determined less by *which* courses they take than by *how* they are taught and *how well* they are taught. (pp. 48–49)

So let's turn to the critical issue of how you will teach your courses. This chapter extends the course design process in Chapter Two into course development: selecting the best teaching methods for enabling students to achieve your learning outcomes. If your course design is your skeleton, your methods are the muscles on the bones. Fortunately, some of your fellow faculty have devised and conducted research on numerous teaching innovations over the past few decades, so you have plenty of worthy options to choose from. Both Part Three of this book, which opens with this chapter, and Part Four focus on a wide range of well-researched methods that we know can generate powerful learning experiences, assuming they are implemented properly and for appropriate purposes. Chapters Twelve through Twenty-Two lay out ground rules for setting up and managing them correctly, and this chapter gives an overview of which methods to use when, where the "when" depends on your learning outcomes.

As Figure 11.1 graphically shows, every aspect of your course should be built on the foundation of your student learning outcomes. These are your ends throughout the term. Your teaching methods

Figure 11.1   The Model of the Perfect Fit in Course and Curriculum Design

Appropriate Assessment of Students' Performance on Outcomes

(the measurement of progress to the ends)

Teaching Methods and Learning Experiences to Help Students Achieve Outcomes

(the means to the ends)

Student Learning Outcomes

(the foundation, the ends)

are the means to your ends. They encompass all the learning experiences you give your students in the form of assignments and activities (active listening is an activity), whether in class or as homework. Your ends should guide your choice of means, right down to each individual class. The most appropriate means will afford your students practice in the performances specified in your learning outcomes—practice specifically in the way you plan to assess student performances for a grade (by multiple-choice items, a case analysis, a literary analysis, a creative multimedia project, a concept map, a diagram, a design, solutions to word problems, a solution to a real-world problem, and so on). Your assessment instruments in turn should measure your students' progress to your ends as directly as possible. These instruments—quizzes, test questions, assignments, and any other course component on which you see student results—should mirror your outcomes very closely.

If your outcomes go beyond students' recognizing and regurgitating correct facts, terms, equations, and algorithms—and they should go beyond these knowledge-level cognitive operations—you should be familiar with multiple means to help your students achieve your ends. As eminent psychologist Abraham Maslow once said, "If your only tool is a hammer, you're apt to go around treating everything as if it were a nail." In the not-so-distant past, faculty knew and used the lecture almost exclusively, and there was

precious little research to suggest that other methods were more effective for most purposes. We have since learned that you can't craft effective learning experiences just by hammering lectures into students' heads. The material doesn't stick well. But now we have a toolbox full of options. As an instructor, one of your most critical tasks is to choose the best tool for the job—or more accurately, choose among the best tools for the job, as you can usually identify several means to reach your ends.

■ TYPES OF TOOLS

A complete teaching toolbox contains three types of tools to select from: course formats, major teaching methods, and teaching "moves." "Teaching moves" refers to the ways you explain and elaborate on material, the learning strategies you share with your class, the short in-class activities and exercises you have students do (interactive lecture breaks, for example), and the questions you ask them to contemplate. You may not think you have control over your formats, but you may be able to negotiate a change.

Formats

A course format defines the course meetings—specifically, the setting and expected activities for the class period. It may be lecture meetings only, lecture meetings with discussion sections, lecture meetings with laboratories, lecture meetings with skill activity sessions, discussion meetings with some lecture, discussion meetings with skill activity sessions, skill activity sessions alone, or seminar. Let us clarify some terms. In a seminar, as opposed to a discussion section, students prepare their contributions in advance, whether research presentations, arguments, points of view, or interpretations. In a skill activity section, students have the chance to practice something, so it may be scheduled in a room other than a regular classroom, such as a computer lab, a language lab, a studio, a stage, a music room, or a clinic with medical equipment or a simulated human body. It may even take place outside or off-campus, perhaps in a botanical garden, a forest, a clinic, or a hospital.

We don't know the direct learning impact of different formats, but we do know quite a bit about the effects of closely related variables: the degree of in-class student activity (or lack thereof; see Chapter One) and class size. Hoyt and Perera (2000) identified not the actual impact of formats but the success that faculty perceive formats having for certain learning objectives. These objectives were somewhat different from the outcomes presented in Chapter Two for course design. In Hoyt and Perera's study, they ranged from "substantive knowledge" (of facts, principles and theories, and applications) to much higher-order abilities such as general cognitive and academic skills (communication and critical thinking), lifelong learning skills (research and interest), personal development (broad liberal knowledge and values development), and other skills and competencies (team skills and creativity). Hoyt and Perera found that faculty consider lecture/discussion, lecture/lab, and lecture/skill activity pretty ineffective—"average" at best—in equipping students to meet these objectives. (Lecture/lab achieved a high average on factual knowledge, as did lecture/discussion on values development.) Discussion/lecture did better on general cognitive and academic skills and personal development (liberal knowledge). Skill activity alone earned high ratings on developing students' communication skills, creative capacities, and liberal knowledge, but average on the other objectives. The

only formats that faculty saw as highly effective on almost all of the objectives were discussion/lecture and seminar. Not surprisingly, both have a great deal of student activity and small-size classes.

You probably think of formats as assigned to you with the courses you teach. Introductory courses are typically lecture based, perhaps with discussion, lab, or skill activity sections, while freshman seminars are set up as seminars or discussion sessions. Courses in the major may be anchored in the lecture, discussion, skill activity, or seminar format. If you believe that a different format from the one currently attached to your course would enhance student learning, make a case to your department chair. Point out that you have learning outcomes that your students are unlikely to achieve because, for all practical purposes, the current format prohibits the effective teaching methods and moves. You have nothing to lose by asking, and you and your students have a great deal to gain.

The next two sections address which teaching methods and moves are most effective for various learning outcomes.

Teaching Methods

The tools in this category comprise major methods—that is, multiweek assignments or in-class activities that require considerable time. We may schedule one on a regular or semiregular basis during a course or devote one or more class periods to it. For instance, we rarely have just one discussion or one small-group activity during a term-long course. If we do plan just one, it probably won't work very well because it will violate the students' expectations. If we choose to give interactive lectures, we probably give many of them. If we use the case method to teach, we probably assign and debrief at least several cases during the term. We may have just one simulation, one substantial problem-based learning assignment, or one service-learning project, but each of these is likely to require students to put in hours of class time or homework.

Before turning to the outcomes each method may serve, let us review the basic definitions of these methods. Most of them merit their own chapter or at least a section of a chapter in Parts Three, Four, or Six of this book.

- *Lecture:* Instructor presenting material and answering student questions that arise (Chapter Twelve)
- *Interactive lecture:* Lecture with two- to fifteen-minute breaks for student activities (such as answering a multiple-choice objective item, solving a problem, comparing and filling in lecture notes, debriefing a minicase, doing a think-pair-share exercise, or a small-group discussion) every twelve to twenty minutes (Chapter Twelve)
- *Recitation:* Students answering knowledge and comprehension questions (Chapter Fourteen)
- *Directed discussion:* Class discussion that follows a more or less orderly set of questions that the instructor has crafted to lead students to certain realizations or conclusions or to help them meet a specific learning outcome (Chapters Thirteen and Fourteen)
- *Writing and speaking exercises:* Any of many informal assignments and activities, usually in-class and ungraded, to help students learn material, clarify their thinking, or make progress on a formal assignment (Chapter Seventeen)
- *Classroom assessment techniques:* Informal assignments and activities, usually in-class and ungraded, to inform the instructor how well students are mastering new material just presented or read; often overlap with writing and speaking exercises (Chapter Twenty-Eight)
- *Group work/learning:* Students doing a learning activity or creating a product in small groups of two to six in or out of class; must be carefully managed by the instructor (Chapter Sixteen)
- *Student-peer feedback:* Students giving one another feedback on a written or an orally presented product, usually a written draft or practice speech (Chapter Seventeen)
- *Cookbook science labs:* Pairs or triads of students conducting a traditional, often predictable experiment following prescribed, cookbook-like procedures (Chapter Twenty-Two recommends and illustrates more effective inquiry-based labs)
- *Just-in-time teaching:* Instructor adjusts class activities and lectures to respond to the misconceptions revealed by students' electronic responses to conceptual questions; an extension of electronic daily quizzes to motivate students to do the readings (Chapters Eighteen and Twenty-Three)
- *Case method:* Students applying course knowledge to devise one or more solutions or resolutions to problems or dilemmas presented in a realistic story or situation; an individual, small-group, or whole-class activity (Chapter Nineteen)
- *Inquiry-based or inquiry-guided learning:* Students learning or applying material in order to meet a challenge, such as to answer a question, conduct an experiment, or interpret data (Chapter Eighteen)
- *Problem-based learning:* Student groups conducting outside research on student-identified learning issues (unknowns) to devise one or more solutions or resolutions to fuzzy problems or dilemmas presented in a realistic story or situation (Chapter Twenty)
- *Project-based learning:* Students (as individuals or in groups) applying course knowledge to produce something, such as a report (written or oral), process or product design, research or program proposal, or computer code; often paired with cooperative learning
- *Role plays:* Students acting out instructor-assigned roles, improvising the script, in a realistic and problematic social or interpersonal situation (Chapter Fifteen)
- *Simulations:* Students playing out, either face-to-face or on computer, a hypothetical social situation that abstracts key elements from reality (Chapter Fifteen)
- *Service-learning with reflection:* Students learning from the experience of performing community service and systematically reflecting on it (Chapter Fifteen)
- *Fieldwork and clinicals:* Students learning how to conduct research and make sound professional judgments in real-world situations

The outcomes we will consider should sound familiar. As you will recall from Chapters One and Two, the first six on this list come from Bloom (1956) and Anderson and Krathwohl (2000), the seventh from Perry (1968), and the last from Nelson (2000):

- *Knowledge/Remembering:* To memorize or recognize facts, terms, principles, or algorithms
- *Comprehension/Understanding:* To translate, restate in one's own words
- *Application/Applying:* To use, apply, make useful
- *Analysis/Analyzing:* To identify and examine components, compare and contrast, identify assumptions, deduce implications
- *Synthesis/Creating:* To make connections, identify new relationships, design something new (new to students)

- *Evaluation/Evaluating*: To make a judgment, assess validity, select, and defend
- *Cognitive Development:* To progress from dualism to multiplicity to relativism to a tentative commitment to the most worthy perspective available; to come to understand the nature of knowledge as inherently uncertain but subject to definite standards of comparison
- *Shift in Mental Models:* to replace a faulty understanding of a phenomenon with the discipline's more valid mental model

Table 11.1 brings these outcomes and the major methods together in answering the question,

Table 11.1 Teaching Methods Found to Be Effective for Helping Students Achieve Different Learning Outcomes

Outcome Method	Knowledge	Comprehension	Application	Analysis	Synthesis	Evaluation	Cognitive Development	Shift in Models
Lecture	X							
Interactive lecture	X	X	a	a	a	a	a	
Recitation	X	X						
Directed discussion		X	a	a	a	a	a	a
Writing/speaking exercises		X	X	X	X	X		
Classroom assessment techniques		X	X	X		X		
Group work or learning		X	a	a	a	a	a	
Student-peer feedback		X		X		X		
Cookbook science labs		X	X					
Just-in-time teaching	X	X						X
Case method			X	X	X	X	X	
Inquiry based or inquiry guided	X[b]	X	X	X	X	X	X	X
Problem-based learning	X[b]		X	X	X	X	X	
Project-based learning	X[b]	X	X	X	X	X		
Role plays and simulations		X	X	X		X		X
Service-learning with reflection			X	X	X	X		X
Fieldwork/clinicals	X		X	X	X	X	X	X

NOTE: An X indicates this method can help students achieve this learning outcome if the method is properly implemented to serve this outcome. Poor implementation or implementation for other ends may mitigate against students' achieving the outcome.
[a]Depends on the lecture-break tasks, the discussion questions, or the group tasks assigned.
[b]The knowledge acquired may be narrowly focused on the problem or project.

"Which methods for which outcomes?" Two caveats are in order. First, this table represents the general findings of a large body of literature on the methods listed. The references are embedded in the chapters and chapter sections on each method. Second, the efficacy of the interactive lecture, directed discussion, and group work depends entirely on the tasks you have students do or the questions you have them discuss. For identifying productive tasks and questions for your outcomes, see Chapters Twelve and Fourteen as well as Exhibit 11.1 in the next section. This table lists short in-class assignments and activities that help students master each of Bloom's cognitive operations.

Teaching Moves

Teaching moves are strategies for clarifying content and giving students practice in thinking about and working with it, as reflected in your learning outcomes. The practice you give them should at least resemble the ways you plan to assess their learning.

Compared to major methods, these mini-methods entail much less time and commitment. You may use a dozen or more of them in a given class period—one to help students recall the readings, the next to clarify a knotty point, another to explain new material, yet another for a lecture break in which students apply the material, and so on. If one doesn't seem to work well, you can immediately try another. When a teaching move involves the students in an activity, not only do they get practice, but you obtain immediate feedback on their misconceptions, misunderstandings, and mastery. In turn, you can give them immediate feedback. Thus, many of these moves serve to assess as well as teach.

Exhibit 11.1 lists effective teaching moves by the learning outcome they serve. Some of them specify what you can do or say in class to familiarize your students with different ways of thinking about and working with the material. The rest are activities and exercises for your students to give them practice and you feedback on their learning. The existing literature addresses these mini-methods only in terms of their relationship to Bloom's cognitive operations (Goodson, 2005). But these operations do represent key learning outcomes and easily map onto Anderson and Krathwohl's (2000). This list is not exhaustive, but it is a rich heuristic device that may inspire you to devise additional teaching moves to serve your purposes.

Exhibit 11.1   Effective Teaching Moves for Six Learning Outcomes (Bloom's Cognitive Operations)

KNOWLEDGE

For You to Do

- Suggest prior knowledge to which students can link new and future information and knowledge.
- Chunk knowledge into coherent groups, categories, or themes.
- Share devices to improve memory such as mnemonic patterns, maps, charts, comparisons, groupings, highlighting of key words or first letters, visual images, and rhymes.
- Point out parts, main ideas, patterns, and relationships within sets of facts or information.

For Students to Do

- Practice recalling and restating information.
- Practice recognizing or identifying information.
- Practice recalling and reproducing information.
- Practice restating concept definitions and principles.

COMPREHENSION

For You to Do

- Outline new or upcoming material in simple form.
- Concept-map or mind-map new or upcoming material.
- Explain with concrete examples, metaphors, questions, or visual representations.

For Students to Do

- Restate or paraphrase and summarize information or knowledge.
- Describe or explain phenomena or concepts using words different from those used in the initial teaching.
- Identify the correct meaning of concepts or terms.
- Add details or explanations to basic content.
- Relate new to previously learned content.
- Construct visual representations of main ideas (mind or concept maps, tables, flowcharts, graphs, diagrams, or pictures).

APPLICATION

For You to Do

- Give multiple examples of a phenomenon that are meaningful to students.
- Define the procedures for use, including the rules, principles, and steps.
- Provide the vocabulary and concepts related to procedures.
- Explain steps as they are applied.
- Define the contexts, problems, situations, or goals for which given procedures are appropriate.
- Explain the reasons that procedures work for different types of situations or goals.
- Ensure students' readiness by diagnosing and strengthening their command of related concepts, rules, and decision-making skills.
- Provide broad problem-solving methods and models.
- Begin with simple, highly structured problems; then gradually move to more complex, less structured ones.
- Use questions to guide student thinking about problem components, goals, and issues.
- Give students guidance in observing and gathering information, asking appropriate questions, and generating solutions.

For Students to Do

- Generate new examples and nonexamples.
- Paraphrase the procedures, principles, rules, and steps for using or applying the material.
- Practice applying the material to problems or situations to gain speed, consistency, and ease in following the problem-solving steps.
- Practice choosing the types of problem-solving strategies for different situations.
- Solve simple, structured problems, then complex, unstructured ones.

- Practice recognizing the correct use of procedures, principles, rules, and steps with routine problems, then complex ones.
- Demonstrate the correct use of procedures, principles, rules, and steps with routine problems, then complex ones.

ANALYSIS

For You to Do

- Point out the important and the unimportant features or ideas.
- Point out examples and nonexamples of a concept, highlighting similarities and differences.
- Give a wide range of examples, increasing their complexity over time.
- Emphasize the relationships among concepts.
- Explain different types of thinking strategies, including how to think open-mindedly, responsibly, and accurately.
- Emphasize persistence when answers are not apparent.
- Ask students questions that require their persistence in discovering and analyzing data or information.
- Encourage students to self-evaluate and reflect on their learning.
- Ask questions that make students explain why they are doing what they are doing.
- Explain and model how to conduct systematic inquiry, detect flaws and fallacies in thinking, and adjust patterns of thinking.

For Students to Do

- Classify concepts, examples, or phenomena into correct categories.
- Summarize different types of thinking strategies.
- Use types of thinking strategies to analyze and evaluate their own thinking.
- Practice choosing the best type of thinking strategy to use in different real-world situations and explaining why their choice is superior.
- Detect and identify flaws and fallacies in thinking.
- Identify and explain instances of open- and closed-mindedness.
- Identify and explain instances of responsible versus irresponsible and accurate versus inaccurate applications of thinking strategies.
- Answer questions that require persistence in discovering and analyzing data or information.

SYNTHESIS

For You to Do

- Promote careful observation, analysis, description, and definition.
- Explain the process and methods of scientific inquiry.
- Explain and provide examples of how to identify a research problem, speculate about causes, formulate testable hypotheses, and identify and interpret results and consequences.
- Model inquiry and discovery processes.
- Encourage independent thinking, and avoid dead ends and simplistic answers.
- Show students examples of creativity to solve problems.
- Encourage students to take novel approaches to situations and problems.
- Explain phenomena using metaphors and analogies.

- Give students examples of reframing a problem—turning it upside down or inside out or changing perceptions about it.
- Explain and encourage brainstorming.
- Pose questions and problems with multiple good answers or solutions.
- Give students opportunities for ungraded creative performance and behavior.

For Students to Do

- Explain their experiences with inquiry activities and the results.
- Resolve a situation or solve a problem that requires speculation, inquiry, and hypothesis formation.
- Resolve a situation or solve a problem requiring a novel approach.
- Design a research study to resolve a conflicting finding.
- Write the limitations section of a research study.
- Write the conclusions section of a research study.
- Develop products or solutions to fit within particular functions and resources.
- Manipulate concrete data to solve challenging thinking situations.
- Practice reframing a problem—turning it upside down or inside out or changing perceptions about it.
- Explain phenomena using metaphors and analogies.

EVALUATION

For You to Do

- Create conflict or perplexity by posing paradoxes, dilemmas, or other situations to challenge students' concepts, beliefs, ideas, and attitudes.
- Explain how to recognize and generate proof, logic, argument, and criteria for judgments.
- Explain and show students the consequences of choices, actions, or behaviors.
- Provide relevant human or social models that portray the desired choices, actions, or behaviors.
- Explain with examples how factors such as culture, experience, desires, interests, and passions, as well as systematic thinking, influence choice and interpretations.

For Students to Do

- Evaluate the validity of given information, results, or conclusions.
- Draw inferences from observations, and make predictions from limited information.
- Explain how they form new judgments and how and why their current judgments differ from their previous ones.
- Identify factors that influence choice and interpretations, such as culture, experience, desires, interests, and passions, as well as systematic thinking.
- Detect mistakes, false analogies, relevant versus irrelevant issues, contradictions, and faulty predictions.
- Critique a research study.
- Use research and analysis to devise the best available solutions to problems, and explain why they are the best.
- Choose among possible behaviors, perspectives, or approaches, and provide justifications for these choices.

Note: Partially adapted from Goodson (2005) with permission.

◼ DANGEROUS KNOWLEDGE?

As we build our knowledge of the effectiveness of different teaching formats, methods, and moves for various learning outcomes, we run out of excuses for relying on traditional lecture. Bok (2006) accuses the faculty of avoiding pedagogical debates for their own self-protection from change:

> It is relatively easy to move courses around by changing curricular requirements. It is quite another matter to decide what methods of pedagogy should be altered. Reforms of the latter kind require much more effort.... To avoid such difficulties, faculty have taken the principle of academic freedom and stretched it well beyond its original meaning to gain immunity from interference with how their courses should be taught.... Teaching methods have become the personal prerogative of the instructor rather than a subject appropriate for collective deliberation. The result is to shield from faculty review one of the most important ingredients in undergraduate education. (p. 49)

Bok's stinging critique of the faculty may be apt, but it also opens a Pandora's box. What if instructors weren't completely free to choose their pedagogy? What if they could choose from only a limited range of methods and moves that were mandated for different learning outcomes? This prospect isn't absurd. After all, don't departments, institutions, and both regional and professional accreditation agencies already mandate learning outcomes? If they mandate the ends of instruction, why shouldn't they mandate the means to those ends? If you regard such intervention as outside interference, consider this: Shouldn't someone be responsible for ensuring that students receive the most effective learning experiences available? If so, should faculty who use methods outside the approved range be disciplined? But then what happens to pedagogical innovation and experimentation? Perhaps we can head off this quandary of questions and the threat of regulation by taking responsibility ourselves for choosing the best teaching strategies.

An instructor's pedagogy also has an impact on her student ratings and comments. While most students do enjoy active learning strategies, some do not (Amador, Miles, & Peters, 2006; Qualters, 2001; Thorn, 2003). In fact, a few of the best teaching methods for helping students acquire high-level thinking skills can lower student ratings (for example, problem-based learning). Some students protest that the methods require too much work, lack sufficient structure, demand more independence than they can or want to manage, or cause undue grade anxiety, since they are being asked to do things they've never done before. Some complain that they have to teach themselves too much and that their instructor isn't doing her job. At the same time, colleges and universities are striving to serve and retain students. In this crunch, which should take higher priority: Student satisfaction or student learning? This is a value matter that only institutions can resolve for themselves. But we can help tremendously by explaining why we choose certain teaching methods and moves over others. When we refer to the research standing behind our selections, we reaffirm to our students our commitment to do the best by them.

CHAPTER 12

Making the Lecture a Learning Experience

Lecturing is the transfer of information from the notes of the lecturer to the notes of the student without passing through the minds of either.

—MORTIMER ADLER, ARISTOTELIAN PHILOSOPHER

Lecture has gotten a bad rap over the past few decades. Although it is just as effective as any other teaching method in conveying factual knowledge, numerous studies find that it falls short in promoting deeper-level student learning and development—specifically, the ability to examine and possibly change attitudes and values, critical thinking and problem-solving skills, the transference of knowledge to new situations, open-minded exploration of controversial or ambiguous material, mastery of a performance technique or technical procedure, improvement in communication skills, personal and social adjustment, motivation for further learning, satisfaction with the course, and retention of knowledge after the course is over (Bligh, 2000; Bonwell & Eison, 1991; Hake, 1998; Jones-Wilson, 2005; McKeachie, Pintrich, Lin, Smith, & Sharma, 1990). In addition, it encourages a surface (superficial, nonconceptual) approach to learning (Canfield, 2002). For deep learning and higher-order thinking outcomes, more student-active methods such as discussion and inquiry-based learning are more successful.

There is more bad news for lecture lovers: from research dating back to the 1920s, lectures have an infamous reputation for being utterly forgettable. Their much-replicated "forgetting curve" for the average student is 62 percent recall of the material just presented, 45 percent recall three to four days later, and only 24 percent recall eight weeks later (Menges, 1988).

Lecture doesn't have to be the mindless, quickly forgotten transmission that Mortimer Adler described. It can be saved—but only if it is used for the right purposes, is carefully prepared and eloquently delivered, and is supplemented with thought-provoking student activities. With lecture, less is more.

■ PURPOSE: TO LECTURE OR NOT TO LECTURE?

As Chapter Eleven advised, student learning outcomes should guide choice of methods. Already listed above are outcomes that lecture doesn't serve well.

113

According to Table 11.1, straight lecture has proven effective only in helping students acquire knowledge, and given its forgetting curve, it hasn't done a very good job of that. Still, knowledge is at the heart of our enterprise. Therefore, for at least segments of a class period, the lecture may be essential. The list below sets out occasions when it is probably the most effective and efficient option (Bligh, 2000; McKeachie, 2002):

- You want to model a problem-solving approach or a kind of higher-order thinking before asking your students to try it themselves.
- You want to provide some quick background knowledge that is not summarized in print.
- You want to adapt very sophisticated knowledge to your students' level and needs in a way that no other available source does.
- You want to present a particular organization of the material that clarifies the structure of the reading, the course, or the field.
- You want to add your personal viewpoint on the material or your own related research.
- You want to update your students with the very latest material, and it is not yet available from another source that is targeted to the students' level.
- You want to pique your students' curiosity and motivation to learn if your style is very expressive.

You will note that some of these occasions are qualified by the lack of other sources. If you can find the same material online or in print, you may want to make it a reading assignment. In fact, some faculty have turned their lectures into homework, posting print versions, videos, or podcasts of them on the course website for students to download. Many of these faculty teach online or hybrid courses, but some just want to reserve their face-to-face class time for student activities.

Do not lecture material that simply duplicates the assigned readings or other course materials. Repetition and redundancy have their place, but student-active exercises can duplicate the material at a higher cognitive level, such as application, analysis, synthesis, and evaluation. Deleting a redundant lecture frees plenty of class time for student activities. Besides, if a lecture primarily repeats the readings, any rational student will decide either to do the readings or to attend lecture (see Chapter Twenty-Three)—no doubt not what you intend.

If you are uncertain of your students' level of expertise, preparation, and interest, have them do one or more classroom assessment exercises (see Chapter Twenty-Eight) before planning your lectures. Otherwise you risk going over the students' heads or boring them with basics.

■ PREPARING AN EFFECTIVE LECTURE

Bligh (2000) lays out several organizational models for lectures, but they share the common ground summarized here.

Class Outcomes

First, determine your student learning outcomes for the class period. What precisely do you want your students to learn that day? How will you express your outcomes to the class? If a lecture serves only one or two of the multiple objectives you have for the class, then it should fill only part of the period.

Overview

Whenever possible, limit one class's lecture to one major topic. Some students find it difficult to pick up a lecture from one period to the next, and global thinkers need to see the big picture before any of the details and examples will make sense. Also lay out a time-content schedule, bearing in mind the two most common lecturing errors: trying to include too much material and delivering the material too fast. While you're lecturing, you will have to proceed slowly enough, including pausing after major points, for students to take notes. So if anything, underbudget content.

To start planning your lecture, you might begin by subdividing the major topic into ten- to fifteen-minute chunks. Then plan student-active breaks of two to fifteen minutes between these chunks. Later in this chapter, you find a wide variety of short break activities that you can use, but feel free to devise your own. Most of them can be (and have been) conducted in large lectures of hundreds of students as well as smaller classes. So class size need not deter you. Finally, allow two to five minutes for some kind of recap activity at the end.

Let us turn to the internal organization of your lecture. The skeleton for any lecture is the introduction, the body, and the conclusion (McKeachie, 2002).

Introduction

The ideal introduction has three parts, the order of which is really an aesthetic decision: (1) a statement that frames the lecture in the context of the course objectives, (2) a statement reviewing and transitioning from the material covered in the previous class period, and (3) an attention grabber for the new material. Effective attention grabbers include an intriguing question the lecture will answer, a story or parable that illustrates the new subject matter of the day, a demonstration of a nonobvious phenomenon, a reference to a current event or movie, a case or a problem that requires the lecture's information to solve, or a strong generalization that contradicts common thought. The idea is to draw in the class with surprise, familiarity, curiosity, or suspense.

Body

The body is your presentation and explication of new material. It is within this section that you subdivide the major topic into minilectures, each of which should revolve around only one major point. There is no best logic to follow in organizing a minilecture except to keep it simple. You can choose from an array of options: deduction (theory to phenomena/examples); induction (phenomena/examples to theory); hypothesis testing (theory to hypothesis to evidence); problem to solution; cause to effect; concept to application; familiar to unfamiliar; debate to resolution; a chronology of events (a story or process)—to name just some common possibilities. To appeal to different learning styles, try to vary your organization from one minilecture to another (see Chapter Twenty-Five).

Organizational Outline

Make whatever organization you select explicit to students. For instance, tell the class, "I am going to describe some common manifestations of dysfunctional family behavior, then give you a definition and general principles that apply to the phenomenon."

It is best to provide a general outline of the main points (only) of your lecture on the board, on an overhead or slide, or in a handout. An outline will ensure that students are following your logical flow, especially if you occasionally refer to it to point out your location in the lecture. It should also highlight new terms you are introducing. However, keep this outline skeletal so students still have to take notes. Research shows that the process of note taking has learning and retention benefits (see the "Teaching Students to Take Good Notes" section later in this chapter.)

In addition, try to integrate as many of these learning aids as you can:

- *Visuals.* As you plan the material, think about how you can convey or repackage it visually—in pictures, photographs, slides, graphic metaphors, diagrams, graphs, and concept or mind maps (spatial arrangements of concepts or stages linked by lines or arrows). Prepare these graphics for presentation to the class. While such visual aids facilitate almost everyone's learning, they can be critical for students with a visual learning style (see Chapters Twenty-Five and Twenty-Six).
- *Examples.* Think about illustrating abstract concepts and relationships with examples. Ideally these examples should be striking, vivid, current, common in everyday life, and related to students' experiences (past, present, or future). Making them humorous also helps students remember them.

- *Restatements*. Consider how you can restate each important point in two or three different ways—in scholarly terms, lay formal language, and informal language. Restatements not only demystify the material, making it more comprehensible, but they also build students' vocabulary and encourage their own paraphrasing of the material.

Conclusion

For learning purposes, the conclusion should be a two- to five-minute recap of the most important points in your lecture. It is too important to be rushed after the bell. You should plan and direct the recap activity, but the students should do it. The prospect of having to retrieve the material helps keep all students on their toes. The recap activity may take the form of an oral summary presented by one or more students, a free-recall writing exercise (see Chapter Seventeen), a classroom assessment technique such as a one-minute paper (see Chapter Twenty-Eight), or a quiz.

In fact, we know that giving a quiz, graded or ungraded, at the end of the class period is a particularly effective means to ensure students retain more of your lecture content. Recall lecture's infamous forgetting curve: 38 percent of the material gone within minutes, 55 percent in three to four days, and 76 percent in eight weeks. Now recall from Chapter One that people learn less by reviewing material and more from being tested or testing themselves on it, as the latter activities involve greater cognitive processing and practice retrieving (Dempster, 1996, 1997; Roediger & Karpicke, 2006). This is why giving some kind of test right after a lecture doubles both factual and conceptual recall after eight weeks (Menges, 1988).

Your Lecture Notes

Your lecture notes should be easy to read at a glance and as sketchy as you can handle. After all, you know the material. So all you need is a map showing your next conceptual destination. Therefore, consider laying out the lecture graphically in flowcharts, concept maps, tree diagrams, Venn diagrams, network models,

and so on, including any visual aids you plan to put on the board. Some instructors like to color-code their notes for quick visual reference. If a graphic organization does not appeal to you, make a sketchy outline of your lecture. But be sure it's very sketchy. In any case, write big and leave a lot of white space.

The habit to avoid is writing out sentences (except direct quotes). That may tempt you to read them in class, in which case you will lose spontaneity, expressiveness, flexibility, eye contact, and, most important, psychological contact with the class, lulling students into a passive, inattentive state of mind (Day, 1980). Confine the words in your notes to key concepts and phrases, transitions to make explicit to the class, and directions to yourself (for example, "board," "pause," "slide," "survey class," "ask class question," "break activity #2—voltage problem").

■ DELIVERING AN EFFECTIVE LECTURE

Actually a lecture can be highly motivational, but its success depends on the lecturer. An expressive, enthusiastic instructor can ignite students' interest in the material, and a reserved, boring one can douse it.

The platform skills that convey energy, dynamism, and charisma can be isolated—they are listed in Chapter Seven—and learned. Public speaking courses and clubs help people develop and practice eye contact, effective verbal pacing and pausing, vocal quality and variety, facial expressions, gestures and movements, lectern and microphone use, visual aid display, and so on. Those who start out weak in these skills but work on them diligently can achieve impressive results within a year.

Some scholars may dismiss such presentation techniques as mere acting. In fact, some people seem to have a knack for them, while others acquire them only with concentration and practice. Acting or not, like it or not, these public speaking techniques have a powerful impact on students' motivation and learning, as well as on their course and instructor evaluations (see Chapter Thirty-Two). But this is true only to the extent that an instructor relies on the lecture format. With the variety of teaching methods available, no instructor need rely on it much at all.

Therefore, instructors have a choice. Those who happen to have an expressive, dynamic public personality or are willing to acquire the trappings of one can afford to use the lecture more in their teaching. (For the sake of student learning, however, even the most charismatic instructor should not depend on it exclusively.) Those who do not project such a persona can avoid lecturing whenever possible and employ more student-active methods. In brief, you should play to your natural and acquired strengths. The wide array of effective teaching methods should put to rest the notion that good teachers are born and not made.

■ INCORPORATING STUDENT-ACTIVE BREAKS: THE INTERACTIVE LECTURE

Well-chosen student-active breaks—coined "brainy breaks" by Rick Beam, academic dean and vice president for academics at Johnston Bible College—comprise the heart of the interactive lecture, transforming the traditional lecture into a series of minilectures.

Attention Span Limits

According to studies cited in Bligh (2000), Bonwell and Eison (1991), and Middendorf and Kalish (1996), a lecture begins with a five-minute settling-in period during which students are fairly attentive. This attentiveness extends another five to ten minutes, and then students become progressively bored, restless, and confused. Focus and note taking increasingly drop—some students effectively fall asleep—until the last several minutes of the period, when they revive in anticipation of the end of class. Bligh reconfirmed this pattern using students' heart rates as a measure of arousal. Even medical students display similar patterns of concentration levels: an increase over about fifteen minutes, followed by a sharp decrease.

This is unsettling, sobering news for the higher education community. After all, if highly motivated learners like medical students demonstrate such a brief attention span in the lecture setting, what can we expect of our undergraduates? No doubt enthusiastic, engaging lecturers can extend that narrow time horizon. But aside from improving our platform skills, what else can we do when we must lecture?

In a word, pause. One study supports the practice of pausing at least three times during each lecture to allow pairs or small groups of students to discuss and clarify the material (Rowe, 1980). Another recommends pausing for two minutes every fifteen to eighteen minutes to permit student pairs to compare and rework their notes (Ruhl, Hughes, & Schloss, 1987). This latter study was designed experimentally with a control group receiving a series of traditional nonstop lectures and a treatment group hearing the same lectures with periodic pauses. Both groups took free-recall quizzes during the last three minutes of each lecture (that is, students individually wrote down everything they could remember from the lecture) and the same sixty-five-item multiple-choice test twelve days after the last lecture. In two different courses repeated over two semesters, the treatment group performed much better than the control group on both the quizzes and the test—better enough to make a mean difference of up to two letter grades (17 percentage points), depending on the cut-off points. Translated into learning terms, sacrificing the least important 12 percent of your lecture content for periodic two-minute pauses can increase the learning of your current C students to that of your current B students and even A students.

Ideas for Student-Active Breaks

During student-active breaks, students should be in some way interacting with the material (and often one another) for brief, controlled periods of time. Add in the appropriate breaks, and suddenly you can help your students achieve almost every type of learning outcomes—those requiring any of Bloom's cognitive operations and those involving cognitive development.

Ideally the breaks should supply students the opportunity to practice performing your learning outcomes or applying the lecture content you just gave. How well they complete the break task should furnish you with a diagnosis of their understanding. After all, you shouldn't move onto the next chunk of material unless students comprehend this one.

To keep the breaks brief and controlled, carefully time-control them. Inform your students that they will have exactly X number of minutes to complete the activity you assign them. Strictly enforced, those limits keep students focused on the task. When in doubt, allocate a little less time than you think some of them will need, but feel free to extend the limit a bit if they are working diligently. To make managing easier, bring a timer or stopwatch to class. Also circulate around the classroom to let students know you are listening to them and are willing to answer any procedural questions.

These breaks work well in any size class. In larger classes, however, having students work with their neighbors (in *ad hoc* pairs or triads) is quicker and easier than having them get into preorganized small groups, unless you arrange for group members to sit together during every class.

Ask students to work and talk as quietly as they can, but expect the classroom to get noisy anyway. After their activity time is up, you can bring even the largest class to silence within seconds by taking this tip from cooperative learning researchers: set the rule that you will raise your hand when the time is up. Tell your students that as soon as they see your hand up, they should immediately stop talking and raise their hands. The rest of the class will quickly follow suit.

Below are some commonly used break activities, along with the number of minutes each typically takes. (They come from Bonwell & Eison, 1991; Cross & Angelo, 1993; McKeachie, 2002; and informal collegial exchanges.) Some of them recommend randomly calling on individual students or groups to

hold them accountable for participating in the activity. Let these examples serve as your inspiration to conceive and experiment with your own innovations:

- *Pair and compare.* Students pair off with their neighbor and compare lecture notes, filling in what they may have missed. This activity makes students review and mentally process your minilecture content. Time: Two minutes.

- *Pair, compare, and ask.* Same as pair and compare but with the addition that students jot down questions on your minilecture content. Students answer one another's questions; you then field the remaining ones. Time: Three minutes, plus one or two minutes to answer questions.

- *Periodic free-recall, with pair-and-compare option.* Students put away their lecture notes and write down the most important one, two, or three points of your minilecture, as well as any questions they have. The first two times you do this, use a slide, overhead, or the board to give instructions. After that, just telling them will do. Again, this activity makes students review and mentally process your minilecture content. Students may work individually, but if they work in pairs or triads, they can answer some of each other's questions. Time: Two minutes, plus one or two minutes to answer students' questions.

- *Reflection/reaction paragraph.* Students individually write out their affective reaction to the minilecture content (or video or demonstration). Ask a few volunteers to share. Time: Three to four minutes.

- *Solve a problem.* Students solve an equational or word problem based on your minilecture. (Chapter Twenty-One describes a problem-solving strategy you can teach them.) They can work individually or, better yet, in *ad hoc* pairs or triads. Randomly call on a few individuals or groups to sample their answers. Time: One to three minutes for problem solving, depending on the problem's complexity, plus one or two minutes for surveying responses.

- *Multiple-choice item.* Put a multiple-choice item, preferably a conceptual one, related to your minilecture on the board, a slide, or an overhead, and give four response options. Survey your student responses (the next section, "Surveying Student Responses: Hands, Flashcards, and Clickers," explains various ways to do this). You can also ask students to rate their confidence level in their answer. Then give them a minute to convince their neighbor of their answer, and resurvey their responses. This activity, developed by Mazur (1997), makes students apply and discuss your minilecture content while it's fresh in their minds, and it immediately informs you how well they have understood the material. You can then clarify misconceptions before proceeding to new material. Time: Three minutes, plus one to two minutes to debrief and answer questions.

• *Multiple-choice test item.* In contrast to the multiple-choice item task above, this one puts students in pairs or small groups to compose multiple-choice items on your minilecture for a test you will give in the future. As we know, this is no easy task, so provide your students some training in good test-item writing. Teach them Bloom's taxonomy. Tell them the characteristics of plausible distractors (see Chapter Twenty-Nine). Show them examples of well-constructed and poorly constructed items, then lower-order recall and higher-order thinking items. Students will be motivated to write test items you will want to use because they will know the answers to the ones they submitted. And you will never have to write multiple-choice items again. Nor will students ever again blame you for items they find tricky, ambiguous, or too hard. Of course, you should reserve the right to tweak their submissions. Time: One to three minutes for each item they write.

• *Listen, recall, and ask; then pair, compare, and answer.* Students only listen to your minilecture—no note taking allowed. Then they open their notebooks and write down all the major points they can recall, as well as any questions they have. Instruct students to leave generous space between the major points they write down. Finally, they pair off with their neighbor and compare lecture notes, filling in what they may have missed and answering one another's questions. Again, this activity makes students review and mentally process your lecture content. Time:

Three to four minutes for individual note writing plus two to four minutes for pair fill-ins and question answering.

• *Pair/group graphic.* Students develop a concept map, mind map, thinking map, graphic organizer, picture, diagram, flowchart, or matrix of your minilecture content in pairs or small groups. What they are actually doing is integrating and reassembling their understanding of the content into a big picture graphic. It is one of the purest constructivist activities you can have them do, and it yields powerful learning benefits, which will be detailed in Chapter Twenty-Six. Because these graphics provide you with deep insight into your students' interpretation of the material, you may want to collect and peruse them. You may also want to return them with some feedback—at the very least, pointing out any misconceptions and oversimplifications they reveal. Time: Three to ten minutes in class.

• *Quick case study.* Students debrief a short case study (one to four paragraphs) that requires them to apply your minilecture content to a realistic, problematic situation. (Chapter Nineteen addresses the case method, including tips on developing your own cases.) Display a very brief case on an overhead or slide; put longer ones in a handout. You may add specific questions for students to answer, or teach your class the standard debriefing formula: What is the problem? What is the remedy? What is the prevention? Instruct students to jot down their answers. Students can work individually or, better yet, in *ad hoc* pairs or small groups. Time: Three to five minutes, depending on the case length and complexity, plus five to ten minutes for class exchange and discussion.

• *Pair/group and discuss.* Students pair off with their neighbor or get into small groups to discuss an open-ended question that asks them to apply, analyze, or evaluate your minilecture content or to synthesize it with other course material. This question should have multiple possible correct answers. (Refer to Chapter Fourteen for helpful questioning schema and question framing techniques.) Have students outline their answers in writing. This activity makes students examine and extend, as well as process, your minilecture content and serves as an effective prelude to a general class discussion. Time: Three to ten minutes, depending on the question's complexity, plus five to ten minutes for class exchange and discussion.

• *Pair/group and review.* Same as above but with an essay question designed for preexam review. Randomly select student pairs or groups to present their answers to the class. Then mock-grade them based on your assessment criteria (explain these before the exercise). You can also have the rest of the class mock-grade these answers to help students learn how to assess their work. Time: Three to ten minutes, depending on the question's complexity, plus five to fifteen minutes for pair/group presentations.

Here are several other break activities that apply to a wide range of content areas. Johnston and Cooper (1997) developed them under the apt name, "quick-thinks." Each takes one or two minutes, plus one to four minutes to survey responses:

• *Correct the error.* Using immediate minilecture content, students correct an error in a statement, equation, or visual that you have intentionally made. The error may be an illogical or inaccurate statement, premise, inference, prediction, or implication.

• *Complete a sentence starter.* Students accurately complete a sentence stem related to your minilecture content. The completed statement may be a definition, a category, a cause-and-effect relationship, an implication, a rationale, or a controversy. Present students with a sentence starter that requires reflection and higher-order thinking, not just rote knowledge, to complete.

• *Compare and contrast.* Students identify similarities or differences between parallel elements in your minilecture, such as theories, methods, models, events, problems, solutions, or artistic or literary works. To comprise a true analysis task, students must work on elements that have not been compared and contrasted in your minilectures or the readings.

• *Support a statement.* Students garner support for a statement—a conclusion, inference, theory, opinion, or description—you present. Sources of support may be your minilecture, the readings, or evidence they generate on their own.

• *Reorder the steps.* Students correctly sequence items that you present to them in mixed order. These items may be elements of a procedure, process, cycle, method, plan, strategy, or technique.

• *Reach a conclusion.* Students logically infer the implications of facts, concepts, or principles drawing from data, opinions, events, or solutions. The inferred conclusions can be probable results, probable causes, or outcomes.

• *Paraphrase the idea.* Students put an idea—a definition, theory, statement, procedure, or description—into their own words. This task can be just a check on their comprehension or a little more when you add the twist of targeting the paraphrase to a specific audience.

Finally, the least cognitively active break is what Kodani and Wood (2007) coin the *seventh inning stretch.* For a few minutes, they play some popular music and have their students just get out of their seats and stretch. Afterward their classes seem more alert. When Kodani and Wood surveyed their classes, their students overwhelmingly appreciated this break and believed it enhanced their learning. But a few would have preferred it to be content focused.

You will find many other options for student-active breaks in Chapter Seventeen (writing-to-learn activities), Chapter Eighteen (learning in groups), and Chapter Twenty-Eight (classroom assessment techniques).

Surveying Student Responses: Hands, Flash Cards, and Clickers

When you develop a lecture break around a multiple-choice item—or for that matter, a true-false item—follow up by surveying your students' responses before and after they discuss their answers with their neighbors. The fact that students commit to an answer makes them more interested in finding out what the correct response is, and the results furnish you with valuable feedback on their understanding.

You can collect those responses in several ways. First, you can ask for a show of hands for each response. While very simple, this option has its weaknesses. In a large class, you can't know for sure whether everyone is participating, and since you don't have time to count all the hands, you may get only a vague measure of the distribution of responses. You have no record of these responses either. One additional problem is that responses are not anonymous, so students may mindlessly change their answers just to follow the crowd.

Second, you can distribute four 8 1/2- by 11-inch "flash cards" (you can use heavy cover stock) of different colors to each student, where each color signifies an answer—for example, red for a, blue for b, yellow for c, and green for d. Then have students put up the color of paper that signifies their response choice. With this alternative, you can get a somewhat better idea of your participation rate and response distribution, especially if you have students put the stock directly in front of their faces. If you see a face, you can coax the student to make a choice. With students' faces covered by their choices, the answers become more anonymous as well. The only problem is that you have no record of the responses.

Third, you can use clickers, more formally known as personal or classroom response systems or voting systems. Students simply push a button indicating their response, and a receiver connected to your computer picks up the signals and immediately tallies all the answers, displaying them in a histogram on your monitor. You then have the option of revealing these results to the class. Of course, this alternative involves more advanced technology, which means that your institution, your students, or both have to pay for the clickers and your receiver. In addition, you have to learn the technology. However, you can tell exactly who isn't participating (and push them to participate) and exactly how the responses distribute, and you can archive the survey results. The process is completely anonymous so only you know how each student is responding. This also means you can take a confidential survey on sensitive attitudinal or behavioral topics. If you think

students may be concerned about your knowing their individual responses, you can turn off your receiver's identification function and tell them that you have.

Almost all of the research on the impact of this lecture break technique—that is, posing a multiple-choice question and surveying student responses before and after a short pair discussion—has been conducted on clickers. Compared to a traditional lecture, incorporating clicker breaks enhances student learning substantially, often by an entire letter grade on tests (Crouch & Mazur, 2001; Deal, 2007; Fagen, Crouch, & Mazur, 2002; Kaleta & Joosten, 2007; Mazur Group, 2008; Reay, Li, & Bao, 2008; additional studies listed at Bruff, 2008). The good news is that lower-tech survey methods, at least flash cards, produce learning gains just as impressive as clickers (Lasry, 2008). The payoff comes from the lecture break activity itself, not the technology. Therefore, the vast majority of the learning-relevant research involving clickers applies to hand raising and flash cards as well.

The student learning benefits of this lecture break technique over traditional lecture derive from its very specific effects. The literature reports that this technique increases class attendance, broadens class participation to literally the entire class, multiplies the chances for both student-to-student and student-to-faculty interaction, affords students regular practice in higher-order thinking, teaches them to critically examine and defend their thinking, improves the formative assessment of learning, provides instant feedback to students and the instructor on their understanding and retention, heightens students' attention and alertness in class (even early and late in the day), enhances their engagement in the material, and develops their metacognition, allowing for mindful and self-regulated learning (Bergtrom, 2006; Bruff, 2009; Crouch & Mazur, 2001; Deal, 2007; Fagen et al., 2002; Kaleta & Joosten, 2007; Mazur Group, 2008; Radosevich, Salomon, Radosevich, & Kahn, 2008). You can also use this technique to assess students' prior knowledge and launch discussion. Clickers offer the additional opportunities to do the following: take attendance instantly, with or without posing a question; grade participation, even in a large class, based on the number of correct responses to questions; play academic games, such as Millionaire; and give objective-item quizzes, as long as considerable cheating isn't likely.

Of course, these benefits depend on the questions; they must require higher-order thinking and problem-solving skills. For example, they may ask students to choose an example of a principle or to choose a principle to explain an example. They may survey an opinion, pose an ethical dilemma, have students classify a concept, or challenge them to make a prediction. (Chapter Fourteen on questioning techniques supplies many more examples.) If clickers collect the responses anonymously, the questions can address controversial or personal matters, such as students' opinions on hot-button issues or private experiences that illustrate a theory, principle, or finding (Bruff, 2007, 2009).

Since this lecture break technique started in large science classes, the STEM fields (science, technology, engineering, and mathematics) already have large online collections of well-tested break questions; start with Databases of Concept Questions at www.skylight.science.ubc.ca/cqdatabases. Bruff (2009) and his website (2008) at www.vanderbilt.edu/cft/resources/teaching_resources/technology/crs_biblio.htm offer other sources of questions for a much wider array of disciplines.

■ TEACHING STUDENTS TO TAKE GOOD NOTES

Many students come to college—and often leave it—with poor note-taking skills. The average student's notes include only 10 percent of the lecture (Johnstone & Su, 1994) and 40 percent of its critical ideas (first-year students, just 11 percent) (Kiewra, 1985, 2005), and only about a third of students take decent notes (Johnstone & Su). One reliable way to get your material into those notes is to write it on the board. But students also make errors copying material, particularly diagrams, equations, numbers, and the

contents of slides and transparencies, through which we often move too quickly. They also tend to leave out the instructor's corrections, descriptions of demonstrations, examples of applications, the structure of arguments, and technical definitions (Johnstone & Su).

And some students don't take notes at all, especially when they have a hard copy of the lecture's presentation slides. But having these slides often gives them a false sense of security that all the material they need to know for the test lies in front of them, and they may think they will remember what they have heard and read at the same time. We must realize that most young students did not take notes in high school. Teachers often provided handouts and gave easy tests. If students succeeded academically without taking notes before, they may question why they should now. So they don't even know that they should take notes, let alone how to take good ones.

Selling Students on Note Taking

Before teaching your students how to take good lecture notes, you have to motivate them to take them, to sell them on the benefits. Fortunately, you can make your case from plenty of research (Carrier, 1983; Johnstone & Su, 1994; Kiewra, 1985, 2005; Potts, 1993; numerous studies cited in Bligh, 2000, and McKeachie, 1994). Students who take their own notes and review them later reap numerous cognitive payoffs over those who just listen. Note taking fosters attention to and concentration on the lecture, accurate judgments about the relative importance of content (from nonverbal cues), understanding of the development and structure of the knowledge, far-transfer application of the material, and deeper cognitive processing. In deeper processing, learners engage in more thoughtful and active listening. They are paraphrasing, interpreting, and questioning, as well as integrating the new material into their organized bank of prior knowledge. Perhaps most compelling to students, taking notes better cements the knowledge in their memories, especially if they review their notes later. This means note takers perform better on all types of tests than non–note takers. Of course, it is just as important that students review their notes, but you can incorporate lecture breaks and end-of-class activities to ensure they review them at least once (see the "Ideas for Student-Active Breaks" section above).

Kiewra (1985) conducted some intriguing research on the relative value of students studying from their own lecture notes versus the instructor's lecture notes. On factual tests, students who studied only the instructor's notes performed better than those who studied only their own notes. In fact, this former group did better even if they did not attend lectures! However, the highest factual test scorers were those who studied both the instructor's notes and their own notes. When students took tests requiring higher-order thinking, the instructor's lecture notes were of no help to them. It seems, then, that for higher-order cognitive outcomes, the greater focus and deeper thought processes that note taking engages really pays off.

Teaching Note Taking

After selling students on note taking, acquaint them with some note-taking systems (Bligh, 2000; Ellis, 2006; Kiewra, 2005). Show them how to make a formal outline with first-order headings, second-order headings, and so on. (Points of equal importance or generality should start at the same distance from the left margin.) Tell them about the Cornell system: drawing a line down each page one-third in from the left, taking lecture notes on the right two-thirds of the page, and reserving the left one-third for reviewing activities, such as condensing the notes and rewriting the most critical content. You might also teach your students how to reorganize their notes into concept maps, mind maps, graphic organizers, matrices, and diagrams so they can take advantage of the learning and memory benefits of visual representation (see Chapter Twenty-Six). No one strategy is equally effective for everyone, so advise students to try out at least a couple.

In addition, explain to your students that the real art of taking notes is putting the most knowledge into the fewest possible words, preferably their own words. It is not transcription. Students should avoid writing complete sentences unless the specific wording is crucial. So tell them to take notes sparingly, dropping all unnecessary words and recording only the words and symbols needed to recall the idea they signify later.

Finally, share with your class some note-taking pointers, such as these (Bligh, 2000; Ellis, 2006; Kiewra, 2005):

- Arrive early to class to warm up your mind. Review your notes from the previous class and the assigned readings. Ask the instructor to clarify what doesn't make sense.
- Avoid cramming your notes or writing too small. Strive for easy readability. Leave a generous left margin for rewriting important words and abbreviated key content later.
- Occasionally glance back over the last few lines of notes you have taken, and rewrite any illegible letters, words, or symbols.
- Make key words, important relationships, and conclusions stand out. Underline, highlight, box, or circle them, or rewrite them in the left margin.
- Organize your notes according to the instructor's introductory, transitional, and concluding words and phrases, such as "the following three factors," "the most important consideration," "in addition to," "on the other hand," and "in conclusion." These phrases signal the structure of the lecture: cause and effect, relationships, comparisons and contrasts, exceptions, examples, shifts in topics, debates and controversies, and general conclusions.
- Identify the most important points by watching for certain instructor cues: deliberate repetition, pauses, a slower speaking pace, a drop in pitch, a rise in interest or intensity, movement toward the class, displaying a slide or transparency, and writing on the board.

- Pay close attention to the instructor's body language, gestures, and facial expressions, as well as changes in pace, pitch, and intonation. The instructor's subtlest actions punctuate and add meaning to the substance of the lecture.
- Whenever possible, draw a picture, concept map, or diagram to organize and abbreviate the relationships in the lecture material. Most people can recall a visual more easily than a written description.
- Develop and use your own shorthand, such as abbreviations and symbols for common or key words—for instance, btw for between, + for and, b/c for because, rel for relationship, df or = for definition, cnd for condition, nec for necessary or necessitates, hyp for hypothesis, Δ for change, T4 for therefore, + for more, − for less, ↑ for increasing, ↓ for decreasing; → for causes, ← for is caused by, and two opposing arrows for conflicts with.
- Take notes quickly and at opportune times. Use the instructor's pauses, extended examples, repetitions, and lighter moments to record notes. You can't afford to be writing one thing when you need to be listening closely to another.
- To help speed your note taking, try different pens until you find an instrument that glides smoothly and rapidly for you.
- If the instructor tends to speak or to move from point to point too quickly, politely ask him or her to slow down. You are probably the most courageous student of many who cannot keep up either.
- If you lose focus and miss part of a lecture, leave a space and ask a classmate, a teaching assistant, or the instructor to help you fill in the blank.
- Separate your own comments and reactions from your lecture notes.
- Review, edit, clarify, and elaborate your notes within twenty-four hours of the lecture, again a week later, and again a month later—even if for just a few minutes. While reviewing, recite, extract, and rewrite the key concepts and relationships. With enough review, the knowledge will become yours forever.

Making Note Taking Easier for Students

We can do a lot to help students take good lecture notes and have already addressed these strategies in detail earlier in this chapter. Still, they are worth highlighting here. For starters, we can organize our lectures clearly and simply, giving each an introduction, a body, and a conclusion and making the organization explicit in class. We can deliver our content using nonverbal cues (vocal variety, gestures, movement) to signal the most important points. We can chunk the content into minilectures, each making one major point, with student-active breaks between them. Finally, we can schedule lecture breaks and end-of-class review activities that allow students to review, fill in, and revise their notes, individually or in pairs (Carter & Van Matre, 1975; Kelly & O'Donnell, 1994; O'Donnell & Dansereau, 1993).

The most effective learning aids we can furnish are skeletal lecture notes that provide just the main headings and subheadings of our lectures and appropriately sized blocks of white space below them. Students need these notes at the beginning of the lecture, so you should post them for downloading on the course website or distribute them as handouts before starting class. With an even sketchy lecture outline in front of them, students tend not to get lost, and they quickly figure out from the amount of white space how much note taking to do on their own. According to research, students not only take better notes on skeletal outlines but also perform better on tests, suggesting they learn more (Cornelius & Owen-DeSchryver, 2008; Hartley & Davies, 1986; Potts, 1993). To make the most of skeletal notes, we can include the type of material that students often miscopy (diagrams, equations, numbers, and the contents of slides and transparencies) and insert a heading and white space for them to record what they frequently leave out: demonstrations, examples of applications, the structure of arguments, and technical definitions (Johnstone & Su, 1994). You can also include the directions or the triggers for lecture-break activities as well as the space to record the discussion, problem solution, answer, graphic, conclusion, most important points, and so on. To prevent that false sense of security that printouts of presentation slides give many students, word-process your skeletal notes.

Whether or not you make skeletal notes for your classes, you might want to display or hand out your own lecture notes just once or twice early in the term to provide students a model of how they should be taking notes.

■ MAKING THE LECTURE EFFECTIVE FOR EVERYONE

To encourage and enable academic success and lifelong learning, we should incorporate as many learning skills, such as lecture note taking, as we can fit into our courses. But for a small subset of students, note taking can actually interfere with their learning and recall. Those with relatively low ability, poor short-term memory, or little prior knowledge of the subject matter are often unable to assimilate new material as quickly as a lecture demands (McKeachie, 2002). They are totally dependent on our instructional aids, such as skeletal notes and student-active breaks like pair and compare that allow them to draw on their neighbor's notes. Try to get these students special help by referring them to your institution's learning skills or academic assistance center. It may offer workshops or one-on one tutoring in note taking.

CHAPTER 13

Leading Effective Discussions

hapter Twelve recommends breaking lectures up with intermittent activities that allow students to work with and assess their understanding of the material. In all but very large classes, one of the easiest and most effective student activities is a well-directed discussion. In smaller classes and seminars, this method may further your learning outcomes and serve as your primary classtime activity. Certainly a "discussion section" should remain true to its name and rely heavily on this format.

Let's define discussion as a productive exchange of viewpoints, a collective exploration of issues. To bear fruit and not degenerate into a free-association, free-for-all bull session, you as the instructor must chart its course and steer it in the right direction. It is your responsibility to plan and control the content and conduct, to keep hot air from blowing it off course. But it is also your responsibility to go with the breezes at least occasionally, to keep it flexible and fluid. Your challenge is to strike that delicate balance between structure and flow. Finding that balance helps you broaden participation and keep all hands on deck.

■ WHEN TO CHOOSE DISCUSSION

When well planned and managed, discussion can help your students achieve every type of learning outcome with the possible exception of knowledge/remembering, and it isn't bad at that either (Bonwell & Eison, 1991; McKeachie, 2002). In fact, discussion shines in developing the skills, abilities, and learning attitudes on which lecture is weak (Bligh, 2000; Bonwell & Eison, 1991; Dallimore, Hertenstein, & Platt, 2008; Delaney, 1991; Ewens, 2000; Forster, Hounsell, & Thompson, 1995; Gilmore & Schall, 1996; Kustra & Potter, 2008; McKeachie, 2002; Robinson & Schaible, 1993; Springer, Stanne, & Donovan, 1999):

- Examining and changing attitudes, beliefs, values, and behaviors

- Exploring unfamiliar ideas open-mindedly
- Deep learning
- Critical thinking
- Problem solving
- Listening actively
- Communicating orally
- Transferring knowledge to new situations
- Retaining the material
- Wanting to learn more about the subject matter

The problem-solving skills that discussion fosters apply not only to math problems but to all kinds of solution-oriented tasks, whether they call for one correct answer, one best answer, or many possible correct answers. Such tasks include resolving ethical dilemmas, designing a research project, explaining deviations from expected results, writing a computer program, solving a case study, evaluating various positions on an issue, analyzing a piece of literature, and developing approaches to tackling real-world social, political, economic, technological, and environmental problems. Because discussion models democracy, it may even promote civic engagement and good citizenship (Brookfield & Preskill, 1999; Lempert, Xavier, & DeSouza, 1995; Redfield, 2000).

One final benefit of discussion for you as well as your class is that across the disciplines, student ratings of instructors vary positively with the amount of time and encouragement an instructor gives to discussion (Cashin, 1988; Cohen, 1981).

Before moving on, we should distinguish discussion from recitation, which is students answering knowledge/remembering and comprehension/understanding questions. By contrast, discussion thrives on higher-order questions (see Chapter Fourteen). But recitation occupies a useful place in helping students achieve several respectable outcomes: recalling and restating knowledge, terms, and facts; speaking the language of the discipline (Leamnson, 1999); expressing important material in one's own words, thereby demonstrating understanding; and practicing what requires drill and repetition to learn. It also helps students retrieve the basic knowledge they need for discussion.

■ HOW TO SET THE STAGE FOR DISCUSSION

The biggest challenge facing you is eliciting broad and active participation. If you can do that, most of the other problems that go wrong in a discussion—domination by one or two students, topical tangents, silent sectors of the room—simply disappear. Just about all the recommendations in this chapter help ensure that all of your students will come to a discussion prepared, comfortable, and willing to contribute.

From the First Day

Students need to be primed for discussion, especially since they spend most of their classroom time passively listening to an instructor and a few particularly loquacious classmates. If you plan to make discussion an integral class activity, even if not a primary one, inform and prepare your students from the first day of class. Let them know the primary ground rule: everyone's participation is expected and no back-benchers will be allowed. Announcing the key role that discussion will play in your course will encourage students to take the activity seriously. So will telling them your reasons for using discussion—for instance, how the research supports its effectiveness in helping them achieve your learning outcomes. Follow up by explaining how class discussions will relate to other parts of the course, such as readings, written assignments, and tests. When you can, build homework, quizzes, and tests around both the readings and the discussions about them.

Explain the true nature of discussion—that it thrives on the expression of different, legitimate points of view. Disagreement enriches the learning experience. In fact, college is all about hearing, "trying on," and appraising different perspectives. So students should listen actively and respectfully to every opinion put on the table, evaluate the evidence for and against that claim, and be prepared with evidence to defend their own positions.

Then lead your class in a discussion—if not about the syllabus (see Chapter Three) then about their prior knowledge of, experience with, and interest in the course material. Try to get every student to say something that day. You might draw students out by directing questions to them individually, such as, "Janet, what interested you in this seminar?" or "Matt, what topics would you like to see addressed in this course?" Cement their participation by having them post extensions of or comments on this first discussion online—to a class blog, wiki, discussion board, or chatroom.

Here are some other first-day primers to break down social barriers from the start. If possible, arrange the seats in a circle so that students can see one another. (It isn't easy to talk to the back of a classmate's head.) Have social or subject-oriented icebreakers the first day of class so students get acquainted (see Chapter Four). They will find it easier to speak out among "friends." Give students index cards to fill out with any information they'd like to share about their learning styles, hometown, personal lives, and career aspirations. To induce them to talk, you might invite them to expand on their index card information. Finally, start calling students by name and helping them learn each others' names by providing name tags or name tents for in-class use.

Continue to nurture the friendly atmosphere you establish on the first day by getting into the habit of casually chatting with students before and after class. If you have the time, make individual or small-group appointments with them early in the term (pass around a sign-up sheet), and include some noncourse conversation on the agenda. Your knowledge of your students will help you pitch the course at the right level as well as develop a solid rapport with your class quickly. If your students are comfortable with you as a person and you feel comfortable with them as well, your discussions will flow more evenly and honestly.

From the start, establish good eye contact and physical proximity with all of your students as equally as possible. A good rule of thumb is to maintain eye contact with one student or, in a large class, a cluster of students for at least three seconds. Your very look makes a student feel included. If your class sits in a circle or around a table, varying where you sit can help you equalize your eye contact and physical proximity. If you do not normally sit down during class, move about the room as much as you can.

Grading on Participation

You may or may not wish to include the quality and quantity of class participation in your final grading scheme. But doing so will increase the likelihood of your students coming to class prepared and participating (Dallimore, Hertenstein, & Platt, 2006). If you do, you should make this very clear in your syllabus and your first-day presentation. Also explain your conception of adequate quality and quantity. To help articulate your standards, put the phrase "class participation grading rubric" in a search engine and peruse the examples your colleagues use.

To head off uneven participation, especially the problem of a couple of dominant students, you can limit the number of contributions each student can make each class before everyone has spoken. To keep track, have students display a colorful sticky note on the front of their desk for each of their contributions. You can combine this system with grading, giving students a participation point for their first two or three comments but no more points for any subsequent ones (Lang, 2008).

Consider the class level and size in deciding the weight to give participation. First-year students may feel comfortable with 20 percent in a class of twenty to twenty-five students but may find it unreasonably stressful in one of forty-five to fifty. More advanced students should be able to handle a higher percentage even in a large class. You might have students vote on the percentage (give them options) and follow the majority rule.

Setting Ground Rules for Participation

How do you foresee conducting class discussions? Students want to know how you will call on them. You have several options: (1) in some predetermined order—perhaps alphabetically, by seating, or by index card order; (2) by raised hands; or (3) cold-calling by random selection, such as shuffling and drawing index cards with students' names or choosing students who haven't spoken recently.

The first method ensures broad participation and preparation, but it creates a stiff, recitation type of atmosphere. In addition, it raises the stress of the student next in line while encouraging others to tune out. Used alone, the raised-hands method keeps the class relaxed but does little to motivate preparation. Most important, participation is bound to be uneven, with a few verbal individuals monopolizing the floor and most students playing passive wallflowers. You may even wind up inadvertently reinforcing social inequities unless you make special efforts to draw out and validate your female and minority students. The third method, cold-calling by random selection, obviously ensures broad participation and motivates preparation, but some instructors resist it for fear it will cause students undue discomfort. Actually there is no evidence to support this concern, at least not for advanced students. In addition, cold-calling combined with graded participation is effective in increasing both the frequency of student contributions and preparation for discussion (Dallimore et al., 2006).

You may want to vary your methods for calling on students. For example, when the raised-hands method fails to generate broad enough participation, you might shift to cold-calling, perhaps targeting students who have been silent for a while.

If you use the cold-calling or predetermined order method, a good ground rule to set is the escape hatch—that is, permitting students to pass on answering a question. It is demoralizing to the class and counterproductive to the discussion to badger, belittle, or otherwise put a person on the spot for not having a comment when you demand it. A student with nothing to say may simply have nothing new to contribute. While it's possible he isn't prepared, he may simply agree with other recent remarks, or may have no questions at the time, or may be having a bad day and not feel like talking. To cover these instances, inform your class that you will occasionally accept responses such as, "I don't want to talk right now" or "Will you please call on me later?"

However, you should make it clear that certain negative behaviors will not be tolerated: purposefully steering the discussion off-track; trying to degenerate it into a comedy act; instigating an inappropriate debate; personally attacking a fellow student; displaying one's temper; asking wheedling, argumentative, or loaded questions; or engaging in more general uncivil classroom behaviors (see Chapter Seven).

A democratic alternative to your setting up civility ground rules is to lead a class discussion on what those rules should be (Kustra & Potter, 2008). Ask the students to recount the qualities of the best discussions they have participated in. How did their classmates behave? How did they show mutual respect? Then ask them about the worst discussions in their educational experience. How did people treat each other? What behaviors induced the silence, anger, or fear of others? From this point, the class can generate their own ground rules, and you can supplement as necessary.

One final rule to set yourself is a reassurance: "The only stupid question is the one you don't ask." Students are downright terrified by the prospect of looking stupid or foolish to you or their peers. They appreciate being told that you will welcome all questions and ensure that they are answered. A similar but modified rule should apply to all answers as well: you will welcome all contributions given with good intentions. But this doesn't mean that you won't correct faulty answers or allow other students to correct them.

Bringing Equity to a Diverse Classroom

If your class is especially diverse or the subject matter of your course encompasses race, ethnicity, and class, it's best to bring differences out in the open early. Brookfield and Preskill (1999) describe several classroom activities that acknowledge and honor diversity. In one of them, "Naming Ourselves," students first reflect on the cultural, racial, ethnic, or socioeconomic group with which they identify. Then they each introduce themselves as members of their group, stating the label they prefer for this group and what their identification means to them—for instance, how it has affected their values, beliefs, language, behavior, and so on. In another, "Expressing Anger and Grief," students get into groups and exchange personal experiences of cruelty set off by racial, ethnic, or class prejudice. Then the group analyzes the stories for common and disparate themes, emotions, and effects.

To ensure gender equity, Brookfield and Preskill (1999) recommend that instructors model and encourage female ways of interacting, such as disclosing personal information, taking risks that could lead to mistakes, and connecting discussion topics with personal experiences. They also offer several classroom exercises and assignments for acclimating students to both male and female ways of talking. One involves the students' making scrapbooks or journals focused on how gender has affected their lives. Another asks students to write down five or so demographic identities or facts about themselves, including gender, and then explain how each has shaped their point of view.

A diverse classroom can introduce controversy and discourse that students may not know how to handle, and you shouldn't assume that they know what civil discourse is. So either you or your students have to establish ground rules for discussion, to include forbidding personal attacks. If the topic may provoke racist or discriminatory remarks, stand poised to intervene and return to the discussion on the subject at hand. Regardless of how you feel about the various positions raised, do not project those emotions to the students who express them. Protect both the attacked and the attacker. Then have the students calm down, step back, and think about what has just happened. You may go from here to turn the situation into a teachable moment. Have students write a reflection paper on the incident expressing not only their feelings but what they learned. Or ask the students involved in the incident to restate and explain their views calmly. Or defer discussing the issue until later, and do bring it up later, after you have a strategy for handling the conflict (Derek Bok Center for Teaching and Learning, 2006).

For more ideas on ensuring equity in your classroom, see the "Inclusive Instruction" section in Chapter One.

■ HOW TO MAXIMIZE PARTICIPATION THROUGH SKILLFUL DISCUSSION MANAGEMENT

Let us consider how to keep a productive discussion going with broad student involvement.

Facilitating Discussion

First and foremost, you are the discussion facilitator. This may seem a trendy term, but it is a fitting one nonetheless. To "facilitate a discussion" means to make it easy for students to participate, and the process can begin before class. By arriving a little early and casually chatting with students as they arrive, you can loosen them up for dialogue. Facilitating also entails starting off the discussion and adding to it when necessary. But once the discussion takes off, it largely involves directing traffic (see the section on this topic below). Still, at all times, you serve as manager-on-call to control the focus, structure, and tone of the exchange.

Depending on the circumstances, you may briefly assume a wide variety of roles: coach, moderator, host, listener, observer, information provider, presenter, counselor, recorder, monitor, instigator, navigator, translator, peacemaker, and summarizer. During particularly animated or contentious exchanges, you may even find yourself playing referee. Congratulate yourself when students start speaking to each other directly rather than through you. Your goal is to make yourself superfluous.

Motivating Preparation

You will find dozens of ways to induce your students to do the readings (see Chapter Twenty-Three), and the following are among them as applied to discussion specifically. Include the reading assignments on the topical agenda of the day they are due. Reading-focused discussions can be enriched by having students take notes on the readings, write a reaction to or a summary of them, draft answers to study questions you have prepared, compose their own written questions on the readings, or make journal entries about their responses to them. Then allow students to use these notes, reactions, questions, and answers in the discussion. They will feel more confident and more willing to participate with a written point of reference in front of them. If you want your students to take notes, compose questions, answer study questions, or keep journals on the readings, collect these regularly or periodically to ensure they are keeping up.

Depending on your discipline, you may also be interested in the following seminar structure, which you can learn more about and watch in process online (SCCtv, Boyer, & Harnish, 2007). Students prepare for class by marking passages in the readings that are puzzling, especially important, or related to other readings or discussion themes. In class, each student in turn reads one passage aloud and explains why she selected it while the rest of the class takes notes. After all the students have shared their passages, each in turn responds to their classmates' choices and insights, recounting what they have found most meaningful, interesting, or novel. Some faculty and their students have found this process highly productive.

Recall that grading on participation and cold-calling motivate students to prepare for discussion. So does calling on students in some predetermined order, but it has weaknesses that cold-calling does not.

Readying the Class

Students come to class with all manner of things on their mind, and the subject matter of your course may not rank among them. So before launching into a discussion, warm up the class to the topic of the day. You needn't follow all the recommendations below, but implementing two or three will make it easier to launch the discussion.

To help students put the upcoming discussion into perspective, begin with a brief review of the previous class period. But draw the highlights out of the students, posing questions like, "What are the major points we covered last time?" Let students refer to, and thus review, their notes.

Then turn the students' attention to the discussion for the day with a road map—that is, an outline on the board, a slide, or an overhead of the day's agenda, outcomes, topics, or the process through which you will guide them. (A list of discussion questions may justify a handout.) In other words, lay out the territory that the class will travel. Not only will you look more organized, you will *be* more organized, and so will the discussion. In addition, you will make it easier for students to take notes on the discussion. It is a technique they find hard to master.

You might also precede the discussion with a few recitation (knowledge/remembering) questions on the readings to refresh your students' memory and get them all on the same page. Or you might have them read important text passages aloud (see the seminar structure described in the previous subsection). Or ask them about their emotional reactions to the readings, such as what the content meant to them or how it made them feel. Another technique that will engage everyone is a writing prompt—that is, a reading-relevant question or provocative statement that students can reflect on and write about for three to five minutes (Jones, 2008). This prompt may be your launch pad for the discussion.

Igniting the Exchange

You have your choice of several proven strategies to stimulate a discussion (Brookfield & Preskill, 1999; Jones, 2008; McKeachie, 2002). One is to start with a common experience, which may be a well-known current event or a classroom experience you have furnished, such as a video, demonstration, or role play. Another is to have students brainstorm what they already know about a topic or what outcomes that they anticipate of a situation or an experiment. A potentially hot ignition switch is to pose a controversial or probing question. You can set up a student debate in advance (see Chapter Fifteen) or play devil's advocate yourself. As some students can interpret your representing "the devil" as manipulative, untrustworthy, and occasionally confusing, it is crucial that you explain what you're doing beforehand. While you're assuming the role, you might even wear a hat or a sign with "Devil's Advocate" written prominently on it.

You can always open a discussion by asking the first in a series of questions you have planned in advance. As we rely on this strategy so extensively, and for good reason, the entire next chapter is devoted to questioning techniques. Not all questions evoke the types of thinking that launch discussions. You will learn about those that do and those that don't.

Motivating Attention

A good discussion relies on all students staying alert and listening carefully. To promote their paying attention, tell students to take notes on the discussion and tell them how to do so. You might start by advising them specifically when to take notes, such as each time a student proffers a new and worthwhile point. It also helps to refer frequently to your discussion road map, write the major points made on the board (another aid for note taking), and ask students to comment on and react to one another's contributions. Of course, if you tell (and remind) students that they will need the content of the discussions to complete assignments and perform well on tests, they are more likely to stay attentive. If some of the discussion takes place in small groups, have a policy of randomly selecting a few groups—and within each group, randomly selecting the spokesperson—to summarize their progress or conclusions.

Ending class with a wrap-up activity on a regular basis can also keep students alert during the whole period. For example, randomly pick a student to summarize the discussion at the end of class, then invite others to add major points. Or conclude class with a classroom assessment technique (see Chapter Twenty-Eight), such as a one-minute paper in which students write down the most important thing they learned that day and any remaining questions or still-confusing point.

Waiting for Responses to Increase Participation

To eliminate needless delays in students' responding, ask only one question at a time. Resist the temptation to pose another related question if you don't get an instant response to the first. Putting multiple questions on the table confuses students.

Once you pose a well-crafted question, allow sufficient time for students to respond—five to fifteen seconds, depending on the difficulty of the challenge. This rule applies no matter what your method of calling on students. While a few members of the class may jump at the chance to say anything, even if it is incorrect, most students need time—more time than we might expect—to think through and phrase a response they are willing to share publicly. After all, they are struggling with new knowledge and thinking in a foreign language—the language of the discipline. So they need time to retrieve and sort through the knowledge for an intelligent response, then figure out how to express it. Extending your wait time from the typical half-second (Stahl, 1994) to just three seconds can dramatically increase the number of students with a response (Rowe, 1974).

If the question is particularly difficult, lengthy, or complex, you might advise students to outline their answer in writing first. Having a response jotted down in front of them will boost their confidence and courage. You may also get higher-quality answers. This way, too, you can feel free to call on anyone—in particular, the quieter students.

Watch for nonverbal cues of students' readiness to respond, especially changes in facial expression. Still, refrain from calling on anyone until you see several raised hands or eager faces. When you have many possible students from whom to select, you can spread the attention and participation opportunities across students who haven't spoken recently.

Breaking the Class into Small Groups

A time-saving way to guarantee a broad response to a question, especially in larger classes, is to break the students into small groups. If you intend to do so only on occasion or as a brief warm-up to a general discussion, you may simply have students cluster themselves into informal, ad hoc "buzz groups" based on seating proximity. If you are setting up long-term formal groups to collaborate on a sizable project outside class (see Chapter Sixteen), you may have students get into these groups. Either way, not only will the groups generate higher-quality answers than will most individuals on their own, but they will give the shyer and more reserved students a safer venue in which to develop their ideas and points of view.

Encouraging Nonparticipants

I have already mentioned several ways to broaden participation: letting students jot down their answer, extending your wait time, and breaking the class into groups to develop responses. You can also monitor participation and actively encourage it where it's lacking. If one side of the room seems too quiet, make a point of saying so, and start directing questions exclusively to those in that area. If an individual is not contributing, use the same tactic, but be extra gentle; you want to avoid putting that person too much on the spot. Another strategy with a quiet student is to ask her to read a passage of text, a question, or a problem aloud. This technique is particularly effective with a passage from a narrative, a play, a poem, or a treatise, and you can follow up by asking the student to interpret or comment on the reading.

Persistent nonparticipation may be a symptom of a deeper problem that calls for a private approach. It is a good idea to have the student see you in your office and tactfully ask why he has been so quiet in class. Accept any answer as legitimate, and then encourage him to become involved. One way to help a student overcome fear is to give him one or more discussion questions in advance of the next class and let him rehearse his answers with you.

Responding to Student Responses

Give approval, verbal or nonverbal, to all student contributions, but with discretion and discrimination. Students want to know how correct and complete their own and their classmates' answers are, but they want you to deliver your judgment in a diplomatic, encouraging way.

Approval can take the form of a nod, an interested or accepting facial expression, your recording the response on the board, or appropriate verbal feedback. Here are some verbal response options you may wish to use:

- *When the answer is correct,* praise according to what it deserves.

- *When the answer is correct but only one of several correct possibilities,* ask another student to extend or add to it. Or frame a question that is an extension of the answer. Avoid premature closure.
- *When the answer is incomplete,* follow up with a question that directs the student to include more—for example, "How might you modify your answer if you took into account the _____ aspect?"
- *When the answer is unclear,* try to rephrase it; then ask the student if this is what she means.
- *When the answer is seemingly wrong,* follow up with one or more gently delivered Socratic questions designed to lead the student to discover his error—for example: "Yes, but if you come to that conclusion, don't you also have to assume _____?" (See the section on the Socratic method in Chapter Fourteen.)
- *When the answer is incomplete, unclear, or seemingly wrong,* invite the student to explain, clarify, or elaborate on it. Or ask other students to comment on or evaluate it. Vary your response to faulty answers so students simply don't translate a stock phrase as, "You're wrong." Avoid identifying and correcting errors yourself for as long as possible.

Directing Traffic

As some of the response options suggest, you often best facilitate by doing and saying very little, acting only as the resource of last resort. You should step in only if no student supplies the needed clarification, correction, or knowledge or if the discussion strays off track. In fact, the successful facilitator's primary task is to direct traffic—that is, to signal students to react to their peers' contributions. When you do respond yourself, try to do it in the form of a thoughtful follow-up question. In addition, whenever you can, refer back to the student's earlier remarks, using the contributor's name.

Your goal is to shift the spotlight from you to your students every chance you get. In addition to inviting students to comment on and extend each other's answers, ask them to address their comments to the classmate to whom they are responding by looking at that person and addressing her by name. For the first few weeks, name tags or tents may be essential. If the class is splitting into camps on an issue, set up a spontaneous debate, allowing students to change their mind in the course of the exchange. For a twist, have each side argue in favor of the opposition. Also bring students center stage when you sense that you are not effectively explaining a point or answering a question. Ask them to help you out and offer their version; they speak one another's language.

What if traffic comes to a screeching halt? If no one says a word after a generous wait time, you might break the silence and tension with a touch of humor: "Helloooooo, is anybody out there?" But you should definitely find out the reason for the silence. Perhaps your question was ambiguous, or your students did not understand the way you phrased it, or they misunderstood your meaning. For your own benefit, ask them to identify the bottleneck.

Wrapping Up

Before moving the discussion onto the next topic, be sure the current one is settled. You might ask if anyone has something to add or qualify. If no one does, ask a student to summarize the main points made during the discussion of the topic. Then move on, making a logical transition to the next topic.

Watch the clock and reserve a few minutes at the end of class to wrap up and summarize the discussion. Some sort of review encourages students to check their notes and fill in important omissions. It also keeps them on common ground. See the "Motivating Attention" section above for several fruitful ways to end a discussion session.

Discussion appeals most strongly to the auditory learning style (see Chapter Twenty-Five), and any one method can get monotonous after a while. So consider varying your participatory strategies to better serve other learning styles, as well as to add spice to life. The many student-active, experiential, and cooperative-learning techniques described in Chapters Fifteen and Sixteen offer stimulating alternatives to the all-class discussion. These include brainstorming, debate, change-your-mind debate, the press conference, the symposium, the panel discussion, role playing, simulations, field and service work, and a wide variety of small-group activities.

Of course, engaging questions and sound questioning techniques can keep the discussion method lively and challenging for weeks on end. They can also inform your quizzes and exams so you can better assess the level of thinking you're trying to foster. So let us turn now to crafting questions.

CHAPTER 14

Questioning Techniques for Discussion and Assessment

Framing questions is a key teaching skill and has been for millennia. Socrates honed it to such a fine art that an entire method of questioning is attributed to him. Sound questioning techniques enhance instruction in several ways:

- Questions launch and carry discussion, one of the oldest and most commonly used student-active teaching techniques (see Chapter Thirteen).
- They promote practice in using disciplinary language, principles, algorithms, and conventions.
- They stimulate the exploratory, critical thinking, and insight in which inquiry-based methods, including Socratic questioning, are grounded (see Chapter Eighteen).
- When used for classroom assessment, questions yield answers that help us gauge what students are learning and whether to review a topic or proceed to the next (see Chapter Twenty-Eight).
- Questions are the major means by which we grade students' performance; the more closely our questions reflect our learning outcomes, the fairer and more useful these grading procedures are (see Chapter Twenty-Nine).

The college teaching literature offers several schemas for organizing and categorizing questions, and the most prominent ones are summarized here. They fall into two categories: those that guide students through a more or less orderly process of inquiry and those that classify questions into more or less useful types. This chapter couches questioning in the contexts of discussion, but later chapters return to using questions for assessment.

■ QUESTIONING AS A PROCESS OF INQUIRY

The most engaging discussions are not just a list of loosely connected questions. Rather, they comprise a purposeful sequence of questions that leads students through a process of thinking about a topic more and more deeply.

Using the Socratic Method

The Socratic method is the most spontaneous questioning technique. You may begin with one planned question to open the dialogue on a given topic, but you frame your succeeding questions according to the answers the students give. In response to your initial question, the student takes a position or point of view. Your next question raises a weakness of or exception to that position, to which the student responds with a defense or a qualification of her original position. The student may also assume a new position. In turn, you respond with another question that reveals a possible weakness of or exception to the defense, the qualified position, or the new position, and the student responds as before. This line of inquiry promotes in students rational thinking, persistence, and pattern recognition across seemingly disparate processes and phenomena (Overholser, 1992). With experience, you should be able to anticipate the blind alleys and misdirections your students will take on specific topics and develop a general discussion plan.

This questioning technique is challenging. Some instructors don't feel comfortable with such a spontaneous, unstructured format for an entire discussion period. Some students don't either; they have a hard enough time taking notes on the most structured discussion. Unless the questions are posed in a light-hearted tone, students can feel as if they are getting hammered and take offense. In addition, questioning one student too long can make the rest of the class tune out. A good situation for the Socratic method is when you are facing a number of students who share the same position. You can then direct each of your questions to a different student. Instructors who play devil's advocate (see Chapter Thirteen) are usually practicing the Socratic method, whether they know it or not (Gose, 2009).

Working Backward from End-of-Class Outcomes

A second strategy, one that has gained the status of a conventional wisdom, is to work backward from one's ultimate learning outcomes for a particular class. It requires advance planning. First, jot down your ultimate outcomes for the class period: the one, two, or three things you want your students to be able to do (classify, explain, analyze, assess, and so on) by

the end of class. For each performance, create one or two key questions that will assess the students' facility. Then for each key question, develop another two or three questions that logically proceed and will prepare the students to answer the key questions intelligently. In other words, work backward from the key questions you want your students to answer well at the end through the questions that will lead them to that facility.

When class begins, launch the discussion with one of the last questions you framed. You can lend structure to the discussion by displaying all the questions (key ones last) on the board, a slide, or an overhead or in a handout, preferably with note-taking space below each question. Still, unless you have framed too many questions, you can afford to be flexible. You can allow the discussion to wander a bit, then easily redirect it back to your list of questions.

The next section on Bloom's hierarchy of questions suggests a logical sequencing scheme for the working-backward strategy.

Guiding Students up Bloom's Hierarchy of Questions

You can view Bloom's (1956) taxonomy of questions as just types or as a hierarchical ladder of cognitive levels for leading your students from knowledge, the lowest-thinking level, to evaluation, the highest. This schema was set out in Chapter Two, where we applied it to developing learning outcomes. The lists of verbs associated with each cognitive operation are just as useful here for framing questions, so refer back to Table 2.1. Also refer to Table 14.1, which furnishes examples of questions at each cognitive level.

To structure a discussion as a process of inquiry, you might start off with knowledge (recitation) questions on the highlights of the previous class or the reading assignment. A factual recall exercise serves as a mental warm-up for the students and gives those who come in unprepared the chance to pick up a few major points and follow along, if not participate later. As you can see in Table 14.1, knowledge questions often ask who, what, where, and when, as well

Table 14.1   Examples of Questions at Each Cognitive Level of Bloom's Taxonomy/Hierarchy

Cognitive Level	Questions
Knowledge	•Who did _____ to _____? •What did you notice about _____? •What do you recall about _____? •What does the term _____ mean? •When did _____ take place? Where did it take place? •How does the process work? (Describe it.)
Comprehension	•In your own words, what does the term _____ mean? •How would you explain _____ in nontechnical terms? •Can you show us what you mean? •What do think the author/researcher is saying?
Application	•What would be an example of _____? •How would you solve this problem? •What approach would you use? •How would you apply _____ in this situation?
Analysis	•How are _____ and _____ alike? How are they different? •How is _____ related to _____? •What are the different parts of _____? •What type of _____ is this? How would you classify it? •What evidence does the author/researcher offer? •How does the author/researcher structure the argument? •What assumptions are behind the argument? •What inferences can you draw about _____?
Synthesis	•What conclusions can you come to about _____? •What generalizations can you make about _____? •How would you design (structure, organize) a _____? •How would you adapt (change) the design (plan) for _____? •How can you resolve the differences (paradox, apparent conflict)? •What new model could accommodate these disparate findings?
Evaluation	•What would you choose, and why? •What are the relevant data, and why? •Why do you approve or disapprove? •Why do you think the conclusions are valid or invalid? •What is your position (opinion), and how can you justify it? •How would you rank (rate, prioritize) the _____? •How would you judge (evaluate) _____?

as how and why when students have already read or been told the correct answer. Avoid questions that call for one- or two-word answers, however; aim for multisentence responses. But do not spend more than several minutes on this level. The boredom potential aside, students will not answer many recitation questions because they may fear their classmates

seeing them as apple polishers—"bailing you out," so to speak. Besides, we have more important critical thinking skills to develop in our students.

Therefore, rapidly move the discussion up the hierarchy through *comprehension* so you can find out whether your students correctly understand the material and can put it in their own words. Draw on the questions in Table 14.1. At this juncture, you can identify and correct any misconceptions they have about the subject matter that might get in the way of their deeper learning. If they do comprehend the material, they should be able to answer *application* questions and think of appropriate examples and use the material to solve problems. If they can do this, they should be ready to progress to *analysis* of the material: distilling its elements; drawing comparisons and contrasts; identifying assumptions, evidence, causes, effects, and implications; and reasoning through explanations and arguments.

Once students have found their way through the material, they are prepared to step outside its confines and attempt *synthesis*. As illustrated in Table 14.1, this type of question calls for integrating elements of the material in new and creative ways: drawing new conclusions and generalizations; composing or designing a new model, theory, or approach; or combining elements from different sources. When students can synthesize material, they have mastered it well enough to address *evaluation* questions. They now can make informed judgments about its strengths and shortcomings, its costs and benefits, and its ethical, aesthetic, or practical merit.

Structured as a hierarchy, Bloom's taxonomy helps rein in students from leaping into issues they aren't yet prepared to tackle. Often students are all too eager to jump to judging material without thoroughly understanding and examining it first. In addition, if you teach the taxonomy to your students, they acquire a whole new metacognitive perspective on thinking processes and levels. If you label the level of your questions, you maximize your chances of obtaining the level of answers you are seeking. Students also quickly learn to classify and better frame their own questions.

The taxonomy should be used flexibly, however. Some discussion tasks, such as debriefing a case (see Chapter Nineteen), may call for an inextricable combination of application, analysis, synthesis, and evaluation. Moreover, a comprehension question in one course may be an analysis task in another. How any question is classified depends on what the

students have previously received as "knowledge" from you and the readings you assign.

TYPOLOGIES OF GOOD DISCUSSION QUESTIONS

There is much more to constructing discussion questions than turning around a couple of words in a sentence and adding a question mark. Well-crafted ones take thought and creativity in order to evoke the same from students. But they all have one feature in common: they have multiple respectable answers. Therefore, they encourage broad participation and in-depth treatment. Often, too, multiple-answer questions spark debate. Welcome the conflict, and let students argue it out. Before letting the issue rest, ask for possible resolutions or analyses of the conflict if they don't evolve on their own.

To help you frame thought-provoking, open-ended discussion questions, several scholars have devised typologies of questions.

McKeachie's Categories

McKeachie (2002) suggests four types of fruitful, challenging questions, which vaguely overlap with Bloom's analysis, synthesis, and evaluation questions:

- *Comparative* questions ask students to compare and contrast different theories, research studies, literary works, and so on. Indirectly, they help students identify the important dimensions for comparison.

- *Evaluative* questions extend comparisons to judgments of the relative validity, effectiveness, or strength of what is being compared.

- *Connective and causal effect* questions challenge students to link facts, concepts, relationships, authors, theories, and so on that are not explicitly integrated in assigned materials and might not appear to be related. These questions are particularly useful in cross-disciplinary courses. They can also ask students to draw and reflect on their personal experiences, connecting these to theories and research findings. When students realize these links, the material becomes more meaningful to them.

- *Critical* questions invite students to examine the validity of a particular argument, research claim, or interpretation. Such questions foster careful, active reading. If the class has trouble getting started, you can initiate the discussion by presenting an equally plausible alternative argument. Asking for comments on what a student has just said is also a critical question. Used in this content, it fosters good listening skills.

Brookfield and Preskill's "Momentum" Questions

Brookfield and Preskill (1999) propose seven types of questions that serve the express purpose of sustaining the momentum of a discussion. These questions are designed to make students probe into issues more deeply, reconsider positions in novel and more critical ways, and stay intellectually stimulated:

- *Questions requesting more evidence.* As the name states, such a question asks a student to defend his position, especially when it comes out of nowhere or another student challenges it as unsupported. The instructor should pose the question in a matter-of-fact way as a simple request for more information—data, facts, passages from the text—so as not to alienate the student.
- *Clarification questions.* This type of question invites the student to rephrase or elaborate on her ideas to make them more understandable to the rest of the class. It may include a request for an example, an application, or a fuller explanation.
- *Cause-and-effect questions.* These questions make students consider the possible causal relationship between variables or events and, in effect, formulate hypotheses. Instructors can use them to challenge a conventional wisdom or introduce the scientific method.
- *Hypothetical questions.* These are "what-if" inquiries that require students to think creatively, to make up plausible scenarios, to explore how changing

the circumstances or parameters of a situation might alter the results. They can induce imaginative thinking and even send a discussion off on fanciful tangents, but students still have to use their prior knowledge and experience to come up with supportable extrapolations. Hypothetical questions can extend cause-and-effect questions. If, for example, the class established the impact of education on income, an instructor could pose this hypothetical scenario to help students define the limits of the relationship: What if everyone in the society got a bachelor's degree? Does that mean that everyone would make the same income?

- *Open questions.* These questions represent the best kind of discussion questions: those with multiple respectable answers. They invite risk taking and creativity in problem solving and have the greatest potential for expanding students' intellectual and affective horizons. No matter how they are phrased, they are truly open only if the instructor welcomes all well-meaning responses and isn't fishing for a preferred answer. She can accept the weaker contributions as opportunities for the students to built and expand on them and follow up with clarification questions, requests for more evidence, cause-and-effect questions, and hypothetical questions.
- *Linking or extension questions.* A high-quality discussion depends on students' actively listening to each other's contributions. Linking or extension questions encourage this by asking students to think about the relationships between their responses and those of their classmates. Often students are building on or bouncing off the previous comments of others, and an instructor can ask questions that help them see and acknowledge the connections. These questions require using students' names. Ideally, they can set off engaging conversations among classmates that don't go through the instructor. They can also launch a collaborative discussion in which students must refer to the previous comments of their classmates when making their own contributions. The resulting discussion is a community product of everyone's ideas cooperatively woven together. Not only does this exercise

give students practice in careful listening and collaborative thinking, but it can also serve as the model of the kind of community-based discussion an instructor may want.

• *Summary and synthesis questions.* To enhance the learning value of discussion, an instructor should end with a few wrap-up questions that ask students to summarize or synthesize the important ideas shared during the exchange. Students have to review and reflect on the discussion, identifying and articulating the intellectual highlights. These questions can take a variety of forms. They can ask outright for the one or two most important ideas that emerged or for some key concept that best encapsulates the exchange. They can ask what points the discussion clarified, what issues remain unresolved, or what topics should be addressed next time to advance the group's understanding.

Gale and Andrews's "High-Mileage" Types

Gale and Andrews (1989) developed categories of questions from classroom observations of discussions and tallied the average number of responses each type evoked. They called this average the "mileage" of each type. Using their results, we can ensure our discussions are lively. Here are the top mileage types, all of which can be pitched at high cognitive levels:

• *Brainstorming questions,* found to yield 4.3 student responses per question, invite students to generate many conceivable ideas on a topic or many possible solutions to a problem—for example: "What issues does Hamlet question in the play?" "What trends starting in the 1960s may have had a negative impact on American public education?" "How might the public be convinced to care about ecological imbalances?" At the start of a brainstorming session, the instructor tells the class to withhold judgment and criticism for the time being and records all the responses on the board, an overhead, a slide, or a flip chart. Only after all brains stop storming do the students begin editing, refining, combining, eliminating,

grouping, and prioritizing, using criteria they generate themselves.

• *Focal questions* elicit an even higher 4.9 responses per question. They ask students to choose a viewpoint or position from several possible ones and support their choice with reasoning and evidence. Students may develop and defend their own opinions, adopt those of a particular author, or assume a devil's advocate stance—for example: "Do you think that Marx's theory of capitalism is still relevant in today's postindustrial societies? Why or why not?" "To what extent is Ivan Illich a victim of his own decisions or of society?" "Is the society in *Brave New World* a utopia, a nightmare of moral degeneration, something between the two?" A variation on a focal question is for you to play devil's advocate on an issue or to make a contentious, controversial statement and invite your students to react against it. But as recommended in Chapter Thirteen, be sure to let your class know exactly what you are doing.

• *Playground questions* hold the mileage record, with an average of 5.1 responses per question. They challenge students to select or develop their own themes and concepts for exploring, interpreting, and analyzing a piece of material—for example, "What do you think the author is saying in this particular passage?" "What underlying assumptions about human nature must this theorist have?" "What might happen if [present a counterfactual]?" When posing such open-ended questions, however, be aware that this type of question can veer the discussion into other topics.

■ POOR QUESTIONS FOR DISCUSSION PURPOSES

It is difficult to fully appreciate highly effective discussion questions without examining the less effective types as well. Gale and Andrews's categories and the classroom research they conducted on discussions provide valuable insight and information on this latter kind too (Gale & Andrews, 1989). Some of these questions have their place, but they tend not to encourage broad participation or higher-order thinking.

Questions Good for Recitation

Some types of questions may flop for discussion but serve the purposes of recitation—that is, knowledge recall and review—quite well:

- *Analytical convergent questions* may elicit complex thought, but they have only one correct answer. So they make students edgy and cut the discussion short as soon as someone gives the right or complete answer. It makes sense that they evoke only 2.0 answers per question. Typically 1.0 of the attempts isn't exactly right or complete. Analytical convergent questions are best used sparingly as knowledge and comprehension warm-ups to get students talking.

- *Quiz show questions* have a short correct answer, such as a person, a place, a date, or a title. They elicit only factual recall and serve poorly as warm-up questions for genuine discussion. Their average mileage is 1.5 responses per question, suggesting that the first "contestant" guesses wrong about half the time. Still many a delightful review session has imitated a quiz show game format, such as *Jeopardy* or *Millionaire,* using exactly this kind of question (Kaupins, 2005).

Questions Good for Nothing

Some types of questions serve no purpose well and can confuse and alienate students. These should be avoided:

- *Fuzzy questions* are too vague and unfocused for students to know how to approach them. They may be phrased unclearly, such as, "Who else knows what else doesn't fall into this category?" Or they may be too global, like, "What about the breakdown of the family?" Students resist taking the risk required to attack such grand questions. Other common fuzzy questions represent well-meaning attempts to help: "Does everyone understand this?" and "Any

questions?" You may occasionally get an honest response, but all too often you find out later that not everyone understood and quite a few students must have had questions. It is usually better to use classroom assessment techniques (see Chapter Twenty-Nine) to answer such concerns.

- *Chameleon* and *shotgun questions* are both a series of weakly related questions fired off one after the other in hopes that one will hit with the students. Chameleons change their topical focus through the series until the last one barely resembles the first, leaving students not knowing which one to try to answer. Shotgun questions may all go off in the same general direction, but they make the instructor look like a "bad shot"—either desperate for a response or confused about the issues. Students become confused and disoriented in the murk of the inquisition, not knowing which in the series to dodge and which to address. The average series yields only 2.3 responses.

- *Programmed-answer questions* sound like open-ended questions on the surface, and indeed they have more than one appropriate answer. But between the lines, the instructor conveys, perhaps unconsciously, having only one specific answer in mind. Students regard this type of question as an unwelcomed challenge to read the instructor's mind. Some even consider it manipulative.

- *Put-down* and *ego-stroking questions* are two sides of the same bad attitude. The former type of question implies that students ought to know the answer or shouldn't have any more questions—for example, "Now that I have explained this topic thoroughly, are there any more questions?" The latter type assumes the superiority of the instructor to the discouragement of the students. An implicit request to "rephrase the answer the way I would say it" douses students' creativity, self-expression, and often their motivation to answer at all.

- *Dead-end questions* are quiz show questions with a yes or no answer. Students simply place their bets. But these questions can easily be transformed into useful types in one of two ways. First, you can often change them into true-false items, having students rephrase false statements to make them true.

Better yet, you can rephrase them by beginning the sentence with a why or a how. With thought now required, students are more likely to participate.

■ TURNING THE TABLES

The person posing the discussion questions need not always be the instructor. If you model good questioning techniques and spend a little time teaching your favorite questioning schema, you can have your students develop discussion and even test questions as homework assignments. You can use the best ones in class and in actual tests and even grade them if you choose. The quality of these questions also tells you how diligently your students are doing their reading (see Chapter Twenty-Three).

The next chapter offers other teaching formats that put the spotlight and the responsibility for learning on students.

CHAPTER 15

Experiential Learning Activities

This chapter covers a potpourri of teaching methods and moves that allow students to discover and construct knowledge by direct experience, either simulated or real. These activities rank even higher than discussion on a continuum of student engagement, ranging from moderately engaging to extremely so, and the intense emotions they often evoke cement the experiences into students' memories. Furthermore, they strongly appeal to the accommodator, diverger, and kinesthetic learning styles (Fleming & Mills, 1992; Kolb, 1984; see Chapter Twenty-Five). Research documents that experiential learning methods, such as simulations, games, and role playing, ensure higher student motivation, more learning at higher cognitive levels, greater appreciation of the subject matter and its utility, and longer retention of the material than does the traditional lecture (Berry, 2008; Bonwell & Eison, 1991; Hertel & Millis, 2002; Howard, Collins, & DiCarlo, 2002; Specht & Sandlin, 1991). These methods also meet a wider range of instructional goals than do less active ones (see Chapters One,

Two, and especially Eleven). We start here with the moderately engaging and move to the more powerful.

STUDENT PRESENTATION FORMATS

Employers place a high priority on communication skills, and many started complaining some years ago that their new college-graduate employees were wanting in these skills. In response, many institutions initiated communication-across-the-curriculum programs, emphasizing not only writing but speaking as well. As a result, oral presentations have become common course components. Formal oral presentations are not in themselves experiential, except to the extent that students learn all the preparation, platform skills, and rehearsal that go into a good presentation. However, oral communication takes many forms, and the activities described in this section give students public speaking opportunities within experiential learning contexts. As such, they add reality and pizzazz to student presentations.

In most cases, you assign or your students select the topic, research area, role, position, or school of thought that they will represent, but in a few cases students play themselves. Often they conduct research and write a paper outside class. However, you can set up some of these activities spontaneously in a well-prepared class. Before you turn students loose to investigate, represent, and question different sides of a controversy, be sure they understand rhetorical structure, the basic rules of evidence, and logical fallacies.

Variations on Debate

Every field has topics amenable to a two-sided (at least) fact-based argument. A debate format need not be any more complex than statements of the affirmative and the negative, plus rebuttals, each with a strict time limit. It is best to assign sides to pairs or triads so students have the chance to consider and discuss points of view other than their own.

A variation on debate that involves the entire class is a *change-your-mind debate*. You designate different sides of the classroom as "for the affirmative" or "for the negative," with the middle as "uncertain/undecided/neutral." Before the debate, students sit in the area representing their current position and can change their seating location during the debate as their opinions sway. After the debate, lead a debriefing discussion focusing on the opinion changers ("What changed your mind?") and the undecided students, who are likely to provide the most objective analysis of both the debate and the issue at hand.

A second variant for a whole-class activity is *point-counterpoint* (Silberman, 1996). Divide your class into groups—as many groups as there are positions on an issue—and tell each group to come up with arguments in favor of its assigned position. Select one student to launch the debate by presenting one argument for his group's stance; then call on each group in turn to give a different argument or counterargument. Conclude with a class discussion comparing the various positions.

Yet another variant is called *structured controversy* or *academic controversy,* in which two pairs in a group of four students formally debate each other on an issue, then switch sides, and finally synthesize a joint position (Johnson, Johnson, & Smith, 1991). Done properly, this activity requires that students conduct considerable outside research and write a final report.

Expert Individuals or Teams

Designate individual students, pairs, or triads to be the class experts on a certain topic, geographical area, body of theory or research, or something else. Following your reference leads, students do outside readings and turn in weekly, annotated bibliographies on their area of expertise. Then you regularly query the "experts" in class, asking for informational updates or about the relevance of their area to the day's discussion.

Dunn (1992) applied this format very effectively in his World Affairs course, where he paired off students as "briefing teams" charged with keeping up on the current affairs of nine world regions. On some days he played the role of a political leader dependent on his students' briefings, especially to lighten the mood when he felt the need to cajole his class into working harder.

Panel Discussion

Four or five students briefly present different points of view on a topic, either their own position or one they are representing. Panel members can play themselves or different noted scholars and historical figures—for example: Freud, Jung, Adler, Skinner, and Rogers in a psychology course; Benjamin Franklin, Thomas Jefferson, Aaron Burr, James Madison, and George Washington in an early American history course. Then the class addresses thoughtful questions and challenges, preferably prepared in advance, to the various panel members.

You can also make the entire class into a panel by calling a town meeting on a multisided issue or complex case (Silberman, 1996). After doing some outside research on the issue or situation, students prepare to voice their views within a time limit you set, following the format that each speaker calls on the next speaker.

Press Conference

You or a student assumes the focal role, posing as a noted scholar, a leader in some realm, or a representative of a particular position or school of thought, while the rest of the class plays investigative reporters, each student or small group with an assigned audience or readership, such as local residents, residents of another area or country, a special interest group, a specific company, or some public agency. These "reporter" students ask probing, challenging questions of the focal person.

Two planning caveats are in order. First, the focal role should represent a broad-ranging, controversial decision or stance. Defining such a role is easy in political science or history, but in other fields, it requires more creative thought. In psychology or sociology, for example, the focal role may be a criminologist or criminal psychologist whose testimony leads to the probation of a violent convict. In economics, the focal role may advocate an uncertain or risky intervention strategy. In the sciences and medical fields, it may stand for a controversial environmental or public health position—perhaps on global warming, endangered species preservation, genetically engineered produce, prescription drug restrictions, human cloning, or the like. Second, in addition to assigning audiences or readerships to the students playing reporters, you can require them to research and write out their questions and challenges in advance. Having them then write a mock article incorporating the press conference is an optional follow-up assignment.

You need not confine the activity to one focal person. You can have a succession of them with different viewpoints and perspectives.

Symposium

Individual students or teams present their independently conducted research papers that express their own ideas. The rest of the class asks probing questions and offers constructive criticism, which is especially useful if students can revise their work. In addition, for each class period, you may assign one or two discussants to interrelate and critique the papers. Discussants should have at least a day or two to review the symposium products in advance.

ROLE PLAYING

You assign students roles in a true-to-life, problematic social or interpersonal situation that they act out, improvising the script. When one player is not supposed to know the full story about another player's intentions, problem, or goals, you should provide written descriptions for each role. You also must decide what information to give to the rest of the class. Following the enactment is a debriefing discussion. It should address how the players felt in their role at crucial junctures, what intentions and interests motivated their actions, what behavioral patterns the rest of the class observed, and how these behaviors reflected concepts and principles addressed in the course.

While role playing relies on make-believe scenarios in the classroom, students learn experientially by identifying with the roles they play and observe. You may also play a role, especially when you want to model certain behaviors (how to conduct a family therapy session, negotiate a contract, mediate conflict, or open a formal meeting, for example).

This technique is used successfully in both therapy and instruction, especially in the humanities, social sciences, counseling, clinical psychology, and nursing. In political science or history, students can take the identity of key leaders or decision makers in a conflict or the role of collective constituencies that face an important task—for instance, landed elites, Tory loyalists, Continental Army soldiers and militia, tradesmen, yeoman farmers, ministers, and lawyers, all responsible for drafting their positions for a state constitutional convention (Frederick, 1991). In almost any discipline or profession, you can provoke discussion by having groups of students enact the violation of an ethical norm. Kraus (2008) had her research methods students role-play violations of the American Sociological Association Code of Ethics, and they found the activity very valuable.

In structuring an original role play, the only rule is to incorporate conflict between the roles and some need for the players to reach a resolution (Halpern & Associates, 1994). Here are some applications to inspire your own ideas:

- Professional (doctor, lawyer, or pastor, for example) and client disagree over an approach to the client's problem.
- Executive promises union negotiator (or up-start worker) a major promotion for keeping quiet about an impending plant closing, a behind-the-scenes corporate takeover, future layoffs, or planned benefit cuts.
- Worker representatives try to convince executives not to close an unprofitable plant.
- Human resource executive must make a tough hiring decision among various male, female, minority, and nonminority candidates with different job qualifications and personalities.
- Politician experiences role conflict between partisan and administrative roles or between ideological stance and the need for campaign funds.
- Couple or family argues over money, (un)employment, discipline of the children, authority, autonomy, communication, moving, in-laws, domestic violence, or alcohol or drug use. This scenario may include a social worker's, physician's, minister's, law enforcer's, lawyer's, or therapist's role.

If you teach a foreign language, feel free to make a role play of any situation your students may encounter while traveling. While they may not learn much through empathy, they will get useful, conversational practice in the target language. If you teach literature, consider casting students in the roles of the characters and letting them play out a hypothetical scene that extends the piece of literature. In other fields, search out case studies that you can adapt to role playing.

■ SIMULATIONS AND GAMES

What simulations and games share is the prospect of winning something desirable, whether that be money, power, territory, profits, being correct, getting one's way, extra credit, candy, or simply a sense of satisfaction. But the biggest win is in learning. Simulations and games can bring the course material to life and emotionally engage an entire class as few other methods can.

Academic Games

Many academic games are modeled on traditional games, such as Bingo and Go Fish, and classic television game shows, such as *Jeopardy, Family Feud, Wheel of Fortune, Password,* and *Who Wants to Be a Millionaire?* Recently some faculty have adapted *Survivor* to subjects as disparate as physiology (Howard et al., 2002) and music theory (Berry, 2008). The questions and answers come from the course material and can easily capture knowledge, comprehension, and application levels of thinking, if not higher. Games provide an effective and painless, even fun, review format (Kaupins, 2005; Moy, Rodenbaugh, Collins, & DiCarlo, 2000), and in this context, students can sometimes submit the questions and even run the game.

Games can also supply a format for almost every class period. After opening her music theory classes with a minilecture, Berry (2008) assigns "tribes" of students their "challenge" for that day, such as a timed workbook exercise on the minilecture topic. The tribe members correct their work and tally their individual and tribal scores with the goal to get the highest possible. Personal pride and peer pressure motivate individual achievement, even though the tribes don't vote off the lowest-scoring member.

Millis (in press) is the definitive contemporary book on academic games. It gives detailed directions on when and how to bring a wide variety of games (not all based on television game or reality shows) into the classroom.

Simulations

By abstracting key elements from reality (Mitchell, 1982), simulations allow students to live out the hypotheses and implications of theories, giving them intense emotional, cognitive, and behavioral experiences that they will otherwise never have. This method developed a strong faculty and student following during the 1970s and the early 1980s around a growing market of simulations of societies, formal organizations, corporations, markets, urban areas, cultures, world politics, and other complex, macro social realms. These were strictly face-to-face enactments of hypothetical social situations, unmediated by computers, some requiring many hours and an array of supporting materials. Many of them resembled role plays involving the entire class. Some of the early simulations that have endured are Barnga and Bafa Bafa, both of which sensitize students to cultural differences and clashes.

Among these early simulations was a variant called a *frame simulation,* which offers the instructor different scenarios or settings to choose from or to develop on her own. These still serve an important instructional purpose, though some have moved onto interactive computer sites. For example, students can play the Prisoner's Dilemma under various conditions and payoff rules that illustrate different psychological and sociological principles (Hyman, 1978, 1981). Another frame simulation, structured like a mock trial, comes with a suite of genuine cases spanning a host of disciplines: environmental protection, industrial safety, medical technology, religious practices, securities markets, affirmative action, community development, and individual rights (Karraker, 1993). For criminal cases, Silberman (1996) invites instructors to create an indictment around different sides of an issue and to set up a trial by jury simulation with the full complement of courtroom roles: judge, prosecuting attorney, defendant, defense attorney, prosecution and defense witnesses, jury members, and friends of the court. In fact, frame simulations can revolve around any decision-making body: a court, a board of directors,

a review board, a legislature, or an administrative agency (Hertel & Millis, 2002).

In addition to the hundreds of tried-and-true face-to-face simulations, computer technology ushered in an expanded selection of new products available either on the Web or in software packages. They range from individual tutorial programs (computer-assisted instruction) to full-blown multimedia simulations. Animated and interactive computer technology opened up elaborate simulations for the sciences and engineering. Among these are hundreds of virtual laboratories allowing students to conduct experiments and manipulate parameters in ways that would be too dangerous or too costly in real life. In hydraulics, for instance, students can solve complex canalization problems by varying the delivery, inflow, outflow, and power of various pumps. In electrical engineering, they can manipulate the performance of an electrical network and study overloading, breaks, and the like. In the health sciences, faculty can program SimMan and other medical software to simulate specific diagnostic situations. To obtain data for diagnosing the symptoms, students can even ask questions of the hypothetical patient and get answers, as well as run hypothetical tests. Biology and environmental sciences have numerous simulations, including Unnatural Selection, SimIlse, and SimWorld, all which realistically mix politics into the controversial decision-making processes. In addition, many of the original face-to-face simulations in the social sciences offer computer versions.

The field of business may have the most simulations, and they tend to be marketed under straightforward titles such as Airline, Corporation, Supply Chain, Manager, Marketer, Human Resource Management, Collective Bargaining Simulated, and Entrepreneur. BusSim has developed a simulation for just about every business specialty.

Simulations are not just for young students. They are mainstays of adult education and job training. The military runs battle simulations, hospitals and emergency response agencies hold disaster preparedness simulations, and even high-level university administration has UNIGAME and Virtual U.

Finding Simulations

Review your learning outcomes and decide what kind of simulation would truly help your students achieve them. Then start looking. You can obtain a simulation in one of three ways: (1) buy one from a commercial distributor (often a publishing house), which can cost up to a few hundred dollars; (2) find one free in a journal (see below) or at a teaching conference, in which case you may have to make or buy any needed materials on your own; or (3) design your own.

If you choose the first option, check the websites of publishers that produce good textbooks or teaching journals in your field. Of course, ask your colleagues as well.

If you choose the second option, start with your own field's teaching journals and the following publications:

- *Decision Sciences: Journal of Innovative Education* published by the Decision Sciences Institute (economics and business disciplines). Available free online at www3.interscience.wiley.com/journal/118499600/home.
- *The International Simulation and Gaming Research Yearbook* published by the Society for Academic Gaming and Simulation in Education and Training as the proceedings of the society's annual conference.
- *Simages,* the online newsletter of the North American Simulation and Gaming Association, which hosts an annual cross-disciplinary conference.
- *Simulation and Gaming: An Interdisciplinary Journal of Theory, Practice and Research,* published by an international consortium of professional associations, including the Association for Business Simulation and Experiential Learning, which also publishes the proceedings of its annual conference.

If you choose the third option, to design your own simulation, follow Hertel and Millis's (2002) advice, keeping in mind your learning outcomes, the number of hours you have available, and the number of students you want to involve. First, look for the real-life or realistic scenarios to structure your simulation around. Good sources are case studies, textbooks, journals, magazines, newspapers, and your personal experience. Next, develop your characters and the interests they will pursue, ensuring conflict or competition among your primary roles. Then fill out the situation with secondary and supporting roles, which the primary characters may use to further their interests. Be sure that none of the acting roles know too much. They have to be challenged and allowed to make bad decisions, even to fail. Finally, select the geographical setting, write the necessary documents, and develop the instructions, action constraints, and procedural rules (Hertel & Millis).

Running Simulations

A simulation and its debriefing take a good deal of class time—at least an hour for the very simplest. In addition, to grab your students' full attention, you should assess them on their performance, with an emphasis on the quality of their strategy, not their oratory. To ensure students get maximum mileage out of the experience, piggyback other assignments onto it, such as readings, outside research (before or during the simulation), an oral presentation, a response paper, or a position paper. Some of these assignments can be graded. To help students gain the most from their experience, require at least some kind of written reflection.

Here is the conventional wisdom for running simulations. First and foremost, be prepared. Read the instructor's manual or directions at least twice at a leisurely pace well in advance. Mark what directions you will give the students at each stage of the simulation. In general, it's best not to give all the instructions at the beginning, because too much information will confuse the students. Rather, parcel them out. List your preclass setup tasks. Know the sequence of events and the schedule of distributing artifacts and materials, but don't hesitate to refer to the manual during the simulation.

Be aware that most facilitators run simulations at too slow a pace. The challenge is to keep the game moving, even if the tempo puts pressure on the students. They need a long enough time to realize the constraints, costs, and benefits of their decision-making options, but not necessarily long enough to answer every question that arises, come to a full consensus, or feel completely comfortable with their decisions. After all, a simulation must imitate life as much as possible. (For more detailed advice, see Hertel & Millis, 2002.)

Debriefing Simulations

The debriefing process is an essential component of a simulation. It disengages students from the emotional aspects of the experience and settles them back into the classroom reality, and it allows them to transform what they experienced into meaningful learning. They should be able to identify the disciplinary concepts and principles illustrated in the simulation and assess their own decision-making abilities. In addition, a debriefing brings out the disparate perceptions, feelings, and experiences each player had (Hertel & Millis, 2002).

So important is the debriefing that you should prepare the discussion questions in advance. They should progress through three phases (Hertel & Millis, 2002). First, ask students to recount their experience and their feelings about it. A successful simulation may evoke some pretty strong emotions, both negative and positive. Second, have them explain their actions within the context of their roles, specifically their intentions and motivations behind their decisions. If different roles had different information, students can reveal what they knew and didn't know, what their goals were, and what strategy they had for attaining them. Finally, return students to their true role as learners with questions that address the connection between their simulated experiences and the concepts, principles, theories, and hypotheses they have studied in your course. Help them translate the concrete into the abstract and derive generalizations related to the subject matter. Hertel and Millis provide a series of debriefing questions suitable for almost any simulation. As recommended above, assigning a follow-up written

reflection will give students the time and emotional distance from the experiences to glean additional insights from it.

■ SERVICE-LEARNING: THE REAL THING

Service-learning is a method by which students acquire various skills and knowledge while working in community service. The current generation of college students is distinguished by its volunteerism and service orientation, which may explain this method's popularity with younger students. Most faculty also find it effective in meeting certain course objectives. According to instructors and "graduates," service-learning is almost uniformly a positive, life-changing experience for students—the kind they never forget. It imparts new knowledge not just in the abstract but in a concrete, real-world context. The experience also stimulates emotions, which strongly enhance learning and retention (see Chapter One) and help students progress toward certain affective, social, and ethical learning outcomes (see Chapter Two), as well almost every higher-order cognitive outcome (see Chapter Eleven).

Service-learning is classic learning by doing, and nothing teaches experientially like direct experience. If you want students to understand the characters in a piece of modern literature, let them talk with the human counterparts. If you want them to comprehend the dynamics of poverty, let them work with the poor and the homeless. If you want them to appreciate the problems and crises of other countries, let them help the émigrés and refugees. If you want them to understand prisoners, children, or any other group, let them spend productive time with some of these people.

Let's examine the accumulated research on the effects of service-learning (Astin, Vogelgesang, Ikeda, & Yee, 2000; Eyler & Giles, 1999). The method has been found to enhance the following:

- Students' personal development (sense of identity and efficacy, spiritual and moral growth)

- Students' social and interpersonal development (leadership, communication, ability to work with others)
- Students' cultural and racial understanding
- Students' sense of civic responsibility, citizenship skills, and societal effectiveness
- Students' commitment to service in their career choice and future voluntary activities
- In many studies, students' academic learning and abilities on some dimensions: writing skills, ability to apply knowledge to the real world, complexity of understanding, problem analysis, critical thinking, and cognitive development (no clear effect on grades, grade point average, or later standardized test scores)
- Students' relationships with faculty
- Students' satisfaction with college and likelihood of graduation
- Relations between the institution and the community.

Another national study (Gray, Ondaatje, Fricker, & Geschwind, 2000; Gray, Ondaatje, & Zakaras, 1999) found more mixed effects. On the positive side, students in service-learning courses were indeed more satisfied with the course than were students in non-service-learning courses. In the same comparison, students perceived that their service-learning experience slightly enhanced their civic engagement, their interpersonal skills, and their understanding of people of different backgrounds from their own. However, they reported no effect on their academic skills (writing, analytical, quantitative, or knowledge) or their professional skills (confidence in their choice of major and career, expectation of graduation, or career preparation). In fact, students who opted out of service-learning felt that they *did* advance their academic and professional skills.

How positive the service-learning experience is depends on several factors. The single most powerful determinant is a student's degree of interest in the subject matter before the experience. Therefore, service-learning is best reserved for upper-level courses in a major (Astin et al., 2000). Other known influences are under the instructor's control: how much students can share and discuss their experiences in class; how much training they have for the experience; how many hours per week they perform service; how well tied the experience is to the course content; and how much written and oral reflection students are asked to do, especially in tying the experience back to the course content (Astin et al., 2000; Gray et al., 1999, 2000; Zlotkowski, 1998).

Implementing Service-Learning

Is service-learning right for your courses? First, examine your learning outcomes. Service-learning is worth considering if you have outcomes that are affective, ethical, or social beyond working effectively in a group, or if your cognitive outcomes are served by students' practicing on an outside clientele. If either of these is true, try to identify community needs that truly complement your subject matter. For example, if you teach children's literature and want your students to be able to critique works from a child's point of view, then their reading books to children makes sense. If you teach public relations, having your students conduct a PR campaign for a local nonprofit organization clearly benefits their learning. If you teach public health or community nursing, your students can better master the subject matter if they plan and implement a community health or health education effort. If you teach political science, your students can learn how to navigate the politics at the various levels of government by conducting partnership projects in your course (Redlawsk, Rice, & Associates, 2009).

Second, be aware of the ethical questions that some service-learning experiences raise, even though requiring them is legal. If the experience involves working for social change, is it appropriate to require students to do this, no matter how they feel about the changes aimed for? Should they have to give service even if their current politics and ethics don't warrant it? Will they be placed in physical danger?

Third, consider your time constraints and commitment. Service-learning requires more planning and coordination than most other methods, especially your first foray into using it. If it fits well in your course and schedule, begin your preliminary tasks at least a couple of months before the term begins. (See Stacey, Rice, & Langer, 1997, a concise and comprehensive instructor's manual.) First, identify one or more appropriate community agencies. You might start with schools, medical and mental health facilities, social service agencies, and the local United Way. Then schedule a face-to-face meeting with the key contact person to find out about the organization's needs and expectations and to explain your own for your course. Ensure that the agency will orient and supervise your students. Alternatively, have students find their own agency and work out the project details, or ask your campus service-learning or voluntary-service center, if you have one, to identify one or more agencies with needs and expectations that will serve your course outcomes.

Then start making course design decisions. Will the service-learning be required, optional, or extra credit? Will you offer an alternative assignment? How much service-learning will be required? Fewer than twenty hours reduces its impact (Gray et al., 2000). What previous course components will be eliminated to make time for service-learning? How much will it count toward the final grade? What will be the requirements of the service-learning experience?

How will you assess and grade it? How will you link the service to the course content? When will you have students discuss their experiences? What writing tasks will you assign for reflection? (Best to have multiple reflection assignments.) How will you grade these reflection assignments? This information will be needed for your syllabus.

Finally, make the necessary logistical arrangements: getting help with liability issues from your institution's risk management office (such as release forms); creating student teams if appropriate (highly advisable to mitigate any physical danger); helping students and the agency coordinate schedules; ensuring students are oriented and supervised at the agency; arranging for student transportation, even if just car pools; and devising a system to monitor students' hours of service.

Additional Guidance

A number of books offer additional guidance for instructors and a wealth of ideas for solid service-learning projects, including exemplars. To stay abreast of the more innovative and successful projects and to share your own with colleagues, see the *Michigan Journal of Community Service-Learning* and the *Journal of Public Service and Outreach*.

CHAPTER 16

Learning in Groups

Every class conveys two lessons: one in the content and another in the teaching method. Student-active techniques send the message that with expert guidance, learners can actively discover, analyze, and use knowledge on their own. With this participatory empowerment, students come to understand that they must assume responsibility for their own learning. One particularly powerful student-active method, when implemented properly, is to put students in pairs or small groups to work and learn together. Our use of it conveys the message that when people work together with a cooperative ethos, they can accomplish much more than they can as individuals working apart—that is, two heads are better than one, three heads are better than two, and for some tasks, four or five heads are best.

■ A GROUP BY ANY OTHER NAME...

This teaching method has become popular enough to take on multiple labels. These days, the most commonly used terms are simply *group work* and *group learning*. Most of the research conducted on it in the 1980s and 1990s relied on the term *cooperative learning* (Millis & Cottell, 1998), which was defined very generally as a structured teaching method where small student groups work together on a common task (Cooper, Robinson, & McKinney, 1993). *Collaborative learning* emerged in the 1990s as the label favored in the sciences and engineering. Following Mazur's (1997) lead, these disciplines also use the terms *peer instruction* and *peer tutoring* when referring to pairs of small groups of students who are explaining their answers to one another. The literature shows no consensus about the difference, if any, among all these terms. However, there is one distinct, highly structured version of group work known as *team learning*. It emphasizes mutual, positive interdependence more than any other version. Students take team as well as individual tests, and their individual accountability and grades rest as much on their team's performance as on their own (Michaelsen, 1997–1998).

Since the terms *group work* and *group learning* are so commonly used, they are the choices here.

The terms *group* and *team* will be used interchangeably, except when referring to *team learning*.

■ THE CASE FOR GROUP WORK

Given how widely used group work is today, it is surprising how slow a start it had in higher education. By 1990, nearly six hundred published studies dating back ninety years had compared the effectiveness of cooperative, competitive, and individual approaches to teaching. Many of these studies found overwhelming support for the superiority of group work, and even those that didn't find support identified no detrimental effects to using it (Johnson, Johnson, & Smith, 1991). Yet group learning met with stiff faculty resistance at first, probably because old teaching paradigms and habits die hard. If we had no trouble learning individually when we were in college, it's hard for us to understand why our students would. This is why the best students can become the worst teachers. Being proud survivors of the lecture method, most of us just can't anticipate where, how, and why our students would have trouble learning our material the same way we did.

In general, the research on the effects of group learning has focused on three fundamental dimensions—achievement/productivity (learning), positive interpersonal relationships, and psychological health—and group work yields positive results on all of them (Johnson et al., 1991; Johnson & Johnson, 1989, 1994; Millis & Cottell, 1998). Astin (1993) studied the effects of 192 environmental factors on various educational outcomes of 27,064 students at 309 institutions. According to his results, the top two influences on academic success and satisfaction are interaction among students and interaction between faculty and students, each a key component of group learning strategies. In fact, both factors rank significantly higher than curriculum and content variables. Light (1990, 1992) reported similar results in the Harvard Assessment Seminars.

Johnson and Johnson (1989) surveyed 193 studies comparing the effects of group versus traditional techniques on student productivity and learning. More than half the literature reported group learning to have the stronger impact, while only 10 percent found individualistic methods more powerful. In addition, group learning enhanced interpersonal attraction in 60 percent of the studies, while competition did so in only 3 percent. A similar literature survey a few years later indicated that group learning is more effective than traditional methods in improving critical thinking, self-esteem, racial and ethnic relations, and positive social behavior (Cooper et al., 1993).

The superiority of group learning seems to hold at all educational levels and across student backgrounds and extends as students mature into adulthood (Johnson & Johnson, 1989, 1994). Disadvantaged students benefit as well. Frierson (1986) documented that minority nursing students who studied cooperatively for their board exams performed significantly better than those who studied alone. After instituting group-based, out-of-class enrichment programs for at-risk calculus students at the University of California, Berkeley, Treisman (1986) found that black students in the program received course grades over one letter grade higher than their nongroup counterparts.

This does not mean that group learning should supplant the interactive lecture, whole-class discussion, experiential learning, and other methods. Variety helps maintain student engagement and ensures reaching students with all learning styles. Moreover, the research indicates that cooperative learning need not be used all the time to have positive effects on student achievement.

A case can also be made against group learning. First, students have to acquire and use some skills and knowledge on their own as individuals. Second, most younger students have been learning in groups all through school, so we are not giving them a totally novel experience in college. What is novel is our expecting them to monitor and sanction each other without the kind of teacher intervention they are used to relying on (Jassawalla, Malshe, & Sashittal, 2008). In fact, some faculty perceive that students have become so close over their school years that they hesitate to evaluate each other's group contributions and performance honestly. Often they cover up for each other, showing more loyalty to their peers than to us. The third downside of group learning is its reliance on the brighter students to teach the slower ones. While you learn a subject most thoroughly by teaching it, many talented students learn very effectively on their own and don't benefit from the reinforcement of teaching it. Furthermore, the time that the brighter students spend tutoring their classmates is time that they are not getting additional challenges and acquiring more advanced knowledge and skills. Group learning clearly benefits average students, but at the cost of the gifted ones.

Therefore, consider group work a supplementary technique suitable for various classroom activities (Millis, 1990). It serves well for many lecture break activities (see Chapter Twelve) and can jump-start class discussion (see Chapters Thirteen and Fourteen). It is also useful for social and subject matter icebreakers (see Chapter Four), experiential learning activities (see Chapter Fifteen), case debriefing (see Chapter Nineteen), problem-based learning (see Chapter Twenty), mathematical problem-solving exercises (see Chapter Twenty-One), science laboratories (see Chapter Twenty-Two), some classroom assessment exercises (see Chapter Twenty-Eight), and review sessions (see Chapter Thirty).

■ CHANGING METHODS, CHANGING ROLES

Group learning casts both students and instructors in different roles from the ones they usually assume in traditional lecture-based classrooms (Johnson et al., 1991; MacGregor, 1990; Millis & Cottell, 1998; Rhem, 1992). Students must move:

- From passive listeners and note takers to active problem solvers, discoverers, contributors, and transformers of knowledge

- From low-to-moderate to high expectations of preparation for class
- From a low-risk, private presence to a high-risk public presence
- From personal responsibility for attendance to community expectation and responsibility
- From individualistic competition among peers to collaboration among group members whose success depends on one another
- From formal, impersonal relationships with peers and instructors to genuine interest in one another's learning and overall well-being
- From viewing instructors and texts as sole authorities to seeing themselves, their peers, and their community as important sources of knowledge

Young first-year students in particular can have a hard time making this adjustment. As group members, they may have experienced uneven workloads, interpersonal conflicts, boredom, exclusion, and even lower grades in elementary and high school where group learning may have been mismanaged (MacGregor, 1990).

In spite of their group experience, your students may know very little about group dynamics, and it is well worth teaching them some basic principles. For instance, acquaint them with communication patterns. Draw a few simple graphics on the board with circles standing for individuals and arrows designating the direction of communication. Show your students one-way and two-way (double-arrow) communication between two individuals, then a group with leader-directed communication (all one-way), and a group with balanced communication (arrows connecting multiple individuals). Finally, have your students sketch the patterns of some of the group communication patterns they have experienced and consider how these patterns affected their participation. Ask them to share their drawings and participation experiences with the class or in their groups. This exercise should sensitize them to the benefits of balanced communication (Kustra & Potter, 2008).

Students may also be unfamiliar with the typical stages of team development—forming, storming, norming, and performing (Tuckman, 1965). If you are putting students in long-term, stable groups, they need to know these stages, especially the fact that storming is normal and not symptomatic of team breakdown.

To give your students a crash course in group dynamics as well as the wisdom and the tools to collaborate successfully, refer them to Kennedy and Nilson's (2008) free online book. It is written simply and is colorfully illustrated for undergraduates.

The instructor's role changes with group learning as well. No longer is it focused on sorting, classifying, and screening out students. Its primary goal is to develop students' competencies and talents as "a guide on the side" instead of "the sage on the stage." In other words, the role shifts from expert/authority figure to facilitator/coach, who unobtrusively circulates, observes, monitors, and answers questions (Millis, 1990). Group work calls for placing much of the responsibility for learning squarely on the students' shoulders. Of course, relinquishing control can be difficult at first for an instructor.

THE SETUP AND MANAGEMENT OF STUDENT GROUPS

Group learning techniques share a number of essential features that you must build into or provide for in the way you assemble groups, design tasks, manage activities, and determine grades (Cooper et al., 1993; Feichtner & Davis, 1984; Felder & Brent, 2001; Johnson et al., 1991; Johnson & Johnson, 1994; Kagan, 1988; Michaelsen, 1997–1998; Millis, 1990; Millis & Cottell, 1998). These features are especially critical for long-term, stable teams.

Positive Interdependence

For a group to function effectively, each member must feel a sense of personal responsibility for the success of his or her teammates. In addition, each member's success must depend at least in part on the group's success. In brief, members must feel they need one another to complete the task at the desired level of quality.

To ensure this element, you can do one or more of the following:

- Assign a group product on which all members sign off and are given a group grade (you can also separately grade individual contributions, if you choose).
- Give group (as well as individual) quizzes and tests that count toward each member's individual grade.
- Allocate essential resources or pieces of information across group members, requiring them to share (materials interdependence).
- Assign each member a different part of the total task (task interdependence).
- Randomly select students to speak for their group.
- Require that all members edit one another's work using Word's Track Changes feature, a wiki, or Google Docs.
- Assign group members different roles. Common roles are recorder, spokesperson, researcher, summarizer, checker/corrector, skeptic, organizer/manager, spy (on the progress of other groups), observer, writer, timekeeper, conflict resolver, and runner/liaison to other groups or the instructor. Less-known ones are coordinator, driver (of the group's operating style), finisher (lends a sense of urgency to the task), implementer (of group decisions), supporter (harmonizer), monitor-evaluator, originator (of ideas), and resource investigator (Belbin, 2004).

Individual Accountability

All members must be held responsible for their own learning as well as for the learning of other group members. At the same time, no member should feel that he or she is giving more (or less) than an equal share of effort to the group task. In other words, no freeloaders, social loafers, or hitchhikers are allowed.

You can build in this element in several ways, some of which overlap with those above:

- Base final grades predominantly on individual quizzes, tests, papers, and other assignments.
- Count the team grades only for students who are passing the individual quizzes, tests, and written assignments.
- Randomly select students to speak for their group.
- Assign group members different roles (see the last subsection for possible roles).
- Assign group members primary responsibility for different parts of the team project, and grade them on their part (for example, one member develops the bibliography, another conducts the research, and another does the write-up).
- Give teams time early in the semester to discuss and agree on what they will do to sanction non-contributing members.
- Allow teams to "fire" a noncontributing member (after a verbal and a written warning).
- Allow an overburdened member to "resign" from a group of freeloaders and seek membership on another team.
- Base a significant portion of the final grade on peer performance evaluations.

This last strategy deserves elaboration. It can be used only when groups have stable memberships over several weeks or months. At the end of the term or the group work unit, have each member assign each of their teammates a letter grade for group contributions, or estimate the percentage of the work they contributed, or allocate a limited number of points across their teammates. If you use percentages or points, you may want to forbid students from giving equal percentages or points across their teammates. It is essential that students have criteria on which to grade their peers, such as attendance, preparation, promptness, leadership, quality of contributions, quantity of contributions, and social skills. If you provide these criteria, be sure to explain them and your peer evaluation policies and procedures before the group work begins. Better yet, have the groups develop their own lists of the criteria that define a good team member. Either way, the peer portion of the final grade should reflect

the amount and importance of group work in the course—at least 10 to 20 percent but no more than 60 percent.

How valid and accurate are peer performance evaluations? Students often give all their teammates high evaluations. Does this reflect the fact that group learning motivates students to prepare and perform more effectively than most other methods, or are students merely covering up for the poor contributors? You have to make the determination based on your own experience at your particular institution. If your students are merciless in penalizing freeloaders, social loafers, slackers, couch potatoes, sandbaggers, control freaks, ego trippers, bullies, whiners, martyrs, and saboteurs, chances are that their positive performance evaluations are valid and accurate. But if you have reason to suspect that freeloaders and other group-pathological types are getting off easy, try this strategy. Have students write peer performance evaluations two, three, or four times during the semester, and schedule them right after major project sections are due. This way any anger or frustration toward errant group members will come out in the heat of the moment. Another way to counter cover-ups is to say you will toss out any peer performance evaluations that give A's to all teams members.

It seems that times have changed in the way students treat freeloaders. Early studies found that group members punished their dysfunctional peers (Ferris & Hess, 1984; Jalajas & Sutton, 1984; Murrell, 1984). However, giving today's younger students the power to sanction social loafing in no way guarantees they will use it when necessary. Quite the contrary, they expect you as the instructor to know about the freeloaders and to administer justice by giving different individual grades on the group product, even if you have explained that their grades will depend solely on quality of the group product (Jassawalla et al., 2008). These students' expectations no doubt reflect their many years in K–12 group work, where teachers handed down the rules of engagement and intervened when violations occurred. So they come to college ill prepared and ill trained for adult-level team dynamics. In other words, we have to dispel them of their immature view of group work and teach them to bear collective responsibilities (Jassawalla et al., 2008).

One Clemson University faculty member, W. H. Warmath Jr. (personal communication, September 19, 2008), successfully instills a more mature understanding of team dynamics in his first-year students. He firmly informs them that their individual project grade will be solely the group grade, that they will be on their own to resolve their group malfunctions, and that he will serve only as a last-resort mediator and only in the presence of the entire group. However, he gives the teams the time and the authority to develop their own contract before they begin their project. In this contract, they must specify exactly when and where they will hold weekly, out-of-class meetings, how they will divide the labor and responsibilities, when sections of the project will be due, and what the sanctions will be for absences from meetings and for not completing assignments on time. Warmath reviews and approves the contracts (or returns them for revision), and all group members sign it. Since he instituted team contracts several years ago, he has counseled only one group, has had no complaints about group-grading policy, and has not heard about any freeloader problems. Oakley, Brent, Felder, and Elhajj (2004) also recommend having groups develop documents detailing team policies and expectations.

Appropriate Group Composition, Size, and Duration

According to the research, groups that are heterogeneous in terms of ability, race, gender, and other characteristics help students develop social skills, understand and get along with individuals of differing social backgrounds, and learn the material better (Heller, Keith, & Anderson, 1992; Heller & Hollabaugh, 1992). When group composition is diverse in ability or content background specifically, the slower students learn from the brighter ones—often better than they do from traditional methods because students seem to speak one another's language.

The brighter ones can benefit too: by teaching the material, they learn it all the better, at least if they didn't learn it thoroughly on their own. Of course, slower students can also hold back the gifted.

Depending on your course, it may be more important that you maximize heterogeneity on a variable other than ability or content background. For example, if you want your groups to debate ideas and critically examine their own, you might want to find out students' views the first week of class (have them do a free-write, for instance) and assign teams based on varying opinions and value systems. Expediency may also have to take priority. If you want teams to meet face-to-face outside class, you may have to consider students' schedules in assigning groups. Finally, be careful to avoid mixing females with a male majority. Heller and Hollabaugh (1992) found that males in the majority tend to dominate and overshadow the females.

The research also indicates that students should not form their own long-term groups. Such a composition only reinforces existing cliques, encourages discussion of extracurricular topics, and can favorably bias the members' peer performance evaluations. But it does reduce intragroup conflict.

Optimal group size varies with the open-endedness of the task. Several group activities described later in this chapter and in Chapter Twelve rely on pairs. But most other activities require groups of three to five to ensure lively, broad participation and prevent freeloading. A threesome seems to be optimal for mathematical and scientific problem-solving tasks that involve alternative means to one correct answer (Heller & Hollabaugh, 1992). Four or five is best for tasks with multiple respectable answers involving brainstorming, interpretation, and problem solving of a "focal" or "playground" nature (see Chapter Fourteen). Still, teams of up to seven members can function effectively and offer the added benefit of greater diversity (Michaelsen, 1997–1998).

Ideal group duration also depends on the task. Long-term group assignments facilitate major projects and ongoing tasks, since duration fosters group loyalty and refines members' cooperative skills. But students can get acquainted with more classmates if groups change with each short-term project or every several weeks. What often happens, however, is that students develop team loyalties quickly and plead to keep the same groups throughout the term.

Ad hoc groups or pairs based solely on seating proximity may be sufficient for occasional problem-solving and discussion assignments. In large classes where space is tight and chairs are immobile, you may feel limited to these groups. But you may be able to overcome such limitations by assigning seats.

Face-to-Face Interaction

Instructors should allocate some class time to team meetings, as experience has shown that you cannot always rely on students to meet and collaborate face-to-face outside class. If they can find a way, they may just divide the labor and go their separate ways, defeating the whole purpose and benefits of group learning. Of course, virtual interaction over email, chatrooms, or discussion boards can and sometimes must substitute for face-to-face meetings. If you have students communicate using your online course management system, you can keep better track of their virtual than their face-to-face meetings.

Genuine Learning and Challenge

The group task must make students learn something, not just do something. It should go beyond what the students have learned in the course and demand group synergy and higher-order thinking processes (application, analysis, synthesis, evaluation) to complete. In addition, it should have either multiple respectable answers or multiple means to the answers and pose a genuine challenge that requires more than one student mind to meet within the given time limit. In brief, it should be a harder task than you'd assign to students working alone.

This setup rule for group work is too often forgotten. Students find doing a routine activity in a group boring busywork. Such a task also undercuts much of the learning payoff of group work. Students learn more not only because they discuss the material

and teach each other but also because they should be tackling a more challenging task than they otherwise would. Anything less also sours the brighter students against working in groups.

Explicit Attention to Collaborative Social Skills

Working together effectively in long-term, stable groups requires certain behaviors of all the individuals involved: attending all meetings, coming prepared to contribute, listening actively, taking turns in talking, not interrupting, encouraging others, cooperating, sharing resources, being open-minded, giving constructive feedback, tactfully defending one's views, compromising, and showing respect for others.

According to cooperative learning proponents, these are acquired skills that you must explicitly foster in as many ways as possible: having the class brainstorm and agree to the qualities of a good teammate; including these skills among your outcomes for group work; including them in your peer evaluation criteria; modeling them yourself; praising students you see practicing them; and, especially, scheduling a few sessions for students to reflect on and process the quality of their group interactions. Young students in particular need occasions for collective reflection and feedback since so many of them depended on their teachers to troubleshoot group problems in primary and secondary school. For them to take responsibility for their team's performance, they have to acquire the courage and communication skills to express criticism constructively to their peers.

Some instructors shy away from overseeing group processing sessions, largely because they don't know how to run one. But it's really quite easy. Processing best begins with students' assessing themselves as teammates, answering questions such as these:

- How many of my group's meetings did I attend?
- How well prepared was I for each meeting? How consistently did I complete whatever task I was assigned to do?
- How well did I listen to others in my group?

- Did I ever interrupt them or get angry with them?
- When I disagreed with one or more teammates, did I try to find common ground or otherwise resolve the conflict? Did I propose or agree to a compromise?
- How much did I comment productively on my teammates' ideas, including giving them praise and encouragement?
- How well did I play my assigned role?
- How consistently did I share my knowledge and resources with my group?

Students should present their self-assessments orally or in writing within their groups. (You can make this a writing assignment.) Then their teammates should provide feedback, couching it in the same terms as a response to the self-assessment. Following this procedure, students are more likely to take the feedback seriously and accept it (Kustra & Potter, 2008).

Do counsel students that the feedback should help their teammates, not hurt them. This is not the time to unload. Rather, they should supply positive as well as negative evaluations. Furthermore, they should describe specific behaviors, not judge the person, and should ask whether he understands the feedback, recalls the behaviors mentioned, or has questions (Kustra & Potter, 2008).

After the individual self-assessments and feedback, the students should address some questions within their groups, and a recorder should take notes:

- How well have we included and encouraged all our members in our discussions?
- How evenly have we shared the work?
- How well have we handled conflict?
- How high-quality has our task performance been?
- How could we accomplish our tasks more effectively?
- How could we function as a group more smoothly?

The recorder should save these notes and read them aloud at the next group processing session.

Then the group members can assess how much they have improved.

Team learning supporters take a different view from the cooperative learning camp. They maintain that students intuitively know from their life experience what defines a good (and bad) team member, and they do not need time to group-process beyond writing peer performance evaluations. If students encounter internal conflicts and inequities, they must resolve them on their own without instructor intervention (which may include firing the offending member). After all, the work world will not be interested in their interactional problems and preferences, and one of your jobs is to prepare them to function effectively as contributing adults.

Which is the wiser position? It depends mostly on the maturity of your students. Many adult learners understand adult team dynamics and already have good interpersonal communication skills, but traditional-age students rarely do. The better position also depends on your personality and background. Some instructors enjoy and do an excellent job of teaching the soft skills, while others feel more comfortable and competent dealing with the hard skills.

■ MANAGEMENT TIPS

Beyond the essential elements already discussed are several standard operating procedures that help ensure student success and make the management of group activities easier and more predictable for you (Cooper et al., 1993; Feichtner & Davis, 1984; Johnson et al., 1991; Millis, 1990).

First and foremost, start small. Begin by trying out a small-scale, pretested technique (like those in the next section) in the class where you feel the most confident. Expect it not to work perfectly—any strategy can fall short the first time tried—and plan for your time estimate to be off one way or another. A safe launching pad is an optional help or review session.

Second, use group learning only with a criterion-referenced grading system (see Chapter

Thirty-One). Grading on a curve (that is, norm-referenced grading) undercuts the spirit of cooperation and the prospect of group success on which group learning relies. An absolute grading scale gives all students an equal chance to achieve.

Third, introduce the activity to your class by explaining your rationale for using it. Without getting technical, mention some of the research that documents its superior effectiveness. Perhaps list the crucial elements of group learning and your objectives for the group work. Also reassure your students that they will not jeopardize their grades or be accused of cheating by helping each other.

Fourth, give groups a specific, structured task that requires a written product to show at the end. The major reasons for group work failure are a lack of organization and specificity in the assignment and the students' confusion over its purpose and expectations. The written end product may be no more formal than handwritten notes for the group's verbal report at the end of the session. It may be a problem solution, a list of ideas, or a group test answer sheet. Or it may be a major team project for which students meet several times over weeks to complete.

A word of warning is in order, however. Feichtner and Davis (1984) present evidence that large-scale, formal group assignments are more problematic than smaller-scale and less formal ones. Specifically, they caution against assigning more than one major group presentation and more than three written papers or reports per term. Otherwise students are more likely to report having a negative group experience. Group tests, however, tend to generate positive experiences (see next section).

Fifth, set and enforce tight time limits and deadlines for task completion, even for short tasks that pairs or groups can complete in a couple of minutes. It is helpful to bring a timer or stopwatch with you to all group work sessions. For tasks of five to fifty minutes, you might give appropriate ten-minute or two-minute warnings. Larger-scale assignments call for firm deadlines for the various subtasks (bibliography, prospectus, data collection, data analysis, outline,

first draft, and so on). It is best to schedule all final product deadlines comfortably in advance of the end of the term. Tight time limits and deadlines help keep teams on task.

Sixth, ensure the assignment of individual roles within each group. Many possible roles were listed above in the section on positive interdependence. At the very least, each group of three or more needs a recorder or spokesperson. Role assignments should rotate at least weekly among the members of stable groups. You can make the first role assignments randomly, or use the following technique for assigning roles in ad hoc groups. After breaking students into groups, tell them to point to one fellow member on the count of three. Assign the student receiving the most points the task of appointing the recorder/spokesperson and any other necessary roles. The element of surprise adds humor to the moment.

Seventh, set the rule of "three before me." That is, you can insist that students take their questions to each other first and not to you until they have asked at least three other students, or accept only group, not individual, questions.

Eighth, set rules to control noise levels and maintain order. Among the most popular ones are "no unnecessary talking" and "only one group member talking at one time." Another helpful hint is to bring the classroom to silence by informing students that you will signal when time is up by raising your hand. They should then stop talking and raise their hands as soon as they see yours up. This technique enables you to silence a large lecture hall in seconds.

Ninth, to ensure that groups have a genuine learning experience, conclude each group session with a means of assessing students' progress or mastery of the material. You might ask for a brief presentation or progress report from each group. Or you can administer a quick quiz or classroom assessment exercise (see Chapter Twenty-Nine). If you choose a quiz, you should set a high standard of mastery that all group members must meet before any of them can leave class. Alternatively, you can select a member from each group at random to take the quiz for the group.

■ TRIED-AND-TRUE GROUP LEARNING STRATEGIES

If you are interested in trying out or extending group learning in your courses, consider experimenting with some of the proven strategies in this section. While the levels of success and usefulness vary by discipline and instructor, you can adjust them or create your own versions to serve your needs. The following sampler comes from several sources, including Cooper et al. (1993), Johnson et al. (1991), Kagan (1988), Michaelsen (1997–1998), Millis (1990), and Millis and Cottell (1998). Many work well as a student-active lecture break (see Chapter Twelve), and some double as a classroom assessment technique (see Chapter Twenty-Eight). Although a few may sound adolescent, all have been used effectively at the postsecondary level:

- *Think-pair-share.* Give students a question or problem and ask them to think quietly of an answer or solution. Have them discuss their responses with their neighbor, and then share them with the class. You can also set the requirement that they come to a consensus or submit one piece of written work as a pair. Set a time limit of one or two minutes for the pair exchange. You can extend this format by having each pair in agreement join another pair in agreement to come to a consensus together.
- *Pairs check.* Partners coach each other on worksheet problems or check their class or reading notes for completeness and accuracy. This two-minute activity is similar to the lecture break pair and compare in Chapter Twelve.
- *T.A.P.P.S. (talking aloud paired problem solving).* Pairs of students solve a problem or resolve a case by taking turns playing different roles—one that talks through the process of reaching a solution, while the other listens, asks questions, and provides feedback.
- *STAD (student teams-achievement divisions).* After a lecture, video, or demonstration, teams of three or four receive a worksheet to discuss and complete. When members feel that they have reached acceptable solutions, you give a brief oral or written quiz to the group, a representative, or each individual member to assess their mastery of the material. In her music theory class, Berry (2008) integrates STAD within the academic game Survivor. For the daily challenges, she distributes workbook exercises for the "tribes" to complete, then administers individual quizzes. These quiz scores are totaled for a tribal score. While tribes don't vote off weak members, students perform diligently due to peer pressure, their personal pride, and their sense of responsibility to their tribe.
- *Jigsaw.* Each member of a "base group" is assigned a mini-topic to research. Students then meet in "expert groups" with others assigned the same mini-topic to discuss and refine their understanding. The base groups re-form, and members teach their mini-topics to their teammates.
- *Structured/academic controversy.* Pairs in a group of four are assigned opposing sides of an issue. Each pair researches its assigned position, and the group discusses the issue with the goal of exposing as much information as possible about the subject. Pairs can then switch sides and continue the discussion.
- *Group investigation.* Assign each group or let each group choose a different topic within a given subject area. Groups are free to organize their work and research methods and even to determine the form of the final product, such as a video, play, slide show, website, demonstration, presentation, or paper.
- *Numbered heads together.* Assign a number to each member of a team of four. Pose a thought question or problem, and allow a few minutes for discussion. Call out a number, designating only students with that number to act as the group spokesperson. This exercise promotes individual accountability.
- *Talking chips.* This method guarantees equal participation in discussion groups. Each group member receives the same number of poker chips (or any other markers, such as index cards, pencils, or pens). Each time a member wishes to speak, he or she tosses a chip into the center of the table. Once individuals have used up their chips, they can no longer speak. The discussion proceeds until all members have

exhausted their chips. Then they reclaim their chips and begin another round.

• *Send a problem.* Each group member writes a question or problem on a flash card. The group reaches consensus on the correct answer or solution and writes it on the back. Each group then passes its cards to another group, which formulates its own answers or solutions and checks them against those written on the back by the sending group. If groups disagree, the receiving group writes its answer as an alternative. Stacks of cards continue to rotate from group to group until they are returned to the original senders, who then examine and discuss any alternative answers or solutions given by other groups.

• *Group tests.* Each student takes a quiz or test individually and hands it in for a substantial portion (one-half or two-thirds) of her quiz or test grade. Then students assemble into groups and take the same quiz or test again as a team, turning it in for the remaining portion of their grade. In most cases, the team scores exceed the individual scores and raise the students' grades. As a near-daily activity in team learning, this technique is called a readiness assessment test (Michaelsen, 1997–1998). Generally the quiz or test is objective, but it doesn't have to be. Groups tests not only give students' quick feedback on their individual thinking and answers, but they also make the students review, discuss, and debate the material, processing it at a higher level. Not surprisingly, this technique improves students'

retention of the course content over individual tests (Cortright, Collins, Rodenbaugh, & DiCarlo, 2003).

■ PREPARING STUDENTS FOR LIFE

Younger college students are intent on learning about the real world they are about to enter, while older ones want to know how they can function more effectively in it at a higher level. As instructors, we need to prepare our students to thrive in this rapidly changing and increasingly challenging world—to make them more knowledgeable citizens, consumers, social participants, appreciators of the arts, and science watchers and supporters, as well as more successful professionals and businesspersons. We select our content with this goal in mind, and we should similarly select teaching methods to reinforce our verbal messages and build the kinds of social skills students will need.

Group collaboration is the way the world works because well-functioning teams generate more innovative and creative ideas and devise better solutions to problems than do individuals with a competitive ethos. In the education we provide students, we need to transform them into high-functioning team members, as both leaders and followers. Therefore, we must implement group learning with care, teaching students to assume collective responsibility and share a collaborative ethos.

CHAPTER 17

Writing-to-Learn Activities and Assignments

Why have your students do in-class or homework-related writing exercises—often called "informal writing"—if you don't grade them? The research gives plenty of reasons. For starters, writing about the material helps students learn it better and retain it longer—whatever the subject and whether the exercise involves note taking, outlining, summarizing, recording focused thought, composing short answers, or writing full-fledged essays. Second, writing is so powerful because it makes students think actively about the material, and depending on your prompt, you can make your students think at any cognitive level you would like. Third, even informal writing can define audience other than the instructor and therefore develop students' sensitivity to the interests, backgrounds, and vocabularies of different readers. A fourth reason is for classroom assessment (see Chapter Twenty-Eight)—that is, to find out quickly, while you're still focusing on a particular topic, exactly what your class is and isn't learning. This way you can diagnose and clarify points of confusion before you give the next exam and move on to other topics (Angelo & Cross, 1993; Cross & Angelo, 1988). In fact, the student feedback and questions that writing exercises provide can plan a good part of your classes for you. Reading short, informal writing assignments that do not require grading takes no more time than any other type of class preparation. Finally, many writing exercises give students the chance to learn about themselves—their feelings, values, cognitive processes, and learning strengths and weaknesses. Younger students in particular need and appreciate such opportunities for self-exploration. This chapter covers a wide variety of writing-to-learn activities and assignments that have proven instructional value (Ambron, 1987; Angelo & Cross, 1993; Cross & Angelo, 1988; Hinkle & Hinkle, 1990; Kalman & Kalman, 1996; Kirkpatrick & Pittendrigh, 1984; Langer & Applebee, 1987; Neal, 2008; Newell, 1984; Wright, Herteis, & Abernehy, 2001; Young, 1997; Young & Fulwiler, 1986).

■ FREEWRITES

Students write about a predetermined topic for a brief, specified number of minutes (one to three) as fast as they can think and put words on paper. The objective is to activate prior knowledge or to generate ideas by free association, disregarding grammar, spelling, punctuation, and the like.

Freewrites serve as effective in-class warm-up exercises. Usually students walk in having forgotten what they discussed in the previous class meeting, the week's reading, and the lab manual instructions. Frequent freewrites on the readings also put students on notice that they had better keep up with the course. Here are some possible freewrite topics:

- "Write down all the important points you remember from last Wednesday's discussion."
- "Summarize the most important points from the readings assigned for today [or from the day's lecture or class activities]."
- "From what you recall from the lab manual, write down what is to be done in lab today, any procedures that confuse you, and what the experiment is expected to create or show."
- Write three key words on the board from the last class or reading and ask students to explain their importance.
- Have students define a concept in their own words, explain the parts of a complex concept, give real-life examples of a concept, or compare concepts from today's class with those from the previous class.
- Write a seed sentence on the board—that is, a major hypothesis, conclusion, or provocative statement related to class or readings—and ask students to write their reactions.
- Have students apply a principle to their own experience.
- Have them write the answer to a question that your last minilecture, your demonstration, a video, or a class activity answered.
- Have them freewrite answers to test review questions to prepare for a tightly timed essay test.

Of course, freewrites needn't be private. Students can share them with one another, in which case the activity is called *inkshedding* (Hunt, 2004). They can trade and comment on one another's freewrites. Their purpose is not to evaluate the other's writing but to understand it. After such an exercise, the class is ready for discussion.

Freewrites can also be assigned as homework. In the *concept assignment,* students read a section or two of a book, then begin freewriting about what they just read and what they don't understand. They read the next section and freewrite again. At the end of the assigned chapter or unit, they write three sentences: one on each of three key concepts they have identified in the readings. Students usually write three or more pages of notes and reflection (Kalman & Kalman, 1996, as applied to physics). The main benefit of concept assignments is getting the students not only to do the readings but to really think about them.

While it is usually best not to grade freewrites, at least not formally, you might collect them and check off those that demonstrate evidence of the student's having listened to the lecture or discussion, done the assigned readings, or studied the lab manual (see Chapter Twenty-Three). You can count freewrites as part of class participation or as ungraded but required assignments.

■ THE ONE-MINUTE PAPER

With books and notebooks closed, students summarize the "most important" or "most useful" points they learned from the day's lecture, reading assignment, laboratory, or discussion. Time permitting, they also write down questions that remain in their minds. Although this is called a "one-minute paper," the exercise usually requires two or three minutes.

Just as freewrites can function as a warm-up, a one-minute paper can serve as a "cool-down." It helps students absorb, digest, and internalize new material, moving it into long-term memory. It also makes them think about the material, especially what they didn't understand, which is precisely what you need to know before wrapping up a topic.

Because one-minute papers are not graded, they are usually anonymous. But you should collect and read at least some of them to find out how well the students grasped the new material. Their summaries and questions will tell you what to review and clarify in the next class.

■ JOURNALS

Students write down their intellectual and emotional reactions to the lectures, discussions, readings, laboratories, solutions to homework problems, or other written assignments. They do this regularly at the end of each lecture, discussion, or lab or while they are doing their assignments outside class. Some instructors require just one weekly journal-writing session, either in class or as handed-in homework, on any or all aspects of a course. Students should have a special notebook solely for their journal.

Journals help students keep up with the course as well as to read and listen actively. They also make students think about the material and what they are learning. It is best, however, to provide students with guidelines on what their journals should address. Here are some possible questions:

- What is new to you about this material?
- What did you already know?
- Does any point contradict what you already knew or believed?
- What patterns of reasoning (or data) does the speaker/author offer as evidence?
- How convincing do you find the speaker's/author's reasoning or data?
- Is there any line of reasoning that you do not follow?
- Is this reasoning familiar to you from other courses?
- What don't you understand?
- What questions remain in your mind?

You should collect and check off journals regularly or intermittently, but you need not grade them. If you do, don't weigh them very much toward the final grade. But do write comments in them to develop a personal dialogue with each student.

■ ONE-SENTENCE SUMMARIES

As an in-class activity or a short homework assignment, students answer these questions on a specific topic in one (long) grammatical sentence: Who Did What to Whom, How, When, Where, and Why (WDWWHWWW)? The topic may be a historical event, the plot of a story or novel, or, by substituting another What for Who/Whom, a chemical reaction, mechanical process, or biological phenomenon.

This technique makes students distill, simplify, reorganize, synthesize, and chunk complex material into smaller, essential units that are easier to manipulate and remember. It is advisable that you do the exercise first before assigning it and allow students twice as much time as it takes you. You can collect and comment on the summaries yourself or have your students exchange them and write comments on each other's.

■ LEARNING LOGS

After each lecture, reading assignment, or problem set, students write two lists: one of the major points they understood and the other of the points they found unclear. Later, at regular intervals, they review their learning logs to diagnose their learning strengths and weaknesses (such as the reasons for repeated errors) and brainstorm ways to remedy these weaknesses. This diagnostic process can be conducted in class where students can discuss their learning pitfalls and share study and problem-solving techniques.

Learning logs serve several worthy purposes. Students isolate and review major points presented in the course. They also identify what they aren't grasping. Finally, and most important for some students, they learn about their own learning styles and ways to enhance their learning. This technique is especially valuable in cumulative subjects in which students do similar graded assignments on a frequent, regular basis.

Do collect and check off learning logs intermittently to ensure students are keeping them up. You might grade them if they comprise a major course assignment.

■ DIALECTICAL NOTES

Students read and take notes on a relatively short, important, self-contained passage that you select from course readings. On the left side of their note paper, they write their reactions to the text as they read it: where they agree, where they disagree, where they are unsure, where they are confused, where they have questions, and so on. At some later time, they review the passage and their left-side notes and write their reactions to these notes on the right side of the note paper.

Students can take dialectical notes in class or as a fairly short homework assignment. You can assign the first part (passage reading and reactions) as homework and do the second part (reactions to reactions) in class. Leave some time between them, however—anywhere from an hour of classroom discussion to a few weeks.

Dialectical notes encourage students to read a text carefully, analyze it critically, and reevaluate their initial reactions to it. These notes also demonstrate the nature and value of scholarly dialogue and debate. In addition, they make superb springboards for discussion. After students get used to the exercise, you might consider collecting and grading their notes.

This technique is especially useful in courses that require close readings of difficult texts, such as philosophy, history, political science, religious studies, law, and social theory. It also adapts easily to problem solving in mathematics, economics, engineering, and physics. Students work the problem in mathematical symbols on the left side of the paper and explain in words what operations they are performing, and why,

on the right side. Later, in small groups, students can read and discuss each other's various approaches and solutions.

■ DIRECTED PARAPHRASING

In their own words, students summarize the content of a reading assignment, a lecture, a discussion, or a lab to a defined audience for a specific purpose. Students can pretend they are writing, for example, to laypersons for the purpose of public education, to public policy makers for the purpose of social change, or to practicing scientists for research purposes.

Because students must paraphrase material, they must work to understand it in depth and internalize it. Also, since they are writing to a specific audience, they must consider the informational, persuasive, and political value of the available knowledge and data—for example, what facts and arguments are important or irrelevant to a given audience.

Directed paraphrasing assignments may be major or minor, in-class or homework, graded or just checked off. Students can also present them orally, and the rest of the class can role-play the audience.

■ LETTERS, MEMOS, NOTES, AND ELECTRONIC POSTS

In the letters home exercise, students paraphrase in informal language what they are learning in a course in the form of a letter to their parents, a sibling, or a friend. This technique helps students see the relationship between course material and projects and their everyday lives. It also gives them the opportunity to describe the material in their own words, and thus to distill, internalize, and remember the major points. Its value as a preexam review exercise is obvious. Letters should at least be collected and checked off.

As in directed paraphrasing, you can vary the audience and purpose for letters, memos, and notes. Students can also write each other or post messages on the class discussion board or blog about a certain reading, a problem they are working on, a design project, or any other assignment they may share as a team or a class. Finally, they can write real or mock letters on some course-related issue to the editor of a newspaper or magazine, a political leader, a young child, or a figure from the past for practice in taking the audience into consideration in their message and writing style.

■ MOCK TESTS

An excellent assignment for getting students to review and really think about the material before a test is to have them make up a test over the material. This exercise can be done in class or as homework, either individually or in groups. However you assign it, students should hear and discuss each other's test questions. The power of this exercise rests in getting students to identify what they believe to be the key concepts and relationships in a body of material. If they miss the mark, they will find out in class before the test.

Before giving your students this assignment, you may want to teach them some questioning techniques, such as Bloom's (1956) taxonomy of cognitive operations (see Chapters Two and Fourteen). You may also find it helpful to specify the test format—so many multiple-choice items, true-false, short answer questions, essays, and so forth. With a little practice, your students may write such good questions that you can use them in your tests. They are motivated to write ones you will want to use because they know the answers to their own questions.

■ DRAFTS FOR PEER FEEDBACK

Prefinal drafts of written work—essays, lab reports, proposals, papers, and the like—that will be turned in later for formal grading fall into a gray category that we might call "writing-to-learn-to-write-better" assignments. Just like professionals, students improve their writing in response to well-informed feedback

on drafts. No doubt you as the instructor can provide the best-informed critique, but students can benefit from peer feedback as well, from both getting it and giving it. Peer feedback not only provides students with more varied, immediate, and frequent feedback than any one instructor can give, but also helps students develop communication, critical thinking, collaboration, and lifelong learning skills (Dochy, Segers, Van den Bossche, & Gijbels, 2003; Topping, 1998).

However, the validity, reliability, and accuracy of peer feedback are uneven, some tainted by personal relationships and traits (such as race) and typically too lenient, superficial, and unfocused (Mowl & Pain, 1995; Orsmond, Merry, & Reiling, 1996). This should not be surprising, as students have loyalties to one another and concerns about criticizing a fellow student's work; lack the disciplinary background to know and apply professional standards, at least in lower-level courses; and give only as much feedback as the questions provided absolutely demand. So in answer to the question, "Is the central idea clear throughout the paper?" most students will say only yes or no and will not reference specific passages unless told to do so.

Instructors can obtain much more valid, neutral, useful, and detailed student peer feedback by putting a different kind of item on the feedback forms. Rather than requiring an evaluation about the adequacy, effectiveness, clarity, or logic of some aspect of the work, you can ask students to identify features or parts of the work, as each student sees them, or give their personal reactions to the work (Nilson, 2002–2003, 2003). For example, instead of forcing a judgment with, "Does the opening paragraph lay out a clear thesis statement for the rest of the paper?" rephrase the question as one requiring simple identification: "What do you think is the thesis of the paper? Paraphrase it below." Rather than asking, "Is the title of the paper interesting, appropriate, and sufficiently focused?" solicit instead students' personal reaction: "What three adjectives would you use to describe the title of the paper?" Rather than requesting an evaluation such as, "How well written is the paper?" give students this innocuous task:

"Highlight any passages you had to read more than once to understand what the writer was saying."

The revised questions are emotionally neutral and require only basic rhetorical knowledge to answer, yet they demand close attention to the work and often references to its particulars. They do not allow students to give biased, uninformed, or superficial feedback. Rather, the responses they solicit tell the writer how readers have understood and reacted to the paper and what they got out of it. If most of the readers did not identify the intended thesis, the writer knows she must strengthen and clarify the thesis statement. If she didn't like the way her readers described her title, she knows she should change it. If they highlighted several passages as hard to read, she knows she needs to work on rewriting those sections. With peer feedback, students find a genuine audience—a role instructors cannot play—and they can come to care about how and what they communicate (Nilson, 2002–2003, 2003).

■ MULTIPLE PURPOSES

Writing-to-learn exercises offer unmatched versatility. Not only do they help students process content, clarify their thinking, and remember their learning, but they can also induce students to pay closer attention in class, do the readings, and think carefully about the material. In addition, they can give you valuable insights into your students' learning. So we will revisit these exercises, perhaps under different names, in later chapters (Twenty-Three and Twenty-Eight) that focus on some of these multiple purposes.

We are not finished with the topic of student writing either. Chapter Twenty-Four will help you teach your students formal modes of writing that conform to the rhetorical and stylistic conventions of your discipline.

PART 4

MORE TOOLS
Teaching Real-World Problem Solving

CHAPTER 18

Inquiry-Guided Learning

Inquiry-guided learning also goes by the names *inquiry-based learning, inquiry learning,* and *guided inquiry*. In addition, it has several definitions in the literature that are not entirely consistent with each other. In Chapter Eleven, it was defined very generally as "students learning or applying material in order to meet a challenge, such as to answer a question, conduct an experiment, or interpret data" so as to accommodate the range of more specific definitions.

■ DEFINITIONS OF INQUIRY-GUIDED LEARNING

According to Hudspith and Jenkins (2001), inquiry-guided learning is "a *self-directed, question-driven search for understanding*" (p. 9). More specifically, they explain it as a process that begins with students exploring a subject for research, then identifying a central research question, developing a research strategy guided by anticipated results, and finally answering the central question with the results. Guiding students

through this entire process might take two terms, Hudspith and Jenkins openly admit. After all, it will take months for students to explore a subject thoroughly enough to come up with decent research questions and narrow their inquiry to one central question. In addition, the instructor must develop and facilitate many training sessions on a list of essential topics and skills: understanding the inquiry process itself, developing researchable questions, anticipating answers, conducting types of research (library, Internet, interviewing), assessing evidence, and writing up or presenting the results.

The definition forwarded by Lee, Green, Odom, Schechter, and Slatta (2004) describes a similar process that starts with students formulating good questions and following the scientific method to answer them. They add that the good questions are likely to lack a single right answer. But the authors also have a very open view of inquiry-guided learning, as they see it happening within the interactive lecture, discussion, group work, and every other student-active teaching method listed in Table 11.1.

In at least some of these situations, however, students are likely to be furnished with questions.

Prince and Felder (2007) do not see students developing questions as a necessary part of the process. Quite the contrary, inquiry-guided learning involves giving students a challenge, such as a question, a hypothesis, or simply data to interpret, and they learn whatever they must to meet that challenge, which may or may not go beyond the course material. The inquiry may have a very narrow scope—for instance, one question that a segment of the lecture raises—or a very broad one entailing a major term project based on outside research. Prince and Felder also consider inquiry-guided learning an umbrella for several major methods—the case method, problem-based learning, discovery learning, project-based learning, and just-in-time-teaching (JiTT)—all of which they call *inductive teaching*. These methods all launch the learning process with a realistic, problematic situation and require that students research and assemble facts, data, and concepts to resolve it.

For purposes here, we will use Prince and Felder's definition of inquiry-guided learning and view the five methods they list as close variations of it. The first two, the case method and problem-based learning, merit their own chapters (Nineteen and Twenty) in this book, as they are complex, well researched, and widely used across the disciplines. The remaining three—discovery learning, project-based learning, and JiTT—require less explanation and are treated within this chapter.

■ THE EFFECTIVENESS OF INQUIRY-GUIDED LEARNING

However you define inquiry-guided learning, its inductive nature makes it a powerful learning method (Bransford, Brown, & Cocking, 1999). It typically involves acquisition and comprehension of knowledge, analysis of data, evaluation of evidence, application of findings to a situation or problem, and synthesis of one or more resolutions. In short, it requires that students engage in multiple modes of higher-order thinking. Some forms of it may even spur cognitive development by introducing students to multiple perspectives on a problem and the uncertainty that arises in choosing among solutions. Compared to lecture-based instruction, it does a much better job of fostering students' academic achievement and improving their critical thinking, problem-solving, and laboratory skills (McCreary, Golde, & Koeske, 2006; Oliver-Hoyo & Allen, 2005; Oliver-Hoyo, Allen, & Anderson, 2004). In addition, engagement in inquiry-guided activities is related to a student's perceived gains in science and technology understanding, intellectual development, and vocational preparation (Hu, Kuh, & Li, 2008; Justice et al., 2007; Pascarella & Terenzini, 2005). To be fair, however, it has a negative effect on perceived gains in general education and personal development, and its positive impacts fade as we move from high-performance to low-performance students (Hu et al., 2008).

Like every other teaching method, the benefits of inquiry-guided learning depend on its implementation. To be effective, students must have sufficient guidance and scaffolding through the inquiry process—that is, explicit directions about what to do and how to do it, assuming they are dealing with new material. In fact, an overwhelming amount of research documents this need, as well as the failure of minimally guided, problem-centered instruction, commonly called *discovery learning* (Aulls, 2002; Kirschner, Sweller, & Clark, 2006; Klahr & Nigam, 2004; Mayer, 2004; Moreno, 2004; National Survey of Student Engagement, 2007). In other words, constructivism has its limits. Students are unlikely to discover the basic principles of science by following the investigative techniques of professional researchers. However, the greater the students' background knowledge in the subject matter, the less guidance they need (Kirschner et al., 2006; Kyle, 1980). With a solid knowledge base, they can start thinking more like experts. They are better able to identify key characteristics of a problem as well as the procedures and algorithms to solve it, thereby drawing on "internal guidance" (Kirschner et al.,

2006). Acquiring this knowledge base may require somewhat more conventional learning strategies.

To make up for a weak or incomplete command of basic knowledge, the literature endorses two forms of guidance. The first form is worked examples, which serve as models of problem-solving schemata for students. They illustrate the procedures and logic for approaching and working through problems (Chi, Glaser, & Rees, 1982). When students can follow a model, they have enough working memory available for processing these procedures and the reasoning behind them. Without worked examples, they have to divert much of their working memory to searching their long-term memory for possible strategies (Kirschner et al., 2006). Numerous studies from the 1980s and 1990s show that students learn more when they can study worked examples before tackling comparable problems on their own (Kirschner et al., 2006).

The second form of guidance is process worksheets. These lay out a proven sequence of problem-solving steps for students to follow, sometimes with hints and rules of thumbs. With this structure, students don't rush headlong into problems without first identifying the useful information they do and don't have, classifying the problem, visualizing it (in mathematics, the physical sciences, and engineering), and performing whatever other steps are prescribed for reasoning through the type of problem. As a result, students display improved task performance (Nadolski, Kirschner, & van Merriënboer, 2005). Chapter Twenty-One recommends teaching students a stepwise schema for solving mathematical problems.

■ OBJECTS AND MODES OF INQUIRY

What might students inquire about? Unless you have the course time to let them explore a new subject and frame research questions, you will have to supply the object of their inquiry. The following are categories of objects that apply to many disciplines, as well as possible questions to pursue (Hudspith & Jenkins, 2001):

- *A phenomenon:* Does it exist? If so, to what magnitude? What are its causes? What are its effects? Examples: black holes, bone cancer, dual coding, election fraud, plate tectonics, near-death experiences, a change in the violent crime rate.

- *The absence of an expected phenomenon:* What prevents (prevented) it from happening? Examples: acceptance of evolutionary theory in the curricula of many K–12 school systems, the worldwide population explosion forecasted in the 1960s, a certain nation's economic collapse.

- *A perceived relationship:* Does it exist? To what extent? To what extent is it causal or spurious? Examples: the links between education and income, religiosity and political affiliation, global warming and human activity, diet and cancer, capital punishment and violent crime rates.

- *A controversy:* What underlies it? Examples: Why do scientists disagree about the cause of the Great Extinction? Why do physicians disagree about the role the mind plays in healing? Why do some people believe that tax cuts on dividends and interest stimulate the economy and others do not?

- *A theory:* How well grounded is it in fact or observation? How well does it explain and predict a phenomenon? How is it related to one or more other theories? Examples: evolutionary biology, the "great man" theory of history, the big bang theory, functionalism/pluralism versus conflict theory/elitism, the theory that Alzheimer's disease is caused by amyloid plaque buildup in the brain.

- *A complex concept:* What is its meaning? How well grounded is it in fact or observation? Examples: addiction, dark matter, genetic marker, constructivism, cultural drift.

- *A process:* How does it work? Examples: How does lupus undermine the immune system? How does economic development lower birth rates? How does the U.S. Census Bureau determine what to ask and how to ask it on the census questionnaire? How do people make decisions about purchasing a house?

- *A solution to a problem:* How can a given problem be solved? Examples: How can we reduce the incidence of AIDS on the African continent? How can we determine whether modern *Homo sapiens* has any Neanderthal DNA?
- *A course of action:* How sound or desirable is it? Examples: producing genetically engineered foods, setting the legal drinking age at twenty-one, allowing electronic machine voting without a paper trail, the U.S. invasion of Iraq, instituting charter schools to spur improvement in the public school system, allowing private corporations to oversee health care, charging illegal immigrant children in-state college tuition

Another way of getting your mind around inquiry-guided activities, especially if you teach in the sciences, engineering, or technical fields, is to consider various modes of inquiry (Arons, 1993). Students can tackle tasks such as these:

- Observe phenomena qualitatively and interpret what they perceive, trying to identify patterns.
- Formulate concepts out of their observations.
- Develop and test models that reflect their observations and concepts.
- Examine a new piece of equipment, and figure out how it works and how it can be used.
- Use a new piece of equipment to make measurements, analyze the data, and present the results.
- Distinguish explicitly between what they have observed and what they are inferring in interpreting the results of observations and experiments.
- Answer probing questions about a given research study, such as, "How do we know . . . ?" "Why do we think . . . ?" and "How strong is the evidence for . . . ?"
- Ask and answer "What will happen if . . . ?" questions (called *hypothetical-deductive reasoning*) about an experiment or other type of research study. If possible, students can follow up by proposing hypotheses and testing them in an experiment that they themselves design.

All of these modes are as useful for the social sciences as they are for the physical and biological sciences. Even those involving physical equipment may apply to psychology, and data-analytical software may be considered a type of equipment.

Inquiry-guided learning is not only for the sciences, however. Perhaps the most varied examples of this method's implementation appear in Lee's edited volume (2004), which showcases the teaching scholarship of North Carolina State University faculty. In addition to inquiry-based courses in food science, microbiology, physics, paper science and engineering, forestry, and psychology, you can read about such courses in history, design, music appreciation, French culture and civilization, and Spanish language. In history, for example, students do what historians do: evaluate and analyze primary sources, then develop logical arguments supporting particular historical interpretations with evidence from their research (Slatta, 2004). In Spanish for Engineers, students research how the Spanish culture influences and informs technology, in history and today (Kennedy & Navey-Davis, 2004). In music appreciation, they investigate the scientific aspects of music (sound, acoustics, hearing, and recording technology) as well as the artistic (musical expression, interpretation, meaning, and value). While the former aspects allow experimentation and testing, the latter, lacking universally agreed-on standards, permit students to develop and defend their own reasoned judgments (Kramer & Arnold, 2004). Across the disciplines, students have the opportunity to learn inductively and critically think their way to their own conclusions.

■ VARIATIONS OF INQUIRY-BASED LEARNING

We already examined discovery learning and had to conclude from the research that this minimally guided, highly constructivist version of inquiry works most effectively for students who already have solid background knowledge and are prepared to practice quasi-professional research methods. So let's turn to JiTT and project-based learning.

JiTT

As a complement to their reading assignments, students receive conceptual questions on these readings, usually multiple choice, shortly before each class through the course management system. (Because this material has not yet been discussed in class, JiTT is considered inductive.) The instructor then designs or adjusts his plan for the upcoming class based on students' answers. The goal is to address and challenge students' misconceptions on the subject matter before they become further ingrained and inhibit learning of new material.

The research on this method attests to its learning effectiveness. Novak, Patterson, Gavrin, and Christian (1999) credited it with reducing attrition by 40 percent and raising students' normalized gains on the Force Concept Inventory by 35 to 40 percent in physics courses that were previously lecture based. A study on a large introductory biology course found comparable and additional benefits to JiTT: higher normalized pretest-posttest gains and lower attrition, plus improved student preparation, study habits, and class participation (Marrs & Novak, 2004). Research in general chemistry and organic chemistry courses also documented higher student achievement and engagement due to JiTT (Slunt & Giancarlo, 2004).

Some instructors are discouraged from trying JiTT because they have to prepare conceptual questions on all the readings. However, these items are the same type as those used in the interactive lecture, and some disciplines, especially the sciences, already have dedicated websites with many conceptual multiple choice questions for collegial use (see Chapter Twelve).

Project-Based Learning

This method comprises a major assignment in which students, often in teams, design or create something, such as a piece of equipment, a product or architectural design, a computer code, a multimedia presentation, an artistic or literary work, a website, or a research study involving the collection, analysis, and presentation of real data. Service-learning projects fall within this category as well. To complete their project, students may draw solely on course material or supplement it with outside research.

Compared to more conventional methods, project-based learning leads to greater improvement in students' conceptual understanding, problem-solving skills, and attitudes about learning, and their performance on content-focused tests is the same or better (Mills & Treagust, 2003; Thomas, 2000). However, a major project shifts students' out-of-class time away from the standard course content to specialized subject matter, so their mastery of the fundamentals often suffers (Mills & Treagust, 2003). In addition, any collaborative problems students encounter on their teams can have high-stakes repercussions that can result in profound dissatisfaction.

Other Techniques

The next two chapters go into much further detail on two more complex and more commonly used inquiry-guided techniques: the case method and problem-based learning. In fact, the case method dates back to the late 1800s, and problem-based learning is at least a few decades old. Both predate the coining of the terms *inquiry-based learning, inquiry learning,* and *guided inquiry* and have a great deal of research documenting their strengths and challenges.

CHAPTER 19

The Case Method

In this complex world full of daunting challenges, students must learn how to solve problems. Different disciplines focus on different types of problems, and different types of problems call for different teaching methods. Both the case method and problem-based learning (in the next chapter) help students learn how to solve open-ended, high-uncertainty problems that have multiple respectable solutions—some better than others, however. These two methods are variants of inquiry-guided learning and are relevant to any discipline with real-world application. Chapter Twenty-One suggests ways to help students reason their way through closed-ended, quantitative problems, as are common in mathematics, physics, engineering, economics, and accounting. Chapter Twenty-Two examines how you can construct laboratories to teach students the real process of scientific problem solving.

The case method exposes students to problematic, real-world situations and challenges them to apply course knowledge to analyze the issues and formulate workable solutions. It is based on real or realistic stories that present problems or dilemmas that are quite well structured but lack an obvious or clear resolution. Cases are usually printed, but some are available dramatized on videotape. Those in Web-based learning objects may add the dramatic realism of interactivity. If canned cases do not suit your instructional purposes, you can always write your own at no cost but your time. Anyone with a bit of storytelling flair should find case writing an entertaining activity. To guide you in writing or selecting cases, this chapter identifies the qualities of a good case and describes the many types of cases.

■ THE EFFECTIVENESS OF THE CASE METHOD

Aside from the fact that students enjoy the case method, good cases are rich educational tools for a host of reasons:

- They require students' active engagement in and use of the material (Sharkey, Overmann, & Flash, 2007).

- They help make up for students' lack of real-world experience.
- They accustom students to solving problems within uncertain, risk-laden environments, thus promoting cognitive development from the dualistic mode of thinking to informed judgments about the best approaches and solutions to difficult problems (Fasko, 2003; Levin, 1997; Lundeberg, Levin, & Harrington, 1999).
- They foster higher-level critical thinking and cognitive skills such as application, analysis, synthesis, and evaluation, all of which come into play in the process of thinking through and developing solutions to a case (Dinan, 2002; Gabel, 1999; Habron & Dann, 2002).
- They raise awareness of the ethical side of decisions (Lundeberg et al., 2002).
- They demand both inductive and deductive thinking, compensating for higher education's focus on the latter.
- They serve as excellent writing assignments, paper topics, and essay questions, as well as springboards for discussion, review, and team activities.
- They increase class attendance (Lundeberg & Yadav, 2006a, 2006b).
- They improve both the students' perceptions of and confidence in their learning, as well as the faculty attitudes about teaching (Lundeberg & Yadav, 2006a, 2006b; Sharkey et al., 2007).
- They enhance students' achievement of their learning outcomes in their instructors' eyes (Lundeberg & Yadav, 2006a, 2006b; Rybarczyk, Baines, McVey, Thompson, & Wilkins, 2007).

On the student-involvement continuum from didactic methods (lecture) on the low end to experiential methods (role plays, simulations, and service-learning, for example) on the high end, the case method falls somewhere in the middle, depending on the case. The more it resembles a simulation, the more experiential the learning. A case more closely approximates a simulation when it is written in the second person (placing the student in the story's key role), the present tense (happening now), and extended stages (see below). But the second person and the present tense don't belong in a case taken from reality. No matter how they are written, cases only approach the experiential (see Chapter Fifteen) because students don't act them out. However, the last type described in this chapter, sequential-interactive, begins to blur the distinction.

■ THE APPROPRIATE SUBJECT MATTER

The case method accommodates all subjects and courses that have a context for application or use. This is why professional schools have adopted it as a central instructional method. Business and law did so decades ago; in fact, the Harvard Business School built a whole curriculum and publishing company around it. Medicine, nursing, clinical psychology, educational administration, and pastoral studies followed. Many engineering specialties have also discovered cases.

The case method is broadly used in many arts and science fields as well, to a greater or lesser degree: music history (Chiaramonte, 1994), philosophy (ethics), economics (macro, legal aspects), political science (policy analysis, public administration, constitutional law), sociology (social problems, criminology, organizations), psychology (clinical, abnormal, organizational behavior), biology (resource management, ecology, paleontology), and scientific methods in general (research study design and implementation to test a given hypothesis). If you teach any of the sciences, you can choose from a huge collection of well-tested cases at this University of Buffalo website: http://ublib.buffalo.edu/libraries/projects/cases/case.html.

Faculty and teaching assistant development has also embraced the method. It uses cases portraying problems that instructors may encounter with classes and individual students—for example, challenges to authority, hostile reactions to sensitive material, accusations of discrimination, grading and academic honesty disputes, and difficulties implementing new techniques.

WHAT MAKES A GOOD CASE

A good case may be written in the second or third person and in the present or past tense, and it may be almost any length. What is important is that it have the following qualities.

Realism

Real or hypothetical, a case should depict a currently relevant situation with which students can empathize or identify. Realism is further enhanced by technical detail, character development, historical context, and extension over time or a decision-making process (see the next section).

Opportunities for Synthesis

Cases should require students to draw on accumulated knowledge of the subject matter to analyze the problems and formulate solutions. Without some review built into the situations, students may forget to apply the basics in real decision-making situations in their careers.

Uncertainty

Although some solutions will be better than others, a case should offer room for multiple solutions and valid debate. Several solutions may be viable, but you may have students select just one course of action and justify their choice. Or you may ask them to rank-order their solutions. The uncertainty surrounding the solutions may be due to uncertainty in the knowledge base (a trait of all bodies of knowledge), information missing in the case (as is often true in reality), or the genuine validity of different approaches to the problem.

Risk

The decisions students make must have some importance, even if it is only hypothetical—for example, a character's employment, health, or life; an organization's survival or success; a country's welfare; the loss of a legal case; or social justice or public security. Something valuable must be at stake.

TYPES OF CASES

A good case may range from brief to very long. *Bullet cases* make one teaching point in just two or three sentences. They serve as good small-group discussion topics and short essay questions. *Minicases* are a tightly focused paragraph or two; if dramatized in a minute or two, they are called *vignettes*. They generate more discussion and analysis than do bullet cases. You can easily modify either type by confining the possible solutions to four or five reasonable options, much like a multiple-choice question. Then students must identify and justify their selection of the best solution (Waterman & Stanley, 2005). On the other extreme are cases that go on for pages. The hundreds of management and business administration cases that the Harvard Business School publishes range from a couple to over forty pages.

Most cases represent a one-time snapshot of a situation and occupy students for fifteen to twenty minutes, a class period or two, or a single homework assignment. But some cases can extend into a continuing story or shift directions according to student decisions.

The former type, a *continuous case*, tells an unfolding story in segments over real or condensed time. As real-life situations usually evolve and change over time, this structure adds realism. For instance, some faculty development cases describe an instructor's shifting relationship with a class over a term, with each minichapter presenting different issues to consider. Some medical and nursing cases follow the progression of a disease or a pregnancy in a hypothetical patient.

The latter type, a *sequential-interactive case,* leads students through a process of narrowing down their solutions or decisions by providing additional information *as the students request it*. Like those on DVD, these cases approach the experiential realism of a simulation. They cast students in the key decision-making role throughout, requiring that at least their minds act it out. Here is an outline of how you can structure such a case across subject matter, with the medical or clinical variant in parentheses:

1. Students study a case giving limited information on the nature or root cause of a problem. First, they brainstorm all interpretations or causes (diagnoses) and their solutions (treatment plans). Then they rank-order the interpretations or causes (diagnoses) according to the ease and feasibility for verifying or eliminating them (ease and safety of testing).

2. Students request specific additional information, beginning with what they have ranked as the easiest and most feasible to obtain (easiest and safest to test), to help them narrow down the possible interpretations or causes (diagnoses).

3. You provide the information they request in turn. (You should have additional information in hand for any likely request.)

4. Students again rank-order the possible interpretations or causes (diagnoses) in light of the new information and repeat step 2.

5. You repeat step 3.

6. Students select the most likely one or two interpretations or causes (diagnoses) and their solutions (treatment plans).

Depending on the subject matter and the problem, you may also want to include the ease and feasibility of implementing a solution (treatment plan) as a rank-ordering criterion. After all, if students identify widespread poverty as the root cause of a problem, they may not be able to develop a workable, action-oriented solution. Alternatively, you may wish to focus attention on the relative importance or likelihood of a cause. The case method is extremely flexible.

■ DEBRIEFING CASES

For cases to function well as homework assignments, paper topics, essay exam questions, or discussion springboards, you must guide students through a productive debriefing. That is, you have to challenge them with good questions about the case—questions that engage them in application, analysis, and synthesis of the material, plus critical evaluation of their proposed interpretations and solutions. Brainstorm, focal, and playground questions admirably serve these purposes (see Chapter Fourteen).

The simplest formula for debriefing a case is problems-remedies-prevention, that is: "What are the problems?" "What are the solutions?" and if applicable, "How could these problems have been prevented?" The structure for sequential-interactive cases given follows this basic formula.

While the problems and solutions are the essential issues, you might ask other questions to direct students back to the course material to find answers. Cases that you debrief following a list a questions are called *directed* (Waterman & Stanley, 2005). Good cases often contain other matters and important details well worth students' consideration—for example: possible reasons behind a character's action or inaction; reasons that such action or inaction fails to solve or even worsens a problem; the impact of the historical context, the organizational culture, or financial constraints; or how the situation might play out if one ingredient were different. Providing your questions in writing will keep the debriefing focused on the key points.

You can launch a case discussion with the entire class (see Chapters Thirteen or Fourteen) or have students discuss a case in groups (see Chapter Sixteen). Using groups offers still more options:

- All groups can work on the same case with the proviso that each group reach a consensus on its answers (otherwise majority rules). This format works well only with cases that can generate widely different interpretations.
- All groups can work on the same case, but with each group addressing different questions.
- After a general class discussion identifying the problems in the case, half the groups address solutions and the other half preventions.
- Each group works on a different case and presents a descriptive summary and debriefing to the rest of the class.

■ A POSTSCRIPT FOR PIONEERS

If the case method is rarely, if ever, used in your field but you can see a place for it in your course, realize that trying it poses very little risk. It is a tried-and-true method in many fields, and course evaluations show that students find it both highly instructive and enjoyable. The key is in the quality of the case. You might show drafts of your own creations to colleagues before using them in class. Remember too that you can continue to improve your cases over time.

CHAPTER 20

Problem-Based Learning

Both the case method and problem-based learning (PBL) present students with real-world, human-situational, open-ended, high-uncertainty, and risky challenges with multiple respectable solutions, some being better than others. However, PBL problems tend to be messier and fuzzier, and the course material alone cannot provide viable solutions. So students must do outside research, which usually makes the problem-solving process a sizable project best conducted by teams of at least four (Duch, Groh, & Allen, 2001).

The McMaster University Medical School in Ontario, Canada, introduced PBL in the late 1960s to move medical education away from straight lecture and memorization tests and toward actual practice. Medical students worked in groups with a precept to discuss, research, and diagnose hypothetical medical cases. From the 1970s on, PBL spread to several dozen North American medical schools (Jonas, Etzel, & Barzansky, 1989; Kaufmann, 1985; Kaufmann et al., 1989; Kirschner, Sweller, & Clark, 2006). But it is applicable in all the same subject areas that the case method is: the social sciences, psychology, history, philosophy, business, law, educational administration, medicine, nursing, clinical fields, the biological and physical sciences, engineering—any discipline or profession that presents unclear and uncertain challenges.

■ HOW PBL WORKS

PBL tends to leave students more or less on their own to research their problem and devise solutions to it. But they can and should follow this series of steps (Amador, Miles, & Peters, 2006; Bridges, 1992; Duch, Allen, & White, 1997–1998; Edens, 2000):

1. Team members review the problem, which is typically ill structured, and clarify the meaning of terms they do not understand.
2. They analyze and define the problem. (You may provide guidance.)
3. They identify and organize the knowledge they already have to solve the problem. This may also

mean identifying and ignoring extraneous information given in the problem.

4. They identify the new knowledge they need to acquire to solve the problem—the learning issues.
5. They organize and rank-order the learning issues and set objectives for outside research. (You may or may not provide references.)
6. They divide the work among themselves.
7. They conduct the assigned research individually by agreed-on deadlines.
8. They continue to meet to share research findings and conduct additional research as needed.
9. They merge their newly acquired and previous knowledge into what they consider to be the best possible solution. (This step qualifies PBL as a constructivist method.)
10. They write up or orally present their solution.

Once the instructor guides students through the basic procedures, the teams should work as independently as possible. Each devises its own internal organization and decision-making rules for evaluating alternative formulations of and solutions to the problem. Members integrate course materials with outside library, Internet, interview, survey, documentary, or field research. Depending on the problem, the assessable product may take the form of a lengthy memo, a report, a budget, a plan of action, or an oral presentation to the class or a hypothetical decision-making body.

Experiential Potential of PBL

While PBL usually doesn't require students to play roles, that's not to say that it can't. Some elaborate PBL problems allow for an optional experiential dimension, which adds an early step: the team members decide on the roles they will play in a kind of open-ended simulation. Students might assume professional roles, such as members of a council with varying political interests to be taken into account. In the lengthy educational administration problem that Bridges (1992) developed, students take the role of

personnel selection committee members, with one acting as project leader, another as facilitator, another as recorder, and the rest as members. He also incorporates specific role plays and mini-simulations, such as conferences, interviews, field observations, in-basket exercises, and progress presentations.

PBL's experiential realism is grounded not only in the problems, activities, and (sometimes) roles, but also in time factors. A project may be designed to proceed in real time. In a multistage rollout problem, the challenge may unfold over time as you supply students with pieces of additional information (Duch et al., 2001). Solving one problem can entail weeks of research and group meetings in and out of class. In fact, a substantial problem can absorb most of a term. But you can find or design problems that take only a week or two to solve.

Assessment of PBL Projects

Beyond balancing group and individual grading (see Chapter Sixteen), you must decide in advance the specific criteria on which you will grade the product and set bottom-line standards for various grades or point ranges. Then you must develop a rubric describing the product for each level of quality on each criterion (see Chapter Thirty-One). You must also convey those criteria and levels to your students before they begin the project so they will have some structure within which to direct their efforts. Appropriate dimensions may include the clarity of the problem definition, the breadth of outside sources used, the feasibility of the solution, the cost-effectiveness of the solution, the extent to which the solution resolves all aspects of the problem, and the rationales for the solution selected.

Because the PBL literature offers little assessment guidance, grading these projects can present challenges. It can be difficult to give them less than an A because the teams are supposed to work independently, so you don't monitor your students as carefully as you might with other teaching methods. Another potential complication stems from the high degree of student engagement. Grading down a project can touch emotional nerves unless you can clearly justify your assessments.

GOOD PBL PROBLEMS AND WHERE TO FIND THEM

Good PBL problems and good cases have the same key characteristics: realism, opportunities for students to synthesize material, uncertainty, and risk—and all the better if they resemble problems that students will experience in their careers (Duch et al., 2001). Some generic workplace problems include managerial miscommunications, low organizational morale, difficult policy implementation, negative public relations, and ethical dilemmas. In addition, a good PBL problem for your particular course is one that gives students practice in the abilities that you targeted in your learning outcomes and directs students to the knowledge you want them to acquire beyond the course material.

You can also judge the quality of problems using Bloom's (1956) taxonomy of cognitive operations (see Chapter Two). A "poor" problem requires only knowledge or comprehension, as do typical end-of-textbook-chapter problems. A "fair" problem adds a story element but entails no more than application. A "good" problem demands analysis, synthesis, and evaluation to solve. It is highly realistic, full of researchable unknowns, and open to more than one solution (Duch & Allen, 1996). Its description is usually much longer as well.

Here's a simple example. Let's say that the readings, lectures, and class activities in a biology course have familiarized students with the structure and function of DNA, the function of various enzymes involved in DNA synthesis and replication, and radio-labeling techniques. The instructor then gives teams this PBL problem: "A rare blood disorder has been identified in a particular family in Europe. [The problem describes the symptoms.] Devise the least expensive method to determine the disorder's cause and to locate the defective gene, and suggest diagnostic tests for identifying potential victims." Solving this problem presumably requires the students

to conduct outside research on topics like blood DNA, DNA research methods, and genetic testing. Once the teams complete their task, they explain their solutions to the class, which then engages in discussion to evaluate the various methods suggested.

Many PBL problems are available in biology (Allen & Duch, 1998; Duch & Allen, 1996; Mierson, 1998). Duch and Allen (1996) also describe one for physics. Bridges (1992) proposes ideas for educational administration problems. Edens (2000) gives brief summaries of ten problems in biology, physics, chemistry, business, art history, educational leadership, medicine, and criminal justice, along with their sources. Finally, you'll find some well-tested problems at two University of Delaware websites: www.udel.edu/pbl and (after you register) https://chico.nss.udel.edu/Pbl/index.jsp. Depending on what knowledge is and isn't included in your course materials, you may also be able to use some of the science cases at the University of Buffalo site: http://ublib.buffalo.edu/libraries/projects/cases/case.html.

THE EFFECTIVENESS OF PBL

Theoretically PBL has very strong credentials. It is based on the well-tested principle of students learning by actively doing (see Chapter One), and they typically get to practice a variety of higher-order and social skills: recording, scheduling, conducting meetings, discussing, prioritizing, organizing, planning, researching, applying, analyzing, integrating, evaluating, making decisions, compromising, cooperating, persuading, negotiating, and resolving conflict. Beyond these basics, you decide and determine what your students will learn to do and what additional knowledge they will acquire by their research in your choice or design of a problem.

According to the research, PBL is especially effective in developing the following abilities in students (Albanese & Mitchell, 1993; Banta, Black, & Kline, 2000; Bridges, 1992; Dochy, Segers, Van den Bossche, & Gijbels, 2003; Edens, 2000; Hintz,

2005; Hung, Bailey, & Johassen, 2003; Lieux, 1996; Mierson & Parikh, 2000; Prince, 2004; Prince & Felder, 2006):

- Teamwork
- Project management and leadership
- Oral and often written communication
- Emotional intelligence
- Tolerance for uncertainty
- Critical thinking and analysis
- Conceptual understanding
- High-level strategies for understanding and self-directed study
- Application (transfer) of content knowledge
- Clinical performance (medical students)
- Application of metacognitive strategies
- Research and information-seeking skills
- Retention of knowledge
- Decision making
- Problem solving (of course), often across disciplines

In addition, PBL activates prior knowledge and imparts new knowledge in the context in which they will later be used. In this way, it builds in enough redundancy to ensure the knowledge is well understood and retained. If the problem mirrors situations that students will encounter in their future occupations, PBL also develops career realism as well as skills (Bridges, 1992).

PBL has its weaknesses and its critics. Implementing it is difficult and time-consuming, starting with finding the right problems to fit your course or writing your own (guidelines are given at the end of the chapter). Given such challenges, fully committed and well-prepared instructors are essential to PBL's success, and their shortage may explain the mixed impact of the method on medical education (Glew, 2003). In addition, when instructors don't provide enough structure and scaffolding, PBL stumbles into the same pitfalls as discovery learning. Students with weaker knowledge backgrounds may require more just-in-time instruction to help them

over problem-solving hurdles (Hmelo-Silver, 2004; Kirschner et al., 2006; see Chapter Eighteen).

Studies of medical students have uncovered performance deficits associated with PBL. While students in a PBL curriculum offer more complex explanations for their diagnoses, their explanations are less coherent and more error prone than those from more traditionally educated students (Patel, Groen, & Norman, 1993). Moreover, PBL-trained students order more unnecessary (and costly) patient tests, spend more hours studying each day, and score lower on basic science exams (Albanese & Mitchell, 1993). As to whether they perform better in a clinical setting, the research yields inconsistent results (Kirschner et al., 2006).

Another unsettled question is whether PBL courses cover less content. Some medical education studies report that PBL courses usually cover 20 percent less content than more traditional ones, and student performance on knowledge-focused standardized tests suffers accordingly (Albanese & Mitchell, 1993). But research on undergraduate PBL courses finds no such content or test performance loss (Banta et al., 2000; Edens, 2000; Hung et al., 2003). Even if such a loss does occur, many PBL enthusiasts may not care because they value application and research skills over content mastery (Biggs, 2003).

■ WHAT STUDENTS THINK

Medical students and faculty prefer PBL to long lectures (Albanese & Mitchell, 1993), but medical students tend to be mature, motivated, self-regulated learners. Many undergraduates feel quite differently about PBL, and their resistance and discomfort constitute another weakness of the method. While students report developing skills such as problem solving, critical thinking, communication, and taking responsibility, they tend to perceive they are working harder but learning less, even though test results don't confirm this (Banta et al., 2000; Edens, 2000; Lieux, 1996). Many students, especially the highest achievers and those in their first year, express frustration with the open-endedness, complexity, and ambiguity of the problems;, the lack of task structure and guidance; and the murky standards for performance (Edens, 2000; Lieux, 1996). Such stressful conditions can breed intragroup conflicts and problems.

This does not mean that PBL courses necessarily get low student ratings and critical comments (Kingsland, 1996; Mierson, 1998; Woods, 1996). But instructors new to PBL may not know how to improvise through unexpected schedule changes or how to handle the student protests and sticky situations that can arise. Such novices may indeed suffer a temporary drop in their ratings (Lieux, 1996). So before you embark on PBL, evaluate how much risk you can afford to take.

■ KUDOS FOR CREATIVITY

When you are looking for PBL problems, start by reviewing those already published. Finding one to fit your course can be difficult. A PBL problem in a colleague's course may be a case in yours because your course materials and activities already address the solutions. Feel free to modify published problems to your purposes, but don't feel constrained to use them at all. Two of the best things about college-level teaching are the creativity and autonomy it allows. Just as you can write your own cases tailored to your course and student needs, you can compose your own PBL problems. This may be your best alternative, if not

your only one, as you maintain full control over your students' learning issues. These learning issues are what distinguish a PBL problem from a case and what push students to practice the highest levels of thinking.

If you want to compose your own PBL problem, follow these steps (adapted from D. Johnston in Biggs, 2003):

1. Identify the concepts, knowledge, and skills required to propose a good solution.
2. Write out your student learning outcomes for the PBL project.
3. Find a real problem that fits your learning outcomes and that your students may encounter in their careers or civic lives.
4. Write your problem as you would a case: in the present tense, with specific data and a practitioner role or multiple roles that students can assume.
5. Consider structuring your problem as an extended rollout type, letting realism be your guide.
6. Define the deliverable—for example, a decision, a lengthy memo, a report, a budget, a plan of action, or a persuasive presentation—and develop a rubric for assessing student products (see Chapter Thirty-One).

After testing out and refining your problem in your course, you can even publish it if you also write a facilitator's guide. Include in the guide the information in the steps above, and add content background for facilitators and suggested resources for students.

CHAPTER 21

Quantitative Reasoning and Problem Solving

Mathematics is an amazing problem-solving tool in physics, chemistry, engineering, computer science, economics, finance, accounting, and, of course, statistics and mathematics. One of the most difficult tasks that instructors face in the quantitatively based fields is teaching students to be good problem solvers using mathematics. Quantitative problem solving is quite a different matter from solving soft, uncertainty-ridden, human-situational problems like the ones the case method and problem-based learning address. Mathematically based problems may have unknowns that require intelligent estimation, but algorithms are usually available to make the estimations and solve the problems themselves. The big question is which algorithms to use for a given problem. In addition, although this type of problem may have different approaches to arriving at a solution, it usually has only one correct answer or a definable range of correct answers. Quantitative reasoning, then, has a more precise process and product than does qualitative reasoning.

In this chapter, we first consider why students find quantitative reasoning so difficult and fraught with pitfalls: their weak conceptual understanding of problems, their reliance on shallow plug-and-chug tactics, their poor problem solving habits, and the common errors that result from their faulty approaches. Then we will look at minor and major changes we can make in our teaching and tutoring that have proven effective in developing students' problem solving and reasoning skills.

■ UNDERSTANDING STUDENTS' PROBLEMS WITH PROBLEMS

Heller, Keith, and Anderson (1992) identify two types of students who are struggling with problem solving in introductory physics. Some students claim to understand the material but not to be able to work the problems. They apparently believe that mathematical problem-solving skills are independent of the physics concepts being taught. Other students say they can follow the problem examples in the text but find the test problems too different and difficult. They seem to view physics as nothing more than a collection of mathematical solutions. Both kinds of struggles may sound familiar to you.

Novice problem solvers of both types often make the same mistakes again and again because they fail to understand the problems conceptually. When confronted with a problem, they try to find another similar problem that either they or their instructor has solved in the past. When they think they have identified such a problem, they use its solution as a template for solving the new problem. Finding a similar solved problem can facilitate solving another, but only if the likeness rests on one or more key concepts or principles. Unfortunately, novices too often choose a template problem based on only a superficial resemblance to the new problem (for example, both involve falling objects). Then in their impatience to find a numerical solution, they dive into algebraic manipulations. They neither qualitatively analyze the situation nor systematically reason through and plan a strategy for solving the problem. When they arrive at any solution, they are satisfied and don't take the time to check it (Heller et al., 1992; Kalman, 2007).

To the extent your students can get the right answers to the problems by whatever means, you might not even notice the shallowness of their understanding. What you may consider a problem in your courses is really only an exercise, since you often give students formulas and specific ways of finding solutions (Zoller, 1987). This kind of problem-solving assignment may not help your students acquire conceptual understanding. Unless the problems you assign elucidate the underlying disciplinary principles and the quantitative reasoning process, your students may merely be going through the motions, repeating the problem-solving pattern you showed them.

A study by Nurrenbern and Pickering (1987) demonstrates the disconnect between problem-solving facility and concept understanding. They found that on a chemistry test covering such standard materials as ideal gas problems and stoichiometry as well as conceptual understanding, students performed well on the math sections but demonstrated little comprehension of the physical chemistry behind the questions. Students picked up on a formula and employed the plug-and-chug tactic of selecting the variables necessary to work a solution without understanding why they chose the variables they did. In essence, they were using nothing more than an algorithm, a set of mechanical rules, to compute the solution.

The plug-and-chug approach can generate additional problem-solving hurdles as well. Students perceive only one way to arrive at a solution, even though there may be several viable alternatives. They also come to expect problems to be easy; after all, the instructor breezes through them and the book examples seem straightforward. Unprepared for hurdles, they become discouraged by difficult problems and stop trying. Then students may mistakenly conclude that only a special few "meant for" the discipline can easily work through problems (Brookhart, 1990).

Not only do most students have poor conceptual understanding of quantitative problems, but they also bring ingrained bad habits to the problem-solving process (Black & Axelson, 1991):

Inaccuracy in Reading

- Failing to concentrate on the meaning of the problem
- Skipping unfamiliar words
- Losing or forgetting one or more facts or ideas
- Failing to reread a difficult passage
- Starting to work the problem before reading all of it

Inaccuracy in Thinking

- Placing speed or ease of execution above accuracy, thus working too rapidly
- Performing a specific operation carelessly
- Interpreting or performing operations inconsistently

- Failing to double-check procedures when uncertain
- Jumping to conclusions

Faulty or Careless Problem Analysis
- Failing to break down complex problems into easily manipulated components
- Failing to draw on previous experience to clarify a difficult idea
- Failing to refer to a dictionary or text glossary when necessary
- Failing to construct diagrams where appropriate

Lack of Perseverance
- Losing confidence and admitting defeat too easily
- Guessing or basing solutions on superficial understanding
- Using algorithms mechanically to arrive at solutions without giving thought to conceptual issues
- Failing to carry out a line of reasoning to completion
- Taking a one-shot approach and giving up if the singular attempt fails

Many of these bad practices result in the common errors that Bridgwood (1999) identifies:

- Conceptual errors due to ignorance or carelessness
- Algebraic errors, especially in cancellation and grouping
- Arithmetic errors due to failure to check one's work

Fortunately, the research suggests strategies to help students acquire conceptual understanding and overcome their faulty problem-solving approaches and bad habits.

■ MODELING EXPERT REASONING

Recall from Chapter Eighteen on inquiry-based learning that novice learners grappling with new material need guidance and scaffolding through the inquiry process—that is, explicit directions about what to do and how to do it. The research recommends two forms of guidance. One form, *worked examples,* provides students with a problem-solving model (Chi, Glaser, & Rees, 1982). Following a logical set of procedures frees up enough of the learners' working memory to let them process the reasoning behind the procedures. We know from numerous studies that students learn more when they can study worked examples before trying to solve comparable problems on their own (Kirschner, Sweller, & Clark, 2006).

So perhaps your first teaching strategy should be modeling new problem-solving procedures—that is, you pose a problem to your students and show them how to work it on the board. However, the way instructors typically do it fails to capture the true problem-solving process. When you work a problem on the board, you are only showing students what experts do when they run through an exercise. You are not actually showing them how to attack a real problem, which involves *quantitative reasoning.* To accomplish this goal, you must model the cognitive processes involved in genuine problem solving and explicitly describe the steps and flow of your thinking. Only then can students grasp the techniques to solving problems and appreciate what these techniques can do for them (Bodner, 1987).

■ TEACHING THE STEPS OF PROBLEM SOLVING

The second form of inquiry guidance that benefits novice learners is *process worksheets*—that is, an optimal sequence of problem-solving steps for students to follow, supplemented by hints and rules of thumbs when available. This reasoning structure improves students' problem-solving performance by making them carefully examine and recast problems in conceptual terms, thus preventing them from rushing headlong into misdirected calculations (Nadolski, Kirschner, & van Merriënboer, 2005). The literature endorses teaching students a tried-and-true method for tackling and solving problems that is adaptable to any quantitatively based discipline (Bodner, 1987; Bridgwood, 1999; Heller et al., 1992; Kalman, 2007; Samples, 1994; Schoenfeld, 1985). The heart of the approach is to make students follow a five-step strategy that requires them to translate the problem systematically into different representations, each more abstract and more mathematically detailed than the last:

Step 1: Visualize the problem. Sketch or diagram the main parts of the problem. Identify the known and unknown quantities and other constraints. Restate the question in different terms to make it more understandable.

Step 2: Describe in writing the principles and concepts at work in the problem. Then translate the diagram into symbolic terms, and symbolically represent the target variable.

Step 3: Plan a solution. Identify the equations necessary to solve the problem and work backward from the target variable to see if enough information is available to arrive at a solution.

Step 4: Execute the plan. Plug in the appropriate numerical values for the variables, and compute a solution.

Step 5: Check and evaluate your solution. Is the solution complete? Are the proper units used? Is the sign correct? Is the magnitude of the answer reasonable?

Bridgwood (1999) surveyed his electrical engineering undergraduates on how helpful they found his similar problem-solving strategy, and they assessed most of the steps as valuable and the overall strategy as well worth using in the future.

Some students may profit from incorporating a few more steps: reading the problem at least twice, preferably aloud, before trying to restate it (step 1); thinking about the relationships among the different pieces of information given before describing the relevant principles and concepts (step 2); if the complexity of the numbers in the problem is getting in the way, substituting simpler numbers before planning the solution (step 3); and pausing while computing

(step 4) to review their intuitive understanding of each concept (Pauk, 2001).

■ TUTORING STUDENTS OUT OF BAD HABITS

Helping your students to identify and overcome poor problem-solving practices and avoid common errors is best done during office hours on a one-on-one or small-group basis following this strategy (Black & Axelson, 1991). First, have your students read a problem aloud and specify what is needed to solve it. Then let them try solving it on their own, insisting that they think through the problem out loud. Talking to themselves makes them slow down and improves accuracy and explicitness. As they attack and proceed through the problem, pose questions that make them examine their reasoning:

- What do you know about the problem?
- What are some possible ways to go about solving it?
- How can you break the problem into smaller steps?
- How did you go from step 1 to step 2?
- What is your reasoning for this step?
- What are you thinking at this point in the process?

The idea is to help students become aware of their problem-solving pitfalls and replace them with more thoughtful metacognitive strategies. So keep the spotlight on the students. If you must model problem-solving procedures, do so sparingly and only to demonstrate the reasoning process, not how to get the answer to any specific problem.

■ ROUTINIZING PEER FEEDBACK

In the mid-1990s, one engineering department in the United Kingdom faced a tough challenge with its mandatory second-year engineering course. Section class size doubled over a short period of time, allowing students to get away with coming unprepared and making grading weekly homework unfeasible. As a result, the average course grade plummeted by 45 percent and the failure rate soared. In response, the engineering faculty reinstituted homework problems but with student peers doing the assessing and grading. Six times during the term, students completed and submitted required problem sheets, which were then randomly redistributed to other students, along with grading directions. During the lecture period, students graded the problem sheets, adding written comments. While these homework grades did not count toward the final grade, not handing in the problems would lead to failing the course (Gibbs, 1999).

This innovation alone raised the average final exam grade from 45 to 75 percent and reduced the failure rate to zero. These stunning results make sense when you consider the learning ramifications of this peer feedback structure. Rather than cramming, students have to practice solving problems fairly evenly during the course. They receive prompt feedback on their homework because by the end of the same class period, they submit it. By grading their peers' problems, they see other, perhaps better, problem-solving approaches. Coming from their peers, the feedback they get has greater impact and may motivate them to try harder and do better. Finally, they practice evaluation skills, which should help them internalize quality control standards (Gibbs, 1999).

Peer assessment accommodates large classes that lack an adequate teaching assistant staff. In the engineering case, the faculty had to sacrifice the better part of six lectures, but the grading could be assigned as homework. While this change would slow the turnaround time to a day or two, the other benefits would still accrue.

■ MAKING PROBLEMS MORE REAL AND CHALLENGING

Heller and Hollabaugh (1992) devised the idea of *context-rich problems* in physics as part of their approach to promote good problem-solving skills. These problems are short stories about real objects and realistic events, more like those that students encounter in the

real world and actually care about. So they incorporate the motivation to understand the problem, perform the calculations, and find a solution. (One such problem involves planning a skateboard stunt, another deciding whether to fight a traffic ticket.) These problems may also have additional characteristics:

- They may not refer specifically to the unknown variable.
- They may include irrelevant information not needed to solve the problem.
- They may require students to supply missing information from common knowledge or educated guessing.
- They do not specifically mention the reasonable assumptions that may be necessary to reach a workable solution.

■ USING THE POWER OF GROUP LEARNING

Context-rich problems are designed to be difficult—too difficult for most students to generate satisfactory answers working on their own. Thus, Heller and Hollabaugh (1992) recommend cooperative problem-solving groups to spread the thinking and reasoning load over several students. Group learning forces students to discuss the physical principles behind the problems and possible strategies to reach a solution. Because students talk out their different ideas and evaluate alternative approaches, they acquire individual problem-solving skills in the process.

To identify the most successful group arrangement and structure, Heller and her associates experimented with different group compositions, including random, homogeneous, and heterogeneous on various variables. Initially they assembled the groups randomly. Then after the first exam, they reconstituted the groups based on abilities, teaming together students of high, medium, and low abilities, as the cooperative learning literature advises (see Chapter Sixteen). Generally students in these heterogeneous ability groups developed their problem-solving skills as fully as did the homogeneous high-ability groups in previous experiments. The optimal group size proved to be three, with members rotating among the roles of manager, skeptic, and checker/recorder. Pairs lacked the critical mass to arrive at more than one or two strategies and were more easily sidetracked onto a fruitless path. On the other hand, groups of four or more gave some members the opportunity to freeload on other members' reasoning. In addition, same-sex groups or groups composed of two females and one male worked best, avoiding the dominance posturing of more than one male in a group (Heller & Hollabaugh, 1992). Chapter Sixteen gives more information on cooperative learning research results and setup methods.

Heller et al. (1992) also found that the students in their experimental program developed higher problem-solving expertise than those taught in the regular lecture and discussion section format with assignments of standard physics problems. They concluded that problem-solving groups working on context-rich problems offer a preferable alternative to the traditional approach (confirming Treisman, 1986). With students relying on each other to resolve their concerns and questions immediately as they arise, groups also free you to circulate and help the students in genuine need.

■ ACCOMMODATING NEW METHODS TO TRADITIONAL SETTINGS

To teach quantitative reasoning and problem solving effectively, you need not completely overhaul your classroom or tutor every student individually. Students do learn problem solving by doing, but they don't learn it by doing it wrong, and very few deduce the real process of problem solving on their own. This is where modeling comes in, as long as you explicate your conceptual-level reasoning. This common method of instruction is perfectly compatible with traditional settings. So is teaching students the five-step strategy of problem solving and insisting that they follow and display it in any homework or in-class problems they hand in. The interactive lecture (see Chapter Twelve) provides an excellent forum for giving students practice in applying the strategy. You can enforce their continuing use of it by instituting peer assessment of homework problems.

Tutoring struggling students during your office hours is traditionally part of the faculty role, but confronting them with questions instead of answers teaches them to think through a problem and monitor their reasoning before moving toward a solution.

If you have the resources to make more substantial course modifications, find or devise concept-rich problems in your field and turn your class into a "studio" in which carefully assembled student triads solve these problems, with you playing the consultant's role. Such real-world problems furnish more interesting, meaningful, and challenging contexts for students to apply and hone their skills, and the group format makes the reasoning processes explicit, generates multiple problem-solving approaches, and weans students away from the mechanical application of algorithms. Even if you cannot replicate the learning environment that Heller and her associates created, you may still be able to organize group problem solving during discussion/recitation sections and review/help sessions.

At the very least, move away from the all-too-standard procedure of letting students passively watch you mechanically solve problems and effortlessly model idealized solutions without explaining the deep reasoning behind what you are doing. Use some class time to let your students tackle problems so you can find out how they approach and solve, or fail to solve, them. Perhaps you can have them display their solutions on the board or project them from a tablet PC, then explain their reasoning to the rest of the class. Students can work individually or in *ad hoc* pairs or triads, as long as they are doing the work.

CHAPTER 22

Problem Solving in the Sciences

While this chapter is written for everyone who teaches a science at the college level, it addresses two frequently distinct audiences: the science faculty and science laboratory instructors, who are often graduate teaching assistants. Only in small colleges do faculty members ordinarily design and conduct the labs that support the lecture part of their course. But dividing the chapter into two sections, one for faculty and the other for teaching assistants (TAs), makes little sense. Even if TAs conduct the lab, it is the faculty who have the power to redesign the labs and define and uphold lab safety standards. While the TAs have little control over the lab agenda and none over the broader course, most of them will soon occupy a position of such control and responsibility for their students' learning.

The physical and life sciences, along with their applied progeny such as engineering and the health sciences, use every inquiry-based, problem-solving teaching method we have examined: the case method, problem-based learning, and quantitative reasoning. Even so, these don't cover all the types of problems that the sciences address. These disciplines have their own unique brand of problems, strategies for solving them, and ways for teaching those strategies.

Most real everyday science involves solving problems in a laboratory, even if the data are collected and partially analyzed in the field. If lab work is so central to science, it should also be in science education. It should imitate the reality of scientific methodology in the lab—that is, devising hypothesis-testing strategies and procedures using reasoning and trial-and-error—on the way to solving the content problem—that is, meeting the experimental objectives with valid and reliable findings.

Since the early 1990s, a different kind of problem solving has been moving into the lecture. The challenges may be case studies, problem-based learning activities, or realistic quantitative word problems, like the context-rich variety mentioned in Chapter Twenty-One. (Recall that these short, real-world cases may include irrelevant information, may require students to draw on common knowledge and make reasonable assumptions, and may not specify the unknown variable.) They can be substantive problems, from a conceptual multiple-choice item used during an interactive lecture break to a lengthier guided inquiry to reveal content that was previously delivered in a lecture.

In this chapter, we review both the lecture-based and the lab-based innovations that are bringing tremendous excitement and success to the field of science education, but not before we look at the failures of traditionally taught science courses, which are still the norm in North America.

WHERE SCIENCE EDUCATION FALLS SHORT

Thanks to two classic works, Tobias (1990) and Seymour and Hewitt (1997), we know quite a bit about why so many students come to dislike, lose interest in, and switch out of the sciences, as well as mathematics and engineering. At the top of the list is poor teaching, manifested as faculty with a weed-out mentality about their courses, poor communication and public speaking skills, attitudes of indifference or even condescension toward students, little understanding of how students learn, and lessons that lack application and illustration—all exacerbated by too much material being crammed into too little time (Seymour & Hewitt). Other influential turn-offs are the heavy reliance on lecture, the emphasis on factual memorization in both teaching and assessment, the predominance of mechanical "how" over more meaningful "why" explanations, the need for quantitative operations, and the focus on technique—all at the expense of theory, creativity, interconnected concepts, and discussion (Tobias).

Although science engages in the discovery and identification of facts, it is not just a mountain of factoids. Yet undergraduate science education often gives that impression. The reason probably lies with science's predominant teaching method: the lecture. It is usually the instructor's technique of choice because it maximizes the amount of factual information that can be conveyed. It also feels comfortable and easy to manage, especially with large classes. The instructor exercises total control while the students merely (one hopes) listen. The lecture has its appropriate uses, but it is not digestible as a steady diet. In physics courses that serve it exclusively, students take away no more than 30 percent of the key concepts, on average, that they didn't already know at the beginning of the course (Hake, 1998). As Chapter Twelve explains, lecturing much beyond fifteen minutes pushes students' ability to process and retain the material and becomes counterproductive. And even fifteen minutes of new science seems to overtax learners' working memories. A series of in-class experiments revealed that only 10 percent of the students could recall a nonobvious fact and illustration of it just fifteen minutes after the professor shared them (Wieman, 2007).

In addition, the lecture does a relatively poor job of teaching students how to do something, such as writing, speaking, reasoning, thinking critically, formulating a hypothesis, solving a problem, or designing and conducting an experiment. Since science combines mental and physical activities, the lecture is not well suited to a lot of it. It is especially ill suited to strongly kinesthetic learners, who are often attracted to science and its professional offshoots (for example, the medical and engineering fields). These learners benefit most from physically acting out or performing the lessons and then identifying the concepts and principles inductively (see Chapter Twenty-Five). In short, they learn best by working in the lab or the field or otherwise solving problems.

Finally, while an excellent lecture can be very motivating, a standard one rarely helps students understand and appreciate the sense of discovery that makes science so stimulating and rewarding.

The laboratory that typically accompanies large lectures also fails to capture the excitement of getting results from a experiment or making a breakthrough on a problem. All too often, labs are treated like second-class, tacked-on learning experiences at best—poorly coordinated with the readings and lectures, hampered by a shortage of functioning equipment, shunted off on poorly paid graduate students, and dulled by cookbook procedures leading to predictable answers that haven't been of scientific interest for decades. In this kind of setting, students are lucky to achieve the comprehension and application learning outcomes that even traditional labs are capable of fostering. Students rightfully come to regard such labs as tedious, irrelevant tasks to hurry through, get done, and forget.

■ HOW TO HELP STUDENTS LEARN SCIENCE: GENERAL ADVICE

Before we examine the revolutionary developments in science lectures and labs, let's introduce some general principles that should guide science education.

First and foremost, instructors have to anticipate and address any misconceptions about the subject matter that students bring into the classroom. These misconceptions are particularly prevalent in the sciences because the layperson's intuitive understandings of natural phenomena are so often wrong. As explained in Chapter One, instructors have to discredit students' faulty conceptions of how the world works while making the scientific explanations more plausible and persuasive and equally comprehensible (Posner, Strike, Hewson, & Gertzog, 1982). Only after students adopt the expert's paradigm can they learn the discipline at a deep, meaningful level, filling in the paradigm with more specific scientific concepts and principles.

Second, students need help filling in the paradigm—that is, acquiring the discipline's hierarchical mental structure of knowledge (Hanson, 2006; Reif & Heller, 1982; Royer, Cisero, & Carlo, 1993; Wieman, 2007). They are not likely to see this hierarchical organization unless we tell them about it explicitly. After all, it took us years to develop it in our own minds because, most likely, no one told us about it when we were in school. Why not alleviate our students' struggle and quicken their learning by showing them how experts structure their vast knowledge? By distinguishing the more general and core concepts and propositions from the condition-specific and derivative ones, a hierarchy reduces the need to memorize while making long-term storage, retrieval, and appropriate application of knowledge much easier (Hanson, 2006; Wieman, 2007).

Third, we need to do whatever we can to reduce the heavy cognitive load that learning science imposes on students. Teaching them the hierarchical structure of the discipline's knowledge helps accomplish this purpose, but we can also show them how to recognize patterns across concepts, principles, and problems and how to chunk knowledge into categories based on such patterns (Hanson, 2006; Wieman, 2007). After showing them, we should give them practice in these mental operations—preferably in small groups to start. Another way of reducing cognitive load is to supplement the verbal delivery of knowledge with visuals—diagrams, figures, flowcharts, concept maps, and the like—and to have students draw their own whenever possible (Hanson, 2006; Wieman, 2007). Not only do graphics package information more efficiently and succinctly than do words, but by their very nature, they also display an organization of knowledge. In fact, visuals facilitate learning in such powerful ways that they merit an entire chapter (Twenty-Six), so we will leave detailed explanations for later.

One final principle to facilitate science education—in fact, learning in any discipline—is to encourage metacognition. That is, students need to acquire the expert's habit of monitoring their own thinking, of honestly assessing how deeply they understand the material (Hanson, 2006; Wieman, 2007). Some teaching techniques build in the process of self-monitoring—for example, group problem solving of context-rich problems, collaborative inquiry-guided learning, and stepwise problem-solving procedures that require students to represent the problem visually and check the answer for plausibility. When working on a challenging, nonroutine task, group members often raise questions that serve to assess each other's understanding.

■ HOW THE LECTURE CAN BE MADE INTO A MEANINGFUL LEARNING EXPERIENCE

An enormous amount of research on science education all leads to the same conclusion: inquiry-guided, problem-focused, and collaborative, alternative teaching strategies are more effective that traditional lecture. That is, students who learn by these newer approaches leave their science course with better skills in higher-order thinking, problem solving, and experimental design (Beichner et al., 2007; Burrowes, 2003; Cortright, Collins, & DiCarlo, 2005; Freeman et al., 2007; Giuliodori, Lujan, & DiCarlo, 2006; Hanson, 2006; Hanson & Wolfskill, 2000; Jones-Wilson, 2005; Knight & Wood, 2005; Lewis & Lewis, 2005; Lord, 1997; McCreary, Golde,- & Koeske, 2006; Oliver-Hoyo & Allen, 2005; Oliver-Hoyo, Allen, & Anderson, 2004; Oliver-Hoyo & Beichner, 2004; Prince & Felder, 2007; Schroeder, Scott, Tolson, Huang, & Lee, 2007; Wieman, 2007; Wilke, 2003; Wilke & Straits, 2001) and stronger conceptual understanding of the content (Crouch & Mazur, 2001; Hanson, 2006; Jones-Wilson, 2005; Oliver-Hoyo & Beichner, 2004; Wieman, 2007). Furthermore, these gains come with no loss in content coverage (Jones-Wilson, 2005) or students' content mastery, whether the class is small or large (Cortright, Collins, & DiCarlo, 2005; Lord, 1997, 1999; Wilke & Straits, 2001).

These alternative strategies vary from relatively small changes, such as interspersing conceptual multiple-choice questions throughout the lecture and having individual students and then groups choose the right answer (Crouch & Mazur, 2001; see Chapter Twelve), to complete course redesigns, such as combining lecture, recitation, and laboratory into a "studio course" (Laws, 1991). Among the minor changes, Wieman (2007) uses clickers in implementing Mazur's peer instruction. In addition, case studies and problem-based learning scenarios, which abound in the sciences, can easily fit into existing courses as in-class activities or homework (see Chapters Nineteen and Twenty). Another moderate change is adding just-in-time-teaching to lectures, as research finds it reduces attrition, raises standardized test scores, and improves student preparation (Marrs & Novak, 2004; Novak, Patterson, Gavrin, & Christian, 1999; see Chapter Eighteen). Yet another relatively modest enhancement is to incorporate experimental demonstrations into the lectures. These may be online interactive simulations that double as virtual labs (Wieman, 2007; see the URLs below for sources) or live experiments (not requiring data collection) that the instructor conducts in front of the class using lab equipment or a computer. Students become involved when they not only watch but also discuss what they have observed and interpret the results. In the course of the discussion, the instructor explains the concepts and principles illustrated and the real-life applications. With the students having time to discuss the experiment, this teaching method is called an interactive lecture demonstration (Sokoloff & Thornton, 1997, 2001).

If you are teaching a lecture course with recitation sessions, you may be able to make those sessions inquiry guided, problem focused, and collaborative by modeling them on *Tutorials in Introductory Physics* (McDermott & Shaffer, 2002). In this format, student groups answer conceptual questions on a worksheet while the instructor or TA rotates around the groups asking them Socratic questions. On occasion, students work with a few simple laboratory items, but the activity is usually paper and pencil. Compared to traditional recitation sessions, the tutorials increase students' learning gains by over 50 percent (Reddish, Saul, & Steinberg, 1997). In lieu of worksheets, you can bring context-rich problems into these sessions. They can be developed for any science or engineering field, and they foster high-level problem-solving skills (Heller & Hollabaugh, 1992).

The most encompassing transformations in science education go under the acronyms of POGIL, which stands for process-oriented guided inquiry learning, and SCALE-UP, short for student-centered active learning environment for undergraduate programs. While the instructor may lecture during some class meetings or give minilectures at the beginning of each class meeting, both innovations entail replacing some lecture periods with hands-on, small-group activities, such as answering critical thinking questions, developing concepts, or inquiry-guided problem solving. Since SCALE-UP places three students around one or more laptops, these triads may also engage in computer-based simulations or hypothesis-testing labs. SCALE-UP instructors call the activities "tangibles" and "ponderables" (Beichner et al., 2007). While the students are working, the instructor and TAs circulate around the class posing Socratic questions. Near the end of the class, at least some of the groups make oral reports, and all turn in written ones or completed worksheets (Beichner et al., 2007; Hanson, 2006). In other words, much of the traditional lecture time is reallocated to small-group tutorials, similar to those described for introductory physics. But the classes may be many times the size of a recitation section.

Both POGIL, which started in chemistry courses, and SCALE-UP, which was introduced in physics, have proved highly successful in promoting student learning. Compared to traditional lecturing and, in one case, interactive lecturing, POGIL has been found to increase student interest in the subject matter, raise student ratings of the instructor and the course, improve learning skills and test performance, and reduce the D-F-W (drop, fail, withdraw) rate—all to statistically significant degrees. In addition, students prefer POGIL to traditional lecturing and deem the activities challenging and valuable for their learning (Hanson & Wolfskill, 2000; Lewis & Lewis, 2005). SCALE-UP has achieved similar significant results: students display enhanced conceptual understanding, better problem-solving skills, higher test scores, and more favorable attitudes toward the discipline (Beichner et al., 2007; Oliver-Hoya & Beichner, 2004). Not surprisingly, POGIL and SCALE-UP have spread to other disciplines. For the sciences and engineering, plenty of appropriate inquiry-guide activities are available on the Web. You may start with the sites listed at the end of the next section.

Bear in mind that SCALE-UP requires some serious investments in new facilities. Short of constructing new buildings, institutions must tear out some of their lecture halls and replace them with large, one-level, "computer-smart" classrooms. These rooms must be furnished with wireless service and large round tables, each with nine movable chairs and electrical outlets. In addition, either the students or the institution have to purchase laptops—at least one for each student triad (Beichner et al., 2007). Class sizes must decrease, as a lecture hall that once held over two hundred students may accommodate only ninety in the SCALE-UP format.

■ HOW THE LAB CAN BE MADE INTO A MEANINGFUL LEARNING EXPERIENCE

All the evidence indicates that traditional lab designs and manuals are outmoded, ineffective, and ripe for replacement with inquiry-guided labs.

The Beginning of a Lab

Recall that science defectors cite a lack of theory and conceptual links as reasons for leaving. When the lab is disembodied from concepts, it lacks meaning and relevance. So it is critical to place it in the bigger scientific picture before proceeding into the actual activities. Given the time constraints of many lab activities, you may be tempted to forgo explaining the objectives to be achieved or the principles to be illustrated and simply launch into the day's work with a brief synopsis of the procedures. While this short-cutting gets students out of the lab more quickly—which they usually appreciate, especially in traditional labs—it robs the lab of its educational value. And it isn't necessary because you can introduce the objectives or principles efficiently while simultaneously preparing students to perform the day's tasks.

Begin a lab by asking students to review the previous week's material. You might have them do a two-minute freewrite to activate their memory (see Chapter Seventeen). After you ask a couple of students to read their responses aloud, tie this particular lab to the course's progression of topics and labs, sketching as cohesive a big picture as possible. Then introduce the day's objectives or principles, eliciting the lab manual information, such as the hypotheses to be tested or questions to be answered, from the students.

The Design of the Lab Itself

In many science courses across the continent, laboratories have been completely revamped to incorporate these characteristics (Felder & Brent, 2001; Howard & Miskowski, 2005; Hufford, 1991; Kimmel, 2002; Laws, 1991; Odom, 2002; Penick & Crow, 1989; Reddish, 2003; Reddish & Steinberg, 1999; Sokoloff & Thornton, 1997):

- They reflect the inquiry-guided learning model—that is, they have students learn or apply material to meet some kind of a challenge, such as to answer questions, solve problems, conduct an experiment, or interpret data. In one way or another, students conduct real scientific investigations, identifying and solving problems the way scientists actually do, only with the instructor's guidance. They must develop their own strategy to test a hypothesis or find answers, along with the procedures to carry it out. The lab manual provides neither, and the lab results are not predictable.
- They focus on developing students' critical thinking, decision making, and complex reasoning skills, including inductive thinking, by giving students opportunities to practice them. In addition to developing an experimental strategy and procedures, they must devise one or more explanations for unexpected results and write them in their lab reports.
- They foster genuine teamwork and collaboration. Since the labs are novel and challenging, students mutually need each other, as they would in a professional setting. In many cases, each lab group turns in one report and shares a group grade. (In Kimmel's labs, students also keep their own individual lab notebook, which is graded.) In addition to sharing their discoveries, results, and conclusions, students may even exchange their lab reports for peer review (Odom, 2002).
- They feature modern technology, such as industry equipment in current use and updated software (for example, spreadsheet, databases, statistical, and mathematical) for analyzing the data and displaying the results.

For clarification, here is an example of an actual inquiry-based lab: a pendulum lab in a sophomore-level calculus-based physics course (Odom, 2002). First, students use their laptops to access the lab manual on the Web. The manual gives a background lesson in the basic mechanics of a pendulum, including the equation to describe its period and the simplified version for small angle approximations (first-order expression). Students then receive the two lab objectives or outcomes:

1. Determine the maximum angle for which the period of a simple pendulum is valid. In other words, ascertain the cutoff angle for when the small angle approximation fails.
2. Use a simple pendulum to determine the value of g, the acceleration due to the earth's gravity.

Each lab group is supplied with equipment: a pendulum stand, clamp, string, and bob (an aluminum rod with its center of gravity marked); a protractor; a computer timing device (on the lab Web page); and meter sticks (located around the classroom). In addition, groups receive ten "nudge" questions to answer and a lab report template (on the Web page) with five problems to solve—all of which lead the students through the process of meeting the lab objectives. They receive no other directions (Odom, 2002). This lab requires about six hours over two weeks. Odom also got rid of the three-hour-a-week-lab restriction that constrains most science curricula.

Innovations such as Odom's are not isolated. Developed by Sokoloff and Thornton (1997), real-time physics labs begin with phenomena and lead students to derive the principles inductively. It relies on the power of small groups answering challenging questions and performing nonroutine tasks with the assistance of a floating instructor or TA. Typically students receive most or all of the data they need electronically, along with analysis tools, so they focus less on collecting data and more on interpreting them. Workshop physics involves an entire curriculum that eliminates the lecture entirely in favor of six hours a week of inquiry-guided labs (Laws, 1991).

The results of these experimental programs have been so positive that the hosting institutions have adopted them into their regular curriculum. Students actually discuss and even argue about the best plan of attack, and they divide the labor on their own. Compared to students in courses with the traditional cookbook labs, they hand in higher-quality lab reports, do significantly better on the tests, have higher final grades, give the course higher evaluations, and enjoy the labs more (Felder & Brent, 2001; Howard & Miskowski, 2005; Hufford, 1991; Kimmel, 2002; Luckie, Maleszewski, Loznak, & Krha, 2004; Odom, 2002; Penick & Crow, 1989). In addition, they make greater improvements in scientific reasoning (Benford & Lawson, 2001), as well as other higher-order thinking skills, such as data analysis and interpretation (Howard & Miskowski, 2005). They retain the lab material longer too (Lord & Orkwiszewski, 2006; Luckie et al., 2004). In Kimmel's labs, the C students show the greatest gains in achievement. In addition, the students' attitudes in his new labs are better than those in the old. Specifically, students are more motivated and more engaged, they perceive they are learning more in the course and the labs, and they assess their team functioning more favorably (Kimmel, 2002).

In the workshop physics curriculum, in particular, students score significantly greater gains on the Force Concept Inventory and the Force Motion Conceptual Evaluation than those in traditional physics classes and measurably greater than those in lecture-based classes supplemented by student-active tutorials (Reddish, 2003; Reddish & Steinberg, 1999; Wittmann, 2001). However, the students' perceptions of the curriculum's effectiveness depend heavily on how well their teams function (Reddish & Steinberg, 1999).

A rich source of inquiry-guided labs, as well as POGIL, SCALE-UP, and tutorial activities, is the Web. You can find numerous learning objects in the forms of virtual labs, field trips, problem scenarios, and simulations for all the science and engineering fields:

Physics: http://phet.colorado.edu (Wieman, 2007)

Chemistry: www.chemcollective.org/find.php (Prince & Felder, 2007)

Biology: www.hhmi.org/biointeractive/vlabs; http://highcred.mcgraw-hill.com/sites/0072437316/student_view0/online_labs.html; www.biologylabsonline.com; http://bio.rutgers.edu; www.phschool.com/science/biology_place/labbench

Zoology: www.abdn.ac.uk/~clt011/zoology/virtuallaboratory

Geology: www.sciencecourseware.org/eecindex.php

Geography: www.abdn.ac.uk/~clt011/geography/virtualfieldtrip

Engineering: www.jhu.edu/~virtlab/virtlab.html; http://virlab.virginia.edu/VL/contents.htm; http://matdl.org/virtuallabs/index.php/Main_Page

Multidisciplinary sites: www.seed.slb.com/science_sectionlanding.aspx?id=26652; www.merlot.org

■ THE ESSENTIALS OF LAB SAFETY AND MANAGEMENT

Unless all your labs are primarily virtual or paper-and-pencil problem solving, safety should be your first priority. With so little lab experience, undergraduates tend to be careless and unaware of the dangers, so you must inform them of hazards and safety measures. They need explicit instructions on proper procedures, especially when working under potentially hazardous conditions. For example, if certain chemicals require special handling or disposal protocols, you must explain the reason in terms that students can understand. For visual and kinesthetic learners, you should demonstrate as well as describe the proper construction and handling of apparatus. As the most experienced scientist in the room, you must also be able to act promptly and effectively in an emergency. Know the standard procedures practiced by your department and your field. If you are unsure of how to proceed in any given situation, ask a(nother) faculty member, a lab staff member, or the departmental safety officer.

Preventing Lab Emergencies

The generic guidelines below apply across the scientific disciplines. Your particular field may call for additional rules:

- Be prepared. Rehearse new or unfamiliar procedures before the lab. Be able to identify pitfalls and problems. If students sense you don't know what you are doing, they will say so on your teaching evaluations.
- Direct students to keep the lab as clean as possible. Not only is this good practice for them, but it also reduces the prep staff's workload.
- Give students dress codes, and show them how to use safety equipment such as goggles and face shields. Then explain the reasons for the rules, and enforce them. Typical clothing codes include long pants, tied-back hair, shoes with tops, no excessively loose clothing, and no encumbering jewelry.
- If your lab has a traditional manual with directions and procedures, you must make your students read the manual carefully before coming to lab. The better informed students are, the smoother and safer the conduct of the lab. Chapter Twenty-Three offers dozens of ways to induce students to do the readings when they are due. (You need

to have input into their lab grade.) You may have to schedule some time at the beginning of lab for a brief accountability activity, such as a quiz, writing exercise, or brief recitation period, but this will take you less time than going over the directions in the manual.

- Discuss procedures thoroughly. You can be redundant where safety is concerned.
- Be especially aware—and continually remind students—of any particularly dangerous procedures.
- Demonstrate proper techniques and correct students when necessary.
- Encourage student questions.
- Move around the lab. While you can't be everywhere at once, be readily available for consultation.

Responding to Medical Emergencies

If you now or ever will supervise a lab, the chances are good that you will face a lab emergency during your career. With some procedural knowledge and preparation, you should be able to handle most situations. In the event of a lab accident, rule number one is to remain calm. Make sure you know the location of the first-aid kit, fire extinguishers, fire blankets, emergency showers and eye washes, bleach solutions, and hazardous waste cleanup kits. Familiarize yourself with the uses of each so that your emergency response will be swift and decisive. Learn first-aid principles, preferably by completing first-aid and CPR certification training courses, whether or not your institution requires it. At the very least, study a first-aid manual such as the one published by the American Red Cross.

If a student is injured in your lab, stop to assess the situation, and then take proper action. Small cuts and scrapes may be inconsequential, requiring nothing more than a bandage. But today due to AIDS, it is best to treat all injuries involving loss of blood as hazardous situations. So do not touch a student who is bleeding unless you are wearing protective gloves.

Isolate the blood spill area, and immediately swab the surface twice with at least a 10 percent bleach solution. Label biohazardous materials accordingly and dispose of properly in accordance with your institution's standards. Contact the student or employee health center for more information on AIDS and how to protect yourself.

Here is a brief quiz presenting several typical lab emergencies that will help you assess your own and your lab TAs' emergency preparedness. How would you or your TA respond to emergencies like these?

- A student tries to force a glass rod into a rubber stopper. The rod breaks, driving the sharp end into the palm of his hand.
- A student wearing a loose sweater is working with a Bunsen burner. As she turns away from the burner, her sleeve catches fire.
- A student spills 12 M HCl on his hand.
- A student tips over a boiling water bath, scalding his feet.
- During an experiment, a student goes into respiratory arrest.
- A student is shocked while plugging an electrical cord into a wall socket.
- A student splashes a large quantity of a corrosive chemical into her eye.
- A student's error releases a massive quantity of bromine gas in the lab.

■ WHY SCIENCE EDUCATION IS SO IMPORTANT

We are forever hearing that our nation is falling behind other countries in scientific literacy at all grade levels and that we are facing a shortage of scientists. At least so far, international scientists have been filling in the openings for scientists and science professors in the United States, but for how long?

If these reasons to improve science education aren't pressing enough, then consider the broader place of science in our country. In a truly enlightened, democratic society, people must be scientifically literate—not only conversant in but also comfortable with science. Everyone who teaches in the sciences and its applied offshoots plays a crucial role in fostering a society that is well informed enough to govern itself intelligently. Self-government requires not only a well-informed populace but also one that can solve its own problems. Problem solving of every type—open-ended and closed-ended, qualitative and quantitative, high-uncertainty and formulaic—is science's stock-in-trade. This fact alone makes science an essential component of higher education. But we have to ensure that students learn how science really proceeds—not like a well-ordered textbook but in a zigzag, trial-and-error, collaborative manner that demands complex reasoning, strategic thinking, and inventiveness.

PART 5

MAKING LEARNING EASIER

CHAPTER 23

Getting Students to Do the Readings

Some faculty say that they don't have the luxury of managing engaging activities in class because so many of their students don't do the readings. These faculty are correct in maintaining that you cannot run a student-active classroom unless your students do the assigned readings on time. Their first exposure to the material must be on their own outside class because if they come to class unfamiliar with the material, they can't do anything with it. In fact, many students seem not to crack a book until right before an exam, by which time many class periods have been dulled by too many "emergency" lectures and too little student participation.

Where these faculty may err is in assuming that just assigning reading should be motivation enough for the students to do them. This may have been the case at one time, but not anymore. Estimated from their performance on pop quizzes, about 80 percent of the students normally did the readings in 1981, but only 20 percent of them did in 1997 (Burchfield & Sappington, 2000). No doubt some faculty also err in believing that their students will learn just as effectively from listening to their lectures as from

doing the readings. Unfortunately, not doing the readings impedes students' learning of the material on a deep level (Fernald, 2004).

In this chapter, we dispassionately examine why students don't do the readings. Students have their reasons, right or wrong, for blowing off the assignments, but we often make it easy for them to so. In fact, we can take measures to encourage them to do the readings—to make it easier for them to get value from their readings—while making it more difficult or costly for them to ignore the readings. In other words, we can better equip them and induce them to do the readings. The tools suggested here may not work on every student, but they will on most. After all, students have a right to fail themselves.

■ WHY STUDENTS DON'T DO THE READINGS

Consider all the reasons that students may habitually not do the readings—at least not when they are due. Don't worry about the student who occasionally doesn't do the readings because of some short-term life interference, and eliminate those who overburden themselves by trying to combine a full course load with more than half-time employment.

Poor Reading Abilities, Habits, and Persistence

Just short of half the high school graduates in the United States do not have the reading skills that college-level work requires (Kuh, Kinzie, Schuh, Whitt, & Associates, 2005). In fact, only 32 percent of these graduates are college ready by the most minimal yardstick, which means having completed the basic college-required courses and having basic literacy skills (Greene & Forster, 2003)—obviously an inadequate definition of "college ready." According to the 2003 National Assessment of Adult Literacy, relatively few students achieve reading proficiency by the end of their higher education—in prose literacy, only 19 percent of those with a two-year degree and 31 percent of those with four-year degrees, and in document literacy, only 16 percent and 25 percent, respectively (Kutner et al., 2007).

Whether as a cause or a result, many students don't seem to enjoy reading, at least not for learning purposes, and do very little of it—much less than earlier students used to. Only 22 percent of seventeen-year olds in the United States read daily in 2004—a drop from 31 percent in 1994—and only half of those eighteen to twenty-four years old read a book of any kind in 2002 (Hallet, 2005). In terms of voluntary reading, those fifteen to twenty-four years old did just seven minutes of it on weekdays and ten minutes of it on Saturdays and Sunday in 2006, while they watched two to two-and-a-half hours of television every day (National Endowment for the Arts, 2007).

One problem that gets in the way of students' reading comprehension and speed is their inability to focus for more than a few minutes (Blue, 2003). They may not realize that reading is not an eye activity but rather a mind activity, and a very engrossing one that demands concentrated attention. With limited reading experience, they lack a sophisticated

vocabulary, which slows their reading speed, impedes their comprehension, and discourages them from further reading (Maleki & Heerman, 1992). So when faced with a reading assignment, many students feel it takes too much time or it's not worth what little they get out of it.

Higher-Priority Activities

Students may also have more compelling or more attractive options for their nonclass time. We can easily understand their obligations to their jobs, their family, other possibly more important courses, and community service arrangements. However, we have to accept the fact they may prioritize socializing (virtual, phone, or face-to-face), fraternity and sorority activities, playing sports and games, watching television, listening to music, surfing the Web, drinking, sleeping, working out, reading a novel or magazine, doing more interesting course work, or engaging in extracurricular activities such as clubs and hobbies. Some of these activities mix well (for example, socializing, drinking, and watching television), making the combination all the more appealing. When you think about it, our courses have a lot of stiff competition for their time.

No Perceived Need

Many college students never or rarely did the readings in middle and high school—and did very well, thank you (Blue, 2003). In fact, two-thirds of the entering first-year students in fall 2003 claimed to have spent less than six hours a week doing homework in their senior year in high school, and almost half of these students graduated from high school with an A average (Higher Education Research Institute, 2004). Furthermore, 70 percent of all students entering college in 2003 rated their academic ability above average or within the top 10 percent of their age group (Higher Education Research Institute, 2004). Since people base their expectations of the present on the past, many students believe that they shouldn't have to work any harder in college than they did in high school, and they see themselves as intelligent enough to slide thorough their college courses. Clearly they consider reading tangential to their learning (Bradley, 2007).

Furthermore, students assess their short-term need to do the readings on time. If they don't have to hand in any homework on the readings, won't be quizzed on the material in class, and won't have to publicly discuss the material, most of them will skip the readings (Nathan, 2005). Students also have fall-back strategies. They think they can skip the readings because they figure they will pick up the gist of them during the next class, especially if you normally lecture. Or their friends will tell them about the class. Or they will go to you to get lecture notes. Or they can read your notes on the course website. Of course, the wisdom of these strategies depends mostly on the instructor.

No Perceived Payoff

Today students are practical instrumentalists. They view college as a means to an end—the end being a high-paying job that can support their consumer habits. This is particularly true of millennials (see Chapter One), but the somewhat older Generation Xers share with them the demand for course material of immediate relevance and utility. Neither generation received the quality K–12 education that taught them to appreciate learning for its own sake, apply themselves to academic pursuits, or defer their gratification for a longer-term purpose. Therefore, they tend to view the assignments, readings, and tests as barriers in their path on their way to a degree and college in general as a game about grades. In their minds, the readings have nothing to do with their aspirations in life or their definition of success. So they are not worth the time and effort, and students seem indifferent to their poor reading skills.

Of course, these young people misperceive the real world. Reading ability correlates with income. In 2003, only 13 percent of the below-basic readers earned $850 a week or more, while almost 60 percent of the proficient readers did (National Endowment for the Arts, 2007). In other words, poor readers become poor students who become poorly paid workers, and good readers become good students who become better-paid workers.

When you examine all the possible reasons that students habitually don't do the reading, they boil down to three: (1) they don't want to (due to poor reading skills or compared to other activities), (2) they don't think they have to, and (3) they really don't have to—that is, they face no dire consequences if they don't.

■ HOW WE CAN EQUIP AND INDUCE STUDENTS TO DO THE READINGS

Let's accept the fact that most students approach the assigned readings with a somewhat cavalier and pragmatic attitude, combined with varying degrees of anxiety and dread. To address this negative posture, we have to see the issue from their point of view given their life circumstances. In particular, we have to avoid projecting our identities and values onto them. When we were in college, most of us ranked among the best students, or we wouldn't have made it into and through graduate school and into the academy. We exceeded the average in our reading abilities and persistence, our enjoyment of the activity, the importance we attach to it, the learning benefits we derive from it, our interest in at least some subjects, and our raw intelligence. At the same time, we probably weren't perfect students ourselves. No doubt we cut some corners, skipped some readings, spent some nights cramming, and prioritized certain extracurricular activities over some of our courses. And we were gifted enough to get away with it.

Here we are years later, happily wedded to our fields and expert readers in them, selecting the readings that we value for our novice students. We may not have noticed that we have internalized a large disciplinary vocabulary that is a foreign language to them. We have also learned a variety of cognitive shortcuts that make our reading easy. For us, a single term may recall an entire mental structure of concepts, principles, assumptions, and implications that enriches our understanding of the sentence and foreshadows the next sentence. The unending flow of meaning allows us to move through the text quickly with unwavering focus. Even our brightest students stumble over technical vocabulary and bring shallow, if any, associations to their academic readings. And they can't possibly appreciate their value or our reasons for selecting them.

Moreover, from our students' standpoint, some of us don't seem very serious about our course readings. We assign them but make little or no effort to sell the students on them. This might not be so odd if everyone else weren't trying to sell them something. Many of us lecture the readings in class, as if we don't expect our students to do them either. In addition, few of us have incentive or sanction mechanisms to hold our students accountable for doing the readings when they are due. A big test is too distant a concern. So why should they do the readings?

Stop Lecturing the Readings

None of the strategies in this chapter for increasing reading compliance will work very well if we continue to lecture the readings. Certainly we should use class time to extend and update the readings and clarify what we know from experience confuses students. But otherwise we should be leading in-class activities on the material, specifically making students practice it, apply it, examine it, and work with it. These activities ensure better learning and retention of the readings while holding students accountable for doing them. (See the "Holding Students Accountable for the Readings" section below.) Just imagine what you and your students could do in class if most of them came prepared!

Teach Students How to Read Academic Material

In view of our students' reading skills, habits, and persistence, we must not assume that they know how to read and study a textbook, a research article, an essay, or a piece of literature. They probably do not know how each genre of assigned reading is organized, what

they should be looking for as they read, how to take notes, and what they should retain for class. We may not be interested in teaching reading skills, but if we don't help our students learn how to navigate reading assignments, they will leave our classes having learned very little, not least of which is how to learn.

Give Students the Grand Tour

Before you give the class a reading assignment from a textbook or other nonfiction book, spend a little time leading students through an exploration of the book's structure and purpose. Of course, you must insist that they bring their books to class for this, which means you must also insist that they buy the required books, which you have a right to do. Have them read the title and the Preface or Foreword and discuss what they think the book is about. Then tell them to examine the Contents pages, and ask them how the book is organized, what its major sections and subsections are, and how they can identify them. If the work is a point-of-view nonfiction book, have students look for the author's thesis, issues, or position and how the book develops it. Not only will this exercise ensure they have the required book, but it will also get them over the hump of opening it and will acquaint them enough with it to get more out of reading it.

Have Students Learn and Use Proven Reading Methods

The simplest proven reading method, at least for factual and problem-solving material, is what is sometimes called active recall or the 3R (read-recite-review) strategy (McDaniel, Howard, & Einstein, 2009; Roediger & Karpicke, 2006). Students read a section of text, then close the book and recite aloud as much as they can remember, and finally reread the section. In other words, they reinforce their reading with saying and hearing the material and practice retrieval with self-testing. In terms of student performance on multiple-choice and problem-solving tests, this technique works as effectively as note taking and exceeds just reading the text multiple times. In addition, it takes less time than note taking (McDaniel et al., 2009; Roediger & Karpicke, 2006).

Similar multiple-step reading strategies date back many decades (for instance, Adler, 1940) and now proliferate on study-skills sites all over the Web. One or more of the steps make excellent writing assignments that students can hand in as proof of their having done the reading. You can select the strategies and tips you find the most effective for your course—some sites recommend different reading techniques for different subjects—and refer your students to them. These are several major sites (active in 2009):

- www.aw-bc.com/etips/usahome/index.html
- www.educationatlas.com/study-skills.html
- www.studygs.net/murder.htm
- www.how-to-study.com/pqr.htm
- www.mindtools.com/rdstratg.html
- www.utexas.edu/student/utlc/learning_resources
- www.ucc.vt.edu/stdysk/stdyhlp.html
- www.studygs.net

The strategies tend to overlap. For example, SQ3R stands for survey-question-read-recall-review, and PQR3 is short for preview-question-read-recite-review. Just about all of them advise students to do the following:

1. Scan the reading to get a sense of what it's about, how it's organized, and where it's going, noting the titles, subtitles, graphics, bold and italicized words, conclusion, and summaries.
2. Review the purpose for reading. (Since few students approach their reading with a purpose, we have to give them one or teach them how to devise their own purpose. See below.)
3. Read with purpose to find what you are looking for, thinking about what you are reading, and paraphrasing what you are finding. (Instructors may incorporate note taking into this step.)
4. Review the main points of the reading. (We may have to induce students to complete this step by

giving them a structured review assignment. See below.)

If you think about these steps, you may realize that you've been following them for years. For example, when you pick up a research article, you don't usually read it straight through from the first word to the last. Rather, you read the abstract, thumb through the pages to glance at the tables and figures, then scan the conclusion, and perhaps work your way back to the results or methods. The last thing you may read is the literature review, which normally comes right after the abstract. This is the way an expert approaches a piece of academic reading, which is quite different from the way one reads a magazine article or a novel. Our students have not yet learned to make the distinctions.

Give Students a Purpose for Their Reading

Having a purpose for reading is the hallmark of the expert reader. When you pick up a scholarly article or book, you're usually looking for something—something relevant to your research, a course you teach, or a long-term interest. One of the reasons that you scan it first is to see if you have a purpose for reading it. If you find you do, your scan informs you where to focus. By contrast, students approach their readings with little or no purpose, except to get it over with. They may not have a preexisting interest in the material, and they probably don't know what they are supposed to look for, which is why they complain that they can't tell what is and isn't important. We don't help them any by telling them that all the material is important.

We must give our students a purpose for the readings, things to look for, or a strategy for devising their own purpose. Possible purposes include seeking answers to the end-of-chapter questions or, better yet, our own study questions. In our own questions, we can direct our students' attention to what we deem important in the readings, what we want them to gain from them. In addition, we can ask students to apply, analyze, synthesize, and evaluate what they are reading, inducing them to deep-process the material, to think practically and critically about it. For a point-of-view nonfiction reading, such as an essay or monograph, we can provide students with several generic thinking questions that ensure solid comprehension and analysis:

- What is the author's position or claim?
- What are the main arguments given in support of this position or claim?
- What evidence or data does the author furnish to support his or her position or claim?
- Evaluate the author's case, identifying any questionable evidence or data, missing information, or flaws in logic or analysis.

In problem-solving disciplines such as mathematics, physics, and engineering, the purpose for reading may be solving the end-of-chapter problems you have assigned. Whatever the purpose, advise students to review the questions or problems before they read so they will be primed to be on the lookout for the answers or the solution strategies as they read.

Alternatively, we can show students how to create their own purpose for reading, especially a textbook: by turning the chapter headings and subheadings into questions for them to answer (Doyle, 2008). For example, if the heading reads "The Causes of Type 2 Diabetes," the question for students to ask themselves and answer is, "What are the causes of type 2 diabetes?" When students scan the assigned reading, they can get a sense of the questions they will be addressing.

To guarantee that students read with the purpose we have in mind, we have to make them write out their answers or solutions and turn them in, either as daily graded homework or in a journal we collect and grade occasionally. While some students may not enjoy reading a text with such care, you can sell them on the idea by telling them that they will never have to read the text again. Don't let the word *grade* scare you. In the section below, "Holding Students Accountable for the Readings," you will see what the term means for you in practice.

Teach Students to Watch for Transitions and Verbal Signals

Without consciously being aware of it, the expert reader homes in on verbal signposts that make logical connections between ideas. These connections provide the key to comprehension, as they build the structure of the knowledge being explained or the arguments being presented. So it is critical that we teach our students to watch for them and ensure they know what the terms mean. Transitions or signal words and phrases fall into several categories (Broderick, 1990; Langan, 2007):

- *Addition* words signal that the author is making multiple points of the same kind. Examples: *also, in addition, another, next, first, second, third, finally, likewise, moreover,* and *furthermore.*
- *Cause-and-effect* words indicate that the author is about to address the results or effects. Examples: *because, since, consequently, therefore, thus, as a result, so that,* and *if-then.*
- *Comparison* words point out a likeness between two ideas. Examples: *like, likewise, similarly, equally, alike, just as,* and *in the same way.*
- *Contrast* words highlight a change in direction or a difference between two ideas. Examples: *but, yet, still, however, in contrast, on the contrary, on the other hand, otherwise, conversely, although,* and *even though.*
- *Emphasis* words tell the reader to pay close attention to a particular idea. Examples: *most of all, above all, a primary concern, a significant factor, a major event, a principal item, a key feature, a distinctive quality, a central issue, in particular,* and *especially valuable/important/vital/relevant.*
- *Illustration* words signal that the author is giving one of more examples to clarify a general point. Examples: *for example, for instance, to illustrate, specifically, like,* and *such as.*

Teach Students to Write Marginalia and to Highlight or Underline Wisely

If your students already have decent academic reading skills, they may not need to write out the answers to study questions to build up their reading skills.

They may be ready for the next level—the level we have mastered. What do we do when we are studying new material? We write marginalia and highlight or underline the most important points. These are advanced reading techniques because they presume the reader can sort out and distill the important points independently. If your students seem halfway prepared to make such judgments on their own, a few in-class practice sessions may ensure their readiness.

Marginalia are notations we write in the margins to summarize the gist of the content or our reactions to a passage of text. Often reviewing our reactions later makes us recall the substance of the text. We can assign our students the task of writing summaries or their reactions or both as homework and can check their compliance by asking them to read their marginalia in class and by providing feedback as needed. To teach them to write useful marginalia, we can impose some rules on what they can write—perhaps three to five words per paragraph. The best readers enrich their marginalia by underlining key words, phrases, and sentences as well.

Underlining or highlighting is an advanced reading technique, but unfortunately some of the poorest readers rely on it. Students typically highlight or underline too much text, which does little to improve their recall of the selected material and actually dulls their recall of unselected material (Kiewra, 2005). As with marginalia, the value of underlining or highlighting depends on the soundness of the reader's judgment in sifting out the important material—the key sentences and ideas. To sharpen our students' judgment, we can lead them through scavenger-hunt exercises to find the main idea in paragraphs. Along the way, we can tell them how textbooks are typically written: the topic sentence is usually the first sentence of a paragraph; if not there, it's probably the last sentence (Doyle, 2008). Weimer (2002) teaches her students intelligent highlighting or underlining in two class periods. She has them mark their readings as homework, then has a discussion about what she selected as important, what they selected, and why. She asks them to explain her decisions as well as to justify their own. Over time, they approach a consensus.

To give marginalia, highlighting, and underlining greater appeal, you can tell your students that these activities, done intelligently, will save them the trouble of having to read the entire text again, as is true with other close-reading methods. But these techniques also require students to buy the assigned books and mark them up, which reduces what little resale value they have. Still, as expert readers, we know that the only way to study a book in depth is to mark it up; it's part of the learning and learning-how-to-learn process. We have the right to require this commitment of our students. If they choose not to make it, they have the option to drop your course.

Require Students to Review Their Readings

Although all the study-skills and reading-skills books and websites recommend taking this final step, students usually don't do it. So we may have to push them to do what is best for them by assigning a homework exercise that makes them consolidate and integrate the new knowledge they have gained in the readings. The simplest review assignment for students is to write out the main points made in the readings and then put them together into a one- or two-sentence summary. Another review strategy, one that requires less writing but more thinking, is to have students draw a concept map or mind map of the readings (Peirce, 2006). This assignment directs their focus to the hierarchical structure of the knowledge. While the readings no doubt give plenty of hints, students must construct their understanding of the organization of the concepts and principles. If it reflects valid understanding, the product gives them a mental structure with which to retain and elaborate on the knowledge. If your students haven't mapped material in other classes, teach them how by modeling the method in class, then having them work in small groups to map a minilecture or reading in class a few times, then assigning mapping as individual homework. (Chapter Twenty-Six examines a variety of graphics aids to learning, including mapping.)

A third type of assignment, called *reflective writing,* relies on freewriting about the readings, section by section (see Chapter Seventeen). Championed by Kalman (2007) for physics courses, this method works well for the sciences and mathematics. Students first read a section or two of the assigned chapter while highlighting, jotting down marginalia, or doing whatever else helps their comprehension. Then for roughly two-thirds of a page, they freewrite about the section—not summarizing it but writing about what it means and then about what they don't understand. By this process, they generate questions to ask in class. In reflective writing, students are reviewing not just the material but also their understanding of it. Kalman grades the freewrites only on completeness, counting them as 20 percent of the course grade. He documents that his students not only master the material better as a result but also come to appreciate the activity by the middle of the term.

Assign Realistic Reading Loads

We have a tendency to assign too much reading for our students, given their reading challenges. Less is more when it comes to reading assignments because student are more likely to complete shorter ones that longer ones (Hobson, 2004). According to one study, when the instructor assigned six different readings, the vast majority of students in the class barely glanced at three of them. They were much more likely to do the readings when only two articles were assigned. Even so, students rarely completed all the readings (Bradley, 2007). Still, the evidence suggests that we should assign as required only the most essential readings. For guidance, we should review our learning outcomes and the fit between the readings and the rest of the course.

We also should take measures to ensure our readings are aimed at students' level—that is, at marginally skilled readers (Hobson, 2004). Even if we teach them how to read the material, they will need practice before they become fluent at it. A few

readability indexes are available on the Web. For example, the Flesch–Kincaid (English) Readability Test, based on word length and sentence length, is explained at http://en.wikipedia.org/wiki/Flesch-Kincaid. When you put text into the calculator at www.standards-schmandards.com/exhibits/rix/index.php, you obtain both a grade-level score and a reading ease score.

Sell the Readings

To an extent, we can make some students want to do the readings simply by promoting them. In the syllabus, we can emphasize how central the readings are to the course. We can explain their purpose, relevance, and high value, as well as our reasons for choosing them over other options. Each day or week, we can preview and promote the upcoming reading assignment, describing what questions it will answer and what value it will hold for their immediate learning and later lives and careers. We can place it in the context of the next class, later assignments, upcoming in-class activities, and the larger course and curriculum. To help get students over the first hump, we can let them start reading key pieces in class (Bean, 1996; Hobson, 2004).

Let's not underestimate the potential impact of such efforts. Students cite their personal desire to learn as their single strongest motivator for doing the readings, far above wanting to participate in discussion or feeling obligated (Bradley, 2007). Chances are we can influence their desire with a short, persuasive pitch.

Hold Students Accountable for the Readings

Making the readings more accessible, doable, and valuable to students may go far. Once students start doing the readings, they may enjoy the learning and sense of achievement enough to continue reading. But these helpful strategies may not go far enough. You may also have to induce students to do the readings for extrinsic reasons—that is, to set up incentives and sanctions related to their own self-interest.

We know that most students are motivated by grades, just as people in general are motivated by material and monetary rewards. We also know that people are motivated by pride. They don't want to look bad in front of others, especially superiors and peers. These two cost-benefit values suggest ways to make students accountable for doing the readings. So whether they want to do them, most students will decide that they have to do them to attain their goals and avoid unpleasant consequences.

This chapter reviews four categories of tools that hold students accountable for the readings: homework on the readings, quizzes on the readings, in-class problem-solving or written exercises on the readings, and oral "performance" on the readings, either prepared or cold-call (impromptu). Abundant research documents that these methods work (Barrineau, 2001; Carney, Fry, Gabriele, & Ballard, 2008; Connor-Greene, 2000; Fernald, 2004; Leeming, 2002; Mazur, 1997; Nathan, 2005; Nilson, 2007b; Ruscio, 2001; Thompson, 2002; Thorne, 2000). In fact, Nathan (2005) claims that students decide if they will do the readings for a given day based on whether they have homework based on the readings to hand in, they will be tested on the material, or they have to speak publicly on the material in class. If none of these conditions applies, Nathan explains, chances are good that most students will skip the readings.

To make any of these tools work effectively as accountability mechanisms, follow these guidelines:

- Use these tools or some combination of them on a regular or near-regular basis on the class days that readings are due. Your students should expect to be held accountable for every reading assignment. Randomly administered (or "chance") quizzes also raise reading compliance (Fernald, 2004; Ruscio, 2002), but not as much as regularly occurring ones (Carney et al., 2008). Generally the more frequent the quizzing, the stronger the inducement to read and the higher the student learning and achievement (Carney et al., 2008; Leeming, 2002).

- Grade the products in some way, even if on an informal scale, such as one to four points, zero or one point, $\sqrt{+}/\sqrt{}/\sqrt{-}$, $\sqrt{}/0$, or P/F. You don't have to grade on quality or provide feedback as you would with a formal assignment. Since you're looking only for evidence of students' having done the readings, you can give full credit to a good-faith effort—that is, one that addresses the readings and meets your length or elaboration requirements. You can assess on these criteria at a glance. At least with homework, as long as you require that students hand it in for every reading, you may get equally good results with grading only some of the homework some of the time as you would with grading all of it all of the time (Carney et al., 2008).
- The grades on the products in total must count significantly toward the final grade. We know that 5 percent is too little (Sullivan, Middendorf, & Camp, 2008) and that 20 percent is an effective incentive (Kalman, 2007).
- Make the readings the only available source of the knowledge in the readings—that is, don't lecture the readings in class or post outlines or summaries of them on the course website.

Pride becomes a powerful secondary motivator when the accountability tool is some sort of oral performance or in-class group work for a group grade. In this latter situation, most students feel a sense of responsibility to their teammates (see Chapter Sixteen).

■ SPECIFIC TOOLS FOR HOLDING STUDENTS ACCOUNTABLE

The tools described here—some obvious, others not—come from a variety of sources, and certain forms of homework also teach students how to read and comprehend the material (see above).

Homework

Some research finds that regular, required homework, even if it is not always graded, motivates students to do the readings more regularly and carefully than does any schedule of quizzes (Carney et al., 2008). With some forms of homework, you may want your students to submit two copies: one for them to refer to and take notes on in class and another to turn in to you for grading. The copy for you may be submitted electronically before class. You may even make the written product a requirement for entering class. The options for homework are almost limitless:

- Notes on or an abstract or summary of the readings (Barrineau, 2001; Kalman, 2007; Kalman & Kalman, 1996; McKinney, 2001; Peirce, 2006)
- An outline, concept map, or mind map of the readings (Peirce, 2006)
- One or more questions on the readings, on cards, or electronically posted (Martin, 2000; McKinney, 2001; Millis & Cottell, 1998). You may ask for specific types of questions (multiple choice, true-false, essay, and so on) for possible use in future tests.
- Answers to study, reading-response, or end-of-chapter questions (Carney et al., 2008; McKinney, 2001; Peirce, 2006). Questions that make students reflect on the personal relevance of the material also enhance their perceptions of their ability to participate productively in class discussions (Carney et al., 2008).
- Solutions to problems.
- Writing-to-learn exercises (see Chapter Seventeen) such as dialectical notes (Peirce, 2006).
- Any type of outside material that illustrates an important point in the readings or an application of them—for example, a magazine or newspaper article, a printed advertisement, a photograph, a website, or an object.

Quizzes

Frequent, regular quizzes are proven accountability tools (Barrineau, 2001; Carney et al., 2008; Connor-Greene, 2000; Mazur, 1997; Nathan, 2005; Nilson, 2007b; Thompson, 2002; Thorne, 2000), and they induce reading compliance more effectively than randomly administered (or chance) quizzes (Carney et al., 2008). These days you can administer

them either in class or online shortly before class. Either way, accountability quizzes should focus only on the major points and concepts in the readings, not details, and the items should be easy for you to grade quickly—either multiple choice or short answer. One study found short answer questions more effective than multiple-choice items in helping students gauge their own learning (Sullivan et al., 2008). Remember that you can grade the answers as simply as acceptable/not acceptable based on the topic they address and their length.

Just-in-time teaching, an inquiry-based method described in Chapter Eighteen, is a type of daily quiz. Students answer conceptual questions, usually multiple choice, online just before each class, giving you enough time to adjust your plan for the day's class to address any comprehension problems students had with the readings. We know this method raises students' level of preparation for class, participation in class, engagement, and achievement (Marrs & Novak, 2004; Novak, Patterson, Gavrin, & Christian, 1999) as long as it appreciably figures into the final grade (Sullivan et al., 2008).

With in-class quizzes, you can save paper by dictating the questions or displaying them on a slide or overhead transparency. You can also have students make up the questions as homework. Finally, you can follow the individual quiz with a group quiz and make the double exercise a real learning experience (Michaelsen, 1997–1998).

In-Class Written Exercises or Problem Solving

These exercises may be any of a wide assortment of writing-to-learn and classroom assessment activities (see Chapters Seventeen and Twenty-Eight)—for example, a one-minute paper, a reading response mini-essay, a summary, or an audience-directed paraphrase—as long as they focus on the readings. They can even be graphical: a summary drawing, a poster, or a concept or mind map of a chapter or book. With problems, students can solve them or design new ones for future tests.

To encourage high-quality work, you might let students use some in-class products as resources for future tests. One summary exercise that is particularly effective at motivating students to study the readings seriously is a "mind dump." After answering any questions on the readings, you allow students five or ten minutes to write everything they can remember from the readings. Then you collect these recollections and return them to their authors at the beginning of tests. While students may have little time to hunt through them during tests, they will feel less anxious and no doubt will have better mastery of the material just for having written about it.

While individual accountability is critical for reading compliance, some of these exercises are adaptable to teams. In fact, the more challenging ones, such as writing high-order multiple-choice items for future tests, may benefit from the synergy of multiple minds. You can find many more group learning activities suitable to most readings in Chapter Sixteen, such as structured controversy, numbered heads together, send-a-problem, talking aloud paired problem solving, and student teams-achievement divisions (STAD).

You will need to keep individual students and groups on task and accountable. So after each exercise or problem, randomly cold-call on several students or groups to read their answer, explain their solution, or display their graphic. If the exercise or problem has one right answer and not everyone comes up with it, don't correct those with wrong answers. Let students with different results debate them. Another accountability measure is having students sign and hand in their exercises or problem solutions. If valid answers emerged during class, you don't have to correct or write feedback to the students. Just check off that they completed the task.

Oral Performances

These are not lengthy oral presentations based on major projects. Rather they are daily recitation or discussion sessions or short impromptu or prepared presentations on the readings. For example, following up in-class written exercises or problem solving by asking some students or groups to explain their results to the class is an oral performance, and many others are possible:

- Randomly call on students to present their homework on the readings (questions, answers to questions, problem solutions, summaries, reading responses, outside material, and so on), either in addition to or instead of handing it in to you. Over the term, you can probably call on all your students at least once, and maybe many times.
- Have students bring in questions on the readings (for future tests, discussion, clarification) and call on other students to answer them.
- Hold regular recitation sessions that start with simple recall questions and move into higher-order discussion questions. The key is to cold-call on students in a way that looks or actually is random. Shaffer (n.d.), for instance, asks his students to print their names on three-by-five-inch cards, which he collects and uses during the semester to pick students to answer questions. At times he shuffles the deck. At other times, he stacks the deck before class. He then grades students' answers on the fly, marking a plus or minus on their card. These oral performances count 15 percent of the course grade and constitute most class periods. Since he calls on thirty to sixty students in a typical class, they get plenty of participation opportunities.
- Use the Socratic method while leading discussions on the readings (see Chapter Fourteen).
- Have speaking-intensive experiential activities in class, such as debates, panels, press conferences, role plays, and simulations that require the knowledge in the readings (see Chapter Fifteen). Though you may not be able to involve all your students equally, you can induce almost all of them to prepare because you might call on any of them to play key roles.

■ MANAGING YOUR WORKLOAD

Before you conclude that accountability tools would generate too heavy a workload for you, consider how much time the tools actually demand and what other tasks they can eliminate. Yes, you will have to find or create short assignments, quiz questions, recitation and discussion questions, or in-class exercises and activities, and you will have to grade them in some fashion. However:

- You can have your students make up questions and problems for you, whether for quizzes, tests, or in-class exercises.
- You can make the grading quick and effortless (Connor-Greene, 2000; Thompson, 2002). With homework, short answer or essay daily quizzes, and in-class exercises and problem solving, you need only check the work for a good-faith effort, and you can grade oral performances on the fly in class.
- You can give fewer major tests and assignments, saving yourself considerable preparation and grading time.
- You can require and collect daily homework on the readings, but you only have to grade some of it some of the time (Carney et al., 2008).
- You need not prepare lectures.

Finally, consider how much more your students will learn and how deeply you can take them into the material if they do the readings on time. Imagine the class discussions and activities you can lead. In fact, most accountability tools serve multiple purposes and can provide a springboard or an entire framework for a student-active class period. Perhaps they can save you time.

CHAPTER 24

Teaching Your Students to Think and Write in Your Discipline

Most of us bemoan the quality of our students' writing. We complain about their apparent ignorance of mechanics, punctuation, spelling, word use, paragraph organization, and the rules of sound sentence structure, and we wonder what they did in their first-year composition class—unless, of course, we teach first-year composition. In fact, whatever writing problems students have tend to get worse as they shift from discipline to discipline (Richardson, 2008). So your students may have learned to write decent papers in composition but produce poorly organized, mechanically marred lab reports, research papers, and literary analyses.

A major reason that students can't write well in a given discipline is that they don't know how to think in the discipline. While thinking may not always be expressed in writing, writing is always an expression of thinking. In fact, writing instruction specialists contend that *writing is thinking* (Bean, 1996; Richardson, 2008). Therefore, when you teach your students to write in your discipline, you are teaching them how to think critically in your discipline. In other words, you are teaching them how your discipline thinks. Only when they can think in the discipline do they have the extra mental energy to tend to grammatical and stylistic conventions (Richardson, 2008).

■ CROSS-DISCIPLINARY COMMONALITIES

Not surprisingly, all of the academic disciplines share a common ground of thought and expression, and the writing-across-the-curriculum movement defined that territory. Toulmin, Rieke, and Janik (1984) offer a particularly useful model of cross-disciplinary reasoning and writing. First, all scholarship states a claim of some kind: a hypothesis, a thesis, a solution, or a resolution. Second, it presents data related to that claim—that is, some kind of factual evidence that may take the form of numerical results of an experiment, inferential statistics from a survey, historical documentation, or quotations from a text. Third, it makes a warrant—that is, as persuasive an argument as possible that the data justify the claim

223

or make this claim superior to competing claims. Scholars then debate the validity of a given claim in terms of the applicability and the quality of its supporting data and the strength of its warrant.

The claim-data-warrant model is simple enough to teach to undergraduates, and it sensitizes them to the need to include all three elements in every piece of formal writing they do. (Student writing is often missing one or two of them.) It also gives them an easy-to-use framework for evaluating scholarly, rhetorical, and expository writing in general, including that of their peers.

However, this cross-disciplinary common ground does not extend very far. The disciplines diverge on the writing formats they follow; the language they use; the organization of the claim, data, and warrant; the forms of data they consider respectable; and their standards for an acceptable warrant (Walvoord & McCarthy, 1991). You cannot improve your students' writing unless you explain the format, language, organization, and so on that your discipline demands and follow up with models, practice assignments, and plenty of feedback (Madigan & Brosamer, 1990).

■ TEACHING CRITICAL THINKING THROUGH THE DISCIPLINE'S METACOGNITIVE MODEL

In general, critical thinking means higher-order thinking, such as more sophisticated cognitive operations described by Bloom (1956), Perry (1968), and Wolcott (2006). But these operations take on more specific definitions in the disciplines, where critical thinking follows the typically unspoken conventions of what constitutes "legitimate" argumentation and evidence. It is the "disciplinary dialect" that a field speaks, the "disciplinary scaffolding" on which the profession constructs knowledge, the "metacognitive model" on which the discipline operates (Nelson, 2000). Thus, one field's critical thinking may be another field's logical fallacy or unjustified conclusion. This is not a problem in itself. The problem is that

we fail to articulate our discipline's metacognitive model to our students (Donald, 2002; Langer, 1992; Nelson, 2000). Maybe it never crosses our minds. Maybe we are so wedded to our model that we forget it isn't common knowledge or common sense. Maybe we assume that students will simply pick it up by osmosis. Some eventually do, of course. Maybe we did. But not everyone does so easily, not without performing poorly in course work along the way. And many students never get it. They major in another field with a disciplinary dialect that they somehow do pick up.

Why not explain your field's metacognitive model to your students up front, especially in introductory courses where their concept is the sketchiest and often the most mistaken? Then you can provide them practice in critically reasoning within the model. Writing is the natural context for their practice because it is the most formal, concrete expression of a student's understanding of the discipline. Almost all of us give graded writing assignments, and they afford students the best feedback on their efforts to communicate in the disciplinary dialect.

■ METACOGNITIVE DIFFERENCES AMONG DISCIPLINES

By way of introduction to disciplinary differences, consider the short-answer or essay-question command that often appears on tests and written assignments: "compare and contrast." In the laboratory sciences this typically means "to list" as many similarities and differences as possible. In the social sciences, it implies "to discuss" as many as possible, referring to theoretical texts and research findings to buttress one's argument. In literature, the command has yet another translation, which is "to analyze" one critical similarity and one critical difference at length, staying close to the texts.

It is little wonder that a literature major in an introductory biology course can write an elegant essay comparing and contrasting plants and animals and never understand why it barely gets a passing grade.

Similarly, the biology major in a literature course may be just as puzzled about why his lengthy list of similarities and differences between *The Grapes of Wrath* and *The Sun Also Rises* receives a D. In fact, it is surprising that as many students figure out these disciplinary nuances as they do.

Based on interviews with college instructors, Langer (1992) outlines the major metacognitive differences among three major disciplinary groups, especially as these differences pertain to the written products expected of students. Donald's (2002) work, also based on faculty interviews, fills in some insightful details, especially within the sciences.

Physical and Biological Sciences and Engineering

Students are supposed to apply hard facts and reliable data to a problem-solving situation, consider possible outcomes, hypothesize the most reasonable prediction, perform a tightly controlled experiment to test the hypothesis, measure the results meticulously, and come to probable, carefully qualified conclusions based on the resulting evidence. Student opinion has little or no place in the process, and students should establish the validity of the source when citing someone else's published conclusions.

A lab write-up or report has a specific format, much like a recipe, that students receive instructions to follow. The task involves selecting the relevant information from lab notes and placing it in the proper categories, following a specific format. Students are expected to include tables, charts, graphs, drawings, and the like to clarify, simplify, and abbreviate the presentation. They should carefully construct and label these visuals. What writing is necessary should be clean, concise, and impersonal, with relatively short, noncomplex sentences. Lists don't even require complete sentences. Usually writing in the passive voice is recommended.

Within the sciences, physics relies heavily on deductive logic to obtain a reasonable, plausible answer within expected limits. On the other end of the continuum, biology students are expected to think inductively, inferentially, metaphorically, and skeptically about their results. Chemistry falls in between. In engineering, students are supposed to use procedural knowledge to solve problems and make design decisions in the absence of complete information (Donald, 2002).

Social Sciences

Most subfields of psychology follow the scientific mode, especially those that rely on the experimental method. However, social scientists rarely have the chance to conduct experiments and instead must rely on surveys, demographic data sets, interviews, and observations, all of which have validity and reliability weaknesses rooted in the data collector or the respondents or subjects. For example, survey and interview respondents are not always accurate or truthful, and those being observed may not behave typically. The styles of analysis of such data rest on questionable assumptions as well. For example, the statistical analyses of large data sets usually assume that the variables of interest are normally distributed, which may or may not be true.

Another difference between the physical and biological sciences and the social sciences lies in the number of acceptable worldviews. While the former adhere to one dominant paradigm, the latter entertain two or three theoretical perspectives (Kuhn, 1970). Sociology, for example, has functionalism and conflict theory, and political science has pluralism and elitism, with major pieces of research usually grounded in one or the other. These pairs comprise competing ideologies with different value-relevant explanations for the unequal distribution of social resources and rewards. They also tend to focus on different questions—in particular, the ones they best answer. To be fair, however, both theoretical sides share one orientation: both look more to the social structure than to individuals to explain human behavior and phenomenon.

Given that the social sciences rely on flawed data and analyses and ideologically shaded theories, the standards for evidence are more relaxed than they are in the physical and biological sciences. Researchers need present only partial, probabilistic explanations, as long as they structure a strong argument and anchor it in the literature. Students in turn must learn to view their own and others' research results as probabilistic, tentative, and subject to debate. To grasp the complex nature of social scientific research with all its sources of inherent uncertainty, students must progress through all of Perry's (1968) stages of undergraduate development.

History-Based Disciplines

Here the focus is on explaining the relationships between contradictory developments and conflicting documentary evidence. Students are expected to examine concrete historical circumstances and to develop defensible stands on controversial issues, drawing on detailed supporting evidence based on valid documentation. Part of this process entails viewing the conclusions of others with a critical eye, distinguishing true from false positions and main points from subpoints.

In essence, the challenge in writing a paper is to argue clearly and convincingly a historical interpretation using concrete factual, contextual evidence. Content is of greater importance than format. As one history instructor describes the rule of thumb, students should "give at least three different types of reasons relevant to the issues and details to support those reasons" (Langer, 1992, p. 79).

The fields within this model include art, music, dance, and literary history, some philosophical studies, the historical specialties in the social sciences, and, of course, history. Law is similar in that an argument is won on the basis of factual evidence and a persuasive analysis of what the facts suggest (Donald, 2002).

Literature

As in the history-based disciplines, students are supposed to interpret literature, but in literary criticism, this means something distinctly different. In the latter, students should interpret the meaning of a piece of literature—that is, how it allegorically or metaphorically reflects some aspect of real life. To infer intelligently what an author may intend, students should draw on the major themes and motifs in literature. But personal opinion is an integral aspect of interpretation; in fact, originality of opinion is prized. But an opinion must also have validity, and validity is derived from specific, supporting references to the text. Therefore, points in the text provide the data or evidence of literary interpretation.

Students are also expected to analyze and evaluate an author's literary style, often comparing and contrasting it with those of other authors. They must incorporate a historical understanding of literary genres and traditions so they know which comparisons and contrasts are interesting. For example, examining stylistic differences between Chaucer and Hemingway might yield an extensive list, but a boring one belaboring the obvious. Of much greater interest are the fewer and more subtle differences between authors who occupy the same or similar literary worlds.

Like the social sciences, the field of literature has no agreed-on approach to analysis and criticism. Rather, the discipline has several competing ones—at the moment, rational, symbolic interpretive, and postmodern—that focus on different dimensions of literature. An English department may have representatives from all three schools of thought on its faculty, so students may learn three different approaches to literary interpretation, never understanding the sources of these differences and completely confused about the discipline's values and standards. Again, it takes a student at an advanced stage of development in Perry's (1968) framework to grasp what a valid literary analysis or criticism constitutes.

An excellent paper then begins with a novel but thematic slant on a piece of literature or a credible analysis of its place within an identifiable school of thought, both strongly supported by details and quotations from the actual work. Thus, content is critical. But more than in other fields, so is the writing style in the paper itself. After all, literature *is* writing, much like science is the scientific method. Those attracted to literature should be extremely literate and literary themselves.

Along with English, foreign languages, and comparative literature, the arts and much of philosophy follow a similar model, perhaps with less exacting standards for students' writing style.

MAKING STUDENTS BETTER THINKERS AND WRITERS

The purpose of this summary was not to tell you what you already know about your field. Rather it was, first, to heighten your awareness of very different heuristics that students may bring into your course from other courses they have taken outside your discipline. Second, it was to help you determine what facets of the disciplinary dialect and scaffolding that you already share with your students and what else they may benefit from learning. Certainly they need to know whether your field has competing schools of thought, and if so, which one you belong to if you expect your students' work to reflect it. In addition, the more they know about your discipline's conventions of argumentation and evidence—the more they can think like a colleague—the better they will perform in your courses, especially in their formal writing assignments.

While you can explain these conventions to your students, Nelson (1993) suggests a one-hour in-class exercise that allows students to "discover" your discipline's metacognitive model on their own, inductively. Pass out a brief essay-type question along with copies of three or four different answers ranging in grades from A to D/F, but with comments and grades removed. (Past exams are excellent sources.) Then break students into small groups and have them figure out which answers are better and in what ways. After they develop a list of criteria (which you should verify in class discussion), assign another essay for them to write, either in class or as homework, following these criteria. According to Nelson, students who have done this exercise report higher-than-expected grades not only in the course in which it is administered but in their other courses as well. For many students, the experience gives them

a whole new gestalt on what disciplines, knowledge, scholarship, and higher education are all about.

TEACHING STUDENTS TO WRITE FOR THEIR FUTURES

Except for students who become academics, few of the writing conventions you teach them will carry them into their careers. The workplace has its own metacognitive mode—yet another dialect, another scaffolding that most of your students will have to learn sooner or later. You can help them learn it sooner in your course, where the costs of error are comparatively low. They need to know that professionals and managers spend much of their workday writing, and even most non-college-educated front-line supervisors spend at least a fourth of their time at work on writing tasks (Mabrito, 1997). No doubt your students will greatly appreciate your instructing them in a skill they will need and use so much. So if any of your courses can accommodate it, you may want to give your students some experience in business/administrative—sometimes called *technical*—writing. Such assignments fit in naturally with simulations, extended cases, problem-based learning, and some service-learning experiences (see Chapters Fifteen, Nineteen, and Twenty), and you can choose among several writing genres: memos and letters; lengthy proposals for new policies, procedures, projects, products, and services; and progress reports on projects and transitions. While the briefer forms make excellent individual tasks, proposals and projects reports are often collaborative products in the business/administrative world and thus should be in a course as well.

This type of writing has distinct features not shared with scholarly kinds (Anson & Forsberg, 1990; Plutsky & Wilson, 2001). Let us examine them in detail.

Specific Audience Pitch

Because a message is always directed to a specific individual or group, either you or your students must clearly define the audience for each assignment.

Students may have to research the literacy level, values, and needs of the audience before they can target their message to it.

Language and Style

Since the audience is usually a nonspecialist in a hectic, pragmatic environment, the language must be nontechnical, accessible, concise, and direct enough to be skimmed. The preferred words and phrases are clean, short, essential, and powerful—chosen to be quickly informative or persuasive. For instance, students should practice replacing prepositional phrases with adjectives and adverbs, wordy constructions like "prior to" and "in the event that" with briefer ones such as "before" and "if," and sentences written in the passive voice with those written in the active voice.

Purpose

With few exceptions, business/administrative communications ask the audience to take some form of action—for example, giving approval, modifying beliefs or values, changing behavior, or parting with money or other resources. Progress reports may ask for more time, more funding, or simply continued faith and support.

Evidence to Justify Purpose

Standard evidence includes observations, repeated events, interviews, small-scale surveys, and printed materials, usually nonacademic. Students can benefit from learning how to collect such data and familiarizing themselves with respected business, administrative, professional, trade, and industry sources.

Format

As in journalistic writing, the purpose and main points appear up front in the introduction. Longer communications such as proposals contain other reader-friendly features that chunk the information: a title page; the Contents page; an executive summary or abstract (one-page maximum) focusing on the purpose and the recommendations; short chapters and sections; abundant headings and subheadings; lists rather than text when possible; graphics such as charts, tables, diagrams, and illustrations to minimize and summarize text; a conclusion listing recommendations; appendixes with nonessential supporting information; and generous white space throughout.

Accuracy and Timeliness

Finally, business/administrative writing must be error free, which means checked for factual accuracy and carefully proofread, as well as submitted on time. If not, the credibility of the writer suffers or, worse yet, the proposal is not even read. Students must come to understand that the real world is much less tolerant and patient than college courses.

■ THE MANY WORLDS OF WRITING

No doubt almost all young students enter college with the mistaken belief that they will learn how to think and write well for all purposes and for all the possible nooks and crannies of the world of work where they could land. Just like dualistic thinking, this belief will die hard in their hearts. But this belief may not die at all if instructors don't explicitly teach and show students the variety of styles and standards of thinking and writing. Students need to know up front that what their literature instructor considers good evidence, argument, and writing style does not carry over completely into their chemistry, political science, or history courses, and that each cluster of disciplines follows its own set of rules and standards. And so do the worlds of private industry and government, where students are most likely to seek employment. If we don't share with them these basic truths, they may come to think that neither academe nor the world beyond it has any standards and conventions at all.

CHAPTER 25

Accommodating Different Learning Styles

People learn, or more precisely prefer to learn, in different ways. Many favor learning by doing hands-on activities, some by reading and writing about a topic, others by watching demonstrations and videos, and still others by listening to a lecture. All of these preferences key into the different ways people learn most easily, commonly known as *learning* or *processing styles*.

Should instructors then teach their material in different ways to cater to these different styles? Maybe they should prepare students for life in the real world by not giving them special treatment. Nevertheless, knowing and being able to take advantage of students' learning-style strengths also helps instructors prepare them for the real world. Particularly now, when our society is concerned with fairness and equality for those of different genders, races, ethnicities, and abilities, teaching to different learning styles is a major facet of equity.

Over the past few decades, the idea of learning styles has spawned a cottage industry. Hall and Mosley (2005) identified seventy-one different learning-style

instruments, most of which have no academic currency. But the approaches, frameworks, models, and typologies of learning styles that do number well over a dozen. They identify individual differences in information processing, orientations to learning, perceived locus of control, types of intelligence, hemispheric dominance, and personality on Jungian and non-Jungian dimensions (Hall & Mosley, 2005; Sarasin, 1998). One that is widely known because some K–12 leaders endorsed it is Gardner's (1993) multiple intelligences, of which there are eight: verbal linguistic, logical-mathematical, musical, spatial, bodily-kinesthetic, interpersonal, intrapersonal, and naturalist. (You can identify your intelligences by taking the inventory free of charge at www.businessballs.com/freematerialsinexcel/free_multiple_intelligences_test.xls.) However, this chapter refers to this model only in passing because teaching to so many intelligences is impractical and because it has no empirical foundation (Morris, 2008).

Rather, we will focus on three other models that are easier to apply, more popular in higher education, and more relevant to college students. Kolb's model of the learning cycle and learning styles (1984) is experiential, Fleming and Mills's VARK model (1992) is sensory based, and Felder and Silverman's Index of Learning Styles (1988) eclectically integrates cognitive, sensory, and experiential elements with one dimension found in the Jungian-based Myers-Briggs Type Indicator, intuitive versus sensing.

■ KOLB'S LEARNING STYLES MODEL AND EXPERIENTIAL LEARNING THEORY

Kolb (1984) developed his model to inform training in private industry and not so much as a piece of scholarship. It has weak predictive validity—too weak even to support its training applications—and low test-retest reliability (research summaries in Felder & Brent, 2005, and Kirschner, Sweller, & Clark, 2006). But the learning cycle Kolb describes maps well onto the structure of the brain (Zull, 2002), and it is still a fixture in the learning styles literature. Because the model is a business tool, the instrument that can "type" a person is available only for purchase at www.haygroup.com/tl/Questionnaires_Workbooks/ Kolb_Learning_Style_Inventory.aspx.

Kolb's Learning Cycle

Kolb portrays the process of meaningful learning as a series of events that integrates the functions of feeling, perceiving, thinking, and acting. The learner moves through a cycle comprising four phases: concrete experience (CE), reflective observation (RO), abstract conceptualization (AC), and active experimentation (AE).

Let us take experiential learners as an illustration. By directly involving themselves in new experiences, these learners enter the first phase of the cycle, designated concrete experience (CE). As they observe others and reflect on their own and others' experiences, they proceed to the reflective observation (RO) phase. Next, they attempt to assimilate their observations and perceptions into logical theories, thus moving into the third phase of abstract conceptualization (AC). When they use concepts to make decisions and solve problems, learners exhibit the final phase of the learning cycle, that of active experimentation (AE).

Individual learners enter the cycle at different points, typically because they prefer the activities associated with a particular part of the cycle. Thus, the various phases of the learning cycle form the basis for categories of learning modes.

The *concrete experience* mode is characterized by a reliance more on feeling than on thinking to solve problems. In this mode, people interpret human situations in a very personal way and focus on the tangible here and now. Intuitive, open-minded, social, and artistic in their information processing, these learners center on knowledge that demonstrates the complex and the unique as opposed to systematic, scientifically derived theories and generalizations.

The *reflective observation* mode is similarly marked by intuitive thinking, but as applied to observing and understanding situations, not solving and manipulating them. Using this mode, a learner is quick to grasp the meanings and implications of ideas and situations and can examine situations and phenomena empathetically from different points of view. Patience, objectivity, and good judgment flourish in this mode.

Reliance on logical thinking and conceptual reasoning characterizes the *abstract conceptualization* mode. It focuses on theory building, systematic planning, manipulation of abstract symbols, and quantitative analysis. This mode can generate personality traits such as precision, discipline, rigor, and an appreciation for elegant, parsimonious models.

Finally, the *active experimentation* mode is directed toward the practical and concrete (like the CE) and rational thinking (like the AC). But its orientation is toward results: influencing people's opinions, changing situations, and getting things accomplished—purely pragmatic applications. This mode fosters strong organizational skills, goal direction, and considerable tolerance for risk.

Now visualize a graph with two axes: the *x*-axis from active (on left) to reflective (on right) and the *y*-axis from abstract (at bottom) to concrete (at top). This arrangement places the concrete experience mode at twelve o'clock, the reflective observation at three o'clock, abstract conceptualization at six o'clock, and active experimentation at nine o'clock. Connecting the modes by arrows going clockwise, you can see Kolb's theoretical learning cycle.

Derived Learning Styles

Kolb went a step further to define a "learning style" and a "learning type" in each quadrant:

- *Accommodators* rely heavily on concrete experience and active experimentation. They enjoy engaging in new and challenging experiences, particularly those requiring hands-on involvement. They attack problems intuitively with a trial-and-error methodology and quite effectively teach themselves through an inquiry-based discovery process. They tend to gravitate toward action-oriented careers such as marketing and sales.
- *Divergers* use concrete experience as well as reflective observation. They examine situations from different angles and like to be personally, even emotionally, involved with their work. They crave to know why things happen as they do. Their major motivator is personal meaning, never competition. They tend to move toward service fields, the arts, and the social sciences.
- *Convergers* rely primarily on their skills of abstract conceptualization and active experimentation in their learning. They are often characterized as asocial and unemotional, preferring to work with things rather than people. What grabs their attention is how things work. They enjoy assignments that require practical applications, experimentation, and, in the end, precise, concrete answers. In general, many engineers and computer scientists fall into this category.
- *Assimilators* combine abstract conceptualization and reflective observation into a style that excels at organization and synthesis. They specialize in integrating large quantities of data into a concise,

logical framework, from which they extrapolate theories and generalizations. These individuals focus on abstract ideas and concepts rather than people or practical applications. Many scientists and academicians are assimilators.

In reality, people's learning styles may shift from situation to situation, encompassing an area that spans two and even three quadrants. So take care not to categorize yourself or others too rigidly.

Teaching to Kolb's Types

When designing a course, you may want to build in a variety of opportunities for students to board the learning cycle: some lessons that are experiential and tangible, some reflective and intuitive, some logical and conceptual, and others applied and practical. The teaching recommendations that follow were developed by Smith and Kolb (1986) and Harb, Terry, Hurt, and Williamson (1995).

Accommodators benefit most from these learning activities:

- Group work
- Discussions and brainstorming sessions
- Projects
- Solving open-ended problems
- Essay tests and assignments
- Inquiry-guided activities
- Making presentations
- Experiential methods such as field trips, role plays, simulations, the case method, problem-based learning, and service-learning

Divergers respond best to:

- Discussions of all types—whole class, small group, and one-on-one
- Group projects
- Essay tests and writing assignments
- Emotionally moving lectures and stories, and interactive lectures
- Experiential methods such as field trips, role plays, simulations, the case method, problem-based learning, and service-learning

Convergers are most successful when taught by:

- Demonstrations
- Inquiry-guided laboratories and other activities
- Objective homework problems and exams
- Computer-aided instruction and simulations
- Assignments involving defining and justifying a model
- Field trips and case studies

Finally, *assimilators* prefer:

- Logical, factual lectures
- Instructor demonstrations and modeling of problem-solving methods (live or video)
- Textbook reading assignments
- Independent data gathering and analysis research or library research

Three of these four types rely heavily on student-active teaching to learn the material. Assimilators do less only because they read and listen actively on their own.

■ FLEMING AND MILLS'S SENSORY-BASED LEARNING STYLE TYPOLOGY

Australian scholars Fleming and Mills (1992) advanced another learning-styles framework that uses a more descriptive classification nomenclature. Here, the terminology reflects the preferred physical sense involved in learning, as reflected in the four categories of read-write, auditory ("aural"), visual, and kinesthetic. Using the first letter of each type (R for "read-write"), Fleming and Mills dubbed their typology "VARK." The model presumes that individuals rely on more than one style. Svinicki tested it statistically and found it has weak validity but endorses its use outside of research:

> Its strength lies in its educational value for helping people think about their learning in multiple ways and giving them options they might not have

considered. . . . Everyone who uses the VARK loves it, and that's a great thing to be able to say. So it is obviously striking a chord with almost everyone who uses it. (Quoted in Fleming & Baume, 2006, p. 6)

You can take the VARK inventory free of charge at www.vark-learn.com/english/page.asp?p=questionnaire, a section of the extensive VARK website.

Read/Write

Students with a read/write learning style excel when asked to read and write about a topic. They rely heavily on recognizing logical, deductive relationships, such as the classic outline form, and they can easily find pattern and flow in a well-constructed lecture or textbook. Their memory structure is more abstract than that of the other styles. They store information as organized sets of symbols, such as outlines, equations, diagrams, and typologies. As you can imagine, these learners do well in the traditional educational setting. The reading and lecture format so common in classrooms is tailor-made for them, and they need no special instructional considerations.

Auditory

Students with an auditory learning style perform well when they are given information in a form they can hear, such as a discussion, a lecture, a debate, or another type of verbal presentation. In fact, they learn best when they can hear themselves express an idea. Consequently they benefit from most standard teaching methods, especially those that require student participation. As they process and store information in chronological relationships, they thrive in fields that base data and analysis on stories, cases, and events, such as history, political science, law, business administration, and literature. Many also have musical talent. Strong auditory learners can retrieve knowledge in "memory tapes" and are aided by mnemonic devices.

Visual

Students who lean more toward visual and kinesthetic styles often face difficulties in the traditional college classroom. Unless they also have a digital or auditory processing style on which to rely, they are often left behind in lecture-based courses, through no fault of their own. So additional forms of stimuli may be necessary in order to optimize their learning experience.

Individuals with a primarily visual learning style rely on their sight to take in information. They work well with maps and rarely forget a face, a scene, or a place. Some gravitate to artistic fields where they can express their flair for design and color. Consistent with their visual nature, these individuals organize knowledge in terms of spatial interrelationships among ideas and store it graphically as static or animated snapshots, flowcharts, pictures, or diagrams. Some even have photographic memories.

With little additional preparation, you can easily supplement your teaching presentations with aids for visual learners. The object is to portray knowledge in two-dimensional spatial relationships that reflect the logical, chronological, or mechanical links among concepts, processes, and events. The less "space" and more connections between two ideas, the more closely related the visual learner will comprehend and remember them.

Among the visuals that this learning style appreciates is the graphic syllabus (see Chapter Three), as well as illustrations, pictures, diagrams, flowcharts, graphs, concept and mind maps, graphic models and organizers, and graphic metaphors. This last type of graphic is a drawing of an analogical relationship, such as a sketch of a building to represent a Marxian view of society, with the basement as the "substructure" and the floors above as the "superstructure."

Visual teaching tools are readily available: the chalkboard, presentation slides, overhead transparencies, and handouts. Some instructional computer software and videotapes also feature outstanding graphical depictions of mathematical, physical, and biological relationships. Using only the least expensive options, you can diagram the relationships among major points in your lectures and the readings. You can add visual components like graphs and histograms to the day's lesson. You can chart complex, logical relationships among overlapping concepts with circle (Venn) diagrams. You can draw flowcharts of multistage assignments, such as the essay-writing process, problem-solving strategies, and laboratory procedures. You can even flow-chart your student learning outcomes from the beginning to the end of the term (see Chapter Two). Since students have such trouble taking notes on class discussions, you might mind-map the ideas as they emerge—that is, diagram the discussion with the central theme as the hub with lines coming off it to the related arguments and points the students make. Then draw secondary lines off each argument or point to the supporting evidence presented (see Chapter Twenty-Six).

Kinesthetic

Those with this learning style benefit most by doing. It uses active involvement as the primary learning mode. Those strong in this style demonstrate superb eye-hand-mind coordination and natural-born mechanical ability. In the recent past, these learners were often maligned and rarely taught their way except in shop or home economics courses. While mechanical skills may seem narrow and unintellectual, kinesthetic individuals make excellent surgeons, dentists, health care professionals, musicians, technicians, engineers, and architects. In processing information, they easily grasp physical interrelationships and store knowledge as experiences with both physical and emotional components.

You can reach strongly kinesthetic students using the same techniques as you do for strongly visually oriented students, as both types relate well to graphic representations of themes and concepts. But since kinesthetic processors also rely heavily on inductive reasoning, they especially benefit from multiple examples and hands-on experiences from which they can formulate general hypotheses and principles on their own. Thus, they learn best from experiential and inductive teaching methods like simulations, role plays, field trips, service-learning, inquiry-guided activities and laboratories, case studies, and problem-based learning, all of which are explained in earlier chapters.

Physical models and analogies are also important learning tools to these students. For instance, an English instructor faced a strongly kinesthetic student with little concept of how to organize the assigned literature review, even after being given oral instructions. So the instructor decided to use a mechanical illustration, which worked. With paper and pencil in hand, she compared the introduction, which contains the thesis, to the motor that drives the paper. The next paragraph contains the points supporting one view, like a series of pulleys all turning in the same direction. The direction of the paper then shifts to the opposing arguments and evidence, much as a mechanical system changes direction if the drive belts are twisted. Finally, in the conclusion, the writer chooses to endorse one direction (side of the argument) or the other.

A section of the VARK website, www.vark-learn.com/english/page.asp?p=helpsheets, lists the most appealing or easiest ways for each of the four sensory-based styles to process new knowledge, study it, and display mastery of it. Refer your students to this source.

■ FELDER AND SILVERMAN'S INDEX OF LEARNING STYLES

While Felder and Silverman (1988) proposed their learning styles model for engineering students, it applies to learners across the disciplines. Furthermore, it is the most scientifically grounded framework of all the major models. The forty-four-item Index of Learning Styles (ILS) questionnaire, developed in 1991 by Felder and Soloman (n.d.-a), has high to moderate construct validity, internal consistency reliability, test-retest reliability, total item correlation, and interscale correlation (Felder & Spurlin, 2005; Litzinger, Lee, Wise, & Felder, 2007;

Zywno, 2003). You can also take it free of charge at www.engr.ncsu.edu/learningstyles/ilsweb.html.

Felder and Silverman (1988) conceive of learning styles as four independent, cognitive continua, each anchored by pure types. One dimension identifies how a student prefers to process information and knowledge: *actively* through physical activity or discussion or *reflectively* through introspection. Another pertains to the sensory mode in which a student prefers to receive information and knowledge: *verbally* in written or spoken words or mathematical equations or *visually* in pictures, graphics, videos, and demonstrations. A third continuum considers the type of information that a student most readily perceives: internally based *intuitive* experiences (hunches, insights, possibilities) or externally based *sensory* experiences. The final dimension focuses on how a student acquires understanding: *sequentially* in incremental steps or *globally* in holistic leaps.

These styles are not meant to be rigid categories. A student may have a strong, moderate, or weak leaning toward one end of a continuum or the other. Furthermore, she may lean in one direction for some tasks and in the other direction for other tasks. The most effective learners and problem solvers tend to cluster around the middle, functioning well in polar styles. Those who strongly prefer one style or another may miss important aspects of learning, such as crucial details, the big picture, alternative approaches, cognitive shortcuts, or possible applications.

The following section provides detailed explanations of these styles and how to teach to them from Felder (1993), Felder and Silverman (1988), and Felder and Soloman (n.d.-b).

Active Versus Reflective

Active learners gain the most out of doing something with the material—discussing it, explaining it to others, applying it, trying things out, experimenting with how things work, or bouncing off ideas. They like to solve problems, evaluate ideas, and design and conduct experiments. They learn best from group work, discussion, problem solving, and experiential and inquiry-guided activities. To study most productively, they should follow up their reading with study group members who take turns explaining different parts of the material to each other. To retain material, they should associate it with ways it can be applied. To prepare for tests, they should work in a group organized around guessing the questions and answering them.

By contrast, reflective learners need some quiet time to process the material internally. With a little thinking time, they can generate good ideas and theories, make up viable models, define problems effectively, and propose possible solutions. While group and experiential activities do not facilitate their learning, we as instructors need only build in brief pauses in the middle of lectures or after classroom activities to allow these learners to process the material. We might also pose reflection questions such as, "What does this all mean?" or "What do you think was the point of this activity?" During recitation and discussion, we should allow at least several seconds of wait time after each question. To study most effectively, reflective learners should work alone and practice summarizing the material and making up and answering questions about it.

Verbal Versus Visual

All people learn better when they receive information and knowledge in both the verbal and the visual modes, and the most facile learners can accommodate input in either mode. But some learners process and remember material better if it is presented in one mode or the other. Visual learners get more out of flowcharts, diagrams, mind and concepts maps, pictures, diagrams, graphs, time lines, matrices, videos, animations, and demonstrations, while verbal learners find it easier to process symbols such as words, whether spoken and written, and equations.

Higher education is designed by and for verbal learners, even though they comprise a minority of the student population. They benefit from listening to lectures, from writing exercises and assignments, and from reading books, handouts, PowerPoint outlines,

and chalkboard writing. If they try, they can figure out how to take decent lecture notes. To prepare for tests, they should write summaries or outlines in their own words or join study groups where they can listen to others explain the material and explain it out loud themselves.

Visual learners are more on their own to make sense of the barrage of verbally presented material they receive. They have to find or create their own graphic representations of the material. They should also highlight their books and notes in various colors representing different topics or themes. But we can do a great deal in our classes to help them by first preparing some graphic representations of the material ourselves, then coaching our students in preparing their own. For more specific recommendations, see the section on the visual learning style in the VARK framework, as well as Chapter Twenty-Six. Since most of our students are visual learners, the efforts we make to reach them can raise our overall class performance.

Intuitive Versus Sensing

Since higher education tends to emphasize concepts and principles, intuitive learners have an edge up because they grasp and remember abstractions, relationships, generalizations, and mathematical formulas quite easily. They tend to work quickly and efficiently and to be innovative and imaginative in the way they conceptualize problems and interpret material. However, they dislike repetition, standard procedures, detail work, "plug-and-chug" courses, and the memorization of facts.

Sensing learners work best with whatever information they receive through their senses from the outside world. So they are comfortable memorizing facts, patiently observing phenomena, carefully tending to details, doing routine assignments, and solving problems by well-established methods. Like active learners, they are practical minded and can remember material better when they can see its connections to the real world in examples or applications. Often averse to complexities and surprises, they can have a lot of trouble on tests that ask them to do more than recognize and regurgitate unless they get a lot of practice performing the higher-order cognitive operations that are required. As instructors, we need to furnish that practice for sensing students and to pepper our lessons with plenty of examples and real-world applications of concepts and principles. We can also advise these learners to study by translating the abstract and general into the concrete and specific, both alone and in study groups.

Sequential Versus Global

Sequential learners represent the majority of students. They learn most easily in linear steps, with each step logically following the one before. They solve problems the same way, following a logical series of steps. While most of us organize our courses sequentially, we can put these learners at a disadvantage if we skip steps or seemingly jump from topic to topic without making explicit connections between them. Many textbooks make the same mistake. Sequential learners study best when they outline the lecture and the readings using their own organizational scheme. Since they can miss the relationships among topics or between new and previously learned knowledge, their learning can be pretty shallow. So we should pose study and discussion questions that make them see these connections. We should also encourage them to enhance their understanding and retention of the material by making these links on their own.

While we are struggling to fully grasp new material, we all experience sudden insights and gestalts that make the pieces fall into place. However, before the flash, sequential learners are usually able to work with the material at some level—enough to do the homework and pass the tests. What marks global learners is their inability to do much of anything with the material until they have made the grand leap to complete understanding. In the meantime, they simply absorb new material as unrelated pieces. Once they grasp the big picture, they may still have trouble with the details, but they may be able to solve complex problems quickly or synthesize ideas

in novel and creative ways, even if they can't explain how they have done it. Interestingly, we can help global learners the same way we can help their sequential counterparts—by helping them see the relationships between new material and what they already know.

Global learners may not know who they are, and just their realizing their need to grasp a subject holistically can help them find ways to facilitate their gestalt. For instance, skimming through a reading assignment before actually reading it (see Chapter Twenty-Three) provides a valuable content overview. Frequently relating new to previously learned material helps a learner capitalize on prior flashes of understanding. In addition, global learners should try immersing themselves in one subject at a time for long study sessions instead of spending short periods with each subject every night.

While neither Felder nor his coauthors mention it, global learners may also profit from some of the same graphic representations of the material that visual learners do—that is, flowcharts, diagrams, graphs, mind and concept maps, matrices, pictures, and animations. As we will see in Chapter Twenty-Six, such graphics can convey the big picture more efficiently and effectively than words ever can.

■ PARALLELS ACROSS LEARNING STYLE MODELS

Clearly none of the three model translates neatly into another. VARK and Felder and Silverman's ILS share the visual style, and the former's Kinesthetic style resembles the latter's Active style. Remember, however, that Felder and Silverman's model posits four independent dimensions on which learners vary, not types of learners. VARK's Read-Write style is roughly comparable to Felder and Silverman's Verbal combined with the Sequential. Some parallels can also be drawn between Kolb's and Felder and Silverman's models. The Diverger suggests a blend of Reflective, Intuitive, and Global learning; the Assimilator appears to be a mixture of the Reflective,

Sensing, and Sequential; the Converger combines the Active and Sensing; and the Accommodator has features of the Active and Intuitive. In summary, each learning style model is distinctive in the cognitive, experiential, or sensory variables it identifies as relevant to learning. Each has different theoretical underpinnings, and one cannot collapse into another. It is not surprising, then, that the models vary in their scientific currency, the Felder-Silverman framework carrying the most. For research purposes, it is the best choice. As heuristic devices to encourage more effective teaching, all the models have value. Draw inspiration from the one or two that resonate most with you.

■ MULTISENSORY, MULTIMETHOD TEACHING: MOST EFFECTIVE FOR ALL

Whatever learning style model you favor, it is important to remember that the students in your classes aren't one type or another. They use multiple learning strategies and rely on multiple input modes. In fact, all students learn more and better from multiple-sense, multiple-method instruction. As noted in Chapter One, people learn best when they receive the new material multiple times and in different ways—that is, through multiple senses and modes that use different parts of their brain (Kress, Jewitt, Ogborn, & Charalampos, 2006; Vekiri, 2002). Teaching to multiple styles and modes can also help you revitalize lesson plans and classroom presentations that have become routine through repetition. Adding visual and kinesthetic components, inquiry-guided activities, group work, and experiential learning may take some time and effort, but the change can avert burnout.

To maximize all of your students' learning and your own professional fulfillment, try to use a rich variety of teaching techniques and learning media in your courses. In addition, acquaint your students with the broad range of learning and studying strategies. Bringing this variety and flexibility into your teaching is the real value of all the learning style models.

CHAPTER 26

Using Visuals to Teach

We humans have relied on our sight for survival more than any other sense. Through most of the ages, we were dependent on it for hunting, fishing, gathering, making fire and tools, determining the edible versus the poisonous, identifying and avoiding predators, planting and harvesting, and reading the sky for the time of day and time of year. At some point, we used our sight to fashion shelters, clothing, and personal decorations and to paint animals on walls of our caves. Even if our eyes could never compete with the eagle's, we were able to distinguish colors, shapes, and distances rather well for a mammal. Besides, we didn't enjoy the olfactory or auditory sentience of so many of our four-legged neighbors. In time, after we refined spoken language and invented the story, we added a strong oral component to our culture. But once we devised writing and later printing, we relied more on sight for communication. Still, reading and writing aren't quite as effortless as spotting a lion. We need the left side of our cerebrum to interpret the symbols our eyes are seeing and to translate our thoughts into visual symbols. Pure visual images, unfettered by text, convey information more directly, efficiently, and quickly.

Visuals, then, can serve our instructional purposes very effectively. They come in many forms—flowcharts, diagrams, graphs, tables, matrices, pictures, drawings, figures, even animations—offering countless options for depicting course material. They can be created and displayed on a computer, but they can be just as powerful when hand-drawn. We can provide them to help students learn and to become accustomed to using visuals, so they can go on to develop graphic representations of their own understanding of the subject matter.

Chapters Two and Three introduced two visual teaching tools: the outcomes map for showing your students' progression through learning outcomes in your course and the graphic syllabus for displaying the topical organization of your course (Nilson, 2007a). Both commonly take the form of a flowchart or diagram to illustrate the sequencing of outcomes or topics over time. Like the most powerful visuals we will examine in this chapter, they provide students with the big picture of your course and the internal structure of its major components, either outcomes or topics. As the next section details, these visual schemata can give students the scaffolding they need to better understand and remember the learning process you have planned for them and your course content.

■ WAYS THAT VISUALS ENHANCE LEARNING

The evidence that graphics of all kinds facilitate comprehension, transfer, and retention of course material has generated a large body of research and several sizable literature reviews (for example, Vekiri, 2002; Winn, 1991). Many of the studies center around specific visual tools, such as concept maps and mind maps, and these will be summarized in the next section on the leading types of graphics. Other research focuses on multimedia learning (Mayer, 2005). More generally, Marzano (2003) documents that "nonlinguistic representations" of material, which include graphics, images, metaphors, and art forms, have an effect size on learning of 0.75, meaning that students exposed to them score 0.75 standard deviations higher on tests than students not so exposed. This effect size is comparable to that of collaborative learning and reinforcement and feedback—too broad and powerful to be due to the subset of students with visual and global learning styles (see Chapter Twenty-Five). So we must turn to cognitive psychology to explain how visuals work for all learners. Specifically, we will look at dual-coding theory, the visual argument theory, and cognitive theory.

Dual-Coding Theory: Redundancy and Reinforcement

Dual-coding theory addresses how visuals work in conjunction with text, which is typically a mode in which students receive material. It posits that the human mind has two memories, the semantic and the episodic, corresponding to the verbal and

visual-spatial systems, respectively (Paivio, 1971). Recent neurological findings that the brain processes and stores verbal and visual-spatial information in separate cognitive systems have lent physiological evidence to this theory (Vekiri, 2002). So when presented with complementary text or audio and visuals, learners process it twice, through both systems, without overloading their working memory (Moreno & Mayer, 1999). As a result, they retain the material better and longer and can access and retrieve more easily than they can when they learn it in just one mode using just one system (Clark & Paivio, 1991; Kosslyn, 1994; Mayer & Gallini, 1990; Mayer & Sims, 1994; Paivio, 1971, 1990; Paivio & Csapo, 1973; Paivio, Walsh, & Bons, 1994; Svinicki, 2004; Tigner, 1999; Vekiri, 2002).

Another way of interpreting dual-coding theory is with reference to brain hemispheres. As the left side of the brain processes verbal symbols and the right side visuals, material presented in both modes activate both sides of the brain, roughly doubling the number of neurons firing and synapses forming.

Of course, the learning and comprehension benefits accrue only if the student receives the verbal and visual versions together and is able to integrate them cognitively (Mayer, 2005). In addition, the visual must clearly and accurately depict the verbal.

The Visual Argument Theory: Greater Efficiency

According to this theory, visuals work so effectively because, compared to text, they convey information more efficiently—that is, visual information requires less working memory and fewer cognitive transformations to process and draw inferences from (Larkin & Simon, 1987; Robinson, Katayama, DuBois, & Devaney, 1998; Robinson & Kiewra, 1995; Robinson & Molina, 2002; Robinson & Schraw, 1994; Robinson & Skinner, 1996; Waller, 1981; Winn, 1987). In other words, it is less taxing on the mind to derive meaning from graphics than from words. In addition, a good graphic does a much better job than text of (1) inducing learners to attend to the conceptual relationships rather than just memorize terms; (2) enabling them to recognize patterns among concepts; (3) helping them elaborate their cognitive schemata by inferring new, complex relationships; and (4) helping them integrate new knowledge into their existing cognitive structures (Hyerle, 1996; Robinson et al., 1998; Robinson & Kiewra, 1995; Robinson & Schraw, 1994; Robinson & Skinner, 1996; Winn, 1991).

According to Larkin and Simon (1987), visuals offer "perceptual enhancement" by communicating information through both their individual components and the spatial organization of those components. As a result, they allow learners to process all the relevant concepts and the relationships among them simultaneously as a whole. This ability facilitates understanding because bodies of knowledge are typically structured as a hierarchy of concepts with relationships among them. So just showing learners a picture of this organization teaches them a great deal about the nature of knowledge—for one, that it is not a list of loosely linked ideas but a tightly structured web of interrelated categories and principles. In addition, the mind need not interpret or infer the conceptual interrelationships because they are transparently displayed in the spatial arrangements, the shapes of the enclosures, the types of lines, the directions of the arrows, the colors, and any other graphic features the designer may use to distinguish causal links and direction, strength of relationship, level of generality, and the like.

Contrast the relatively effortless, holistic learning that visuals allow with the slower and more complicated process of extracting information from printed material. Text unfolds components and interrelationships among them linearly, sequentially, one piece at a time, as though they comprise a list. The mind must then interpret the pieces and connections and, to integrate and retain the knowledge, reconstruct the hierarchical organization, hopefully discerning the superordinate from the subordinate concepts, the more general and abstract from the more specific and concrete, exactly the way the text intended. The task demands a great deal of working memory and several cognitive transformations, allowing plenty

of room for misunderstandings, shifts in meaning, and just plain error. In the meantime, the mind is too occupied to think very much about the material it is translating, such as to link it to prior knowledge, question it, draw inferences from it, trace its implications, or apply it toward solving a problem. Going back over the text to find specific information also takes more time and cognitive energy than does locating it on a graphic. The reader has to search through paragraphs, if not pages, or refer to the Contents page or the index (Larkin & Simon, 1987; Veriki, 2002).

McMaster University professor Dale Roy (cited in Gedalof, 1998) demonstrated the superior efficacy of graphics on a faculty audience, a group highly skilled in processing text. He asked participants to prepare a brief oral presentation, which included developing one text-based and one visual transparency. After the participants delivered their minilesson, he had the rest of the audience reconstruct it. Consistently the faculty were able to reproduce almost all of the visual material but no more than half of the text-based presentation.

Cognitive Theory: The Big Picture

The "How Structure Increases Learning" section in Chapter One already addressed the critical importance of learners' seeing the organized big picture of knowledge, which includes recognizing patterns in how the world works. It is having this big picture of our field that makes us experts. In our mind's eye, this structure resembles a complex web of patterns that our contemporary and ancestral colleagues have identified and verbalized. It equips us with an intricate filing system that enables us to easily assimilate new information and to store and retrieve from a vast collection of concepts, facts, data, and principles (Alexander, 1996; Anderson, 1993; Carey, 1985; Chi, Glaser, & Rees, 1982; Novak, 1977; Reif & Heller, 1982; Royer, Cisero, & Carlo, 1993). We developed this schema over many years of intensive study—probably the hard way without the help of conceptual maps.

Without such a valid and robust mental structure, our students are disciplinary novices. They bring to our courses little background knowledge, no filing system for new knowledge, and often faulty models and misconceptions about the subject matter (Svinicki, 2004). After all, the mind is so wired to seek patterns that it can make mistakes in its quest. Students are unfamiliar with the hierarchy of concepts and principles, cannot discern patterns and generalizations, and lack the algorithms that facilitate applying knowledge to solving conceptual problems (DeJong & Ferguson-Hessler, 1996; Kozma, Russell, Jones, Marx, & Davis, 1996). As a result, they wander through a knowledge base picking up pieces of it on a superficial level, memorizing isolated facts and terms, and using trial-and-error to solve problems and answer questions (Glaser, 1991). What they need to advance beyond novice is an empirically grounded big picture of the hierarchical structure of the body of knowledge—one convincing enough to override their misconceptions, as well as accurate and comprehensive enough to accommodate new knowledge and multiple conceptual networks (Baume & Baume, 2008; Posner, Strike, Hewson, & Gertzog, 1982). This is their entrée into expert thinking and a framework for deep, meaningful learning. In fact, students can't really learn and get beyond memorizing without it. The mind depends on organization; it acquires and stores new knowledge only if it perceives its organization and its logical place within the mental structure of prior knowledge (Anderson, 1984; Baume & Baume, 2008; Bransford, Brown, & Cocking, 1999; Reif & Heller, 1982; Rhem, 1995; Royer et al., 1993; Svinicki, 2004; Zull, 2002). While global learners may need this schema up front more than other learning style types (see Chapter Twenty-Five), cognitive theory tells us that we are all global learners as we approach the expert level.

Since the chances are very slim that our students will independently build such cognitive schemata in a semester or two of casual study, we would be wise to furnish them with relevant structures of our discipline, with valid, ready-made frameworks for filing this content (Kozma et al., 1996). They need to internalize this scaffolding—especially at the introductory level, where they have little prior knowledge of the subject matter on which to map new knowledge—before we elaborate it with details, conditions, and qualifications (Ausubel, 1968; Carlile & Jordan, 2005; Zull, 2002). In addition, we should help students become aware of any faulty mental models they may harbor and guide them in reconciling these with more accurate cognitive structures. Specifically, we can give them practice in reinterpreting their prior observations and experiences. Otherwise, if all we impart are masses of content, they will graduate mentally unchanged and uneducated, with only memory traces of their college years.

Because mental structures of knowledge are so crucial to our students' learning, we need to convey them in the most transparent and efficient way possible. We know that the cognitive models of experts like ourselves look like hierarchical networks of complexly interrelated concepts and principles. Many types of visuals are similarly structured to display component parts in hierarchical or weblike arrangements. Therefore, well-crafted graphics should do an excellent job of depicting disciplinary schemata. The next section examines four types that are suitable to the task.

■ TYPES OF VISUALS FOR LEARNING

Ausubel (1968) coined the term *advance organizer* more than four decades ago to apply to any graphic that would offer an opening overview of a lesson, whether a flowchart, diagram, chart, table, matrix, web, map, figure, or something else. In this section we focus on the major types of graphics that spatially display the relationships among ideas and concepts. Such visuals can serve as an advance organizer, a constructivist assignment for student groups or individuals, or a planning and memory aid for managing projects, solving problems, running meetings, organizing papers and presentations, integrating and summarizing material, and even writing creative works (Buzan, 1974; Svinicki, 2004; Wycoff, 1991). In other words, we can use graphics not only to help students acquire and retain knowledge but also to teach them tools that will facilitate their work in college and beyond and engage the creativity of the visual-holistic side of the brain. In addition, having students draw their own graphics can make excellent homework assignments—for example, summarizing their understanding of the readings or reviewing for tests—as well as challenging group activities during class and even test questions. The products can help you diagnose students' misconceptions and assess their conceptual, analytical, and synthesis skills without your having to read essays.

Concept Maps

A concept is a human-defined pattern or common ground across a category of objects, events, or properties. For instance, concepts that represent objects include "force," "light," "food," "population," "weather," "pressure," and "energy." Examples of those describing events are "rain," "photosynthesis," "osmosis," "conversion," "fission," and "marriage." Among those designating properties are "taste," "density," "life-giving," "volume," and "texture." A concept map graphically displays the hierarchical organization of several (up to twenty or so) concepts and often examples of them, from the most inclusive/general/broad/abstract concept at the top to the most exclusive/specific/narrow/concrete concepts at the bottom. Therefore, it frequently looks like a network or spider web, typically pyramidal in overall shape, in which the lines link concepts or ideas to one another. When Angelo and Cross (1993) suggested using such maps as a classroom assessment technique (see Chapter Twenty-Eight), they described them as "drawings or diagrams showing mental connections that students make between a major concept . . . and other concepts they have learned" (p. 197). These connections may be categorical, causal, or logical relationships or even comparisons and contrasts. They may also designate a process or sequence of events, in which case they may resemble a chain or flowchart. Because of the many possible links, the lines between concepts should usually be labeled to specify the relationship.

You can teach your students how to draw a concept map by having them follow these steps (Wandersee, 2002b):

1. Identify key concepts, perhaps twelve to twenty, from the readings, your last lecture, or another source.
2. Write each concept on a small index card or sticky note.
3. Identify the main topic or concept, and place it at top center. This is called the *superordinate* concept. It is either the most inclusive, general, broad, or abstract or the first stage in a process or sequence.
4. Rank-order or cluster all the remaining ideas, called *subordinate* concepts, from the most inclusive, general, broad, or abstract, placing these higher up and closer to the main concept, to the most exclusive, specific, narrow or concrete, placing these lower down. In the case of a process or sequence, order the concepts chronologically. The object is to structure the concepts and their interrelations correctly.
5. Arrange the concepts in a linkable hierarchy.
6. Draw the entire hierarchy on a piece of paper with enclosures around the concepts and linking lines that are labeled to specify the relationship. The linked concepts together with the labeled link is called a *proposition*. Because the map's presumed direction is downward, arrows are not necessary.
7. Check for cross-links (connections going across the branches), draw in these links as dotted lines, and label them.

Figure 26.1 shows several examples of very simple concept maps with just two or three concepts and one or two links. In a real class, these maps would be only part of a larger map. Figure 26.2 elaborates the very simple map in which "population" is the superordinate concept, extending it by seven additional concepts arranged on three levels. Where a concept falls in the hierarchy depends on the lesson. In one map a concept may be superordinate and in another subordinate. As Figure 26.3 illustrates, "photosynthesis" may be on the lowest (fourth) level in a concept

Figure 26.1   Examples of Very Simple Concept Maps

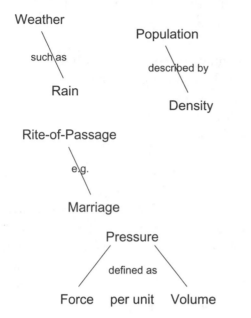

2. The number of valid propositions (links between concepts)
3. The number of valid levels in the hierarchy
4. The number of valid cross-links
5. The number of valid examples

Therefore, you can instruct students to draw a map with a given number of concepts interrelated with a given number of links, spanning a given number of hierarchical levels, with a given number of cross-links and examples. Novak and Gowin (1984), who devised the leading scoring model for concept maps, recommends giving one point for each valid link, five points for each valid level, ten points for each valid cross-link, and one point for each valid example. Quicker still is a computer-based technique that scores maps by the number of links and the geometrical distances between concepts (Taricani & Clariana, 2006).

Many researchers have found that concept maps facilitate students' mastery of content and development of cognitive skills. In fact, concept maps have proven their value in some of the most challenging subjects, such as accounting (Leauby & Brazina, 1998), applied statistics (Schau & Mattern, 1997), biology (Briscoe & LaMaster, 1991; Cliburn, 1990; Kinchin, 2000, 2001; Wallace & Mintzes, 1990), chemistry (Regis & Albertazzi, 1996), conceptual astronomy (Zeilik et al., 1997), geoscience (Rebich & Gauthier, 2005), marine ecology (Beaudry & Wilson, 2010), mathematics

map that starts with "energy," ranking below "light" and "life-giving," but "photosynthesis" can also be a superordinate concept, in which case "light" may be subordinate.

Concept maps are quite easy to write instructions for and to assess, which is why they make good gradable assignments and tests. The key evaluative dimensions are:

1. The number of concepts included, unless you provide them

Figure 26.2   Concept Map of "Population" with a Total of Nine Concepts

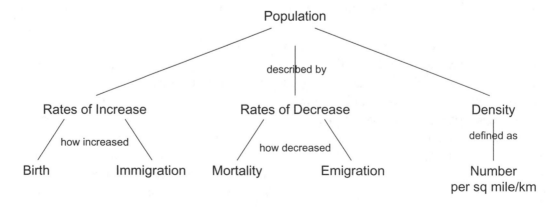

Figure 26.3 Two Simple Concept Maps Illustrating How Concepts in One Map Can Change Levels in Another Map

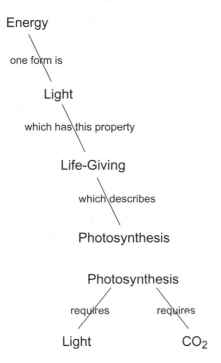

(Brinkmann, 2003), medicine (Hoffman, Trott, & Neely, 2002; McGaghie, McCrimmon, Mitchell, Thompson, & Ravitch, 2000; West, Pomeroy, & Park, 2000), and nursing (Baugh & Mellott, 1998; King & Shell, 2002; Schuster, 2000; Wilkes, Cooper, Lewin, & Batts, 1999), among others. In Zeilik et al.'s (1997) experimental study, the astronomy students who developed concept maps scored higher than the control group on three kinds of conceptual examinations: one measuring the ability to relate concepts, another of multiple-choice items designed to identify faulty models, and a third fill-in-the-blank concept map. Among the skills that concept maps are known to enhance are postsecondary reading comprehension (Katayama, 1997; Mealy & Nist, 1989; Robinson & Kiewra, 1995; Robinson & Schraw, 1994), writing (Beaudry & Wilson, 2010), critical thinking (King & Shell, 2002; Nixon-Cobb, 2005; Schuster, 2000; West et al., 2000; Wilkes et al., 1999), and problem solving (Baugh & Mellot, 1998; Beissner, 1992; Kalman, 2007; Okebukola, 1992).

Of course, the effectiveness of concept maps, like every other teaching tool, depends on how it is used, and instructors have often maximized their interactive, constructivist potential by having students develop them along with the instructor or in peer groups, as well as alone. When students draw the maps, they are actively constructing their own knowledge (Kinchin, 2000, 2001), clarifying and organizing it (Hoffman et al., 2002; McGaghie et al., 2000), reinforcing their understanding of the material, and integrating it with prior knowledge (Plotnick, 2001). In addition, they are making explicit to both the instructor and themselves any misconceptions they may have and the progress they are making in correctly and complexly structuring the subject material (Romance & Vitale, 1997; Vojtek & Vojtek, 2000). Concept maps work well for most knowledge construction tasks because all but the process variety presume an overall hierarchical structure of carefully integrated elements (Anderson, 1984; Leichhardt, 1989; Plotnick, 1996; Romance & Vitale, 1999). As we will see, mind maps presume the same but have a different look and layout.

Mind Maps

Mind maps are the more colorful and whimsical cousin of concept maps. The mind-mapping method was developed by Buzan (1974) for note taking. Over the years, Ellis (2006) and authors of other college-success books popularized it as a technique for organizing course material for study, review, and paper writing. It follows steps similar to concept mapping:

1. Write the central concept, topic, or idea in the center of a large piece of paper, the board, or a landscape-set screen. This is the *primary* idea.
2. Identify up to six or seven closely related concepts, topics, or ideas (for example, subordinate concepts, subtopics, properties, descriptors), and write each of them on the end of a thick line (with arrows) radiating from the center. Use key words only (the briefest and sharpest expression of the idea). These are the *secondary* ideas.

3. For each secondary concept, topic, or idea, identify up to six or seven closely related subordinate concepts, subtopics, or ideas (properties, descriptors, examples, or the like), and write each of them on the end of a thinner line (arrows are optional) radiating from the secondary idea. Again, use key words. These are the *tertiary* ideas.

4. Look for cross-relationships, and draw thin lines between related ideas.

5. Add color, suggestive icons, and appropriate symbols. Color-code the lines and key words by secondary–idea branch.

A couple of examples will bring the power of mind maps to light. Figure 26.4 is a graphic syllabus of the advanced corporate finance course designed and taught by Ernest N. Biktimirov, a finance professor at Brock University in St. Catharines, Ontario, Canada. He has used mind maps and other visual tools extensively in his teaching. His course, the primary idea, is graphically conveyed with a drawing of a check. It has three major segments (the secondary ideas): an overview of financial markets and instruments, symbolized by the struggle between the bear and the bull; portfolio theory, represented by a briefcase full of money; and financial instruments, illustrated by an investment certificate. These visual representations capture the major topics in an eye-catching way. The chapters addressing these topics are the tertiary ideas.

Figure 26.5 shows a more elaborate, icon-rich mind map that Biktimirov created to summarize course material on futures contracts and make it memorable for his students. In the center he represents the primary idea, types of futures contracts, by an Unidentified Flying Object and a crystal ball to communicate two ideas: in a futures contract, a buyer and a seller agree on a price today for a future transaction; and the prices of futures contracts

Figure 26.4   Mind-Mapped Graphic Syllabus of Advanced Corporate Finance Course
Source: Created by Ernest N. Biktimirov. Reprinted with his permission.

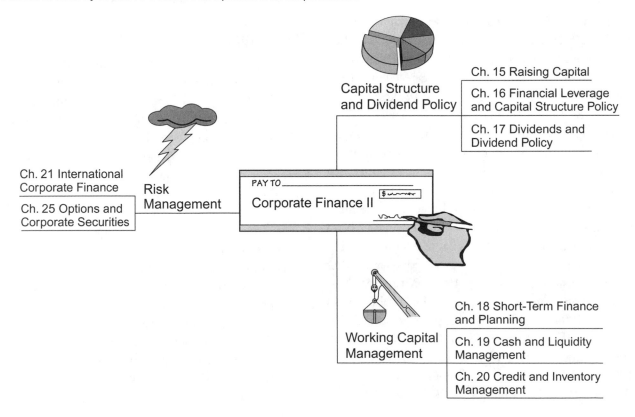

Figure 26.5 Mind Map of Types of Futures Contracts
Source: Created by Ernest N. Biktimirov. Reprinted with his permission.

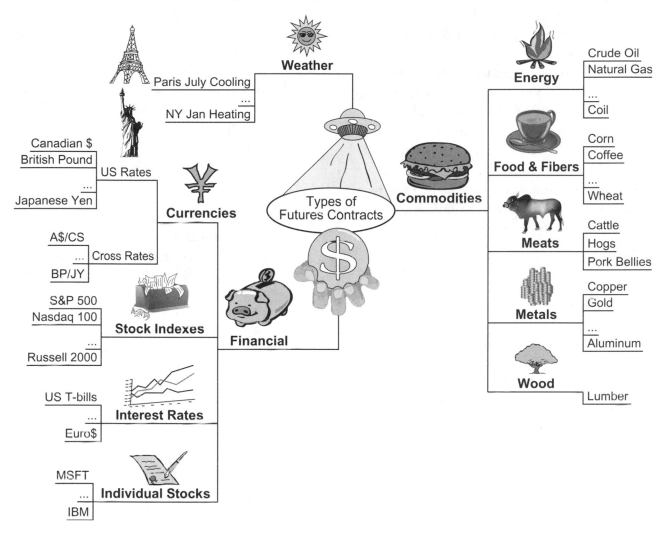

on different underlying assets help investors forecast the futures prices of these assets (E. N. Biktimirov, personal communication, April 13, 2009). Radiating from the center are three lines, one for each type of contract (secondary ideas): commodities, of which there are five types (tertiary ideas); weather, which affects cooling to heating needs all over the world (tertiary ideas); and financial, of which there are four types (tertiary ideas). The connection between each idea and its visual representation is transparent and sometimes amusing—for example, a piggy bank symbolizing financial types of futures contracts. This mind map extends out to quaternary ideas

on the commodities branch and quinary ideas on the financial branch. It would be easy to recast this graphic as a concept map, but the end product wouldn't be nearly as visually evocative without the icons.

While not as well researched as concept maps, mind maps have proven to be effective learning tools in business (Driver, 2001), business statistics (Sirias, 2002), economics (Nettleship, 1992), executive education (Mento, Martinelli, & Jones, 1999), finance (Biktimirov & Nilson, 2006), marketing (Eriksson & Hauer, 2004), and optometry (McClain, 1987). In another study, fifty second- and third-year medical students who used mind mapping as a study aid improved their factual recall of their readings one week later (Farrand, Hussain, & Hennessy, 2002). Mind maps can be graded the same way as concept maps.

Although the secondary and tertiary ideas radiate out from the center of a mind map, this graphic reflects a hierarchy of ideas. But unlike a concept map, it uses icons, symbols, color, and line thickness to communicate meaning and does not normally label the lines. Of course, you and your students can mix and match features of concept and mind maps to serve your learning purposes. Similarly, graphic syllabi and outcomes maps may also incorporate the visual cues of mind maps. Such colorful and whimsical touches not only add fun to instructional materials but also contribute to learning and retention. Specifically, unexpected novelty and humor attract attention and arouse emotions, releasing neurotransmitters from the limbic system that reinforce associated synaptic connections (Leamnson, 2000; Mangurian, 2005; see Chapter One). Besides, such personal extras testify to your sense of humor, creativity, openness to new ideas, and comfort with students and yourself.

Concept Circle Diagrams

The least well known of the graphics we will look at here, concept circle diagrams illustrate the relationships among concepts in terms of the distances and the overlaps among circles and the relative sizes of the circles. When drawn by the instructor, they can disentangle complex conceptual interrelationships for the students and serve as a memorable image. Of course, students can create their own to clarify their understanding of conceptual interconnections, in which case they should also entitle their diagram and write an accompanying sentence or two to explain its meaning (Wandersee, 2002a).

Here are some basic guidelines for creating these diagrams (Wandersee, 2002a):

1. The relative sizes of the circles reflect the relative importance, quantities, variable values, or level of generality of the concepts.
2. A smaller circle drawn within a larger one indicates that the latter concept encompasses the former.
3. Partially overlapping circles mean that one concept includes some but not all instances of the other concept.
4. Superimposed circles show that the concepts are equivalent and share all the same instances.
5. Completely separate circles denote unrelated or independent concepts.
6. Broken circles convey that the conceptual boundaries are not well understood.
7. Adding color enhances the diagram, especially when the colors of overlapping areas accurately reflect the combination of the circle colors.
8. Detail in a diagram can be shown by projecting out a new diagram of an enlarged section of the original diagram (called "telescoping").

Venn diagrams, which illustrate overlapping concepts and categories by overlapping circles, are the most widely used kind of concept circle diagrams. The simplest example is two partially overlapping circles. How much they overlap depends on the content. If you wish to show the relationship between deviant behavior and illegal behavior, you might overlap the circles about a quarter of the way because some deviant behavior is not illegal (for instance, cross-dressing) and some illegal behavior is not deviant (for example, exceeding the speed limit by five or ten miles per hour).

The more complex Venn diagram showcased in Figure 26.6 demonstrates the full potential of this type of graphic. It illustrates the complicated relationships among different classifications of explicit, first-order, ordinary differential equations (ODEs). Its creator, Daniel D. Warner, professor of Mathematical Sciences at Clemson University, designed it for his sophomore course for engineering and science majors on differential equations and his calculus course for life science majors. He gives it to his students along

Figure 26.6 Concept Circle Diagram (Venn Diagram) for the Classification of Explicit, First-Order, Ordinary Differential Equations

Source: Created by Daniel D. Warner. Reprinted with his permission.

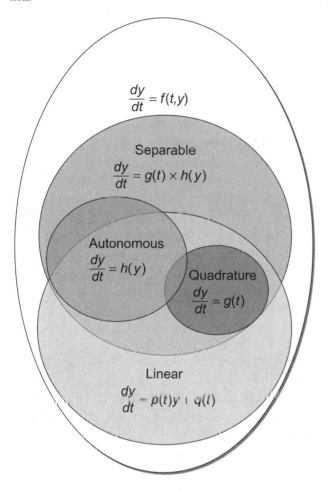

with the assignment of constructing an example of an ODE that is exclusive to each portion of the diagram. (Possible correct answers are in brackets, where a, b, r, N, and Ta are constants.) As the diagram has eight portions, the solution involves eight different ODEs (D. D. Warner, personal communication, April 8 and 16, 2009):

1. General and neither separable nor linear [$dy/dt = a + b \cos(t) \exp(y)$]
2. Separable and neither autonomous nor linear [$dy/dt = a \cos(t) \sin(y)$]
3. Linear and not separable [$dy/dt = a - y/(b - t)$, a mixing model, or $dy/dt = -m \, g \, t - b \, y$, like an object falling with air resistance]
4. Autonomous and not linear [$dy/dt = r \, (1 - y/N) \, y$, logistic growth]
5. Autonomous and linear but not quadrature [$dy/dt = r \, y$, Malthusian growth, or $dy/dt = r \, (Ta - y)$, Newton's law of cooling]
6. Quadrature and not autonomous [$dy/dt = r \, t + a$, variable velocity, constant acceleration]
7. Linear and separable but neither autonomous nor a quadrature [$dy/dt = (t + a) \, (y - b)$]
8. Autonomous and quadrature (a very small set, but not empty) [$dy/dt = r$, constant velocity].

Another type of concept circle diagram is the context map (Hyerle, 1996), which is composed of two or more concentric circles. The outer circles represent the contexts, settings, environments, or frames of reference of the inner circles or the external influences on the inner circles. For instance, sociologists sometimes use a context map to show the different levels of socialization that affect the individual. If you place individuals in the innermost circle, their primary groups—immediate and near-immediate family, close friends and neighbors, and one's minister—occupy the closest concentric circle because these groups have the most direct impact on the focal person. In the next concentric circle are secondary groups, with which an individual may occasionally have direct contact of a more formal type. These include most relatives, school and work associates, colleagues, fellow church members, distant friends, acquaintances, most neighbors, and people with whom one does business. While their influence on the individual is weaker, they often have indirect effects through members of the primary group. The outermost concentric circle represents the broader society, which socializes the individual both directly—through the mass media, political institutions, law enforcement, and economic markets, for instance—and indirectly through its impact on the secondary and primary groups.

Table 26.1   Matrix Comparing and Contrasting Aspects of the Major Wars of the United States in the Twentieth and Twenty-First Centuries

	Duration (Years or Months)	Causes	How Started	Positive Effects for United States	Negative Effects for United States
World War I					
World War II					
Korean War					
Vietnam War					
Desert Storm					
Iraq War					

Since concept circle diagrams can take on several shapes and forms, no scoring formula is available. However, Wandersee (2002a) suggests several evaluative dimensions to consider when assessing a student product: (1) its legibility, clarity, and interpretability; (2) the relevance of the concepts selected to the assignment; (3) the validity of the relationships shown among concepts; (4) the relevance of the title to the diagram; (5) the accuracy and fit of the written explanation; and (6) the appropriate use of graphic options, such as color and telescoping.

Matrices

Matrices may be the least constructivist visual of those considered here, as they are constrained by a table-like format. Yet they can transform linear text and notes into much more useful two-dimensional schemata that invite comparing and contrasting objects, concepts, or categories by any number of properties. As text or notes alone are not set up to engage higher-order thinking, students usually wind up just memorizing them. Matrices also enhance storage and retrieval (Atkinson et al., 1999; Derry, 1984). Kiewra (2005) strongly recommends matrices as learning devices for organizing, analyzing, reviewing, and remembering material, and he furnishes examples that display categories of literature, different schedules of psychological reinforcement, properties of various biological species, and types of atomic particles. If used for assessment purposes, matrices are easy to score on a cell-by-cell basis.

Table 26.1 shows a data retrieval matrix comparing and contrasting aspects of the six major wars in which the United States has fought during the twentieth and twenty-first centuries. The matrix asks students to identify the length of each war, the causes, the precipitating incidents, and the positive and negative impacts on the country. The level of thinking required to complete it depends partially on what the students can and cannot gather directly from course materials. For instance, if the materials have provided the effects of these wars but have not distinguished the favorable from the unfavorable effects, students must evaluate the broader, longer-term ramifications of each war on the country.

■ THE FUTURE OF VISUALS IN TEACHING AND LEARNING

Due to the dominance of television, movies, video games, and the Internet, our culture has been deemphasizing text to communicate information in favor of graphics for decades (Fischman, 2001; Hartman, 2006). The millennial generation has grown up with the full dose of these visual media, and as far as we can tell, subsequent generations will too. This "visual explosion," as Felten (2008, p. 60) terms it, has spread from the popular culture into the scholarly arena. We can now use high-quality digital libraries and galleries—historical, scientific, and artistic—and educational resources, such as those archived at www.merlot.org, www.brocku .ca/learningobjects/flash_content, www.wisc-online .com/, www.shodor.org/interactivate, and www4 .uwm.edu/cie/learning_objects.cfm?gid=55. Many of these resources showcase the power of adding interactivity and animation to the graphics, generating many of today's cutting-edge teaching tools in distance education and computer-assisted instruction: learning objects, virtual and augmented realities, and simulations. These may come to dominate the educational media, elevating visual literacy to an essential skill for understanding and interpreting complex sets of information (Avgerinou & Ericson, 1997; Hodgins, 2000). Such innovations represent just a few of the new high-tech instructional tools, the topic of the next chapter.

One more benefit of graphics—this one particularly important in the global village we now inhabit—is that they communicate across cultures. Many of the conventions used in visuals—such as spatial proximity among closely related elements and the use of arrows to indicate direction or movement—seem to be universal, anchored in the basic human processes of visual perception (Tversky, 1995, 2001).

CHAPTER 27

Using Instructional Technology Wisely

Teaching at its best requires that we consider every educational tool at our command to give our students the richest educational experience possible. After focusing on a wide variety of face-to-face teaching methods and moves, we now turn to integrating technology into courses to enhance students' learning. Although hybrid and online courses share forms of instructional technology, this chapter does not address distance learning per se. But there are many available books, articles, and training programs that do.

As Chapter Twenty-Five points out, students prefer different learning modalities to varying extents. Some students learn most easily by listening and discussing, some by reading and writing, others through graphic representations, and still others by hands-on experience. Since the traditional college classroom is strongly geared to the digital and auditory learning styles, students who are more visually or kinesthetically oriented are often at a disadvantage. Visual aids and simulated experiences, ranging from low-tech chalkboards and flip charts to the most advanced computer simulations and interactive learning modules, help these students excel while reinforcing everyone's learning.

■ RELIABLE LOW-TECH TOOLS FOR THE CLASSROOM

Let's begin with the lowest-tech, most readily available visual aids. They have been around for a long time, and for good reason.

The Ubiquitous Board

You and your students grew up with it. It's in almost every classroom in the nation—though no classroom seems to have enough of them. You might even have one in your office. It now comes in a few colors and a modern, glossy white version with marker pens. In fact, it's so familiar to all of us in the educational sector that we rarely consider how to use it most effectively. All we notice are the times when it's used ineffectively, which is when we can't see or follow what is written on it.

Just because the board represents an old technology doesn't make it an outdated one. It holds at least two benefits for our students. First, it slows us down—both our speaking pace and our movement through the material—giving students a few more precious moments to follow and absorb what we are saying and doing. We might not notice it, but we often speed through the material when we are working off prepared slides or transparencies. Second, while writing on the board, most of us do a better job of modeling our thought processes. We explain them while they unfold. By contrast, PowerPoint slides are designed for lists of items, not cognitive processes.

Below are a few guidelines for board use, which are perhaps intuitive yet all too frequently forgotten (Bartlett & Thomason, 1983):

- Write neatly, legibly, and large, as much as possible on a horizontal (versus diagonal) line, and only on areas visible to all students. If board writing is not your forte, shift to printing. Be very careful with your spelling, especially if you hold students responsible for theirs.
- Use thick chalk in a large classroom, such as "railroad crayon."
- Use different colors of chalk and markers for complex diagrams and drawings to facilitate students' visual understanding of the parts of a process, stages of development, sections of a specimen, and so on.
- Write what you can before class to save time and energy during class.
- Outline material on the board rather than writing sentences, and use symbols and abbreviations wherever possible. Not only does this practice save you time and board space, but it also helps students increase their note-taking efficiency. In addition, try to write quickly so you don't lose students' attention.
- Use the board as an organizational tool, working from far left to right and numbering points as you develop them. Divide different topics with lines or

spaces, but do connect related ideas with lines as well. Underline new terms when defining them. During pauses, step back to evaluate your board work, and correct and clarify points as required.

- Be complete in your presentation, defining critical new terms, giving all steps in a solution, and labeling all parts of your diagrams and technical drawings.
- Practice writing while looking over your shoulder toward the class. At least try to avoid spending much time with your back to the class. During the moments that you must, don't bother talking; your students may not hear you. It is better to pause, turn around, and explain the material while you are making eye contact with the class.
- Ask students occasionally whether they can see your board work. Over an hour, your handwriting may change, or the glare from the windows may settle on different spots.
- Coordinate your words and your board work to reinforce each other. It is best to introduce new material verbally, then outline it on the board, then explain what you have outlined. If you have written out major topics or questions, point to each one as you shift the discussion to it. Also refer to the board regularly to reinforce important points.
- Use the board to record discussion contributions. You can reduce redundancy and help students learn to take notes on discussion.
- Ask the class before you erase something to make sure that everyone has been able to copy it. (Ever hear the horror story of the math professor who wrote on the board with the right hand and followed closely with an eraser in the left?) If someone needs an extra moment, you might move on to a different part of the board, if available, or use the pause productively to ask or answer questions.
- Bring students to the board to display their answers to problems, discussion questions, and the like. They will be less shy about coming up if you begin this routine early in the term and you assign the problems or questions to small groups.

Students don't mind publicly presenting a group solution.

- Avoid wearing very dark clothes on a heavy chalkboard-work day. Or judiciously try to avoid leaning against the chalkboard. They may call it "dustless" chalk, but it isn't!

The Flip Chart

Heavily used at conferences and in boardrooms, the flip chart is rarely seen in a classroom. Yet it has great teaching potential in smaller classes, where it has some advantages. For one, you can write out much of your material in advance and in any color marker. Then you can annotate it and add to it during class. For another benefit, you can preserve the material, both what you prepare and what evolves during a class, from term to term. Finally, rather than erase, you can tear off pages and tape them wherever you want. It may be worth the minor investment to buy your own flip chart or easel and large pad. Some of the same guidelines for board use apply.

The Overhead and the Document Projectors

An overhead projector displays on a screen only what is on a transparency, while a document projector, a much newer technology, displays whatever is on a transparency, piece of paper, or anything else that fits over the plate. For the most part, computers have replaced these projectors, but they still have their place. The guidelines for their use are similar to those for board use. For instance, if you use marker pens on your transparencies or documents, make sure that the colors you select are easily discernible, and be careful to allow students adequate time to assimilate and take notes on the projected material. These projectors have additional intricacies and guidelines for effective use (Head, 1992; Rogers, 1993), which we will see apply to presentation software slides as well:

- Use images and graphics freely. These projectors are perfect for showing concept and mind maps,

symbols, graphs, charts, pictures, tables, matrices, and diagrams.

- Focus on only one concept in a transparency or document, and keep the images as simple as possible. Avoid clutter and multiple images.
- Use key words, not complete sentences, as headings and subheadings to focus students' attention on concepts and relationships.
- Keep the information on each transparency or document to a minimum, not to exceed seven lines of seven words each. More than this is difficult for students to process. Furthermore, the print should be large and clearly legible—at least three-sixteenths of an inch character height. Smaller print may be hard to read from the back of even a small room. For a substantial data set, you may wish to project just a title and to distribute handouts with the actual data—the same for complex graphs, tables, and diagrams.
- Use a pointer, such as a pencil or a laser, rather than your finger.
- Never stand between the projector and the projected images. Doing so blocks the image and is distracting to the class.

Overhead projectors have a few additional rules for use (Head, 1992; Rogers, 1993):

- Design your transparencies to project horizontally on the screen rather than vertically if possible. The horizontal format fits better on the square screen. In fact, the screen often crops off the lower fourth of a vertical transparency.
- Consider using overlays for sequential diagrams, such as when you want to illustrate a process or when you want to reuse some of your transparencies in other contexts. Mathematics, physics, and economics present excellent opportunities for overlaying transparencies. Start with the basic axes, add the curves, then add symbols and explanations. The biological sciences often use overlays to show a succession of specimen sections.
- Eliminate glare by using tinted transparencies instead of the standard clear ones. A soft yellow film

is particularly easy on the eyes. Brighter colors such as green or red can be interjected for emphasis.

- Turn off the projector lamp when not in use, even if you are still talking. This way students stay focused on what you are saying instead of the glaring empty screen.

THE CHOICE OF HIGH-TECH ALTERNATIVES

High-tech has come to mean "computer based," and some of the highest-tech options have grown out of Web 2.0 (really just extended uses of the "old" Web). Our younger students simply assume the existence of personal computers. According to Junco and Mastrodicasa's (2007) survey of 7,705 college students in the United States, 97 percent own a computer, 94 percent own a cell phone, 76 percent use instant messaging and 15 percent of these users are online 24/7, 75 percent are on Facebook, 60 percent own an iPod or its equivalent, 34 percent get their news mostly from the Web, 49 percent download music using peer-to-peer file sharing, 44 percent read blogs, and 28 percent have their own blogs.

Still, the old rule holds true: instructors should choose a technology for sound pedagogical reasons (Albright & Graf, 1992; Knapper, 1982), not just because they think their students think it's cool. After all, computers are only a tool—one most frequently used for communication, business, and data management—and only one of many tools for effective instruction. We can become so fascinated with the bells and whistles that we forget the lower-tech ways to accomplish the same objective just as well. Interestingly, the sound pedagogical reasons that faculty gave for using advanced technology in the 1980s (Lewis & Wall, 1988) still apply:

- A technology may help achieve certain course goals and facilitate certain instructional tasks that are impossible to accomplish otherwise. For instance, a virtual world or learning object may allow students to experience distant times, places, and events to which they lack direct access. For another example, a Web-based simulation may give students the chance to perform lab experiments and procedures that would be too dangerous or too expensive to do in reality, such as surgeries, hazardous chemical procedures, and molecular biology experiments.

- A technology may provide the best available or the only realistic means for you to demonstrate a phenomenon. For instance, chemistry and physics instructors can use a digital simulation or animation to show an atomic structure or a chemical or physical force interaction. Such applications are particularly effective when the phenomenon in question is too large, too small, or too dynamic to convey with printed media, static diagrams, or hand gestures.

- A technology may allow students to drill and practice at their own pace. No one instructor can regularly give every student individual instruction, although we try to do so when necessary. Computer-based tutorials can function in our place, without the time and patience limitations that afflict us mere mortals.

- A technology may help students acquire the technological literacy that their future occupations will require. By learning to use a type of program—spreadsheet, database, information management, statistical analysis, form development layout and design, photography, sound, video, publishing, website development, mathematical, drafting, engineering, and the like—students overcome their anxieties as well as their ignorance and broaden their employment prospects. While the software will probably advance in a couple of years, it is easier to master a new version after having used the previous one.

- A technology may enhance your own and your students' productivity by reducing the time spent on routine record keeping and communication. Grading and attendance records, for example, are most easily managed on a spreadsheet or on the learning management system (Blackboard, for example). Posting announcements, assignments, handouts, and grades on the learning management system saves class time. Sometimes you can even word-process your comments on written assignments and essay exams, since students' papers and responses often display similar strengths and weaknesses.

• A technology may afford you and your students unique conveniences. Various forms of electronic communication facilitate collaboration with and among your students—for instance, team and class discussion boards, wikis, blogs, Del.icio.us, Diingo, and the Track Changes tool on Microsoft Word. Using one or more of these tools, teams of students can collaborate, exchange files and Web resources, and edit projects online at any time. Putting a class journal on a discussion board, wiki, or blog encourages timely and thoughtful responses. Using email, you and your students can confer privately with one another outside class and your office hours.

New technologies give greater latitude in developing your courses but also demand greater care in choosing and using the various technologies appropriately. While just about everyone has used the easier or more ubiquitous types of technology, some of the more advanced kinds require the newest computer hardware, which may be too expensive for many students. Other types have substantial learning curves that drain precious in-class and out-of-class time from your content.

Students have their own views on the instructional value of various technologies. In a Harvard University (2008) survey, those with experience in using a tool not surprisingly rated its utility higher. Students also said they appreciated the conveniences of online course materials—in particular, syllabi with links to readings and resources—and recorded lectures they can replay at any time. In addition, they liked online discussion forums, blogs to connect course material with current events, and foreign video clips on YouTube for learning languages (Harvard University, 2008). In a national survey (Young, 2004), however, students found most online discussion and chat useless, especially when not moderated by the instructor, while course websites and interactive features like preclass online testing on the readings registered high praise. Most of the students'

complaints were about the ways faculty fumbled with and misused technology, especially presentation software, a topic addressed later in the chapter. An even larger national survey found that most students prefer a blend of face time with the instructor and moderate use of technology (Kiernan, 2005).

Let us now take a look at some of the most pedagogically relevant high-tech instructional tools.

■ LEARNING MANAGEMENT SYSTEMS

Also called "course management systems," these are actually packages of instructionally useful software. Some of their tools are designed to streamline the instructor's duties—such as an online syllabus template, a spell-checker, automatic test grading, and a grade book linked to a spreadsheet program. Other features facilitate and expand opportunities for communication and interaction with and among students, extending the classroom beyond its walls and scheduled meeting times.

Among the best-known brands of learning management systems are Blackboard, Moodle, Desire2Learn, eTEA, and Sakai. (You can run product comparisons at www.edutools.info/item_list .jsp?pj=4.) Institutions often purchase one system or select an open-source system for its entire faculty, so you probably will not have a choice. However, these are the online tools that are bundled in a good product:

• Announcements page
• A course site template with subtemplates for the syllabus, course calendar, pop-up glossary, and class roster
• Space for posting course materials (text, graphics, multimedia), such as the syllabus, handouts, assigned readings, lecture notes, student presentations, and directions for assignments
• Space for links to library reserve materials
• Drop-box for homework assignments and take-home tests

- Online testing (timed, untimed, and multiple-tries option)
- Automatic grading (of closed-ended items)
- Grade book (Excel compatible)
- Automatic test feedback to students (on closed-ended items)
- Student survey template
- Student Web page templates
- Spell-checker
- Online help and search
- Email, with a mass mailing option for the instructor
- Class and team discussion boards with threaded discussion options
- Live chatrooms
- Blogs
- Wikis

The last five tools are forms of electronic communication that can augment classroom learning and help develop students' cognitive skills in important ways. The fact that the type of communication is somewhat anonymous and not face-to-face reduces many students' self-consciousness and defensiveness, thereby fostering their involvement and participation. It can also enhance problem-solving skills and creativity (Gallupe & Cooper, 1993) and even stimulate clearer and deeper thinking. As students have to write their questions and responses and frame their messages for clarity and conciseness, the medium encourages more careful and critical thought and clearer writing (Bellman, 1992). But perhaps most obvious, electronic interaction extends your students' learning beyond the classroom, increasing student-active time on task.

The rest of this section elaborates on certain tools in learning management systems that deserve closer examination. We explore blogs and wikis later in the chapter under "Web 2.0 Tools."

Space to Post Course Material

For distance learning students, you have to post all your course materials. But if your course Web presence is a hybrid enhancement of a live course,

consider the impact of posting materials before you do so. Of course, students love the one-stop convenience of obtaining all the course materials whenever and wherever they want (Harvard University, 2008; Young, 2004). But both you and they may pay a price.

If you post your syllabus and assignments and modify them during the term, many students may not notice the changes, not even after alerts on the announcements page. It is safest to alert students to the changes in class or on email. Posting homework assignments, study questions, review sheets, and the like in advance rarely presents problems, but be careful not to post homework solutions and answers until after you grade and return the students' work. Of course, putting up test questions and answers renders those items unusable in the future.

What about posting your complete lecture notes, slide presentations, and class exercises and activities? If you do, you will not have students who miss classes coming to you for information and materials. But unless you make every class more valuable than the documents you post, your live attendance and even participation are likely to drop (Young, 2004).

Many students claim that they benefit from downloading lecture notes and presentation slides before class so they can listen more intently and write fewer of their own notes. Some contend that reading the notes and slides reinforces hearing them (Clark, 2008). But these arguments have a few holes. How deeply are students processing a lecture when they are just following along with prepackaged material? If they are not taking notes, they are not judging what is more or less important, translating the material into their own words, or distilling it down to an abbreviated version (see Chapter Twelve). In addition, reading and hearing words both involve receiving material verbally, essentially in the same modality, so this redundancy does little to enhance learning (Kress, Jewitt, Ogborn, & Charalampos, 2006; Tulving, 1985; Vekiri, 2002). Not surprisingly, then, handouts that duplicate the lecture presentation seem not to increase student learning or improve exam performance (Kinchin, 2006; Noppe, Achterberg, Duquaine, Huebbe, & Williams, 2007).

Therefore, post selectively. If you will lecture, the best document to post in advance is a skeletal outline of your lecture. You can create it in a word processing or a presentation program. Allow plenty of white space between major topics, and advise your students to print it out and bring it to class for note taking. It will enable them to follow your organization. In fact, skeletal notes are the most effective learning aid you can furnish to students for lectures. Because these aids improve note taking, students perform better on tests, suggesting they learn more (Cornelius & Owen-DeSchryver, 2008; Hartley & Davies, 1986; Potts, 1993; see Chapter Twelve). You should also post complex visuals so students don't have to draw them, as well as equations, formulas, and the like that invite copying errors. In brief, feel free to post in advance any materials that are supplementary to, not redundant with, your classes.

But then again, consider the exciting possibilities of making all your lectures outside reading, listening, or viewing assignments (see the "Podcasts and Vodcasts" section below). You then liberate hours and hours of valuable class time for all the discussion, debate, writing-to-learn exercises, group work, simulations, games, and other student-active methods that you may have wanted to integrate into your course but never had the time to include.

Online Preclass Quizzes

Easily administered from a learning management system, regular online quizzes can serve as an incentive for students to keep up with the readings (see Chapter Twenty-Three) or as an inquiry-based diagnostic technique to assess your students' understanding and plan class around clearing up their misconceptions (see Chapter Eighteen). The latter use is called just-in-time-teaching. Research attests that this method raises students' level of preparation for class, participation, engagement, and achievement (Bowen, 2006; Marrs & Novak, 2004; Novak,

Patterson, Gavrin, & Christian, 1999), as long as the quizzes figure substantially into the final grade (Sullivan, Middendorf, & Camp, 2008). Students seem to know the positive effects of online quizzes on their motivation, engagement, and learning, and they endorse them as a wise use of instructional technology (Young, 2004).

Class Email

Email is a one-to-one or one-to-many (through multiple receivers, cc's, or lists) asynchronous communication system by which a sender accesses a mainframe system and leaves a message to be read by one or more receivers at remote locations. One-to-one email with your students can substitute for live office hours and after-class exchanges but without the restrictions of time and place. Your students can contact you individually and confidentially with their questions, to which you can reply individually. This option also saves class time that would otherwise go to individual student questions, concerns, and Socratic dialogue. Using the attachment tool, students can email you homework assignments, papers, and presentations if you don't want to use the drop-box. The mailing list option also saves class time, as you can send your entire class housekeeping messages, reminders, study questions, assignments, tips on doing the readings, and connections between the course material and current events—all in one mailing (Bowen, 2006).

A word of warning: some students, especially younger ones, keep very late hours and may not realize that you might not. They may email you with questions, especially right before tests, in the middle of the night, anticipating a prompt reply. Or they may expect you to be online evenings, weekends, and whenever else they are. In your syllabi (see Chapter Three) you should set explicit limits with your classes about your online availability.

If you distribute a class list of email addresses, your students can also communicate with one another, but you will not be able to monitor them unless they "cc" their course-relevant messages to you.

Discussion Boards

Like email, this form of communication is asynchronous; messages can be sent and retrieved at any time. In addition, they appear on a permanent running record. Once posted, messages cannot be deleted or modified, so you can monitor and, if you wish, grade your students' participation. This type of communication is strictly one-to-many, but "many" can be a small group if you make team discussion boards. Since a class may be discussing a number of topics at any given time during the course, it is best to have threaded discussions where contributions are clearly labeled and organized by topic.

If online discussion will comprise a serious, graded part of your course, you'll need to develop some explicit standards and procedures like these:

- Explain to your students the importance of online discussion in their achieving the learning outcomes of the course (see Chapter Two).
- Decide how the discussion topics or questions will be generated.
- Establish replies as important contributions (Knowlton, Knowlton, & Davis, 2000).
- Explain the difference between high-quality and low-quality contributions, and show examples of both types.
- Define and insist on proper netiquette.
- Give credit to students who answer other students' questions before you do (B. E. Weaver, personal communication, November 15, 2002).
- Even if you set a minimum rate or number of contributions or grade on quantity, also take quality into account when grading.
- Include peer evaluation of student contributions in the grading.
- Model appropriate participation; do not dominate or direct too much (Knowlton et al., 2000).
- Ask questions to encourage clarification, elaboration, and correction (Knowlton et al., 2000).
- Over time shift your role from a participant to a facilitator who may, for instance, synthesize students' contributions around key points (Knowlton et al., 2000).

Chatrooms, Conferencing Software, and MOOs

Synchronous, real-time communication systems like these are less popular than email and discussion boards for several reasons:

- They strongly privilege those who think and type fast.
- They require synchronized schedules of participation.
- They invite netiquette violations, especially chatrooms.
- They encourage free-for-all bull sessions that may wander off the main topic.
- They allow pairs and triads to splinter off into private side conversations.

Still, if somewhat controlled, these tools can play a critical educational role. Team chatrooms can facilitate small-group collaboration, and the instructor can participate. In addition, with conferencing software, you and your students can set up topical folders and share any type of computer file. MOOs (multiple-user object-oriented environments) add graphical interfaces to text-based chat and even allow video- and audio-streaming of lectures and class activities. If you intend to use these tools for discussion, consider explicitly setting up standards and procedures similar to those for discussion boards.

■ LECTURE-RELATED SOFTWARE

While reading this section, keep in mind that a little lecture goes a long way. In fact, only a little lecture, a minilecture, serves instructional purposes effectively (see Chapter Twelve).

Presentation Software

While not interactive, presentation software like PowerPoint can enhance the visual quality and impact of lectures and professional presentations. It allows you to create and project text integrated with images, animations, Web resources, and video clips—all in full color—as well as sound. Even if you intend to display only text and images, this software gives you greater flexibility than overhead transparencies because you can highlight the text or zoom in on the section of the image you are explaining. In addition, you can save and post the presentation for students to download before the live lecture or to review later. If you want to write or draw on your slides, which can be particularly helpful when teaching mathematics, engineering, and the physical sciences, you should project your presentation onto a Smartboard (an interactive white board) or from a tablet PC. Using these technologies, you can save your annotations and digitally distribute the modified slides to your class.

While presentation software is almost essential for conveying knowledge at a distance, it is easy to overuse it in the classroom, especially for text. Such software is merely a complement to lecture and just as student-passive as lecture. So you need to interject student-active breaks within your presentations. You can sprinkle in occasional questions for reflection, discussion (whole class or small group), or informal writing. You can insert short cases or problems to give students practice in application. Or you can strategically place concept-oriented multiple-choice questions to assess students' understanding. Fortunately, clickers are designed to interface with PowerPoint (see Chapter Twelve).

Design Guidelines

Presentation software shines when used to show visually intensive or multimedia material. But when you do make text slides, keep in mind the same rules that apply to text in lower-tech instructional aids, like the overhead and the document projectors (above). Focus on only one concept per slide, use key words rather than complete sentences, and keep the information on each slide to an absolute minimum. Use the templates to help you arrange your information in a logical and pleasing way. Make only your major points on the slides; don't just dump your notes on them. And never read them in class. To students, these are among the most egregious abuses of the software

(Young, 2004). In addition, presentation software may require lower classroom lighting than do overhead transparencies, so it can encourage some students to fall asleep in class.

One more rule applies: restrain yourself from getting wildly elaborate with color combinations, backgrounds, clip art, slide transitions and builds, and attention-grabbing special effects. In instruction, the fewer the glitzy distractions and the simpler the visuals, the better. It is also advisable to keep the same colors and backgrounds throughout a presentation. Nevertheless, students appreciate your mixing in graphics, animations, and Web links and your displaying some design flair with color, pleasing composition, and varying slide layouts. Some students depend on the slides and their movement to stimulate their attention (Clark, 2008).

Student Presentations

Presentation software is for your students' use as well. It encourages them to incorporate multimedia vitality and richness into their class presentations and offers you and your students the freedom to view them outside class. A slide presentation can be run at any time, preserved and revised indefinitely, and integrated into a student's e-portfolio.

Podcasts and Vodcasts

Some faculty record the audio of their lectures as a podcast, allowing their students to listen to them on their computers, cell phones, or MP3 players whenever they want. A few even video-record their lectures as a "vodcast" so their students can similarly view them electronically at their convenience. Both forms allow playback at any time. Special pod-catching software (for example, Camtasia and Echo 360) digitally records the presentations and publishes them on the Internet, then delivers them through a feed to the computers or mobile devices of student subscribers.

The intention of the technology is for students to review lectures, not for them to skip the live presentation and just listen to it or watch it whenever. No doubt, students use podcasts and vodcasts both ways. These recordings do not capture student activities during the class very well and may not pick them up at all, and faculty have no way of monitoring whether students outside the classroom are doing the activities.

Still, this technology has rich potential. Just as you can post your lecture notes on your course website and make them a reading assignment, so can you make your recorded lectures listening or viewing assignments and free class time for student questions and activities. Campus events—such as speeches, debates, radio shows, interviews, ceremonies, and performances—can also be recorded and syndicated the same way, permitting you to assign such events whenever they occur, without concern about your students' or your own scheduling conflicts.

■ WEB RESOURCES

A good reason to have a course website is to incorporate links to other relevant sites. The Web contains a wealth of free resources that you may want your students to read, view, hear, critique, analyze, play, or respond to as an assignment or for course-related research. Because this electronic space is so vast, your campus library or instructional technology center may offer Web-search workshops that can save you hours, even days, of roaming around on a browser. Good browser search engines can also direct you to worthy sites. Perhaps most valuable are your colleagues' referrals to resources in specialized areas. You can post your request for recommended sites on one of your discipline's teaching-focused listservs. Also see the discipline-specific sites listed on the Web page of Clemson University's Office of Teaching Effectiveness and Innovation at www.clemson .edu/OTEI/resources/instructional.html.

Many of the educational computer programs and multimedia presentations that were once sold on CD-ROMs have moved to the Web. (But don't forget to mine the CD-ROM that comes with your textbook.) They usually feature imaginative, high-quality graphics—some with sound, animation, or video—creating a multisensory learning experience that speaks to all learning styles (Lamb, 1992; also see

Chapter Twenty-Five). Many arrange the material nonlinearly and interactively, allowing students to select different learning paths based on the decisions they make earlier in the presentation. Thus, students can pursue the topics of greatest interest of them. With more control over their learning process, they should feel greater ownership of the material. In addition, these resources are accessible to students anytime, anywhere, from any computer terminal with a browser, and they usually contain links to more online sources of relevant information.

Teaching and Learning Tools

Among the Web's resources are an amazing array of free digital teaching and learning tools. Many of these fall under the general category of learning objects, which are self-contained, self-paced, reusable, digital lessons on specific topics; the best of them are animated and interactive. Others of those listed here are simply learning resources:

- Realistic demonstrations, animated or on video (for example, cellular processes at www.cellsalive .com for biology, bioengineering, and the health professions)
- Performances (musical, dramatic, dance, sport)
- Virtual science laboratories for hazardous or costly procedures and experiments (for example, the Chemistry Collective at www.chemcollective.org; see Chapter Twenty-Two for more)
- Case studies
- Simulations (for example, in business, management, sociology, urban planning, political science, environmental studies, biology)
- Setups for experiments student can run on each other (for example, the Senses Challenge on perception at www.bbc.co.uk/science/humanbody /body/interactives/senseschallenge)
- Drills and exercises for remediation, practice, or review (for example, mathematics, reading, foreign languages)
- Teacher resources for K–12 and special education (presentations, exercises, and other activities)
- "Tests" of greater or lesser validity on learning styles, temperament and personality, aptitudes,

career preferences, political ideology, leadership style, and other human dimensions—many free
- Research-worthy multimedia materials

Collections for Multimedia Research

Let's look first at the research-worthy multimedia sites. Here are some extensive, cross-disciplinary collections that you can safely send your students to, and all of them have existed for many years:

- Calisphere at www.calisphere.universityofcalifornia.edu: a huge collection of websites, scholarly materials, images, electronic books, data, and statistics
- Open Learning Initiative at www.cmu.edu/oli/index.shtml: access to publicly available online courses and course materials in a wide range of academic fields
- CSERDA Metadata Catalog at www.shodor.org/refdesk/Catalog: a searchable repository of Web-based teaching materials for mathematics, computer science, and the sciences
- Internet Archive at www.archive.org/index.php: a collection of Internet sites and digitized cultural artifacts (images, audio files, animations); also courses, study guides, assignments, and recorded lectures under Education
- MERLOT (Multimedia Educational Resource for Learning and Online Teaching) at www.merlot.org: thousands of annotated links to free learning materials, most peer reviewed, including entire courses, databases, presentations, and collections
- National Science Foundation Internet Library at http://nsdl.org/index.php: rich and technologically sophisticated instructional materials for the sciences, mathematics, public health, economics, and other fields
- Online Books Page at www.digital.library.upenn.edu/books: access to over thirty-five thousand free books on the Web
- New York Public Library Digital Collections at www.nypl.org/digital: a vast collection of culturally significant images, audio files, videos, books, and literary works.

- Notre Dame's OpenCourseWare at http://ocw.nd.edu: lecture transcripts, syllabi, and other instructional materials in history and the social sciences
- Smithsonian Institution at www.si.edu: virtual access to the world's largest museum (actually nineteen museums), nine research centers, and the National Zoo
- World Lecture Hall at http://wlh.webhost.utexas.edu: access to courses and their materials from around the world in all disciplines

Learning Objects

Depending on the specific object, learning objects can serve multiple purposes. They can make eye-catching demonstrations to spark up your presentations, whole-class activities, or teacher education resources. They can also make appealing student assignments as well as in-class activities in a computer lab or a laptop classroom (see the next section). Since they provide lessons, students can learn on their own and at their own pace by playing or running them any number of times. Both faculty and students perceive learning objects to be powerful teaching and learning tools (Fontana, 1991; Howard-Rose & Harrigan, 2003; Ip, Morrison, & Currie, 2001; Moore, 2003–2004), and one study supports that they are, especially for the students who need the most help (Biktimirov & Nilson, 2007).

Learning objects are housed in open learning object repositories, many of which are searchable by discipline. In some cases, you must join a community. One of the repositories listed below even provides annotated links to additional repositories:

- MERLOT (Multimedia Educational Resource for Learning and Online Teaching) at www.merlot.org: thousands of interactive case studies, simulations, games, and animations for almost every discipline
- Brock University at www.brocku.ca/learning objects/flash_content: twenty high-quality simulations, games, animations, and exercises for English, finance, German, management, mathematics, and psychology

- Wisconsin Online Resource Center at www.wisc-online.com: over twenty-three hundred animations, games, and interactive exercises for many content areas as well as for cognitive, communication, and social skills
- Shodor Interactivate at www.shodor.org/interactivate: interactive lessons and exercises for the sciences and especially mathematics
- University of Wisconsin, Milwaukee Center for International Education at www4.uwm.edu/cie/learning_objects.cfm?gid=55: learning objects for global studies and a few more for the social sciences, plus an annotated listing of dozens of learning object repositories across the disciplines

"Link Rot"

One reason to add links to your course Web page is to avoid violating copyright laws and guidelines (see Chapter Six). But in relying on links for required readings and activities, you encounter another problem, one particularly serious for distance learning courses: "link rot." The links may or may not be there the next time you teach the course, or even later in the term when your students get to them. In three graduate-level biochemistry courses at the University of Nebraska at Lincoln, half of the links disappeared in less than five years (Kiernan, 2002). The only way around link rot is to make online copies of the Web materials and make course links to the copies rather than the originals. But doing this legally requires the written permission of the creators of the materials and may entail a fee (Kiernan, 2002; see Chapter Six).

◼ LAPTOPS IN THE WIRELESS CLASSROOM

During the past decade or so, several universities, law schools, and business schools mandated that all their students have laptop computers and bring them to class, but very few of these institutions set up training programs and incentives for faculty to teach student-actively with laptops. Not surprisingly, most of the mandates were quickly aborted or went on to yield poor to mixed results (Bugeja, 2007; Foster, 2008b; "Georgia System Ends Laptop Program with Debt and Claims of Success," 2001; Mangan, 2001; Olsen, 2001, 2002). Eventually the faculty got fed up with too many students wandering off to renegade sites to do noncourse-related things during classes.

Using Laptops in Class Productively

The few successful pioneers in laptop pedagogy have important lessons to share. Lesson 1 is that faculty need training in how to make good pedagogical classroom use of laptops and how to manage student use of them. Just letting students use them to take notes invites abuse. (Registered disabled students or their note takers are excepted.) Instructors have to seek out or develop useful activities for students to do during class, and as we saw in the previous section, the Web holds some amazing learning experiences. In addition, students may benefit by doing some course work during class because you are nearby to lend help and they can most easily collaborate. Weaver and Nilson (2005) suggest these fruitful uses of laptops in class:

- Students work on online simulations, virtual laboratories, case studies, exercises, or problems, whether instructor developed, in an instructional software package, or on the Web (see "Web Resources" above).
- Students work on individual or team projects online (for example, websites, presentations, or e-portfolios).
- Students analyze a digitized performance.
- Students complete one or more self-assessment instruments (listed in the "Web Resources" section above).
- You facilitate a workshop on writing, research methods, Web page evaluation, Web page development, problem solving, or some other skill, during which students try out the recommended procedures and get quick feedback from you and one another.

- Students conduct Web-based research on a specific topic, then present and pool their findings. Documentary, experimental, survey analysis, and even field research are possible.
- Using a class discussion board, blog, or wiki, students discuss a complex question or issue that you have posted. Students then have a record of the discussion.
- Students exchange their drafts of assignments to give and receive peer feedback.
- While students are watching an in-class demonstration, a live performance, a video, or a student presentation, they record and post their observations, questions, and evaluative feedback. The learning management system's survey tool can be used to make these posts anonymous if preferred.
- You or a student conducts a class survey of opinions, attitudes, beliefs, experiences, or reactions. The survey may also be a classroom assessment activity (see Chapter Twenty-Eight), such as an anonymous ungraded quiz, or it may provide you with midterm feedback on the course.
- Students take timed online quizzes, assuming you implement ways to discourage cheating—for example, making the quizzes low stakes and proctoring judiciously. Students can get nearly instantaneous feedback on online objective tests.
- Students can take in-class essay tests with minimal cheating if they can't read each other's monitors.
- You hold class outside the classroom—at field research or observation sites, in the library, in a gallery or museum, or even in a local coffee shop for the atmosphere.

How essential are laptops to the classroom activities listed above? Certainly laptops enable computer-driven activities without holding class in a computer lab, which usually doesn't allow the instructor and the students to see each other. It is true that some of these activities are quite possible with only low-tech tools. However, laptops enhance the speed and efficiency of these tasks while saving reams of paper and preparing students for an increasingly laptop-oriented work world. They also allow you to extend some of the activities listed above that can capture a student's monitor for projection. You can find many more innovative and productive ideas for using laptops in class in a wide range of disciplines in Nilson and Weaver (2005). Every idea was assessed and found to improve student learning, engagement, or motivation.

Laptop technology is advancing every year. Products are getting lighter, faster, and more reliable, and their battery life is increasing. Furthermore, tablet PCs have extended their utility. As their pedagogical use is in its infancy, laptops and tablet PCs invite more creative experimentation.

Keeping Students on Task

Generally students feel comfortable learning with laptops, but many prefer doing other things with their laptops in class: surfing the Web, shopping, game playing, doing email, talking in chatrooms, trading stocks online, instant messaging with a friend, blogging, twittering, or even viewing pornography. No matter what students may believe, research documents that multitasking is mostly wishful thinking (Crenshaw, 2008; Loukopoulos, Dismukes, & Barshi, 2009). No one can concentrate on two activities, neither of which is semiautomatic like driving, at the same time.

Because part of our job is to attract and maintain our students' attention, we need to remove all the classroom distractions and occasions for incivility that we can. Here is a list of ways to discourage laptop abuse (Weaver & Nilson, 2005):

- Institute strict course policies for laptop use and put them in your syllabus—for instance: "Students should keep their laptops closed unless they are doing an online task that I have assigned. Anyone caught at a renegade site during class will be marked absent for the day."
- Tell students that laptop abuse is discourteous and distracting to their classmates, not to mention discourteous to you.
- Tell them that research shows—and it does—that laptop abuse lowers grades (Fischman, 2009)—just

one more piece of evidence that multitasking is a myth.

- Tell them when to open and close their laptops.
- Whenever possible, have students work on their laptop assignments in groups of three. No one wants to watch someone else shop, play, chat, email, and the like, and three students will seldom be able to agree on a renegade Internet site.
- Set specific objectives for students to accomplish in their in-class laptop assignments and hold them accountable—for example, randomly ask individuals or teams to report their progress to the entire class.
- Set tight time limits for these assignments.
- Walk around the room and stand in the back to watch the students' monitors during these assignments.
- Have students bring their laptops to class only on certain days, and tell them explicitly not to bring them the other days.

Experimenting with Mobile Devices

A few universities are making classroom use of cell phones and BlackBerries, which now have many of the capabilities of laptops but are much smaller and lighter. However, they cannot accommodate certain kinds of software and are not designed for substantial, in-depth writing. Most important, an instructor cannot even see them, let alone monitor and control student use, except in a small class. This is why many faculty require students to turn off and put away these devices during class. Be aware of these pitfalls if you want to experiment with them in the classroom.

■ WEB 2.0 TOOLS

Web 2.0 is simply an extension of the "old" World Wide Web equipped with new software that facilitates communication, commentary, file exchange, and collaboration. Some tools require add-ons (free downloads for the basic utility) to user computers and mobile devices.

Blogs

Also called a "weblog," it is a frequently updated personal website where the "owner" shares opinions, passions, happenings, links, and the like, similar to a journal or a diary. Posts are very easy to make, and only the blog owner can change them. While a stripped-down site is free, it lacks the features that some bloggers may want, such as the abilities to design the site, invite commentators, and post images, audio files, and videos. The host (for example, Blogger, Livelogcity, Livejournal, Squarespace, and WordPress) will also use a free site to display advertising.

Of course, most learning management systems have built-in blogs for your class as a group and each student in it, and these typically have all the features that you and your students are likely to need. Since they are quasi-public (open to the class and specific individuals granted permission), many students do some of their most conscientious writing on blogs and enjoy adding multimedia to their posts. Individual blogs are particularly well suited to journaling. You can also use the class blog like a discussion board and require that students make a specified number of posts on whatever topics. However, blogs do not offer topical threading. Blogs can also be a source of up-to-date reading material. You and your students can sign up to receive updates of the blogs of political and cultural leaders, corporations, nonprofit organizations, action groups, and social forums. (They usually offer syndication, which means they use RSS feed to inform subscribers by email.) If you are going to use blogs, however, you must integrate them into other aspects of the course.

Of course, students need an incentive to post regularly to a class-related blog, just as they do to post to a discussion board. Although you need to check that students have made a post, you need not grade every contribution. You can, for example, have students write a self-assessment of their posts around midterm, comparing theirs to the best ones they have read in the class. This exercise tends to improve the quality of posts in the second half of the course. Then at the end of the term, you can ask students to select and submit their best three posts for a grade (Lang, 2008).

Higdon and Topaz (2009) adapted blogging to just-in-time-teaching. They have their students post to their individual blog their answers to two questions on the readings—the first about the most difficult part of the material and the second about the most interesting part, the material's connection to prior knowledge, or its relevance to their intellectual or career interests. (The first question resembles a standard classroom assessment technique that we cover in the next chapter.) Students submit their responses the night before class and email the link to the blog's RSS feed to the instructor, who (for convenience) aggregates the posts onto a wiki (see below). The instructor scans and grades the responses, looking for common difficulties and themes, then adapts the upcoming class to clear the bottlenecks. According to Higdon and Topaz, just-in-time blogging enhances their students' conceptual understanding, their time on task out of class, their metacognitive reflection on the material, and their ability to transfer knowledge to real-world applications.

Wikis

A wiki is an ever-evolving, collaboratively developed website that allows users to add, remove, edit, revise, update, and make comments to the content, usually including text, images, video, audio files, video, and links. Its capabilities make it ideal for collaborative writing assignments, research, portfolios, and other projects, and the format encourages sharing, reflection, and continual assessment (Madigan, 2006). All the versions of and changes to the document are recorded and attributed, so all users (including the instructor) can easily find out who made what change when and, if expected in the comments, why. Thus, wikis build in accountability.

Wiki space—free or paid, public or private—is available from many dozens of hosts, called "wiki farms," listed at http://c2.com/cgi/wiki?WikiFarms, but most learning management systems also offer it, restricted to students and invited guests. You can

allocate wikis across individual students and teams and to the entire class. You can also allocate read-only and edit rights to each one, allowing students to read but not to modify each other's wikis (Konieczny, 2007). With edit rights to every class wiki, you can also provide students with formative feedback as their product develops (Madigan, 2006). Multiple-page wikis are organized by content. While wikis are user friendly and intuitive, you can find video tutorials at sites such as www.youtube.com/watch?v=-dnL00TdmLY&feature=related, as many students will need an orientation. In fact, you might create a class wiki with wiki instructions and ask students to add tips (Allwardt, 2009).

Scott Moore, professor of business at the University of Michigan, has made extensive course use of classwide wikis for class notes and test questions (Moore, 2009). For each class, he assigns one student the task of taking notes on the class wiki, allowing other members of the class to make corrections and additions. He also invites students to make up and post objective test items (with answers), which others can then improve or elaborate. Students can check and study from the items any time they want, and Moore uses about half of them for actual tests.

While students are motivated to visit Moore's class wiki, they may not find some wikis so obviously useful. Some students back away from discussing difficult topics or critiquing the work of their peers, so you may have to require and monitor regular participation, specify appropriate dimensions for critiquing, and promote and reward serious discussion and constructive criticism (Allwardt, 2009). Like every other student discussion tool, you have to be involved with it to make it a success.

Social Bookmarking Tools

Social bookmarking tools help users to accumulate and organize websites by topic. Therefore, it can facilitate collaborative research that depends on a large number of Web-based sources—in other words, when you or your students outgrow your long lists of browser favorites. The simplest social bookmarking tool is Del.icio.us, which allows users to categorize, annotate, save, manage, and share sites from a centralized collection. It is an add-on you download onto your browser. You can import your "favorites" into your Del.icio.us collection, and your collection is available from any computer with Web access. For the software and text instructions on how to use it, go to http://delicious.com/help. Instructional videos are available at www.youtube.com/watch?v= PIkMS-Co8Vc&feature = related and www.youtube .com/watch?v=meyiH9E60hY&feature=related%20 percent20Diigo.

Diigo does what Del.icio.us does and more. Users can highlight material on bookmarked websites, add "sticky notes," and create groups to pool resources on specific topics. In addition, they can easily post their findings to their blog (even set up automatic daily posting), send multiple annotated and highlighted pages in one email, and post to social networking sites such as Twitter and Facebook. The free browser add-on is available at http://help.diigo.com and video instructions at http://help.diigo.com /home/get-started. YouTube also offers video tutorials at www.youtube.com/watch?v=meyiH9E60hY &feature=related (also includes Del.icio.us), www .youtube.com/watch?v=0RvAkTuL02A, and www .youtube.com/watch?v=kcecBgRd3ig&eurl=http:// blog.diigo.com.

Social Networking Tools

This kind of tool allows you to set up your own social network, which could comprise the students in one of your courses or a broader special interest group. Over 113,000 of these networks exist (as of spring 2009). For educational purposes, a network can define a learning community. Like a face-to-face community, its value depends on the meaningful participation of all users, which can be hard to motivate among students without the instructor's monitoring and intervening. But compared to some other social platforms, networks offer some of the features in Facebook and MySpace that personalize the virtual interaction, so they overcome some of the social roadblocks of online learning. Among your

software options are OpenSocial (also called Ning, which is the name of the company that created it), OpenID, OAuth, Microformats, and Jobber. Video tutorials on OpenSource abound, but you might start with the one at www.youtube.com/watch?v= lVIYhdaavsw. A tutorial on several programs is at www.youtube.com/watch?v=6SYnlH5FXz0&feature =channel.

Twitter is a microblogging and social network utility designed to send and receive very short messages (140 characters long) called "tweets." It is too simple to require instructions; all you need do is sign up for a free account at http://twitter.com. The video tutorial at www.youtube.com/watch?v= ddO9idmax0o explains the typical way people use it: to update what they are doing for the purpose of staying in touch with others. While its instructional value is debatable, it does enable you to connect with your students with bite-size text messages. So you can use it to make quick announcements ("No class today due to snow") and to remind students of upcoming tests and assignments, reaching those who rely almost exclusively on text messaging. You can also incorporate links into your messages, enabling you to publicize a current event or new development relevant to your course.

Because Twitter allows discussion to run parallel to the lecture, a few faculty have experimented with it as a "back channel" during class. Proponents claim it engages students and reduces the social distance between them and the instructor. In addition, students who wouldn't speak up in a large class can tweet their questions, which a teaching assistant can answer immediately or the instructor can do so after class. However, students can't pay attention in class while they are texting, and often the Twitter exchanges roam far off class topics (Young, 2009; Zax, 2009). No doubt some students text to nonclass sites.

Virtual Worlds

Because virtual worlds imitate three-dimensional reality, they offer unique opportunities for experiential learning. The most heavily populated virtual world at the moment is Second Life. If your computer has enough bandwidth to accommodate it, you can join and explore this world by downloading the software, registering, and taking an avatar at http://secondlife.com. A basic membership is free. You can learn all the technical how-to's in short videos accessible at http://secondlife.com/showcase/tutorials, but bear in mind that depending on your objectives for use, the learning curve can be steep. Find out first whether your institution has its own island. If so, you can "landmark" it as "home" and use its space for meeting with others.

As with the Web, it is impossible to keep up with all the new developments and activities in Second Life, but these are among its applications in higher education:

- As a virtual classroom for synchronous meetings in distance learning and hybrid courses. In strictly online courses, synchronous meetings can be difficult to arrange.
- As a place for virtual office hours, consultations, team meetings, and the like.
- As a social laboratory in which students can observe human behavior and conduct small-scale experiments on economic, social, and psychological phenomena (Conklin, 2007).
- As a forum for practicing written and oral communication in a foreign language with native speakers.
- As a role-playing forum for practicing social and interpersonal skills (Walker, 2009)
- For simulations and re-creations, such as businesses, scientific phenomena (such as the cell, basic genetics, and planets), art galleries, historical scenes, geographic sites, theatre performances, and experiments (Conklin, 2007).

For ideas on how to teach in or with Second Life, go to the free online *Journal of Virtual Worlds Research* at http://jvwresearch.org and "101 Uses for Second Life in the College Classroom" by M. S. Conklin at www.dokimos.org/secondlife/education.

■ LOOKING AHEAD

It is almost impossible to forecast the future of instructionally relevant technology. Every few years bring new waves of recording and Internet-based innovations, and this chapter skimmed only the most popular ones up through 2009. Here are some safe predictions, however: in one form or another, the ubiquitous board will stay with us indefinitely. So will electronically delivered and enhanced instruction. But (ironically) the higher-tech tools and software will likely be obsolete in a few years, having been superseded by another version, product, or utility that accomplishes the same purposes in some better way.

The younger generation may drive the changes. After all, it didn't take long for texting and twittering to replace instant messaging on the cutting edge of routine communication. Younger instructors and early adopters will take to the changes naturally, comfortably, and quickly, but many older faculty, not being digital natives, will experience future shock. If they feel pressured to adopt newfangled technologies, they should review the "sound pedagogical reasons" for doing so given early in this chapter. If the new technology meets one or more of those standards, they should consider embracing it. They should also feel free to ask others for help and training. After all, instructional technology is a complex, specialized field in which expertise and proficiency require a graduate degree, plus a commitment to lifelong learning. Few people can pick it up and stay current on their own. You can (try to) keep abreast of the latest high-tech improvements and innovations by following publications like *Syllabus, E-Learning, EDUCAUSE Review, IEEE Computer Graphics and Applications, Innovations,* the *Journal of Virtual Worlds Research,* the *International Journal of Mobile Learning,* the *International Journal of E-Learning,* the *Journal of Educational Multimedia and Hypermedia,* the *Journal of Interactive Learning Research,* and the *International Journal of Instructional Technology and Distance Learning.*

PART 6

ASSESSING LEARNING OUTCOMES

CHAPTER 28

Assessing Student Learning in Progress

No doubt you can recall classes when you would have liked to have known what your students were learning from your lesson and whether you should proceed with the next one. Perhaps you found out what they missed from a test you gave three weeks later. Obviously it is much more cost-effective to assess your students' learning while in progress, before their shortfalls in understanding adversely affect their grades and motivation. Such information can also help you evaluate, and ultimately enhance, your teaching effectiveness. It can even direct your students to the areas on which they need to focus their studying. We call this useful feedback to both you and your students *formative assessment,* as it helps to shape and focus your subsequent teaching and their subsequent learning. Its goal is always to help students learn better (Prégent, 1994).

■ CLASSROOM ASSESSMENT TECHNIQUES

Classroom assessment techniques (CATs) were developed precisely to serve these purposes (Angelo, 1991a; Cross & Angelo, 1988). You can use them regularly or intermittently without violating the structure and content of your course and quickly identify trouble spots your class is encountering. Knowing what your students did not absorb the first time through the material, you can turn around a potentially disappointing situation. Perhaps classroom assessment is not all that much different from the informal, sometimes unconscious gauges you already use, such as reading your students' expressions and body language and asking and answering questions. But these are unreliable and rarely encompass the whole class. CATs formalize and systematize the process, ensuring that you assess all your students. Given their purpose, they are especially appropriate for student-active lecture breaks, but they make stimulating warm-up activities at the beginning of class and good wrap-up exercises at the end of class.

All good CATs share these features (Angelo & Cross, 1993):

- *Learner centered.* While it is no substitute for appropriate teaching methods or graded examinations, classroom assessment aims to help students learn better. It can help them improve their study habits and their listening skills and push them to correct their mental model of the discipline

- *Teacher directed.* You have total freedom to decide what will be assessed, how it will be assessed, how the results will be analyzed, and how they will affect further actions. Be sure, then, that your CATs address factors that you are willing and able to change or improve.

- *Mutually beneficial.* As students actively participate in the process of classroom assessment, CATs reinforce their learning of material. Like the student-active lecture breaks described in Chapter Twelve and the writing-to-learn exercises covered in Chapter Seventeen, good CATs make your students review, retrieve, apply, analyze, synthesize, or evaluate the material in your lectures, classroom activities, and reading assignments as well as their prior learning experiences. Furthermore, because classroom assessment underscores your interest in your students' progress, it can also boost student motivation. In turn, you benefit from the feedback on the effectiveness of your teaching methods and moves.

- *Formative.* Unlike summative evaluations such as graded quizzes, tests, and assignments, CATs are usually anonymous, ungraded, and geared strictly toward student learning.

- *Context specific.* CATs work differently in different classes. Since you know your classes best, you can tailor CATs to their specific personality and needs, as well as to your discipline, materials, time constraints, and educational priorities.

- *Ongoing.* Ideally CATs provide a continual educational feedback loop, informing you about your students' learning, to which you in turn adjust your teaching, back and forth, until the end of the term.

- *Rooted in good teaching practice.* Classroom assessment builds on current teaching practices, making them more systematic, effective, and flexible. For example, by using a simple diagnostic pretest, you can find out how well prepared your students are to tackle your learning outcomes. You can then pitch your presentations to their actual level, covering more or less material than you might have otherwise.

Angelo and Cross (1993) suggest a three-step plan for successfully launching classroom assessment. First, *start small*. Select one class in which you are confident things are going well and do a simple, short, low-effort CAT—for example, the one-minute paper, the one-sentence summary, directed paraphrasing, or the muddiest point. Second, *give detailed directions and a rationale*. Tell students what you are doing and why. They will need explicit instructions and the assurance that their responses will be anonymous and used solely for mutual improvement. Allocate a few extra minutes the first time through any CAT. Finally, *respond to the information you gather*. After you have reflected on your students' responses, take some time to share them with your class. If you decide to modify your teaching as a result, tell your students what you will do differently and why. Equally important, give them pointers on how they can improve their learning.

Selecting Appropriate CATs

Different CATs are designed to measure students' progress in different types of learning. So before selecting a CAT, consider which type you wish to assess (Angelo, 1991b). *Declarative learning* is "learning what"—that is, learning the facts and principles of a given field. In terms of Bloom's (1956) taxonomy of cognitive operations (see Chapters Two and Fourteen), declarative learning focuses on knowledge and comprehension at the lower-level end of the scale. *Procedural learning* is learning how to do something, from the specific tasks of a given discipline to universal skills such as writing, critical thinking, and reasoning. Its emphasis is application. The third type, *conditional learning,* is learning when and where to apply the acquired declarative knowledge and procedural skills. Too often taught only implicitly through example and modeling, it can be better taught explicitly using the case method, problem-based learning, role playing, simulations, and service-learning (see Chapters Fifteen, Nineteen, and Twenty). While conditional learning clearly entails application, it also involves analysis and synthesis. Finally, *reflective learning* is learning why, which engages students in analysis, synthesis, and evaluation. It directs their attention to their beliefs, values, and motives for learning about a particular topic. Without this reflection, higher education is little more than job training.

Some Tried and True CATs

Chapter Seventeen introduced several popular CATs that also serve as writing-to-learn exercises: the one-minute paper, the one-sentence summary, directed paraphrasing, dialectical notes, and learning logs. Angelo and Cross (1993; also Cross & Angelo, 1988) describe dozens of other techniques, among which are the following.

Background Knowledge Probe: Moderate Instructor Effort and Low Student Effort

This is essentially a diagnostic pretest to administer on the first day of class or when you begin a new unit of instruction. It can consist of two or three short answer or essay questions or fifteen to twenty multiple-choice items about students' attitudes and understanding.

This CAT provides information not only on your students' prior knowledge but also on their motivation, beliefs, values, misconceptions about the subject matter, and, if you use open-ended questions, their writing skills. The results also tell you what material to cover and what existing knowledge you can use to map on new knowledge. Finally, probes activate students' prior knowledge, readying them for additional learning.

Focused Listing: Low Instructor and Student Effort

You can use this technique to activate students' prior knowledge before you teach a topic and to help them review afterward. Direct students' attention to a single important name, concept, or relationship, and ask them to list as many related concepts and ideas as they can. You might limit the exercise to two to three minutes or five to ten items. With these constraints, the results give you a pretty accurate picture of the features students identify and recall as salient and not just those they think you want to hear.

Memory Matrix: Moderate Instructor Effort and Low Student Effort

Memory matrices stress recall of course material, but they also require students to organize it in a graphic framework you provide. Start by drawing a matrix with content-appropriate row and category headings. Leave sufficient space for several one-word or phrase responses in each cell. Distribute copies for your students to fill in, with a limit on the number of items they can write in each cell. This limit keeps students from stalling in search of the one best answer. Collect and examine the matrices for completeness and correctness.

Memory matrices show you how your students organize knowledge and whether they properly associate principles and concepts. In addition, matrices help visual learners excel, facilitate students' retrieval of large amounts of information, and are easy to evaluate.

Muddiest Point: Low Instructor and Student Effort

Very simply, ask your students to write down what they perceived as the muddiest point in a lecture, an assigned reading, a video, a demonstration, a discussion, and so on. Reserve some time at the end of class to ask and answer questions; then collect the student responses. You can clarify the muddy points during the next class.

Perhaps the easiest CAT to implement, you can use it on the spur of the moment. Struggling students who are not comfortable asking questions publicly find it to be a lifeline. In addition, it enables you to see the material through your students' eyes, reminding you of the many different ways they process and store information. Finally, knowing that they will have to identify a muddy point induces students to pay closer attention in class. And when the time comes for the CAT, they have to review whatever learning experience they are reflecting on.

Concept Maps: Medium to High Instructor and Student Effort

Covered in detail in Chapter Twenty-Six, concept maps are diagrams that spatially show the mental connections (labeled lines) that students make among various concepts (written in circles). They help visual learners get their minds around abstract relationships and give you a graphic view of your students' organization of the knowledge. For instance, you might ask your students to concept-map the process of photosynthesis, the structure of the U.S. government, or the dynamics of racism.

If your students are not accustomed to drawing maps, diagrams, and flowcharts, work through an example or two with the class. Start by writing a focal concept on the board, then ask your students to brainstorm related concepts and terms, beginning with primary (closest) associations, then secondary and tertiary ones.

Paper or Project Prospectus: Moderate to High Instructor and Student Effort

A prospectus is a detailed plan for a project or paper—perhaps even a rough draft—that focuses students on the topic, the purpose, the issues to address, the audience, the organization, and the time, skills, and other resources needed—in fact, whatever

guidelines you provide for the final product. First, students need to understand these guidelines—that is, the important facets and likely pitfalls of the assignment. For the prospectus itself, you might compose a list of three to seven questions that students must answer. Of course, advise students not to begin substantive work on their actual assignment until they receive feedback on their prospectus from you and possibly other students. This CAT is a major assignment in itself, so you may want to make it required and grade it, but without counting it heavily toward the final grade.

The prospectus accommodates many different types of assignments and teaches crucial, transferable planning and organizational skills. In addition, it gives students early enough feedback to help them produce a better product.

Everyday Ethical Dilemmas: Moderate to High Instructor and Student Effort

For this CAT, you begin by locating or creating a brief case study that poses an ethical problem related to the material (see Chapter Nineteen). Then write two or three questions that force students to take and defend a position. Let your students turn in their written responses anonymously, thus giving you an honest overview of the prevailing class opinions and values. Students will need some time to reflect and develop their arguments, so you might assign this CAT as homework.

This CAT encourages students to try on different values and beliefs, thus helping them develop moral reasoning skills. It also affords you probing, personal glimpses into your students' ethical and cognitive maturity. With these insights, you can foster their continuing growth by introducing values and opinions that they have not yet considered.

Self-Confidence Surveys: Low to Medium Instructor and Student Effort

As the name implies, this CAT consists of a few simple questions about your students' confidence in their ability to perform course-related tasks. Design a brief, anonymous survey focusing on specific skills and tasks. Find the low-confidence areas in the results, and give additional instruction and practice accordingly. Self-confidence surveys help you identify your students' areas of anxiety and establish the minimal levels of self-confidence necessary for success in the course.

Punctuated Lectures: Low Instructor and Student Effort

After your students listen to your lecture or demonstration, stop for a moment and ask them to reflect on what they were doing during your presentation and how it helped or hindered their understanding. Have them anonymously write out and turn in their reflections. After reading their responses, offer suggestions on how they can improve their listening and self-monitoring skills. Through your feedback, this CAT helps students hone these skills, both of which are highly transferable. It also better acquaints you with your students' processing styles and pitfalls.

Application Cards: Low Instructor and Student Effort

After a lecture segment, demonstration, or video on procedure, principle, or theory, have students write down on a card or piece of paper one or more real-world applications of the material. As you read through them, select the best ones from a wide range of examples to read to the class at the next meeting. This CAT gives students practice in transferring knowledge to useful applications.

RSQC2 (Recall, Summarize, Question, Connect, and Comment): Low to Medium Instructor and Student Effort

This technique assesses your students' recall, comprehension, analysis, synthesis, and evaluation of recent material. Begin by having students list the most important points they can remember from the previous class (or the assigned reading). Second, ask them to define as many terms as they can in one-sentence summaries. Third, have them write one or two questions about each point that still confuses them. Fourth, ask them to connect each important point

they identified with either other important points or your learning outcomes for them. Finally, have them write an evaluative comment about the course, the class period, or the material (for example, "What I enjoyed most/least...") "What I found most/least useful..."). Each of the five activities requires at least two minutes. If you can spare the time, let students compare their responses among themselves. Of course, feel free to pick and choose the activities you find most useful.

RSQC2 gives you timely feedback on what your students consider important material and what they value about your course. By having them recall the previous class and make connections, this CAT also builds bridges between old and new material.

◾ FORMATIVE FEEDBACK

Formative feedback is the sum of recommendations we give students for improving their work at an early stage, with the expectation that they will revise it accordingly. When you comment on drafts of papers or projects or you have your students comment on each other's drafts, you are providing formative feedback. If you attach a grade to such drafts, it should be mainly to motivate student effort during the work's development and should count only for a portion of the work's final grade.

This type of feedback benefits both you and your students in several ways. For them, it encourages steady writing and work habits, it gives them criteria on which to improve their work and their communication skills, and it teaches them the professional creation process, which always involves extensive revision. For you, it yields much better student products, practically eliminates plagiarism, and changes your role from judge to facilitator.

These suggestions will make formative assessments of papers and projects more productive:

- Strictly enforce deadlines for students to find topics, gather resources, develop an outline, and submit a first draft. Formative assessment takes time.

- Comment more on major writing issues, such as content, reasoning, and organization, and less on style and grammar.
- Make your comments constructive, personalized, and informal. Give praise where deserved, because students often do not know what they are doing right.
- Involve your students in providing useful, valid, and objective peer feedback by preparing a list of nonevaluative questions that ask students to identify features or parts of the work, as each student sees them, or to give their personal reactions to the work (Nilson, 2002–2003, 2003). Chapter Seventeen furnishes details.
- If you think your students are cognitively and emotionally mature enough to appraise each other's work, teach them to do so by modeling and explaining the process. Provide your own detailed comments on the drafts of the first paper, review your feedback methods with your class, then oversee their comments on the drafts of the second paper. After that, students should be able to provide decent peer feedback on their own.
- Make sure students understand that formative feedback focuses on major problems in their work and that making the suggested changes does not guarantee them an A.

■ STUDENT PORTFOLIOS

While very different from anonymous, one-time CATs, student portfolios allow you to assess and document your students' progress across written products without attaching grades. A portfolio is a collection of samples of a student's work during the term, one that you and she may assemble together, along with her written reflections on the products or her own intellectual progress through writing them. It may take the form of a notebook or folder or a website; if the latter, it is called an electronic portfolio or e-portfolio. The samples may be the student's best work, the widest variety of her good work, or the history of one or more major pieces of work—such as notes, outlines, peer and instructor reviews, and multiple revisions in response to those reviews (Bernhardt, 1992; Zubizarreta, 2009). You grade only the total portfolio and the student's reflections, typically at the end of the course.

Beginning in the 1980s, student portfolios started to acquire a strong following among English instructors from primary through postsecondary levels. Those who use them testify that portfolios encourage constructive dialogue between students and the instructor and motivate students to attempt more varied and adventuresome writing, take instructor and peer feedback seriously, and revise their work, often several times. Instructors in many disciplines, even mathematics and business, have developed their own versions of the portfolio, most of which encourage more creative demonstrations of learning than do traditional assignments and tests (Belanoff & Dickson, 1991; Crowley, 1993; Zubizarreta, 2009).

Consider, for example, the imaginative range of assessment artifacts that a mathematics portfolio can contain: samples of journal entries; written explanations for each mathematical step of a complex problem solution; a mathematics autobiography focusing on changing attitudes and new insights; multiple solutions to a challenging problem, each reflecting a different approach; an elegant proof, either intuitive or formal depending on the student's abilities; student-developed lesson plans for teaching a particular mathematical concept; student-developed word problems; student-drawn visual representations of problems; student-made concrete representations; and reviews of mathematical books and journal articles—all in addition to examples of traditional student output, such as tests, quizzes, and homework (Crowley, 1993; Stenmark, 1989, 1991).

Portfolios are not without their problems, however. For example, postponing gradings until the end of the course will not necessarily save you grading time. Quite the contrary. While you may not have to affix letters or points to students' work until the end, you will probably assign more and more varied writing projects and put more time and effort during the term into giving formative feedback and holding student conferences on each project. Without this detailed, personalized feedback, none of the potential benefits of portfolios will accrue. In addition, you will otherwise suffocate at the end of the course under an avalanche of paper or Web pages filled with only vaguely familiar writing samples. In the terms used above to describe CATs, portfolios entail very high effort on both your own and your students' part (Bernhardt, 1992; Zubizarreta, 2009).

Another serious problem for many students is the lack of grading during the term. Often they are anxious not knowing where they stand and how they are doing, and some need to know early in the term to decide whether to stay in the course. Academic regulations may not even allow such postponement of grades. At some universities, faculty are required to disclose midterm grades or to submit deficiency reports on students earning a C− or lower, and curriculum committees will not approve new courses unless a substantial part of the final grade is determined by the middle of the term.

A final challenge with using portfolios pertains to grading standards. If a portfolio contains only students' best work, how can anyone in the class not receive a good grade? But the converse problem also arises: some instructors resist assigning deservedly low grades to students who have worked so hard during the term. Even with herculean effort, some students barely pass a course, and it can be very difficult for an instructor to break the bad news to them after all the time spent counseling and conferencing with them.

Therefore, before adopting student portfolios, consider the following issues about delayed grading: how your students might respond to it, if your institution's academic regulations accommodate it, and whether you can uphold your quality standards in

spite of it. Then ask yourself if you can make the time to give your students' work the detailed, ongoing feedback that is required.

■ EXTENDING CLASSROOM ASSESSMENT TO CLASSROOM RESEARCH AND THE SCHOLARSHIP OF TEACHING AND LEARNING

If you are collecting and examining systematic data on the teaching effectiveness or student appeal of one method over another, why not write up and publish your more interesting results? This type of research is the backbone of the college teaching field, as well as the foundation of this book. It has been labeled "classroom research" and "action research," but it is now most commonly called "the scholarship of teaching and learning." You probably already know how to conduct this kind of research, especially if you are in psychology, education, or one of the social sciences. Research on teaching typically relies on a quasi-experimental or a survey design, or it describes and assesses an innovative method or curriculum (Nilson, 1992). The proper design may require your collaborating with colleagues who are teaching the same or similar courses (Cross, 1992) or your conducting a longitudinal study of classes before and with the "treatment."

If you plan to conduct a survey of your students or use student products for your research, you must contact your university's research compliance office at least a few weeks before you begin and inquire about having your research plan reviewed by its Institutional Review Board (IRB). Typically IRBs grant classroom research an exemption, but you need evidence of its review. A violation can cost your institution federal funding.

In addition, you probably have some background reading to do. Much of the scholarship of teaching and learning is anchored in learning theory or cognitive psychology, and your particular research topic may have already inspired a body of literature. You can search for relevant articles—and find publication outlets—in the hard copy and electronic journals and newsletters on college teaching. Some specialize in a given discipline, a few in a specific teaching method (such as cooperative learning or instructional technology), but most are general. Although each journal favors one or two types of articles, they collectively publish standard research studies, literature reviews with insightful conclusions, evaluative descriptions of teaching innovations (how-to articles), philosophical statements, and analyses of current educational policies, problems, and trends (Nilson, 1992). You should skim recent issues of several journals to find those that publish manuscripts

similar to yours. Look for such periodicals in your institution's main library, education library, or teaching center library, and find electronic journals (some are free) using a Web search engine.

Research on teaching is not new. Decades before Cross and Angelo (1993) started promoting the idea, economics and physics ushered in scholarly, scientific inquiry into student learning and achievement, the most important outcome we can assess. These fields have been on the forefront ever since, largely because its members have been able to agree on the learning outcomes for certain courses and to develop standardized tests to measure their attainment. Until other disciplines can reach a similar consensus, their research predicting to student learning will be limited to small classroom samples.

CHAPTER 29

Constructing Summative Assessments

A *summative assessment* is a performance evaluation that is intended to establish a recorded, final judgment about the performer's competence. By contrast, *formative assessment,* as we saw in the previous chapter, is intended to furnish helpful feedback to the performer. A summative judgment may take the form of a grade, score, rating, ranking, or personnel decision. Typically much of the final grade that we give students is based on summative assessment instruments called tests or exams, the shorter version of which are called quizzes, and writing assignments, which may also use visual or sound media in addition to writing. This chapter summarizes the best practices in test construction and techniques for designing meaningful summative assessments—first objective test items and then essay tests and writing assignments. In addition, it examines the advantages and disadvantages of all types of test items.

■ GENERAL TESTING GUIDELINES

Summative assessment is serious business to your institution and especially to your students. If they are consistently performing poorly on your tests, you might find the reasons in this section.

It's All About Outcomes

As Chapter Two explains, teaching at its best begins with developing and sequencing assessable student learning outcomes, then selecting the teaching formats, methods, and moves that are most effective for helping students achieve those outcomes. Excellent teaching also entails appropriate assessment—specifically, constructing instruments that measure, as directly as possible, the students' success in achieving those outcomes. In the end, all three phases of instruction—outcomes setting, teaching, and assessing—should be woven into a multifaceted arrangement of interdependent parts, each reflecting and reinforcing the others.

Therefore, before you begin writing a quiz or an exam, think seriously about what you are trying to accomplish with it. A test can assess just short-term memory skills or the abilities to comprehend, apply, analyze, synthesize, and evaluate the material as well (Bloom, 1956; see Chapters Two and Fourteen). Review your learning outcomes, and identify each one's cognitive level. If they focus primarily on knowledge, comprehension, and application, then so should your test questions. Unless you have taught your students and given them practice in thinking at the higher levels, questions pitched at these levels will not measure your students' attainment of your outcomes. In other words, your tests will not be valid (Jacobs & Chase, 1992; Suskie, 2004; Walvoord & Anderson, 1998). In addition, your students will be doomed to perform poorly.

Lessons Learned by Experience

The following recommendations represent much of the conventional wisdom on test construction (Jacobs & Chase, 1992; Lacey-Casem, 1990; Ory & Ryan, 1993; Suskie, 2004; Walvoord & Anderson, 1998).

- *Test early and often.* Frequent testing yields benefits for both you and your students. Early testing furnishes students with feedback they can use to optimize their course performance. Frequent testing gives them more opportunities for success, reducing the penalties for any single poor performance. It also enhances the reliability of your overall assessment—that is, its stability, repeatability, and internal consistency. Over more test items and occasions, the effects of random errors, such as students' misinterpretations and distractions, tend to weaken.

One recent experimental study on two sections of a social statistics course backs up these claims (Myers & Myers, 2007). Both sections had the same content, instructor, and textbook, but the control

section had only two midterms and a final and the experimental section had biweekly exams and the same final. The students in the experimental section scored one letter grade (ten percentage points) higher on their biweekly exams and a grade and a half (fifteen percentage points) higher on their final than did the students in the control section. Moreover, the control section had a withdrawal rate of 11 percent versus the experimental section, which had no withdrawals. The course and the instructor evaluations also differed markedly, with the experimental section getting much higher ones.

- *Compose test questions immediately after you cover the material in the class.* The material and the cognitive levels at which you taught it are fresh in your mind. Practiced regularly, this strategy ensures you a stock of questions to use when quiz and exam times arrive. Alternatively, you can have your students develop these questions at the end of class or as homework. They will want to compose clean, challenging ones to increase the odds that theirs will appear on a future test. After all, they know the answers to the ones they made up.

- *Give detailed, written instructions for all tests.* Remind students about your and your institution's policies on academic dishonesty (see Chapter Eight). Also specify how much time the test is allotted, how many questions of each type, how many points each item is worth, where to record answers, whether to show work, and whether books, notes, or calculators can be used. Do not assume that your students committed all this information to memory just because you announced it in class, in a handout, or somewhere on the learning management system.

- *Start the test with some warm-up questions.* Asking a few easy questions at the beginning of an exam gives students some low-stress practice in retrieving the material and builds their confidence.

- *Have another instructor evaluate the test for clarity and content.* This is a particularly good idea if you are somewhat inexperienced at teaching or at the type of items you are using. You may have written a quiz or exam that seems crystal clear to you, only to find out later that certain items were double-barreled, ambiguously phrased, or awkwardly constructed. Writing good test items is a hard-to-learn craft, and you need not learn it all by bad experience.

• *Proofread the test form for errors.* Check for spelling and grammar mistakes, split items (that is, items that begin on one page and continue on the next), inconsistencies and errors in format, missing or ambiguous instructions, and inadequate space for constructed responses. It is best to have another set of eyes—those of a colleague, your teaching assistant, your supervising professor, or even a friend or family member—proofread the test form too.

• *After the test, conduct an item analysis of your new objective items.* If your completions, true-false, matching, multiple-choice, and multiple true-false items are machine- or computer-graded, check whether the overwhelming majority of your students missed certain questions. If so, these items are suspect, so you should examine them carefully for unclear or ambiguous wording. Check also for any items that all or almost all the students answered correctly. These items are also suspect because they failed to discriminate the more from the less knowledgeable students. They probably were too obvious or easy to guess right due to unintentional cuing in the wording. This type of item analysis is the basic one. To refine your analysis, you have to be able to identify the best 10 to 15 percent of your students in the class, in which case you must have either tested the class previously or accessed all your students' academic records. Either way, your best students' item responses become your point of comparison. If all or almost of them missed an item, it is probably faulty. If they answered an item correctly and only a few in the rest of the class did, it is highly discriminating.

■ OBJECTIVE TEST ITEMS

In general, summative assessment instruments come in two types: *objective* and *constructed response,* otherwise known as essay questions or writing assignments

(Ory & Ryan, 1993). The objective varieties—completion (fill-in-the-blank), true-false, matching, multiple choice, and multiple true-false, the least known and used on the list—are typically test questions. Known for measuring knowledge and comprehension, most types can also assess higher-order thinking very efficiently. Since most objective items can be graded by a scanning machine or a computer, they make regular assessment in large classes possible. However, none can measure students' abilities to create, organize, communicate, define problems, or conduct research.

Inexperienced instructors may think that objective questions are easy to construct, but unambiguous and discriminating ones take time and thought. Professional test writers may produce only eight or ten usable questions a day. However, be wary of test bank items that come with your textbook. They are rarely, if ever, composed by professionals, and they tend to tap only factual knowledge, sometimes of the trivial variety.

The rest of this section lays out the advantages and disadvantages of each type of objective item and furnishes guidelines for constructing them (Brookhart, 1999; Gronlund & Waugh, 2009; Jacobs & Chase, 1992; Jacobsen, n.d.; Lacey-Casem, 1990; Ory & Ryan, 1993; Suskie, 2004). Each type has its place, and some students do better with some types of questions than with others. Using a variety of questions on an exam allows students to feel more secure with the test format. Remember that you can teach your students to write good questions before the test.

Completion (Fill-in-the-Blank)

These items measure only how well students have memorized facts, terms, and symbols, but some material is so basic that students have to be able to reproduce it. This type of item is well suited to mathematical problems—assuming you do not need to see how your students arrived at the answer—because they have only one exact right answer and students can't work backward from given options, as they can from multiple-choice items. However, in other fields, the one right answer may have several acceptable versions. If the correct answer is John Fitzgerald Kennedy, you might consider John F. Kennedy, John Kennedy, Jack Kennedy, J. F. Kennedy, Kennedy, J.F.K., and some of the possible misspellings of Kennedy acceptable. In such cases, you cannot computer-score completion items unless you can anticipate and specify every possible variation of the correct answer that you will accept as right. Your alternative is to restrict all fill-ins to one word and insist on the correct spelling.

Advantages

- Easy to prepare and grade
- Assesses knowledge, recall, and vocabulary well
- Eliminates guessing
- Can test a lot of material in a short time

Disadvantages

- Cannot assess higher levels of cognition
- Highly structured and inflexible; may require an all-or-nothing response
- Not useful as a diagnostic tool
- May include grammatical clues
- Difficult to construct so that the desired response is unambiguous
- Difficult to grade if more than one version of the right answer may be correct

Construction

- Allow thirty seconds to one minute per item.
- Use clear wording to elicit a unique response.
- Avoid grammatical cues. Use *a/an* and *is/are,* for instance, to reduce cluing.
- Omit only significant words from the statement.
- Omit words from the middle or end of a statement, not the beginning.
- Make all fill-in lines the same length.
- Place the response lines in a column to the left or right to facilitate grading.
- Use familiar language that is similar to what you and the readings have used to explain the material.

True/False

This type of item encourages guessing because students have a fifty-fifty chance of getting an item right. It also tends to focus on recall of terms and facts, sometimes trivial ones. You can eliminate both limitations by having students correct false statements. But then you cannot use a machine or computer to grade these items; the job will fall to you.

Advantages

- Usually easy to prepare and grade
- Can test a lot of material in a short time
- Can tap higher levels of cognition by having students correct the false statements
- Useful as a diagnostic tool if students correct the false statements

Disadvantages

- High guessing factor for simple true-false questions
- May be difficult to think of unequivocally true or false statements
- Encourages instructors to test trivial factual knowledge
- Often fails to discriminate the more from the less knowledgeable students because the best students may see too many nuances, read in multiple meanings, or conceive of exceptions
- May be ambiguous
- May include verbal clues (for example, questions with *usually, seldom,* and *often* are frequently true, while those with *never, always,* and *every* are commonly false).

Construction

- Allow thirty seconds to one minute per item.
- Use only statements that are entirely true or entirely false.
- Focus each statement on a single idea or problem.
- Write positive statements. Negative and double-negative statements are confusing.

- Avoid verbal cues to the correct answers (for example, *usually, seldom, often, never, always,* and *every*).
- Use familiar language that is similar to what you and the readings have used to explain the material.
- Roughly balance the number of true and false answers.
- Avoid always making true statements long and false statements short, or vice versa. Students quickly pick up on these patterns.
- Avoid direct quotes from lectures or readings requiring only rote memorization.
- Add higher-level cognitive challenge and assessment validity by having students rewrite false statements to make them true.
- Allow students to write a rebuttal to your marking their answer wrong for a small percentage of the items.

Matching

One way of looking at matching items is as a set of multiple-choice items that share the same set of responses (Suskie, 2004). The key to composing them is to assemble homogeneous items in the stimulus or question column with homogeneous items in the response or option column, such that every response is plausible for every stimulus. Common matches include theories with their originator, people with their major achievement or work, causes with their effect, terms with their definitions, foreign words with their translation, and pieces of equipment, tools, lab apparatus, or organs with their use or function. If you wish, you can list stimuli with multiple correct responses; just inform students that some items may have more than one answer or specify the number for each stimulus. Check to see whether the testing tool in your learning management system can grade multiple-answer matching items.

Matches can also involve visuals, such as concepts or chemicals with their symbol, pictures of objects with their name, or labeled parts in a picture with their function. In fact, if your matching responses are embedded in one large graphic, such as a representation of a cell, a part of human anatomy, an electrical system, or a machine, you can have students describe a process by specifying a sequence of responses (Laird, 2004). Again, find out if your electronic testing tool accommodates multiple-answer items.

The examples thus far assess only lower-level thinking, but you can test higher-order cognitive skills by having students match causes with *likely* effects, concepts with *new* examples of them, and *new* hypothetical problems with concepts, tools, or approaches needed to solve them. Of course, "new" examples or problems need just be new to your students.

Advantages

- Easy to grade
- Assesses knowledge and recall well and can assess higher levels of cognition
- Relatively unambiguous
- Can test a lot of material in a short time

Disadvantages

- Difficult to construct a common set of stimuli and responses
- High guessing factor
- Not useful as a diagnostic tool

Construction

- Allow thirty seconds to one minute per item.
- Keep stimuli and responses short and simple.
- List the possible responses in some logical order, alphabetical or chronological, to reduce student search time.
- Add challenge and reduce process-of-elimination thinking by inserting one or more unmatchable responses or one or more responses that match more than one stimulus. Just be sure to add this statement to the directions: "Some responses may be used more than once and others not at all."
- To add even more challenge, include a few stimuli that require multiple responses or a sequence

of responses. Inform your students by adding this or a similar statement to the directions: "Some items require multiple responses or a sequence of responses describing a process."

- Limit the list of stimuli and responses to fifteen or fewer.
- Keep all stimuli and responses on one page.
- If students write down their response choice, have them use capital letters to avoid ambiguity.

Multiple Choice

No doubt multiple-choice items are the most popular type of objective test item in North America. Educational Testing Services and publishers' test banks rely on them heavily. You would think good ones would be easy to write, but they aren't. A solid, clean multiple-choice question avoids two tricky pitfalls: diverting a knowledgeable student away from the correct response and cluing a poorly prepared student toward the correct response (Suskie, 2004). Faulty phraseology and construction can do either. Test bank items that accompany textbooks usually avoid these flaws, but they do so at the cost of challenging students and assessing their higher-order thinking. To meet these higher standards, you have to search out proven, concept-oriented multiple-choice items or compose your own. If your area is the sciences, you should be able to find some high-quality items in the Databases of Concept Questions at www.skylight.science.ubc.ca/cqdatabases. Otherwise, search using "'clicker questions' + teaching" and look for your discipline. But don't be discouraged from writing your own and teaching your students how to write good ones.

One way to guarantee that your multiple-choice questions will assess higher-order thinking is to compose what are called *scenario-based* (Instructional Assessment Resources, University of Texas at Austin, 2007) or *simulation-like* (Thalheimer, 2002) items, or *interpretive exercises* (Suskie, 2004). These are a series of multiple-choice items based on a new (to the students), realistic stimulus—a table, graph, diagram, flowchart, drawing, photo, map, schematic, equation, data set, description of an experiment, statement, quotation, passage, poem, situation, short case, or the like—that students must interpret intelligently to answer the items correctly. The process of interpreting and reasoning from the stimulus normally requires—in addition to knowledge—comprehension, application, analysis, synthesis, or evaluation. If you prefer, you can look at the types of thinking involved as interpretation, inference, problem solving, generalization, and conclusion drawing. This type of multiple-choice question frequently appears in professionally written standardized tests, such as the Scholastic Assessment Test and the Graduate Record Examination, and licensing exams, such as the National Council of Licensure Examinations for registered nurses and practical nurses. Here are two college-level examples (reprinted with permission from the Division of Instructional Innovation and Assessment, University of Texas at Austin, 2007), the first of which focuses on an experiment and the second, on a situation or minicase. Correct answers are marked with an asterisk.

Scenario 1: Statistics

Two researchers were studying the relationship between amount of sleep each night and calories burned on an exercise bike for 42 men and women. They were interested if people who slept more had more energy to use during their exercise session. They obtained a correlation of .28, which has a two-tailed probability of .08. Alpha was .10.

1. Which is an example of a properly written research question?
   a. Is there a relationship between amount of sleep and energy expended?*
   b. Does amount of sleep correlate with energy used?
   c. What is the cause of energy expended?
   d. What is the value of rho?
2. What is the correct term for the variable amount of sleep?
   a. Dependent*
   b. Independent
   c. Predictor
   d. y
3. What is the correct statistical null hypothesis?
   a. There is no correlation between sleep and energy expended.
   b. Rho equals zero.*
   c. R equals zero.
   d. Rho equals *r*.
4. What conclusions should you draw regarding the null hypothesis?
   a. Reject*
   b. Accept
   c. Cannot determine without more information
5. What conclusions should you draw regarding this study?
   a. The correlation was significant
   b. The correlation was not significant.
   c. A small relationship exists.*
   d. No relationship exists.

Scenario 2: Biology

One day you meet a student watching a wasp drag a paralyzed grasshopper down a small hole in the ground. When asked what he is doing, he replies, "I'm watching that wasp store paralyzed grasshoppers in her nest to feed her offspring."

1. Which of the following is the best description of his reply?
   a. He is not a careful observer.
   b. He is stating a conclusion only partly derived from his observation.*
   c. He is stating a conclusion entirely drawn from his observation.
   d. He is making no assumptions.
2. Which of the following additional observations would add the most strength to the student's reply in question 1?
   a. Observing the wasp digging a similar hole
   b. Observing the wasp dragging more grasshoppers into the hole

 c. Digging into the hole and observing wasp eggs on the paralyzed grasshopper*

 d. Observing adult wasps emerging from the hole a month later

3. Both of you wait until the wasp leaves the area, then you dig into the hole and observe three paralyzed grasshoppers, each with a white egg on its side. The student states that this evidence supports his reply in question 1. Which of the following assumptions is he making?

 a. The eggs are grasshopper eggs.

 b. The wasp laid the eggs.*

 c. The wasp dug the hole.

 d. The wasp will return with another grasshopper.

4. You take the white eggs to the biology laboratory. Ten days later, immature wasps hatched from the eggs. The student states that this evidence supports his reply in question 1. Which of the following assumptions is he making?

 a. The wasp dug the hole.

 b. The wasp stung the grasshoppers.

 c. The grasshoppers were dead.

 d. A paralyzed grasshopper cannot lay an egg.*

Whether you use this type of multiple-choice item or the standard kind, these are the plusses and minuses and, if you or your students write them, the best practices in constructing them:

Advantages

- Easy and quick to grade
- Reduces some of the burden of large classes
- Can assess knowledge, comprehension, application, analysis, synthesis, and evaluation and do so more efficiently than constructed response questions
- Useful as a diagnostic tool since students' wrong choices can indicate weaknesses and misconceptions
- Familiar to students

Disadvantages

- Difficult and time-consuming to construct
- Can be ambiguous to students
- Encourages students to find the correct answer by process of elimination

Construction

- Estimate one to two minutes for students to answer each question.
- Address one problem or concept per question.
- Strive for clarity and conciseness; avoid wordiness.
- Include in the stem any words that may repeat in the response alternatives.
- Avoid lifting phrases directly from your lecture or the readings and reducing the thinking required to simple recall.
- Still, use familiar language that is similar to what you and the readings have used to explain the material.
- Make *no, not, never, none,* and *except* stand out by italicizing, bolding, and underlining them.
- Write the correct response first, then the distractors.
- One way to develop the distractors is by juggling the elements of (or the variables in) the correct response. For example, if you have students interpret a table from which they should conclude that more industrialized nations have lower birthrates

and infant mortality rates than less industrialized nations, the elements (or variables) are a nation's degree of industrialization, birthrate, and infant mortality rate. You can mix these variables together in an assortment of ways. You might also use other variables that students often confuse with the elements—for instance, population growth, which some students mistakenly equate with birthrate.

- Make all responses equally plausible and attractive. Absurd options only make guessing easier.
- Make all responses grammatically parallel and about the same length.
- Present the options in some logical order, alphabetical or chronological, to reduce the possibility of cuing students or falling into a pattern.
- Avoid grammatical cues to correct answers.
- Use three to five responses per item—six at the outside.
- Make sure each item has only one correct or clearly best response. Questions with multiple correct answers confuse students (but see the "Multiple True-False" section next).
- Incorporate graphics where appropriate.
- If you want to use "none of the above" or "all of the above," use it liberally, not just when that answer is correct. These options discriminate the more from the less knowledgeable students; even the "all of the above" option makes an item more challenging to students (Huang, Trevisan, & Storfer, 2007).

Scenario-based or simulation-like multiple-choice items (or interpretive exercises) have a few additional construction guidelines:

- Give students prior practice in interpreting the types of stimuli you put on the test and in performing the cognitive operations each item requires.
- Minimize interlocking items—that is, items that responding to correctly requires having responded correctly to previous items in the series.
- Longer and more complex stimuli should yield a longer series of multiple-choice questions.
- If you start looking for good stimuli, you will find them; they are all around you.
- Be creative with the stimuli and use different kinds.

Multiple True-False

Perhaps the least used, least known, and yet statistically strongest objective test question is the multiple true-false item. Like a multiple-choice item, it has a stem and a list of responses, and it may (or may not) involve interpreting a stimulus. But students do not select one right response; they decide whether each option is true or false in relation to the stem. Therefore, a multiple true-false item is flexible enough to accommodate multiple correct answers. Here is an example with the true and false responses marked:

When constructing a completion (fill-in-the-blank) test item, it is recommended that you:

T 1. Allow thirty seconds to one minute for students to answer each item.
F 2. Locate the word(s) to fill in at the beginning of the sentence, not in the middle or at the end of it.
F 3. Vary the length of the fill-in lines according to the length of the correct answer.
T 4. Omit only significant words from the sentence to complete.

Note that a single stem, one multiple true-false item, presented four decision points—two incorrect distractors and two correct responses. In essence, it created four separate objective items, and it did so very efficiently using no more words than for one item. With ten stems, then, you can easily generate forty to fifty items, and a test with fifty items is much more reliable than one with only ten. In summary, multiple true-false items are more flexible, more efficient, and more reliable than multiple-choice and most other objective test items (Ebel, 1978; Frisby & Sweeney, 1982).

Multiple true-false items share a great deal with true-false and multiple-choice questions in terms of their advantages, disadvantages, and construction guidelines. However, they have a few of their own:

Advantages

- Superior flexibility, efficiency, and reliability
- Easier and quicker to develop a multiple true-false test than a multiple-choice test
- Adds challenge and eliminates process-of-elimination thinking

Disadvantage

- One faulty stem undercuts the value of multiple items.

Construction

- Take extra care to write clear, concise, unambiguous stems.
- Be sure the distractors are clearly true or false in relation to the stem.
- Consider allowing students to write a rebuttal to your marking their answer wrong for a small percentage of the items.

Short Answer

Instructors typically use a short-answer question to test recall, comprehension, or application. Given its length limitation, it does not allow students to construct or justify a deeply considered response.

Advantages

- Easy to construct
- Can assess recall, comprehension, and application
- Requires a command of vocabulary or problem-solving skills
- Very useful as a diagnostic tool
- Encourages instructors to give students individual feedback

Disadvantages

- Time-consuming to grade given the amount of knowledge usually tested
- Difficult to standardize grading due to variability across answers

Construction

- Estimate two to five minutes per item.
- Be very specific and concise in identifying the task that students are to perform. See the advice below for constructing essay questions and writing assignments.
- Use familiar language that is similar to what you and the readings have used to explain the material.
- Indicate whether diagrams or illustrations are required or are acceptable in place of a written answer.
- Require students to show their work for full credit on problems.
- Leave an appropriate amount of space for the answers. Too much space invites students to write too much.

■ CONSTRUCTED RESPONSE INSTRUMENTS: ESSAY QUESTIONS AND WRITING ASSIGNMENTS

A constructed response instrument is an interrogatory statement (a question) or an imperative statement (a task description) that an instructor composes to assess student achievement of one or more learning outcomes. The responses are student structured and written in multiple complete sentences, and each is uniquely original or at least different from each other. In addition, the question or task has multiple respectable answers or responses that only a specialist in the subject matter can fairly assess. Stalnaker (1951) proposed this strict definition for essay questions, but it applies just as well to good writing assignments.

For our purposes here, let's use the term *writing assignment* to cover any assignment with a significant writing component, even one that incorporates other media. Therefore, the term includes a video production if it has a script and a multimedia e-portfolio if it integrates reflection. If you drop Stalnaker's requirement for multiple complete sentences, even complex graphics, such as concept maps, mind maps, and concept circle diagrams (see Chapter Twenty-Six), can qualify as essay questions or writing assignments.

Constructed response instruments, especially essay tests, have been misnamed "subjective" (as opposed to "objective"). This poorly chosen descriptor makes a mockery of professional judgment and gives students the mistaken impression that faculty have no clear standards for evaluating their written work. We do have standards, of course, but they often do not boil down to a dualist right or wrong answer. Moreover, each of us may prioritize different criteria on given essay questions and assignments. This is why we should explain our grading criteria and standards to students at the same time we talk about the test or the assignment (see Chapter Thirty-One).

By Stalnaker's (1951) strict definition, an essay must demand higher-order thinking; it cannot ask students merely to regurgitate material from class or the readings, even in their own words. By extrapolation, an application question or task must use problems, cases, diagrams, graphs, data sets, and the like that the students have not seen before. Therefore, this set of questions does not constitute an essay question, let alone a good writing assignment: "What are the six major capital budgeting techniques? Define them (you need not give their formula). Under what two categories are they normally grouped? Categorize all six techniques." Every introductory finance textbook supplies the answers to these questions. This next set is less clear: "What is the difference between experimental research and survey research? What do they have in common?" If the course addressed experimental research and survey research independently and never drew comparisons or contrasts between the two methods, then this set indeed qualifies as an essay question or a suitable writing assignment.

Even with the time-saving grading methods that Chapter Thirty-One recommends, constructed responses take more time and effort to grade than do objective test items. You must interpret your students' sometimes rambling thoughts, distracting grammar and spelling, and confusing punctuation, and then evaluate variable content. So you should be efficient in your use of essay tests and writing assignments. You need use them only when the learning outcomes you are assessing indicate higher-order thinking that requires construction, as opposed to selection, of an answer. (Even in this case, you can assign a graphic like a concept or mind map for some tasks.) If your outcome allows students either to construct or to select the answer, then you have your choice of an essay test question, a writing assignment, or one or more objective test items. If your outcome calls only for selection, then you might as well use objective test items (Reiner, Bothell, Sudweeks, & Wood, 2002).

Essay questions and writing assignments share most of the same advantages, disadvantages, and construction guidelines, which are listed below. Those that apply only to essay test questions are marked with a †.

Advantages

- Quick and relatively easy to construct (but specify exactly what you want students to do, following the guidelines in the next section)
- Encourages students to study in a deeper, more integrated manner†
- Discourages last-minute cramming†
- Can assess all types of higher-order thinking
- Can assess students' abilities to logically compose and present an argument
- Can assess their reasoning skills (you get inside their heads)
- Can assess them authentically—that is, on tasks that they are likely to do in real-world work
- Can encourage creativity and originality
- Requires students to really know the material
- Gives practice in writing
- Makes cheating more difficult and reduces its incidence†
- Encourages instructors to give students individual feedback

- Varies the type of assessment from objective tests (yet yields the same student rankings as do multiple-choice tests, according to Jacobs & Chase, 1992)†

Disadvantages

- More time-consuming to grade than objective items (but see Chapter Thirty-One for ways to cut that time)
- Difficult to standardize grading because of variability across answers as well as length of answers (but see Chapter Thirty-One for ways to handle the variability)
- Cannot test broad content with any one question†
- Penalizes students who read or work slowly, have poor writing skills, or are nonnative English speakers
- Can mislead students if they do not understand the verbs used in the questions or don't read the entire question very carefully
- Encourages grading protests if the scoring may seem subjective, inconsistent, or unjustified (but see Chapter Thirty-One for ways to nearly eliminate protests)
- Easy to make a question or task too broad for students to zero in on the answer
- Allows students to pick up credit for bluffing and padding
- Produces poor, hasty writing, and students do not learn to improve it†

Construction

- Specify exactly what you want the students to do, following the guidelines in the next section.
- Estimate fifteen minutes to one hour per essay question.†

- Put on the test your estimate of how long an answer should take students, helping them budget their time wisely.†
- Give the point value for each essay.†
- Give several shorter essay questions rather than one or two long ones. This strategy covers more material and spreads the risk for students.
- Consider giving students a choice among several essay questions. Having options lowers their anxiety and lets them show you the best of what they have learned.
- If you let students choose among several questions, limit their choices—for example, to five out of seven options rather than five out of ten.

Making Essay Questions and Writing Assignments Specific Enough

Be specific and concise in describing the task you want students to perform or the answer you expect to the questions you ask. Identify the key points that students should address. You might even specify the cognitive operations and the general content that students should use in their responses. Rather than beginning a question with an interrogative pronoun such as *why, how,* or *what,* start with a descriptive verb (see Chapter Thirty for a list of common test and assignment verbs and their definitions) and state exactly how elaborate the answer should be and, to an extent, how it should be organized (Reiner et al., 2002)—for instance: "*Describe three ways* that social integration could break down in the modern world, according to Durkheim. Then *assess* how closely *each one* applies to the United States today."

All you have to do is to decide exactly how you would like an excellent answer to read. Then you can transform a vague question like, "What were the causes of the collapse of the Ming dynasty?" into a well-defined, multistage task:

Select *three key* causes of the collapse of the Ming dynasty, and decide which was *most* important, which was *second* in importance, and which was *last* in importance. Write a paragraph on each cause, not only describing its impact on the Ming dynasty, but also arguing why you rank-order it as you do. Explain any interrelationships that exist among the causes.

By incorporating the proper procedure to follow, the instructions reinforce students' understanding of historical interpretation and analysis while assessing their ability to do it. Similarly, the rudderless task, "Explain Shakespeare's view of women as reflected in his plays," can be elaborated into a review of basic literary analysis:

> Pick *three* of Shakespeare's plays that feature women in major roles, and analyze these characters to identify *four* patterns in his views of women. Consider not only what these female characters do and say but also what other characters do and say to them.

If the content lends itself, it is also an excellent strategy to situate an essay question or writing assignment in a novel (but not foreign) problem (Reiner et al., 2002). Problem-focused assessment gives students practice in real-world application and for this reason is authentic. You can take a theoretical task such as, "Explain how a nurse should handle a person who threatens suicide," and place it in a realistic situation:

> In the emergency department, a patient tells the nurse that he plans to commit suicide and agrees to a voluntary admission to the psychiatric unit. What specific issues should the nurse discuss with the patient when he asks, "How long do I have to stay there?" (Adapted from http://findarticles.com /p/articles/mi_qa3689/is_200408/ai_n9444981.)

The last example of an essay question or writing assignment that needs and gets a makeover asks students to perform a low-level and vaguely stated task: "Summarize the most important trends in social inequality that we have seen in the United States since the 1960s." The revision assumes that students can perform this low-level task and requires that they analyze and synthesize that knowledge in a new way to address a contemporary real-world paradox:

> Recall the trends in social inequality that we have seen in the United States since the 1960s. Also recall that during this time (1) the relationship between educational and income attainment has been consistently positive and (2) educational attainment has increased. Then how is it possible that the distributions of income and wealth have become more polarized over this time period? Resolve this apparent contradiction, taking into account other major determinants of income, the role of the occupational structure, and the type of economy in the United States.

With direction, organization, and hints in the instructions, you can equip your class to perform truly high-order cognitive operations. But do remember that you have to give your students plenty of prior practice in the types of thinking you ask them to do in graded assessments. If you identify these types of thinking from the start in your learning outcomes, you will be able to select and implement the teaching formats, methods, and moves that will create the learning experiences to give your students the practice they need.

If you want to use an essay question or give a writing assignment that students may view as controversial or value based, do assure them in advance that you will assess their work strictly on the validity of their arguments, the strength of their evidence, or the quality of their presentation—not the opinion or viewpoint they express. Be sure to incorporate whatever grading dimensions you define in your grading rubric (see Chapter Thirty-One).

Ideas for Good Essay Questions and Writing Assignments

For a little inspiration, consider how you might adapt these general ideas for engaging essay questions and writing assignments to your course material:

- Discuss the relevance of course material to a life decision.
- Argue against a position you believe in.
- Set the conditions under which a relationship or concept does and does not apply.
- What if _____ (a specific change occurs, time or place shifts, or an assumption is violated)? Would a relationship still hold? How would it be changed?
- Push an idea to its limits, to the point of absurdity.
- Determine whether a problem can or cannot be solved given available information.
- Separate relevant from irrelevant information to solve a problem.
- Break a problem into subproblems.
- Explain a specific complex phenomenon to a twelve year old.
- Design a study to test a relationship.
- Consider why a relationship may be causal or spurious.
- Suggest reasons that different research studies may obtain different results.
- Design a study to reconcile different results across different studies.
- Imagine you are a _____ with the following problem to solve: _____. Draw on course material to structure an approach to the problem or to propose a solution.

- Design a society, government, private or public organization, or funding agency to accomplish a certain purpose.

■ TESTS AND ASSIGNMENTS: THE ULTIMATE TEACHING EVALUATIONS

The time and effort invested in writing a good test or assignment are not without reward. It is heartening to see your students perform well on a challenging task or to receive a compliment on the task from a student. Both indicate that your test or assignment was a worthwhile learning experience as well as a fair evaluation.

But even more important, the tests and assignments you design are the most important instruments you have for assessing your teaching effectiveness. For your sake as well as your students', they should measure what you set out to teach. Student, peer, and self-evaluations are other instruments, and student opinions of your success generally carry the most weight. But they merely take the place of the only real teaching evaluation, which is how much students have learned.

In the best of all possible educational worlds, each major exam would be tested to ensure high reliability and validity, and each assignment would be reviewed and enhanced by your peers. Then student performance would be used to evaluate the instructor's teaching success relative to other instructors teaching the same course. Of course, such an ideal could come to pass only if faculty could agree on standardized learning outcomes, content, assignments, and testing instruments for each course—a notion that goes against academic freedom and autonomy. Still, how well your students perform on summative assessments is the best data you can use for your personal self-assessment of your teaching.

CHAPTER 30

Preparing Students for Tests

Recall your undergraduate days. Did you ever experience anxiety or a sense of dread when your professors announced an exam? Did you ever walk into a test feeling pretty well prepared, only to freeze when you saw the first question? Did you ever leave an exam thinking that you aced it, only to be sorely disappointed in your grade? If even one of these situations rang true, you can probably empathize with some of the emotions your students are experiencing now.

The first question you usually hear when you announce an upcoming exam is, "What will be on the test?" While this is not a valid question, another common query, "What will the test format be?" is perfectly valid. We'd like to believe that students will perform well on any type of test with adequate study. But different types of exams call for different types of study strategies, and most students learn based on how they are tested (Wergin, 1988). Factual memorization for a recall-oriented objective test takes a different kind of study effort from that for analyses of problems or situations. It is that latter type of studying that helps students develop critical thinking skills, and they need experience in the higher cognitive processes of analysis, synthesis, and evaluation. In fact, students perform better on the multiple-choice portion of a test if they know there will be an essay question on it (Drake, 2009). In other words, studying to use higher-order thinking on a test better prepares a learner to perform whatever level of cognitive operation is required. Of course, multiple-choice items can call for much more thought than just recall and comprehension.

TEST PREPARATION MEASURES

If we accept that tests can be instruments of instruction as well as evaluation, then preparing students to perform well on tests is also an excellent teaching strategy. Here are some easily implemented ways to help students get ready for exams.

Reading and Review Strategies

You begin preparing your students for tests from the very first day by teaching them proven techniques for taking notes on your lectures and class activities, provided in Chapter Twelve, and for reading academic material effectively, given in Chapter Twenty-Three. Of course, students should review the relevant readings and their notes before a test. More than 80 percent of the studies conducted on reviewing lecture notes find that the activity enhances test performance (Bligh, 2000). But just reading notes over, even multiple times, will not help much for the test. As research cited in Chapter Twenty-Three indicates, the quickest, most efficient, and most effective way to study written material, at least for factual and problem-solving tests, is "active recall" or the 3R (read-recite-review) strategy (McDaniel, Howard, & Einstein, 2009; Roediger & Karpicke, 2006). According to this method, students read a section of their text or notes, then put the material away, recite aloud as much as they can remember, and finally reread the section. In addition to reinforcing their reading by restating and hearing the material, students practice retrieval with self-testing, which is exactly the skill they will need during the test.

Study Groups

Several of the chapters in this book point out how groups facilitate learning. Study groups that meet regularly outside class are also very helpful (Hufford, 1991; Treisman, 1986). Since member commitment can make or break them, consider formalizing them by having students sign up for such groups early in the term. Then distribute a list of all the groups with their members' names and contact information.

Review Sheets

This study aid helps many students prepare for a test, especially first-year and second-year students who do not yet know what college-level assessment involves. You can make a review sheet as simple as a list or outline of important topics that you have emphasized, but this alone will not tell students how to study this content.

Students gain much more from a sample test or a list of review questions. These questions should mirror your student learning outcomes and represent the variety of item formats that will appear on the test. If you plan to use some factual and terminological multiple-choice questions on the test, then put some of those items on the review sheet. If you intend to test analysis and synthesis, develop some questions that require those same cognitive operations. This method demands much more of your time and effort because you do not want to duplicate the sample items on the real test. But it is highly effective, and you can draw appropriate items from previous tests.

Perhaps the best option for students is what is called a "test blueprint" (Questionmark Corporation, 2000; Suskie, 2004), and it can also help you design a test that assesses your students' achievement of your outcomes. So have your syllabus and outcomes map handy. To make a test blueprint, begin by listing all the major content areas that your test will address; then designate their relative importance by the percentage of the test (or number of points) to be devoted to each area. Within each content area, write down what you want students to be able to do or demonstrate, using action verbs and avoiding internal-states verbs such as *know, understand, realize,* and *appreciate* (see Chapter Two). These statements should reflect your student learning outcomes, though perhaps on a more microlevel than in your syllabus or outcomes map. Finally, allocate points or items across these outcome statements according to how central they are in this part of the course. In other words, instead of just listing concepts for students to "know," tell them more specifically that, for instance, they should be able to *recognize* the definitions, purposes, and examples of a list of concepts and be able to *reproduce* a given list of principles. Then let these statements serve as the blueprint for your test questions.

Review Sessions

About three-quarters of the students say that they want a pretest review session (Mealy & Host, 1993), so you may want to schedule one during a class or outside class, as do many instructors. But it is likely to work well only if students have already made significant progress in their independent or small-group studying. Therefore, you should make it clear that you will not be summarizing the past few weeks of lectures and readings or dispensing the answers to the review questions.

The most productive way to conduct a review session is to insist that students come prepared to ask specific questions on the material and answer any review questions on their own. With respect to their questions, always ask the class for answers before answering them yourself. With respect to the review questions, have the entire class participate in brainstorming and refining the answers, and assign different questions to small groups and have them develop and orally present their answers. Invite other students to evaluate the group's answers, and then offer your own assessment.

Chapter Twelve describes another version of this format called *pair/group and review*, in which student pairs or small groups develop answers to review questions, after which you randomly select a few of them to present their answers to the class. You then mock-grade them and explain your assessment criteria or, better yet, have the rest of the class mock-grade the answers to help students learn how to assess their own work.

One more variation, this one tailored to an essay test, is the *question shuffle* (Millis, 2005). Students attending the review session must bring in two essay questions, each on an index card, that they think would be appropriate for the test. They pair off, review their four questions, and select the best two. Then all the pairs circulate for a few moments, shuffling their two cards among other pairs. From the two questions they wind up with, the pairs select one to answer, and each student writes out an answer

within a time period that replicates what the test will allow for such a question. This activity furnishes a test-taking rehearsal, which generally reduces anxiety and enhances performance. The students in each pair compare and evaluate their different approaches to the question, giving them practice in critical thinking. As time permits, you can repeat the "shuffle." You can then collect the questions (and responses) and use the best ones on the test. Not only does this review exercise supply you with an already-vetted test (or discussion) question bank, but it also serves as a classroom assessment technique (see Chapter Twenty-Eight), informing you about your students' understanding of the material to be tested and possibly giving you the chance before the test to clear up their misconceptions and help them improve their essay writing (Millis, 2005).

Help Sessions or Course Clinics

This measure takes the review session one step further by establishing weekly meetings of one or more hours during which you or your teaching assistant answers questions. A regularly scheduled meeting motivates students to keep up with the course and not wait until the last minute to cram for a test. It also reduces stress by encouraging students to study without the impending threat of an exam.

Definitions of Key Test Terms

Students, especially in their first year, often do poorly on tests because they are not exactly sure what a question, especially an essay question, is asking them to do. They do not know what the verb designating the task means, at least not the way we use the verb. This sometimes explains why some students fail to follow directions. So it may be safest to provide them with written definitions of common test verbs, along with review questions that give them practice in the cognitive operations. Therefore, consider sharing the definitions below with your classes (Anderson & Krathwohl, 2000; Ellis, 2006; Lacey-Casem, 1990; Moss & Holder, 1988; Reiner, Bothell, Sudweeks, & Wood, 2002):

- *Analyze:* Break something down into parts, such as a theory into its components, a process into its stages, or an event into its causes. Analysis involves characterizing the whole, identifying its parts, and showing how the parts interrelate.
- *Assess/criticize/critique/evaluate:* Determine or judge the degree to which something meets or fails to meet certain criteria. If not provided in the question, develop criteria for making judgments.
- *Categorize/classify:* Sort into major, general groups, or types that you name or identify.
- *Compare/contrast:* Identify the important similarities and differences between two or more elements in order to reveal something significant about them. Identify similarities if the command is to compare and differences if it is to contrast.
- *Create/devise:* Put together, organize, or reorganize elements to make a new approach, product, process, or solution.
- *Defend/justify:* Give good reasons to support a position, and explain how or why something happened.
- *Define/identify:* Give the key characteristics by which a concept, thing, or event can be understood. Place it in a general class; then distinguish it from other members of that class.
- *Describe:* Give the characteristics by which an object, action, process, person, or concept can be recognized or visualized.
- *Develop:* Create, elaborate on, or make more effective, detailed, or usable.
- *Discuss/examine:* Debate, argue, and evaluate the various sides of an issue.
- *Explain/justify:* Give the basic principles of or reasons for something; make it intelligible. Explanation may involve relating the unfamiliar to the more familiar.
- *Generate:* Think up, devise, or brainstorm good ideas or alternatives.
- *Infer:* Logically conclude on the basis of what is known.
- *Interpret/explain:* State what you think the author or speaker of a quotation or statement means, and why.

- *Illustrate:* Use a concrete example to explain or clarify the essential attributes of a problem or concept, or clarify a point using a diagram, chart, table, or other graphic.
- *List/enumerate:* Give the essential points one by one, in a logical order if applicable. It may be helpful to number the points.
- *Outline/review/state:* Organize a description under main points and subordinate points, omitting minor details and classifying the elements or main points.
- *Predict:* Infer from facts, trends, or principles what will happen in the future.
- *Propose:* Suggest or present for consideration.
- *Prove/validate:* Establish that something is true by citing factual evidence or giving clear, logical reasons.
- *Summarize:* Briefly restate the main points.
- *Synthesize:* Put together elements in a new way so as to make a novel theory, approach, product, process, or solution.
- *Trace:* Describe the course or progress of a phenomenon, trend, or development.

ANXIETY-REDUCTION MEASURES

Moderate anxiety is normal before a major test and indeed can motivate and energize students. From their review of the test anxiety literature, Mealy and Host (1993) identified three types of anxious students. Those of the first type lack adequate study skills and are aware of the problem; they are not well prepared for exams and worry about performing poorly. The second group comprises students who have adequate study strategies but become severely distracted during a test. Other research confirms these two categories of anxious students (Naveh-Benjamin, McKeachie, & Lin, 1987). The final type consists of students who mistakenly believe that they have adequate study skills but do poorly on exams, then wonder what the problem could be. They may blame instructors and "unfair exams" for their falling short of their high expectations.

Mealy and Host (1993) also asked students how an instructor can affect their anxiety before, during, and after a test. They received four kinds of responses:

1. Seventy-five percent of the students want their instructor to conduct some kind of review before the test and are less anxious after attending one. They feel more confident if they are sure they have correct information in their notes.
2. Students become stressed when their instructor tells them that the test will be hard. They do not mind a challenging exam, but they want to hear how they should study, followed by some words of reassurance.
3. Most students get nervous when their instructor walks around the room during a test and looks over their shoulders. While this may keep cheating in check, it also raises the anxiety of stress-sensitive students.
4. Many students resent interruptions during a test. Even if their instructor breaks in just to correct or clarify an exam item, it throws off their train of thought.

In summary, taking measures to prepare your students for tests, such as providing quality review sheets and review sessions, along with building their self-confidence and minimizing test interruptions, will help allay their test anxiety. So will these actions:

- Have your test schedule written in your syllabus, and stick to it.
- Have in your syllabus a clear grading system and your policies on missed quizzes and tests.
- Consider dropping your students' lowest test or quiz score from your final grade calculations; anyone can have a bad day or a legitimate reason for missing a class.

- Test frequently, reducing the relative weight of each test so that one poor performance will not cost students dearly.
- Tailor your tests to the time allotted. If it takes you so many minutes to complete one of your tests, figure that it will take your students three times as long. Not being able to finish a test discourages students, even if you tell them they are not expected to finish it.
- Teach students relaxation techniques, such as deep breathing, counting to ten, and visualizing a successful test session (Ellis, 2006; Hebert, 1984).

Occasionally you may have a student for whom test anxiety is a debilitating problem. Refer this individual to your institution's counseling center, as you should for other emotional and psychological problems, or the learning skills and academic assistance center.

■ WHAT THE EFFORT IS WORTH

Taking measures to prepare your students for a test is one way to ensure that they review, synthesize, and retain the material. Some of these measures can also help you better plan and organize a test so that it assesses exactly what you want to assess. Whatever else you can do to reduce your students' test anxiety allows them to better demonstrate their actual learning and gives you a more valid assessment of their understanding. It is only by seeing their honest achievement that you can appraise how successful your teaching has been. In your performance review, you may also want to use some of your students' tests to document your teaching effectiveness, a topic addressed in Chapter Thirty-Two.

CHAPTER 31

Grading Summative Assessments

rading is a task you may view with dread and disdain, as the vast majority of your colleagues do. But it furnishes essential feedback to your students on their performance and, to a certain extent, to you on your teaching effectiveness. Of course, grades cannot provide the whole picture on your teaching because assessment standards vary radically across the academy and some students are unable or unwilling to learn, no matter what you do.

■ THE MEANING OF GRADES

Historically, grading is a relatively new phenomenon in the academy (Hammons & Barnsley, 1992). Yale University was the first American institution to assign grades, starting in 1783. To classify student performance, faculty used Latin descriptors ranging from the exceptional *optime* to the dismal *pejores*. In 1800, Yale adopted a numerical scale of 0 to 4, thus initiating the grade point average. Later the College of William and Mary adopted a similar scheme. In 1850,

the University of Michigan introduced a pass/fail system that set the passing grade minimum at 50 percent. In 1883, Harvard began using letter grades. This system soon swept the country, but with tremendous disagreement on the grade cut-off points. For instance, Mount Holyoke established the failing grade at 75 percent, while Michigan maintained the 50 percent standard. Interestingly, Harvard set the lowest failing mark, just 26 percent. Higher education eventually closed the discrepancies in the scale but has otherwise made few major changes in this system, except to add "plus" and "minus" modifiers, and not at all institutions (Hammons & Barnsley, 1992).

Faculty, students, parents, and businesspeople do not agree on the meaning of grades (Pollio & Humphreys, 1988). For instance, when asked how long the impact of receiving a C versus an A would last, a full 53 percent of the faculty respondents expected it would last at least two to five years. So did a third of the parents and businesspeople. But only 14 percent of the students surveyed agreed, and 45 percent anticipated no impact at all. While

301

many students may not want to believe that grades are important to their futures, one of your major responsibilities is to evaluate their achievement and assign grades accordingly. In addition, you are responsible for upholding the value of the grading currency—that is, combating grade inflation. So it is worth reviewing the level of performance each grade represents:

- An A signifies an exceptional level of achievement. The student displays a superb command of the subject matter and can creatively apply it at many different levels. A students tend to be committed, motivated, and cognitively gifted.
- A B indicates a good but not outstanding level of achievement. B students demonstrate a decent grasp of the material and the ability to apply at several but not all levels.
- A C represents a fair level of achievement. The student shows some mastery of the material and a narrow application range. This grade may indicate poor study skills, a lack of motivation or interest, or low ability. Some C students get by on their decent test-taking skills.
- A D means that the student has little or no true understanding of the subject area and may not be motivated or able to learn it.
- An F denotes a performance below the level of random chance. The student lacks interest, motivation, or ability.

■ SUMMATIVE ASSESSMENTS AND GRADING SYSTEMS

Summative assessment occurs at the end of a learning process, which may occur after a section of a course or at the end of the course. It typically follows one of two basic grading systems (Hammons & Barnsley, 1992; Ory & Ryan, 1993; Prégent, 1994; Wergin, 1988): norm-referenced or criterion-referenced grading.

Norm-Referenced Grading

The first type of summative grading system, commonly called grading on a curve, assesses each student's performance relative to all other students' performances. Its relative nature gives it some serious flaws. First, the more strictly that faculty implement it, the more it places students in competition with each other for class ranking. Therefore, you cannot expect students to work cooperatively together in graded group work. Second, it statistically assumes a bell-shaped ("normal") distribution of student scores—a phenomenon that doesn't always occur. Third, the grades the system yields are unrelated to any absolute performance standard. So if all students in a class perform poorly, some inadequate performances will receive an A anyway. Conversely, in a high-achieving class, some good performances will unjustly get a C.

Nevertheless, this system also has its strengths. The best and worst performances set the parameters within which other performances are judged, so an instructor can give a very challenging test without unduly lowering his students' grades or an easy one while still differentiating the quality of student performance. It also ensures any class grade point average an instructor considers reasonable, so it can combat grade inflation.

In the past couple of decades, norm-referenced grading has fallen into disfavor for at least a couple of reasons. For one, higher education has widely embraced group work, and for another, it no longer aims to screen out the low achievers. The retention rate has replaced the attrition rate as an institution's badge of honor.

Criterion-Referenced Grading

This second type of grading system requires instructors to set absolute standards of performance (grading criteria) in advance, giving all students sole responsibility for their own grades. Compared to norm-referenced, criterion-referenced grading better serves the purpose of assessing how well students achieve given learning outcomes. It allows the possibility that all students will attain A's or, conversely, that all students will fail. In addition, it does not discourage cooperation and collaboration among students.

To be sure, criterion-referenced grading has its drawbacks. In particular, it is difficult to develop meaningful, valid standards for assigning grades based on absolute knowledge acquisition (Ory & Ryan, 1993). Instructors who are unfamiliar with their student population may have no idea how scores will distribute on any given test or assignment. (As the nightmare goes, all the scores cluster around 95 percent or all lag below 70.) But with more experience, instructors learn how to design and grade tests and assignments to differentiate performances.

■ THE QUALITIES OF A SOUND GRADING SYSTEM

A sound grading scheme is accurate, consistent, and valuable to learning. Larger classes require special efforts to ensure these qualities, especially consistency. Following these guidelines should enhance the soundness of your grading system (Jacobs & Chase, 1993; Lacey-Casem, 1990; Ory & Ryan, 1993; Walvoord & Anderson, 1998):

Accuracy

- A final course grade based on many and varied assignments and tests
- Well-constructed quizzes and tests reflecting your student learning outcomes (see Chapter Twenty-Nine)
- Point values on tests that reflect the relative importance of the concepts, principles, and relationships
- Clear and unambiguous written instructions for tests and assignments
- Grading keys and rubrics that, where appropriate, allow the possibility of more than one correct answer

- Validity across items, which means discarding an objective test item that practically all the students missed (see item analysis in Chapter Twenty-Nine)
- Grading standards appropriate for the level of your students

Consistency

- Clearly written grading keys and rubrics for assessing responses, particularly if multiple graders are involved
- Consensus among multiple graders, which will require discussion of problematic answers
- Maintenance of student anonymity to avoid grading biases

Learning Value

- Sharing studying, writing, problem-solving, and test-taking techniques with your class
- Providing a grading rubric (defined in the next section) before an essay test or the due date of a writing assignment or a detailed grading key when returning tests
- Going over your rubric with students to ensure they understand it
- Supplying samples of exemplary work and helping students understand what makes them excellent, preferably before the essay test or due date
- For writing assignments, allowing students to make revisions after providing formative assessments on first drafts
- Commenting as generously as your time allows, including on what the student did right (Too many negatives are overwhelming and counterproductive.)
- Making specific comments, not a cryptic "What?" or "?"
- Identifying a few key areas for improvement, especially those emphasized in your grading rubric, and specific remediation methods
- Directing comments to the performance, not the student
- Reviewing exams when you return them so that students understand what you wanted and how

they can improve their performance, with a focus on frequently made errors

- Referring some students to your institution's academic assistance center for special help

GRADING CONSTRUCTED RESPONSES AND PAPERS

Grading answers to constructed response questions requires considerable thought and strategy to ensure accuracy and consistency within reasonable time frames. You can choose from three popular grading methods (Ory & Ryan, 1993; Rodgers, 1995; Stevens & Levi, 2005; Suskie, 2004; Walvoord & Anderson, 1998): atomistic, holistic, and analytical grading.

Atomistic Grading

This grading technique follows a key. To develop one, you first list the components of an ideal response or paper, then allocate point values among the components. As you read a student's work, you mentally check off the components on your list or write the number of points earned next to the component on the student's work. You typically give partial credit to an incomplete or partially correct answer. Then you total the point values for the grade. This approach helps inexperienced instructors become accustomed to the quality range of student work and the grading process.

This method is content focused and serves well for grading tests and assignments that require only knowledge or low-level comprehension and have one correct response. It can also be used with criteria that have fairly clear standards of right and wrong: trueness to specified format, organization, quality of data or evidence, logic of reasoning, style (sentence structure, word choice, and tone), and mechanics (grammar, punctuation, and spelling). You can easily keep track of four or five dimensions and, if you wish, give each a different point value or weight—for example, twenty points for content, fifteen for organization, ten for style, and five for mechanics,

for a total of fifty points. In terms of allocating points on such criteria, this method resembles analytical grading, addressed later in the chapter.

Do explain your general assessment dimensions and their point values to your class in advance, perhaps when you give the assignment or conduct a review for the test. Your students need to know and understand the criteria on which you will evaluate their work.

Atomistic grading takes a great deal of time because it requires attention to minute detail and because most instructors feel obligated to explain what is wrong or missing on each student's work. It may be more efficient to show students a copy of the key when returning the test or paper. While atomistic grading seems highly objective, it still invites grading protests and "point-mongering," especially for partial credit. It often involves hair-splitting the total point value for a question into fractions for flawed answers. If an instructor could be totally consistent in hair-splitting points, students might not try to argue for a point or two more. But student answers are unique, and no key can cover every possible imperfection. In addition, it is difficult to remember precisely how one graded a similarly but not identically flawed response twenty or thirty papers ago. Consistency across multiple graders can also be difficult to maintain. Perhaps a more serious weakness in atomistic grading is its rigidity when applied to essays and assignments that require higher-level thinking and have multiple respectable answers. The key can quickly become unruly if you try to lay out standards for grading every possible acceptable response, and it may not include all such responses.

Holistic Grading

Over the years, this method has been called global grading and single impression scoring. As the name implies, an instructor grades a student-constructed response on her overall evaluation of its quality. The technique is relatively quick, efficient, reliable, and fair when backed by instructor experience, practice, and familiarity with the student performance range at the institution. In addition, it easily accommodates essays and assignments that demand higher-order thinking and have multiple respectable responses.

With inductive holistic grading, which is suitable for small classes, you read quickly through all the responses or papers, rank each above or below the ones you have already read, from best to worst, and then group them for assigning grades. Finally, you write up descriptions of the quality of each group and give them to students when you return their work. To personalize the feedback, you can add comments to each student's sheet or highlight the most applicable parts of the appropriate description. While the descriptions are customized to the student products, this schema presents a couple of problems. Because it relies on the instructor's comparative evaluations of students' responses and papers, it contains an element of norm-referenced grading (curving). Moreover, students cannot know in advance the dimensions on which their instructor will assess their work.

With deductive holistic, grading, which is one suitable for any size class, students do know in advance and in some detail how their work will be evaluated. At the same time you compose the writing assignment or essay question, you decide the four or five dimensions on which you will assess the student product. Four or five criteria are a reasonable number to explain to your students and to remember while you are grading. Furthermore, your students cannot do their best on more than a handful of dimensions at one time. We carry around in our heads twenty or more criteria on which we judge scholarly work, all of which come out when we read a journal article or book in our discipline. But students cannot work on so many in one assignment or essay; they don't even know what all these criteria are. Besides, it is unfair to them to critique their novice efforts on the full array of professional dimensions, even if we don't expect high performance. So select just a few as the most important skills for students to demonstrate in any given piece of work, and forget the rest. You can focus on other dimensions in other assignments and essays.

Your relevant assessment criteria will vary according to your discipline, the course level, the nature of your material, and the task you are assigning. Here are just some of the many possible options:

- Satisfying the assignment, following directions (particularly salient for first-year students)
- Recall of facts, figures, definitions, equations, or text material
- Proper use of technical terminology
- Demonstration of accurate understanding of the materials and texts
- Proper references to texts and other sources
- Organization, conformity to the required organizing framework of format
- Precision of measurement, quality of data
- Specification of limits, qualifications to results, and conclusions
- Clarity of expression or explanations
- Conciseness, parsimony
- Strength or tightness of arguments (internal consistency, evidence, and logic)
- Mechanics (spelling, grammar, and punctuation)
- Writing style, as suitable to the discipline and assignment
- Creativity of thought, design, or solution

After choosing the criteria of interest, you then write out descriptions of what the student product will look like at the different levels of quality. If you are assigning letter grades, you will describe the qualities of A, B, C, D, and F work on the dimensions you selected for the assignment or essay. If you are allocating points, you will describe the work for each point or range of points. You might link words to the letter grades or point ranges, such as *exemplary, competent, developing,* and *unacceptable.* The document you generate is called a *rubric,* defined as an assessment and grading tool that lays out specific expectations for an essay or assignment (writing, speaking, multimedia, and so on) and describes each level of performance quality on selected criteria. In holistic grading, these descriptions take the form of paragraphs in which each sentence typically addresses a different dimension in the rubric.

An example should clarify. Let's say our assignment is to write a classic five-paragraph essay arguing in favor of norm-referenced grading or criterion-referenced grading, drawing on several readings on the topic. Let's assume our rubric focuses on satisfying the assignment (with an emphasis on following the classic five-paragraph essay format), demonstrating an accurate understanding of the readings, backing one's argument with evidence from the readings, and mechanics. The holistic rubric would look like this:

- An A essay strictly follows the classic five-paragraph essay format, stating the thesis (position) in the first paragraph, providing evidence in each of the next three paragraphs, and concluding with a summary or synthesis. It consistently makes appropriate and accurate references to the readings. It also provides all the evidence available in the readings to support its argument. Finally, it contains no more than two spelling, punctuation, or grammatical errors.
- A B essay follows the classic five-paragraph essay format with no more than one minor deviation. While generally accurate in referring to readings, it shows a thin, incomplete, or shaky understanding of some readings in a couple of places. It also misses some parts of the readings that would lend evidence to the argument. It contains no more than several spelling, punctuation, or grammatical errors.
- A C essay breaks significantly from the classic five-paragraph essay format—perhaps failing to state a clear position in the first paragraph, mixing arguments across paragraphs, or closing with a new argument or information. While it refers to the readings, it demonstrates a spotty or superficial understanding of them. It also misses opportunities to use them for evidence. It contains quite a few spelling, punctuation, or grammatical errors, though not enough to make parts of it incomprehensible.
- A D essay does not follow the classic five-paragraph essay format—failing either to state a

clear position or to use the rest of the essay to bring evidence from the readings to support it. It demonstrates little understanding or knowledge of the readings. In addition, it draws little relevant evidence from them. The frequent errors in spelling, punctuation, and grammar are distracting or render the essay incomprehensible in places.
- An F essay fails to address the assignment in topic or format, or the frequent errors in spelling, punctuation, and grammar render the essay incomprehensible, or it is not turned in.

Distribute copies of these performance descriptions to your students along with the assignment directions or review sheet (preferably a test blueprint, as described in Chapter Thirty), and explain them with examples. This way students will know to concentrate on the dimensions that are most important to you and will understand the quality of work you expect. To save paper and increase the odds that they will study your rubric again, you might ask them to attach the document to the product they hand in. (Of course, this does not apply to electronic turn-ins.) Then you need not hand back another copy with their work.

When you grade the essays or papers, you decide which performance description best fits the work and write that grade on the paper or essay. That is really all you have to do, and this can reduce your grading time to a fraction of what atomistic grading requires. The rubric explains the reasons for the grade, although you should write personal comments as well, as time permits.

The literature offers examples of holistic rubrics written in paragraphs for many types of assignments: letters (Montgomery, 2002); portfolios (Stevens & Levi, 2005); oral presentations, class participation, and journals (Baughin, Brod, & Page, 2002); essay tests and Web page designs (Brookhart, 1999); and mathematical problem solving (Baughin, Brod, & Page, 2002; Benander, Denton, Page, & Skinner, 2000; Montgomery, 2002). As these models demonstrate, it is important not to abbreviate the descriptions of the B, C, and D products because students are likely to focus only on the description of their own grade. However, the description of F work may be briefer because such serious shortcomings often transcend the rubric.

This holistic approach shortchanges students in one way, however: although the rubric provides an overall rationale for each grade, it does not furnish much feedback on the specific dimensions. After all, it is quite possible, using the example above, that a student's paper might contain elements of two, three, or even more performance levels—for example, following the organizational format perfectly but demonstrating a poor understanding and use of the readings throughout and containing a moderate number of mechanical errors. In this case, a holistic description is of little help to you or the student, especially as formative feedback, and rarely does it incorporate strategies for improvement. Of course, you can always write personalized comments on each student's work and underline or highlight the salient qualities in the performance quality descriptions. But then you may sacrifice much of the efficiency and time-saving advantages of holistic grading. As a result, many instructors favor a synthetic approach that combines some of the specificity of atomistic grading with the efficiency and professional judgment involved in the deductive holistic method.

Analytical Grading: The Effective Synthesis of Atomistic and Holistic

This grading technique follows the procedures of deductive holistic grading—focusing on four or five assessment criteria, writing descriptions for each performance level, and providing students with the rubric in advance—and shares the advantage of speed and efficiency. But rather than writing an overall description of the student product for each performance level, you write a brief description for each performance level on each criterion, and you assess the product not overall but independently on each criterion. Then you either total or average the points gained or the letter grades earned across

all the criteria to derive an overall grade. (Because you are working across dimensions, a point system may be easier.) This grading method certainly requires you to write more descriptions than does the holistic method—as many as the number of performance levels times the number of criteria—and you may find yourself writing more extensive or specific descriptions. However, these furnish your students more detailed instructions, expectations, and feedback as well as clearer justification for your assessment.

While you can write the descriptions in full sentences and even paragraphs, you can also use more succinct phrases. You can also display the rubric in an easy-to-read matrix or table for clarity, listing the assessment dimensions down the left side of the page to define rows and the levels of performance, such as possible numbers of points or letter grades, across the top to create columns. The cells contain your descriptions of the performance quality on each dimension. For purposes of illustration, let's return to that essay assignment arguing in favor of norm-referenced grading or criterion-referenced grading and transform the holistic rubric shown above into an analytical one (Table 31.1). (Only holistic rubrics with well-defined, consistent dimensions easily convert into an analytical version.)

When you use your rubric to grade, first test it out on three or four pieces of student work. While you are ethically bound not to make substantive changes, you may tweak it if needed. As you read a student product, mark (underline, highlight, check, star, or circle) the applicable phrases in the descriptions on the student's copy of the rubric. This grading method accommodates the wide differences in a student's performance across criteria. Then either calculate the point total or letter grade or eyeball it from the distribution of your markings, and write that in a discrete place on the student work. Add your personalized comments on the work or the rubric only as your time permits. If you have composed a good rubric, you should not have much more to say. Finally, return the work with the student's copy of the rubric.

Table 31.1   Analytical Grading Rubric for a Hypothetical Essay Assignment

Grade Criteria	A	B	C	D	F
Format	Follows the classic five-paragraph essay format strictly, stating the thesis (position) in the first paragraph, providing evidence in each of the next three paragraphs, and concluding with a summary or synthesis	Follows the classic five-paragraph essay format with no more than one minor deviation	Breaks significantly from the classic five-paragraph essay format—failing to state a clear position in the first paragraph, mixing arguments across paragraphs, or closing with a new argument or information	Does not follow the classic five-paragraph essay format—failing either to state a clear position or to use the rest of essay to bring evidence from the readings to support it	Fails to address the assignment in topic or format, or frequent errors in spelling, punctuation, and grammar render the essay incomprehensible, *or* not turned in
Command of readings	Consistently makes appropriate and accurate references to the readings	Generally accurate in referring to readings, but shows a thin, incomplete, or shaky understanding of some readings in a couple of places	Refers to the readings but demonstrates a spotty or superficial understanding of them	Demonstrates little understanding or knowledge of the readings	
Evidence from readings	Provides all the evidence available in the readings to support its argument	Provides evidence available in the readings, but misses some parts that would lend evidence to the argument	Misses opportunities to use the readings for evidence	Draws little relevant evidence from the readings	
Mechanics	No more than two spelling, punctuation, or grammatical errors	No more than several spelling, punctuation, or grammatical errors	Quite a few spelling, punctuation, or grammatical errors, though not enough to make parts of it incomprehensible	Frequent errors in spelling, punctuation, and grammar that are distracting or render the essay incomprehensible in places	

With a little experience, you will be able to develop rubrics quickly and at the same time that you design an assignment or write an essay test question. For the latter use, you can prepare a generic rubric that doesn't give away the question. When students can work on an assignment or study for a test with the rubric in front of them, they are less likely to explain away a poor performance with, "I didn't know what he wanted." You will find more examples of analytical rubrics in matrix/table form than any other kind, and models are available for every grading purpose. Look in the assessment literature (for example, Baughin et al., 2002; Brookhart, 1999; Leahy, 2002; Montgomery, 2002; Rodgers, 1995; Stevens & Levi, 2005; Suskie, 2004; Walvoord & Anderson, 1998) and on dedicated websites, such as RubiStar (http://rubistar.4teachers.org), Teach-nology (www.teach-nology.com/web_tools/rubrics), iRubric (www.rcampus.com/rubricshellc.cfm?mode=gallery&sms=home&srcgoogle&gclid=CNSCsu3PmZMCFQv_sgodPBO_xA), and Tech4Learning (http://myt4l.com/index.php?v=pl&page_ac=view&type=tools&tool=rubricmaker). All of these sites feature not just models but also rubric generators, allowing you to create your own for specific assignments. For many types of assignments, RubiStar, for instance, offers a drop-down menu of appropriate criteria to choose from. When you select a dimension, it displays descriptions of four quality levels, which you can then edit to your needs. While designed primarily for and by K–12 teachers, most of the models and generated rubrics apply to college-level work with little or no modification. The next chapter contains another example of an analytical rubric, and this is one you can use to guide you in writing a statement of your teaching philosophy.

■ GRADING LAB REPORTS

While this is a specialized kind of grading for a specialized kind of writing, all guidelines for grading constructed responses still apply. The questions below are also important to take into consideration across all lab reports:

- How well does the student understand the problem, and how properly does she address it?
- How clearly does she state the hypothesis?
- How does she present the results? Does the presentation follow the instructions? Are *all* the results included?
- How clear are the student's logic and organization?
- How strong are her analytical skills in the results and discussion?
- How solid is her grasp of the scientific method?

In lower-level science courses, you can help your students write better lab reports by providing them with samples of quality scientific writing—perhaps model lab reports from other courses—to familiarize them with the proper format and content. You can also have them organize their reports with an outline or flowchart and practice write the various sections.

Another excellent way to help your students produce good reports is to give them the grading rubric in advance. Rodgers (1995) developed a detailed analytical rubric, presented in an easy-to-read matrix, to grade his students' chemistry lab reports. His rubric has a daunting twenty-one assessment dimensions, but they fall within four more general criteria—focus, appearance, content, and structure—and have only three levels of point allocations: 2, 4, and 6.

For example, under "focus," Rodgers (1995, p. 21) has nine dimensions:

1. Understanding experimental objectives
2. Abstract describes what was done and major results
3. Unnecessary statements or observations in the procedure
4. Depth of introduction
5. Tone
6. Suggestions for improvement, further study in conclusions
7. Effort to relate the experiment to other known chemical principles
8. Shows detailed understanding of scientific method
9. Student distinguishes between a theory and a proof

This many dimensions seems high, but many of the cells have only one- or two-word descriptors—for dimension 1, "very clear," "demonstrated," or "unsophisticated"; for dimension 7, "clear," "vague," or "none"; for dimension 9, "yes," "yes," or "no." Even when the descriptor is considerably longer, it is very easy to simply check, circle, or highlight the most appropriate option. At the end, the grader totals the points accumulated across all twenty-one dimensions by calculating or eyeballing.

Rodgers (1995) recorded how long it took to grade a lab report using his old atomistic method versus his new method. He timed both himself and his trained teaching assistants. The results were quite startling. His previous grading technique required fifteen to twenty minutes per report, while the new one took only three and a half minutes (for him) to four minutes (for his teaching assistants) per report. In other words, atomistic grading took four to five times longer than analytical. Rodgers was pleased with the reliability and overall grading results.

■ HOW TO GRADE MECHANICS QUICKLY WHILE ENSURING STUDENTS LEARN THEM

With any grading method involving multiple criteria, be careful to distinguish among your various evaluative dimensions. For example, try not to let a poor grammatical construction devalue a good idea—assuming, of course, you can decipher the idea despite the construction. Still, because poor mechanics can hide a good idea, you should consider assessing your students' spelling, grammar, punctuation, sentence structure, and word choice as a separate dimension. Many instructors decide to avoid grading mechanics, even though they bemoan their students' writing—or perhaps because they do. Those who have tried assessing writing will tell you that it is a lost cause, that they spent laborious hours copyediting their students' work and their students neither looked carefully at their corrections nor improved their writing.

Indeed, grading mechanics this way is a lost cause. Once you return an essay test or written assignment with a grade on it, students will read the rubric description associated with their grade and your written comments but will give scant attention to your copyediting, even if their poor mechanics cost them points. Most of our scrawls make little sense to them. Besides, the work already has a grade, so what's the point?

Happily, you can grade mechanics, and do it in a fraction of the time it takes to copyedit the work, *and* ensure that students learn some grammar, spelling, punctuation, and sentence structure rules along the way and use what they learn in their subsequent writing. When you make an assignment, tell students that you will be grading their mechanics by choosing one page from their work—but you will not tell them which page in advance—to note their mechanical errors. You determine how many errors on the page will affect the grade in what ways and state that in your rubric—for example, up to five errors merit twenty points (total possible) for mechanics, five to ten errors merit fifteen points, ten to fifteen errors merit ten points, fifteen to twenty errors merit five points, and more than twenty errors merit no points. On that page, you will be placing a check mark at the end of a line for every grammar, spelling, punctuation, and sentence structure error in that line without identifying what the error is or correcting it.

After returning the graded work to your students, make the required follow-up assignment of identifying and correcting all the mechanical errors (or as many as students can) they have made on that page to gain back a portion of the points they lost. They will get credit only for accurate corrections. Refer them to one or more English language or writing handbooks. (The Web has a variety of free ones, including *The Writing Handbook* at www.lz95.org /LZHS/wcenter/Handbook.pdf, World-English at www.world-english.org/writing.htm, and the University of Wisconsin-Madison Writing Center's Writer's Handbook at http://writing.wisc.edu /Handbook.) To motivate students to get the mechanics right the first time, give them only partial credit for each correction, certainly no more than half the value of the points they lost. Instruct them to make their corrections on the actual page of the paper in a different color ink (or pencil) from black and the color you used for grading. Give them three to four days to complete this follow-up assignment. They will learn their mistakes and how to correct them through the process of discovery. When you collect these corrected pages, you need only look at the number of check marks you made in the margin and the corrections made. Moreover, students will remember the errors they identified, researched, and corrected and will not want to repeat the same errors again. If on the average they learn just a dozen new punctuation, grammar, and sentence structure rules, that is a dozen rules they otherwise would not learn at all.

In the next writing assignment, grade on mechanics the same way, selecting a different page for noting mechanical errors. Chances are that you will see fewer errors than before and, for each student, different ones from those you marked before. This time students will learn a few more rules for good writing. With just a few writing assignments and a modest amount of your time, your students will radically improve their writing.

Identify students who are not native English speakers, and be more lenient in grading their work. Note only the more important errors rather than overwhelm them. If advisable, refer them to your institution's writing or academic assistance center for individual help. In fact, refer any student with a serious writing problem to such a center. Every college and university has a range of specialized campus resources that can support you and your students; they are well worth exploring (see Appendix).

■ OUTCOME-BASED GRADING

Back in the 1970s and 1980s, a few progressive faculty experimented with a student-centered alternative to traditional grading called "contract grading." At the beginning of the course, students individually contracted or committed to complete specific assignments during the term for a specific final grade. Aside from the instructor's logistic challenge of monitoring a different set of requirements for each student, the system resulted in too many A's being given for subpar work and fell into disrepute.

However, a revised version of contract grading, one more appropriately called "outcome-based grading," that overcomes the pitfalls of the original has emerged and has been successfully adopted by faculty across the disciplines (Codde, 1996; K. Kegley, personal communication, February 17, 2005; Leff, n.d.; Weimer, 2002). In this new version, the instructor lays out the terms by which the students will earn grades, which promotes high standards, and assigns grades according to how well students fulfill certain work requirements, as specified in the syllabus or in assignment directions. In operational terms, students receive grades based on the number of assignments and often on the specific assignments they complete at a satisfactory level by given due dates. That is, they earn higher grades by jumping more hurdles, presumably showing evidence of more learning, or jumping higher hurdles, presumably showing evidence of more advanced learning, or jumping both more and higher hurdles. While students must aim for a specific grade to decide how much and which work they will complete, they wind up with the final grade they earn during the term.

What about students who try to jump a hurdle but for one reason or another fail to solve the problem, complete the assignment, or satisfy the requirements? In this case, they receive no credit for that hurdle. Because of the dire consequences of substandard work, outcome-based grading requires you to define exactly what jumping a hurdle means. That is, you must write very specific assignment directions and an up-or-down, one-level rubric for what acceptable work entails—perhaps obtaining the correct answer to a problem (and showing one's work), answering a list of questions, completing specific sections, writing so many words or pages, or satisfying whatever criteria will guide students to meet your expectations. You might even recommend how many hours students should put into a given assignment. Of course, you may set the bar as high as you believe that your students can reach, which can mean raising it—that is, for example, making what you consider B work in a traditionally graded course "acceptable," rather than C work. If you will grade an assignment on how advanced the level of learning a student demonstrates, you must convey exactly what you mean by "more advanced"—perhaps higher-order cognitive skills in Bloom's (1956) hierarchy, or higher-stage thinking in Perry's (1968) schema of undergraduate development, or higher-step skills in Wolcott's (2006) framework of critical thinking.

This type of grading may sound rigid and harsh, but it need not be. When students turn in unacceptable work for the first assignment, you can return it to accustom students to this new grading system. K. Kegley (personal communication, February 17, 2005) recommends building in flexibility with a token system. Starting the course with three tokens, each student can use one to revise and resubmit an unacceptable assignment, to be absent from class without penalty, or to obtain a one-day emergency extension. She also offers rewards for still having tokens at the end of the term, such as exempting the final exam or adding points to course grade.

Enhanced with some flexibility, outcome-based grading offers some advantages over traditional grading (Codde, 1996; Hiller & Hietapelto, 2001; K. Kegley, personal communication, February 17, 2005; Leff, n.d.; Warrington, Hietapelto, & Joyce, 2003; Weimer, 2002). Being menu driven and learner centered, students have choices about whether to complete or not to complete at least some assignments (and tests) or how much effort to allocate to an assignment. Therefore, they are more likely to see their grade as their own responsibility, not as a punitive faculty action or a capricious whim of the fates. This view should increase their sense of internal locus of control as well as their motivation because feelings of volition, choice, and self-determination motivate people to pursue a goal (Bandura, 1997; Wigfield & Eccles, 2000). Furthermore, if the requirements for success are clear to students, they should feel less anxious about their grade, more oriented to learning, and freer to take risks and be creative within the parameters of the

assignment (Dweck & Leggett, 1988). No wonder most students prefer outcome-based to traditional grading once they experience it.

■ RETURNING STUDENTS' WORK

To protect students' privacy, return their work in any order except grading rank, and record points and grades inside the test or paper—never where they can be seen. Under the provisions of the Buckley Amendment (the Family Educational Rights and Privacy Act), it is illegal to publicly display scores or grades with any identifying information, including entire or partial social security numbers.

Grade and return tests and assignments as promptly as you can; students cannot learn from your feedback on a piece of work they have long forgotten. Allow class time for review, questions, and problem-solving exercises so students can learn what they did not the first time. It is best not to proceed to new material until students assure you that they understand what they did wrong. Some instructors give a statistical grading summary showing the distribution of points, the class mean and median, the standard deviation, and the cut-off lines for grades (already built into the criterion-referenced system). No doubt these data increase students' interest in elementary statistics, but they also encourage "point mongering" around the cut-off lines.

This brings us to the unpleasant topic of grade disputes. No matter how carefully you grade, a few students will be dissatisfied with their scores. The holistic and analytical grading methods discourage (but do not prevent) such challenges because, unlike atomistic grading, they rely heavily on professional judgment, which is too sophisticated for most students to debate against. Rule number one is never to discuss a grade with an emotional student. Rather, require him to cool off and to submit his case for a grade change formally in writing (not by email) with justifications citing specific material in the readings or your lectures, within a time limit of forty-eight to seventy-two hours. Students who cannot make a case in two or three days probably do not have one.

Alternatively, agree to regrade the entire test or paper, which means you may find a grading error that does not work in the student's favor. Or agree to regrade the item in question, but should you find no cause for a point change, you will subtract the number of points disputed. However you decide to respond to grade challenges, clearly state your policy in your syllabus and stick to it.

■ HELPING STUDENTS USE YOUR FEEDBACK TO IMPROVE

The purpose of feedback is to help the recipient perform some skill better, yet it does not always succeed. The section on grading mechanics describes a two-stage assessment procedure that builds in motivation for students to use your feedback. Unless you follow up an assignment with another one that makes your students examine and learn from their errors, you should not assume that they will use your feedback to improve their performance next time. So consider having them write a summary of the feedback contained in your rubric and comments, along with an explanation of how they will use it to improve their next assignment or essay test. This strategy has yielded good results and will make the energy you put into furnishing feedback worthwhile (Doyle, 2008).

Even with such a follow-up assignment, other factors can undermine the value and impact of our feedback (Falkenberg, 1996). For whatever reason, a student may not be capable of meeting the higher standards our feedback sets as a goal. If so, all the feedback in the world will fail. A second possibility is that a student may not agree with our performance standards, in which case it falls on us to change her mind. But can we? For instance, faculty and students have quite different definitions of cheating and plagiarism and the stage at which they become unethical (see Chapter Eight). Thus far, we have not found successful ways to convince students to adopt our values. Many students also believe that we should grade them not just on performance but also on effort, and some maintain they are entitled to an A just for showing up

in class or paying tuition. In this case, we can force our standards, but have we gained converts? Another area of disagreement is writing standards. Students who in our view write poorly may argue that they have always written this way and have gotten good grades and been understood by their friends. We can tell them that the workplace will expect a writing style closer to our criteria, but will they believe us? They may also oppose our scientific perspectives on religious grounds, pitting our material against their years of socialization. Rather than challenging their beliefs, we may be able to persuade them to accept and compartmentalize science as a separate worldview.

Two other dynamics may explain why our feedback fails (Falkenberg, 1996). First, a student may not correctly perceive our performance standards. For example, we may counsel a student that he frequently writes sentence fragments, but if he continues to write them, he may not yet understand what a sentence fragment is. We can overcome this barrier by clarifying our standards in different words, providing more models, or tutoring the student individually. Second, a student may not correctly evaluate her performance against our standards, and one of several reasons may be behind it. If it is because of simple error, all we need do is to supply additional feedback that gives new information or an alternative interpretation. But the block may represent ingrained error—that is, she has been performing the skill wrong for so long that it feels right to her. Even so, we can probably reach her by furnishing more models and tutoring. However, if the student is too immature to accept criticism or out of touch with reality, there is really nothing we can do (Falkenberg, 1996). This may explain the students we have known who have cut classes, turned in failing work, and refused our help.

When we can intervene, we should enlist other students to help us. Often they furnish the additional clarification, information, interpretation, models, and even tutoring, especially when they work in small groups to provide peer feedback on their drafts of assignments. We should also refer students to campus resources such as the writing or the academic assistance center.

■ THE REAL MEANING AND LIMITS OF GRADES

In the best of all possible worlds, we would not give grades at all. Rather we would furnish our students with individual feedback on how to improve their work. So we should keep grades in perspective and see them for what they are: an institutionally mandated shorthand used to screen, sanction, motivate, and reward—with mixed results. What grades cannot do is to inspire students to want to learn. That admirable task is ours, and our success depends on our teaching methods and moves, our motivational strategies, our enthusiasm, our rapport with students, and other qualities and behaviors that we examine in the next and final chapter.

CHAPTER 32

Evaluating and Documenting Teaching Effectiveness

Over the past couple of decades, teaching effectiveness has come to weigh more heavily in the faculty review process, including tenure and promotion decisions, in North American colleges and universities. With this trend has come an increasing emphasis on student ratings and the development of additional ways to document teaching success. This chapter summarizes the major research findings on the validity and reliability of student ratings, which almost all institutions use to measure teaching effectiveness, and suggests ways that you can improve yours. Then it presents guidelines for writing your teaching philosophy and documenting your teaching effectiveness in teaching and course portfolios. Finally, it reviews two systems for evaluating teaching effectiveness in formal faculty reviews, both of which take more than student ratings into account. As it turns out, evaluating teaching turns out to be more complex than judging the merits of a faculty member's research or service. So let's begin by looking at how it is defined and measured.

■ DEFINING AND MEASURING TEACHING EFFECTIVENESS

Teaching effectiveness is an instructor's degree of success in facilitating student learning. In general, the more material and skills students learn, the higher the cognitive, affective, ethical, social, and psychomotor levels at which they learn it, and the better they can communicate what they have learned, the more effective an instructor's teaching is. More specifically, the better the students achieve an instructor's learning outcomes and the more students who do so, the more effective her teaching is.

It is simple enough to propose this formal definition, but how are we to measure student learning? While we do this in our tests and assignments, we rarely use standardized assessment instruments across different sections and terms of the same course—and for good reason. First, some faculty would consider being required to do so as impinging on their academic freedom and autonomy as we currently define them. Second, it would tempt instructors to teach to the test—a good consequence only if the tests validly assessed all of their student learning outcomes. But typically these instruments are too objective and fact heavy to test all the cognitive, affective, ethical, social, and psychomotor skills that so many courses aim to help students develop. Third, no single instruments can capture the complexity of the learning process. The instructor is only one among many factors that affect the depth and breadth of student learning in a given course. Beyond her influence are the student's intelligence, energy level, interest, attitudes toward work, out-of-class commitments, family background, and previous schooling (Arreola, 2007). A final reason is that few disciplines have developed standardized assessment tests of what students should gain from a given course. Even the notable exceptions, physics and economics, have such instruments only for their lowest-level courses

But because institutions eschew standardized assessments, they cannot directly measure teaching effectiveness or directly compare the relative effectiveness of different instructors. Rather, most of them rely heavily on student ratings and written comments, which together constitute "students' evaluations" about the course and the instructor. Numerical ratings in particular permit quick and easy analysis and comparison. But how justified are institutions in using student ratings as a surrogate for student learning? The next section tackles this question.

■ STUDENT EVALUATIONS

Student evaluations directly tap students' perceptions and affective reactions to an instructor and a course, specifically their satisfaction with them. (This variable may be of greater interest than learning to administrators who are striving for customer satisfaction.) Obviously satisfaction is not the same as learning, even if they are related. In addition, the forms that collect these data often have flawed, homespun items with questionable validity and reliability (Nuhfer, 2003). So we don't know how well the research on student

ratings, which has generally used well-tested questionnaires, applies at many institutions.

Moreover, what relationships do exist between direct measures of student learning and student ratings (satisfaction) are grounded largely in research that was conducted in the 1970s and 1980s (Cashin, 1988; Cohen, 1981; Feldman, 1989). Since then, the college student population has markedly changed on many dimensions: demographics, values, attitudes, motivations, aspirations, percentage employed, preparation for college, and reasons for attending college. Certainly such profound shifts should have an impact on students' assessment of the instructors, perhaps for the more critical. If we could replicate the best of the many "old" studies with today's students, our conclusions on the merits of student evaluations would stand on much firmer grounds. All this is to say that extrapolating yesterday's research findings to today involves a leap of faith.

How Valid Are Student Ratings?

To assess *validity* means to find out how well we are measuring what we intend to measure. Two concerns are paramount in determining the validity of student ratings: how effectively they serve as an indicator of student learning or achievement and what biases may reduce that effectiveness. The closer the relationship is between student ratings and learning, and the fewer and weaker the biases in ratings, the more valid ratings are and the better they serve as proxies for direct measures of learning.

A vast literature on the evaluation of teaching—research with which few instructors are familiar—supports the claim that student ratings (not necessarily the written comments) are sufficiently valid to be used in faculty reviews. This assumes, of course, that an institution is using a statistically solid rating instrument tested for validity and reliability, which is frequently not the case (Arreola, 2007; Nuhfer, 2003). The evidence in favor of student ratings is found in two meta-analyses conducted by Cohen (1981) and Feldman (1989). Synthesizing the results of dozens of rigorous studies, both reported that student achievement on an external exam (a direct measure of learning) correlates decently with student ratings of specific facets of teaching effectiveness (mean $r = .57$ to $.38$)—in particular, the instructor's ability to explain clearly, his good use of class time, preparation, course organization, students' perceived learning gains, instructor's stimulation of interest in the subject, and his ability to motivate students to do their best. Learning and the overall (also called "global") ratings of instructor effectiveness and the course also correlated moderately ($r = .44$ and $.47$, respectively; Cohen, 1981). Instructor friendliness, personality, rapport, and the like related more weakly to achievement ($r = .31$; Cohen, 1981). Bear in mind that these correlations are moderate at best and are derived from large data sets. You cannot use them to predict how much a class has learned from only the instructor's student ratings. Therefore, while over many faculty and classes, higher ratings result in more learning, or vice versa, student ratings are a poor stand-in for learning in any one class.

Recent research has uncovered one source of interference between learning and ratings. A number of students—and that's all it takes to affect ratings—object to active learning strategies, student-centered courses, and an emphasis on critical thinking, and they accordingly penalize instructors on the evaluation forms (Edens, 2000; Lieux, 1996; Rhem, 2006; Thorn, 2003; Weimer, 2002).

Biases affect validity, but some of the variables that correlate most strongly with ratings, those characterizing the instructor's persona, may or may not be biases. As you may recall, Chapter Seven recommends projecting a certain instructor persona to reduce classroom incivilities. The same persona also seems to enhance ratings, and among its most potent facets are enthusiasm/expressiveness, warmth, and self-esteem (Erdle & Murray, 1986; Feldman, 1986). The first two traits positively color even peer assessments of an instructor's teaching. Some scholars argue that enthusiasm constitutes a bias because it is unrelated to learning as tested by multiple-choice tests (Williams & Ceci, 1997). However, enthusiasm, self-confidence, and warmth toward the audience

characterize an engaging lecturer and a competent professional public speaker (see Chapter Twelve). Such qualities build trust with the audience and attract and maintain its attention. In addition, an instructor's stimulation of student interest in the course and subject matter, which often stems from his enthusiasm and his sensitivity to and concern with class progress, which often accompanies warmth, correlates with student learning, though not strongly (Feldman, 1989, 1998a, 1998b). On balance, then, instructor enthusiasm/expressiveness, warmth, and self-esteem are more components of effective teaching than they are interference.

Let's examine another reputed bias in student ratings. Many instructors believe that grading more leniently raises their ratings, and some respectable research backs up their claim (Greenwald & Gillmore, 1997; Johnson, 2003). The correlation between grades (actual or expected) and overall student ratings, while not strong, varies somewhat across studies ($r = .33$ in Greenwald & Gillmore, 1997; $r = .10$ to $.30$, according to Feldman, 1998b). Whatever the size of the relationship, we have no statistically respectable method to draw a definitive conclusion about what is apparently causing the increase in ratings on either the individual or the class level. Is it grades, or is it one or more variables closely associated with grades? Clearly grades and learning are linked. We also know certain precursors to both greater learning and higher grades, such as students' prior interest in the subject matter, motivation to learn, and academic commitment. In fact, these precursors are also correlated with student ratings, about as much as instructor behaviors are. So are higher ratings due to higher grades, or are they due to greater learning and its precursors? If it is the latter, then ratings reflect what they should. In fact, all six of these variables are sufficiently interrelated that we cannot isolate the independent effects of one variable on another (Abrami, Dickens, Perry, & Leventhal, 1980; Cashin, 1995; Howard & Maxwell, 1980, 1982).

Running counter to the grading leniency hypothesis are findings, both decades old and recent, that students give higher ratings in more challenging courses in which they have to work hard (Beyers, 2008; Centra, 1993; Dee, 2007; Marsh & Dunkin, 1992; Martin, Hands, Lancaster, Trytten, & Murphy, 2008; Sixbury & Cashin, 1995). It seems then that watering down a course and its workload will not boost student ratings.

What about other biases? Aleamoni (1999), Cashin (1988, 1995), and Feldman (1986, 1992, 1993/1998b) separate myth from reality in their comprehensive literature reviews. First presented are the variables that have been found not to affect student ratings in a statistically significant and consistent way.

Instructor Characteristics

1. Gender (also see Centra & Gaubatz, 1999; Feldman, 1992, 1993; Nilson & Lysaker, 1996)
2. Age and experience (but d'Apollonia & Abrami, 1997, report that rank, experience, and autonomy modestly bias ratings upward)
3. Personality (as measured by a personality inventory; this is not "persona")
4. Research productivity ($r = .12$, Feldman, 1987)

Student Characteristics

1. Gender
2. Age
3. Level (freshman to senior)
4. Grade point average
5. Personality (as measured by a personality inventory)

Course and Administrative Variables

1. Class size
2. Time of day the course is taught
3. Time during the term the evaluations are collected

But some genuine biases *do* exist (Aleamoni, 1999; Cashin, 1988, 1995):

Instructor Characteristics

1. Status has an impact in that regular faculty tend to get higher ratings than teaching assistants do.

Student Characteristics

1. Prior interest in the subject matter. The higher the students' prior interest in the subject matter, the higher their ratings of the course and the instructor.
2. Academic commitment. The more willing students are to put noninstructor-induced effort into their learning—that is, the more motivated they are to work—the higher their ratings of the course and the instructor.
3. Reason for taking the course. Holding course and instructor characteristics constant, students give higher ratings to courses they take voluntarily (electives) and lower ratings to those they take to fulfill a requirement (for instance, general education). These higher or lower ratings also extend to the instructor. However, what is voluntary and what is not is often in the eye of the beholder. Given a choice of a hundred courses that satisfy a general education requirement, does a student view his selection as elective or required?

Course and Administrative Variables

1. Course level. Higher-level courses, especially graduate level, tend to receive higher ratings.
2. Discipline. Humanities courses receive higher ratings than social science courses, which in turn receive higher ratings than science, technical, engineering, and mathematics (STEM) courses. But the research only suggests possible reasons for these differences. We know that humanities instructors exhibit a broader range of teaching behaviors that are positively related to student ratings (for example, interactivity, rapport with class, making the material relevant) than do social and natural science instructors, who focus more on structuring and pacing the subject matter (Murray & Renaud, 1996). But other possible reasons include the greater difficulty of STEM courses (Johnson, 2003) and the more immediate and obvious personal relevance of humanities and social science courses.
3. Student anonymity. Signed ratings are higher than anonymous ones for obvious reasons.

4. Presence of the instructor. The instructor's presence while students are filling out the forms biases ratings upward.
5. Perceived purpose of the evaluation. Students rate more generously if they believe their ratings will be used for personnel decisions than if they believe their ratings are only for instructor self-improvement.

How Reliable Are Student Ratings?

In assessing reliability, three criteria are very important: consistency, stability, and generalizability. The consistency of student ratings—that is, the agreement between raters—is quite high, increasing from moderately high to very high with class size. In Cashin and Perrin's (1978) study, average item reliability in a class of ten students was .69, but it increased to .89 in a class of forty. In Sixbury and Cashin's (1995) replication, the reliability figures were the same or higher. Stability, which indicates the concurrence of ratings over time, is also high. In a longitudinal study conducted by Marsh and Overall (1979; Overall & Marsh, 1980), student ratings collected at the end of a semester were compared against ratings collected at least one year after graduation. The average correlation of the ratings was .83, showing a high level of stability. Finally, generalizability, defined as the concurrence of ratings for the same instructor in different teaching situations, is very good. Marsh (1982) compared the ratings of the same instructor teaching the same course in different semesters, the same instructor teaching different courses, different instructors teaching the same course, and different instructors teaching different courses. The correlations for the same instructor-same course were quite high (.71) and much higher than those for the same course-different instructor (.14). An instructor's effectiveness apparently crosses course boundaries as well, since the same instructor-different course correlation was .52 versus the much lower different instructor-different course correlation of .06. More recent research (Albanese, 1991; Hativa, 1996) has found higher correlations of .87 to .89 between

an instructor's student ratings from one year to the next.

In using student ratings for personnel decisions, Cashin (1988, 1995) recommends using data from multiple terms and multiple courses to obtain a more reliable picture of teaching effectiveness. If an instructor teaches only one course, then consistent ratings from two terms may be sufficient. For instructors with more responsibilities, however, ratings from two or more courses for every term taught over the past two or more years provide a better assessment. For fair and comprehensive instructor reviews, the ratings of courses with fewer than fifteen students should be supplemented with other assessment material.

How to Improve Your Student Ratings

Start by reviewing the statistical summaries and student comments from your previous evaluations. It is best to do this with your department chair, a trusted colleague, or a staff member from your institution's teaching center. Look for repeated areas of criticism—pay no attention to isolated complaints—and try to identify patterns and trends. Does class size, level, or subject matter seem to make a difference? Bear in mind the biases in student ratings and mentally correct for them. Remember that these questionnaires collect students' perceptions and affective reactions, not objective reality. You might not think you behaved a certain way (for example, condescending, impatient, disorganized) that alienated your students, but you apparently did or said something that gave them that impression. What could that be?

Then consider the factors related to ratings that you can and cannot control. For instance, you cannot change your discipline, the specific subjects you teach, the required or elective nature of your courses, or the size of your classes. Nor can you affect your students' prior interest in the subject matter, their academic commitment, or their motivation to take your course. But you can make changes in the clarity of your explanations, your use of class time, your preparation (real and apparent), the organization of your course (even if it is just making that organization more apparent to students with a graphic syllabus and an outcomes maps), and your public speaking skills (see Chapter Twelve). You can enhance your persona by projecting more enthusiasm, energy, relaxed self-confidence, authority, and in-command leadership—qualities that will stimulate students' interest in the material and maintain their respectful attention (see Chapters Seven and Twelve). You can also add warmth, empathy, and caring to your persona by learning students' names, encouraging their success, smiling, and exhibiting a few other simple behaviors, which will motivate students to do their best (see Chapters Five and Seven). You can help students see how much they are learning by having them reflect and write about their newly acquired or improved skills. You can explain to them how important their evaluations are to you personally and to your institution. You can replace some major tests with daily quizzes (see Chapter Twenty-Three). This book presents a wealth of teaching methods and moves that can improve your ratings as well as your students' learning. Just give a major innovation two or more terms to show positive results.

In addition, try to gather student feedback far enough in advance of the official evaluation process to fine-tune your courses. You can write up, administer, and analyze your own midterm student evaluations, including items similar to those on your institution's or department's official ratings form, as well as others of concern to you. Alternatively, you can ask your teaching center to conduct a small-group instructional diagnosis (class interview) in your classes. Research shows that soliciting early student feedback and having an interpretive consultation with a specialist result in significantly higher student evaluations at the end of the term (Cohen, 1980).

Students seem to take the opportunity to give their instructors midterm feedback more seriously than they do end-of-term teaching evaluations. After all, they stand to benefit from the former, while the latter come too late to improve their learning experience. You can pick and choose among the changes they request, explaining to them why you

are making some changes and not others. In fact, you can address many of their concerns not by changing anything but by providing your reasons for the teaching and assessment decisions you have made. Again, this book supplies plenty of research-based rationales for effective choices.

■ PEER, ADMINISTRATIVE, AND SELF-EVALUATIONS

Dozen of studies conducted in the 1970s and early 1980s (for example, Aleamoni, 1982; Bergman, 1980; Centra, 1975, 1979; Greenwood & Ramagli, 1980) came to these conclusions about self-evaluations of teaching and peer and administrative evaluations based on classroom observations:

- Self-evaluations do not correlate much with any other type of evaluation.
- Self-evaluation and peer evaluations based on classroom visits are much more generous than student ratings.
- Among peer evaluators who visit a classroom for observational purposes, interrater reliability (that is, consensus) is low.
- Peer and administrative evaluations based on classroom visits are so highly correlated as to be almost redundant.
- All three relate very little to student learning and only modestly to student ratings.

The literature also consistently argues that none of these types of evaluations should be used as the sole teaching evaluation tool, and they should not replace student ratings and comments. In fact, peer and administrative evaluations based on classroom observations should not be used for promotion and tenure reviews at all, unless:

- The observers are formally trained in classroom observation and the use of the evaluation form.
- They meet with the instructor beforehand to discuss his teaching philosophy, preferred methods,

characteristics of the course and students, and learning outcomes for the course and the specific class.

- They observe the instructor's class at least seven or eight times during the term.
- They schedule the classroom visits with the instructor in advance.

Some of these conditions are very difficult for busy faculty, department chairs, and deans to meet, but such a professional observation program has been developed and tested (Millis, 1992).

Of course, feedback from more casual peer and administrative classroom observations is not only harmless but potentially useful for formative purposes. Peers in particular have the expertise to advise on the course content, book selections, online resources, possible demonstrations and class activities, and the technical aspects of instructional design, such as the syllabus and assignments. However, students are the more relevant judges of instructional design (the completeness of the syllabus, the clarity of the course organization, and the learning effectiveness of assignments and activities), instructional delivery (the use and organization of class time, communication and presentation skills, the clarity of explanations, and the degree of student activity and engagement), and their perceived learning (the challenge of tests and assignments, perceived achievement of outcomes, and interest in learning more about the subject matter).

■ DOCUMENTING YOUR EFFECTIVENESS

Numerous studies document that student ratings provide meaningful assessment data that should be used in faculty reviews, but *without exception* they recommend including other teaching-related data as well (Aleamoni, 1999; Arreola, 2007; Berk, 2005; Cashin, 1988, 1995; Centra, 1999; McKeachie, 2002; Nuhfer, 2003; Seldin, 2004). While some departments and institutions request additional materials, you should always submit more than your student

ratings; the reviewers will look at whatever you supply. Besides, current students are in no position to judge your course content, every facet of your instructional design and delivery, or the longer-term impact of your teaching.

Although submitting the documents and materials described in this section cannot guarantee you a faculty position, tenure, or promotion, they do make the academic reward system more responsive to teaching achievements (Seldin, 2004). Their use in whole or in part is gaining acceptance because they complement the student ratings data and fit easily into current hiring and review procedures. Perhaps most important, they motivate faculty and administrators to talk about teaching, thereby promoting reflection, innovation, and improvement.

The Teaching Philosophy

This one- to two-page single-spaced statement is often a required part of an academic job application and faculty review materials, including a teaching portfolio. It does not document your teaching effectiveness as much as it proves you have reflected on your teaching and are committed to an effective strategy. There is no simple formula for writing a teaching philosophy, but certain conventions apply. Following an essay format with an introduction and conclusion, it is a personal statement incorporating both cognitive and affective elements written in the first person. It also contains all or most of the facets of a philosophy: (1) a theory of how reality works—in this case, a theory of teaching and learning; (2) an informed and systematic rationale for why you do what you do—in this case, the way you teach; and (3) a system of principles or values that guides living and action—in this case, that shapes or drives your teaching. While nontechnical, the statement must demonstrate an understanding of how students learn and practical knowledge of at least a few student-active teaching methods.

Several scholars have proposed lists of questions that a teaching philosophy should address (for example, Berke & Kastberg, 1998; Chism, 1997–1998; Johnston, 2003; Schönwetter, Sokal,

Friesen, & Taylor, 2002). A careful analysis of their recommendations reveals their near total concurrence on what you should provide: your theory of how learning occurs and how teaching can foster it; the values, goals, or ideals that motivate you to teach; and the specific teaching methods you use, linking them to your learning theory or your motivating values, goals, or ideals, or both. The scholars just phrase the questions differently, and one trigger may resonate more with you than others. For example, Berke and Kastberg ask you to identify the notions about learning that make you teach the way you do; Johnston wants you to address the conditions under which students best learn; and Schönwetter et al. ask you to define *teaching* and *learning*. Berke and Kastberg elicit your motivations for teaching by asking why you teach, and, if you are experienced, why you still teach. They probe for answers among your desires, beliefs, values, and hopes for what students will gain from your teaching. Johnston wants to know what you are trying to accomplish in your teaching, and how your approaches reflect who you are. In one way or another, all of these scholars ask for descriptions of and rationales for your teaching methods and the learning experiences you create for students. Indeed, all philosophies describe what one does in the classroom, even if some focus more on the theory and others on the motivation to teach. One global question that Berke and Kastberg pose could frame an entire teaching philosophy: What is your conception of a great teacher, and what are you doing to become one?

Some instructors can identify a key belief that is central to how they teach. If you can do this, you can generate a statement of your teaching philosophy just by answering these questions: What assumptions about teaching, learning, students, education, and the like underlie your key belief? What values, principles, goals, or ideals does it reflect or spring from? What does it imply for your classroom teaching?

If you are having troubling articulating key beliefs, a theory of teaching and learning, or your motivations for teaching, complete one or more of these free online teaching inventories: the Teaching Goals Inventory at http://fm.iowa.uiowa.edu/fmi/xsl/tgi/data_entry.xsl?-db=tgi_data&-lay=Layout01&-view; the Grasha-Reichman Teaching Style Inventory at http://longleaf.net/teachingstyle.html; and the Teaching Perspectives Inventory (TPI) at www.teachingperspectives.com. In addition to finding out more about your own teaching identity, you will learn descriptively rich terms for various teaching aims, styles, and approaches that you can use in your statement.

If appropriate, two other topics also belong in a teaching philosophy. First, you should at least mention any research on teaching you have done, even if you have not published it. If you have published it, refer your reader to the section of your curriculum vita where you list it. Second, you should explain, if possible, any problematic student evaluations you have received in recent years. As mentioned earlier in this chapter, some students have been known to penalize instructors who teach student-actively, emphasize critical thinking, or use student-centered practices. If your evaluations have suffered for any of these reasons and you have continued to teach the way you do because you know it is most effective for student learning, then state this in your philosophy as an illustration of your strong educational principles.

Make your statement inviting. Do not try to cram in more text by covering all the available white space. Leave margins of at least one inch and use eleven- or, preferably, twelve-point type. Write clearly, simply, and with conviction, and use transitions generously to shepherd your readers through the document. Once you have a decent draft of your statement, appraise it against the teaching philosophy rubric in Table 32.1, and revise it to meet the specifications and qualities under "Excellent."

The Teaching Portfolio

This is a collection of materials that you assemble to highlight your major teaching strengths and achievements, comparable to your publications, grants, and scholarly honors in your research record (Seldin, 2004). It provides a comprehensive, factual base to

Table 32.1   Rubric for Assessing and Revising a Statement of Teaching Philosophy

	Excellent	Needs Some Revision	Needs Considerable Revision	Needs a Complete Rewrite
Content; coverage of essential topics	Thoroughly and thoughtfully presents a theory of teaching and learning, teaching values, goals, and ideals, and compatible teaching methods.	Addresses the three essential topics but does so too briefly or superficially.	Fails to address one of the three essential topics.	Fails to address two of the three essential topics.
Balance of personal and professional	Well balanced; formal in tone but maintains the sense of "I."	Occasionally too informal or too impersonal.	Often lapses into an inappropriate informality or loses the sense of "I."	A personal stream of consciousness or a totally impersonal essay with no sense of "I."
Structure and organization	Essay is coherent with a clear introduction, a strong conclusion, and logical transitions between paragraphs and sentences.	Essay is generally coherent but lacks either a clear introduction or a strong conclusion. Has some logical transitions between paragraphs and sentences.	Essay lacks a coherent structure and organization. Some paragraphs seem out of place, unconnected to the surrounding text. Lacks either a clear introduction or clear conclusion, or conclusion is very weak. Has few logical transitions between paragraphs and sentences.	Essay is incoherent and unstructured. Lacks a clear introduction, a clear conclusion, and logical transitions between paragraphs and sentences.
Writing style and mechanics (grammar, punctuation, and spelling)	Writing is clear, concise, and smooth. It follows the rules of standard English. Each sentence is connected to the ones before and after. Varied sentence structure. Very few, if any, mechanical errors.	Writing follows the rules of standard English with few errors in sentence structure and syntax. Sentences are usually connected. Some minor mechanical errors.	Writing violates some rules of standard English and is sometimes awkward and difficult to understand. Some sentences seem unconnected and out of place. Frequent mechanical errors.	Writing often violates the rules of standard English and is generally awkward and difficult to understand. Sentences are unconnected. Monotonous sentence structure. Numerous mechanical errors.
Presentation and length	Neatly typed, single-spaced, twelve-point type, not cramped. Optimal length: one to one and a half pages, possibly two pages if very experienced.	A bit too long or too short.	Somewhat too long or too short.	Sloppy, double-spaced, type too small, cramped, or much too long or too short.

develop self-assessment and improvement efforts and for peers and administrators to make sound hiring, promotion, and tenure decisions. The five- to ten-page statement that you write presents both basic information about your teaching responsibilities and your critical, improvement-driven analysis of the content you selected to put in the appendixes, such as your teaching contributions, professional activities, course materials, student ratings, and peer feedback.

While faculty most often put together a teaching portfolio for a formal personnel review, your purpose will influence what you include and how you organize it. To ensure objectivity in selecting materials, prepare your portfolio in consultation with a mentor, a trusted colleague, your department chair, or a teaching center consultant. Your partner can help you focus on the important questions: What is the purpose of the portfolio? What information will your audience find useful? Which areas of your teaching best serve your purpose? What is the best way to present and analyze the information? What additional information do you need, and how can you obtain it? For instance, reviewers involved in personnel decisions will be looking to see that you accurately represent your teaching responsibilities, that your teaching goals fit with the department's and institution's, that you have sought peer input, and that your students have left your courses both satisfied and more knowledgeable.

Approach assembling the teaching portfolio as a step-by-step process (Seldin, 2004), starting with a teaching statement. First, summarize your teaching responsibilities in a few paragraphs, describing the types of courses you teach, your student learning outcomes, your approach to course design, your expectations for student progress, and your assessment strategies. Then explain and prioritize your criteria for assessing your teaching effectiveness along with your reasons for choosing these criteria. They should coincide with your teaching style and responsibilities and reflect the purpose of the portfolio. For instance, if you particularly want to demonstrate your improvement, then rank your participation in teaching workshops and programs high. Finally, make a list

of the materials and data that support your criteria, such as student assignments, journals, test results, ratings, and the like, and gather these artifacts for the appendixes. In your statement, refer readers to these items as examples or evidence.

Institutions that use teaching portfolios vary somewhat in the required components and preferred organization. For example, yours may want you to integrate your teaching philosophy, five-year teaching goals, self-evaluation, course updates and improvements, and teaching-related professional activities into your teaching statement. Or it may recommend that you accompany each item in the appendixes with a paragraph of two linking it to your teaching responsibilities, your criteria for effectiveness, and other information you provide in your teaching statement. So check first with your department chair.

If not incorporated into your teaching statement, these items probably belong in your appendixes:

- Your teaching philosophy
- Your teaching goals for the next five years
- A brief self-evaluation with your teaching improvement strategies and efforts, including the teaching center services, workshops, and programs you have taken advantage of
- Descriptions of improvements and updates in your course assignments, materials, and activities
- A list of your teaching-related professional activities, such as instructional research (the scholarship of teaching and learning), publications, journal editing and reviewing, conference presentations, and invited teaching workshops (include abstracts or reprints of your published research on teaching and summaries of your unpublished research in the appendixes)
- Syllabi and other important course materials (a DVD of one of your class periods is optional)
- A list of students you have advised or supervised in research projects
- Teaching awards, honors, and other types of recognition, such as teaching committee appointments

- Student ratings and comments from all your courses

Ask whether your department or institution would like any of these testimonial-type supporting materials:

- Statements from peers or administrators who have observed your teaching
- Statements from peers who have reviewed your course materials
- Statements from peers on how well you have prepared your students for more advanced courses
- A statement from your chair or supervisor about your past and projected departmental contributions
- Statements from employers about graduates who studied a great deal with you
- Statements from service-learning clients on the impact of your student projects
- Statements from your advisees and research mentees about how you have influenced them
- Statements and letters, solicited and unsolicited, from former students about your longer-term teaching impact

Finally, your reviewers may be interested in more data from and about your students:

- Student feedback or evaluation summaries that reflect improvement, perceived learning, or satisfaction—aside from student ratings and comments
- Samples of student work on graded assignments (include samples of varying quality with your feedback and your reasons for the grades you assigned)
- Surveys of student knowledge at the beginning and the end of a course
- Improvements in students' attitudes about the subject matter, as documented by final reflection or personal-growth essays or by attitudinal surveys you administer at the beginning and the end of the course

- Students' opinions of their success in achieving your learning outcomes (extra student ratings form item)
- A list of your successful mentees in the discipline
- Information on how you have influenced students' postgraduate and career choices
- Students' scores on standardized tests, especially the sections of national and licensing exams that reflect your courses

You can read examples of high-quality teaching portfolios in Seldin (2004) or at www.ilr.cornell.edu/TAC/toolbox/portfoli/examples.html.

The Course Portfolio

This collection of materials summarizes how you planned, taught, managed, and currently evaluate a particular course, so you might assemble one on every course you regularly teach. Not as widely used as a teaching portfolio, a course portfolio contains many of the same materials but organizes them around a course rather than your teaching career. It also serves the same purposes of promoting self-assessment and improvement and encouraging sounder hiring, promotion, and tenure decisions with respect to teaching effectiveness (Cerbin, 1994; Hutchings, 1998).

These are the kinds of documents that belong in a course portfolio (Cerbin, 1994; Hutchings, 1998):

- Course syllabus, with student learning objectives and outcomes
- Brief description of course's content and its place in the curriculum
- Important handouts
- Annotated list of teaching methods
- Descriptions of assignments, if not in the syllabus
- Laboratory exercises or problem sets
- Descriptions of special class activities, such as simulations, role plays, case studies, problem-based learning projects, laptop exercises, service-learning assignments, guest speakers, and field trips
- Samples of graded student work

- Assessment instruments: quizzes, tests, and major classroom assessment techniques
- Results of midterm student feedback
- Summaries of the teaching center services, workshops, and programs you took advantage of to improve this course
- End-of-term student ratings and written comments
- Feedback from any peer or administrator classroom observations
- A reflective narrative of several pages

This last element is the most important. The document should incorporate some of the material listed above and refer to the rest. You might organize it around these course topics (Cerbin, 1994, 1995):

- *Design.* Why did you organize the course the way you did? How does it reflect your teaching philosophy and serve your student learning outcomes? How does it help you meet the course's major challenges?
- *Enactment.* What did the students experience during the course? What are the reasons behind your important assignments, class activities, and assessment strategies? (Including a DVD of your major class activities is optional.)
- *Results.* What did students learn in the course? How did they change? What did they not achieve that you hoped they would?
- *Evaluative analysis.* What is your overall assessment of the course and your teaching of it? What will you change to improve it?

■ COMPREHENSIVE APPROACHES TO FACULTY EVALUATION

The traditional way of appraising faculty performance has weighted research far more heavily than teaching, has relied almost exclusively on student ratings to assess teaching effectiveness, and has followed idiosyncratic procedures. Some institutions have responded by adopting one of two comprehensive systems for evaluating faculty performance, both suitable for promotion and tenure.

Glassick, Huber, and Maeroff (1997) build their system around six standards for judging all forms of scholarship—discovery, integration, application, and teaching:

- Clear and realistic goals, objectives, and purpose to the work
- Adequate preparation in skills, resources, and background knowledge
- Appropriate methods properly and flexibly implemented to meet the goals
- Significant results and impact; achievement of the goals
- Effective presentation; clear and honest communication to the intended audience
- Reflective critique; evaluation of the results with plans for improvement. (Reprinted with permission of John Wiley and Sons, Inc.)

In fact, funding agencies, journal editors and reviewers, and faculty review bodies already use these standards, at least implicitly, in assessing research proposals, manuscripts, and publications. While Glassick et al. (1997) do not flesh out their system down to specific indicators and measures, they do suggest how we can easily apply these same standards in evaluating teaching:

- To assess goals, peers examine the student learning outcomes in the syllabi, the teaching philosophy, and any portfolio statement or narrative.
- To assess preparation, peers examine the currency and appropriateness of the course content and readings in the syllabi.
- To assess methods, peers examine the appropriateness of the teaching and assessment methods chosen (in the syllabi, teaching philosophy, and teaching or course portfolio).
- To assess results, peers examine student performance on assessment instruments and other available indicators of learning, as well as student ratings on items relevant to perceived learning, challenge, interest, and motivation to learn.

- To assess presentation, peers examine student ratings on communication-relevant items.
- To assess reflective critique, peers examine the teaching philosophy, any portfolio statement or narrative, and any other self-assessment document.

Arreola's (2007) system, now used in whole or part at hundreds of North American institutions, includes detailed, step-by-step guidelines for implementing it on a comprehensive scale, starting with these departmental decisions:

Step 1. Determine and list all the faculty activities worth evaluating at your institution: research, teaching, advising, community service, professional service, university service, and so on.

Step 2. Weight the importance of each activity in percentages that add up to 100 percent.

Step 3. Define each activity as a list of components—that is, observable or documentable products, performances, and achievements. For example, a department may agree to define teaching in terms of content expertise, instructional design skills, instructional delivery skills, impact on student learning, and course management.

Step 4. Weight the components of each role, again in percentages.

Step 5. Determine the best sources of evaluation information—for example, students, department peers, outside peers in specialized areas, the department chair, or someone else.

Step 6. Weight each information source by appropriate worth. (A spreadsheet can do all the arithmetic required in steps 2, 4, and 6).

Step 7. Determine how to gather the information from each source, such as by using forms or questionnaires.

Step 8. Select or design the appropriate policies, procedures, protocols, and forms for your system. Model forms are readily available in Chism (1999) and Arreola (2007).

Once the department sets the parameters and implements the system, each faculty member under review ends up with a rating, usually between 1.0 and 4.0 or between 1.0 and 5.0, that represents the collective judgment of that individual's performance in each faculty role. These numbers are weighted (as in step 2) and added to create an overall composite rating (OCR). The OCR is then compared against the evaluative standards set by the top-level administration. Therefore, faculty are not compared against each other but against an absolute standard. In a 1.0 to 4.0 system where 1.0 denotes "unsatisfactory" and 4.0 means "exemplary" or "exceptional," 3.0 may designate the "acceptable" level. This system easily adapts to any review—tenure, promotions, raises, and post-tenure.

The key—and the challenge—to instituting any comprehensive faculty evaluation system is forging a departmental consensus on appropriate faculty activities, their relative value, the relative value of their components, and the relative value of their information sources. The decision-making process is all about values, bringing them out from under the table and laying them out on the table.

Some academics have complained that such systems undermine professional and administrative judgment, but all they really do is eliminate a review party's discretion to say one thing and do another—for example, to claim to value teaching and service but to decide the fate of faculty careers solely on the research record. By demanding integrity and making the review process transparent, such systems can only benefit those who value, practice, and document teaching at its best.

■ COMPLEX BEYOND MEASURE

Evaluating and documenting teaching effectiveness is genuinely hard. It requires considerable evidence just to show that you are trying to excel in your teaching. Even if you administer standardized tests to demonstrate your students' learning, you will obtain limited data because the best of them cannot tap into noncognitive outcomes and all possible cognitive ones. Moreover, the evidence that a teaching philosophy, a teaching portfolio, or a course portfolios presents is "soft"—not the kind that would stand up under scientific scrutiny or in a court of law. The reviewers must arrive at a judgment based on the preponderance of evidence and the precedents set by faculty who were recently reviewed at their own and comparable institutions.

The fact is that teaching represents a relationship—not a single relationship but one between the instructor and every student in every one of her classes over many terms. Superimposed on these many relationships are those among all of her students who ever interacted in a class. What instrument, what assembly of data can possibly capture this elusive, multilayered, multifaceted transaction in which one individual tries to induce other individuals to process new knowledge, acquire new skills, and change their thinking? The "other individuals," the students, each bring their own unique backgrounds, abilities, aptitudes, attitudes, interests, and aspirations to the table, and the "one individual," which is you, can motivate, persuade, explain, inspire, and nurture learning only as far as each student will allow. You can't bring everyone with you, but if you strive for teaching excellence, you can bring most students with you—enough to give your professional life magnificent meaning.

Instructional Support and Resources at Your Institution

Teaching well at the college level starts with becoming familiar with your institutional environment. Instructors, especially new ones, need to realize that they cannot and should not try to handle all the many challenges of their jobs single-handedly. Every college and university is a large, multilayered organization—a few rivaling small cities in size and complexity—each with its own unique subculture, norms and values, official power structure, informal power networks, and infrastructure of services and support units. Even seasoned faculty in a new institution feel unsettled as they anticipate unfamiliar policies, forms, procedures, expectations, and types of students.

Most colleges and universities offer a wealth of instructional support services and resources—the library and computer services being among the most obvious. But the instructional help available from some individuals and units may not be obvious from their titles or names alone. The people and campus offices described here are well worth your getting to know. The referral services they provide can save you

countless hours, and the information they furnish can prevent costly, however innocent, mistakes.

For Faculty, Students, and Staff

Colleagues, especially senior ones, are perhaps the most conveniently located and sometimes the most knowledgeable sources of information on discipline-specific issues, including how best to teach certain material, what to expect of students in specific courses, how to motivate students in a given subject, how to locate appropriate guest speakers, how to prepare for tenure and other faculty reviews, how to obtain special services or funding, and what assistance to request from department support staff. Colleagues are also excellent sources of informal feedback on teaching; most will be happy to serve as a classroom observer or teaching videotape reviewer. (Also see the information below on teaching centers.)

Department chairs can offer broader, departmental perspectives on discipline-specific issues. They are especially well informed on departmental curriculum matters and can advise on proposals to develop new courses and revise established ones. They may also provide the best counsel on standards and procedures for promotion and tenure. Finally, since they have the opportunity to study the teaching evaluations of all the courses and sections in the department, chairs can help interpret the student ratings and written comments, as well as suggest ways to improve them.

The *dean's office* of your college, school, or division can advise you about promotion and tenure matters, student characteristics, curriculum issues, and course design and development from a still broader perspective. Demographic and academic data about the student body will prove particularly valuable in helping you decide on the objectives, design, content, and techniques for each of your courses. You will also need information about curriculum policies and procedures: What general education or breadth requirements do your courses satisfy? What percentage of students will enroll in a particular course because they are required to take it? How do you propose and get approval for a new course? What components and assignments must a course have to qualify for "honors," "writing," or any other special designation? Finally, the dean's office may be the place to turn for help with classroom matters—for example, if the classroom you are assigned doesn't meet your class size, ventilation, or technological needs, or if you need a room reserved for special class activities and sessions. In large universities, departments may control a set of classrooms and handle such matters.

The *library* is not just a place to find books anymore. Having adapted to the technological age in record time, libraries have expanded into one-stop shops for electronic information, as well as print resources, and librarians have evolved into the sentinals of information literacy.

You don't have to go to the library for many of these resources. Just visiting its Web page will give you easy access to an impressive range of academic search engines, indexes, and databases, such as Lexis-Nexis, InfoTrac, OneFile, Ingenta, Web of Science, and EBSCO Host, which allow you to find scholarly publications by subject, author, publication type, and

other criteria. These resources can also help your students broaden their research horizons beyond Google, and librarians will teach your class how to use them for the assignments you have in mind.

While libraries still provide traditional services, the card catalogue, library requests, and interlibrary loan are usually online. Beyond print and electronic resources, libraries also maintain a collection of instructionally useful videos, CDs, and DVDs.

A *teaching, faculty development, or instructional development center* has become an increasingly common resource on research- as well as teaching-oriented campuses. It usually provides instructional consultation and training services to faculty and teaching assistants, such as classroom videotaping, classroom observations, class interviews (often in a small-group format called a small group instructional diagnosis), midterm student evaluations, advisory consultations, orientations for new instructors, teaching workshops, and assistance in classroom research (also called action research and the scholarship of teaching and learning). Often these centers also maintain a library, run lecture series, publish a newsletter and teaching handbook, consult to departments and colleges on curricula and assessment, award minigrants for teaching innovations and travel to teaching conferences and workshops, and maintain a Web page with links to online teaching resources. Some house language testing and training programs for international teaching assistants.

On a number of campuses, these centers also offer consultations and training in instructional technology, such as the most effective pedagogical applications and the how-to's of available software (see Chapter Twenty-Two). Certainly those with "instructional development" or "technology" in the title do, and these may housed within larger technology units. But most campuses have specialized, stand-alone teaching centers.

A *center for academic computing, information technology, or instructional technology* is the most likely unit to handle the computing needs of faculty, as well as students and staff, from setting up email accounts to replacing old terminals. Its major functions are client support in both hardware and software and training workshops in commonly used office, technical, and instructional software. This support usually includes buying the software and licenses and installing the software on request. Almost all campuses have some brand of course management software, such as Black-board, which is currently the most popular.

In the past decade, these centers transformed many traditional classrooms into smart classrooms equipped with software-rich computer terminals, LCD projectors, VCRs, CD-ROM and DVD players, and Ethernet connections. In some cases these classrooms have laptop stations rather than computers. Scheduling, maintaining, and updating these classrooms is a full-time job. Some centers oversee mandated or voluntary laptop programs, which may entail training the faculty in their technical and pedagogical use, training the students, leasing the laptops or negotiating purchasing deals, and servicing the laptops, as well as retrofitting classrooms with wireless connections.

Centers vary in how much instructional design they do for faculty who are teaching wholly and partly online. On one extreme, some universities expect instructors to learn the necessary software for Web page design, animation, photo and video digitizing and editing, and so forth in specialized workshops and on their own. On the other extreme are the institutions that employ instructional designers to do all the technical work for the faculty. Most fall in between.

A *women's center* often provides a wider variety of services than the lecture series, library, and support groups that you would expect. It is well worth asking if the one on your campus also sponsors self-development and health workshops, career planning forums, book and study groups, and writers' groups. No doubt it offers legal and policy information about sexual harassment as well as emotional support for those who may have a complaint. However, complaints are probably processed by the equal opportunity unit described below.

Multicultural and racial/ethnic cultural centers may be a richer instructional resource than one might expect—and an essential one on today's highly diverse campuses. They usually offer symposia and lectures on cultural topics and coordinate multicultural celebrations and commemorations. Many of them maintain libraries of print materials and videos—most valuable if you are teaching multicultural subjects—and a few sponsor art exhibits and musical performances. Typically they also provide support services for students of color.

Of particular value to faculty and staff are cultural awareness programs, including diversity training workshops. These centers can also answer your private questions about the minority student population on your campus and cultural differences among various groups. They will help you resolve any concerns about relating to students of color in the classroom.

An *international center* typically administers study-abroad and international internship programs and sets up new ones to meet the demands of the rapidly changing world economy. For example, many universities have recently added programs in China, Southeast Asia, and India. Often in conjuction with an area studies center, this kind of unit also equips the students and faculty traveling abroad with some basic global competencies, such as information on the social and cultural differences between Americans and natives of a host country.

The center also provides acculturation counseling and support for international students and their families, as well as legal advice on visas, work permits, taxes, and others areas. On some campuses, the international center is also responsible for English as a Second Language testing and courses.

An *equal opportunity center* may go by any number of titles, but you should look for key words such as "opportunity development," "affirmative action," "equality," "equity," and "civil rights." Its purpose is to coordinate state and federally mandated programs designed to ensure equal opportunities for minorities, women, individuals with disabilities, and other disadvantaged groups. It also serves as a source of information for students, faculty, and staff who may have questions or complaints related to equal opportunity in education, employment, and campus programs and activities. If a complaint is judged valid, it will also advise on grievance procedures.

Sexual harassment falls under the equal opportunity umbrella. Often in collaboration with a women's center (see above), an equal opportunity office disseminates information on the legal definition of sexual harassment, the institution's policy regarding it, specific types of harassment behavior, its prevalence, its prevention, procedures for filing a complaint or a grievance, and confidential support and counseling services.

A *disabilities center* identifies students with learning as well as physical disabilities and usually issues written certification of these disabilities for instructors. As required by the Americans with Disabilities Act of 1990, this type of center ensures that people with disabilities have equal access to public programs and services. Therefore, it also recommends the special accommodations, if any, that instructors should make for identified students in their teaching and testing.

Most accommodations are minor (for example, an isolated test environment or a longer test period), and the center may provide special facilities for them, such as proctored testing rooms. In any case, it will advise the instructor about exactly what accommodations are needed. For hearing-impaired classroom students, the instructor may have to stand or sit where the student can lip-read. For visually impaired classroom students, you may have to vocalize or verbally describe any visual materials you present or distribute to the class. Appropriate testing may require you to make a large-print copy of the exam or allow the students use of a reader, scribe, or computer during the test.

Online learning demands more extensive adaptations, but usually the student's own specialized computer hardware and software will take care of most access problems. Still, instructors must be mindful to keep Web pages uncluttered and to provide captions or transcripts for audio materials and text alternatives for visual materials.

Just for Students

The centers described may serve your own or your students' needs. Let's consider now the units and individuals that specialize in serving students. Students seeking general academic counsel should be referred to their academic advisers; those requesting information or assistance with respect to a specific course should be sent to the instructor or the department. At times, however, students need help with other problems—some that most instructors are ill equipped to address. These include learning disabilities, math or test anxiety, severe writing problems, poor study and test-taking skills, weak academic backgrounds, emotional difficulties, and career planning questions. These cases call for a referral to a unit in the next group.

Almost all campuses have a facility designed to help students improve their academic skills. It is often called a *learning, learning skills, learning resources, academic assistance,* or *academic support center,* and its services typically include individual counseling in academic skills, individual and small-group tutoring, workshops in learning strategies (for example, reading skills, study skills, note taking, test preparation, and test taking). Some tutoring may be geared to specific courses or subject matter known to give students trouble, such as calculus, chemistry, physics, biology, economics, and foreign languages. This type of center may also offer English as a Second Language testing and courses.

A *writing or communication program* may be housed in a learning center or comprise its own stand-alone unit. It is likely to provide individual or small-group tutoring in the mechanics of grammar and punctuation, as well as the structure of exam essays, short papers, critical papers, and research papers. It may even schedule formal writing workshops. Staff are trained not to outline or edit student work, but rather to show students how to master the stages of the writing process on their own.

If "communication" is in the title, the unit may be one of a small but growing number of centers that also help students improve their public speaking and presentation skills. These are usually associated with an active speaking- or communication-across-the-curriculum program.

A *psychological* or *counseling center* is the place to refer students who manifest any type of psychological or emotional disorder. As students usually show signs of trouble only in more private environments, Chapter Nine on office hours lists the behaviors to watch out for. This type of unit gives free individual counseling for psychological, emotional, and sometimes academic problems, and it may coordinate group programs for personal growth, self-improvement, and self-awareness. If it is associated with a medical facility or it has a physician on staff, it may also prescribe drugs.

A *career center* helps students identify and achieve their occupational goals. It typically provides assessment tests in skills and interests and resources for career exploration, as well as information on internship opportunities and summer jobs. Workshops on job search strategies, résumé preparation, communication and decision-making skills, and job interview techniques may also be available. Some centers hold campus job fairs and help graduates obtain jobs.

All of these campus units will welcome your requests for further information and will point you to their Web page or mail you their brochures, newsletters, and any other materials they furnish for students. They are well worth learning about because they are service centers with a service orientation. They exist to meet your and your students' needs—instructional, professional, or personal. Unless their resources are already stretched beyond capacity, they actively pursue and benefit from increasing use. So if they can make your life as an instructor easier or more fulfilling, if they can save you class and office hour time, if they can handle any of the many student requests and problems that pass through your office door, by all means take advantage of their invaluable services.

Abrami, P. C., Dickens, W., Perry, R., & Leventhal, L. (1980). Do teacher standards for assigning grades affect student evaluations of instruction? *Journal of Educational Psychology, 72,* 107–118.

Adler, M. J. (1940). *How to read a book: The art of getting a liberal education.* New York: Simon & Schuster.

Albanese, M. A. (1991). The validity of lecturer ratings by students and trained observers. *Academic Medicine, 66* (1), 26–28

Albanese, M. A., & Mitchell, S. (1993). Problem-based learning: A review of the literature on its outcomes and implementation issues. *Academic Medicine, 68,* 52–81.

Albright, M. J., & Graf, D. L. (Eds.). (1992). *New directions for teaching and learning: No. 51. Teaching in the information age: The role of educational technology.* San Francisco: Jossey-Bass.

Aleamoni, L. M. (1982). Components of the instructional setting. *Instructional Evaluation, 7* (1), 11–16.

Aleamoni, L. M. (1999). Student rating myths versus research facts: An update. *Journal of Personnel Evaluation, 13* (2), 153–166.

Alexander, P. (1996). The past, the present, and the future of knowledge research: A reexamination of the role of knowledge in learning and instruction. *Educational Psychologist, 31* (2), 89–92.

Allen, D. E., & Duch, B. J. (1998). *Thinking toward solutions: Problem-based learning activities for general biology.* New York: Saunders College Publishing.

Allen, R. D. (1981). Intellectual development and the understanding of science: Applications of William Perry's theory to science teaching. *Journal of College Science Teaching, 10,* 94–97.

Allen, W., Epps, E., & Haniff, N. (1991). *College in black and white: African American students in predominantly white and historically black public universities.* Albany, NY: SUNY Press.

Allwardt, D. (2009, April). *Using wikis for collaborative writing assignments: Best practices and fair warnings.* Poster session presented at the 3rd annual Innovations in Teaching Forum, Western Illinois University, Macomb.

Altman, H. B., & Cashin, W. E. (1992). *Writing a syllabus* (IDEA Paper No. 27). Manhattan: Kansas State University, Center for Faculty Evaluation and Development.

Altschuler, G. (2001, January 7). Battling the cheats. *New York Times Magazine,* p. 15.

Amador, J. A., Miles, L., & Peters, C. B. (2006). *The practice of problem-based learning: A guide to implementing PBL in the college classroom.* Bolton, MA: Anker.

Ambron, J. (1987). Writing to improve learning in biology. *Journal of College Science Teaching, 16,* 263–266.

335

Anderman, L., Freeman, T., & Mueller, C. (2007). The "social" side of social context: Interpersonal and affiliative dimensions of students' experiences and academic dishonesty. In E. Anderman & T. Murdock (Eds.), *Psychology of academic cheating* (pp. 203–228). Burlington, MA: Elsevier.

Anderson, J. A., & Adams, M. (1992). Acknowledging the learning styles of diverse populations: Implications for instructional design. In L. Border & N.V.N. Chism (Eds.), *New directions for teaching and learning: No. 49. Teaching for diversity* (pp. 19–33). San Francisco: Jossey-Bass.

Anderson, J. R. (1993). Problem solving and learning. *American Psychologist, 48* (1), 35–57.

Anderson, L. W., & Krathwohl, D. R. (2000). *A taxonomy for learning, teaching, and assessment: A revision of Bloom's taxonomy of educational objectives.* White Plains, NY: Longman.

Anderson, R. C. (1984). Some reflection on the acquisition of knowledge. *Educational Researcher, 13* (2), 5–10.

Angelo, T. A. (1991a). Introduction and overview: From classroom assessment to classroom research. In T. A. Angelo (Ed.), *New directions for teaching and learning: No. 46. Classroom research: Early lessons from success* (pp. 7–15). San Francisco: Jossey-Bass.

Angelo, T. A. (1991b). Ten easy pieces: Assessing higher learning in four dimensions. In T. A. Angelo (Ed.), *New directions for teaching and learning: No. 46. Classroom research: Early lessons from success* (pp. 17–31). San Francisco: Jossey-Bass.

Angelo, T. A., & Cross, K. P. (1993). *Classroom assessment techniques: A handbook for college teachers* (2nd ed.). San Francisco: Jossey-Bass.

Anson, C. M., & Forsberg, L. L. (1990). Moving beyond the academic community: Transitional stages in professional writing. *Written Communication, 7* (2), 200–231.

Arocha, J. F., & Patel, V. L. (1995). Novice diagnostic reasoning in medicine: Accounting of clinical evidence. *Journal of the Learning Sciences, 4,* 355–384.

Arons, A. B. (1993). Guiding insight and inquiry in the introductory physics lab. *Physics Teacher, 31* (5), 278–282.

Arreola, R. A. (2007). *Developing a comprehensive faculty evaluation system: A guide to designing, building, and operating large-scale faculty evaluation systems* (3rd ed.). Bolton, MA: Anker.

Aslanian, C. B. (2001). *Adult students today.* New York: College Board.

Astin, A. W. (1993). *What matters in college: Four critical years revisited.* San Francisco: Jossey-Bass.

Astin, A. W., Vogelgesang, L. J., Ikeda, E. K., & Yee, J. A. (2000). *How service learning affects students.* Los Angeles: University of California, Higher Education Research Institute.

Atkinson, R. K., Levin, J. R., Kiewra, K. A., Meyers, T., Kim, S., Atkinson, L., et al. (1999). Matrix and mnemonic text-processing adjuncts: Comparing and combining their components. *Journal of Educational Psychology, 91,* 342–357.

Aulls, M. W. (2002). The contributions of co-occurring forms of classroom discourse and academic activities to curriculum events and instruction. *Journal of Educational Psychology, 94,* 520–538.

Ausubel, D. (1968). *Educational psychology: A cognitive view.* New York: Holt.

Avgerinou, M., & Ericson, J. (1997). A review of the concept of visual literacy. *British Journal of Educational Technology, 28* (4), 280–291.

Baldwin, R. G. (1997–1998). Academic civility begins in the classroom. *Essays on Teaching Excellence, 9* (8), 1–2.

Ballantine, J., & Risacher, J. (1993, November). *Coping with annoying classroom behaviors.* Paper presented at the 13th annual Lilly Conference on College Teaching, Oxford, OH.

Ballard, M. (2007). Drawing and questioning the syllabus. *The National Teaching and Learning Forum, 16* (5), 5–6.

Bandura, A. (1977). Self-efficacy: Toward a unifying theory of behavioral change. *Psychological Review, 84* (2), 191–215.

Bandura, A. (1997). *Self-efficacy: The exercise of control.* New York: Freeman.

Banta, T. W., Black, K. E., & Kline, K. A. (2000). PBL 2000 plenary address offers evidence for and against problem-based learning. *PBL Insight, 3* (3). Retrieved January 5, 2001, from www.samford.edu/pbl.

Barnett, D. C., & Dalton, J. C. (1981). Why college students cheat. *Journal of College Student Personnel, 23,* 545–551.

Barrineau, N. W. (2001). Class preparation and summary note cards. *The National Teaching and Learning Forum, 10* (4), 5–6.

Bartlett, A. A., & Thomason, M. A. (1983). Legibility in the lecture hall. *Physics Teacher, 21* (8), 531.

Baugh, N. G., & Mellott, K. G. (1998). Clinical concept mapping as preparation for student nurses' clinical experiences. *Journal of Nursing Education, 37* (6), 253–256.

Baughin, J., Brod, E. F., & Page, D. L. (2002). Primary trait analysis: A tool for classroom-based assessment. *College Teaching, 50* (2), 75–80.

Baume, D., & Baume, C. (2008). *Powerful ideas in teaching and learning.* Wheatley, UK: Oxford Brookes University.

Baxter Magolda, M. B. (1992). *Knowing and reasoning in college: Gender-related patterns in students' intellectual development.* San Francisco: Jossey-Bass.

Bean, J. C. (1996). *Engaging ideas: A professor's guide to integrating writing, critical thinking, and active learning in the classroom.* San Francisco: Jossey-Bass.

Beaudry, J., & Wilson, P. (2010). Concept mapping and formative assessment: Elements supporting literacy and learning. In P. L. Torres & C. V. Marriott (Eds.), *Handbook of research on collaborative learning using concept mapping* (pp. 449–473). Hershey, PA: Information Science Reference.

Beichner, R. J., Saul, J. M., Abbott, D. S., Morse, J. J., Deardorff, D. L., Allain, R. J., et al. (2007). *The student-centered activities for large enrollment undergraduate programs (SCALE-UP) project.* Retrieved November 5, 2008, from www.per-central.org/document/ServeFile.cfm?ID=4517 &DocID=183.

Beissner, K. L. (1992). Use of concept mapping to improve problem solving. *Journal of Physical Therapy, 6* (1), 22–27.

Belanoff, P., & Dickson, M. (1991). *Portfolios: Process and product.* Portsmouth, NH: Boynton/Cook & Heinemann.

Belbin, R. M. (2004). *Team roles at work.* Amsterdam: Elsevier.

Bellman, B. L. (1992). Computer communications and learning. In M. J. Albright & D. L. Graf (Eds.), *New directions for teaching and learning: No. 51. Teaching in the information age: The role of educational technology* (pp. 55–63). San Francisco: Jossey-Bass.

Benander, R., Denton, J., Page, D., & Skinner, C. (2000). Primary trait analysis: Anchoring assessment in the classroom. *Journal of General Education, 49* (4), 280–302.

Benford, R., & Lawson, A. E. (2001). Relationships between effective inquiry use and the development of scientific reasoning skills in college biology labs. *Report to the National Science Foundation,* Grant DUE 9453610.

Bergman, J. (1980). Peer evaluation of university faculty. *College Student Journal, 14* (3), 1–21.

Bergtrom, G. (2006). Clicker sets as learning objects. *Interdisciplinary Journal of Knowledge and Learning Objects, 2.* Retrieved September 1, 2008, from http://ijklo.org /Volume2/v2p105–110Bergtrom.pdf.

Berk, R. A. (2005). Survey of 12 strategies to measure teaching effectiveness. *International Journal of Teaching and Learning in Higher Education, 17* (1), 48–62.

Berke, A., & Kastberg, S. S. (1998, March). *Writing a teaching philosophy: The beginning of a teaching portfolio.* Paper presented at the 19th annual meeting of the Sharing Conference of the Southern Regional Faculty and Instructional Development Consortium, Kennesaw, GA.

Bernhardt, S. A. (1992). Teaching English: Portfolio evaluation. *Clearing House, 65* (6), 333–334.

Berry, P., Thornton, B., & Baker, R. (2006). Demographics of digital cheating: Who cheats, and what we can do about it. In M. Murray (Ed.), *Proceedings of the Ninth Annual Conference of the Southern Association for Information Systems* (pp. 82–87). Jacksonville, FL: Jacksonville University, Davis College of Business.

Berry, W. (2008). Surviving lecture: A pedagogical alternative. *College Teaching, 56* (3), 149–153.

Beyers, C. (2008). The hermeneutics of student evaluations. *College Teaching, 56* (2), 102–106.

Biggs, J. (2003). *Teaching for quality learning at university* (2nd ed.). Berkshire, UK: Society for Research into Higher Education and Open University Press.

Biktimirov, E. N., & Nilson, L. B. (2003). Mapping your course: Designing a graphic syllabus for introductory finance. *Journal of Education for Business, 78* (6), 308–312.

Biktimirov, E. N., & Nilson, L. B. (2006). Show them the money: Using mind mapping in the introductory finance course. *Journal of Financial Education, 32,* 72–86.

Biktimirov, E. N., & Nilson, L. B. (2007). Adding animation and interactivity to finance courses with learning objects. *Journal of Financial Education, 33*, 35–47.

Black, B., & Axelson, E. (1991). Teaching students to solve problems. In *The University of Michigan TA guidebook* (pp. 41–46). Ann Arbor: University of Michigan.

Blandford, S. (2000). *Managing professional development in school.* London: Routledge.

Bligh, D. A. (2000). *What's the use of lectures?* San Francisco: Jossey-Bass.

Bloom, B. (1956). *Taxonomy of educational objectives: The classification of educational goals. Vol. 1: Cognitive domain.* New York: McKay.

Bloom, B. (1984). The 2 sigma problem: The search for methods of group instruction as effective as one-on-one tutoring. *Educational Researcher, 13* (6), 4–16.

Blue, T. (2003, March 14). "I don't know HOW to read this book!" *The Irascible Professor.* Retrieved October 16, 2006, from http://irascibleprofessor.com/comments-03–14–03-epr.htm.

Bodner, G. (1987). The role of algorithms in teaching problem solving. *Journal of Chemical Education, 64* (6), 513–514.

Boice, R. (1996). Classroom incivilities. *Research in Higher Education, 37* (4), 453–485.

Boice, R. (2000). *Advice for new faculty members: Nihil nimus.* Needham Heights, MA: Allyn & Bacon.

Bok, D. C. (2006). *Our underachieving colleges.* Princeton, NJ: Princeton University Press.

Bonwell, C. C., & Eison, J. A. (1991). *Active learning: Creating excitement in the classroom* (ASHE-ERIC Higher Education Report No. 1). Washington, DC: George Washington University, School of Education and Human Development.

Bourland, J. (1996, March). Hollywood hustle. *Parenting, 53,* 29.

Bowen, J. A. (2006). Teaching naked: Why removing technology from your classroom will improve student learning. *The National Teaching and Learning Forum, 16* (1), 1–5.

Brabrand, C. (Co-producer/Writer/Director), & Andersen, J. (Co-producer). (2006). *Teaching teaching and understanding understanding* [DVD]. Denmark: University of Aarhus and Daimi Edutainment.

Bradley, K. (2007). Reading noncompliance: A case study and reflection. *MountainRise, 4* (1). Retrieved November 24, 2008, from http://mountainrise.wcu.edu/archive/vol4no1/html/bradley.pdf.

Bransford, J. D., Brown, A. L., & Cocking, R. R. (1999). *How people learn: Brain, mind, experience, and school.* Washington, DC: National Academy Press.

Brauchle, K. C. (2000). Plagiarism and the Internet: Cut and paste your way to success. *The National Teaching and Learning Forum, 10* (1), 10–11.

Braumoeller, B. F., & Gaines, B. J. (2001). Actions do speak louder than words: Deterring plagiarism with the use of plagiarism-detection software. *PS: Political Science and Politics, 34* (4), 835–839.

Bridges, E. M. (1992). *Problem-based learning for administrators.* Eugene, OR: ERIC Clearinghouse on Educational Management.

Bridgwood, M. A. (1999). Guidelines for communication and engineering problem solving at the basic level. *IEEE Transactions on Professional Communication, 42* (3), 156–165.

Brinkmann, A. (2003). Mind mapping as a tool in mathematics education. *Mathematics Teacher, 96*, 96–101.

Brinson, J. D., & Radcliffe, M. F. (1996). *Multimedia law and business handbook.* Menlo Park, CA: Ladera Press.

Briscoe, C., & LaMaster, S. U. (1991). Meaningful learning in college biology through concept mapping. *American Biology Teacher, 53* (4), 214–219.

Broderick, B. (1990). *Groundwork for college reading.* West Berlin, NJ: Townsend Press.

Brookfield, S. D., & Preskill, S. (1999). *Discussion as a way of teaching: Tools and techniques for democratic classrooms.* San Francisco: Jossey-Bass.

Brookhart, S. M. (1999). *The art and science of classroom assessment: The missing part of pedagogy* (ASHE-ERIC Higher Education Report, 27[1]). Washington, DC: George Washington University, Graduate School of Education and Human Development.

Brookhart, V. (1990). *Problem solving in science.* Unpublished manuscript.

Brooks, R. P. (1987). Dealing with details in large classes. In M. Weimer (Ed.), *New directions for teaching and learning: No. 32. Teaching large classes well* (pp. 9–44). San Francisco: Jossey-Bass.

Bruff, D. (2007). Clickers: A classroom innovation. *Thriving in Academe, 25* (1), 5–8.

Bruff, D. (2008). *Classroom response system ("clickers") bibliography*. Retrieved September 1, 2008, from www.vanderbilt.edu/cft/resources/teaching_resources /technology/crs_biblio.htm.

Bruff, D. (2009). *Teaching with classroom response systems: Creating active learning environments*. San Francisco: Jossey-Bass.

Bugeja, M. J. (2007, January 26). Distractions in the wireless classroom. *Chronicle of Higher Education*. Retrieved April 28, 2009, from http://chronicle.com/jobs/news /2007/01/2007012601c.htm.

Bunn, D. N., Caudill, S. B., & Gropper, D. M. (1992). Crime in the classroom: An economic analysis of undergraduate student cheating behavior. *Journal of Economic Education, 23* (3), 197–207.

Burchfield, C. M., & Sappington, J. (2000). Compliance with required reading assignments. *Teaching of Psychology, 27* (1), 58–60.

Bureau, D., & McRoberts, C. (2001). Millennials: The corrective generation? *Perspectives*, 8–12.

Burrowes, P. A. (2003). A student-centered approach to teaching general biology that really works: Lord's constructivist model put to a test. *American Biology Teacher, 65* (7), 491–502.

Buzan, T. (1974). *Use your head*. London: BBC.

Cameron, B. J. (1993). *Teaching at the University of Manitoba*. Manitoba, Canada: University of Manitoba Teaching Services.

Cameron, J., & Pierce, W. D. (1994). Reinforcement, reward, and intrinsic motivation: A meta-analysis. *Review of Educational Research, 64*, 363–423.

Canfield, P. J. (2002). An interactive, student-centered approach to teaching large-group sessions in veterinary clinical pathology. *Journal of Veterinary Medical Education, 29* (2), 105–110.

Carey, S. (1985). Are children fundamentally different kinds of thinkers and learners than adults? In S. F. Chapman, J. W. Segal, & R. Glaser (Eds.), *Thinking and learning skills* (Vol. 2, pp. 485–517). New York: Basic Books.

Carlile, O., & Jordan, A. (2005). It works in practice but will it work in theory? The theoretical underpinnings of pedagogy. In G. O'Neill, S. Moore, & R. McMullan (Eds.), *Emerging issues in the practice of university teaching* (pp. 11–25). Dublin: All Ireland Society for Higher Education.

Carlson, S. (2005, October 7). The Net Generation goes to college. *Chronicle of Higher Education*, p. A34.

Carnevale, D. (1999, November 12). How to proctor from a distance: Experts say professors need savvy to prevent cheating in online courses. *Chronicle of Higher Education*, pp. A47–A48.

Carney, A. G., Fry, S. W., Gabriele, R. V., & Ballard, M. (2008). Reeling in the big fish: Changing pedagogy to encourage the completion of reading assignments. *College Teaching, 56* (4), 195–200.

Carrier, C. A. (1983). Notetaking research implications for the classroom. *Journal of Instructional Development, 6* (3), 19–26.

Carroll, J. (2003a, May 2). Dealing with nasty students: The sequel. *Chronicle of Higher Education*, p. C5.

Carroll, J. (2003b, October 14). Constructing your in-class persona. *Chronicle of Higher Education*. Retrieved October 14, 2003, from http://chronicle.com/jobs/2003/10 /2003101401c.html.

Carter, J. F., & Van Matre, N. H. (1975). Note taking versus note having. *Journal of Educational Psychology, 67* (6), 900–904.

Case, K., Bartsch, R., McEnery, L., Hall, S., Hermann, A., & Foster, D. (2008). Establishing a comfortable classroom from day one: Student perceptions of the reciprocal interview. *College Teaching, 56* (4), 210–214.

Cashin, W. E. (1979). *Motivating students* (IDEA Paper No. 1). Manhattan: Kansas State University, Center for Faculty Evaluation and Development.

Cashin, W. E. (1988). *Student ratings of teaching: A summary of the research* (IDEA Paper No. 20). Manhattan: Kansas

State University, Center for Faculty Evaluation and Development.

Cashin, W. E. (1995). *Student ratings of teaching: The research revisited* (IDEA Paper No. 32). Manhattan, KS: Kansas State University, Center for Faculty Evaluation and Development.

Cashin, W. E., & Perrin, B. M. (1978). *Description of a standard form data base* (IDEA Technical Report No. 4). Manhattan: Kansas State University, Center for Faculty Evaluation and Development.

Centra, J. A. (1975). Colleagues as raters of classroom instruction. *Journal of Higher Education, 46* (1), 327–337.

Centra, J. A. (1979). *Determining faculty effectiveness.* San Francisco: Jossey-Bass.

Centra, J. A. (1993). *Reflective faculty evaluation: Enhancing teaching and determining faculty effectiveness.* San Francisco: Jossey-Bass.

Centra, J. A., & Gaubatz, N. B. (1999). *Is there gender bias in student evaluations of teaching?* Princeton, NJ: Educational Testing Service.

Cerbin, W. (1994). The course portfolio as a tool for continuous improvement of teaching and learning. *Journal of Excellence in College Teaching, 5,* 95–105.

Cerbin, W. (1995). Connecting assessment of learning to the improvement of teaching. *Assessment Update, 7* (1), 4–6.

Chi, M.T.H., Glaser, R., & Rees, E. (1982). Expertise in problem solving. In R. Steinberg (Ed.), *Advances in the psychology of human intelligence* (pp. 7–76). Mahwah, NJ: Erlbaum.

Chiaramonte, P. (1994). The agony and the ecstasy of case teaching. *Reaching Through Teaching, 7* (2), 1–2.

Chism, N.V.N. (1997–1998). Developing a philosophy of teaching statement. *Essays on Teaching Excellence, 9* (3), 1–2.

Chism, N.V.N. (1999). *Peer review of teaching: A sourcebook.* Bolton, MA: Anker.

Chung, C., & Hsu, L. (2006). Encouraging students to seek help: Supplementing office hours with a course center. *College Teaching, 54* (3), 253–258.

Clark, J. (2008). PowerPoint and pedagogy: Maintaining student interest in university lectures. *College Teaching, 56* (1), 39–45.

Clark, J. M., & Paivio, A. (1991). Dual coding theory and education. *Educational Psychology Review, 3* (3), 149–210.

Cliburn, J. W. (1990). Concepts to promote meaningful learning. *Journal of College Science Teaching, 19* (4), 212–217.

Codde, J. R. (1996). *Using learning contracts in the college classroom.* Retrieved February 25, 2005, from www.msu.edu/user/coddejos/contract.htm.

Cohen, P. A. (1980). Effectiveness of student-rating feedback for improving college instruction: A meta-analysis of findings. *Research in Higher Education, 13* (4), 321–341.

Cohen, P. A. (1981). Student ratings of instruction and student achievement: A meta-analysis of multi-section validity studies. *Review of Educational Research, 51,* 281–309.

Collison, M. (1990a, January 17). Apparent rise in students' cheating has college officials worried. *Chronicle of Higher Education,* pp. A33–A34.

Collison, M. (1990b, October 24). Survey at Rutgers suggests that cheating may be on the rise at large universities. *Chronicle of Higher Education,* pp. A31–A32.

Conklin, M. S. (2007). *101 uses for Second Life in the college classroom.* Retrieved April 10, 2009, from http://trumpy.cs.elon.edu/metaverse.

Connor-Greene, P. (2000). Assessing and promoting student learning: Blurring the line between teaching and learning. *Teaching of Psychology, 27* (2), 84–88.

Cooper, J. L., Robinson, P., &. McKinney, M. (1993). Cooperative learning in the classroom. In D. F. Halpern & Associates, *Changing college classrooms* (pp. 74–92). San Francisco: Jossey-Bass.

Cornelius, T. L., & Owen-DeSchryver, J. (2008). Differential effects of full and partial notes on learning outcomes and attendance. *Teaching of Psychology, 35* (1), 6–12.

Cortright, R. N., Collins, H. L., & DiCarlo, S. E. (2005). Peer instruction enhanced meaningful learning: Ability to solve novel problems. *Advances in Physiology Education, 29* (2), 107–111.

Cortright, R. N., Collins, H. L., Rodenbaugh, D. W., & DiCarlo, S. E. (2003). Student retention of course content is improved by collaborative-group testing. *Advances in Physiology Education, 27* (3), 102–108.

Crenshaw, D. (2008). *The myth of multitasking: How "doing it all" gets nothing done.* San Francisco: Jossey-Bass.

Cross, K. P. (1988). In search of zippers. *AAHE Bulletin, 40* (10), 3–7.

Cross, K. P. (1992). Classroom assessment/classroom research: Four years into a hands-on movement. *The National Teaching and Learning Forum, 1* (6), 1–3.

Cross, K. P., & Angelo, T. A. (1988). *Classroom assessment techniques: A handbook for faculty.* Ann Arbor: University of Michigan, National Center for Research to Improve Postsecondary Teaching and Learning.

Crouch, C. E., & Mazur, E. (2001). Peer instruction: Ten years of experience and results. *American Journal of Physics, 69,* 970–977.

Crowley, M. L. (1993). Student mathematics portfolio: More than a display case. *Mathematics Teacher, 86* (7), 544–547.

Dallimore, E. J., Hertenstein, J. H., & Platt, M. B. (2006). Non-voluntary class participation in graduate discussion courses: Effects of grading and cold-calling on student comfort. *Journal of Management Education, 30* (2), 354–377.

Dallimore, E. J., Hertenstein, J. H., & Platt, M. B. (2008). Using discussion pedagogy to enhance oral and written communication skills. *College Teaching, 56* (3), 163–170.

Daniels, A. C. (2000). *Bringing out the best in people: How to apply the astonishing power of positive reinforcement.* New York: McGraw-Hill.

Daniels, A. C., & Daniels, J. E. (2004). *Performance management: Changing behavior that drives organizational effectiveness* (4th ed.). Atlanta, GA: Performance Management Publications.

d'Apollonia, S., & Abrami, P. (1997). Navigating student ratings of instruction. *American Psychologist, 52* (11), 1198–1208.

Davidson, H. (2008). *Welcome to Hall Davidson's site.* Retrieved August 20, 2008, from www.halldavidson.com.

Day, R. S. (1980). Teaching from notes: Some cognitive consequences. In W. J. McKeachie (Ed.), *New directions for teaching and learning: No. 2. Learning, cognition, and college teaching* (pp. 95–112). San Francisco: Jossey-Bass.

Deal, A. (2007, November). *Classroom response systems* (Teaching with Technology White Paper). Retrieved September 1, 2008, from www.cmu.edu/teaching /resources/PublicationsArchives/StudiesWhitepapers /ClassroomResponse_Nov07.pdf.

Deci, E. L. (1971). Effects of externally mediated rewards on intrinsic motivation. *Journal of Personality and Social Psychology, 18* (1), 105–115.

Deci, E. L., Koestner, R., & Ryan, R. M. (1999). A meta-analytic view of experiments examining the effects of extrinsic rewards on intrinsic motivation. *Psychological Bulletin, 185,* 627–668.

Dee, K. C. (2007). Student perceptions of high course workloads are not associated with poor student evaluations of instructor performance. *Journal of Engineering Education, 96* (1), 69–78.

DeJong, T., & Ferguson-Hessler, M. G. (1996). Types and quality of knowledge. *Educational Psychologist, 8* (2), 105–113.

Delaney, E. (1991). Applying geography to the classroom through structured discussions. *Journal of Geography, 90* (3), 129–133.

Dempster, F. N. (1996). Distributing and managing the conditions of encoding and practice. In E. L. Bork & R. A. Bork (Eds.), *Human memory* (pp. 197–236). Orlando, FL: Academic Press.

Dempster, F. N. (1997). Using tests to promote classroom learning. In R. F. Dillon (Ed.), *Handbook on testing* (pp. 332–346). Westport, CT: Greenwood Press.

Derek Bok Center for Teaching and Learning, Harvard University. (2006). *Tips for teachers: Teaching in racially diverse college classrooms.* Retrieved September 2, 2008, from http://isites.harvard.edu/fs/html/icb.topic58474/TFTrace .html.

Derry, S. J. (1984). Effects of an organizer on memory for prose. *Journal of Educational Psychology, 76,* 98–107.

Dinan, F. (2002). Chemistry by the case. *Journal of College Science Teaching, 32* (1), 36–41.

Dochy, F., Segers, M., Van den Bossche, P., & Gijbels, D. (2003). Effects of problem-based learning: A meta-analysis. *Learning and Instruction, 13*, 533–568.

Donald, J. (2002). *Learning to think: Disciplinary perspectives.* San Francisco: Jossey-Bass.

Doyle, T. (2008). *Helping students learn in a learner-centered environment: A guide to facilitating learning in higher education.* Sterling, VA: Stylus.

Drake, R. (2009, February). *Essay preparedness and student success.* Poster session presented at the annual Lilly South Conference on College Teaching, Greensboro, NC.

Driver, M. (2001). Fostering creativity in business education: Developing creative classroom environments to provide students with critical workplace competencies. *Journal of Education for Business, 77*, 28–33.

Duch, B. J., & Allen, D. E. (1996). Problems: A key factor in PBL. *About Teaching, 50*, 25–28.

Duch, B. J., Allen, D. E., & White, H. B., III. (1997–1998). Problem-based learning: Preparing students to succeed in the 21st century. *Essays on Teaching Excellence, 9* (7), 1–2.

Duch, B. J., Groh, S. E., & Allen, D. E. (2001). *The power of problem-based learning.* Sterling, VA: Stylus.

Dunn, J. P. (1992). Briefing teams in world affairs class. *College Teaching, 41* (2), 61–62.

Dweck, C., & Leggett, E. (1988). A social-cognitive approach to motivation and personality. *Psychological Review, 95*, 256–273.

Ebel, R. L. (1978). The effectiveness of multiple true-false test items. *Educational and Psychological Measurement, 38* (1), 37–44.

Edens, K. M. (2000). Preparing problem solvers for the 21st century through problem-based learning. *College Teaching, 48* (2), 55–60.

Eisenberger, R., & Cameron, J. (1996). Detrimental effects of reward: Reality or myth? *American Psychologist, 51*, 1153–1166.

Ellis, D. (2006). *Becoming a master student* (11th ed.). Boston: Houghton Mifflin.

Emett, R. C., & New, D. A. (1997, October). *Opening the world to your students without feeling like a criminal: Legal aspects of creating educational multimedia.* Paper presented at the annual meeting of the Professional and Organizational Development Network in Higher Education, Haines City, FL.

Erdle, S., & Murray, H. G. (1986). Interfaculty differences in classroom teaching behaviors and their relationship to student instructional ratings. *Research in Higher Education, 24* (2), 115–127.

Ericksen, S. C. (1974). *Motivation for learning: A guide for the teacher of the young adult.* Ann Arbor: University of Michigan Press.

Eriksson, L. T., & Hauer, A. M. (2004). Mind map marketing: A creative approach in developing marketing skills. *Journal of Marketing Education, 26* (2), 174–187.

Ewens, W. (2000). Teaching using discussion. In R. Neff & M. Weimer (Eds.), *Classroom communication: Collected readings for effective discussion and questioning* (pp. 21–26). Madison, WI: Atwood.

Eyler, J., & Giles, D. E., Jr. (1999). *Where's the learning in service-learning?* San Francisco: Jossey-Bass.

Fagen, A. P., Crouch, C. H., & Mazur, E. (2002). Peer instruction: Results from a range of classrooms. *Physics Teacher, 40*, 206–209.

Falkenberg, S. (1996). *The feedback fallacy.* Retrieved May 1, 2006, from http://people.eku.edu/falkenbergs/feedback.htm.

Farrand, P., Hussain, F., & Hennessy, E. (2002). The efficacy of the "mind map" study technique. *Medical Education, 36*, 426–431.

Fasko, D. (2003, April). *Case studies and method in teaching and learning.* Paper presented at the annual meeting of the Society of Educators and Scholars, Louisville, KY.

Featherstone, B. J. (1999). *The millennial generation: Leading today's youth into the future.* Salt Lake City, UT: Deseret Books.

Feichtner, S. B., & Davis, E. A. (1984). Why some groups fail: A survey of students' experiences with learning groups. *Organizational Behavior Teaching Review, 9* (4), 58–73.

Felder, R. M. (1993). Reaching the second tier: Learning and teaching styles in college science education. *Journal of College Science Teaching, 23* (5), 286–290.

Felder, R. M., & Brent, R. (2001). Effective strategies for cooperative learning. *Journal of Cooperation and Collaboration in College Teaching, 10* (2), 67–75.

Felder, R. M., & Brent, R. (2005). Understanding student differences. *Journal of Engineering Education, 94* (1), 57–72.

Felder, R. M., & Silverman, L. K. (1988). Learning and teaching styles in engineering education. *Engineering Education, 78* (7), 674–681.

Felder, R. M., & Soloman, B. A. (n.d.-a). *Index of Learning Styles (ILS).* Retrieved December 31, 2008, from www4.ncsu.edu/unity/lockers/users/f/felder/public/ILSpage.html.

Felder, R. M., & Soloman, B. A. (n.d.-b). *Learning styles and strategies.* Retrieved December 31, 2008, from www4.ncsu.edu/unity/lockers/users/f/felder/public/ILSdir/styles.htm.

Felder, R. M., & Spurlin, J. (2005). Applications, reliability, and validity of the Index of Learning Styles. *International Journal of Engineering Education, 21* (1), 103–112.

Feldman, K. A. (1986). The perceived instructional effectiveness of college teachers as related to their personality and attitudinal characteristics: A review and synthesis. *Research in Higher Education, 24* (2), 129–213.

Feldman, K. A. (1987). Research productivity and scholarly accomplishment of college teachers as related to their instructional effectiveness: A review and exploration. *Research in Higher Education, 26* (3), 227–298.

Feldman, K. A. (1989). The association between student ratings of specific instructional dimensions and student achievement: Refining and extending the synthesis of data from multisection validity studies. *Research in Higher Education, 30* (6), 583–645.

Feldman, K. A. (1992). College students' view of male and female college teachers: Part I— Evidence from the social laboratory and experiments. *Research in Higher Education, 33* (2), 317–375.

Feldman, K. A. (1993). College students' view of male and female college teachers: Part II— Evidence from students' evaluations of their classroom teachers. *Research in Higher Education, 32* (2), 151–211.

Feldman, K. A. (1998a). Effective college teaching from the students' and faculty's view: Matched or mismatched priorities? In K. A. Feldman & M. B. Paulsen (Eds.), *Teaching and learning in the college classroom* (2nd ed., pp. 215–240). Needham Heights, MA: Allyn & Bacon.

Feldman, K. A. (1998b). Identifying exemplary teachers and teaching: Evidence from student ratings. In K. A. Feldman & M. B. Paulsen (Eds.), *Teaching and learning in the college classroom* (2nd ed., pp. 391–414). Needham Heights, MA: Allyn & Bacon.

Feldmann, L. J. (2001). Classroom civility is another of our instructor responsibilities. *College Teaching, 49* (4), 137–141.

Felten, P. (2008). Visual literacy. *Change, 40* (6), 60–63.

Ferguson, M. (1989). The role of faculty in increasing student retention. *College and University, 69,* 127–134.

Fernald, P. S. (2004). The Monte Carlo quiz. *College Teaching, 52* (3), 95–99.

Ferris, W. P., & Hess, P. W. (1984). Peer evaluation of student interaction in organizational behavior and other courses. *Organizational Behavior Teaching Review, 9* (4), 74–82.

Fink, L. D. (2003). *Creating significant learning experiences: An integrated approach to designing college courses.* San Francisco: Jossey-Bass.

Fischman, G. E. (2001). Reflections about images, visual culture, and educational research. *Educational Researcher, 30* (8), 28–33.

Fischman, J. (2009, March 16). Students stop surfing after being shown how in-class laptop use lowers test scores. *Chronicle of Higher Education.* Retrieved April 27, 2009, from http://chronicle.com/blogPost/Students-Stop-Surfing-After/4576.

Fleming, N. D., & Baume, D. (2006). Learning styles again: VARKing up the right tree! *Educational Development, 7* (4), 4–7.

Fleming, N. D., & Mills, C. (1992). Not another inventory, rather a catalyst for reflection. In D. H. Wulff & J. D. Nyquist (Eds.), *To improve the academy: Vol. 11. Resources for faculty, instructional, and organizational development* (pp. 137–155). Stillwater, OK: New Forums Press.

Fontana, L. A. (1991). The Civil War interactive. *Instruction Delivery Systems, 5* (6), 5–9.

Forster, F., Hounsell, D., & Thompson, S. (1995). *Tutoring and demonstrating: A handbook*. Edinburgh, UK: University of Edinburgh, Center for Teaching, Learning, and Assessment.

Foster, A. (2008a, January 17). Despite skeptics, publishers tout new "fair use" agreements with universities. *Chronicle of Higher Education*. Retrieved August 20, 2008, from http://chronicle.com/daily/2008/01/1279n.htm.

Foster, A. (2008b, June 13). Law professors rule laptops out of order in class. *Chronicle of Higher Education*, p. A1.

Frand, J. (2000, September–October). The information-age mindset: Changes in students and implications for higher education. *EDUCAUSE Review*, 15–24.

Frederick, P. (1991). Active learning in history classes. *Teaching History: A Journal of Methods, 16* (2), 67–83.

Freeman, S., O'Connor, E., Parks, J. W., Cunningham, M., Hurley, D., Haak, D., et al. (2007). Prescribed active learning increases performance in introductory biology. *Cell Biology Education, 6*, 132–139.

Friedman, P., Rodriguez, F., & McComb, J. (2001). Why students do and do not attend classes: Myths and realities. *College Teaching, 49* (4), 124–133.

Frierson, H. T. (1986). Two intervention methods: Effects on groups of predominantly black nursing students' board scores. *Journal of Research and Development in Education, 19*, 18–23.

Frisby, D. A., & Sweeney, D. C. (1982). The relative merits of multiple true-false achievement tests. *Journal of Educational Measurement, 19* (1), 29–35.

Frymier, J. R. (1970). Motivation is what it's all about. *Motivation Quarterly, 1*, 1–3.

Gabel, C. (1999, March). *Using case studies to teach science*. Paper presented at the annual meeting of the National Association for Research in Science Teaching, Boston.

Gale, R. A., & Andrews, J.D.W. (1989). *A handbook for teaching assistants*. San Diego: University of California, Center for Teaching Development.

Gallupe, R. B., & Cooper, W. H. (1993). Brainstorming electronically. *Sloan Management Review, 33*, 27–36.

Gardner, H. (1993). *Frames of mind: The theory of multiple intelligences*. New York: Basic Books.

Gedalof, A. J. (1998). *Green guide: No. 1. Teaching large classes*. Halifax, Canada: Society for Teaching and Learning in Higher Education.

Georgia System ends laptop program with debt and claims of success. (2001, June 1). *Chronicle of Higher Education*, p. A27.

Gibbs, G. (1999). Using assessment strategically to change the way students learn. In S. Brown & A. Glasner (Eds.), *Assessment matters in higher education: Choosing and using diverse approaches* (pp. 41–53). Buckingham, UK: Society for Research into Higher Education and Open University Press.

Gigliotti, R. J., & Fitzpatrick, D. R. (1977). An investigation into the factors accounting for college student interest in courses. *Educational Research Quarterly, 2* (1), 58–68.

Gilmore, T. N., & Schall, E. (1996). Staying alive to learning: Integrating enactments with case teaching to develop leaders. *Journal of Policy Analysis and Management, 15* (3), 444–457.

Giuliodori, M. J., Lujan, H. L., & DiCarlo, S. E. (2006). Peer instruction enhanced student performance on qualitative problem-solving questions. *Advances in Physiology Education, 30*, 168–173.

Glaser, R. (1991). The maturing of the relationship between the science of learning and cognition and educational practice. *Learning and Instruction, 1* (1), 129–144.

Glassick, C. E., Huber, M. T., & Maeroff, G. I. (1997). *Scholarship assessed: Evaluation of the professoriate*. San Francisco: Jossey-Bass.

Glew, R. H. (2003). The problem with problem-based medical education: Promises not kept. *Biochemistry and Molecular Biology Education, 31* (1), 52–58.

Gogel, H. K. (1985). Faculty office hours. *Journal of Medical Education, 60*, 242–245.

Golding, T. L. (2008). Bonuses of a bonus assignment! *Teaching Professor, 22* (6), 5.

Gonsalves, L. M. (2002). Making connections: Addressing the pitfalls of white faculty/black male student communication. *College Composition and Communication Online, 53*, 435–465.

Gonzalez, V., & Lopez, E. (2001). The age of incivility: Countering disruptive behavior in the classroom. *AAHE Bulletin, 55* (8), 3–6.

Goodson, L. (2005, March). *Content, presentation and learning activities*. Paper presented at the 26th annual meeting of the Sharing Conference of the Southern Regional Faculty and Instructional Development Consortium, Lake Junaluska, NC.

Gordon, L. (1990, November 22). Study finds cheating joins 3 Rs as a basic college skill. *Los Angeles Times*. Retrieved October 13, 2009, from http://articles.latimes.com/1990–11–22/news/mn-6949_1_student-cheating.

Gose, M. (2009). When Socratic dialogue is flagging: Questions and strategies for engaging students. *College Teaching, 57* (1), 45–49.

Grant-Thompson, S., & Atkinson, D. (1997). Cross-cultural mentor effectiveness and African American male students. *Journal of Black Psychology, 23*, 120–134.

Gray, M. J., Ondaatje, E. H., Fricker, R. D., & Geschwind, S. A. (2000). Assessing service-learning: Results from a survey of "Learn and Service American Higher Education." *Change, 32* (2), 30–39.

Gray, M. J., Ondaatje, E. H., & Zakaras, L. (1999). *Combining service and learning in higher education: Summary report*. Santa Monica, CA: Rand.

Greene, J. P., & Forster, G. (2003). *Public high school graduation and college readiness rates in the United States* (Education Working Paper No. 3). Retrieved August 6, 2007, from www.manhattan-institute.org/html/ewp_03.htm.

Greenwald, A. G., & Gillmore, G. M. (1997). No pain, no gain? The importance of measuring course workload in student ratings of instruction. *Journal of Educational Psychology, 89* (4), 743–751.

Greenwood, G. E., & Ramagli, H. J., Jr. (1980). Alternatives to student ratings of college teaching. *Journal of Higher Education, 51* (6), 673–684.

Gronlund, N. E., & Waugh, C. K. (2009). *Assessment of student achievement* (9th ed.). Needham Heights, MA: Allyn & Bacon.

Grunert, J. (1997). *The course syllabus: A learning-centered approach*. Bolton, MA: Anker.

Grunert O'Brien, J., Millis, B. J., & Cohen, M. W. (2008). *The course syllabus: A learning-centered approach* (2nd ed.). San Francisco: Jossey-Bass.

Guo, S., & Jamal, Z. (2007). *Green guide: No 8. Cultural diversity and inclusive teaching*. Ontario, Canada: Society for Teaching and Learning in Higher Education.

Habron, G., & Dann, S. (2002). Breathing life into the case study approach: Active learning in an introductory natural resource management class. *Journal on Excellence in College Teaching, 13* (2/3), 41–58.

Hake, R. R. (1998). Interactive-engagement vs. traditional methods: A six thousand-student survey of mechanics test data for introductory physics courses. *American Journal of Physics, 66*, 64–74.

Hall, E., & Mosley, D. (2005). Is there a role for learning styles in personalised education and training? *International Journal of Lifelong Learning, 24* (3), 243–255.

Hall, R. M., & Sandler, B. R. (1982). *The classroom climate: A chilly one for women?* Washington, DC: Association of American Colleges.

Hallet, V. (2005, July 25). The power of Potter: Can the teenage wizard turn a generation of halfhearted readers into lifelong bookworms? *U.S. News & World Report*. Retrieved October 16, 2006, from www.usnews.com/usnews/culture/articles/050725/25read.htm.

Halpern, D. F., & Associates. (1994). *Changing college classrooms*. San Francisco: Jossey-Bass.

Hammons, J. O., & Barnsley, J. R. (1992). Everything you need to know about developing a grading plan for your course (well, almost). *Journal on Excellence in College Teaching, 3*, 51–68.

Haney, W., & Clarke, M. (2007). Cheating on tests: Prevalence, detection, and implications for on-line testing. In E. Anderman & T. Murdock (Eds.), *Psychology of academic cheating* (pp. 255–288). Burlington, MA: Elsevier.

Hanson, D. (2006). *Instructor's guide to process-oriented guided-inquiry learning*. Stony Brook, NY: Stony Brook University.

Hanson, D., & Wolfskill, T. (2000). Process workshops: A new model for instruction. *Journal of Chemical Education, 77* (1), 120–129.

Harb, J. N., Terry, R. E., Hurt, P. K., & Williamson, K. J. (1995). *Teaching through the cycle: Applications of learning style theory to engineering education at Brigham Young University.* Provo, UT: Brigham Young University Press.

Harding, T., Mayhew, M., Finelli, C., & Carpenter, D. (2007). The theory of planned behavior as a model of academic dishonesty in engineering and humanities undergraduates. *Ethics and Behavior, 17* (3), 255–279.

Harper, G. K. (2001). *Crash course in copyright.* Retrieved June 18, 2004, from www.utsystem.edu/OGC/Intellectual Property/cprtindx.htm.

Hartley, J., & Davies, I. K. (1986). Note-taking: A critical review. *Programmed Learning and Educational Technology, 15,* 207.

Hartman, J. L. (2006, June). *Teaching and learning in the Net Generation.* Plenary session presented at the annual meeting of the Association of American University Presses, New Orleans, LA.

Harvard University. (2008). *Instructional technology survey.* Cambridge, MA: Harvard University, Department of Romance Languages and Literatures.

Hativa, N. (1996). University instructors' ratings profiles: Stability over time and disciplinary differences. *Research in Higher Education, 37* (3), 341–365.

Head, J. T. (1992). New directions in presentation graphics: Impact on teaching and learning. In M. J. Albright & D. L. Graf (Eds.), *New directions for teaching and learning: No. 51. Teaching in the information age: The role of educational technology* (pp. 17–31). San Francisco: Jossey-Bass.

Hebert, S. W. (1984). A simple hypnotic approach to treat test anxiety in medical students and residents. *Journal of Medical Education, 59,* 841–842.

Heller, P., & Hollabaugh, M. (1992). Teaching problem solving through cooperative grouping. Part 2: Designing problems and structuring groups. *American Journal of Physics, 60* (7), 637–644.

Heller, P., Keith, R., & Anderson, S. (1992). Teaching problem solving through cooperative grouping. Part 1: Group vs. individual problem solving. *American Journal of Physics, 60* (7), 627–636.

Hersch, P. (1998). *A tribe apart: A journey into the heart of American adolescence.* New York: Ballantine.

Hertel, J. P., & Millis, B. J. (2002). *Using simulations to promote learning in higher education.* Sterling, VA: Stylus.

Higdon, J., & Topaz, C. (2009). Blogs and wikis as instructional tools: A social software adaptation of just-in-time-teaching. *College Teaching, 57* (2), 105–109.

Higher Education Research Institute. (2004, January 26). *Political interest on the rebound among the nation's freshmen, UCLA survey reveals.* Retrieved November 21, 2008, from www.gseis.ucla.edu/heri/03_press_release.pdf.

Hiller, T. B., & Hietapelto, A. B. (2001). Contract grading: Encouraging commitment to the learning process through voice in the evaluation process. *Journal of Management Education, 25* (6), 660–684.

Hinkle, S., & Hinkle, A. (1990). An experimental comparison of the effects of focused free writing and other study strategies on lecture comprehension. *Teaching of Psychology, 17,* 31–35.

Hintz, M. M. (2005). Can problem-based learning address content and process? *Biochemistry and Molecular Biology Education, 33,* 363–368.

Hmelo-Silver, C. E. (2004). Problem-based learning: What and how do students learn? *Educational Psychology Review, 16,* 235–266.

Hobson, E. H. (2002). Assessing students' motivation to learn in large classes. *American Journal of Pharmaceutical Education, 56,* 82S.

Hobson, E. H. (2004). *Getting students to read: Fourteen tips* (IDEA Paper No. 40). Manhattan: Kansas State University, Center for Faculty Evaluation and Development.

Hodgins, H. W. (2000). *Into the future: A vision paper.* Retrieved December 12, 2006, from www.learnativity.com /download/MP7.PDF.

Hoffman, E., Trott, J., & Neely, K. P. (2002). Concept mapping: A tool to bridge the disciplinary divide. *American Journal of Obstetrics and Gynecology, 187* (3), 41–43.

Howard, D. R., & Miskowski, J. A. (2005). Using a module-based laboratory to incorporate inquiry into a large cell biology course. *Cell Biology Education, 4,* 249–260.

Howard, G. S., & Maxwell, S. E. (1980). The correlation between student satisfaction and grades: A case of mistaken causation? *Journal of Educational Psychology, 72* (6), 810–820.

Howard, G. S., & Maxwell, S. E. (1982). Do grades contaminate student evaluations of instruction? *Research in Higher Education, 16* (2), 175–188.

Howard, M. G., Collins, H. L., & DiCarlo, S. E. (2002). "Survivor" torches "Who wants to be a physician?" in the educational games ratings war. *Advances in Physiology Education, 26*, 30–36.

Howard-Rose, D., & Harrigan, K. (2003, August). *CLOE learning impact studies lite: Evaluating learning objects in nine Ontario university courses.* Paper presented at the MERLOT International Conference, Vancouver, Canada.

Howe, N., & Strauss, W. (2000). *Millennials rising: The next great generation.* New York: Vintage.

Hoyt, D. P., & Perera, S. (2000). *Teaching approach, instructional objectives, and learning* (IDEA Research Report No. 1). Manhattan, KS: IDEA Center.

Hu, S., Kuh, G., & Li, S. (2008). The effects of engagement in inquiry-oriented activities on student learning and personal development. *Innovative Higher Education, 33* (2), 71–81.

Huang, Y., Trevisan, M. S., & Storfer, A. (2007). The impact of the "all-of-the-above" option and student ability on multiple choice tests. *International Journal for the Scholarship of Teaching and Learning, 1* (2), 1–13.

Hudspith, B., & Jenkins, H. (2001). *Green guide: No 3. Teaching the art of inquiry.* Ontario, Canada: Society for Teaching and Learning in Higher Education.

Hufford, T. L. (1991). Increasing academic performance in an introductory biology course. *BioScience, 41* (2), 107–108.

Hung, W., Bailey, J. H., & Johassen, D. H. (2003). Exploring the tensions of problem-based learning: Insights from research. In D. S. Knowlton & D. C. Sharp (Eds.), *New directions for teaching and learning: No. 95. Problem-based learning in the information age* (pp. 13–24). San Francisco: Jossey-Bass.

Hunt, R. (2004). *What is inkshedding?* Retrieved September 22, 2008, from www.stthomasu.ca/~hunt/dialogic/whatshed.htm.

Hutchings, P. (1998). Defining features and significant functions of the course portfolio. In P. Hutchings (Ed.), *The course portfolio: How faculty can examine their teaching to advance practice and student learning* (pp. 13–18). Washington, DC: American Association for Higher Education.

Hutton, P. A. (2006). Understanding student cheating and what educators can do about it. *College Teaching, 54* (1), 171–176.

Hyerle, D. (1996). *Visual tools for constructing knowledge.* Alexandria, VA: Association for Supervision and Curriculum Development.

Hyman, R. T. (1978). *Simulation gaming for values education: The prisoner's dilemma.* Washington, DC: University Press of America.

Hyman, R. T. (1981). *Using simulation games in the college classroom* (IDEA Paper No. 5). Manhattan: Kansas State University, Center for Faculty Evaluation and Development.

Instructional Assessment Resources, University of Texas at Austin. (2007). *Assess students: Scenario-based approach.* Retrieved December 22, 2009, from www.utexas.edu/academic/diia/assessment/iar/students/plan/method/exams-mchoice-scenario.php.

Intrinsic motivation doesn't exist, researcher says. (2005, May 17). *PhysOrg.com.* Retrieved June 16, 2008, from www.physorg.com/news4126.html.

Ip, A., Morrison, I., & Currie, M. (2001). *What is a learning object, technically?* Retrieved May 1, 2006, from http://users.tpg.com.au/adslfrcf/lo/learningObject(WebNet2001).pdf.

Jacobs, L. C., & Chase, C. I. (1992). *Developing and using tests effectively: A guide for faculty.* San Francisco: Jossey-Bass.

Jacobsen, M. (n.d.). *Multiple choice item construction.* Retrieved December 22, 2009, from http://people.ucalgary.ca/~dmjacobs/portage.

Jalajas, D. S., & Sutton, R. I. (1984). Feuds in student groups: Coping with whiners, martyrs, saboteurs, bullies, and deadbeats. *Journal of Management Education, 9* (4), 94–102.

Jassawalla, A. R., Malshe, A., & Sashittal, H. (2008). Student perceptions of social loafing in undergraduate business classroom teams. *Decision Sciences Journal of Innovative Education, 6* (2), 403–426.

Johnson, C., & Ury, C. (1998). Detecting Internet plagiarism. *The National Teaching and Learning Forum, 7* (4), 7–8.

Johnson, C., & Ury, C. (1999). Preventing Internet plagiarism. *The National Teaching and Learning Forum, 8* (5), 5–6.

Johnson, D. W., & Johnson, R. T. (1989). *Cooperation and competition: Theory and research.* Edina, MN: Interaction Books.

Johnson, D. W., Johnson, R. T., & Smith, K. A. (1991). *Active learning: Cooperation in the college classroom.* Edina, MN: Interaction Books.

Johnson, R. T., & Johnson, D. W. (1994). An overview of cooperative learning. In J. Thousand, A. Villa, & A. Nevin (Eds.), *Creativity and collaborative learning* (pp. 31–44). Baltimore: Brookes Press.

Johnson, V. E. (2003). *Grade inflation: A crisis in college education.* New York: Springer-Verlag.

Johnston, K. M. (2003). *"Why do I have to change the way I learn just to fit the way you teach?" Steps to creating a teaching philosophy statement.* Workshop conducted in the Michigan State University Teaching Assistant Program, East Lansing.

Johnston, P. (2005, August 10). Dressing the part. *Chronicle of Higher Education.* Retrieved August 10, 2005, from http://chronicle.com/article/Dressing-the-Part/44918.

Johnston, S., & Cooper, J. (1997). Quick-thinks: The interactive lecture. *Cooperative Learning and College Teaching, 8* (1), 2–6.

Johnstone, A. H., & Su, W. Y. (1994). Lectures— A learning experience? *Education in Chemistry, 35,* 76–79.

Jonas, H., Etzel, S., & Barzansky, B. (1989). Undergraduate medical education. *Journal of the American Medical Association, 262* (8), 1011–1019.

Jones, E. B. (2004). Culturally relevant strategies in the classroom. In A. M. Johns & M. K. Sipp (Eds.), *Diversity in the classroom: Practices for today's campuses* (pp. 51–72). Ann Arbor: University of Michigan Press.

Jones, R. C. (2008). The "why" of class participation: A question worth asking. *College Teaching, 56* (1), 59–62.

Jones-Wilson, T. M. (2005). Teaching problem-solving skills without sacrificing course content: Marrying traditional lecture and active learning in an organic chemistry class. *Journal of College Science Teaching, 35* (1), 42–46.

Jordan, D. (1996, February). *Copyright and multimedia.* Paper presented at the 17th annual meeting of the Sharing Conference of the Southern Regional Faculty and Instructional Development Consortium, Baton Rouge, LA.

Josephson Institute. (2008). *The ethics of American youth: 2006.* Retrieved August 8, 2008, from http://character counts.org/programs/reportcard/2006/index.html.

Junco, R., & Mastrodicasa, J. (2007). *Connecting to the Net Generation: What higher education professionals need to know about today's students.* Washington, DC: Student Affairs Administrators in Higher Education.

Justice, C., Rice, J., Warry, W., Inglis, S., Miller, S., & Sammon, S. (2007). Inquiry in higher education: Reflections and directions in course design and teaching methods. *Innovative Higher Education, 31* (4), 201–214.

Kagan, S. (1988). *Cooperative learning.* San Juan Capistrano, CA: Resources for Teachers.

Kaleta, R., & Joosten, T. (2007, May 8). Student response systems: A University of Wisconsin study of clickers. *EDUCAUSE Center for Applied Research, 10.* Retrieved September 1, 2008, from http://net.educause.edu/ir/library/pdf/ERB0710.pdf.

Kalman, C. S. (2007). *Successful science and engineering teaching in colleges and universities.* Bolton, MA: Anker.

Kalman, J., & Kalman, C. S. (1996). Writing to learn. *American Journal of Physics, 64,* 954–956.

Karabenick, S. A., & Knapp, J. R. (1988). Help seeking and the need for academic assistance. *Journal of Educational Psychology, 80* (3), 406–408.

Karraker, M. W. (1993). Mock trials and critical thinking. *College Teaching, 41* (4), 134–137.

Katayama, A. D. (1997, November). *Getting students involved in note taking: Why partial notes benefit learners more than complete notes*. Paper presented at the annual meeting of the Mid-South Educational Research Association, Memphis, TN.

Kaufman, A. (1985). *Implementing problem-based medical education*. New York: Springer.

Kaufman, A., Mennin, S., Waterman, R., Duban, S., Hansbarger, C., Silverblatt, H., et al. (1989). The New Mexico experiment: Educational innovation and institutional change. *Academic Medicine, 64,* 285–294.

Kaupins, G. (2005). Using popular game and reality show formats to review for exams. *Teaching Professor, 19* (1), 5–6.

Kellogg, A. (2002, February 15). Students plagiarize online less than many think, a new study finds. *Chronicle of Higher Education*. Retrieved November 19, 2009, from http://chronicle.com/article/Students-Plagiarize-Online-/24131.

Kelly, A. E., & O'Donnell, A. (1994). Hypertext and study strategies of pre-service teachers: Issues in instructional hypertext design. *Journal of Educational Computing Research, 10* (4), 373–387.

Kennedy, A., & Navey-David, S. (2004). Inquiry-guided learning and the foreign language classroom. In V. S. Lee (Ed.), *Teaching and learning through inquiry: A guidebook for institutions and instructors* (pp. 71–79). Sterling, VA: Stylus.

Kennedy, F., & Nilson, L. B. (2008). *Successful strategies for teams: Team member handbook*. Retrieved November 24, 2009, from www.clemson.edu/OTEI/documents/TeamworkHandbook.pdf.

Kerkvliet, J. (1994). Cheating by economics students: A comparison of survey results. *Journal of Economic Education, 25* (2), 121–133.

Kerkvliet, J., & Sigmund, C. L. (1999). Can we control cheating in the classroom? *Journal of Economic Education, 30* (4), 331–334.

Kibler, W. L. (1992, November 11). Cheating: Institutions need a comprehensive plan for promoting academic integrity. *Chronicle of Higher Education*, pp. B1–B2.

Kiernan, V. (2002, April 10). Nebraska researchers measure the extent of "link rot" in distance education. *Chronicle of Higher Education*. Retrieved January 2, 2009, from http://chronicle.com/article/Nebraska-Researchers-Measur/1877.

Kiernan, V. (2005, November 25). Students desire balance of technology and human contact, survey suggests. *Chronicle of Higher Education*. Retrieved April 24, 2009, from http://chronicle.com/article/Students-Desire-a-Balance-o/11687.

Kiewra, K. A. (1985). Providing the instructor's notes: An effective addition to student notetaking. *Educational Psychologist, 20,* 33–39.

Kiewra, K. A. (2005). *Learn how to study and SOAR to success*. Upper Saddle Creek, NJ: Pearson Prentice Hall.

Kimmel, R. M. (2002). Undergraduate labs in applied polymer science. *Proceedings of the 2002 American Society for Engineering Education Annual Conference and Exposition*, American Society for Engineering Education, Session #1526.

Kinchin, I. M. (2000). Concept mapping in biology. *Journal of Biological Education, 34* (2), 61–68.

Kinchin, I. M. (2001). If concept mapping is so helpful to learning biology, why aren't we all using it? *International Journal of Science Education, 23* (12), 1257–1269.

Kinchin, I. M. (2006). Developing PowerPoint handouts to support meaningful learning. *British Journal of Educational Technology, 37,* 33–39.

King, M., & Shell, R. (2002). Teaching and evaluating critical thinking with concept maps. *Nurse Educator, 27* (5), 214–216.

Kingsland, A. J. (1996). Time expenditure, workload, and student satisfaction in problem-based learning. In L. Wilkerson & W. Gijselaers (Eds.), *New directions for teaching and learning: No. 68. Bringing problem-based learning to higher education: Theory and practice* (pp. 73–82). San Francisco: Jossey-Bass.

Kirkpatrick, L. D., & Pittendrigh, A. S. (1984). A writing teacher in the physics classroom. *Physics Teacher, 22* (3), 159–164.

Kirschner, P. A., Sweller, J., & Clark, R. E. (2006). Why minimal guidance during instruction does not work: An analysis of the failure of constructivist, discovery, problem-based, experiential, and inquiry-based teaching. *Educational Psychologist, 41* (2), 75–86.

Klahr, D., & Nigam, M. (2004). The equivalence of learning paths in early science instruction: Effects of direct instruction and discovery learning. *Psychological Science, 15*, 661–667.

Kleiner, C., & Lord, M. (1999, November 22). The cheating game. *U.S. News & World Report*, 55–66.

Kloss, R. J. (1994). A nudge is best: Helping students through the Perry schema of intellectual development. *College Teaching, 42* (4), 151–158.

Knapper, C. K. (1982). Technology and teaching: Future prospects. In C. K. Knapper (Ed.), *New directions for teaching and learning: No. 9. Expanding learning through new communication technologies* (pp. 81–90). San Francisco: Jossey-Bass.

Knight, J. K., & Wood, W. B. (2005). Teaching more by lecturing less. *Cell Biology Education, 4*, 298–310.

Knowlton, D. S., Knowlton, H. M., & Davis, C. (2000). The whys and hows of online discussion. *Syllabus: New Directions in Educational Technology, 13* (10), 54–58.

Kobrak, P. (1992). Black student retention in predominantly white regional universities: The politics of faculty involvement. *Journal of Negro Education, 61*, 509–530.

Kodani, C. H., & Wood, M. (2007). The benefits of music and stretching in maintaining student attention. *Teaching Professor, 21* (6), 5.

Kohn, A. (1993). *Punished by rewards*. Boston: Houghton Mifflin.

Kolb, D. A. (1984). *Experiential learning: Experience as the source of learning and development*. Upper Saddle River, NJ: Prentice Hall.

Konieczny, P. (2007). Wikis and Wikipedia as a teaching tool. *International Journal of Instructional Technology and Distance Learning, 4* (1). Retrieved April 24, 2009, from www.itdl.org/Journal/Jan_07/article02.htm.

Kosslyn, S. M. (1994). *Image and brain: The resolution of the imagery debate*. Cambridge, MA: MIT Press.

Kozma, R. B., Russell, J., Jones, T., Marx, N., & Davis, J. (1996). The use of multiple linked representations to facilitate science understanding. In S. Vosniadou, E. DeCorte, R. Glaser, & H. Mandl (Eds.), *International perspectives on the design of technology-supported learning environments* (pp. 41–60). Mahwah, NJ: Erlbaum.

Kramer, J., & Arnold, A. (2004). Music 200 "Understanding Music": An inquiry-guided approach to music appreciation. In V. S. Lee (Ed.), *Teaching and learning through inquiry: A guidebook for institutions and instructors* (pp. 41–50). Sterling, VA: Stylus.

Krathwohl, D. R., Bloom, B. S., & Masia, B. B. (1999). *Taxonomy of educational objectives: Book 2. Affective domain*. Reading, MA: Addison-Wesley.

Kraus, R. (2008). You must participate: Violating research ethical principles through role play. *College Teaching, 56* (3), 131–136.

Kress, G., Jewitt, C., Ogborn, J., & Charalampos, T. (2006). *Multimodal teaching and learning: The rhetorics of the science classroom*. London: Continuum.

Kristensen, E. (2007). *Teaching at the University of Ottawa: A handbook for professors and TAs* (5th ed.). Ottawa, ON: University of Ottawa, Centre for University Teaching.

Krupnick, C. G. (1985). Women and men in the classroom: Inequality and its remedies. *Journal of the Harvard-Danforth Center: On Teaching and Learning, 1*, 18–25.

Kuh, G., Kinzie, J., Schuh, J., Whitt, E., & Associates. (2005). *Student success in college: Creating conditions that matter*. San Francisco: Jossey-Bass.

Kuhn, T. S. (1970). *The structure of scientific revolutions* (2nd ed.). Chicago: University of Chicago Press.

Kustra, E.D.H., & Potter, M. K. (2008). *Green guide: No 9. Leading effective discussions*. Ontario, Canada: Society for Teaching and Learning in Higher Education.

Kutner, M., Greenberg, E., Jin, Y., Boyle, B., Hsu, T., & Dunleavy, E. (2007). *Literacy in everyday life: Results from the 2003 National Assessment of Adult Literacy*. Washington, DC: U.S. Department of Education, National Center for Education Statistics.

Kyle, W. C., Jr. (1980). The distinction between inquiry and scientific inquiry and why high school students should be cognizant of the distinction. *Journal of Research on Science Teaching, 17*, 123–130.

Lacey-Casem, M. L. (1990). Testing students' learning and grading tests and papers. In L. B. Nilson (Ed.), *Teaching techniques: A handbook for TAs at UCR* (pp. 34–46). Riverside, CA: University of California, Teaching Assistant Development Program.

Laird, R. (2004). Heuristic models/concept maps in neuroanatomy instruction. *The Teacher, 6* (1&2), 17–25.

Lamb, A. C. (1992). Multimedia and the teaching-learning process in higher education. In M. J. Albright & D. L. Graf (Eds.), *New directions for teaching and learning: No. 51. Teaching in the information age: The role of educational technology* (pp. 33–42). San Francisco: Jossey-Bass.

Lang, J. M. (2008). *On course: A week-by-week guide to your first semester of college teaching.* Cambridge, MA: Harvard University Press.

Langan, J. (2007). *Reading and student skills* (8th ed.). New York: McGraw-Hill.

Langer, J. A. (1992). Speaking of knowing: Conceptions of understanding in academic disciplines. In A. Herrington & C. Moran (Eds.), *Writing, teaching, and learning in the disciplines* (pp. 69–85). New York: Modern Language Association of America.

Langer, J. A., & Applebee, A. N. (1987). *How writing shapes thinking.* Urbana, IL: National Council of Teachers of English.

Larkin, J. H., & Simon, H. A. (1987). Why a diagram is (sometimes) worth ten thousand words. *Cognitive Science, 11,* 65–99.

Lasry, N. (2008). Clickers or flashcards: Is there really a difference? *Physics Teacher, 46,* 242–244.

Laws, P. (1991). Calculus-based physics without lectures. *Physics Today, 12,* 24–31.

Leahy, R. (2002). Conducting writing assignments. *College Teaching, 50* (2), 50–54.

Leamnson, R. (1999). *Thinking about teaching and learning: Developing habits of learning with first year college and university students.* Sterling, VA: Stylus.

Leamnson, R. (2000). Learning as biological brain change. *Change, 32* (6), 34–40.

Leatherman, C. (1996, March 8). Whatever happened to civility in academe? *Chronicle of Higher Education,* p. A21.

Leauby, B. A., & Brazina, P. (1998). Concept mapping: Potential uses in accounting education. *Journal of Accounting Education, 16* (1), 123–138.

Lee, V. S. (Ed.). (2004). *Teaching and learning through inquiry: A guidebook for institutions and instructors* (pp. 3–16). Sterling, VA: Stylus.

Lee, V. S., Green, D. B., Odom, J., Schechter, E., & Slatta, R. W. (2004). What is inquiry-guided learning? In V. S. Lee (Ed.), *Teaching and learning through inquiry: A guidebook for institutions and instructors* (pp. 3–16). Sterling, VA: Stylus.

Leeming, F. C. (2002). The exam-a-day procedure improves performance in psychology classes. *Teaching of Psychology, 29* (3), 210–212.

Leff, L. L. (n.d.). *Contract grading in teaching computer programming.* Retrieved December 18, 2008, from www.wiu.edu/users/mflll/GRADCONT.HTM.

Leichhardt, G. (1989). Development of an expert explanation: An analysis of a sequence of subtraction lessons. In L. Resnick (Ed.), *Knowing, learning, and instruction* (pp. 67–125). Mahwah, NJ: Erlbaum.

Lempert, D., Xavier, N., & DeSouza, B. (1995). *Escape from the ivory tower: Student adventures in democratic experiential education.* San Francisco: Jossey-Bass.

Levin, B. (1997, March). *The influence of context in case-based teaching: Personal dilemmas, moral issues or real change in teachers' thinking?* Paper presented at the annual meeting of the American Educational Research Association, Chicago.

Levin, J. (2001, December). *Developing a learning environment where all students seek to excel.* Faculty workshop conducted at Clemson University, SC.

Levine, A., & Cureton, J. S. (1998). *When hope and fear collide: A portrait of today's college student.* San Francisco: Jossey-Bass.

Lewes, D., & Stiklus, B. (2007). *Portrait of a student as a young wolf: Motivating undergraduates* (3rd ed.). Pennsdale, PA: Folly Hill Press.

Lewis, R. J., & Wall, M. (1988). *Exploring obstacles to uses of technology in higher education: A discussion paper.* Washington, DC: Academy for Educational Development.

Lewis, S. E., & Lewis, J. E. (2005). Departing from lectures: An evaluation of a peer-led guided inquiry alternative. *Journal of Chemical Education, 82* (1), 135–139.

Lieux, E. M. (1996). Comparison study of learning in lecture vs. problem-based format. *About Teaching, 50* (1), 18–19.

Light, R. J. (1990). *The Harvard Assessment Seminar, first report: Explorations with students and faculty about teaching, learning, and student life.* Cambridge, MA: Harvard Graduate School of Education.

Light, R. J. (1992). *The Harvard Assessment Seminar, second report: Explorations with students and faculty about teaching, learning, and student life.* Cambridge, MA: Harvard Graduate School of Education.

Lin, Y., McKeachie, W. J., & Kim, Y. C. (2001). College student intrinsic and/or extrinsic motivation and learning. *Learning and Individual Differences, 13* (3), 251–258.

Litzinger, T. A., Lee, S. H., Wise, J. C., & Felder, R. M. (2007). A psychometric study of the Index of Learning Styles. *Journal of Engineering Education, 96* (4), 309–319.

Lord, T., & Orkwiszewski, T. (2006). Didactic to inquiry-based instruction in a science laboratory. *American Biology Teacher, 68* (6), 342–345.

Lord, T. R. (1997). A comparison between traditional and constructivist teaching in college biology. *Innovative Higher Education, 21* (3), 197–216.

Lord, T. R. (1999). A comparison between traditional and constructivist teaching in environmental science. *Journal of Environmental Education, 30* (3), 22–28.

Loukopoulos, L. D., Dismukes, R. K., & Barshi, I. (2009). *The multitasking myth (Ashgate studies in human factors for flight operators).* Burlington, VT: Ashgate.

Lovett-Hooper, G., Komarraju, M., Weston, R., & Dollinger, S. (2007). Is plagiarism a forerunner of other deviance? Imagined futures of academically dishonest students. *Ethics and Behavior, 17* (3), 323–336.

Lowery, J. W. (2001). The millennials come to campus. *About Campus, 6* (3), 6–12.

Luckie, D. B., Maleszewski, J. J., Loznak, S. D., & Krha, M. (2004). Infusion of collaborative inquiry throughout a biology curriculum increases student learning: A four-year study of "Teams and Streams." *Advances in Physiology Education, 28* (4), 199–209.

Lundeberg, M. A., Levin, B., & Harrington, H. (1999). *Who learns what from cases and how? The research base for teaching and learning with cases.* Mahwah, NJ: Erlbaum.

Lundeberg, M. A., Mogen, K., Bergland, M., Klyczek, K., Johnson, D., & MacDonald, E. (2002). Fostering ethical awareness about human genetics through multimedia-based cases. *Journal of College Science Teaching, 32* (1), 64–69.

Lundeberg, M. A., & Yadav, A. (2006a). Assessment of case study teaching: Where do we go from here? Part I. *Journal of College Science Teaching, 35* (5), 10–13.

Lundeberg, M. A., & Yadav, A. (2006b). Assessment of case study teaching: Where do we go from here? Part II. *Journal of College Science Teaching, 35* (6), 8–13.

Mabrito, M. (1997). Writing on the front line: A study of workplace writing. *Business Communication Quarterly, 60,* 58–70.

MacGregor, J. (1990). Collaborative learning: Reframing the classroom. *Chalkboard, 2,* 1–2.

Madigan, D. (2006). *The technology literate professoriate: Are we there yet?* (IDEA Paper No. 43). Manhattan: Kansas State University, Center for Faculty Evaluation and Development.

Madigan, R., & Brosamer, J. (1990). Improving the writing skills of students in introductory psychology. *Teaching of Psychology, 17,* 27–30.

Maleki, R. B., & Heerman, C. E. (1992). *Improving student reading* (IDEA Paper No. 26). Manhattan: Kansas State University, Center for Faculty Evaluation and Development.

Mangan, K. S. (2001, September 7). Business schools, fed up with Internet use during classes, force students to log off. *Chronicle of Higher Education,* p. A43.

Mangurian, L. P. (2005, February). *Learning and teaching practice: The power of the affective.* Paper presented at the annual Lilly Conference on College Teaching South, Greensboro, NC.

Marrs, K. A., & Novak, G. (2004). Just-in-time teaching in biology: Creating an active learner classroom using the Internet. *Cell Biology Education, 3,* 49–61.

Marsh, H. W. (1982). The use of path analysis to estimate teacher and course effects in student rating of instructional effectiveness. *Applied Psychological Measurement, 6,* 47–59.

Marsh, H. W. (1984). Experimental manipulations of university student motivation and their effects on examination performance. *British Journal of Educational Psychology, 54,* 206–213.

Marsh, H. W., & Dunkin, M. (1992). Students' evaluations of university teaching: A multidimensional perspective. In

J. C. Smart (Ed.), *Higher education handbook of theory and research* (Vol. 8, pp. 143–233). New York: Agathon.

Marsh, H. W., & Overall, J. U. (1979). Long-term stability of students' evaluations: A note on Feldman's "Consistency and variability among college students in rating their teachers and courses." *Research in Higher Education, 10,* 139–147.

Marsh, H. W., & Roach, L. A. (1997). Making student evaluations of teaching effectiveness effective: The critical issues of validity, bias, and utility. *American Psychologist, 52,* 1187–1197.

Martin, G. I. (2000). Peer carding. *College Teaching, 48* (1), 15–16.

Martin, H. H., Hands, K. B., Lancaster, S. M., Trytten, D. A., & Murphy, T. J. (2008). Hard but not too hard: Challenging courses and engineering students. *College Teaching, 56* (2), 107–113.

Marzano, R. J. (2003). *What works in schools: Translating research into action.* Alexandria, VA: Association for Supervision and Curriculum Development.

Mayer, R. E. (2004). Should there be a three-strikes rule against pure discovery learning? The case for guided methods of instruction. *American Psychologist, 56,* 14–19.

Mayer, R. E. (2005). Introduction to multimedia learning. In R. E. Mayer (Ed.), *The Cambridge handbook of multimedia learning* (pp. 1–15). Cambridge: Cambridge University Press.

Mayer, R. E., & Gallini, J. K. (1990). When is an illustration worth ten thousand words? *Journal of Educational Psychology, 82* (4), 715–726.

Mayer, R. E., & Sims, V. K. (1994). For whom is a picture worth ten thousand words? Extensions of a dual coding theory of multimedia learning. *Journal of Educational Psychology, 86* (3), 389–401.

Mazur, E. (1997). *Peer instruction: A user's manual.* Upper Saddle River, NJ: Prentice Hall.

Mazur Group. (2008). *Publications: Peer instruction.* Retrieved September 1, 2008, from http://mazur-www .harvard.edu/publications.php?function=search&topic=8.

McCabe, D. L. (2005). Cheating among college and university students: A North American perspective. *International Journal for Educational Integrity, 1* (1). Retrieved August 14, 2008, from www.ojs.unisa.edu.au/index .php/IJEI/article/viewFile/14/9.

McCabe, D. L., & Pavela, G. (2000). Some good news about academic integrity. *Change, 32* (5), 32–38.

McCabe, D. L., & Pavela, G. (2004). Ten principles of academic integrity: How faculty can foster student honesty. *Change, 36* (3), 10.

McCabe, D. L., & Trevino, L. K. (1996). What we know about cheating in college: Longitudinal trends and recent developments. *Change, 28* (1), 28–33.

McCabe, D. L., & Trevino, L. K. (1997). Individual and contextual influences on academic dishonesty: A multi-campus investigation. *Research in Higher Education, 38* (3), 379–396.

McCabe, D. L., Trevino, L. K., & Butterfield, K. D. (1999). Academic integrity in honor code and non-honor code environments: A qualitative investigation. *Journal of Higher Education, 70* (2), 211–234.

McClain, A. (1987). Improving lectures: Challenging both sides of the brain. *Journal of Optometric Education, 13,* 18–20.

McCreary, C. L., Golde, M. F., & Koeske, R. (2006). Peer instruction in the general chemistry laboratory: Assessment of student learning. *Journal of Chemical Education, 83* (5), 804–810.

McDaniel, M. A., Howard, D. C., & Einstein, G. O. (2009). The read-recite-review study strategy: Effective and portable. *Psychological Science, 20* (4), 516–522.

McDermott, L., & Shaffer, P. (2002). *Tutorials in introductory physics.* Upper Saddle River, NJ: Prentice Hall.

McGaghie, W. C., McCrimmon, D. R., Mitchell, G., Thompson, J. A., & Ravitch, M. M. (2000). Quantitative concept mapping in pulmonary physiology: Comparison of student and faculty knowledge structures. *Advances in Physiology Education, 23* (1), 72–80.

McKeachie, W. J. (1994). *Teaching tips: Strategies, research, and theory for college and university teachers* (9th ed.). Lexington, MA: D. C. Heath.

McKeachie, W. J. (2002). *Teaching tips: Strategies, research, and theory for college and university teachers* (11th ed.). Boston: Houghton Mifflin.

McKeachie, W. B., Pintrich, P. R., Lin, Y-G., Smith, D. A., & Sharma, R. (1990). *Teaching and learning in the college classroom: A review of the literature* (2nd ed.). Ann Arbor: University of Michigan, National Center for Research to Improve Postsecondary Teaching and Learning.

McKinney, K. (2001). *Responses from the POD Network discussion list on encouraging students to prepare for class.* Retrieved March 30, 2002, from www.cat.ilstu.edu /teaching_tips/handouts/pod.shtml.

Mealy, D. L., & Host, T. R. (1993). Coping with test anxiety. *College Teaching, 40* (4), 147–150.

Mealy, D. L., & Nist, S. L. (1989). Postsecondary teacher directed comprehension strategies. *Journal of Reading, 32* (6), 484–493.

Menges, R. J. (1988). Research on teaching and learning: The relevant and the redundant. *Review of Higher Education, 11*, 259–268.

Mento, A. J., Martinelli, P., & Jones, R. M. (1999). Mind mapping in executive education: Applications and outcomes. *Journal of Management Development, 18* (4), 390–407.

Meyers, S. A. (2003). Strategies to prevent and reduce conflict in college classrooms. *College Teaching, 51* (3), 94–98.

Meyers, S. A., Bender, J., Hill, E. K., & Thomas, S. Y. (2006). How do faculty experience and respond to classroom conflict? *International Journal of Teaching and Learning in Higher Education, 18* (3), 180–187.

Michaelsen, L. K. (1997–1998). Keys to using learning groups effectively. *Essays on Teaching Excellence, 9* (5), 1–2.

Middendorf, J., & Kalish, A. (1996). The "change-up" in lectures. *The National Teaching and Learning Forum, 5* (2), 1–4.

Mierson, S. (1998). A problem-based learning course in physiology for undergraduate and graduate basic science students. *Advances in Physiological Education, 20* (1), S16–S27.

Mierson, S., & Parikh, A. A. (2000). Stories from the field: Problem-based learning from a teacher's and a student's perspective. *Change, 32* (1), 20–27.

Miller, J. M., & Chamberlin, M. (2000). Women are teachers, men are professors: A study of student perceptions. *Teaching Sociology, 28*, 283–298.

Milliron, V., & Sandoe, K. (2008). The Net Generation cheating challenge. *Innovate: Journal of Online Education, 4* (6). Retrieved August 14, 2008, from www.innovateonline .info/index.php?view=article&id=499&action=article.

Millis, B. J. (1990). Helping faculty build learning communities through cooperative groups. In L. Hilsen (Ed.), *To improve the academy: Vol. 9. Resources for faculty, instructional, and organizational development* (pp. 43–58). Stillwater, OK: New Forums Press.

Millis, B. J. (1992). Conducting effective peer classroom observations. In D. Wulff & J. Nyquist (Eds.), *To improve the academy: Vol. 11. Resources for faculty, instructional, and organizational development* (pp. 189–206). Stillwater, OK: New Forums Press.

Millis, B. J. (2005). *Question shuffle.* Retrieved May 8, 2009, from http://teaching.unr.edu/etp/teaching_tips /indexttips.html.

Millis, B. J. (in press). *Using academic games to promote learning.* Sterling, VA: Stylus.

Millis, B. J., & Cottell, P. G., Jr. (1998). *Cooperative learning for higher education faculty.* Phoenix, AZ: American Council on Education and Oryx Press.

Mills, J. E., & Treagust, D. F. (2003). Engineering education: Is problem-based or project-based learning the answer? *Australasian Journal of Engineering Education.* Retrieved October 4, 2008, from www.aaee.com.au /journal/2003/mills_treagust03.pdf.

Mitchell, P. D. (1982). Simulation and gaming in higher education. In C. K. Knapper (Ed.), *New directions for teaching and learning: No. 9. Expanding learning through new communications technologies* (pp. 57–67). San Francisco: Jossey-Bass.

Mixon, F. G., Jr. (1996). Crime in the classroom: An extension. *Journal of Economic Education, 27* (3), 195–200.

Montgomery, K. (2002). Authentic tasks and rubrics: Going beyond traditional assessments in college teaching. *College Teaching, 50* (1), 34–39.

Moore, A. H. (2003–2004). Great expectations and challenges for learning objects. *Essays on Teaching Excellence, 1* (4), 1–2.

Moore, S. (Speaker). (2009). *Scott Moore: Using technology and collaboration to engage students* (Video). Ann Arbor:

University of Michigan, Center for Research on Learning and Teaching. Retrieved April 24, 2009, from www.crlt.umich.edu/faculty/Thurnau/ThurnauVideos.php.

Moore, V. A. (1996). Inappropriate challenges to professional authority. *Teaching Sociology, 24*, 202–206.

Moreno, R. (2004). Decreasing cognitive load in novice students: Effects of explanatory versus corrective feedback in discovery-based multimedia. *Instructional Science, 32*, 99–113.

Moreno, R., & Mayer, R. E. (1999). Cognitive principles of multimedia learning: The role of modality and contiguity. *Journal of Educational Psychology, 91* (2), 358–368.

Morris, C. (2008). *Critiques of Howard Earl Gardner's multiple intelligences theory.* Retrieved December 31, 2008, from www.igs.net/~cmorris/critiques.html.

Moss, A., & Holder, C. (1988). *Improving student learning: A guidebook for faculty in all disciplines.* Dubuque, IA: Kendall/Hunt.

Mowl, G., & Pain, R. (1995). Using self and peer assessment to improve students' essay writing: A case study from geography. *Innovations in Education and Training International, 32* (4), 324–335.

Moy, J. R., Rodenbaugh, D. W., Collins, H. L., & DiCarlo, S. E. (2000). Who wants to be a physician? An educational tool for reviewing pulmonary physiology. *Advances in Physiology Education, 24* (1), 30–37.

Murray, H. G., & Renaud, R. D. (1996). Disciplinary differences in classroom teaching behaviors. In M. Marincovich & N. Hativa (Eds.), *New directions for teaching and learning: No. 64. Disciplinary differences in teaching and learning: Implications for practice* (pp. 31–39). San Francisco: Jossey-Bass.

Murray, M. (1991). *Beyond the myths and magic of mentoring: How to facilitate an effective mentoring program.* San Francisco: Jossey-Bass.

Murrell, K. L. (1984). Peer performance evaluation: When peers do it, they do it better. *Journal of Management Education, 9* (4), 83–85.

Myers, C. B., & Myers, S. M. (2007). Assessing assessments: The effects of two exam formats on course achievement and evaluation. *Innovative Higher Education, 31*, 227–236.

Nadelson, S. (2007). Academic misconduct by university students: Faculty perceptions and responses. *Plagiary, 2* (2), 1–10.

Nadler, A. (1983). Personal characteristics and help-seeking. In B. M. DePaulo, A. Nadler, & J. D. Fisher (Eds.), *New directions in helping: Vol. 2. Help-seeking* (pp. 303–340). Orlando, FL: Academic Press.

Nadolski, R. J., Kirschner, P. A., & van Merriënboer, J.J.G. (2005). Optimizing the number of steps in learning tasks for complex skills. *British Journal of Educational Psychology, 84*, 429–434.

Nathan, R. (2005). *My freshman year: What a professor learned by becoming a student.* Ithaca, NY: Cornell University Press.

National Association of Student Affairs Professionals in Higher Education. (2007). *Profile of today's college student.* Retrieved May 1, 2008, from www.naspa.org/profile/results.cfm.

National Endowment for the Arts. (2007). *To read or not to read: A question of national consequence.* Washington, DC: Author.

National Survey of Student Engagement. (2007). *Experiences that matter: Enhancing student learning and success.* Bloomington: Indiana University, Center for Postsecondary Research and Planning.

Naveh-Benjamin, M., McKeachie, W. J., & Lin, Y. (1987). Two types of test-anxious students: Support for an information processing model. *Journal of Educational Psychology, 79* (2), 131–136.

Neal, E. (2008, June). *Teaching critical thinking.* Workshop presented at the South Carolina Higher Education Summer Institute for Teaching and Learning, Greenville.

Nelson, C. (1993, November). *Fostering critical thinking and mature valuing across the curriculum.* Workshop presented at the 13th Annual Lilly Conference on College Teaching, Oxford, OH.

Nelson, C. E. (2000). How can students who are reasonably bright and who are trying hard to do the work still flunk? *The National Teaching and Learning Forum, 9* (5), 7–8.

Nemire, R. E. (2007). Intellectual property development and use for distance education courses: A review of law, organizations, and resources for faculty. *College Teaching, 55* (1), 26–30.

Nettles, M. (1988). *Towards black undergraduate student equality in American higher education.* Westport, CT: Greenwood Press.

Nettleship, J. (1992). Active learning in economics: Mind maps and wall charts. *Economics, 28*, 69–71.

Newell, G. E. (1984). Learning from writing in two content areas: A case study/protocol analysis. *Research in the Teaching of English, 18*, 265–287.

Nicholls, G. (2002). Mentoring: The art of teaching. In P. Jarvis (Ed.), *The theory and practice of teaching* (pp. 132–142). Sterling, VA: Stylus.

Nilson, L. B. (1981). *The TA handbook: Teaching techniques and self-improvement strategies.* Los Angeles: University of California, Department of Sociology, TA Training Program.

Nilson, L. B. (1992). Publishing research on teaching. In A. Allison & T. Frongia (Eds.), *The grad student's guide to getting published* (pp. 123–130). Upper Saddle River, NJ: Prentice Hall.

Nilson, L. B. (2002). The graphic syllabus: Shedding visual light on course organization. In D. Lieberman & C. Wehlburg (Eds.), *To improve the academy: Vol. 20. Resources for faculty, instructional, and organizational development* (pp. 238–259). Bolton, MA: Anker.

Nilson, L. B. (2002–2003). Helping students help each other: Making peer feedback more valuable. *Essays in Teaching Excellence, 14* (8), 1–2.

Nilson, L. B. (2003). Improving student peer feedback. *College Teaching, 51* (1), 34–38.

Nilson, L. B. (2007a). *The graphic syllabus and the outcomes map: Communicating your course.* San Francisco: Jossey-Bass.

Nilson, L. B. (2007b). Best practices: Students *will* do the readings; Issues to consider: Holding students accountable: The options are endless, the results unexpectedly positive. *Thriving in Academe, 25* (3), 7.

Nilson, L. B., & Jackson, N. S. (2004). Combating classroom misconduct (incivility) with bills of rights. *Proceedings of the 4th Conference of the International Consortium for Educational Development.* Ottawa, ON, Canada.

Nilson, L. B., & Lysaker, J. T. (1996, Spring/May). The gender factor in teaching evaluations: Beyond economics. *American Economics Association 1996 Committee on the Status of Women in the Economics Profession Newsletter,* 5–7.

Nilson, L. B., & Weaver, B. E. (Eds.). (2005). *New directions for teaching and learning: No. 101. Enhancing learning with laptops in the classroom.* San Francisco: Jossey-Bass.

Nixon-Cobb, E. (2005). Visualizing thinking: A strategy that improved thinking. *Teaching Professor, 19* (1), 3, 6.

Noppe, I., Achterberg, J., Duquaine, L., Huebbe, M., & Williams, C. (2007). PowerPoint presentation handouts and college student learning outcomes. *International Journal for the Scholarship of Teaching and Learning, 1* (1). Retrieved April 24, 2009, from http://academics .georgiasouthern.edu/ijsotl/v1n1/noppe/IJ_Noppe.pdf.

Novak, G. M., Patterson, E. T., Gavrin, A. D., & Christian, W. (1999). *Just-in-time teaching: Blending active learning with Web technology.* Upper Saddle River, NJ: Prentice Hall.

Novak, J. D. (1977). An alternative to Piagetian psychology for sciences and mathematics education. *Science Education, 61*, 453–477.

Novak, J. D., & Gowin, B. D. (1984). *Learning how to learn.* Cambridge: Cambridge University Press.

Nowell, C., & Laufer, D. (1997). Undergraduate student cheating in the fields of business and economics. *Journal of Economic Education, 28* (1), 3–12.

Nuhfer, E. B. (2003). *Of what value are student evaluations?* Retrieved November 17, 2008, from www.isu.edu/ctl /facultydev/extras/student-evals.html.

Nurrenbern, S., & Pickering, M. (1987). Concept learning versus problem solving: Is there a difference? *Journal of Chemical Education, 64* (6), 508–510.

Nyquist, J., & Wulff, D. (1996). *Working effectively with graduate assistants.* Thousand Oaks, CA: Sage.

Oakley, B., Brent, R., Felder, R. M., & Elhajj, I. (2004). Turning student groups into effective teams. *Journal of Student Centered Learning, 2* (1), 9–34.

Oblinger, D. (2003). Boomers, Gen-Xers, and millennials: Understanding the "new students." *EDUCAUSE Review, 38* (4), 36–40, 42, 44–45.

Odom, C. D. (2002, April). *Advances in instructional physics laboratories at Clemson University*. Colloquium presented at the College of Engineering and Sciences, Clemson University, SC.

O'Donnell, A., & Dansereau, D. F. (1993). Learning form lecture: Effects of cooperative review. *Journal of Experimental Education, 61* (2), 116–125.

Office of Educational Development. (1985). Preventing student academic dishonesty. *Tools for teaching*. Berkeley: University of California.

Okebukola, P.A.O. (1992). Can good concept mappers be good problem solvers in science? *Research in Science and Technological Education, 10* (2), 153–170.

Oliver-Hoyo, M., & Allen, D. (2005). Attitudinal effects of a student-centered active learning environment. *Journal of Chemical Education, 82* (6), 944–949.

Oliver-Hoyo, M., Allen, D., & Anderson, M. (2004). Inquiry-guided instruction. *Journal of College Science Teaching, 33* (6), 20–24.

Oliver-Hoyo, M., & Beichner, R. (2004). SCALE-UP: Bringing inquiry-guided methods to large enrollment courses. In V. S. Lee (Ed.), *Teaching and learning through inquiry: A guidebook for institutions and instructors* (pp. 51–69). Sterling, VA: Stylus.

Olsen, F. (2001, September 21). Chapel Hill seeks best role for students' laptops. *Chronicle of Higher Education*, p. A31.

Olsen, F. (2002, January 11). Duke U. decides against requiring freshmen to own laptops. *Chronicle of Higher Education*, p. A44.

Orlans, H. (1999). Scholarly fair use: Chaotic and shrinking. *Change, 31* (6), 53–60.

Orsmond, P., Merry, S., & Reiling, K. (1996). The importance of marking criteria in peer assessment. *Assessment and Evaluation in Higher Education, 21* (3), 239–249.

Ory, J. C., & Ryan, K. E. (1993). *Survival skills for college: Vol. 4. Tips for improving testing and grading*. Thousand Oaks, CA: Sage.

Overall, J. U., & Marsh, H. W. (1980). Students' evaluations of instruction: A longitudinal study of their stability. *Journal of Educational Psychology, 72*, 321–325.

Overholser, J. C. (1992). Socrates in the classroom. *College Teaching, 40* (1), 14–19.

Owens, R. E. (1972). How important is motivation in college learning? *Kansas State University Teaching Notes, 2*, 2–3.

Paivio, A. (1971). *Imagery and verbal processes*. New York: Holt.

Paivio, A. (1990). *Mental representations: A dual coding approach*. New York: Oxford University Press.

Paivio, A., & Csapo, K. (1973). Picture superiority in free recall: Imagery and dual coding? *Cognitive Psychology, 5*, 176–206.

Paivio, A., Walsh, M., & Bons, T. (1994). Concreteness effects on memory: When and why? *Journal of Experimental Psychology: Learning, Memory, and Cognition, 20* (5), 1196–1204.

Panitz, T. (1999). The motivational benefits of cooperative learning. In M. Theall (Ed.), *New directions for teaching and learning: No. 78. Motivation from within: Encouraging faculty and students to excel* (pp. 59–67). San Francisco: Jossey-Bass.

Pascarella, E. T., & Terenzini, P. T. (2005). *How college affects students: A third decade of research*. San Francisco: Jossey-Bass.

Patel, V. L., Groen, G. J., & Norman, G. R. (1993). Reasoning and instruction in medical curricula. *Cognition and Instruction, 10*, 335–378.

Pauk, W. (2001). *How to study in college*. Boston: Houghton Mifflin.

Paulsen, M. B., & Feldman, K. A. (1999). Student motivation and epistemological beliefs. In M. Theall (Ed.), *New directions for teaching and learning: No. 78. Motivation from within: Encouraging faculty and students to excel* (pp. 17–25). San Francisco: Jossey-Bass.

Pavela, G. (2008, June 5). Classroom honor codes. *Association for Student Judicial Affairs Law and Policy Report: No. 291*.

Peirce, W. (2006). *Strategies for teaching critical reading*. Retrieved December 19, 2008, from http://academic.pg.cc.md.us/~wpeirce/MCCCTR/critread.html.

Penick, J. E., & Crow, L. W. (1989). Characteristics of innovative college science programs. *Journal of College Science Teaching, 19* (1), 14–17.

Perlmutter, D. D. (2008a, April 18). Are you a good protégé? *Chronicle of Higher Education*, p. C1.

Perlmutter, D. D. (2008b, June 19). Supervising your graduate assistants. *Chronicle of Higher Education*. Retrieved August 20, 2008, from http://chronicle.com/article /Supervising-Your-Graduate-A/45859/.

Perrine, R. M., Lisle, L., & Tucker, D. L. (1995). Effects of a syllabus offer of help, student age, and class size on college students' willingness to seek support from faculty. *Journal of Experimental Education, 64*, 41–52.

Perry, W. G. (1968). *Forms of intellectual and ethical development in the college years: A scheme.* New York: Holt, Rinehart, & Winston.

Perry, W. G. (1985). Different worlds in the same classroom. *Journal of the Harvard-Danforth Center: On Teaching and Learning, 1*, 1–17.

Plotnick, E. (1996). *Trends in educational psychology.* Syracuse, NY: ERIC Clearinghouse on Information and Technology. (ERIC Document Reproduction Service No. ED398861)

Plotnick, E. (2001). A graphical system for understanding the relationship between concepts. *Teacher Librarian, 2* (4), 42–44.

Plotz, D. (1999, September 17). The American teen-ager: Why Generation Y? *Slate Magazine.* Retrieved October 14, 2009, from www.slate.com/id/34963/.

Plutsky, S., & Wilson, B. A. (2001). Writing across the curriculum in a college of business and economics. *Business Communication Quarterly, 64* (4), 26–41.

Pollio, H. R., & Humphreys, W. L. (1988). Grading students. In J. H. McMillan (Ed.), *New directions for teaching and learning: No. 34. Assessing students' learning* (pp. 85–97). San Francisco: Jossey-Bass.

Posner, G. J., Strike, K. A., Hewson, P. W., & Gertzog, W. A. (1982). Accommodation of a scientific concept: Towards a theory of conceptual change. *Science Education, 66* (2), 211–227.

Potts, B. (1993). Improving the quality of student notes. *Practical Assessment, Research, and Evaluation, 3* (8). Retrieved August 19, 2007, from http://PAREonline.net /getvn.asp?v=3&n=8.

Poythress, K. (2007, May 25). Cheating rampant on college campuses, survey reveals. *CNS News Culture.* Retrieved August 14, 2008, from www.cnsnews.com /public/content/article.aspx?RsrcID=7446.

Prégent, R. (1994). *Charting your course: How to prepare to teach more effectively.* Madison, WI: Magna.

Prince, M. (2004). Does active learning work? A review of the research. *Journal of Engineering Education, 93* (3), 223–231.

Prince, M., & Felder, R. M. (2006). Inductive teaching and learning methods: Definitions, comparisons, and research bases. *Journal of Engineering Education, 95* (2), 123–138.

Prince, M., & Felder, R. M. (2007). The many faces of inductive teaching and learning. *Journal of College Science Teaching, 36* (5), 14–20.

Profile of undergraduate students, 2003–4. (2007, August 31). *Chronicle of Higher Education Almanac Issue 2007–8,* p. 17.

Qualters, D. M. (2001). Do students want to be active? *Journal of the Scholarship of Teaching and Learning, 2* (1), 51–60.

Questionmark Corporation. (2000). *Writing test blueprints and test items.* Retrieved May 1, 2009, from http://tryout .questionmark.com/learningcafe/1846070911/writing_ blueprints_test_items.ppt.

Radosevich, D. J., Salomon, R., Radosevich, D. M., & Kahn, P. (2008). Using student response systems to increase motivation, learning, and knowledge retention. *Innovate, 5* (1). Retrieved October 4, 2008, from www.innovateonline .info/index.php?view=article&id=40&action=article.

Raines, C. (2002). *Connecting generations: The sourcebook for a new workplace.* Menlo Park, CA: Crisp Publications.

Raymark, P., & Connor-Greene, P. (2002). The syllabus quiz. *Teaching of Psychology, 29* (4), 286–288.

Reay, N. W., Li, P., & Bao, L. (2008). Testing a new voting machine question methodology. *American Journal of Physics, 76* (2), 171–178.

Rebich, S., & Gauthier, C. (2005). Concept mapping to reveal prior knowledge and conceptual change in a mock summit course on global climate change. *Journal of Geoscience Education, 53* (4), 355–365.

Reddish, E. F. (2003). *Teaching physics with the physics suite.* Hoboken, NJ: Wiley.

Reddish, E. F., Saul, J. M., & Steinberg, R. N. (1997). On the effectiveness of active-engagement microcomputer-based laboratories. *American Journal of Physics, 65,* 45–54.

Reddish, E. F., Saul, J. M., & Steinberg, R. N. (1998). Students' expectations in introductory physics. *American Journal of Physics, 66* (3), 212–224.

Reddish, E. F., & Steinberg, R. N. (1999). Who will study physics, and why? *Physics Today, 52,* 24–30.

Redfield, J. (2000). On discussion teaching. In *Teaching at Chicago: A collection of readings and practical advice for the beginning teacher.* Retrieved September 2, 2008, from http://teaching.uchicago.edu/handbook/tac10.html.

Redlawsk, D. P., Rice, T., & Associates. (2009). *Civic service: Service-learning with state and local government partners.* San Francisco: Jossey-Bass.

Regis, A., & Albertazzi, P. G. (1996). Concept maps in chemistry education. *Journal of Chemical Education, 73* (11), 1084–1088.

Reif, F., & Heller, J. I. (1982). Knowledge structure and problem solving in physics. *Educational Psychologist, 17,* 102–127.

Reiner, C. M., Bothell, T. W., Sudweeks, R. R., & Wood, B. (2002). *Preparing effective essay questions: A self-directed workbook for educators.* Stillwater, OK: New Forums Press.

Rhem, J. (1992). Conference report: Cooperative learning as a teaching alternative. *The National Teaching and Learning Forum, 2* (1), 1–2.

Rhem, J. (1995). Going deep. *The National Teaching and Learning Forum, 5* (1). Retrieved December 21, 2006, from www.ntlf.com/html/pi/9512/article2.htm.

Rhem, J. (2006). The high risks of improving teaching. *The National Teaching and Learning Forum, 15* (6), 1–4.

Richardson, J. (2006, July 19). Office hours alfresco. *Chronicle of Higher Education.* Retrieved August 13, 2008, from http://chronicle.com/jobs/news/2006/07/2006071901c.htm.

Richardson, M. (2008, November 7). Writing is not just a basic skill. *Chronicle of Higher Education,* p. A47.

Rice, R. E., Sorcinelli, M. D., & Austin, A. E. (2000). *Heeding new voices: Academic careers for a new generation.* Washington, DC: American Association for Higher Education.

Rigby, C. S., Deci, E. L., Patrick, B. C., & Ryan, R. M. (1992). Beyond the intrinsic-extrinsic dichotomy: Self-determination in motivation and learning. *Motivation and Emotion, 16* (3), 165–185.

Roach, K. D. (1997). Effects of graduate teaching assistant attire on student learning, misbehaviors, and ratings of instruction. *Communication Quarterly, 45* (3), 125–142.

Robinson, B. D., & Schaible, R. (1993). Women and men teaching "Men, Women, and Work." *Teaching Sociology, 21,* 363–370.

Robinson, D. H., Katayama, A. D., DuBois, N. E., & Devaney, T. (1998). Interactive effects of graphic organizers and delayed review of concept application. *Journal of Experimental Education, 67* (1), 17–31.

Robinson, D. H., & Kiewra, K. A. (1995). Visual argument: Graphic organizers are superior to outlines in improving learning from text. *Journal of Educational Psychology, 87* (3), 455–467.

Robinson, D. H., & Molina, E. (2002). The relative involvement of visual and auditory working memory when studying adjunct displays. *Contemporary Educational Psychology, 27* (1), 118–131.

Robinson, D. H., & Schraw, G. (1994). Computational efficiency through visual argument: Do graphic organizers communicate relations in text too effectively? *Contemporary Educational Psychology, 19,* 399–414.

Robinson, D. H., & Skinner, C. H. (1996). Why graphic organizers facilitate search processes: Fewer words or computationally efficient indexing? *Contemporary Educational Psychology, 21,* 166–180.

Rodgers, M. L. (1995). How holistic scoring kept writing alive in chemistry. *College Teaching, 43* (1), 19–22.

Roediger, H. L., III, & Karpicke, J. D. (2006). The power of testing memory: Basic research and implications of the educational practice. *Perspective on Psychological Science, 1* (3), 181–210.

Rogers, K. A. (1993, August). Using the overhead. *Toastmaster,* 27–29.

Romance, N. R., & Vitale, M. R. (1997, April). *Knowledge representation systems: Basis for the design of instruction for undergraduate course curriculum.* Paper presented at the 8th National Conference on College Teaching and Learning, Jacksonville, FL.

Romance, N. R., & Vitale, M. R. (1999). Concept mapping as a tool for learning. *College Teaching, 4* (2), 74–79.

Ross, R. H., & Headley, E. L. (2002). Training new college professors to teach more effectively: What role does the case method play? *Journal on Excellence in College Teaching, 13* (2/3), 119–129.

Rowe, M. B. (1974). Wait time and rewards as instructional variables: Their influence on language, logic, and fate control: Part 2, rewards. *Journal of Research in Science Teaching, 11* (4), 291–308.

Rowe, M. B. (1980). Pausing principles and their effects on reasoning in science. In F. B. Brawer (Ed.), *New directions for community colleges: No. 8. Teaching the science* (pp. 27–34). San Francisco: Jossey-Bass.

Royce, A. P. (2000). *A survey of academic incivility at Indiana University: Preliminary report.* Bloomington: Indiana University, Center for Survey Research.

Royer, J., Cisero, C. A., & Carlo, M. S. (1993). Techniques and procedures for assessing cognitive skills. *Review of Educational Research, 63,* 210–224.

Ruhl, K. L., Hughes, C. A., & Schloss, P. J. (1987). Using the pause procedure to enhance lecture recall. *Teacher Education and Special Education, 10,* 14–18.

Ruscio, J. (2001). Administering quizzes at random to increase student reading. *Teaching of Psychology, 28* (3), 204–206.

Ryan, A. M., Pintrich, P. R., & Midgley, C. (2001). Avoiding seeking help in the classroom: Who and why? *Educational Psychology Review, 13* (2), 93–114.

Ryan, R. M., & Deci, E. L. (2000). Intrinsic and extrinsic motivations: Class definition and new directions. *Contemporary Education Psychology, 25* (1), 54–67.

Rybarczyk, B., Baines, A., McVey, M., Thompson, J., & Wilkins, H. (2007). A case-based approach increases student learning outcomes and comprehension of cellular respiration concepts. *Biochemistry and Molecular Biology Education, 35,* 181–186.

Sadker, M., & Sadker, D. (1992). Equitable participation in college classes. In L.L.B. Border & N.V.N. Chism (Eds.), *New directions for teaching and learning: No. 49. Teaching for diversity* (pp. 49–55). San Francisco: Jossey-Bass.

Samples, J. W. (1994). We want them to learn; sometimes we need to teach them how. *Connexions, 6* (2), 2.

Sarasin, L. C. (1998). *Learning styles perspective: Impact in the classroom.* Madison, WI: Atwood.

Sass, E. J. (1989). Motivation in the college classroom: What students tell us. *Teaching of Psychology, 16* (2), 86–88.

SCCtv, Boyer, M., & Harnish, J. (Co-producers/Writers/Directors). (2007). *Seminar: A skill everyone can learn.* Seattle, WA: University of North Seattle Community College.

Schau, C., & Mattern, N. (1997). Use of map techniques in teaching applied statistics courses. *American Statistician, 51,* 171–175.

Schneider, A. (1999, January 22). Why professors don't do more to stop students who cheat. *Chronicle of Higher Education,* pp. A8–A10.

Schneps, M. H., & Sadler, P. M. (Co-producers). (1988). *A private universe* (Videocassette). Cambridge, MA: Harvard-Smithsonian Center for Astrophysics.

Schoenfeld, A. H. (1985). *Mathematical problem solving.* Orlando, FL: Academic Press.

Schönwetter, D. J., Sokal, L., Friesen, M., & Taylor, L. L. (2002). Teaching philosophies reconsidered: A conceptual model for the development and evaluation of teaching philosophy statements. *International Journal for Academic Development, 7* (1), 83–97.

Schroeder, C. C. (1993). New students—New learning styles. *Change, 25* (5), 21–26.

Schroeder, C. M., Scott, T. P., Tolson, H., Huang, T., & Lee, Y. (2007). A meta-analysis of national research: Effects of teaching strategies on student achievement in science in the United States. *Journal of Research in Science Teaching, 44* (10), 1436–1460.

Schuster, P. M. (2000). Concept mapping: Reducing clinical care plan paperwork and increasing learning. *Nurse Educator, 25* (2), 76–81.

Seldin, P. (2004). *The teaching portfolio: A practical guide to improved performance and promotion/tenure decisions* (3rd ed.). Bolton, MA: Anker.

Seymour, E., & Hewitt, N. M. (1997). *Talking about leaving: Why undergraduates leave the sciences.* Boulder, CO: Westview Press.

Shaffer, L. (n.d.). *Texts and teaching.* Retrieved December 19, 2008, from http://faculty.plattsburgh.edu/lary.shaffer/texts%20and%20teaching.html.

Sharkey, L., Overmann, J., & Flash, P. (2007). Evolution of a course in veterinary clinical pathology: The application of case-based writing assignments to focus on skill development and facilitation of learning. *Journal of Veterinary Medical Education, 34* (4), 423–430.

Silberman, M. (1996). *Active learning: 101 strategies to teach any subject.* Needham Heights, MA: Allyn & Bacon.

Simon, J. (Producer). (1992). *Thinking together: Collaborative learning in the sciences* [Videocassette]. Cambridge, MA: Harvard University, Derek Bok Center for Teaching and Learning.

Sirias, D. (2002). Using graphic organizers to improve the teaching of business statistics. *Journal of Education for Business, 78,* 33–37.

Sixbury, G. R., & Cashin, W. E. (1995). *Description of database for the IDEA diagnostic form* (IDEA Technical Report No. 9). Manhattan: Kansas State University, Center for Faculty Evaluation and Development.

Slatta, R. W. (2004). Enhancing inquiry-guided learning with technology in history courses. In V. S. Lee (Ed.), *Teaching and learning through inquiry: A guidebook for institutions and instructors* (pp. 93–102). Sterling, VA: Stylus.

Slunt, K. M., & Giancarlo, L. C. (2004). Student-centered learning: A comparison of two different methods of instruction. *Journal of Chemical Education, 81* (7), 985–988.

Smith, D. M., & Kolb, D. A. (1986). *User's guide for the Learning-Style Inventory: A manual for teachers and trainers.* Boston: McBer.

Sokoloff, D., & Thornton, R. (1997). Using interactive lecture demonstrations to create an active learning environment. *Physics Teaching, 35,* 340–347.

Sokoloff, D., & Thornton, R. (2001). *Interactive lecture demonstrations.* Hoboken, NJ: Wiley.

Sorcinelli, M. D. (1994). Dealing with troublesome behaviors in the classroom. In K. W. Prichard & R. M. Sawyer (Eds.), *Handbook of college teaching: Theory and applications* (pp. 365–374). Westport, CT: Greenwood Press.

Specht, L. B., & Sandlin, P. K. (1991). The differential effects of experiential learning activities and traditional lecture classes in accounting. *Simulation and Gaming, 22* (2), 196–210.

Spence, L. D. (2001). The case against teaching. *Change, 33* (6), 11–19.

Springer, L., Stanne, M., & Donovan, S. (1999). Effects of small-group learning on undergraduates in science, mathematics, engineering, and technology: A meta-analysis. *Review of Educational Research, 69* (1), 21–51.

Staats, S., Hupp, J. M., Wallace, H., & Gresley, J. (2009). Heroes don't cheat: An examination of academic dishonesty and students' views on why professors don't report cheating. *Ethics and Behavior, 19* (3), 171–183.

Stacey, K., Rice, D., & Langer, G. (1997). *Academic service-learning: Faculty development manual.* Ypsilanti: Eastern Michigan University, Office of Academic Services.

Stage, F. K., Kinzie, J., Muller, P., & Simmons, A. (1999). *Creating learning centered classrooms: What does learning theory have to say?* Washington, DC: ERIC Clearinghouse on Higher Education.

Stahl, R. J. (1994). *Using "think time" and "wait time" skillfully in the classroom.* (ERIC Document Reproduction Service No. ED370885)

Stalnaker, J. M. (1951). The essay type of examination. In E. F. Lundquist (Ed.), *Educational measurement* (pp. 495–530). Washington, DC: American Council on Education.

Stenmark, J. K. (1989). *Assessment alternatives in mathematics: An overview of assessment techniques that promote learning.* Berkeley, CA: EQUALS, Lawrence Hall of Science and California Mathematics Council.

Stenmark, J. K. (1991). *Mathematics assessment: Myths, models, good questions, and practical suggestions.* Reston, VA: National Council of Teachers of Mathematics.

Stevens, D. D., & Levi, A. J. (2005). *Introduction to rubrics.* Sterling, VA: Stylus.

Strauss, W., & Howe, N. (2003). *Millennials go to college: Strategies for a new generation on campus.* Washington, DC: American Association of Collegiate Registrars and Admissions Officers.

Sullivan, C. S., Middendorf, J., & Camp, M. E. (2008). Engrained study habits and the challenge of warm-ups in just-in-time teaching. *The National Teaching and Learning Forum, 17* (4), 5–8.

Svinicki, M. (2004). *Learning and motivation in the postsecondary classroom.* Bolton, MA: Anker.

Suskie, L. (2004). *Assessing student learning: A commonsense guide.* Bolton, MA: Anker.

Taricani, E. M., & Clariana, R. B. (2006). A technique for automatically scoring open-ended concept maps. *Educational Technology Research and Development, 54* (1), 65–82.

Taylor, M. L. (2006). Generation NeXt comes to college: 2006 updates and emerging issues. In *A collection of papers on self-study and institutional improvement* (Vol. 2, pp. 48–55). Chicago: Higher Learning Commission.

Teaching Assistant Program, Michigan State University. (n.d.). *MSU thoughts on teaching #10: What undergraduates say are the most irritating faculty behaviors.* Retrieved July 24, 2008, from http://tap.msu.edu/PDF/thoughts/tt10.pdf.

Teaching notes. (1992, February 26). *Chronicle of Higher Education,* p. A35.

Thalheimer, W. (2002). *Simulation-like questions: The basics of how and why to write them.* Retrieved March 5, 2005, from www.work-learning.com/ma/pp_wp002.asp.

Theall, M., & Franklin, J. (1999). What have we learned? A synthesis and some guidelines for effective motivation in higher education. In M. Theall (Ed.), *New directions for teaching and learning: No. 78. Motivation from within: Encouraging faculty and students to excel* (pp. 97–109). San Francisco: Jossey-Bass.

Thomas, J. W. (2000). *A review of research on project-based learning.* San Rafael, CA: Autodesk Foundation.

Thompson, B. (2002, June 21). If I quiz them, they will come. *Chronicle of Higher Education,* p. B5.

Thorn, P. M. (2003). *Bridging the gap between what is praised and what is practiced: Supporting the work of change as anatomy and physiology instructors introduce active learning into their undergraduate classroom.* Unpublished doctoral dissertation, University of Texas, Austin.

Thorne, B. M. (2000). Extra credit exercises: A painless pop quiz. *Teaching of Psychology, 27* (3), 204–205.

Tigner, R. B. (1999). Putting memory research to good use: Hints from cognitive psychology. *College Teaching, 47* (4), 149–152.

Tobias, S. (1990). *They're not dumb, they're different: Stalking the second tier.* Tucson, AZ: Research Corporation.

Toombs, W., & Tierney, W. (1992). *Meeting the mandate: Renewing the college and department curriculum* (ASHE-ERIC Higher Education Report No. 91–6). Washington, DC: Association for the Study of Higher Education.

Topping, K. (1998). Peer-assessment between students in colleges and universities. *Review of Educational Research, 68,* 249–276.

Toulmin, S., Rieke, R., & Janik, A. (1984). *An introduction to reasoning* (2nd ed.). New York: Macmillan.

Treisman, P. U. (1986). *A study of the mathematics performance of black students at the University of California, Berkeley.* Unpublished doctoral dissertation, University of California, Berkeley.

Tucker, P. (2006). Teaching the millennial generation. *Futurist, 40,* 1.

Tuckman, B. (1965). Developmental sequence in small groups. *Psychological Bulletin, 63* (6), 384–399.

Tulving, E. (1985). How many memory systems are there? *American Psychologist, 40,* 385–398.

Turner, C.S.V., & Myers, S. L., Jr. (2000). *Faculty of color in academe: Bittersweet success.* Needham Heights, MA: Allyn & Bacon.

Tversky, B. (1995). Cognitive origins of conventions. In F. T. Marchese (Ed.), *Understanding images* (pp. 29–53). New York: Springer-Verlag.

Tversky, B. (2001). Spatial schemas in depictions. In M. Gattis (Ed.), *Spatial schemas and abstract thought* (pp. 79–111). Cambridge, MA: MIT Press.

University of Minnesota Libraries. (2007). *Copyright scenarios.* Retrieved August 20, 2008, from http://blog.lib.umn.edu/copyinfo/scenarios/.

Urdan, T. (2003). Intrinsic motivation, extrinsic rewards, and divergent views of reality. [Review of the book *Intrinsic and extrinsic motivation: The search for optimal motivation and performance*]. *Educational Psychology Review, 15* (3), 311–325.

Vekiri, I. (2002). What is the value of graphical displays in learning? *Educational Psychology Review, 14* (3), 261–312.

Vella, J. (1994). *Learning to listen, learning to teach: The power of dialogue in educating adults.* San Francisco: Jossey-Bass.

Vojtek, B., & Vojtek, R. (2000). Technology: Visual learning—This software helps organize ideas and concepts. *Journal of Staff Development, 21* (4). Retrieved December 3, 2007, from www.nsdc.org/library/publications/jsd/vojtek214.cfm.

Walker, V. L. (2009). 3D virtual learning in counselor education: Using Second Life in counselor skill development. *Journal of Virtual Worlds Research, 2* (1). Retrieved April 24, 2009, from http://journals.tdl.org/jvwr/article/view/423/463.

Wallace, J. D., & Mintzes, J. J. (1990). The concept map as a research tool: Exploring conceptual change in biology. *Journal of Research in Science Teaching, 27* (10), 1033–1052.

Waller, R. (1981, April). *Understanding network diagrams.* Paper presented at the annual meeting of the American Educational Research Association, Los Angeles. (ERIC Document Reproduction Service No. ED226695)

Walvoord, B. E., & Anderson, V. J. (1998). *Effective grading: A tool for learning and assessment.* San Francisco: Jossey-Bass.

Walvoord, B. E., & McCarthy, L. P. (1991). *Thinking and writing in college: A naturalistic study of students in four disciplines.* Urbana, IL: National Council of Teachers of English.

Wandersee, J. (2002a). Using concept circle diagramming as a knowledge mapping tool. In K. Fisher, J. Wandersee, & D. Moody (Eds.), *Mapping biology knowledge* (pp. 109–126). Dordrecht, Netherlands: Springer Netherlands.

Wandersee, J. (2002b). Using concept mapping as a knowledge mapping tool. In K. Fisher, J. Wandersee, & D. Moody (Eds.), *Mapping biology knowledge* (pp. 127–142). Dordrecht, Netherlands: Springer Netherlands.

Warrington, A. C., Hietapelto, A. B., & Joyce, W. B. (2003, August). *Contract grading: Impact on student learning and motivation in accounting and management classes.* Poster session presented at the annual meeting of the American Accounting Association, Honolulu, HI.

Wasley, P. (2008, February 29). Antiplagiarism software takes on the honor code. *Chronicle of Higher Education,* p. A12.

Waterman, M. A., & Stanley, E. (2005). *Case format variations.* Retrieved October 10, 2008, from http://cstl-csm.semo.edu/waterman/cbl/caseformats.html.

Watkins, D. (1982). Identifying the study process dimensions of Australian university students. *Australian Journal of Education, 26*(1), 76–85.

Watson, D. L., & Stockert, N. A. (1987). Ensuring teaching and learning effectiveness. *Thought and Action: The NEA Higher Education Journal, 3* (2), 91–104.

Weaver, B. E., & Nilson, L. B. (2005). Laptops in class: What are they good for? What can you do with them? In L. B. Nilson & B. E. Weaver (Eds.), *New directions for teaching and learning: No. 101. Enhancing learning with laptops in the classroom* (pp. 3–13). San Francisco: Jossey-Bass.

Weimer, M. (2002). *Learner-centered teaching: Five key changes to practice.* San Francisco: Jossey-Bass.

Wergin, J. F. (1988). Basic issues and principles in classroom assessment. In J. H. McMillan (Ed.), *New directions for teaching and learning: No. 34. Assessing students' learning* (pp. 71–83). San Francisco: Jossey-Bass.

West, D. C., Pomeroy, J. R., & Park, J. K. (2000). Critical thinking in graduate medical education: A role for concept mapping assessment? *Journal of the American Medical Association, 284* (9), 1105–1110.

Western Kentucky University Counseling and Testing Center. (2008). *Faculty/staff.* Retrieved August 14, 2008, from www.wku.edu/Dept/Support/StuAffairs/COUNS/resources/facultyStaff.html.

Whitley, B. E., Jr. (1998). Factors associated with cheating among college students: A review. *Research in Higher Education, 39* (3), 235–274.

Wieman, C. (2007). Why not try a scientific approach to science education? *Change, 39* (5), 9–15.

Wiesman, D. W. (2006). The effects of performance feedback and social reinforcement on up-selling at fast-food restaurants. *Journal of Organizational Behavior Management, 24* (6), 1–18.

Wiesman, D. W. (2007, April). *Achieving classroom civility through positive reinforcement: As easy as ABC.* Paper presented at the International Conference on College Teaching and Learning, Jacksonville, FL.

Wigfield, A., & Eccles, J. (2000). Expectancy-value theory of achievement motivation. *Contemporary Educational Psychology, 25,* s68–s81.

Wilhoit, S. (1994). Helping students avoid plagiarism. *College Teaching, 42* (4), 161–164.

Wilke, R. R. (2003). The effect of active learning on student characteristics in a human physiology course for non-majors. *Advances in Physiology Education, 27* (4), 207–223.

Wilke, R. R., & Straits, W. J. (2001). The effects of discovery learning in a lower-division biology course. *Advances in Physiology Education, 25* (2), 62–69.

Wilkes, L., Cooper, K., Lewin, J., & Batts, J. (1999). Promoting science learning in BN learners in Australia. *Journal of Continuing Education in Nursing, 30* (1), 37–44.

Williams, W. M., & Ceci, S. J. (1997). "How am I doing?" Problems with student ratings of instructor and courses. *Change, 29* (5), 13–23.

Wilson, J. H., & Taylor, K. W. (2001). Professor immediacy as behaviors associated with liking students. *Teaching of Psychology, 28,* 136–138.

Wilson, M. A. (2008). *Syllabus for History of Life (Geology 100), Department of Geology, The College of Wooster.* Retrieved May 1, 2008, from www.wooster.edu/geology /HOL.html.

Winn, W. (1987). Charts, graphs, and diagrams in educational materials. In D. M. Willows & H. A. Houghton (Eds.), *The psychology of illustration* (Vol. 1, pp. 152–198). New York: Springer-Verlag.

Winn, W. (1991). Learning from maps and diagrams. *Educational Psychology Review, 3* (3), 211–247.

Wittmann, M. (2001). *Real-time physics dissemination project: Evaluation at test sites.* Retrieved October 30, 2005, from http://perlnet.umephy.maine.edu/research /RTPevaluation1.pdf.

Wlodkowski, R. J. (1993). *Enhancing adult motivation to learn: A guide to improving instruction and increasing learner achievements.* San Francisco: Jossey-Bass.

Wolcott, S. (2006). *Steps for better thinking performance patterns.* Retrieved January 2, 2009, from www.wolcottlynch .com/EducatorResources.html.

Woods, D. R. (1989). Developing students' problem-solving skills. *Journal of College Science Teaching, 19,* 108–110.

Woods, D. R. (1996). Problem-based learning for large classes in chemical engineering. In L. Wilkerson & W. Gijselaers (Eds.), *New directions for teaching and learning: No. 68. Bringing problem-based learning to higher education: Theory and practice* (pp. 91–99). San Francisco: Jossey-Bass.

Wright, W. A., Herteis, E. M., & Abernehy, B. (2001). *Learning through writing: A compendium of assignments and techniques.* Halifax, Canada: Dalhousie University, Office of Instructional Development.

Wueste, D. E. (2008, August). *Ethics across the curriculum.* Faculty seminar conducted at Clemson University, SC.

Wycoff, J. (1991). *Mind mapping: Your personal guide to exploring creativity and problem solving.* New York: Berkley Books.

Young, A. P. (1997). *Writing across the curriculum* (2nd ed.). Upper Saddle River, NJ: Prentice Hall.

Young, A. P., & Fulwiler, T. (1986). *Writing across the disciplines: Research into practice.* Upper Montclair, NJ: Boynton/Cook.

Young, J. R. (2003, August 8). Sssshhh. We're taking notes here. Colleges look for new ways to discourage disruptive behavior in the classroom. *Chronicle of Higher Education,* p. A29.

Young, J. R. (2004, November 12). When good technology means bad teaching. *Chronicle of Higher Education,* p. A31.

Young, J. R. (2009, November 22). Teaching with Twitter: Not for the faint of heart. *Chronicle of Higher Education.* Retrieved November 30, 2009, from http://chronicle.com/article/Teaching-With-Twitter-Not-/49230/.

Zax, D. (2009, October). Learning in 14-character bites. *ASEE Prism*. Retrieved November 30, 2009, from http://bit.ly/7bbPG5.

Zeilik, M., Schau, C., Mattern, N., Hall, S., Teague, K. W., & Bisard, W. (1997). Conceptual astronomy: A novel model for teaching postsecondary science courses. *American Journal of Physics, 6* (10), 987–996.

Zlotkowski, E. (Ed.). (1998). *Successful service-learning programs: New models of excellence in higher education*. San Francisco: Jossey-Bass.

Zoller, U. (1987). The fostering of question-asking capacity. *Journal of Chemical Education, 64* (6), 510–512.

Zubizarreta, J. (2009). *The learning portfolio: Reflective practice for improving student learning* (2nd ed.). San Francisco: Jossey-Bass.

Zull, J. E. (2002). *The art of changing the brain: Enriching the practice of teaching by exploring the biology of learning*. Sterling, VA: Stylus.

Zywno, M. S. (2003). A contribution to validation of score meaning for Felder-Soloman's Index of Learning Styles. *Proceedings of the 2003 American Society for Engineering Education Annual Conference and Exposition* (Session 2351). Washington, DC: American Society for Engineering Education.

Note to index: An *e* following a page number denotes an exhibit on that page; an *f* following a page number denotes a figure on that page; a *t* following a page number denotes a table on that page.